Theorizing
the City

Theorizing the City

The New Urban Anthropology Reader

EDITED BY SETHA M. LOW

RUTGERS UNIVERSITY PRESS
New Brunswick, New Jersey, and London

04-33647(3)

Second paperback printing, 2002

Library of Congress Cataloging-in-Publication Data

Low, Setha M.
    Theorizing the city : the new urban anthropology reader / Setha M.
Low.
      p. cm.
    Includes bibliographical references.
    ISBN 0-8135-2719-8 (cloth : alk. paper). — ISBN 0-8135-2720-1
(pbk. : alk. paper)
      1. Cities and towns. 2. Urban anthropology. 3. Sociology, Urban.
I. Title.
HT119.L67 1999
307.76—dc21   99-17712
                                                             CIP

British Cataloging-in-Publication data for this book is available from the
British Library

To Joel
for bringing me to New York City

Epigraph

Lunch with Giambattista Nolli

Architect and surveyor of *Pianta Grande di Roma*, the first modern city map, 1748. "Despite praise heaped on the work by everyone from the pope on down, it was not a financial success. . . . After two years, most engraved copies were still unsold."

Remember when we two young architects
measured a street with a dozen crooked houses?
I draw all Rome now, every way-out quarter,
the Pope himself signed me a pass, I enter
everywhere. Yes, even cloistered convents.

All Rome's my universe, I extend my chain,
slice ground and figure, figure and ground, survey.
The riverbanks and cypresses, you'll know,
Nature I've sketched in realistic style,
the plan's all new, stretched flat on twelve wide sheets.

"Lacks charm," a colleague carps, he can't see grid
as science. "No taste, no style," a rival sneers.
"Buy it," the pilgrim friars beg their abbots.
Craving the martyrs' tombs and holy relics,
they swear the saints themselves guide my *bussola*!

No one has ever drawn a map like mine,
or understood its mathematic power,
or counted up its thousand uses—taxing,
policing, buying, selling, spying, wooing—
that's not to mention ordinary viewing.

You build, my friend, you know our art is urban.
Just four *zecchini*. No? I wager you—
I'm sure to win your hard-earned money—
one day we'll all own city maps in Rome.
So please, be one of the first, put down your cash!

Dolores Hayden, 1998

Contents

ACKNOWLEDGMENTS AND PERMISSIONS   XI

Introduction. Theorizing the City   1
SETHA M. LOW

Part I The Divided City

1 The Changing Significance of Race and Class in
an African American Community   37
STEVEN GREGORY

2 Creating Family Forms: The Exclusion of Men and
Teenage Boys from Families in the New York City
Shelter System, 1987–1991   67
IDA SUSSER

3 Fortified Enclaves: The New Urban Segregation   83
TERESA P. R. CALDEIRA

Part II The Contested City

4 Spatializing Culture: The Social Production and
Social Construction of Public Space in Costa Rica   111
SETHA M. LOW

5   Landscape and Power in Vienna: Gardens
    of Discovery   138
    ROBERT ROTENBERG

    Part III   The Global City

6   Personal Relations and Divergent Economies: A
    Case Study of Hong Kong Investment in South China   169
    JOSEPHINE SMART AND ALAN SMART

7   Wholesale Sushi: Culture and Commodity in
    Tokyo's Tsukiji Market   201
    THEODORE C. BESTOR

    Part IV   The Modernist City

8   The Modernist City and the Death of the Street   245
    JAMES HOLSTON

9   The Power of Space in the Evolution of an
    Accra *Zongo*   277
    DEBORAH PELLOW

    Part V   The Postmodern City

10 Making Place in the Nonplace Urban Realm:
    Notes on the Revitalization of Downtown Atlanta   317
    CHARLES RUTHEISER

11 Discourses of the City: Policy and Response in
    Post-Transitional Barcelona   342
    GARY MCDONOGH

12 Spatial Discourses and Social Boundaries:
    Re-imagining the Toronto Waterfront   377
    MATTHEW COOPER

    BIOGRAPHICAL NOTES   401
    INDEX   405

Acknowledgments and Permissions

I am grateful for the support of many people. Gloria Levitas coedited an earlier version of this book, which included urban fiction, and encouraged me to write an urban ethnography reader. Martha Heller and Marlie Wasserman of Rutgers University Press were enthusiastic about the project from the beginning. Also at Rutgers, Marilyn Campbell answered my technical questions and helped with assembling the text; Brigitte Goldstein and Tricia Politi saw the project through production. Willa Speiser copyedited with a careful eye. Graduate students who attended the "Anthropology of the City" seminar at the Graduate School and University Center of the City University of New York added their substantive interests and theoretical concerns. Dolores Hayden inspired me with her poetry and work on the power of place. And Joel Lefkowitz provided the emotional and editorial support needed to complete the endeavor.

I would particularly like to thank my colleagues who contributed their work, and their publishers who granted permission for the articles and book chapters to be reprinted in this volume:

Setha M. Low, "The Anthropology of Cities: Imagining and Theorizing the City." Excerpts reprinted with permission from the *Annual Review of Anthropology*, volume 25, copyright © 1996 by Annual Reviews.

Steven Gregory, "The Changing Significance of Race and Class in an African-American Community." Reprinted by permission of the American Anthropological Association from *American Ethnologist* 19, no. 2 (May 1992). Not for further reproduction.

Ida Susser, "Creating Family Forms: The Exclusion of Teenage Boys in the New York City Shelter System, 1987–1991." Reprinted by permission of Sage Publications, Ltd., from *Critique of Anthropology* 13, no. 3 (1993).

Teresa P. R. Caldeira, "Fortified Enclaves: The New Urban Segregation." Reprinted by permission of the University of California Press from *City of Walls: Crime, Segregation, and Citizenship in São Paulo*, forthcoming.

Setha M. Low, "Spatializing Culture: The Social Production and Social Construction of Public Space in Costa Rica." Reprinted by permission of the American Anthropological Association for *American Ethnologist* 23, no. 4 (November 1996). Not for further reproduction.

Robert Rotenberg, "Gardens of Discovery" from *Landscape and Power in Vienna*. Reprinted with permission of Johns Hopkins University Press.

Josephine Smart and Alan Smart, "Personal Relations and Divergent Economies." Reprinted with permission for one-time use, nonexclusive world English rights, not extending to electronic formats by Blackwell Publishers for *International Journal of Urban and Regional Research* 15 (1991).

James Holston, "Introduction and The Death of the Street" from *The Modernist City*. Reprinted with permission of the University of Chicago.

Deborah Pellow, "The Power of Space in the Evolution of an Accra Zongo." Reprinted with permission from *Ethnohistory* 38, no. 4 (1991).

Charles Rutheiser, "Making Place in the Nonplace Urban Realm: Notes on the Revitalization of Downtown Atlanta." Reprinted with permission of The Institute, Inc. from *Urban Anthropology and Studies of Cultural Systems and World Economic Development* 26, no. 1 (1997).

Gary McDonogh, "Discourses of the City: Policy and Response in Post-Transitional Barcelona." Reprinted by permission of the American Anthropological Association from *City and Society Annual Review* 5, no. 1 (June 1991). Not for further reproduction.

Matthew Cooper, "Spatial Discourses and Social Boundaries: Re-Imaging the Toronto Waterfront." Reprinted by permission of the American Anthropological Association from *City and Society Annual Review 1994*. Not for further reproduction.

Theorizing
the City

SETHA M. LOW

Introduction: Theorizing the City

This introduction begins with a query about why the city has been undertheorized within anthropology. Urban theory has been left to sociologists, cultural geographers, urban planners, and historians, all of whom bring their distinct disciplinary skills to this endeavor (Zukin 1991, 1995; Smith 1984; Soja 1989; Harvey 1990; Sassen 1991; Castells 1989; Cronon 1991; Hayden 1995). It becomes clear, however, from the following historical overview and review of contemporary research, that the problem is not really an absence of the city in anthropological theory but rather that this line of inquiry has not had a major theoretical impact.

It is also worth questioning why an anthropological voice is not often heard in the urban studies discourse even though many anthropologists have contributed actively to theory and research on urban poverty, racism, globalization, and architecture and planning. Stack (1996), Bourgeois (1995a), Susser (1991), and Newman (1992) argue that while anthropological data are essential to understanding urban problems, anthropologists have been hesitant to participate in, if not totally absent from, urban public policy debates. In this introduction I address both of these queries by reviewing the urban anthropological literature, identifying the images and concepts that organize this inquiry, and highlighting anthropological contributions to urban theory in order to position the ethnographic studies presented in this volume within the broader discourse of urban studies and urban policy.

This introduction, however, does not argue for an essentialism of the city (Lynch 1994, Zenner 1994) but is, rather, in favor of attending to the social relations, symbols, and political economies that are most manifest in the city. In earlier reviews, Fox (1972, 1977), Jackson (1985), and Gulick (1989) advocated an anthropology *of* the city, rather than *in* the city arguing that this distinction "is not trivial or hairsplitting" (Gulick 1989, xiv).

Theorizing the city, however, is a necessary part of understanding the changing postindustrial/advanced, capitalist/postmodern world in which we live. The city as a site of everyday practice provides valuable insights into the linkages of these macro processes with the texture and fabric of human experience. The city is not the only place where these linkages can be studied, but the intensification of these processes—as well as their human outcomes—occurs and can be understood best in cities. Thus, the "city" as presented in this volume is not a reification but the focus of study of cultural and sociopolitical manifestations of urban lives and everyday practices illustrated by urban ethnographies.

Historical Overview

The historical trajectory begins with the Chicago School in the 1920s and 1930s and the development of an urban ecological perspective (Park and Burgess 1974). The city is theorized as being made up of adjacent ecological niches occupied by human groups in a series of concentric rings surrounding the central core. Class, occupation, worldview, and life experiences are coterminous with an inhabitant's location within this human ecology. Social change occurs through socioeconomic transitions of these areas in an ever-downward spiral toward the inner city. Research strategies focus on participant observation as a method of uncovering and explaining the adaptations and accommodations of urban populations to these microenvironments. Contemporary researchers, such as the sociologists Anderson (1990) and Wacquant (1994), both of whom trained at the University of Chicago and studied the Afro-American ghetto experience in Chicago, continue to draw upon this body of work for theoretical and methodological inspiration.

A second major influence was a series of community studies undertaken as part of the Institute of Community Studies program of policy and planning research on the slum clearance and replacement of housing in London, England, and Lagos, Nigeria. These studies, beginning in the 1950s and continuing through the present (Young and Willmott 1957, Marris 1962, 1995), theorized the city as made up of a series of urban "communities," based on extended family relations and kinship networks. Coincidentally, the Tavistock Institute of Human Relations published Bott's (1957) study of the social networks of middle-class

English families, which drew upon discussions with anthropologists at the University of Manchester (Gluckman 1971). The methodological contribution of network analysis as the basis for studying the social organization of city residents was widely used to understand the rapidly urbanizing populations of Africa (Mitchell 1969) and Latin America (Lomnitz 1977), as well as by North American researchers interested in the interconnections and interdependencies of family and household relationships among the urban poor (Stack 1974, 1996). Network studies have become more elaborate and quantitative but they still provide an important methodological strategy and theoretical model for urban researchers (Laguerre 1994b, Kadushin and Jones 1992, Liebow 1989).

Studies of planned physical and social change in Latin American low-income residential neighborhoods (Lobo 1983, Logan 1984), as well as studies of the planning and design of new towns such as Ciudad Guyana (Peattie 1972) and Brasilia (Epstein 1973) provided further ethnographic examples of local as well as national and international conflict over planning goals. These studies identified foreign capital investment (Peattie 1987) and the power/knowledge of the technologies of planning and architecture (Rabinow 1989) as antithetical to producing a humane environment for local populations and workers. Studies of urban renewal (Greenbaum 1993) and community rebuilding after natural disasters (Oliver-Smith 1986) further contributed theoretical understandings of how the dynamics of redevelopment processes often exclude the psychosocial needs of residents. Anthropological analyses of the conflicts that emerge among government institutions, planning experts, and local communities set the stage for contemporary poststructuralist studies of urban struggle for land tenure rights (Holston 1995) and adequate housing (Low 1988, Low and Chambers 1989), as well as for studies of planning and architecture as instruments of social control (McDonogh 1991, Plotnicov 1987).

Another theoretical force has been the cumulative work of Leeds (1973), more recently published in a posthumous volume (Sanjek 1994). Although Leeds's work concentrated on supralocal and local linkages and the nation/state level of analysis, the majority of his fieldwork dealt with the city as the point of articulation of these complex relationships. Anthropologists continue to utilize Leeds's theoretical model of the flow of goods, cash, labor, and services between metropole and countryside in their analyses of the city (Guldin 1989,1992).

The most important theoretical transition, however, occurred in the 1980s with the introduction of the study of the political economy of the city. Susser's (1982) landmark ethnography of a Brooklyn working-class neighborhood, Hannerz's theoretical monograph (1980), and Mullings's

(1987) critique of the study of cities in the United States ushered in a decade of critical studies of the structural forces that shape urban experience. The social organizational paradigm that dominated earlier studies was superseded by a political economy paradigm (Walton 1993, Sanjek 1990). These studies theorize the city by examining the social effects of industrial capitalism and deconstructing the confusion of urbanism with inequality and alienation (Mullings 1987, Ong 1987).

The final development in this theoretical trajectory is what Jacobs (1993) has called representational cities—an approach in which messages encoded in the environment are read as texts. Jacobs argues that "ethnographic studies were commonly prescribed the role of rendering more real the exotic and marginalized, but were seen to have little value in terms of the modern project of theory-building" (1993, 828). Radicalized urban ethnography, however, makes possible a link between everyday practices and the broader processes of class formation. According to Jacobs (1993), new cities require new forms of analysis in which the urban built environment becomes a discursive realm. Within anthropology this representational approach is reflected in Holston's (1992) analysis of the planning and architecture of Brasilia, in which the city is read as an ideological tract of an imagined socialist utopia, and in Dorst's (1990) postmodern ethnography of the re-creation of the history and landscape of Chadds Ford, Pennsylvania.

The correspondence of academic training with the geographical area of study has also contributed to continuities of research and theory within culture regions. The tradition of British social anthropology in Africa has created a history of studies that focus on social relations in the city—exchanges, political alliances, market relationships, and network analyses that form the core of contemporary theoretical work (Barnes 1986, MacGaffey 1987, Peil 1991, Moore 1994). Other continuities include studies of *favelas*, shantytowns, and *turgurios* in the urban periphery, and the informal economy in Latin America (Safa 1986, Kasarda and Crenshaw 1991); Japanese studies that focus on work organization (Hamabata 1990, Kondo 1990, Sumihara 1993, Bestor in press), and Chinese studies that emphasize urban hierarchies (Guldin 1993, Jankowiak 1993).

Thus, the historical development of the anthropological study of the city has produced a number of theoretical approaches that continue to be drawn upon by urban anthropologists. These approaches include urban ecology models; community, family and network analyses; studies of the power/knowledge of planning and architecture; supralocal/local linkage analyses; and political economic, representational, and discursive models of the city.

Imagining the City: Metaphors and Images

Contemporary studies, however, are much more diverse and do not fall neatly into these categories. This section, therefore, presents recent literature on the anthropology of cities through a series of images and metaphors. These images of the city are meant to be heuristic and illuminating, neither all-encompassing nor mutually exclusive. The images should not be confused with previous evolutionary schemes or the development of urban typologies (Gulick 1989, Fox 1977). They provide a guide to the diverse ideas, concepts, and frameworks that authors use to analyze and write about the city and should be considered different lenses that offer the reader as well as the writer other ways to communicate about an often elusive and discursively complex subject.

Twelve images are explored for their theoretical relevance. Four of them focus on social relational processes—the ethnic city, the divided city, the gendered city, and the contested city; three focus on economic processes—the deindustrialized city, the global city, and the informational city; three images emphasize urban planning and architectural approaches to urban analysis—the modernist city, the postmodern city, and the fortress city; and two reflect religious and cultural aspects of urban life—the sacred city and the traditional city. Five of these images organize the contents of this volume. Articles and book chapters were selected from the divided city, the contested city, the global city, the modernist city, and the postmodern city to illustrate the kind of detailed ethnography and integrative theory that characterizes contemporary urban anthropology.

Social Relations

The Ethnic City. As illustrated by the difficulties of the protagonist in the movie *Little Odessa* (1994), set in the Russian immigrant community of Brighton Beach, Brooklyn, it is often impossible to escape the pressures of one's cultural group when one stays—and trying to leave can lead to unexpected, and sometimes unfortunate circumstances. *Little Odessa* depicts one of the mythic images of an East Coast ethnic city. This image, which has deep historical roots, is currently popular as a result of the increased attention given to ethnic politics and ethnically based urban social movements. Edited volumes that enumerate the multiplicity of immigrant groups that coexist within large U.S. cities (Foner 1987, Sutton 1987, Chavez 1990, Lamphere 1992) and ethnographies that portray the differences in the structure of opportunity (Fernandez Kelly 1993a), access to power by generation (Kasinitz 1992), location of headquarters and subsidiary relations (Laguerre 1994a), and self-conscious creation of collective identities (Liebow) define the parameters of group success and failure in this urban model.

There are two dominant streams of research in the study of the ethnic city: (1) the ethnic city as a mosaic of enclaves that are economically, linguistically, and socially self-contained as a strategy of political and economic survival (Zhou 1992, Portes and Stepick 1993); and (2) studies of ethnic groups that may or may not function as enclaves but are defined by their location in the occupational structure (Margolis 1994), their position in the local immigrant social structure (Markowitz 1993), their degree of marginality (Mahler 1995), or their historical and racial distinctiveness as the basis of discrimination and oppression (Kwong 1987, Chen 1992, Fong 1994). The concept of the ethnic enclave has been criticized as often being assumed rather than empirically verified (Pessar 1995); nonetheless, this concept has generated a productive stream of theorizing (Portes and Zhou 1993, Portes and Schauffler 1994). The studies of urban ethnic communities, although part of the continuing tradition of anthropological community studies, contribute less to the ongoing development of a theory of the ethnic city but provide important insights into collective ethnic politics.

One book that has received considerable attention is Portes and Stepick's *City on the Edge* (1993), a study of the development of Miami, Florida, as a city of competing ethnic enclaves. Historically dominated by the white middle class, the cultural hegemony of Miami has more recently shifted into the hands of Cuban-born immigrants; Spanish has become the *lingua franca* of commerce and sociopolitical networks. Cuban-born immigrants have been singularly successful in manipulating the local power structure and media to create a new kind of ethnic politics in which the oppressed have become the oppressor.

Probably the most ambitious research program has been Lamphere's (1992) Ford Foundation project on the changing relations between established residents and newcomers in Miami, Chicago, Houston, Philadelphia, Monterey Park (California), and Garden City (Kansas). The studies identify quite different strategies in the development of ethnic politics: Horton (1995) discusses the "voluntary construction of ethnicity" (1995, 234) of the Chinese majority and Latino newcomers in Monterey Park; Stull (1990, and with Broadway and Griffith 1995) emphasizes class-based perceptions of ethnic identity in Garden City; Goode and Schneider (1994) frame their study in terms of racial as well as ethnic divisions in Philadelphia.

Goode and Schneider's depiction of Philadelphia is particularly noteworthy in that it provides an assessment of the political and economic processes that segregate Philadelphia's neighborhoods. Although Goode and Schneider use the term racially "divided city," their research suggests that new immigrants who are settling in older divided communities are in fact reconfiguring the city into ethnically diverse neighborhoods. An ethnically based real estate market has developed as well as specialty shopping areas, local ethnic associations, and a variety of ethnic festivals. Philadelphia is an interesting case that draws upon two complementary images: it is a historically diverse city known for its neighborhoods dotted with churches and synagogues marking ethnic differences, and it is a city divided into racial territories of black and white (Koptiuch 1991).

The Divided City. This image conjures up the Berlin wall (Borneman 1991) and the current socioeconomic division between East and West Berlin (Borneman 1997). But within anthropology it evokes hidden barriers of race and class encoded in metaphors of "uptown" and "downtown," "upscale" and "ghetto," and, particularly within cities of the United States, of black and white. McDonogh (1993) theorizes the experience of being black and Catholic in the divided city of Savannah as "characterized by a continuous tension among discourses that sustain stereotypes, delimit social groups, and shape the activities of citizens who participate in urban cultures" (1993, 65). Keith and Cross (1993), on the other hand, argue that the divided city has restored the cultural primacy of the urban as a culture and cash nexus or "city as playground." In this image, the division is between the white cultural playgrounds and the abandoned black residential areas so clearly seen in cities such as Washington, D.C., Los Angeles, and New York.

The processes that produce the divided city have been studied primarily in U.S. cities and focus on different aspects of racism and racial segregation (Williams 1992). Williams's exploration of the displacement of blacks through gentrification and other real estate activities, and Greenbaum's (1993) study of housing abandonment provide the ethnographic explanations for the more theoretical overviews of American residential apartheid (Massey and Denton 1993, Bullard, Grigsby, and Lee 1994). According to Massey and Denton (1993) the continued high level of residential segregation experienced by blacks in American cities is an example of racial prejudice and discriminatory real estate practices and mortgage structures designed to insulate whites from blacks. Gregory (1992, 1998, and this book, chapter 1) notes that a shift from race-based to class-based politics is even separating the residences of low-income blacks in Queens from middle-class blacks, who are increasingly adopting the political values of white homeowners.

Anthropologists, however, have explored other avenues of theorizing the divided city and the economic, social, and political consequences of racism. Page (1994) has developed the concept of "white public space" to analyze how white institutions control even the production of "blackness." Within her white public space, even efforts by black entrepreneurs to serve their own people and culture are co-opted by the white power structure that dominates the economic and communication systems utilized by the black community. Sacks (1997) explains race, class, and gender relations through the metaorganization of capitalism, which she defines as a materially based and state-reinforced social and cultural construction. Fernandez-Kelly (1993b) explains the divided city through the unequal distribution of "cultural capital," the symbolic repertory whose meanings individuals learn and use as members of particular social networks, and "social capital," the relations of reciprocity between individuals and groups. Cultural and social capital are defined by physical vectors such as urban space and by collective constructions such as social class, race, and gender, and thus are toponomical, dependent on physical and social location.

Other anthropologists have theorized the unequal distribution of material resources and urban services as a reflection of the "major cleavage between those able to augment their basic needs through labor market participation at a wage high enough to insulate them from the vagaries of state budget crises and those who remain on state services just to survive" (Jones, Turner, and Montbach 1992, 112). Susser (1991, and this book, chapter 2) points to the separation of mothers and male children as perpetuating the dismantling of the black family and increasing vulnerability of black male children. Jones (1993), on the other hand, demonstrates that even though mothers want their children to achieve, the material bases for social reproduction are not available to support such desires. Ogbu (1991) and George (1992) identify the failure of city schools to provide educational environments that affirm and allow black and other minority student achievements.

The most extreme image of the divided city is Wacquant's (1994) concept of the hyperghetto, a racially and socioeconomically segregated section of the inner city characterized by the depacification of everyday life, desertification of organizations and institutions, social dedifferentiation, and informalization of the economy. Wacquant (1993) compares the stigma and racial division of South Side Chicago's Black Belt with the Parisian Red Belt of the urban periphery that "highlights the distinctively racial dimension of inner city poverty in the United States" (Wacquant 1993, 380). Mingione (1993) comments on the "Americanization" of poverty in European cities meaning the increasing racialization and ghettoization of the European poor.

Other researchers, however, argue that the South Side of Chicago is a special case, and that New York's Harlem and Los Angeles's South Central are not experiencing these desertification and depacification processes. The work of Newman (1992, 1996a, 1996b) and George (1992) refutes the generalizations of Wacquant and Wilson (1989) and instead identifies an increase in the number of local churches, the development of new Afrocentric schools, and a reappropriation of identity politics based on positive black images.

In Latin America the image of the divided city refers to number of fortified residential enclaves found in the cities where walls, surveillance technologies, and armed guards separate the upper and middle classes from the poor. Caldeira (1996, and this book, chapter 3) identifies the role these enclaves play in the spatial segregation and transformation of the quality of public life by comparing Brazilian cities and Los Angeles. Justified by increasing fear of violence and street crime, fortified enclaves have become status symbols and instruments of social separation dividing cities in areas of ostentatious wealth and extreme poverty (Caldeira, this volume).

The Gendered City. The city has been perceived primarily as a male place in which women, "along with minorities, children, the poor, are still not full citizens in the sense that they have never been granted full and free access to the streets . . . and they have survived and flourished in the interstices of the city, negotiating the contradictions of the city in their own particular way" (Wilson 1991, 8). The life within these interstices makes up the gendered city, theorized by feminists (Wilson 1991, Spain 1992, Massey 1994, Hayden 1995) and feminist anthropologists (di Leonardo 1993) as a place of work, struggle, and strife.

The majority of anthropological studies have focused on women's work and workplaces in the informal sphere: the market (Clark 1994, Harrison 1991), homework (White 1994), and domestic service (Gill 1994, Repak 1995). With the increasing feminization of key sectors of the informal economy and the informalization of economic and political processes in Third World cities, more women are finding themselves supporting their children as street vendors ("higglers") in Jamaica (Harrison 1991), market women in West Africa (Clark 1994), pieceworkers in urban Turkey (White 1994), and domestic workers in Bolivia. Repak (1995) argues that the structural forces in El Salvador of no rural jobs, low marriage rates, and multiple partners have produced a gender-specific migration of women as a low-wage labor source of domestics for District of Columbia households. This historical-structural theory of "gendered labor recruitment" explains why single women come, but it is their newly acquired values of freedom, growth, and individual achievement that explain why they stay.

Another way of conceptualizing the gendered city has been to document and theorize women's urban protests against their "silencing" in urban public high schools (Fine 1992), their exclusion from the sites of knowledge acquisition in Sudan and New York (Katz 1993), their control by traditional and Western hegemonies in Cairo (Macleod 1991), and their invisible practices of resistance (Aretxaga 1997). Hayden (1995) is particularly concerned about the absence of physical and spatial markers of women's contributions. In *The Power of Place* she explores the forgotten histories of the women who built and nourished Los Angeles. Redevelopment schemes erase the cultural, architectural, and spatial remains of ordinary people, leaving an urban landscape that provides no place memories for women, immigrants, and other minorities (Low 1996a, Hayden 1995, Boyer 1994).

The Contested City. The West Indian Labor Day Parade in Brooklyn (Kasinitz 1992), the Mummer's New Year Parade in Philadelphia (Davis 1986), the Halloween Parade in Greenwich Village (Kugelmass 1994), and Las Fallas in Valencia (Lawrence 1992)—these events, which temporarily invert the urban power structure through symbolic control of the streets, are well-known images of "the contested city" (Low 1996a). The growing attention to the masquerade politics of urban cultural movements (Cohen 1993) and to Castells's (1983) work on urban social movements (Banck and Doimo 1989), however, has produced a much broader range of contemporary examples of urban struggle and resistance. These poststructural analyses of race, class, gender, and ethnic politics theorize the city as the site of ongoing urban conflicts about the provision of the material basis for social reproduction: quality of life (Jones and Turner 1989), access to land (Barriga 1995), and neighborhood control of affordable housing (Beck 1992). Historical studies of Central Park in New York City (Rosenzweig and Blackmar 1992) and of Barcelona (Kaplan 1992) also record the solidarity of class and gender in the struggle to control land and labor.

Resistance, however, is not always a process of active contestation. Pred (1992) and Banck (1993) emphasize how simply naming streets can be an act of political struggle. The reconstruction of urban space, street name revision, and battles for street control are important areas for the study of ideological domination and anti-hegemonic discourse (O'Connor 1990, Aretxaga 1997)). In urban high schools, resistance has been explored through the concept of "silencing," a theoretical vehicle for understanding how it is that "language, representations, and even the forms of resistance permitted or not" (Fine 1991, 9) shape patterns of social injustice. Even the publication of an anthropological monograph can be an act of cultural resistance when the author is a member of the resisting group—the Dalits in India—and the work identifies the violence against the Dalits from inside the culture (Ram 1995).

Ethnographic approaches to the study of urban space are another way to explore the theoretical implications of the contested city. I (Low 1996b and this book, chapter 4) explore the concept of "spatializing culture" by locating social relations and social practice in space, both physically and metaphorically. By focusing on the contestation of the design form and meaning of two plazas in San José, Costa Rica, I illuminate how people work out larger conflicts stemming from the growing impact of globalization, increased tourism, and loss of cultural identity within the relative safety of urban public space.

Rotenberg, on the other hand, is concerned with identifying conflicting forms of metropolitan knowledge. "Metropolitan knowledge is a subset of the knowledge people gain from their lived experience and value socialization" (Rotenberg and McDonogh 1993, xii) that city dwellers share because they live in dense and specialized concentrations of people, information, built form, and economic activity. Rotenberg (1993) introduces this concept in his discussion of the "salubrity of sites" as a way of understanding how metropolitan knowledge is made manifest on the urban landscape. In *Landscape and Power in Metropolitan Vienna* (1995) and in this volume (chapter 5) he elaborates the idea by tracing the history of conflict over the open spaces and gardens in Vienna and documenting how these spaces have become a spatial template of urban symbolic contestation.

The contested city also provides a site for methodological innovation. Burawoy and others (1991) used the "modern metropolis" as a participant observation laboratory for students who produced urban ethnographies based on theories of power and resistance. With a team of professors and graduate students, Abu-Lughod (1994) has written a "collective ethnography" of New York City's Lower East Side in "an effort to produce a new type of community study . . . able to capture the economic and social complexities found in our newest forms of inner-city neighborhoods, zones that have lost their common culture and consensus and have become, instead, contested turf of diverse groups which intermingle in physical space but which pursue disparate lifestyles and, often, conflicting goals" (1994, 5). Not only have these inner-city neighborhoods become arenas for struggle with outsiders, such as developers and city government officials, but they are also sites of conflict for the subgroups that live within its boundaries.

Economics

The Deindustrialized City. Michael Moore's underground film *Roger and Me* (1989) tells the story of the closing of the General Motors automobile factory in Flint, Michigan, and the resulting unemployment of workers, disinvestment in the community, declining standard of living, and subsequent deterioration of family and personal life. The story is a common one: deterioration of a city because of the closing or relocation of industries that had been the sole employers in working-class towns. The forces of globalization, new forms of flexible capital, and new venues of cheap labor have accelerated the number of these closings and their socially deleterious effects.

Anthropologists have theorized the plight of residents by documenting the consequences of deindustrialization on the lives of the working-class men and women. Pappas (1989) focuses on the effects of the closing of the Seiberling plant of the Firestone Tire and Rubber company in the industrial town of Barberton, Ohio. His ethnography sensitively depicts the reaction of the displaced workers who once had a modicum of affluence and security. Nash (1989), in her comprehensive historical-structural analysis of the economic and social decline of Pittsfield, Massachusetts, theorizes the response to deindustrialization in terms of the construction of community and corporate hegemony. When General Electric announced downsizing and the subsequent closing of local plants, the discourse between employees and management began to change and issues of corporate responsibility, social contract, and community welfare took on new meaning. Nash concludes that "General Electric consciously used the threat and actual practice of moving production elsewhere when they recognized the strength of nationally organized unions. . . . Their growing global investments were as much an attempt to control the labor movement in their domestic plants as to take advantage of cheap labor in export processing plants or branches within low-wage countries" (324).

Other anthropologists have looked at the costs of deindustrialization in terms of its impact on residents in New York City suburbs (Newman 1993), immigrants in Philadelphia (Koptiuch 1991), and Afro-Americans in Chicago's ghettos (Wacquant and Wilson 1989). Deindustrialization has contributed to the hyperghettoization of the city (Wacquant and Wilson 1989) and the "withering" of the middle-class American dream (Newman 1993).

The Global City. New York, Tokyo, and London are cited as the preeminent global cities—centers of technology, financial production, and support services (Sassen 1991) in which translocal economic forces have more weight than local policies in shaping urban economies (Sassen 1990). These three cities have "undergone massive and *parallel* changes in their economic base, spatial organization, and social structure" in order to accommodate their "command post" functions as key locations for markets, finance and special services, and sites of production and innovation. The resulting polarization of the city and the economy, the internationalization and "casualization" of labor, and deterritorialization of the social organization of work and community, are products of the same post-Fordist forces that have reshaped the deindustrialized city (Sassen 1991, 4).

Global forces are also reshaping regional systems of cities and hinterlands. Along the United States–Mexico border a distinct category of global city, the "border metropolis," is being created (Herzog 1990). These border cities are characterized by their commuting populations and transnational character (Herzog 1991, Arreola and Curtis 1993). Globalization in the Hong Kong–South China region, however, has developed different social and spatial characteristics. Smart and Smart (1991, and this book, chapter 6), explore how Hong Kong investments in South China are negotiated based on gift exchange grounded in social relationships and familial ties. These socially mediated investments successfully integrate the South China economy and political system with the Hong Kong globalized economy without the problems of the direct investment practices of other capitalist nations.

The term "world city" has also been used to describe the changing economies of large central cities from a world systems perspective (Wallerstein 1990). Friedmann (1995), summing up a decade of research, argues that world cities: (1) articulate local economies in a global economy; (2) provide a space for capital accumulation that excludes the world as a whole; (3) are locations of intense economic and social interaction; (4) are hierarchically arranged within the world system order; and (5) constitute a social class—the transnational capitalist class. Another manifestation of the global city is the "dual city" (Mollenkopf and Castells 1991) made up of upper-class and upper-middle-class professionals who act as a group in pursuing their own political ends and who effectively diffuse the political influence of more pluralistic neighborhoods.

Anthropologists have explored the consequences of globalization from a variety of perspectives: Rothstein and Blim (1991) examine new industrialization in the Third World and the creation of the "global factory." Watson (1997) has brought together studies of McDonald's as this global company has penetrated the markets of East Asia. Bestor (this book, chapter 7) explores the impact of globalization on the local urban

economy through his study of the Tsukiji wholesale fish market in Tokyo and the commodification of fish within Japan's food culture.

Anthropological contributions, however, have primarily focused on
transnational perspectives on migration (Glick Schiller, Basch, and Blanc-
Stanton 1992) in which issues of race, class, ethnicity, and nationalism
are reconsidered (Georges 1992, Charles 1992, Lessinger 1992, Ong 1992).
Everything from drug trafficking by gangs (Harrison 1989) to selling hats
in Harlem made in Africa and emblazoned with Malcolm Xs (Coombe
and Stoller 1994) is transformed by the transnational web of international
capitalism. Transnational forces are also changing the "social, territorial, and cultural reproduction of group identity" (Appadurai 1991, 191)
in such a way that landscapes of group identity are deterritorialized. The
shifting terrain of public culture is constantly redefining the local in terms
of the global. This new world of cultural ebb and flow, however, has
probably been captured more adequately in the media-based image of
the informational city.

The Informational City. In *The Informational City* (1989), Castells describes another kind of dual city, one in which space flows supersede
the meaning of the space of places. Space flows, however, are based on
the principles of information-processing activities, rather than on the
everyday spaces of living and working. The resulting meaninglessness
of everyday places and political institutions is resented and resisted
through a variety of individual and collective strategies. People attempt
to reaffirm their cultural identity, often in territorial terms, by "mobilizing to achieve their demands, organizing their communities, and stak-
ing out their places to preserve meaning, to restore whatever limited
control they can over work and residence" (Castells 1989, 350).

Castells (1996) further outlines his theory of the informational society as a world in which control of knowledge and information will
decide who holds power. Communications technology and media control of images, representations, and public opinion, as well as the increasing ability of computer networks to allow the individual to create
personal image representations, illustrate the growing tension between
globalization and individualization. Individuals react by representing
their values and interests through the reassertion of primary identities
of self-identified communities, resulting in the rejection of other communities, increasing racism, and xenophobia.

The image of the informational city from an ethnographic perspective, however, suggests that the emphasis on adaptive, continuous change
is creating an everyday concept of the "flexible body"(Martin 1996); that
new forms of inequality—in poverty, education, immigrant experience,

and communication—are being produced; and that the dynamics of the new identity making are, in fact, dialectical rather than unidimensional processes (Low 1996a).

Hannerz (1992) theorizes another version of an informational society, this one based on cultural flows organized in terms of states, markets, and movements. Here the city is the center of cultural growth, the place where the interplay of the centralizing agencies of culture—schools and media—and the decentralizing forces of the diversity of subcultures are located. Hannerz's work, in contrast to that of Castells, emphasizes the theoretical working out of the linkages between local experience and these global cultural flows.

Urban Planning and Architecture

The Modernist City. Brasília is the archetypal modernist city based on the CIAM (Congrès Internationaux d'Architecture Moderne) premise of social transformation and executed by the force of a strong central government. Brasília's design was supposed to integrate the disparate classes and colors of Brazil's complex social structure while at the same time revitalizing the economy through the creation of new jobs and industries in the central part of the country. Brasília was conceived by President Kubitschek as an attempt to celebrate Brazil's arrival as a modern country, ready to take its proper place in the world system and global economy. As a symbolic statement it was successful, but as a city its abstracted modern architecture and idealist plan came into conflict with the needs and desires of its people. This story is the substrate of Holston's architectural ethnography, *The Modernist City* (1989; see also this volume, chapter 8), and the one on which he builds an effective anthropological critique of Brasília's plan and architecture as a basis for deconstructing the underlying cultural assumptions of this monumental urban project. Holston's (1995) critique of modernist planning has led him to search for a new social imagination, one that provides "spaces of insurgent citizenship" that will provide new sources of legitimation and political participation.

The modernist city is most often theorized as "the colonial city" (Wright 1991, King 1990), where modern technologies of planning and architecture are employed to build new societies and indoctrinate citizens within the spatial confines of rationally planned towns. Mitchell's (1989) *Colonizing Egypt* and Rabinow's (1989) *French Modern* both theorize the "enframing" of power relations that become reflected in colonial spatial configurations and visual perspectives. Low (1993, 1995) provides examples of how colonial power relationships are materialized by examining the impact of the Spanish colonial system of spatial organization on the Latin American grid plan town and plaza. Pellow (1991; this volume, chapter 9) goes farther by employing both historical and ethnographic analyses to explore the consequences of the British colonial spatial system on the everyday lives of residents in the *zongos* of Accra, Ghana. King (1990), on the other hand, links colonialism with the broader issues of urbanism and the world economy.

Certainly the analysis of the political role of planning and of vested local interests has become a critical part of any study of urbanization and the politics of development in Third World countries such as Ghana (Campbell 1995) and China (Davis, Kraus, Naughton and Perry 1995) as these countries struggle to modernize. But ethnographies draw a more complex picture of the representation of modernity; for example, Ossman (1994) argues that television images are manipulated as a contestation of traditional culture and convey individuals' desire for freedom from local convention.

The Postmodern City. The movie *Pulp Fiction* (1994) reflects the space-time compression theorized by Harvey (1990) and Giddens (1990) by moving the characters back and forth through time, not via the narrative device of flashbacks but with casual ease, telling a fragmented and elliptical story that can have various endings. The sense that there is no need to explain this new phenomenology of unmarked transitions and shifting boundaries suggests that Quentin Tarantino has already arrived in a postmodern era.

Jameson (1984) argues that late capitalism has a distinctive cultural logic that is reshaping the form and functioning of the city. Boyer (1994) calls it the "city of illusion," Zukin (1995) the "city of cultural consumption," and Rutheiser (1997, and this book, chapter 10) calls it a "non-place urban realm" where the packaging of cities as commodities creates the "city of scenographic sites" (Boyer 1994). The postmodern city has burst on the academic scene, physically produced by late capitalist urban space and conceptually produced by a new type of knowledge, thinking, and representation (Watson and Gibson 1995, King 1996).

MacCanell identifies California as the center of postmodern "consciousness-for-itself. . . . Virtually the entire postmodern literature that emphasizes the *simulacrum*, historical rupture, valorization of surfaces, and the death of the subject attempted to qualify itself as California ethnography" (1992, 183). Similarly, Soja's influential *Postmodern Geographies* (1989) focuses on sites in Los Angeles and Orange County. Nonetheless, some of the most important anthropological depictions of postmodernity have focused on other places.

Dorst's extraordinary analysis of Chadds Ford, Pennsylvania, as an image, idea, ideological discourse, and assemblage of texts—a written suburb—and of the preservation of Chadds Ford as a representative display of a place that exists putatively only in Andrew Wyeth's paintings, demonstrates the theoretical power of ethnography when applied to a postmodern site. Dorst employs the concept of postmodern hyperspaces constructed to behave like depthless surfaces to explain the visual impact of the mirror-glass surface of the Brandywine Museum and its enframed scenes (1989, 108).

Fjellman, on the other hand, takes on the ultimate city of illusion: Walt Disney World in Orlando, Florida. He argues that it has become the major middle-class pilgrimage center in the United States, "partly because of the brilliance of its cross-referential marketing and partly because its utopian aspects appeal strongly to real peoples' real needs in late capitalist society" (1992, 10). The cinema structures one's experience there, with activities constructed as movie scenes: thus, all experience is made up of surfaces similar to the "veneer" and "vignette" of Dorst's Chadds Ford.

Another anthropological approach has been to theorize the "imagineering" of the postmodern city, as in Rutheiser's (1997) study of how Atlanta's nondistinctive identity was "repackaged" for the 1996 Olympics into an image of "traditional urbanity" (this book, chapter 10). McDonogh (1991, and this book, chapter 11), on the other hand, explores the ideological impact of Olympics planning on the reconstitution of public space and citizenship in Barcelona. Sieber (1991) has been concerned with how postindustrial port cities use the revitalization of the waterfront to create downtown tourist sites with middle-class images of housing complexes and shopping malls, while Cooper (1994, and this book, chapter 12) traces the transformation of spatial ideologies for imagining the Toronto waterfront. Ruble (1992) critiques the reshaping of the image of a provincial Russian city in the postsocialist transition. In each of these revitalization schemes, histories and monuments of public memory are manipulated to create a seamless presentation of the city's revalorized cultural heritage (Sieber 1990, Norkunas 1993, Boyer 1992).

Hong Kong has also been identified as an important site of postmodernity. The four eroding ecologies of the merchant city, the industrial city, the financial city, and the capital city have created colonial spaces with working-class conditions adjacent to commodity spaces with new towns and high-rise buildings (Cuthbert 1995). The contradictions of these spaces can be seen on any Sunday when groups of Filipina domestic workers picnic on blankets, filling the cement sidewalks and streets because the city will not provide public parks and recreation; during the week a staggering number of street hawkers sell their wares next to transnational corporate buildings (Smart 1989). The skyscraper architecture of Hong Kong has been derived from modernist ideas of town planning, but these buildings are transformed by the hyperdensity of the site (Abbas 1994). Dovey (1992) argues that these corporate towers are produced by the forces of creative destruction that are so emblematic of the condition of postmodernity (Harvey 1990).

The Fortress City. Imagine private police guarding New York City's wealthy Upper East Side, or private highways running along the median strip of Los Angeles's freeways (*New York Times*, 2 January 1996, A1, C33). Remember the fortified encampments of futuristic films such as *Mad Max* (1979), *The Road Warrior* (1981), and *Mad Max Beyond Thunderdome* (1986) or the underground prison of "Twelve Monkeys" (1996). These are all images of the fortress city, conceived of by Davis (1990) and modeled on Los Angeles.

Davis's (1990) fortress city is drawn from his radical history of the development of Los Angeles, in which he traces the control of media, seizure of land, busting of unions, rigging of water rights, and exclusion of minorities from political participation, all of which have resulted in the destruction of public space. Davis explains that the resulting militarization (1992) took a long time to develop, with many periods of working-class and minority resistance producing minor successes. However, the riots in South Central Los Angeles and movies such as *Boyz in the Hood* (1991) suggest that unequal social relations solidified with the continued infusion of capital from moviemaking businesses and Pacific Rim financial services, which accelerated land speculation, development, and housing price increases.

An explanation of the social production of the fortress city is found in Fainstein's study of the logic of large development projects in such cities as New York and London: "This built environment forms contours which structure social relations, causing commonalities of gender, sexual orientation, race, ethnicity, and class to assume spatial identities. Social groups, in turn, imprint themselves physically on the urban structure through the formation of communities, competition for territory, and segregation—in other words, through clustering, the erection of boundaries, and establishing distance" (1994, 1).

Large mixed commercial and residential development projects reinforce the segregation of the divided city, further cutting off communities by visual boundaries, growing distances, and ultimately walls. Merry (1990) argues that in middle-class and upper-middle-class urban neighborhoods, residents seek privacy because they desire peace and can afford it. She found these neighborhoods marked by patterns of staying away, of building fences, of cutting off relationships, and of moving out in response to problems and conflicts. At the same time, she found that "the government has expanded its regulatory role. . . . Zoning laws, local police departments, ordinances about dogs, quiet laws, laws against domestic and interpersonal violence, all provide new forms of regulation of family and neighborhood life" (1993, 87).

In this fortress city youth gangs and homeless youth are part of the new social imaginaries: "new social subjects are created and create themselves in and through the social space of the city" (Ruddick 1996). Space takes on the ability to confirm identity (Low 1996a), and gangs compete for limited urban spaces (Jankowski 1991) as institutional and private forces increasingly constrain and structure the lives of street addicts and other marginalized groups within the public arena. (Waterson 1993, Hagan and McCarthy 1997).

Within this context, acts of violence and crime are increasingly feared. Anderson (1990) discusses the "streetwise" behavior of Philadelphians in which residents cross the street when faced with oncoming young black males. Wacquant (1995) portrays the perceived isolation of families in Chicago's Black Belt, where the streets are deserted and no longer patrolled by police. Bourgois (1996) describes the fear and sense of vulnerability experienced by El Barrio residents and by anthropologists faced with the everyday violence of those who sell crack in East Harlem, New York City. Afro-American adolescents in Baltimore perceive this violence as both within and against their communities (Kaljee, Stanton, Ricardo, and Whitehead 1995), while Bourgois (1995b) argues that a structural economic analysis is simply not accepted by suburbanites and black and Latino working poor urbanites.

The majority of studies of the fortress city have focused on Los Angeles, Chicago, and New York, even though the United States does not have a monopoly on this type of social and physical development. In fact, it is surprise at the presence of walls, fences, and residential segregation within the context of the myth of democracy and equal housing opportunity that prods researchers to examine this image more closely. Brazil, however, also offers examples of fortification and urban violence to match any U.S. venue (Scheper-Hughes 1992, Caldeira, 1996). Banck (1994) documents the growing fear with the increased differentials of consumption by class. Linger (1992) has written an ethnography about *brigas*, violent confrontations that are a kind of cultural performance that take place during Carnival. The fortress city is on the horizon as a new-built form and device of social control that should be studied as part of our inquiry into the city of the twenty-first century (Blakely and Snyder 1977, Low 1977).

Religion and Culture

The Sacred City. Levy's (1990) insightful and exhaustive account of Hinduism and the organization of the traditional Newar city of Bhaktapur theorizes the city as a "mesocosm," an essential middle world that symbolically mediates between the cosmological universe and the experience of everyday life. Levy describes Bhaktapur as an archaic city, one that uses "marked" symbols to solve the problem of communication at the urban scale, and he provides an elaborate analysis of how these symbolic forms, such as sacrifice, mystery religion, festival calendars, and the pantheon of divinities, work to order a very large and complex city. For Levy, civic life is a "choreographed ballet" (1990, 17) of religious observance and practice. Parish, also working in Bhaktapur, reiterates that the city is a sacred setting for collective ritual, "a mandala of shrines" (1994, 21) that embodies the Hindu religious system and cosmology within which individuals locate and create moral selves. Lynch (1996) also examines the construction of identity but in the Hindu city of Mathura, where ancestral place becomes a metaphor for the self-identity of the Chaubes, a community of priests who act as guides and ritual specialists performing the necessary rites for pilgrims at Krishna's birthplace.

The image of the sacred city is clearly theorized through its symbolic form in Hindu (Lynch 1996, Levy 1990, Parish 1994) and Islamic cities (Abu-Lughod 1987, Reeves 1995), but there are other aspects of urban sacredness. Ethnographic studies of religion as a basis of urban resistance movements (Burdick 1993, Reeves 1995), as a basis for class politics (Taylor 1994), as an expression of gay identity (Shokeid 1995), and as a vehicle of immigrant survival (Brown 1991) suggest that urban religion plays a variety of roles in the lives of urban residents. Reeves in particular argues that religion as a form of urban resistance goes unnoticed in Northern Egypt and therefore is not controlled or countered. Burdick's work in Brazil, however, suggests that there are many religious discourses in the urban arena, some of which produce strong counterreactions.

The Traditional City. A few studies focusing on cities in Japan, India, and China are concerned with the maintenance of "tradition" within the urban context. While they do not contribute directly to a theory of the city, these studies investigate dimensions of urban life that are often overlooked by other researchers.

Bestor's (1989, 1992) work on a shitamachi neighborhood in Tokyo and Robertson's (1991) study of newcomers in a small Japanese city portray urban experience as a struggle for balance between maintaining tradition and the pressures of rapid social change. Kondo's (1990) work is a particularly revealing examination of the relationship of work and self-concept, in which a person's occupational status may come into conflict with traditional values and sex role obligations. Japanese urban studies are also concerned with the maintenance of traditional forms of status privilege and status recognition, both in business (Hamabata 1990, Sumihara 1993) and among the nobility (Lebra 1993). A fascinating study of a Mongol city in China also focuses on the many details of urban social hierarchies and provides insights into the management of marriage and romance within this traditional setting (Jankowiak 1993).

Indigenous studies of urban processes, although not readily available in the United States, provide an important window into indigenous conceptualizations of urban problems and culturally significant themes. Edited volumes by indigenous authors on urban anthropology in China (Guldin and Southall 1993) and on urban sociology in India (Rao, Bhatt, and Khadekar 1991) include a number of articles emphasizing ongoing conflicts between the desire to preserve cultural traditions and the reality of rapid social change.

Conclusions

The anthropological literature on the city incorporates a number of paradigms from other disciplines. The influence of political economy, architectural and planning theory, cultural studies, urban sociology, and cultural geography can be seen in the increasing attention to economic, political, and discursive models of the city. At the same time, poststructural and postmodern perspectives have recast the kinds of questions and modes of inquiry used to study the city.

The dominant research trends in urban anthropology are currently poststructural studies of race, class, and gender in the urban context; political economic studies of transnational culture; and studies of the symbolic and social production of urban space and planning. These three trends are highlighted in this book. Gregory (1992 and this book, chapter 1), Susser (1993 and this book, chapter 2), and Caldeira (1996 and this book, chapter 3) draw upon analyses of race, class, and gender to describe the divided city. Low (1996 and this book, chapter 4) and Rotenberg (1995 and this book, chapter 5) utilize poststructural concepts of contestation and resistance as well as the social production and symbolic meaning of the built environment to characterize the contested city. Smart and Smart (1991 and this book, chapter 6) and Bestor (chapter 7) focus on the political economy of urban markets and social networks to discuss the global city. Holston (1989 and this book, chapter 8) and Pellow (1991 and this book, chapter 9) rely on spatially informed critiques of history and planning to illustrate social relations in the modernist city. Rutheiser (1997 and this book, chapter 10), McDonogh (1991 and this book, chapter 11), and Cooper (1994 and this book, chapter 12) employ discursive theories of the social production of urban space and city planning to critique the postmodern city.

A number of theoretically useful images and metaphors of the city also have been identified. Some of these images—the divided city and the global city—have had a clear theoretical impact on the body of research and have provided the basis for ongoing theoretical projects. For instance, the global city has focused attention on the unique roles that cities play in the development of transnational cultures and traditions (Bestor, Smart and Smart). Other images suggest future research endeavors. For instance, the contested city is a powerful image for poststructural studies that enriches anthropological theorizing about conflict and resistance in both the public and private urban realms (Low, Rotenberg).

Some areas of anthropological theory have been more influential within the broader discourse of urban studies and urban policy. The anthropological take on globalization has been to focus attention on the transnational aspects of migration, culture making, and identity management, and on the shifting cultural environments and meanings that contextualize (and decontextualize) behavior (Smart and Smart, Pellow). Anthropologists offer an experience-near critique of city life that provides a more complex understanding of the differences between cities' and residents' responses to racial segregation and class inequality (Gregory, Susser). Anthropological critiques of planning and design projects provide a methodology and theoretical framework for decoding the ideological intentions and material consequences of architectural plans and landscape designs (Holston, McDonogh, Rutheiser, Cooper, Low, Rotenberg). And anthropological studies that link the macro processes of cultural hegemony with the micro processes of resistance and social transformation within the context of deindustrialization and globalization demonstrate that these linkages can be made through a combination of sophisticated theorizing and empirical fieldwork (Holston, Caldeira, Low, Rotenberg, Gregory, Susser, Rutheiser, Cooper, McDonogh). The contributions of anthropological fieldwork still retain the power to demonstrate the how, why, and when of urban processes, but are even more effective when linked to theoretical frameworks that provide a grounding for further study and discussion.

The chapters that follow ground recent research trends and theory in the context of eleven specific cities on five continents, over a range of historical periods. A number of the studies were conducted in the United States: Steven Gregory and Ida Susser both worked in contemporary New York City, while Charles Rutheiser studied Atlanta, Georgia, during the three decades that led up to the 1996 Summer Olympics. Another North American contribution is Matthew Cooper's study of waterfront development in Toronto, Ontario, Canada. European studies include Robert Rotenberg's historical analysis of gardens in Vienna, Austria, and Gary McDonogh's study of the discourses of city planning in Barcelona, Spain. Three studies focus on Latin America: my study of the plaza in San José, Costa Rica, and two studies of Brazil—Teresa Caldeira's research on fortified enclaves in São Paulo, and James Holston's historical analysis of the building of Brasília. Asia is represented by two contributions: Ted Bestor's study of the Tokyo fish market and Josephine and Alan Smart's study of investment relationships between Hong Kong and South China. There is one African contribution, Deborah Pellow's study of Accra, Ghana, which traces the history and contemporary use of the *zongo*. Each of these studies identifies what urban anthropological research and theory can contribute to an understanding of the city within a culturally distinct urban, national, and transnational context.

Bibliography

Abbas, A. 1994. Building on disappearance: Hong Kong architecture and the city. *Public Culture* 6:441–459.

Abu-Lughod, J. L. 1987. The Islamic city: Historic myth, Islamic essence, and contemporary relevance. *International Journal of Middle Eastern Studies* 19:155–176.

———. 1994. *From urban village to East Village: The Battle for New York's Lower East Side.* Oxford: Blackwell.

Altman, I., and S. M. Low. 1992. *Place attachment.* New York: Plenum.

Anderson, E. 1990. *Streetwise: Race, class and change in an urban community.* Chicago: University of Chicago Press.

Appadurai, A. 1991. Global ethnoscapes: Notes and queries for a transnational anthropology. In *Recapturing anthropology*, edited by R. Fox. Pp. 191–210. Santa Fe, N. M.: School of American Research.

Aretxaga, B. *Shattering silence: Women, nationalism, and political subjectivity in Northern Ireland.* Princeton, N.J.: Princeton University Press,

Arreola, D. D., and J. R. Curtis. 1993. *The Mexican border cities.* Tucson: University of Arizona Press.

Banck, G. A. 1993. Signifying urban space: Vitória, Brazil. In *Urban Symbolism*, edited by P. J. M. Nas. Pp. 104–115. Leiden: E. J. Brill.

———. 1994. Mass consumption and urban contest in Brazil: Some reflections of lifestyle and class. *Bulletin of Latin American Research* 13:45–60.

Banck, G. A., and A. M. Doimo. 1989. Between utopia and strategy: A case study of a Brazilian urban social movement. In *Urban social movements in the Third World*, edited by F. Schuurman and R. V. Naerssen. Pp. 125–150. London: Routledge.

Barnes, S. 1986. *Patrons and power: Creating a political community in metropolitan Lagos.* Bloomington: Indiana University Press.

Barriga, M. D. 1995. The politics of urban expansion in Mexico City: Of *ejido* urbanization in the Ajusco foothills, 1938–1990. *Urban Anthropology* 24:363–396.

Beck, S. 1992. *Manny Almeida's Ringside Lounge: The Cape Verdean's struggle for this neighborhood*. Providence, R. I.: Gávea-Brown.

Bestor, T. C. 1989. *Neighborhood Tokyo*. Stanford, Calif.: Stanford University Press.

———. 1992. Conflict, legitimacy, and tradition in a Tokyo neighborhood. In *Japanese social organization*, edited by T Sugiyama. Pp. 23–47. Honolulu: University of Hawaii Press.

———. 1993. Rediscovering shitamachi: subculture, class and Tokyo's "traditional" urbanism. In *The cultural meaning of urban space*, edited by R. Rotenberg and G. W. McDonogh. Pp. 47–60. Westport, Conn.: Bergin and Garvey.

———. In press. *Tokyo's marketplace: Culture and trade in the Tsukiji wholesale fish market*. Stanford, Calif.: Stanford University Press.

Blakely, E. J., and M. G. Snyder. 1997. *Fortress America: Gated communities in the United States*. Washington, D.C.: Brookings Institution Press.

Borneman, J. 1991. *After the wall: East meets West in the new Berlin*. New York: Basic Books.

———. 1997. *Settling accounts: Violence, justice, and accountability in postsocialist Europe*. Princeton, N.J.: Princeton University Press.

Bott, E. 1957. *Family and social network: Roles, norms and external relationships in ordinary urban families*. London: Tavistock.

Bourgois, P. 1995a. *In search of respect: Selling crack in El Barrio*. Cambridge: Cambridge University Press.

———. 1995b. The political economy of resistance and self–destruction in the crack economy. In *The anthropology of lower income urban enclaves*, edited by J. Freidenberg. Pp. 97–118. New York: New York Academy of Sciences.

———. 1996. Confronting anthropology, education, and inner-city apartheid: Ethnographic vulnerability in El Barrio. *American Anthropologist* 98, no. 2: 1–10.

Boyer, M. C. 1992. Cities for sale: Merchandising history at South Street Seaport. In *Variations on a Theme Park*, edited by M. Sorkin. Pp. 181–204. New York: Noonday Press.

———. 1994. *The city of collective memory*. Cambridge, Mass.: MIT Press.

Brown, K. M. 1991. *Mama Lola: A voudou priestess in Brooklyn*. Berkeley: University of California Press.

Bullard, R. D., J. E. Grigsby III, and C. Lee. 1994. *Residential apartheid: The American legacy*. Los Angeles: Center for Afro-American Studies Urban Policy Series.

Burawoy, M., et al. 1991. *Ethnography unbound: Power and resistance in the modern metropolis*. Berkeley: University of California Press.

Burdick, J. 1993. *Looking for God in Brazil: The progressive catholic church in urban Brazil's religious arena*. Berkeley: University of California Press.

Caldeira, T. 1996. Fortified communities. *Public Culture* 8:303–328.

Campbell, J. 1995. Urbanization, culture, and the politics of urban development in Ghana, 1875–1980. *Urban Anthropology* 23:409–450.

Castells, M. 1983. *The city and the grassroots*. Berkeley: University of California Press.

———. 1989. *The informational city: Information technology, economic restructuring and the urban-regional process*. Oxford: Blackwell.

———. 1996. Networks, flows, and the new social system: Working notes for a theory of the informational society. *Critique of Anthropology* 16:9–38.

Charles, C. 1992. Transnationalism in the construct of Haitian migrants racial categories of identity in New York City. In *Towards a transnational perspective on migration: Race, class, ethnicity and nationalism reconsidered*, edited by N. Glick Schiller, L. Basch, and C. Blanc-Stanton. Pp. 101–124. New York: New York Academy of Sciences.

Chavez, L. R. 1990. Immigrants in U.S. cities. *Urban Anthropology* 19:1–184.

Clark, G. 1994. *Onions are my husband: Survival and accumulation by West African market women*. Chicago: University of Chicago Press.

Chen, H. S. 1992. *Chinatown no more: Taiwan immigrants in contemporary New York*. Ithaca, N.Y.: Cornell University Press.

Cohen, A. 1993. *Masquerade politics: Explorations in the structure of urban cultural movements*. Berkeley: University of California Press.

Coombe, R., and P. Stoller. 1994. X marks the spot: The ambiguities of African trading in the commerce of the black public sphere. *Public Culture* 7:249–274.

Cooper, M. 1994. Spatial discourses and social boundaries: Re-imagining the Toronto waterfront. *City and Society Annual Review* 1994:93–117.

Cooper, M., and M. C. Rodman. 1992. *New neighbours: A case study of cooperative housing*. Toronto: University of Toronto Press.

Cronon, W. 1991. *Nature's metropolis: Chicago and the great west*. New York: W. W. Norton.

Cuthbert, A. 1995. Under the volcano: Post-modern space in Hong Kong. In *Postmodern cities and spaces*, edited by S. Watson and K. Gibson. Pp. 138–148. Oxford: Blackwell.

David, S. G. 1986. *Parades and power: Street theatre in nineteenth century Philadelphia*. Philadelphia: Temple University Press.

Davis, D.S., R. Kraus, B. Naughton, and J. Perry. 1995. *Urban spaces in contemporary China: The potential for autonomy and community in post-Mao China*. Cambridge: Cambridge University Press.

Davis, M. 1990. *City of quartz: Excavating the future in Los Angeles*. London: Verso.

———. 1992. Fortress Los Angeles: The militarization of urban space. In *Variations on a Theme Park*, edited by M. Sorkin. Pp. 154–180. New York: Noonday Press.

di Leonardo, M. 1993. What a difference political economy makes: Feminist anthropology in the postmodern era. *Anthropology Quarterly* 66: 76–80.

Dorst, J. D. 1989. *The written suburb: An American site, an ethnographic dilemma*. Philadelphia: University of Pennsylvania Press.

Dovey, K. 1992. Corporate towers and symbolic capital. *Environment and Planning B: Planning and Design* 19:173–188.

Epstein, D. 1973. *Brasília, plan and reality: A study of planned and spontaneous urban development*. Berkeley: University of California Press.

Fainstein, S. S. 1994. *City builders: Property, politics and planning in London and New York*. Oxford: Blackwell.

Fernandez Kelly, M. P. 1993a. Rethinking citizenship in the global village: Reflections on immigrants and the underclass. New York: Russell Sage Foundation. Working paper no. 38.

———. 1993b. Towanada's triumph: Unfolding the meanings of adolescent pregnancy in the Baltimore ghetto. New York: Russell Sage Foundation. Working paper no. 40.

Fine, M. 1991. *Framing dropouts: Notes on the politics of an urban public high school*. Albany, N.Y.: State University of New York Press.

———. 1992. *Disruptive voices: The possibilities of feminist research*. Ann Arbor: University of Michigan Press.

Fjellman, S. M. 1992. *Vinyl leaves: Walt Disney World and America*. Boulder, Colo.: Westview.

Foner, N. 1987. *New immigrants in New York*. New York: Columbia University Press.

Fong, T. P. 1994. *The first suburban Chinatown: The remaking of Monterey Park, California*. Philadelphia: Temple University Press.

Fox, R. 1972. Rational and romance in urban anthropology. *Urban Anthropology* 1:205–233.

Fox, R. 1977. *Urban anthropology: Cities in their cultural settings.* Englewood Cliffs, N.J.: Prentice Hall.

Friedmann, J. 1995. Where we stand: A decade of world city research. In *World cities in a world system*, edited by P. L. Knox and P. J. Taylor. Pp. 21–47. Cambridge: Cambridge University Press.

George, L. 1992. *No crystal stair: African-Americans in the city of the angels.* London: Verso.

Georges, E. 1992. Gender, class, and migration in the Dominican Republic: Women's experiences in a transnational community. In *Towards a transnational perspective on migration: Race, class, ethnicity and nationalism reconsidered*, edited by N. Glick Schiller, L. Basch, and C. Blanc-Stanton. Pp. 81–100. New York: New York Academy of Sciences.

Giddens, A. 1990. *The consequences of modernity.* Stanford: Stanford University Press.

Gill, L. 1994. *Precarious dependencies: Gender, class and domestic service in Bolivia.* New York: Columbia University Press.

Ginsburg, F. 1991. Indigenous media: Faustian bargain or global village? *Cultural Anthropology* 6: 95–114.

Glick Schiller, N., L. Basch, and C. Blanc-Stanton. 1992. *Towards a transnational perspective on migration: race, class, ethnicity and nationalism reconsidered.* New York: New York Academy of Sciences.

Gluckman, M. 1971. Preface to *Family and social network.* 2d ed. E Bott. Pp. xiii–xxx. New York: New Press.

Goode, J., and J. A. Schneider. 1994. *Reshaping ethnic and racial relations in Philadelphia: Immigrants in a divided city.* Philadelphia: Temple University Press.

Greenbaum, S. D. 1993. Housing abandonment in inner-city black neighborhoods: A case study of the effects of the dual housing market. In *The cultural meaning of urban space*, edited by R. Rotenberg and G. W. McDonogh. Pp. 139–156. Westport, Conn.: Bergin and Garvey.

Gregory, S. 1992. The changing significance of race and class in an African-American community. *American Ethnologist* 19:255–274.

———. 1998. *Black Corona.* Princeton, N.J.: Princeton University Press.

Guldin, G. E. 1989. The invisible hinterland: Hong Kong's reliance on southern Guangdong Province. *City and Society* 3:23–39.

———. 1992. *Urbanizing China.* New York: Greenwood Press.

Guldin, G. E., and A. Southall. 1993. *Urban anthropology in China.* Leiden: E. J. Brill.

Gulick, J. 1989. *The humanity of cities: An introduction to urban societies.* Granby, Mass: Bergin and Garvey.

Hagan, J., and B. McCarthy. 1997. *Mean streets.* Cambridge: Cambridge University Press.

Hamabata, M. M. 1990. *Crested kimono: Power and love in the Japanese business family.* Ithaca, N.Y.: Cornell University Press.

Hannerz, U. 1980. *Exploring the city.* New York: Columbia University Press.

———. 1992. *Cultural complexity: Studies in the social organization of meaning.* New York: Columbia University Press.

Harrison, F. V. 1989. Drug trafficking in world capitalism: A perspective on Jamaican posses in the U. S. *Social Justice* 16: 115–131.

———. 1991. Women in Jamaica's urban informal economy: insights from a Kingston slum. In *Third World women and the politics of feminism*, edited by C. T. Mohanty, A Russo, and L. Torres. Pp. 173–196. Bloomington: Indiana University Press.

Harvey, D. 1990. *The condition of postmodernity: An enquiry into the origins of cultural change.* Cambridge: Basil Blackwell.

Hayden, D. 1995. *The power of place.* Cambridge, Mass.: MIT Press.

Herzog, L. A. 1990. Cross-national urban structure in the era of global cities: The US-Mexico transfrontier metropolis. *Urban Studies* 28:519–533.

———. 1991. The transfrontier organization of space along the U.S.–Mexico border Mexico. *Geoforum* 22:255–269.

Holston, J. 1989. *The modernist city: An anthropological critique of Brasília.* Chicago: University of Chicago Press.

———. 1991. The misrule of law: Land and usurpation in Brazil. *Comparative Studies in Society and History* 33:695–725.

———. 1995. Spaces of insurgent citizenship. *Planning Theory* 13: 35–51.

Hopper, K. 1991. Symptoms, survival and the redefinition of public space. *Urban Anthropology* 20:155–175.

Horton, J. 1995. *The politics of diversity: Immigration, resistance and change in Monterey Park, California.* Philadelphia: Temple University Press.

Jackson, P. 1985. Urban ethnography. *Progress in Human Geography* 10: 157–176.

Jacobs, J. 1993. The city unbound: Qualitative approaches to the city. *Urban Studies* 30: 827–848.

Jameson, F. 1984. Post-modernism, or the cultural logic of late capitalism. *New Left Review* 146:53–92.

Jankowiak, W. 1993. *Sex, death, and hierarchy in a Chinese city.* New York: Columbia University Press.

Jankowski, M. S. 1991. *Islands in the street: Gangs and American urban society.* Berkeley: University of California Press.

Jones, D. J. 1993. The culture of achievement among the poor: the case of mothers and children in a Head Start program. *Critique of Anthropology* 13:247–266.

———, and J. T. Turner. 1989. Housing and the material basis of social reproduction: political conflict and the quality of life in New York city. S. Low and E. Chambers, *Housing, culture and design: A comparative perspective.* Pp. 13–42. Philadelphia: University of Pennsylvania Press.

———, J. Turner, and J. Montbach.1992. Declining social services and the threat to social reproduction: an urban dilemma. *City and Society* 6:99–114.

Kadushin, C., and D. Jones. 1992. Social networks and urban neighborhoods in New York City. *City and Society* 6:58–75.

Kaljee, L. M., B. Stanton, I. Ricardo, and T. L. Whitehead. 1995. Urban African American adolescents and their parents: Perceptions of violence within and against their communities. *Human Organization* 54:363–372.

Kaplan, T. 1992. *Red city, blue period: Social movements in Picasso's Barcelona.* Berkeley: University of California Press.

Kasarda, J., Crenshaw, E. M. 1991. Third World urbanization: Dimensions, theories, and determinants. *Annual Review of Sociology* 17:467–501.

Kasinitz, P. 1992. *Caribbean New York: Black immigrants and the politics of race.* Ithaca, N.Y.: Cornell University Press.

Katz, C. 1993. Growing girls/closing circles: limits on the spaces of knowing in rural Sudan and United States cities. In *Full circles: Geographies of women over the life course,* edited by C. Katz and J. Monk. Pp. 88–106. London: Routledge.

Keith, M., and M. Cross. 1993. *Racism, the city and the state.* New York: Routledge.

King, A. D. 1990. *Urbanism, colonialism and the world economy: Culture and spatial foundations of the urban world system.* New York: Routledge.

———. 1996. *Re-presenting the city.* London: Macmillan.

Kondo, D. 1990. *Crafting selves: Power, gender, and discourse.* Chicago: University of Chicago Press.

Koptiuch, K. 1991. Third Worldizing at home. *Social Text* 9:87–99.

Kugelmass, J. 1994. *The Greenwich Village Halloween parade*. New York: Columbia University Press.

Kwong, P. 1987. *The new Chinatown*. New York: Hill and Wang.

Laguerre, M. S. 1994a. Headquarters and subsidiaries: Haitian immigrant family households in New York City. In *Families in the United States: A multicultural perspective*, edited by R. L. Taylor. Pp. 47–61. Englewood Cliffs, N.J.: Prentice-Hall.

———. 1994b. *The informal city*. New York: St. Martin's Press.

Lamphere, L. 1992. *Structuring diversity: Ethnographic perspectives on the new immigration*. Chicago: University of Chicago Press.

Lawrence, D. 1992. Transcendence of place: The role of La Placeta in Valencia's Las Fallas. In *Place attachment*, edited by I. Altman and S. M. Low. Pp. 211–230. New York: Plenum.

Lebra, R. S. 1993. *Above the clouds: Status culture of the modern Japanese nobility*. Berkeley: University of California Press.

Leeds, A. 1973. Locality power in relation to supralocal power institutions. In *Urban Anthropology*, edited by A. Southall. Pp. 15–41. New York: Oxford University Press.

Leone, M. P. 1995. A historical archaeology of capitalism. *American Anthropologist* 97:251–268.

Lessinger, J. 1992. Investing or going home? A transnational strategy among Indian immigrants in the United States. In *Towards a transnational perspective on migration: Race, class, ethnicity and nationalism reconsidered*, edited by N. Glick Schiller, L. Basch, and C. Blanc-Stanton. Pp. 53–80. New York: New York Academy of Sciences.

Levy, R. 1990. *Mesocosm: Hinduism and the organization of a traditional Newar city in Nepal*. Berkeley: University of California Press.

Liebow, E. D. 1989. Category or community? Measuring urban Indian social cohesion with network sampling. *Journal of Ethnic Studies* 16:76–100.

———. 1991. Urban Indian institutions in Phoenix: Transformation from headquarters city to community. *Journal of Ethnic Studies* 18:1–27.

Linger, D. T. 1992. *Dangerous encounters: Meanings of violence in a Brazilian city*. Stanford, Calif.: Stanford University Press.

Lobo, S. 1983. *A house of my own: Social organization in the squatter settlements of Lima, Peru*. Tucson: University of Arizona Press.

Logan, K. 1984. *Haciendo Pueblo: The development of a Guadalajaran suburb*. Tuscaloosa: University of Alabama Press.

Lomnitz, L. A. 1977. *Networks and marginality: Life in a Mexican shantytown*. New York: Academic Press.

Low, S. M. 1988. Housing organization and social change: A comparison of programs for urban reconstruction in Guatemala City. *Human Organization* 47:15–24.

———. 1993. Cultural meaning of the plaza: The history of the Spanish American gridplan-plaza urban design. In *The cultural meaning of urban space*, edited by R. Rotenberg and G. W. McDonogh. Pp. 75–94. Westport, Conn.: Bergin and Garvey.

———. 1995. Indigenous architecture and the Spanish American Plaza in Mesoamerica and the Caribbean. *American Anthropologist* 97:748–762.

———. 1996a. A response to Castells: An anthropology of the city. *Critique of Anthropology* 16: 57–62.

———. 1996b. Spatializing culture: The social production and social construction of public space in Costa Rica. *American Ethnologist* 23:861–879.

———. 1997. Urban fear: Building the fortress city. *City and Society Annual Review*, 53–72.

————, and E. Chambers. 1989. *Housing, culture and design: A comparative perspective*. Philadelphia: University of Pennsylvania Press.

Lynch, O. 1994. Urban anthropology, postmodernist cities, and perspectives. *City and Society Annual Review*, 35–52.

————. 1996. Contesting and contested identities: Mathura's chaubes. In *Narratives of agency*, edited by W. Dissanayake. Pp. 74–103. Minneapolis: University of Minnesota Press.

MacCannell, D. 1992. *Empty meeting grounds: The tourist papers*. London: Routledge.

MacGaffey, J. 1987. *Entrepreneurs and parasites: The struggle for indigenous capitalism in Zaire*. Cambridge: Cambridge University Press.

Macleod, A. E. 1991. *Accommodating protest: Working women, the new veiling and change in Cairo*. New York: Columbia University Press.

Mahler, S. J. 1995. *American dreaming: Immigrant life on the margins*. Princeton, N.J.: Princeton University Press.

Margolis, M. L. 1994. *Little Brazil: An ethnography of Brazilian immigrants in New York City*. Princeton, N.J.: Princeton University Press.

Markowitz, F. 1993. *A community in spite of itself: Soviet Jewish émigrés in New York*. Washington, D.C.: Smithsonian Institution Press.

Marris, P. 1962. *Family and social change in a African city: A study of rehousing in Lagos*. Northwestern University Press.

————. 1995. Knowledge and persuasion: Research at ICS. In *Young at eighty: The prolific public life of Michael Young*, edited by G. Gench, T. Flower, and K. Gavron. Pp. 75–83. Manchester, U.K.: Carcanet Press.

Martin, E. 1996. Flexible bodies in a society of flows. *Critique of Anthropology* 16:49–56.

Massey D. 1994. *Space, place, and gender*. Minneapolis: University of Minnesota Press.

Massey, D., and N. Denton. 1993. *American apartheid: Segregation and the making of the underclass*. Cambridge: Harvard University Press.

McDonogh, G. W. 1991. Discourses of the city: Policy and response in post-transitional Barcelona. *City and Society* 5:40–63.

————. 1993a. *Black and Catholic in Savannah, Georgia*. Knoxville: University of Tennessee Press.

————. 1993b. The geography of emptiness. In *The cultural meaning of urban space*, edited by R. Rotenberg and G. W. McDonogh. Pp. 3–16. Westport, Conn.: Bergin and Garvey.

Merry, S. 1990. *Getting justice and getting even*. Chicago: University of Chicago Press.

————. 1993. Mending walls and building fences: Constructing the private neighborhood. *Journal of Legal Pluralism* 33:71–90.

Mingione, E. 1993. The new urban poverty and the underclass. *International Journal of Urban and Regional Research* 17:319–428.

Mitchell, T. 1988. *Colonizing Egypt*. Cambridge: Cambridge University Press.

Mollenkopf, J, and M. Castells. 1991. *Dual city: Restructuring New York*. New York: Russell Sage Foundation.

Moore S. F. 1994. *Anthropology and Africa: Changing Perspectives on a changing scene*. Charlottesville and London: University Press of Virginia.

Mullings, L. 1987. *Cities of the United States: Studies in urban anthropology*. New York: Columbia University Press.

Nash, J. 1989. *From tank town to high tech: The clash of community and industrial cycles*. Albany, N.Y.: State University of New York Press.

Newman, K. S. 1992. Culture and structure in *The Truly Disadvantaged*. *City and Society* 6:3–25.

————. 1993. *Declining fortunes: The withering of the American dream.* New York: Basic Books.

————. 1996a. Place and race: Mid-life experience in Harlem. In *The Idea of Middle Age*, edited by R. Shweder. Chicago: University Chicago Press.

————. 1996b. Working poor: Low wage employment in the lives of Harlem youth. In *Transitions through Adolescence: Interpersonal Domains and Context*, edited by J. J. Graber and A. Peterson. New York: Erlbaum Associates.

Norkunas, M. 1993. *The politics of public memory.* Albany, N.Y.: State University of New York Press.

O'Connor, R. A. 1990. Place, power and discourse in the Thai image of Bangkok. *Journal of the Siam Society* 78:61–73.

Ogbu, J. 1991. *Minority status and schooling.* New York: Garland.

Oliver-Smith, A. 1986. *The martyred city: Death and rebirth in the Andes.* Albuquerque: University New Mexico Press.

Ong, A. 1987. *Spirits of resistance and capitalist discipline.* Albany, N.Y.: State University of New York Press.

————. 1992. Limits to cultural accumulation: Chinese capitalists on the American Pacific Rim. In *Towards a transnational perspective on migration: Race, class, ethnicity and nationalism reconsidered*, edited by N. Glick Schiller, L. Basch, and C. Blanc-Stanton. Pp. 125–144. New York: New York Academy of Sciences.

Ossman, S. 1994. *Picturing Casablanca: Portraits of power in a modern city.* New York: Doubleday.

Page, H, and R. B. Thomas. 1994. White public space and the construction of white privilege in the U.S. health care: Fresh concepts and a new model of analysis. *Medical Anthropology Quarterly* 81:109–116.

Pappas, G. 1989. *The magic city: Unemployment in a working-class community.* Ithaca, N.Y.: Cornell University Press.

Parish, S. M. 1994. *Moral knowing in a Hindu sacred city: An exploration of mind emotion, and self.* New York: Columbia University Press.

Park, R, and E. Burgess. 1974 edition. *The City.* Chicago: University Chicago Press.

Peattie, L. R. 1972. *The view from the barrio.* Ann Arbor: University of Michigan Press.

————. 1987. *Planning: Rethinking Ciudad Guyana.* Ann Arbor: University of Michigan Press.

Peil, M. 1991. *Lagos: The city is the people.* Boston: G. K Hall.

Pellow, D. 1991. Chieftaincy and the evolution of an Accra *zongo. Ethnohistory* 38: 414–450.

Pessar, P. 1995. The elusive enclave: Ethnicity, class and nationality among Latino entrepreneurs in greater Washington, D.C. *Human Organization* 54:383–392.

Plotnicov, L. 1987. The political economy of skyscrapers: an anthropological introduction to advanced industrial cities. *City and Society* 1:35–51.

Portes, A., and R. Schauffler. 1994. Language and the second generation: Bilingualism yesterday and today. *International Migration Review* 28:641–661.

Portes, A., and A. Stepick. 1993. *City on the edge: The transformation of Miami.* Berkeley: University of California Press.

Portes, A., and M. Zhou. 1993. The new second generation: Segmented assimilation and its variants. *The Annals of the American Academy of Political and Social Sciences* 530: 74–96.

Pred, A. 1992. Languages of everyday practice and resistance: Stockholm at the end of the nineteenth century. In *Reworking Modernity*, edited by. A. Pred and M. Watts. Pp. 118–154. New Brunswick, N.J.: Rutgers University Press.

Rabinow, P. 1989. *French modern: Norms and forms of missionary and didactic pathos.* Cambridge, Mass.: MIT Press.

Ram, N. 1995. *Beyond Ambedkar: Essays on Dalits in India.* New Delhi: Har-Anand Publications.

Rao, M. S. A., C. Bhatt, and L. N. Khadekar. 1991. *A reader in urban sociology.* 2d ed. Delhi: Orient Longman.

Reeves, E. B. 1995. Power, resistance and the cult of Muslim saints in a northern Egyptian town. *American Ethnologist* 22:306–323.

Repak, T. A. 1995. *Waiting on Washington: Central American workers in the nation's capital.* Philadelphia: Temple University Press.

Robertson, J. 1991. *Native and newcomer: Making and remaking a Japanese city.* Berkeley: University of California Press.

Rodman, M., and M. Cooper. 1995. Housing cultural difference: questions of power and space in developing Canadian non-profits and co-ops. *Canadian Journal of Urban Research* 4, no. 1:93–111.

Rosenzweig, R., and E. Blackmar. 1992. *The park and the people: A history of Central Park.* Ithaca, N.Y.: Cornell University Press.

Rotenberg, R. 1992. *Time and order in metropolitan Vienna.* Washington, D.C.: Smithsonian Institution Press.

———. 1993. On the salubrity of sites. In *The cultural meaning of urban space*, edited by R. Rotenberg and G. W. McDonogh. Pp. 17–30. Westport, Conn.: Bergin and Garvey.

———. 1995. *Landscape and power in metropolitan Vienna.* Baltimore: The Johns Hopkins University Press.

Rotenberg, R., and G. W. McDonogh. 1993. *The cultural meaning of urban space.* Westport, Conn.: Bergin and Garvey

Rothstein, F. A., and M. L. Blim. 1991. *Anthropology and the global factory: Studies of the new industrialization in the late twentieth century.* Westport, Conn.: Bergin and Garvey.

Ruble, B. 1992. Reshaping the city: The politics of property in a provincial Russian city. *Urban Anthropology* 21:203–233.

Ruddick, S. 1996. *Young and homeless in Hollywood: Mapping social identities.* New York: Routledge.

Rutheiser, C. 1993. Mapping contested terrains: Schoolrooms and streetcorners in urban Belize. In *The cultural meaning of urban space*, edited by R. Rotenberg and G. W. McDonogh. Pp. 103–120. Westport, Conn.: Bergin and Garvey.

———. 1996. *Imagineering Atlanta: The politics of place in the city of dreams.* New York: Verso Press.

———. 1997. Making place in the nonplace urban realm: Notes on the revitalization of downtown Atlanta. *Urban Anthropology* 26, no. 1:9–42.

Sacks, K. B. 1997. *Race, class, gender and the Jewish question.* New Brunswick, N.J.: Rutgers University Press.

Safa, H. I. 1986. Urbanization, the informal economy, and state policy in Latin America. *Urban Anthropology* 15:135–163.

Sanjek, R. 1990. Urban anthropology in the 1980s: A world view. *Annual Review of Anthropology* 19:1151–186.

———. 1994. *Cities, classes, and the social order: Anthony Leeds.* Ithaca, N.Y.: Cornell University Press.

Sassen, S. 1990. Economic restructuring and the American city. *Annual Review of Sociology* 16:465–490.

———. 1991. *The global city: New York, London, Tokyo.* Princeton, N.J.: Princeton University Press.

Scheper-Hughes, N. 1992. *Death without weeping: The violence of everyday life in Brazil.* Berkeley: University of California Press.

Shokeid, M. 1995. *Gay synagogue in New York.* New York: Columbia University Press.

Sieber, R. T. 1990. Selecting a new past: Emerging definitions of heritage in Boston Harbor. *Journal of Urban and Cultural Studies* 1:101–122.

———. 1991. Waterfront revitalization in postindustrial port cities of North America. *City and Society* 5:120–136.

Smart, J. 1989. *The political economy of street hawkers in Hong Kong.* Hong Kong: Centre of Asian Studies.

Smart, J., and A. Smart. 1991. Personal relations and divergent economies: A case study of Hong Kong investments in South China. *International Journal of Urban and Regional Research* 15, no. 2:216–233.

Smith, N. 1984. *Uneven development: Nature, capital and the production of space.* Oxford: Basil Blackwell.

Smith, N., and C. Katz. 1993. Grounding metaphor: Towards a spatialized politics. In *Place and the politics of identity*, edited by M. Keith and S. Pile. Pp. 67–83. London: Routledge.

Soja, E. 1989. *Postmodern geographies: The reassertation of space in critical social theory.* New York. Verso.

Spain, D. 1992. *Gendered spaces.* Chapel Hill: University of North Carolina.

Stack, C. 1974. *All our kin: Strategies for survival in a black community.* New York: Harper and Row.

———. 1996. *Call to home: African Americans reclaim the rural South.* New York: Basic Books.

Stull, D. 1990. When the packers came to town: Changing ethnic relations in Garden City, Kansas. *Urban Anthropology* 19:303–425.

Stull, D., M. J. Broadway, and D. Griffith. 1995. *Any way you cut it: Meat processing and small-town America.* Lawrence: University of Kansas Press.

Sumihara, N. 1993. A case study of cross-cultural interaction in a Japanese multinational corporation in the United States. In *Diversity and differences in organizations*, edited by R. R. Sims and R. F. Denneby. Pp.136–147. Westport, Conn.: Quorum Books.

Susser, I. 1982. *Norman Street.* New York: Oxford University Press.

———. 1991. The separation of mothers and children. In *Dual city: Restructuring New York*, edited by J. Mollenkopf and M. Castells. Pp. 207–224. New York: Russell Sage Foundation.

———. 1993. Creating family forms: The exclusion of men and teenage boys in the New York City shelter system 1987–1991. *Critique of Anthropology* 13: 267–285.

Sutton, C. R., and E. M. Chaney. 1987. *Caribbean life in New York City.* Staten Island, N.Y.: Center for Migration Studies.

Taylor, C. 1994. *The black churches in Brooklyn.* New York: Columbia University Press.

Wacquant, L J. D. 1993. Urban outcasts: Sigma and division in the black American ghetto and the French urban periphery. *International Journal of Urban and Regional Research* 17:366–383.

———. 1994. The new urban color line: The state and fate of the ghetto in post-Fordist America. In *Social theory and the politics of identity*, edited by C. Calhoun. Pp. 231–276. Oxford: Blackwell.

———. 1995. Dangerous places: Violence and isolation in Chicago's black belt and the Parisian red belt. In *Urban poverty and family life in Chicago's Inner City*, edited by W. J. Wilson. Oxford: Oxford University Press.

Wacquant, L. J. D., and W. Wilson. 1989. The cost of racial and class exclusion in the inner city. *Annals of the American Academy of Political and Social Science* 501:8–25.

Wallerstein, I. 1990. Culture as the ideological battleground of the modern world-system. *Theory, Culture and Society* 7:31–56.

Walton, J. 1993. Urban sociology: the contribution and limits of political economy. *Annual Review of Sociology* 19:301–320.

Waterson, A. 1993. *Street addicts in the political economy.* Philadelphia: Temple University Press.

Watson, J. L. 1997. *Golden arches east: McDonald's in East Asia.* Stanford, Calif.: Stanford University Press.

Watson, S., and K. Gibson. 1995. *Postmodern cities and spaces.* Oxford: Blackwell.

White, J. 1994. *Money makes us relatives: Women's labor in urban Turkey.* Austin: University of Texas Press.

Williams, B. 1992. Poverty among African Americans in the urban United States. *Human Organization* 51:164–174.

Wilson, E. 1991. *The sphinx in the city: Urban life, the control of disorder, and women.* Berkeley: University of California Press.

Wright, G. 1991. *The politics of design in French colonial urbanism.* Chicago: University of Chicago Press.

Young, M., and P. Willmott. 1957. *Family and kinship in East London.* Middlesex, U.K.: Penguin.

Zenner, W. 1994. Nominalism and essentialism in urban anthropology. *City and Society Annual Review,* 53–66.

Zhou, M. 1992. *Chinatown: The socioeconomic potential of an urban enclave.* Philadelphia: Temple University Press.

Zukin, S. 1991. *Landscapes of power: From Detroit to Disney World.* Berkeley: University of California Press.

———1995. *The cultures of cities.* Oxford: Blackwell.

PART I

The Divided City

STEVEN GREGORY

1

The Changing Significance of Race and Class in an African American Community

The post–civil rights era has witnessed the growth of the black middle class and increased class strati-fication in African American communities. This chapter examines how state-sponsored reforms associated with civil rights era activism restruc-tured political power in an African American community, shifting the focus of neighborhood activism from institutions and strategies that em-phasized a race-based definition of political interests and identity to-ward those that privilege the discourse and claims of the black middle class. It argues that civil rights era reforms disproportionately empow-ered middle-class homeowners, enabling them to translate economic gains into political power and, in the process, to rearticulate the significance of race and class in community politics. A young black stockbroker once explained to me the difference between his own neighborhood, East Elmhurst, and southeast Queens, a black community situated at the op-posite end of the county. "Southeast Queens is a black community," he began. "It has a black consciousness. We in East Elmhurst are people who live with blacks but in a white community. We think outside of our community." The stockbroker went on to explain that the middle-class residents of East Elmhurst did not act politically as a "black com-munity." Rather, because they shared "middle-class values" with the residents of neighboring white communities, they tended to organize around issues that had more to do with their interests as homeowners than with interests that could be associated with race. The paradoxical notions of living with blacks but in a "white community" and of "thinking outside" one's own community seem to confound, if not undermine, the significance of the concept "black community," pitting consciousness against racial topography in a manner that exposes the interplay of race and class in its most ambiguous form.

East Elmhurst and the adjoining neighborhood of North Corona form the largest concentration of African Americans in northern Queens, with a black population of 20,197, accounting for 79 percent of the area's total population of 25,456 (U.S. Bureau of the Census 1981, 3A). The two neighborhoods have a common history and common institutions and are generally considered by residents and nonresidents alike to be a single black community, referred to as Corona-East Elmhurst or East Elmhurst-Corona, depending on where the speaker resides. Despite these commonalities, the two neighborhoods diverge along an axis that has increasingly made its influence felt since World War II. Whereas East Elmhurst is primarily a working- to middle-class community of homeowners, North Corona is working-class to poor and composed largely of renters.

In this chapter, I examine the impact that changes in race and class relations associated with civil rights era reforms have had on the political life of Corona-East Elmhurst. I argue that increased class stratification within this community, coupled with the political empowerment of its middle-class residents through state-sponsored political reforms, resulted in a shift in the focus of neighborhood activism from institutions and strategies that emphasized a race-based definition of political interests and identity toward those privileging the economic interests and political orientation of black middle-class homeowners.

The Changing Class Structure of the African American Community

Researchers have debated the degree to which classes have stratified among African Americans (Farley 1984, Kilson 1981, Pickney 1984, Shulman 1981, Willie 1989), with much of the recent debate gravitating around the work of William Julius Wilson, who focused attention on changes in black class structure in his analysis of the changing significance of race in American society (1978) and his study of the intensification and persistence of black poverty in inner cities (1987). Since 1940, Wilson observes, the black occupational structure has exhibited a "consistent pattern of job upgrading," leading to growth in the ranks of the black working and middle classes (1978,129). However, this job mobility, promoted by fair employment legislation and economic growth, has not benefited all sectors of the black population equally: structural changes in the economy following World War II decreased the number of entry-level jobs for poorly educated, low-skilled African

Americans at the very time that their more educated and skilled counterparts were experiencing unprecedented upward job mobility (Wilson
1978). Thus, despite gains made by the black workforce in recent decades, Wilson observes that there has been "an uneven development of
economic resources in the black community" and that the income gap
between the black poor and higher-income groups has widened
(1978:134).[1] Wilson also points to what he sees as the rise of a persistent form of poverty that is concentrated in the inner cities and linked
to an array of social problems unprecedented in black community life
(1987). The emergence of an "underclass" presents a paradox to be
untangled, and Wilson offers it as a challenge to proponents of the "discrimination thesis," who emphasize the contemporary role of racial discrimination in perpetuating black poverty. Backers of this thesis, Wilson
writes, "find it difficult to explain why the economic position of poor
urban blacks actually deteriorated during the very period in which the
most sweeping antidiscrimination legislations and programs were enacted and implemented. Their emphasis on discrimination becomes even
more problematic in view of the economic progress of the black middle
class during the same period" (1987, 30).

Wilson's explanation of this paradox rests in part on his analysis of
structural changes in the economy, which, he argues, undermined the
period's gains for the black poor. But to this macroeconomic argument
Wilson adds a sociological one that sets out to relate changes in the black
occupational structure to the concentration and persistence of black poverty
in inner cities. It is the latter argument, brought to bear on the problem
of inner-city poverty, that provides the context for Wilson's investigation of the changing class structure within black communities,

In Wilson's view, changes in the black occupational structure not
only widened the income gap between the poor and the middle classes
but also provoked demographic and institutional changes in black communities. Analyzing Chicago census data, Wilson argues that the concentration of poor households in inner-city neighborhoods is tied to an
outmigration of working and middle-class families (1987, 55):

> In the 1940s, 1950s, and as late as the 1960s such communities
> featured a vertical integration of different segments of the urban
> black population. Lower-class, working-class, and middle-class
> black families all lived more or less in the same communities
> (albeit in different neighborhoods), sent their children to the
> same schools, availed themselves of the same recreational
> facilities, and shopped at the same stores. Whereas today's black
> middle-class professionals no longer tend to live in ghetto neigh-

borhoods and have moved increasingly into mainstream occupations outside the black community, the black middle-class professionals of the 1940s and 1950s (doctors, teachers, lawyers, social workers, ministers) lived in higher-income neighborhoods of the ghetto and serviced the black community. Accompanying the black middle-class exodus has been a growing movement of stable working-class blacks from ghetto neighborhoods to higher-income neighborhoods in other parts of the city and to the suburbs. In the earlier years, the black middle and working classes were confined by restrictive covenants to communities also inhabited by the lower class: their very presence provided stability to inner-city neighborhoods and reinforced and perpetuated mainstream patterns of norms and behavior. (1987, 7)

Wilson (1987) argues that the exodus of nonpoor African American families removed a critical social buffer: that could have mitigated the socioeconomic consequences of prolonged joblessness during the 1970s and early 1980s. The exodus of working- and middle-class people not only weakened community institutions but also divested the inner cities of the kind of "mainstream role models that help keep alive the perception that education is meaningful, that steady employment is a viable alternative to welfare, and that family stability is the norm, not the exception" (1987, xx).[2]

Wilson's portrayal of the changes in African American communities in recent decades raises important questions regarding the process and effects of class stratification in these communities. For example, was the breakdown of "vertical integration" in African American communities chiefly the result of an exodus of middle- and working-class families? If so, where did the nonpoor go, given evidence indicating that there has been little decline in residential segregation in the post–civil rights era?[3]

These questions are especially troublesome given Wilson's focus, when discussing black class structure, on explaining poverty in inner-city areas that "are populated almost exclusively by the most disadvantaged segments of the black community" (1987, 8).[4] Are these areas of concentrated poverty typical of inner-city African American communities? If not, what has been the impact of changes in class structure on communities not characterized by such concentrated poverty? How has class stratification affected the institutions and political activism of such communities? And lastly, what effects are changes in class structure having on the significance of race in community politics? In the following sections I explore some of these issues by examining the process and effects of class stratification in Corona-East Elmhurst. Ethnographic data from this community present a case study that contrasts with Wilson's model of black class stratification.

First, although class stratification has increased in Corona-East Elmhurst, it has not produced an "exodus" of the nonpoor; rather, it has exacerbated social and political cleavages within this community, as middle-class residents have gained access to mainstream channels of political power and, in the process, have rearticulated their political interests, ideologies, and alliances along class lines. Thus, whereas Wilson approaches black class stratification as a spatial segregation of income groups (the "exodus" model), I want to direct attention to how class stratification has interacted with state-sponsored reforms (such as the War on Poverty and political decentralization) to restructure the social and institutional basis of political power in this community. In contrast to Wilson's economistic treatment of class differences among African Americans (see Reed 1988), I want to focus attention on how these differences are enacted within a political field.

Second, Wilson's analysis of black class stratification discounts the significance of race for the black nonpoor by treating class stratification and racial oppression as "inversely related processes" (Shulman 1981, 22). Thus, despite his assertion that racism remains significant in the "sociopolitical order," Wilson assumes that race loses its significance for members of the middle class who have been able to leave ghetto neighborhoods for "higher-income neighborhoods in other parts of the city" (1987, 7). This "seesaw" approach to the relationship between race and class not only minimizes the effects of contemporary racism on all classes within the African American population but also fails to take account of the diverse ways in which race and class intersect in specific sociopolitical contexts.

The "Golden Age"

African American families began settling in Corona at the turn of the twentieth century. Many of the early arrivals were skilled workmen, household workers, and professionals leaving areas of black settlement in Manhattan in search of homeownership and better living conditions in Queens. These black newcomers settled on the northern fringe of Corona, a farming and light manufacturing settlement not far from Newtown, the center of one of the five original townships on Long Island (Seyfried 1986).

The parents of Jacob Govan, for example, moved in 1892 from Harlem to Corona, where they purchased a house lot to build on. Jacob's father had migrated to New York City from Virginia in the 1880s. While working as a custodian at the Negro YWCA in Manhattan, the elder Govan learned boiler engineering and became the first black licensed engineer in New York City. Govan's mother was a live-in household worker for a wealthy family in Westchester County.

Harriet Hill's family moved from Manhattan to Corona in 1905, renting an apartment in a house owned by Italian immigrants. Along with a group of Corona's early black arrivals, Harriet's father, a carpenter, organized the community's first black church in 1916. Like Harriet's father, the other founding members of the Corona Congregational Church were skilled workmen, upper-echelon service workers, and professionals, the kind of people who formed what Bart Landry has termed "the old black elite" (1988).

Before World War II, African Americans lived throughout North Corona alongside European immigrants. As their number grew during the 1920s and 1930s, black "Coronaites" organized churches, social clubs, and other voluntary associations while maintaining strong social and cultural ties to Harlem. Before the Great Depression, North Corona could be viewed as a middle-class suburb of Harlem—a connection that was strengthened when the building of the Triborough Bridge in 1939 provided a direct road link between northern Queens and Harlem.

Older residents of Corona often speak of the period between the world wars as a "Golden Age," a time when the area boasted a "better class of people" and "good society." One resident who had moved to Corona in 1926 described the community as "hoity-toity," noting that his parents were refused an apartment by its black owner because they had too many children and did not attend the Abyssinian Baptist Church, the spiritual center of black middle-class life in New York City during the period.

The focal point of black community life in Corona was the church, and in particular the Corona Congregational Church. Under the leadership of the Reverend George W. Hinton, the Corona Congregational Church organized youth clubs, Bible schools, and a literary circle and provided relief services during the Great Depression. When the 1939 World's Fair was held in nearby Flushing Meadows, Hinton organized a campaign to house black Fair visitors who were excluded from the area's segregated hotels. Corona's Congregationalists were soon joined by Baptist and African Methodist congregations.

Between 1930 and 1940, Corona's black population increased by nearly 50 percent to 4,327, and the community began to exert the political influence that its growing number implied. Democratic politicians based in Corona Heights, a largely Italian community to the south, lured Corona blacks away from the Republican party with job opportunities.

Black political clubs established patron-client relations with white political "kingpins" and secured patronage in exchange for Corona's growing black vote. Hinton pressured city officials to hire black workers at LaGuardia Airport, which was completed in 1939. A prominent black realtor and "race man" organized boycotts of white-owned businesses that would not hire blacks. And in 1949, a Corona chapter of the National Association for the Advancement of Colored People (NAACP) was formed.

During the 1940s, African American families began settling in East Elmhurst, an affluent area to the north of Corona, bordering on Flushing Bay. Doctors, entertainers, realtors, and other members of Corona's old black elite bought houses in an area of Ditmars Boulevard which, skirting Long Island's North Shore, became known as the "black Gold Coast." Residence in East Elmhurst became associated with elite status—it was seen as being a cut above middle-class life in Corona, which was perceived by many to be deteriorating. One longtime black resident of Corona, a doctor and the son of a merchant seaman, linked the decline of the area to an influx of southern migrants before World War II: "The transition of Corona was devastating to watch. When they opened [La Guardia Airport], they brought a lot of blacks from Newark, New Jersey, over here to work at the airport. That's when this town started going down the hill. That influx of blacks. Nothing to say about southerners, but most of them were southerners from Newark who came up here to take the jobs. And then the whole atmosphere of the community started to change."

By 1950 the black population of Corona-East Elmhurst had reached nearly 10,000 and accounted for 26 percent of the area's total population (Hart, Krivatsky, and Stubee 1970). Those who arrived during the 1940s and 1950s were more economically diverse than their largely working and middle-class predecessors had been. Many had arrived directly from the South in search of defense industry jobs during the war and of manufacturing jobs in the prosperous postwar economy. Housing in black sections of Corona deteriorated as single-family homes were converted into rooming houses and apartment buildings to absorb the new arrivals. This rapid increase in population density strained the community's social service infrastructure, prompting the City Planning Commission to report later that "since 1950, the northern area of Corona has absorbed a large percentage of Negroes with serious problems of social disorder" (City Planning Commission 1963).[5]

Rapid population growth coupled with an increase in social problems associated with overcrowded housing and poor social services promoted a spatial differentiation of the community along the lines of class and race. On the one hand, black middle-class families began selling or renting their homes in Corona and buying in East Elmhurst and other areas of Queens and Long Island. On the other, middle-class whites in East Elmhurst joined white families in North Corona in an exodus to the suburbs. Between 1950 and 1960, for example, 70 percent of Corona's white residents left the neighborhood. White businesses fled black areas, leading to the deterioration of Northern Boulevard, the community's once-vibrant commercial strip. One black resident reported that a white grocer had told her at the time that he was leaving because "he didn't want to sell black-eyed peas and grits."

By 1960 the black population of Corona-East Elmhurst had reached 20,793 and accounted for more than 50 percent of the total (Hart, Krivatsky, and Stubee 1970). As white families fled predominantly black areas, a color line was defined, distinguishing North Corona and East Elmhurst from what was coming to be called "Italian Corona" to the south. Italian and black youth gangs skirmished along Roosevelt Avenue, the boundary separating the two neighborhoods. Junction Boulevard, the recognized border between Corona-East Elmhurst and predominantly white Jackson Heights to the west, became known as the "Mason-Dixon line" when white parents there fought against a plan to desegregate the area's schools.

The hardening of this color line coincided with a differentiation of the black community itself along a boundary perceived to separate the middle-class homeowners of East Elmhurst from the largely working-class and poor renters of North Corona. In an effort to legitimize this distinction, residents of East Elmhurst pressured the Postal Service to have their neighborhood assigned a separate zip code. Although the border, like the socioeconomic differences between the two areas, remained vague, the symbolic distinction from "Corona" became increasingly meaningful as a marker of status to the homeowners of "East Elmhurst."[6] One woman who had moved with her family to East Elmhurst from Corona in 1952 remarked that "if you didn't have a college degree, [the neighbors] would walk all over you." She added: "I was surrounded by people who owned their own businesses and they got to putting on airs. I told them, 'I pay the same taxes as you all do, I go to the bank just like you, I throw out just as much garbage as you do, and I do just as much for my children as you do.' That stopped them."

During the 1950s, residents of East Elmhurst and Corona formed block and civic associations, which paralleled the declining white homeowner associations in the area. In 1952, a number of these block associations were united under the umbrella of the East Elmhurst-Corona Civic Association.[7] The Civic Association, today composed primarily of

East Elmhurst homeowners, saw as its principal goal the preservation of the community against the neighborhood decline that was being experienced in Corona. In 1961, largely as a result of pressure applied on city officials by civic and church groups, Corona was declared an Urban Renewal Area by the City Planning Commission. A City Planning Commission report summarizing a public hearing held at this time underscored the role played by homeowners in defining the community's urban renewal priorities: "A theme common to many speakers was the difficulty faced by homeowners in securing loans to improve their properties. Five speakers asked that special financial assistance be provided to homeowners for making improvements. . . . One speaker suggested that difficulties in obtaining improvement funds had played a significant role in the conversion of larger homes by property owners in the area into small apartments" (1963, 7).

The emergence of a form of activism tied to the interests of homeowners and organized into a block and civic associational structure gave institutional form to class divisions within the community, creating an effective organizing base for the growing middle class, one that linked their activism directly to their interests as property owners. This is not to say that these homeowner associations ignored issues of importance to poor and low-income residents of the community. As we shall see, both block and civic associations played leading roles in addressing the community's needs for social services, urban renewal, and political empowerment. However, as these groups gained access to political power through civil rights–era reforms, the interests of their middle-class property owners would increasingly come to dominate the community's political agenda and resources.

Civil Rights, Community Renewal, and Political Reform

In 1957, Martin Luther King, Jr., spoke at a rally in Queens sponsored by the Jamaica, Queens, branch of the NAACP. A local newspaper reported the next day: "Nonviolent resistance to segregation was urged last night in Queens by the man who persuaded 50,000 Montgomery, Alabama, Negroes to quit riding segregated buses" (*Long Island Star Journal* 1957). For residents of Corona and East Elmhurst who attended the rally that night, the message struck home. Politically powerless and alarmed by the deterioration of their neighborhood and its schools, black residents of Corona-East Elmhurst mobilized.

In 1958, a civil rights activist from Louisiana was appointed pastor of the Corona Congregational Church. The new pastor was elected president of the local chapter of the NAACP, and the Corona Congregational

Church once again became the focal point of community activism. The church invited civil rights activists from the South to speak at community events about their organizing experiences. In 1963, a church-sponsored political committee unsuccessfully ran its pastor for city councilman-at-large against a conservative Republican. "The greatest domestic issue facing our country, our city, and our borough since 1860," began a letter sent to local clergy before the election, "is the moral issue of Civil Rights." It went on: "We appeal to you, as a moral leader in your community, to join with us in our campaign to help rid our city of this dangerous cancer of bigotry and race hatred, with all its explosiveness. We now have the political means of doing something about this moral issue" (Independent Citizens' Committee 1963).

The Corona Congregational Church was not alone in the struggle for political power, integrated schools, and community renewal. Ad hoc political action committees convened representatives of local churches, civic associations, and political clubs to coordinate voter registration drives and pressure city officials for community development funds. Parents organized to improve the quality of local schools, supporting the demand for "community control" during the Ocean Hill-Brownsville school crisis of 1968 (see Ravitch 1988), as well as a controversial plan to desegregate the community's schools by "linking" them to schools in neighboring, predominantly white communities. In the late 1960s, a chapter of the Black Panther party was formed in Corona. Residents report that its organizers included members of local youth gangs from poor sections of Corona who had taken up the call for "Black Power" and become active in community politics. Other Corona youth joined or attended the Nation of Islam's Queens mosque, located in Corona, where Malcolm X had taken up residence in 1959.

Political activism in Corona-East Elmhurst from the mid-1960s to the 1970s was characterized by coalition building, often cutting across class and ideological lines. For example, when the 1968 teachers' strike threatened to close local schools, members of the Black Panther party demonstrated together with middle-class parents from East Elmhurst. On another occasion, the Panthers and civic groups staged a demonstration to move city officials to install traffic lights at a dangerous intersection. And in the early 1970s block and civic associations worked together with local clergy, parents' groups, and militants to pressure the city to fund a community library specializing in African American cultural education.

Civil rights era activism interacted with state-sponsored political reforms to fundamentally restructure political life in Corona-East Elmhurst. New institutions were created and the function and significance of old ones transformed as residents organized to address community issues while pursuing the new avenues of political power and community control that had been opened through local and national struggles. Through the War on Poverty, community organizations were formed and funded to organize job training, day care, and other social service programs. The Civic Association and the NAACP sponsored publicly funded day care centers. A number of community development corporations were consolidated under the umbrella of Elmcor Youth and Adult Services, a multiservice community agency providing job training, drug rehabilitation, and other social services. These government-funded organizations created a new social service infrastructure within the community, one that could bring more resources to bear on community needs than had the churches and voluntary organizations before it.

Political decentralization, accelerated by reforms instituted under the administration of Mayor John Lindsay and local demands for "community control," led to the creation of quasi-governmental citizens' advisory boards intended to bridge the gap between local communities and city government (see Katznelson 1981). Black residents of Corona-East Elmhurst were appointed and elected to participate in new community institutions, such as the community board, the police precinct council, and the local community school board.

Lastly, voter registration drives of the 1960s educated and mobilized black voters, making them a force to be reckoned with by white politicians. Black political clubs riding a wave of civil rights activism were organized to run "independent" Democrats against the "machine" candidates of the powerful Northside Democratic Club based in "Italian" Corona Heights. In 1974 Corona-East Elmhurst elected Helen Marshall, a former PTA activist, to be its first black district leader. In 1980 Marshall was elected to the New York State Assembly. The insurgent politics of the 1960s, empowered by civil rights activism and reform movement agitation, had given way to incorporation into the regular politics of the Queens County Democratic organization.

One result of the civil rights era developments was a shift in the focus of neighborhood activism from the traditional, relatively autonomous centers of associational life in the black community to institutions linked to government agencies, service bureaucracies, and mainstream political parties. Churches, independent political clubs, and other voluntary associations that had formerly played leading roles in organizing and directing political power saw these roles diminish as opportunities for political participation appeared elsewhere.

The viability of the new centers of political activism depended less on a neighborhood unity conceived of and mobilized on the basis of race—the common experience of racial discrimination—than on the ability of tightly organized interest groups to bring pressure to bear on public officials through mainstream channels of political power. On the one hand, the geographic boundaries of these new centers of political activism did not correspond to those of the "black community": residents of Corona-East Elmhurst shared state assembly, community board, and other governing districts with neighboring white communities. As a result, black community leaders found themselves serving as minorities on predominantly white "local" governing bodies.

On the other hand, decentralization and participation in the political mainstream tended to fragment community issues, restricting their consideration to the purview of specialized administrative bodies. Problems in the schools, for example, fell under the jurisdiction of the local community school board. Housing and zoning problems became the concern of the community board. The distribution of community development block grants was delegated to an area policy board. Each of these local governing bodies had its own peculiar electoral or appointment process, meeting schedule, and decision-making procedure. The bureaucratization of local decision making not only rendered the mechanics of political participation confusing, if not incomprehensible, to most community residents, but also diminished the significance of the "black community" as a political entity with unique and interrelated concerns.

Katznelson writes of decentralization: "At issue was the attempt to take the radical impulse away from the politics of race by the creation of mechanisms of participation at the community level that had the capability to limit conflicts to a community orientation, to separate issues from each other, and to stress a politics of distribution—in short, to reduce race to ethnicity in the traditional community-bounded sense. The new institutions of decentralized schools, neighborhood government, local planning, and the like were developed to perform the functions for blacks and their political blocs that party machines had performed for white ethnics" (1981, 177).

Thus, civil rights era activism, which had galvanized political support for community issues around the common experience of racial oppression and a common sense of black identity, provoked institutional reforms that undermined the significance of race in local politics. By fragmenting the political identity of the black community, decentralization and political inclusion "depoliticized" the issue of race. Corona-East Elmhurst remained a "black community," but its leaders and institutions were increasingly unable to mobilize it as such. For as we shall see, the new mechanisms of political participation proved to be disproportionately responsive to the interests and institutions of the black middle-class homeowners of East Elmhurst.

Poverty and Property

The War on Poverty program in Corona-East Elmhurst led to the creation of special service organizations bureaucratically tied to government agencies. Poverty, once addressed as a civil rights issue affecting the community as a whole, was reduced to an administrative problem to be managed by the professional staff of the community development corporation. Moreover, the viability of these organizations depended less on the mobilization of neighborhood residents than on the tactical support of local politicians. As a former pastor of the Corona Congregational Church put it, "The loyalty of the people went to Borough Hall, rather than to the church and what it was doing."

One result of the bureaucratization of the community's social service infrastructure was indeed the transfer of decision-making authority to "Borough Hall." Community organizations were not only dependent on government service bureaucracies for funding but also constrained to define and address community needs in a manner consistent with the policy priorities of their funding sources (see Piven and Cloward 1971). An equally important effect of this institutional specialization was to remove the problem of poverty—and, by extension, the interests of the poor—from the purview of community-based institutions which, like the churches and civic groups, had hitherto played prominent roles in addressing the needs of the poor and conceptualizing their problems. It was not that the membership and leaders of these groups had lost interest in the "plight of the poor"; rather, their roles in both defining and mobilizing residents to act on the issue of poverty were obviated by the rise of the antipoverty program—development that transferred these roles from local community activists to professional public policy planners.

The bureaucratization of the community's social service infrastructure also tended to increase the social and, one might say, psychological distance between the community's middle-class residents and its low-income residents by differentiating the institutional contexts in which the interests of the two groups were articulated and addressed. The community corporations served as a kind of institutional buffer between the middle class and the poor, linking the latter as clients to external service bureaucracies rather than to institutional bases in the community.

The executive director of one of the community's largest development corporations, someone who had once been active in the Black Panther party, observed: "I'm thinking about the clients we serve and how they might even begin to interact with the upper-class blacks and there's no type of connection. Their paths never cross anymore. The only possible connection might be in the church, where you might have this grassroots person still attending this church. But other than that there's little opportunity for them to meet."

The polarization of interests among the community's organizations gave institutional form to class divisions in the community. Although these divisions had existed before, political interests and ideologies had often cut across class lines. Faced with political exclusion and systematic racial discrimination, people had perceived social, economic, and political struggles to be "race issues," presupposing a unity of interests, if not always of action.[8] Thus, major struggles in Corona-East Elmhurst during the period of civil rights activism had brought together a broad, interclass coalition of civic, church, and political groups.

As Michael Omi and Howard Winant have noted, the racial politics of the 1950s and 1960s, which foregrounded race as a unifying principle of black identity and political action, experienced a sharp decline during the 1970s: "After initial victories against segregation were won, one sector of the movement was thus reconstituted as an interest group, seeking an end to racism understood as discrimination and prejudice, and turning its back on the oppositional 'politics of identity.' Once the organized black movement became a mere constituency, though, it found itself locked in a bear hug with the state institutions whose programs it had itself demanded, while simultaneously isolated from the core institutions of the modern state" (1986, 108).

In the wake of civil rights era reforms, and with the War on Poverty being waged by the community's development corporations, the activism of the middle-class homeowners of East Elmhurst gravitated around territorially organized block and civic associations—groups that more directly expressed their interests and potential political influence as property owners. And it was through these block and civic associations that the occupational mobility of the community's growing black middle class in the 1980s was translated into unprecedented local political power.

The Politics of Homeownership

The political reforms of the civil rights movement tended to benefit middle-income African Americans more than it did members of low-income groups. As Wilson has argued, the more educated and skilled working and middle classes were better positioned than the low-income groups to exploit newly created job opportunities in the government and corporate sectors and thereby realize limited gains in income and economic security (1981). In Corona-East Elmhurst class played an equally important role in determining how political power was restructured in the aftermath of civil rights era reforms. Occupational mobility interacted with state-sponsored institutional reforms to enable the black middle class of East Elmhurst to translate economic gains into political influence. This empowerment of the black middle class, although rooted in the civil rights era struggles, was realized through a form of activism associated less with the politics of race than with the "quality-of-life" interests and ideology of the middle class (see Sanjek in press). The nexus of this political conversion was homeownership, the symbol and embodiment of middle-class wealth and aspirations.

The neighborhood deterioration that had alarmed the middle class of Corona and East Elmhurst during the 1950s had by no means been arrested by the 1980s. Rather, the problems of poverty and neighborhood decline had been separated, institutionally if not conceptually, into two components: on the one hand, the need to address the housing, employment, and other social service needs of the poor; and on the other, the need to "defend" the community from the effects of this poverty within—crime, drug abuse, homelessness, and other manifestations of "urban blight." During the era of civil rights activism, these two faces of poverty had been approached as one: both poverty and neighborhood deterioration were understood to be the result of racial discrimination. And both, it was believed, could be solved through black political empowerment.

"Why, one may ask, was it necessary to form such an organization?" began a pamphlet describing the founding of a black reform Democratic club in Corona in 1962: "The only truthful answer could be—it grew out of the need for political representation, recognition, and consideration. That is, consideration as it pertains to patronage and other benefits which normally accrue from political participation. Plus the consideration of community problems which were brought about due to the lack of political representation" (Julian I. Garfield Democratic Association 1962, 11).

Denied political power and participation on the basis of race, activists viewed the benefits of political representation as undifferentiated by class. With the institutionalization of the antipoverty program, however, the plight of the poor became the privileged concern of the community development corporation. The growing black middle class of East Elmhurst, no longer subjected (at least overtly) to systematic discrimination at the workplace, focused its activism on protecting its neighborhood from crime, drug abuse, and other social problems associated with poverty.

For along with a modicum of economic prosperity and security the black middle class had gained access to channels of political participation and influence that could be used to pursue its class interests as such, relatively unhindered by the arbitrary exercise of racism. These political resources—effective participation in electoral politics and in the organs of decentralized city government—proved to be disproportionately responsive to the interests of middle-class homeowners, organized into tightly knit networks of block and civic associations. The formation of these property-owning groups and their empowerment within the framework of community politics institutionalized class divisions within the black community. In contrast to the community's churches, for example, these block and civic associations mobilized residents around the specific interests of property owners: interests that not only were territorially defined and circumscribed but, equally important, also reflected material and symbolic relations to the neighborhood that were strongly influenced by housing tenure.

Block associations, which the area's state assemblywoman, Helen Marshall, once referred to as the "building blocks of the community," crisscross East Elmhurst and to a lesser extent Corona, forming microconstituencies that directly link the political and economic interests of homeowners to everyday, face-to-face relations of familiarity and cooperation. Of the sixty or so block associations active in Corona-East Elmhurst, the majority are located in East Elmhurst.[9] Whereas roughly 24 percent of East Elmhurst's block faces are organized by block associations, only 12 percent of the block faces in Corona are. The differing roles played by the block associations in the two communities can be correlated with differences in housing tenure.

Block data from the 1980 U.S. census reveal a higher rate of owner-occupied housing in East Elmhurst than in Corona. For example, 74 percent of the blocks listed in East Elmhurst census tracts show rates of owner occupancy of 50 percent or more—that is, on those blocks at least 50 percent of the housing units are occupied by their owners. On the other hand, only 15 percent of Corona's blocks exhibit owner occupancy rates of 50 percent or more. At the other end of the scale, 18 percent of the blocks listed in the Corona census tracts show owner occupancy rates of less than 25 percent, whereas only three percent of the East Elmhurst blocks do (U.S. Bureau of the Census 1981, 1B).

A number of researchers have examined the relationship between homeownership and neighborhood activism (see, for example, Cox 1982; Harvey 1978; Kemeny 1980; Lowe 1977). Cox, after analyzing survey data gathered in Columbus, Ohio, concluded, "Homeownership does have substantial effects upon neighborhood activism, effects that are enhanced in the presence of neighborhood problems" (1982, 122). "The option of relocation as opposed to activism affects homeowners rather differently from the way it does renters. For the homeowner, transaction costs may be considerable. Selling a house is often a lengthy, tedious and costly process involving making the house available for viewing, negotiating with would-be buyers, carrying out small repairs regarded as necessary to clinch the sale, as well as a substantial commission for the realtor" (1982, 117–118).

For the black homeowners of East Elmhurst, racism in white residential communities—underscored in the 1980s by a number of highly publicized racially motivated attacks on blacks in predominantly white neighborhoods—added a social surcharge to the costs of relocation. Thus, the transaction costs of relocation interacted with racism in white residential communities to set limits on the spatial mobility of black middle-class homeowners. Caught in this double bind, between the social and economic costs of relocation on the one hand and the threat of neighborhood deterioration on the other, the homeowners of East Elmhurst organized to defend their hard-earned "quality of life." Residential discrimination and the threat of racial violence therefore served to reinforce the tenure-based propensity for activism of East Elmhurst's middle class.[10]

The black civic associational networks that appeared in East Elmhurst during the 1950s and 1960s added an interest-based dimension to the spatial segregation of the community along class lines. East Elmhurst emerged in the aftermath of the civil rights era not merely as a middle-class section of a black community but as a distinct "community of interest" with its own activist infrastructure and interests to be defended. These interests were closely associated with homeownership and, specifically, with the social and economic investment in the built environment that such tenure implies.[11]

Today, the block associations of East Elmhurst serve as skirmish lines: front lines of defense against threats to the neighborhood's quality of life. They provide interlocking networks of communication for disseminating news and for alerting residents to neighborhood problems. And, as tightly organized microconstituencies, they can act to pressure community leaders and public officials to respond to their interests and concerns. Generally these concerns focus on the block and its immediate environs; potholes in the street, poor garbage collection, and rashes of car break-ins are typical of the issues that incite block association activism. In other cases a more organized threat, such as a merchant's or public agency's plan to locate an undesirable business or facility in the neighborhood, will catalyze block association activism.

For example, only days after it was formed, the Ninety-ninth Street Block Association of East Elmhurst was faced with a crisis. Members of the association had learned that a not-for-profit corporation planned to open a diagnostic center for foster care children in a two-family building on their street. The association called a public meeting at the local office of the area's state assemblywoman. Representatives of the not-for-profit sponsor and the New York City Human Resources Administration—which would fund and monitor the facility—were invited to attend.

About thirty-five residents of Ninety-ninth Street gathered at Assemblywoman Marshall's storefront office on the evening of the meeting. Some had come directly from work: others had walked the short distance to the office in small groups of friends, family, and neighbors. Folding chairs were brought out to seat the overflow crowd. A few latecomers stood in the open doorway, waiting with arms folded for the meeting to begin. "No way they're gonna put that thing here," one woman said. "And right there next to the school?" added a second, raising her eyebrows Most of the residents were middle-aged, and women were a clear majority. They eyed with suspicion the three representatives of the foster care agency, whose business suits and briefcases more than their race disclosed their identity.

With awkward solemnity, the block association's officers took seats at a folding table facing the restless audience. The association's president, a West Indian man in his mid-forties, convened the meeting and introduced the association's "chaplain," who was to give the invocation. Those present were asked to rise and bow their heads as the chaplain gave thanks for "the large turnout and the unity of our association." He asked that God continue to protect the neighborhood and its residents.

One of the sponsors was then asked to describe the proposed facility. The diagnostic center, she reported, would house about twelve children between the ages of eight and twelve for a period of three months. Once the three-month period of diagnostic evaluation was concluded, the children would be referred elsewhere for additional services. Anticipating the fears and concerns of the association's members, she concluded: "The children staying at our facility will be compatible with the children already in the neighborhood. There will be no drug abusers, retarded, or antisocial types."

After her presentation, members of the association posed a battery of questions: "How many supervisors will there be?" "Will the supervisors be qualified?" "What about the parents who abandoned the children—will they be allowed to visit?" "Where will the children who stay in the home play?" "How can these children be normal after all they've been through?" The agency's representatives skillfully parried each question with assurances drawn from well-prepared notes. One man, apparently frustrated by the direction the meeting was taking, stood and said bluntly: "These are problem children—we as a block of people don't want this type of building on our block. This is a private neighborhood—there are no big public buildings. What happens when your kids meet our kids?"

"That's very sad," a representative responded glibly, "because what we do keeps neighborhoods together." She then alluded to the insensitivity of the not-in-my-back-yard, or "NIMBY," attitude, concluding, "These kids are the kids who become problems if they are not helped." The allusion to NIMBY called to mind similar controversies, most of which involved middle-class white communities opposing the location of low-income housing, homeless shelters, and other facilities in their communities. Since the beneficiaries of such projects are often African Americans and members of other minority groups, the accusation of insensitivity carried with it an ironic twist that resonated as a subtext during the meeting: how could a "black community" oppose a facility that was intended to serve a minority population?

The executive director of Elmcor, the neighborhood's principal community development corporation, stood to address the issue of insensitivity. "This community is very sensitive to the needs of people," she observed. Members of the association nodded their heads in agreement. "That's demonstrated by the number of facilities we already have. This community is already oversaturated. Do we want another?" she asked, surveying the audience with a quick glance. "No, we've had enough," a young woman stated. Elmcor's director then turned back toward the agency representatives. "This is not a NIMBY—our yard is already full."

The members of the block association felt that the representatives of the foster care agency were mixing apples with oranges, juxtaposing the immediate, block-focused concerns of residents with abstract, bureaucratic notions of "community" and "sensitivity." The abstract concept of community, once the object of Great Society reform, had lost the legitimacy conferred on it by civil rights era activism. The representatives of the foster care agency were speaking a different language—a language rooted in the bureaucratic discourse of "downtown." The residents of Ninety-ninth Street were black, but the meaning of "blackness" no longer resonated with the racial politics and discourse of the 1960s; it was instead firmly situated in their quality-of-life concerns as middle-class homeowners.

When the meeting was about to end. the block association's president rose and addressed the three representatives. "Enough has been said," he concluded, slapping the palm of his hand against the table. "The neighborhood is infested enough. We would like you to find somewhere else for the home."

The Ninety-ninth Street Block Association's opposition to the placing of a foster care facility on its block illustrates the important organizing role that block associations play in community life; as territorially organized interest groups ("blocks of people"), block associations are able to muster the support of community leaders and exert considerable influence in defining the community's interests and political agenda. But equally important, the association's resistance to the foster care facility illustrates how the bureaucratization of social services has sharpened the perception of class divisions within the black community by framing poverty (and its associated social issues) as an abstract problem imposed on the community by "outside agencies." In opposing "your children" to "our children," members of the association were portraying the "disadvantaged" as outsiders to East Elmhurst. In short, in the discourse of homeowner politics, the poor had become the Other—the object rather than the subject of neighborhood activism. Many black residents of Corona feel that East Elmhurst's activist networks are not responsive to the needs and interests of lower-income groups. A resident of North Corona who ran unsuccessfully for district leader in the 1960s recalled the reaction of her neighbors when their block suffered a crime spree: "When they stole us all blind around here—stole all the flowers and plants and even stole my stone lions out here in front—my neighbors said, 'If we lived in East Elmhurst, we wouldn't have that. See the rich people in East Elmhurst, they could put anything out. They must all have guns or something—nobody steals from them.' And I said, 'I got news for you. They steal over there too.' And they said, 'Yeah, well, they don't worry. They don't even care what happens to us—they hoping it happens to us.'"

Although the power and influence that block associations wield in this micropolitical context are considerable, their importance within the larger framework of community politics should not be minimized. Involvement in a block association is often a resident's first experience of neighborhood activism. Not only are the interests expressed through such associations "closest to home," but participation in a block association requires less travel and inconvenience than involvement in other community institutions. The block association is therefore a recruiting base for neighborhood activists, a place where residents learn the nuts and bolts of community politics and the often bewildering procedural mechanics of municipal service bureaucracies. Many residents who hold positions in other, more broadly based neighborhood groups began their activist careers in block associations. Frequently, such community leaders remain active in their block associations after assuming positions of greater responsibility.

Involvement in a block association, however, is not only a learning experience or basic training for participation in community politics. More important, such involvement integrates residents into the informal social networks that constitute the fabric of local politics (Stone 1989). These informal social ties, which Guest and Oropesa have called "localized friendships," motivate people to act collectively: "Due to their integration into social networks, individuals with localized friendships are likely to be influenced by others arguing for collective action. In this sense, individuals with highly localized friends may be mobilized because they are part of a two-step flow of communication, involving the transmission of ideas from opinion leaders to the rest of the population" (1986, 567).

This exchange of information is especially pronounced or, perhaps better, "block focused" in the case of homeowners. Topics such as property taxes, home contractors, tenants, and the maintenance of streets, sidewalks, and trees by municipal agencies are central to the discourse of homeowners by virtue of the homeowners' investment in the physical environment—symbolic as well as material relation to the block in particular and the neighborhood in general. As a number of researchers have suggested, homeowners tend to experience the boundary between the home and the neighborhood as blurred, porous, and vulnerable. The perception that the community is a vulnerable extension of the private space of the home attunes the property owner to signs of "decay" in the urban landscape. Poor garbage collection, abandoned cars, and potholes in the street are not mere inconveniences but highly charged signifiers of disorder that speak to the social, economic, and moral well-being of the family and community. Homeowners become adept at reading such signs of the community's quality of life, and through participation in block associations they share the information gleaned.[12]

The political power of individual block associations is strengthened through their participation in the East Elmhurst-Corona Civic Association, which transforms local block issues into quality-of-life concerns of the neighborhood as a whole. In this way, the Civic Association is able to link the mobilizing efficiency of its constituent block associations to an institutional structure sufficient in size and visibility to bring pressure to bear on local politicians and municipal authorities and get results.

The East Elmhurst-Corona Civic Association has proven to be the most powerful neighborhood interest group in Corona-East Elmhurst and, with an average meeting attendance of fifty to seventy-five persons, is strongly supported by residents. Like the block associations, the Civic Association focuses primarily on quality-of-life issues. Over the years it has fought the Port Authority over the expansion of La Guardia Airport, won concessions from hotel developers in the airport area, lobbied successfully with civic associations in surrounding white communities for the cleanup of Flushing Bay, and resolved numerous quality-of-life problems brought before it by its constituent block associations. Civic Association meetings are held at the La Guardia Airport Holiday Inn on the northern fringe of East Elmhurst. The right to hold meetings at the hotel was one of the concessions granted to the Civic Association by the Holiday Inn Corporation in return for support of a zoning variance required in order to build on the site.

The popular support enjoyed by the Civic Association rests on its capacity to apply pressure to politicians, municipal officials, and members of the business community to resolve community problems, such as poor garbage collection and inadequate police protection. In return, these public and private officials use the Civic Association as a forum for assembling and negotiating community support for public policy and business initiatives. Together with these officials, the Civic Association and its broadly affiliated membership can be regarded as what Stone has termed an "urban regime"—a loosely structured governing coalition that cooperates in the day-to-day governance of the community (1989).

Perhaps the best way to disclose how the Civic Association works with municipal officials, businesspeople, and local politicians would be to describe a Civic Association meeting held in April 1989. The meeting was attended by about sixty women and men, most if not all of whom were East Elmhurst homeowners. Many Civic Association members are also active in other community institutions, and there is a strong tendency for such activism to overlap with Civic Association membership. Many people regard involvement in the Civic Association as a prerequisite to becoming a community leader. Community leaders, whether politicians or members of the clergy, are often evaluated by the frequency with which they are seen at Civic Association meetings.

The Civic Association meeting was opened with a prayer asking for protection of the community. After the minutes of the previous meeting had been read and approved, the president gave a report summarizing developments in the neighborhood since the last meeting. First on his list were ongoing negotiations with Field Associates, a hotel development firm that had recently purchased the Holiday Inn and was in the process of constructing a new luxury hotel in East Elmhurst. As with the Holiday Inn Corporation, the Civic Association had demanded that the development firm provide amenities in return for the right to "come into our community." Although the Civic Association has no formal authority to sanction development (let alone deny or approve zoning variances), its ability to enlist the support of local politicians and the community board provides it with an effective means of exerting influence. Moreover, the overlapping memberships that Civic Association activists hold in other community institutions, such as the NAACP, local political clubs, and community churches, constitute a tightly knit network of civic cooperation that can be rapidly mustered in times of crisis.

Representatives from Field Associates had attended a number of Civic Association meetings in the past to answer complaints about hazardous and unsightly conditions resulting from construction at the new hotel site. Many of these complaints had been brought to the attention of the Civic Association by the Ditmars Boulevard Block Association (the hotel was being constructed in its neighborhood), whose president was a member of both the Civic Association and the community board. Monthly meetings between the development company and a Civic Association committee had culminated in agreement on a number of concessions to be granted to the community: the developer would give preference to residents of North Corona, East Elmhurst, and Jackson Heights (the neighborhoods included in the community board) when hiring staff for the new hotel, and Field Associates would establish a scholarship fund for residents interested in studying hotel-related subjects.

After the president's report, two guest speakers were introduced, representing the sanitation and the police department respectively. The first representative, the Department of Sanitation's community liaison for the area, gave a presentation on his agency's efforts to serve East Elmhurst better. His presentation exemplified the discourse of quality-of-life politics and, in particular, the symbolic importance that physical environment holds for homeowners.

The liaison, an African American man in his thirties, began by citing statistics on the number of summonses that had been issued by inspectors in East Elmhurst for "behavioral incidents"—that is, for failures to sweep the fronts of homes and businesses. Continuing in a more philosophical vein, he observed: "Garbage is no longer out of sight, out of mind. There is a moral breakdown in our society that includes crime, drugs, garbage . . . everything. It is the younger kids who don't care about your house and don't have values and morals." Two block association presidents then questioned the representative about erratic garbage collection on their blocks and the procedure for getting rid of abandoned cars. One woman asked what she could do about neighbors who walked their dogs in front of her house and did not "scoop." She was particularly frustrated, she said, because the neighbors in question were otherwise "very respectable people."

The next speaker was a young African American police officer from the local precinct's crime prevention squad. He discussed the precinct's attempts to stop drug use in a residential building in Corona that was being used as a "crack den." A number of arrests had been made, but since the building was privately owned the police could not legally close it. He suggested that the block and civic associations pressure the community board to have the building closed by the city. The chairman of the board of the League for Better Community Life complained that his group had done everything it could and nothing had worked (the crack house was located next to the League's day care center). The police officer responded by repeating that arrests had been made and that the community had to apply more pressure. "Arresting people is no panacea," he observed. "We have to change the attitude of people—society has to do something." The woman whose prayer had opened the meeting responded, "Yeah, you can shoot them all!"

The April 1989 Civic Association meeting underscores not only the power and influence that the block and civic associations of East Elmhurst are able to exert on corporations, municipal authorities, and politicians (an influence far exceeding that of other community institutions), but also the increasingly important role that quality-of-life politics is playing in rearticulating the interests and political identity of black middle-class residents.[13] Crime, drugs, and urban decay are no longer spoken about as "social problems" resulting from poverty, racial discrimination, and injustice (the discourse of 1960s racial politics); rather, framed by the institutions and discourse of middle-class activism, these social problems appear as radically "other." In short, given the empowerment of middle-class homeowners through block and civic associational activism, the exercise of political power in Corona-East Elmhurst is increasingly being structured by interests defined on the basis of class rather than race.

This is not to say that race today plays merely an epiphenomenal role in the political discourse and practice of East Elmhurst: rather, the significance of race has changed as the political identity and the interests of the "black community" have been rearticulated in a new class structure and political context. The tension resulting from this rearticulation of the significance of race and class in community politics was reflected in a decision made by the Civic Association to fight the establishment of a home for mentally disabled adolescents in East Elmhurst.

This incident must be read against a backdrop of similar incidents that have occurred in white communities, involving the establishment of low-income housing or housing for what are euphemistically called "special" populations. In many such cases, the community resisting the housing or facility has been charged with racism, since low-income and special-needs populations are often conflated with minorities. For example, less than a year before the Civic Association reached its decision, residents of a white section of Flushing firebombed a house that the city had purchased in order to shelter homeless infants. Many people perceived the firebombing as a "racial incident," and a march against racism, led by a local black minister, was later held in Flushing.[14]

The East Elmhurst-Corona Civic Association met to consider the proposal for the group home in the summer of 1988. Marshall invited representatives from the social service agency sponsoring the group home to present their plan. After the presentation of the plan, the members of the Civic Association were invited to question the group home's sponsors. One resident asked, "Shouldn't you come to the community first before you go into contract [to buy the house]?" The representative responded with a question: "Do you ask permission from neighbors when you move into a new neighborhood? We see our home as one big family." This response provoked an angry outburst from the audience, since it seemed to conflate the establishment of the group home with the experience of black families moving into segregated white neighborhoods. Marshall tried to restore calm, assuring the audience that the area's community board would hold a public hearing later in the month.

"What guarantee does the community have that the residents won't be a problem?" a middle-aged woman asked. "They will not be a detriment to the community," the representative responded curtly. "Will there be drug testing?" a young woman asked. "The residents will be mentally retarded adolescents and not drug addicts," came the response.

The audience again erupted in anger. "No way! We have enough problems with our own families," one man stated. A second shouted, "I don't want them; I live two doors away. They should be institutionalized." He added menacingly, "I'm a pretty good shotgun artist." "How can you force this on us when we don't want it?" A woman continued. "Why don't you put it next to where you live? You put it in the heart of the community, instead of outside. Our property values will go down." Another woman agreed: "There will be twenty outsiders in the middle of the block with kids. How do you expect us to accept the tearing apart of the fabric of our community? This is basically a business and a quality-of-life decision for us."

Marshall, again trying to calm the audience, stood and addressed the representative: "You see, Mr. Farnum, this is a black community and everyone has put their life investments into this community. We care so much [about disadvantaged people] that we already have 481 beds [for special populations]. We did our share, but the city didn't do its share."

The audience applauded her comments enthusiastically, seeming to respond to the statement that East Elmhurst was a "black community"—or, perhaps better, to the relation between this statement and the decision that they were about to make. For in her use of the term, she appeared to be mediating a contradiction between "care for the disadvantaged" and the interests of property owners. The significance of the term "black community," rescued by ambiguity, seemed to link two contradictory notions: that of a "community of the disadvantaged" being dumped on by municipal authorities and that of a community protecting its interests against a threat posed by the "disadvantaged." For the homeowners of East Elmhurst, the meaning of race, of the "black community," no longer fit neatly and unambiguously into the racial discourse of civil rights era activism—it had come to embrace, albeit tenuously, the interests of the black middle class.

Twenty minutes later, after the representatives from the social service agency had left, the president of the Civic Association stood solemnly to address the audience, as if to explain to the members why they themselves had opposed the group home. "We do care," he said earnestly, "but we have to care about the whole community." What remained in doubt as residents quietly left the meeting room, however, was the identity of that "whole community."

Conclusion

In this chapter, I have argued that Wilson's "exodus model" of black class stratification minimizes the continuing significance of race for the black nonpoor and neglects the political effects of class differentiation within African American communities. In Corona-East Elmhurst, processes of class stratification interacted with state-sponsored reforms to reshape political interests, power relations, and ideologies along class lines. I do not mean to suggest that race is declining in significance in the lives of the black middle class—as if, to recall Shulman, class stratification and racial oppression were "inversely related processes." Residential segregation, bias at the workplace, and the threat of racial violence continue to constrain the black middle class.[15] Moreover, race remains important in the construction and elaboration of black middle-class identities. I do mean to suggest that for the homeowners of East Elmhurst, class-based interests, ideologies, and political alignments are playing an increasingly important role in defining what it means to be black and middle-class in the post–civil rights era political landscape.

Acknowledgments

Research for this article was funded with support from the National Research Council and the National Science Foundation. I thank Roger Sanjek, Mary Anne Clawson, and the *American Ethnologist* reviewers for comments on earlier drafts.

Notes

1. Wilson notes that during the 1970s the movement of blacks to higher-paying jobs slowed considerably because of economic recession (1978, 130). Bart Landry also points to a decline in the growth rate of the black middle class during the recession years of the 1970s, but he stresses white resistance to equal employment opportunities for blacks in the face of increased job competition (1988, 75–76). In short, Landry places greater emphasis on the continuing significance of racial discrimination in the workplace, particularly during periods of intense job competition.

2. See Reed (1988) for a critique of Wilson's use of the notion of "mainstream role models" and his deployment of the language of social pathology to describe underclass deviation from those models. In a later article, Loïc J. D. Wacquant and Wilson advance the concept of "social capital"—that is, the social resources that individuals can draw upon "by virtue of being socially integrated into solidary groups, networks, or organizations" (1989, 22). With this concept, Wilson seems to shift his emphasis from the role of working- and middle-class people as normative models for behavior to the role of the social resources that such people can provide through both informal and formal means.

3. Using the index of dissimilarity (a statistical measure of segregation) to analyze census data for the years 1960, 1970, and 1980, Reynolds Farley and Walter R. Allen observed relatively small changes in segregation in a study of the twenty-five U.S. cities with the largest black populations in 1980. Farley and Allen conclude that their data "suggest that a continuation of the trends of the 1970s will leave blacks highly segregated in the foreseeable future" (1987, 145). Moreover, Farley and Allen discount the influence of economic status on patterns of residential segregation: "Blacks are thoroughly segregated from whites regardless of how much income they obtained or how many years they spent in school. The segregation score for families in the $50,000 and over range—79—is close to that for poverty-level families—76 for families with incomes under $5,000" (1987, 150).

4. See Gephart and Pearson (1988) for a discussion of the problems involved in defining and conceptualizing the underclass.

5. Corona has historically suffered from poor social services, particularly in terms of recreational facilities for children. A report published in 1946 by the Urban League of Greater New York concluded: "The survey of recreational facilities within Corona reveals the meagerness of resources. . . . [A]fter-school facilities during the greater part of the year, are all but non-existent, the libraries are not equipped to do community work, and scouting is poorly developed" (Urban League 1946, 96). Before the 1960s, what services did exist were provided by churches and, to a lesser extent, local black voluntary associations.

6. Older residents of Corona-East Elmhurst often remark that East Elmhurst was not considered a distinct neighborhood until the late 1940s. Northern Boulevard was the perceived boundary between Corona and East Elmhurst until the 1970s. Today, most residents of East Elmhurst see Astoria Boulevard, farther to the north, as the dividing line. In short, the neighborhood boundary

is fluid and contingent on where the speaker resides, as well as on the subjective perception of class differences between the two areas.

7. Some neighborhood activists have told me that the founders of the Civic Association had originally intended to limit membership to residents of East Elmhurst but, under pressure from neighborhood activists in both Corona and East Elmhurst, eventually broadened the group's purview to include Corona.

8. After an NAACP meeting, one neighborhood activist and veteran of the civil rights movement told me, "The civil rights movement was the worst thing that ever happened to us. That's right—the worst thing. Sure we got some rights, but it split our community apart."

9. This estimate is based on a list of block associations prepared by the local state assemblywoman's office during the 1980s. Although block associations do exist in North Corona, I have a sense that they are declining in both number and relative importance. Several of the Corona block associations included on the list exist in name only.

10. Some residents of East Elmhurst report, for example, that African Americans are discriminated against when they attempt to buy cooperative apartments in neighboring Jackson Heights, a predominantly white, middle-class community. A recent article published in a New York City–based community affairs magazine reported that despite a growing population of Asian and Hispanic immigrants, the black population of Jackson Heights remained very small. The director of fair housing for the city's Commission on Human Rights said to Lisa Glazer, the article's author, "Openness to diversity often stops at people of color who are black. We see increases in integration in neighborhoods with a small number of blacks, where blacks aren't seen as a threat. We've definitely gotten complaints from Jackson Heights" (Glazer 1990).

11. Brett Williams, for example, discusses the contrasting ways in which homeowners and renters experience the boundary between the inside and the outside of the home: "[T]enants find telling the places where they see owners—outdoors but in charge, on their porches, in their yards, shoveling the snow from a small patch of sidewalk. These transitional spaces highlight the easy movement outdoors and back inside that tenants lack, for they must negotiate buffer zones such as hallways, elevators, and stairwells" (1985, 254).

12. This reading of the signs of community decay is sometimes conducted in an organized manner. I once accompanied the president of the Civic Association on a tour of East Elmhurst during which we systematically recorded the number and location of faded parking signs. A number of residents had complained at Civic Association meetings that they were being given parking tickets unfairly, since the parking signs were unreadable. During the tour, we surveyed a grid of about fifty block faces, noting in the process abandoned cars, sites of illegal dumping, and other signs of neighborhood decay to be reported at the next meeting of the Civic Association.

13. Omi and Winant define rearticulation as "a practice of discursive reorganization or reinterpretation of ideological themes and interests already present in the subjects' consciousness, such that these elements obtain new meanings or coherence" (1986, 173).

14. This incident became known as the "boarder baby" firebombing and resulted in the arrests of three residents of the block where the planned facility was to be located (Stein 1987). Three days after the arrests, Timothy Mitchell, pastor of the Ebenezer Missionary Baptist Church of Flushing, led members of his church on a march in the Flushing neighborhood in order, as he put

it, to "express outrage" over the bombing. Speaking to a crowd of white residents, Mitchell said: "If these were white babies, you would be over here bringing baby clothes to these children." Residents shouted in response, "Don't turn this into a racial issue" and "It's not a racial issue" (Hernandez 1987, 35).

15. For example, in the summer of 1989 a young African American couple from East Elmhurst was attacked by a group of white men while stopped at a toll booth on the New Jersey Turnpike. Since the victims were successful professionals (an investment banker and a lawyer), many residents perceived the incident as a reflection of the precarious position of the black middle class. Moreover, the young man who was attacked was the grandson of the president of the local NAACP and the son of the first African American to have been elected to the local community school board.

References

City Planning Commission. 1963. *Corona-East Elmhurst area extension: Urban renewal designation.* New York: City Planning Commission.

Cox, Kevin R. 1982. Housing tenure and neighborhood activism. *Urban Affairs Quarterly.* 18, no. 1:107–129.

Farley, Reynolds. 1984. *Blacks and whites: Narrowing the gap?* Cambridge: Harvard University Press.

Farley, Reynolds, and Walter R. Allen. 1987. *The color line and the quality of life in America.* New York: Russell Sage Foundation.

Gephart, Martha A., and Robert W. Pearson. 1988. Contemporary research on the urban underclass. *Social Science Research Council Items* 42, no. 1/2:1–10.

Glazer, Lisa. 1990. Integration: Myth and reality. *City-Limits* 15, no. 7:16–21.

Guest, Avery M., and R. S. Oropesa. 1986. Informational social ties and political activity in the metropolis. *Urban Affairs Quarterly* 21, no. 4:550–574.

Hart, Robert L., Adam Krivatsky, and William Stubee. 1970. *Local area study: Jackson Heights, Corona, East Elmhurst, Elmhurst.* New York: Department of City Planning.

Harvey, David. 1978. Labor, capital and class struggle around the built environment in advanced capitalist societies. *In Urbanization and conflicts in market societies,* edited by. K. R. Cox. Pp. 9–37. New York: Methuen.

Hernandez, Evelyn. 1987. Black church rallies in Flushing. *New York Newsday,* 4 May, 7, 35.

Independent Citizens' Committee for the Election of Rev. Robert D. Sherard. 1963. Letter, 24 October. Typescript, files of the author.

Julian I. Garfield Democratic Association. 1962. *The second anniversary testimonial and awards banquet honoring Corinne K. Harris.* Corona, N.Y.: Julian I. Garfield Democratic Association.

Katznelson, Ira. 1981. *City trenches: Urban politics and the patterning of class in the United States.* New York: Pantheon.

Kemeny, Jim. 1980. Home ownership and privatization. *International Journal of Urban and Regional Research* 4:372–388.

Kilson, Martin. 1981. Black social classes and intergenerational poverty. *Public Interest* 64:58–78.

Landry, Bart. 1988. *The new black middle class.* Berkeley: University of California Press.

Long Island Star Journal. 1957. King asks non-violence in anti-bias fight. *Long Island Star Journal,* 13 November, 5.

Lowe, Philip D. 1977. Amenity and equity: A review of local environmental pressure groups in Britain. *Environment and Planning* 9:35–58.

Omi, Michael, and Howard Winant. 1986. *Racial formation in the United States.* New York: Routledge and Kegan Paul.

Pickney, Alphonso. 1984. *The myth of black progress.* New York: Cambridge University Press.

Piven, Frances Fox, and Richard A. Cloward. 1971. *Regulating the poor.* New York: Pantheon.

Ravitch, Diane. 1988. The great school wars. New York: Basic Books.

Reed, Adolph, Jr. 1988. The liberal technocrat. Review of *The truly disadvantaged* by William Julius Wilson. *The Nation* 246 (6 February):167–170.

Sanjek, Roger. In press. The organization of festivals and ceremonies among Americans and immigrants in Queens, New York. In *To make the world safe for diversity: Towards an understanding of multi-cultural societies*, edited by A. Daun, B. Ehn, and B. Klein. Stockholm: Swedish Institute and Museum of Immigrants.

Sevfried, Vincent F. 1986. *Corona: From farmland to city suburb, 1650–1935.* Garden City, N.Y.: Edgian.

Shulman, Steven. 1981. Race, class and occupational stratification: A critique of William J. Wilson's *The declining significance of race. Review of Radical Political Economy* 13, no. 3:21–31.

Stein, Sharon. 1987. Three Queens neighbors arrested in "boarder baby" house fire. *New York Newsday*, 1 May, 5, 25.

Stone, Clarence N. 1989. *Regime politics: Governing Atlanta 1946–1988.* Lawrence: University of Kansas Press.

Urban League of Greater New York. 1946. *Aspects of Negro life in the Borough of Queens, N.Y.C.* New York: Urban League of Greater New York.

U.S. Bureau of the Census. 1981. *Census of population and housing, 1980: Summary tape files 1B & 3A. New York State.* Washington, D.C.: Bureau of the Census.

Wacquant, Loic J. D., and William Julius Wilson. 1989. The cost of racial and class exclusion in the inner city. *Annals of the American Academy of Political and Social Science* 501:8–25.

Williams, Brett. 1985. Owning places and buying time: Class, culture, and stalled gentrification. *Urban Life* 14, no. 3:251–273.

Willie, Charles. 1989. *Caste and class controversy on race and poverty: Round two of the Willie/Wilson debate.* New York: General Hall.

Wilson, William Julius. 1978. *The declining significance of race.* Chicago: University of Chicago Press.

_____. 1981. The black community in the 1980s: Questions of race, class and public policy. *Annals of the American Academy of Political and Social Science* 454:28.

_____. 1987. *The truly disadvantaged.* Chicago: University of Chicago Press.

IDA SUSSER

2 | Creating Family Forms

*The Exclusion of Men
and Teenage Boys from
Families in the New York
City Shelter System,
1987–1991*

The term "underclass" (Wilson 1987; Ricketts and Sawhill 1988) and its relationship to the 1960s concept of "culture of poverty" has been a source of controversy (Jones 1993; Maxwell 1993). William Julius Wilson, a widely recognized sociologist, at first used the term but has since abandoned "underclass" and now refers to the "urban poor." However, we still need to reconceptualize the urban poor in order to avoid implying an illusory separation between poor and not poor. An emphasis on separateness obscures rather than illuminates analysis of the dynamic processes of capitalism (Vincent 1993). Whereas terms such as "underclass" emphasize the social isolation of poor people, they neglect the institutional connections that bind members of different income groups together: through work in the formal and informal economies and through social service institutions (Mollenkopf and Castells 1991). Research suggests that it is precisely the interaction with and active intervention of government institutions, schools, health care, police, and shelters for the homeless that limit and reshape the lives of the poor, whether we label them unemployed working class, urban poor or "underclass." For homeless people in New York City, the experience of poverty reflects the constant interplay between institutional regulations and poor people's strategies of adaptation and resistance to such constraints.

Much of the discussion of the underclass and poverty centers around the family or household structure: questions of female-headed households, teenage mothers, absent fathers, abandoned and neglected children (Zinn 1989). The research presented here suggests that such family strategies must be analyzed within the context of the historically specific constraints of institutions serving the poor.

The presence of these constraints is not a new observation. These constraints have been noted for some time in the literature concerning poor and minority families in the United States (Piven and Cloward 1971, Stack 1974, Susser and Kreniske 1987, Abramovitz 1988, Block et al. 1988). However, in examining the shelter system in New York City, we see the reemergence of old patterns in new institutions.

Family Form and Institutional Dynamics

The data from the shelters suggest that United States society has at least two models of family that are fostered by social and government institutions.

One model is the generally noted nuclear family, which has been the target of much discussion and criticism by feminists and other social researchers. Clearly, this model has never allowed for the range of households found in the United States (Cole 1986, Rapp 1987, Mullings 1989, Susser 1989). Nevertheless, much research has documented the ways in which government institutions, such as schools, social security, and other entitlements have assumed the natural existence of the nuclear family and treated household units as if they were constructed in this way (Abramovitz 1988). Indeed, government-guaranteed housing loans for working people who could afford a mortgage were also predicated on the nuclear family (Edel, Sclar, and Luria 1984). Cultural explanations have drawn on this model of the nuclear family to describe "American kinship" (Schneider 1968). Households that do not conform to this cultural expectation have been classified as "broken" if not pathological.

The second model of the U.S. family is the model for poor households. This model separates the father from the mother and their young children. It treats the mother and children as a family unit. Research on the shelter system suggests that, far from imposing a nuclear family model on the poor household, some institutions are in fact imposing a female-headed household as the model for poor people when they receive government subsidies. This tendency was first documented in analysis of public assistance programs such as Aid to Families with Dependent Children (AFDC), which provided funds preferentially for women and children. The original version of this program, Aid to Dependent Children (ADC), was instituted by the 1934 Social Security Act. One might attribute the current bias in public assistance to its emergence during that time. However, the imposition of the model becomes dramatically apparent in an examination of the new institutions that have been created in the 1980s to shelter homeless "families."

It is not suggested here that regulations directly construct family patterns. Variations in household structure have not been found to directly parallel variations in public assistance (Ellwood and Summers 1986, Wilson and Neckerman 1986). Nevertheless, the historical consistency in models of family life that accompany government assistance for poor people contrast strikingly with programs designed to provide financial assistance to higher-income households.

The Structuring of Households

Based on a study of household structure and gender as observed in the New York City shelter system between 1987 and 1991, this chapter documents the institutional processes that divide poor families. It also documents the ongoing struggle among the families themselves to provide for children and improve their own living conditions under difficult circumstances.[1]

Much research has demonstrated the economic factors that have structured poor households and left young women largely responsible for child rearing (Stack 1974, Wilson 1987, Dehavenon 1990, Susser 1986). The shift of industrial work out of the metropolitan Northeast has decreased the availability of well-paid, stable, unionized manufacturing work for men and women (Bluestone and Harrison 1982). At the same time, the growing service economy of the advanced capitalist city, supplemented by an informal economy of sweatshops and nonunionized work, has provided low-paid insecure employment for women, immigrants, and members of U.S. minority groups (Sassen 1991). Homicide rates, military service, and incarceration have reduced the number of men available for marriage among low-income populations (Dehavenon 1993). In addition, studies from the 1960s to the 1990s have documented the difficulties that confront men in their attempt to maintain nuclear households in the face of poverty, unemployment, and racial discrimination (Liebow 1967, Sullivan 1990). It is within the context of the persistent assaults on employment and household income that have confronted families in New York City in the last two decades that the impact of homeless shelters on family life and the construction of social supports must be analyzed.

Homelessness

Conceptually, the experience of homelessness must be seen as one aspect of the life of the poor of New York City in the 1980s and 1990s. Data indicate that many working people became homeless in the 1980s and that some, despite being homeless, worked in both the formal and informal economy (Susser and Gonzalez 1992). By 1988, there were two hundred thousand names on the waiting list for apartments in New York City housing projects (Barbanel 1988). Many poor New Yorkers shared their apartments with people who later became homeless (known in New York City as "doubling up"). In 1992, one study found four-fifths of the families asking for shelter had spent the previous night doubling up (Dehavenon 1992). Similarly, many poor New Yorkers experienced intermittent homelessness (Dehavenon 1992).

Thus, it is analytically misleading to view "the homeless" as a category separate from other poor people in New York City. To categorize a person as "homeless" carries the implication that this is a permanent characteristic rather than an experience through which s/he is passing temporarily. Like the use of the term "underclass," such an approach leads to static analyses of "the homeless" as a reified group. It fails to further our understanding of the processes that lead to loss of a home and the ongoing problems of poverty faced by both "homed" and "homeless."

History of Homelessness in New York City

Homelessness in New York City followed the fiscal crisis of 1975 and the ensuing changes in social services and public policy. In 1969, there were only thirty homeless families to be found in New York City; by 1985 there were five thousand (New York State Department of Social Services 1988). The category "homeless" was not used in New York City until the late 1970s. At that time, the increasing number of people living in the streets combined with the disastrous living circumstances of homeless families became a major political issue (Baxter and Hopper 1981, Hopper and Cox 1982, Hopper 1987).

By 1988, 15,600 people, including 10,000 children, lived in eighty-two hotels for homeless families citywide (New York State Department of Social Services 1988). In addition, estimates have suggested that approximately 23,000 "single" adults slept in shelters run by the city each night (*New York Times* 1987). Since the populations were transient and many people never entered publicly regulated shelters but slept instead in subways, railway stations, parks, and a wide variety of claimed spaces, estimates of the total numbers of people homeless in the city each night ranged between 35,000 and 100,000. The range in these figures indicates the extent to which people moved in and out of homelessness over the course of a year. Thus, a very conservative estimate would be that 100,000 to 200,000 New York City residents experienced at least one night of homelessness in one year. In 1987, 1.7 million people lived below the poverty line in New York City (Community Service Society 1989 3). Thus, one can calculate that homelessness was experienced by about 5 percent of poor people in the city in that year.[2]

While we can trace the appearance of "homelessness" to the years of the 1975 fiscal crisis, during New York City's period of recovery from 1979 to 1989 we see a continued increase in homelessness and poverty. In the 1980s, the number of poor people in New York City rose from 1.4 million to 1.7 million (Community Service Society 1989, 3–8). In line with these shifts, the numbers of homeless people also rose dramatically.

Thus, homelessness, as we now recognize it, is a recent product of the shifting economy of New York City reflecting basic changes in the national economy. Homelessness was the underside of the economic resurgence that accompanied the development of New York City as an international corporate center in the 1980s (Hopper, Susser, and Conover 1987, Mollenkopf and Castells 1991, Sassen 1991, Susser 1991). Almost 500,000 service and clerical jobs were created in New York City in the 1980s. However, the continuing loss of well-paying manufacturing work, rising prices in real estate, reductions in social services, the decrease in the value of public assistance, and the cessation of federal construction of housing combined to create a new experience of poverty (Marcuse 1985, Drennan 1991, Mollenkopf and Castells 1991, Susser 1991). Such changes resulted in the actual loss of shelter for many New Yorkers.[3]

In response to growing national concern, political exposure, and legal action by and for homeless people, the New York City administration and a variety of voluntary agencies and churches began to organize temporary shelters (Hopper and Cox,1982). Armories, schools, and hospitals were converted by the New York City Human Resource Administration into mass dormitories for the homeless. Managers of rundown hotels often were paid three thousand dollars per month to provide single rooms for homeless families, thus creating the miserable settings commonly known as "homeless hotels" (Kozol 1988, Christiano and Susser 1989).

The Shelter System and the City's Response to Homelessness

As homelessness became more routine and the numbers of men, women, and children seeking shelter overwhelmed the existing public assistance offices, new Emergency Assistance Bureaus (EABs) were created. To prevent people sleeping overnight in public assistance offices, the Emergency Assistance Bureaus operated after hours to assign families to emergency housing (Dehavenon 1990, 1992).

As hundreds of people continued to congregate and sleep in public locations such as Grand Central Terminal and the Port Authority Bus Terminal, such agencies were forced to confront the issue of homelessness. In an unsuccessful effort to reduce the large population sleeping in and around the bus terminals every night, the Port Authority of New York and New Jersey facilitated the establishment of "drop-in centers" where people could spend time but not sleep.

Initially, access to shelters varied as some settings accepted people from specific neighborhoods while others only accepted those assigned by centralized bureaus. Eventually, regulations about access to shelters were implemented. People were assigned to shelters throughout the city without regard for the neighborhood in which they had lived or the schools children attended.

While the numbers of homeless families have been increasing, the response of the New York City administration has vacillated over time in line with political realities. Between 1987 and 1990, first Mayor Edward Koch and then Mayor David Dinkins made much-publicized efforts to close down the most infamous "homeless hotels." Between 1988 and 1991, in response to political pressure and court orders, homeless families were moved to the top of the waiting list for New York City publicly owned housing (Barbanel 1988). As one result of this revised policy, approximately seven hundred families were moved out of a hotel in downtown Manhattan where we were conducting fieldwork. Some were transferred to another hotel in Times Square, while others were moved into transitional housing organized by voluntary agencies. Many were moved into apartments around the city.

However, in 1991, after four years of effort to move people out of "homeless hotels" the city was once again placing families in hotels. A family was required to prove six to twelve months of homelessness before becoming eligible for assignment to public housing (Dehavenon 1992). Doubled-up families (those sharing apartments with other families) were assigned first option for city apartments. Thus, "homeless hotels" did not disappear. The process of homelessness or the need to pass through homelessness to find an apartment in New York City continued unabated (Dehavenon 1992).

Gender and Shelter in New York City

As the shelter system materialized, certain patterns emerged concerning gender expectations and the structuring of families. Such patterns, while apparently varying from site to site, were in fact significant for their consistency with the public assistance regulations of the pre-homeless era with respect to the ways they divided families.

The Shelter System: Divisions by Age and Gender

Access to shelters in New York City was largely determined by sex, age, mental status, and family structure. "Single" men were usually assigned to large barracks in the city's armories. In such places up to seven hundred cots were lined up in the main halls (for a more detailed description of such a shelter, see Susser and Gonzalez 1992). "Single" women without children were assigned to other armories. Adults defined as single (any adults without children accompanying them) had no access to the hotels and voluntary-agency settings to which families were sometimes assigned. Men were not allowed in women's barracks, and women were not allowed to enter the halls where men slept. Shelters were also provided specifically for mentally ill women, although they were not permitted to live with their children. Other gender-specific shelters served the older population of men and women, and various small church spaces provided nightly beds for a few men and women together.

One of the few "shelter creations" where men and women without children were allowed to meet indoors were the "drop-in centers." In these newly invented forms, no one was supposed to sleep overnight. A "drop-in" center usually provided chairs, tables, and a television. Sometimes caseworkers and counselors were present. People were allowed to visit the center twenty-four hours a day. However, no one was permitted to lie down to sleep and no space was provided for possessions. People were offered gender-specific assignments as buses left the drop-in centers in the early evening. Those found sleeping on floors or tables were awakened during the night by shelter guards.

Women with young children were often assigned, like "single" men and women, to large congregate sleeping shelters. However, this was supposed to be a temporary measure. If they were fortunate, women with young children might be sent to stay in "homeless hotels"; if they were even more fortunate, they might be allocated "transitional" housing run largely by voluntary associations.

Homeless Hotels

Privately owned hotels where the New York City Human Resources Administration placed families seeking shelter were commonly known as homeless hotels. Such hotels had little to recommend them (Kozol 1988, Christiano and Susser 1989). Rooms were arranged along dark, poorly lit corridors with crumbling paint. Many elevators did not work, and people were forced to climb dangerous stairwells with loose railings. Inside the rooms themselves, beds took up most of the space, and frequently bathroom facilities were out of order. Security was lax. We were told by public health nurses in several hotels that they made their visits in the mornings (if at all) because they were afraid to walk down the corridors later in the day. Residents reported in interviews that rats were entering some of the rooms and that some had entered children's cots. During the 1980s some services and programs had been implemented. Caseworkers assisted people with public assistance applications and applications for housing. Public health service nurses checked with pregnant women and new mothers to see if medical appointments had been scheduled and kept. In some hotels day care programs and other services had been provided in response to residents' demands (Mathieu 1990).

In homeless hotels, rooms were usually allocated to women with children. If husbands were listed as recipients of public assistance in the household, they, too, were allowed to stay in the hotel. Many more men were in evidence here than in transitional housing. Frequently, however, due to the complexity and biases of public assistance regulations, men were not authorized to accompany women and children to the hotels.

Transitional Housing

In the transitional housing, which was the most humane offered up to 1991, women and children were allocated rooms with beds and bathroom facilities. No cooking facilities were provided, however, and cooking was not officially permitted in rooms. Women were assigned to caseworkers who assisted in filing applications for public assistance and housing. Frequently, day care for young children, substance abuse counseling, and access to medical care was arranged.

Multiple restrictions determined access to transitional housing. In 1992, only 9 percent of families seeking shelter at emergency assistance bureaus were assigned to transitional housing (Dehavenon 1992). Nevertheless, such placements were much sought after by women in need of shelter. Transitional housing was selected for women with less substance abuse and fewer family problems than the general population of homeless families. Women who did not attend required substance abuse seminars or group meetings or failed to conform to other regulations could be evicted.

Most transitional housing had regulations concerning the age and gender of children permitted to reside there. One such institution housed only mothers with daughters under eighteen and sons under twelve. Men were allowed to visit at certain hours in the basement. They were never allowed in women's rooms. Another transitional facility only housed women with children under nine years old. In this facility, there were no visiting hours for men and they were not allowed to enter the institution at all, unless as employees. Visiting female relatives, such as grandmothers, were not allowed into the shelter unless they had a scheduled appointment. One woman told a fieldworker that her mother had been turned away at the door of the shelter because she had not formally arranged a visit. Women and children stayed in these facilities from six months to over a year.

A Comparison of Homeless Hotels and Transitional Housing

One major difference between homeless hotels and transitional housing was the level of security. It was possible for men not officially listed as residents to find their way into hotels, whereas this was highly unusual in transitional housing. By 1990, the main institutions created for homeless people where men and women could live together with their children were the notorious homeless hotels. Even in this case, most men had to sneak into the rooms against regulations. It is significant, in light of descriptions of absent fathers and young boys concerned with sexual prowess rather than responsibility found in discussions of the underclass (for example Anderson 1989), that the institutional separation and exclusion of males from the household structure started at an early age in the shelter system. In transitional housing, teenage girls were often allowed to stay with their mothers, but teenage boys were never admitted. If a woman accepted such housing she had to give up her older boys to foster care or the supervision of relatives. Private hotels had no such regulations. However, in the course of fieldwork in one hotel, a researcher was informed that the "manager" who runs the hotel, "doesn't allow teenagers." This rule clearly referred to young boys, as numerous teenage mothers were permitted to live in this hotel.

Men's Participation in Family Life in a Mid-Manhattan Hotel

In order to examine household relations, we document the multiple parenting roles of men observed in a mid-Manhattan hotel. In such hotels, men did come into the building, albeit illegally or after harassment at the entrance. This will be compared with the experiences of families in transitional housing from which men and boys were categorically excluded.

The impact of hotel regulations on family life is evidenced by the experiences of one household in 1989. Dawn, a thirty-six-year-old African American woman had been assigned a room in the hotel.[4] She had two teenage children, a girl and a boy, and a three-month-old infant girl. The boy of fifteen was officially living with his grandmother, although he visited the hotel daily. The father of the infant took care of all three children while Dawn was away. She attended data entry classes on week-day nights. The father was not officially allowed in the hotel and was frequently stopped by security guards at the front door. The family was awaiting renovation of an assigned apartment where, according to Dawn, they were to be reunited. In the meantime, both the teenage boy and the baby's father were formally excluded from participation and coop-eration in family life.

In a conversation with a public health nurse who was checking the immunization record and clinic visits of the baby, Dawn stated, "I am so angry that sometimes I feel like killing myself." The nurse invited her to come to the nurses' office and talk to someone when she felt this way. Staff in the hotel, although overworked and not always support-ive, were an important source of assistance for residents. However, as this example makes evident, under the debilitating conditions of home-lessness, a mother with a newborn baby was unable to mobilize social supports that would otherwise be available to her. In addition, she had been placed in a hotel far from friends and relatives and the concern for security made visits difficult. Regulations excluded the youngest child's father from her household.

In the same hotel in the fall of 1989, fieldworkers observed fathers sharing a variety of tasks. Fathers collected children from the day care center in the hotel. They stayed with children in their rooms while the mother was out. They met children at school and brought them back to the hotel. They cared for infants and young children when their moth-ers were ill. In general, men assisted in family life.

Even unrelated men sometimes assisted families. For example, Anne had lived in the hotel for one and a half years. She shared her room with her twin five-year-old sons, a seventeen-year-old daughter, and the daughter's baby. When asked by a fieldworker if she felt threatened by the men in the hallways, she said no. She claimed that people knew and respected her. She explained that the men who spent their time "hanging out" in the hallway did not harass her and sometimes even helped her. She recalled the following incident, to demonstrate her sense of the supportiveness of the men who congregated in the corridor out-side her door.

Concerned about a sick child, Anne ran out of her room to telephone for medical assistance. One of the men in the corridor called out to her, "What's up mama, where are you running to?" When she explained,

"Please do me a favor, call an ambulance, one of my boys is sick," he reassured her, "Don't worry mama, I'll take care of it."

In spite of the obvious integration of men in the family lives of hotel residents, negative stereotypes were prevalent. A teenage boy with a baseball bat greeted a public health nurse in the corridor of the hotel. In another setting baseball might have been seen as a predictable activity for a young boy. However, as he went by, the nurse commented to a fieldworker, "He was probably on his way to beat someone up."

Robberies occurred frequently in the hotels, and rapes and stabbings were not uncommon. Under these conditions, men who congregated in the stairwells, lobbies, and corridors were suspect. Some were known to residents as drug dealers. When we talked with residents, they speculated that guards allowed drug dealers and criminals through the security checkpoint in the lobby because they feared them or because they received payments. Male family members, on the other hand, were often stopped and harassed at the hotel entrance.

The Exclusion of Men from Transitional Housing

In contrast to the ambiguous status of men in privately run hotels, men and teenage boys were categorically excluded from most transitional settings. Since women were frequently battered or victimized by husbands and male companions, one might expect that they sought this separation. However, women in transitional settings spent weekends with men. They sent children to stay with their fathers as well as with relatives on the fathers' side. They also brought their children to meet with men on the steps outside the shelter. Constant discussion in the shelters referred to husbands or male companions.

In at least one situation, the legal marriage of a woman with two children fell apart during the enforced separation of transitional housing. As the separation continued for more than six months, the father began to suspect his wife of infidelity and became alienated from her and their children. Thus, in the transitional housing, women were deprived of the company and assistance with child care that men were sometimes able to provide in the privately run hotels.

Men and Families

In spite of their official absence from statistics and measures of households among the poor, men were certainly present among the families of the homeless. As soon as the women with whom we worked were relocated to apartments, men appeared in their homes.

But within the institutions, both hotels and transitional housing, men and young boys were relegated to the status of criminals and reduced to sneaking in illegally (in the hotels) or shut out all together (in the transitional housing).

Research in a shelter for "single" men indicated that many men spent weekends visiting girlfriends, wives, and children (Susser and Gonzalez 1992). However, the overall impact of the shelter system was to separate households and undermine whatever cooperation or mutual responsibilities might have been developed among men, women, and children.

The exclusion of young boys and men from the family has been documented in public assistance programs since AFDC was implemented (Stack 1974, Abramovitz 1988). Research among poor residents of New York City between 1975 and 1978 documented the harassment of young men when they applied for relief. Even twelve-year-old boys were dropped from public assistance rolls because of bureaucratic hurdles (Susser 1982, Susser and Kreniske 1987).

In the extreme case of homelessness, young boys were cast out by regulations that, while confusing and varied, followed regular patterns. Boys were seen as criminals and a danger to society from a young age. They were subject to pressures that separated them from household and family, and, unlike their sisters, they could not anticipate assistance for rearing children. As they grew older, boys were portrayed as absent fathers or seen as unmotivated in terms of marriage and family commitments. However, these portrayals cannot be clearly understood without an analysis of the ways in which boys are excluded from participation in family life and the regulatory hurdles that men had to surmount in order to take on fatherhood.

As this brief outline of the structure of the shelter system illustrates, once people lost their homes, or in fact became financially dependent on the state through public assistance, "families" were defined as women and young children, and men were excluded from participation.

Conclusion

Among their many effects, shelters prevented mothers from mothering. Frequently, mothers were encouraged to entrust their children to some form of foster care in order to find a nightly bed in the shelters assigned to single women. As a result, many children were separated from brothers and sisters and placed in foster homes (for discussion of these issues see Dehavenon 1990 and Susser 1991). In hotels and transitional housing, although women could keep their children with them, they were not permitted to cook, and decisions about schedules and housing were made for them. Factors such as these might be expected to affect the way or the extent to which a woman could perform her role as mother.

Among middle-income residents of the United States, there are tasks expected of fathers as well as mothers. This is not the case among the poor and homeless in New York City. Fathers were defined out of the picture.

If we note the duties carried out by men in a mid-Manhattan hotel, under discouraging circumstances, we can see that men, women, and children suffer from the enforced separation. Children spent hours in staff offices as the staff were forced to substitute a bureaucratic network for family, friends, and neighbors. Nevertheless, requests for assistance with child care from shelter staff were frowned upon. Shelter administrators and caseworkers evaluated women poorly as mothers because they arrived late to pick up children or left them unsupervised in their rooms. On three occasions, we observed caseworkers informing women that another infraction of the rules, which involved collecting children late from child care, would result in the removal of the children from the mother's care. Many women in the hotels and transitional settings had already been reported to child welfare agencies and were being observed for future problems. This was known as "having an open case." Women with "open cases" lived under the threat of losing their children to foster care for infractions of shelter regulations, but they were deprived of the assistance that many men gave, when permitted. They were also deprived of previous friendships and the support of extended family members, both men and women. Women were then criticized for not being able to rear their children alone.

Thus, the separation of men and women was likely in the long run to contribute also to the loss of children by desperate mothers. Certainly, such enforced separation, in addition to lack of work, housing, and financial hardship, contributed to the destruction of nuclear households.

Thus, institutions that served the homeless of New York City redefined family life to exclude men and teenage boys. Data from shelters suggest that consistent barriers militate against the formation of nuclear households among poor people in the United States. Even where direct exclusion does not take place, barriers indicate symbolic separation and criminalization of boys and young men. Clearly, poor households and people without homes are in desperate need of government assistance. Still, at the least, we need to understand why services replicate the patterns of the past in consistent age and gender-specific ways. Such patterns reflect the need for control and regulation of the unemployed poor. In addition, they might be seen as contributing to the perpetuation of a hegemonic ideology that informs the formulation of models of the ideal family by class, race, and gender.

Notes

I would like to acknowledge the encouragement and assistance of Dr. Anke Ehrhardt, director, and Dr. Zena Stein, codirector, of the HIV Center for Clinical and Behavioral Studies, Columbia University, New York City, Grant No. MH43520 NIMH/NIDA, and of Eliecer Valencia and Ezra Susser from the Columbia-Presbyterian Psychiatric Shelter Program. I would also like to thank John Kreniske and two reviewers for editorial comments.

1. Alfredo Gonzalez, Yvonne LaSalle, Anne Christiano, Sheryl Heron, and Gwendolyn Martinez assisted in this research and spent time in various settings. During the course of the research, Yvonne LaSalle, Gwendolyn Martinez, and I visited transitional housing over the period of a year, talked with administrators, caseworkers, women, and children; we observed many activities. Fieldworkers spent many hours, several days a week, talking with women in their rooms and observing and talking with women and children in the various public areas of the shelters. Alfredo Gonzalez spent three months observing a drop-in center and interviewing homeless men and women who spent time there. He and another researcher spent four months visiting and interviewing families, caseworkers, and public health nurses in a hotel where homeless people had been placed. Researchers also spent over a year conducting fieldwork in a men's shelter. In general, fieldworkers visited the same people many times over and developed informal relationships with both staff and residents in the various settings. The data presented here are based on analysis of field notes, and discussions with fieldworkers as well as my own observations and fieldwork.

2. The poverty level is a federal index developed to classify families or related individuals as poor or nonpoor.

3. For a detailed analysis of the impact of these changes in one New York City neighborhood, see Mullings and Susser (1992).

4. All names of shelter residents have been changed to protect their identity and preserve confidentiality.

References

Abramovitz, M. 1988. *Regulating the lives of women.* Boston: South End Press.

Anderson, E. 1989. Sex codes and family life among poor inner-city youths. *Annals of* the *American Academy of Political Science* 501.

Bailey, T., and R. Waldinger. 1991. The changing ethnic/racial division of labor. In *The dual city,* edited by J. Mollenkopf and M. Castells. New York: Russell Sage Foundation

Barbanel, J. 1988. Hotel shelters to end by '90 Koch says: Families move to top of housing projects list. *New York Times,* 2 August, B1.

Baxter, E., and K. Hopper. 1981. *Private lives/Public spaces.* New York: Community Service Society of New York.

Block, F., R. Cloward, B. Ehrenreich, and F. Piven. 1988. *The mean season.* New York: Pantheon.

Bluestone, D., and B. Harrison. 1982. *The deindustrialization of America.* New York: Basic Books.

Christiano, A., and I. Susser. 1989. Knowledge and perceptions of HIV infection among homeless pregnant women. *Journal of Nurse-Midwifery* 34:318–22.

Cole, J., ed. 1986. *All American women.* New York: Free Press.

Community Service Society. 1989. *Poverty in New York City, 1985–1988.* New York: CSS.

Dehavenon, A. 1990. *The tyranny of indifference.* New York: The Action Research Project on Hunger, Homelessness and Family Health.

———. 1992. *Promises! Promises! Promises! The failed hopes of New York City's homeless families in 1992.* New York: The Action Research Project on Hunger, Homelessness and Family Health.

———. 1993. Where did all the men go? An etic model for the cross-cultural study of the causes of matrifocality. In *Where did all the men go? Female-headed households cross-culturally,* edited by J. Mencher and A. Okongwu. Boulder, Colo.: Westview Press.

Drennan, M. 1991. The decline and rise of the New York economy. In *The dual city,* edited by J. Mollenkopf and M. Castells. New York: Russell Sage Foundation.

Edel, M., E. D. Sclar, and D. Luria. 1984. *Shaky palaces.* New York: Columbia University Press.

Ellwood, D., and L. Summers. 1986. Poverty in America: Is welfare the answer or the problem? In *Fighting Poverty,* edited by S. Danziger and D. Weinberg. Cambridge: Harvard University Press.

Hopper, K.(1987. The public response to homelessness in New York City: The last hundred years. In *On being homeless: Historical perspectives,* edited by Rick Beard. New York: Museum of the City of New York.

Hopper, K., and L. Cox. 1982. Litigation in advocacy for the homeless: The case of New York City. *Development: Seeds of Change* 2:57–62.

Hopper, K., E. Susser, and S. Conover. 1987. Economics of makeshift: Deindustrialization and homelessness in New York City. *Urban Anthropology* 14:183–236.

Jones, Delmos. 1993. The culture of achievement among the poor: The case of mothers and children in a head-start program. *Critique of Anthropology* vol.13, 3:247–267.

Kozol, J. 1988. *Rachel and her children.* New York: Crown.

Liebow, E. 1967. *Tally's corner.* Boston: Little, Brown.

Marcuse, P. 1985. Gentrification, abandonment and displacement: Connections, causes and policy responses in New York City. *Journal of Urban and Contemporary Law* 28:193–240.

Mathieu, A. 1990. Parents on the move. Ph.D. diss., New School for Social Research, New York.

Maxwell, Andrew. 1993. The underclass, "social isolation" and "concentration effects": The "culture of poverty" revisited. *Critique of Anthropology* vol. 13, 3: 231–247.

Mollenkopf, J., and M. Castells. 1991. *The dual city.* New York: Russell Sage Foundation.

Mullings, L. 1989. Gender and the application of anthropological knowledge to public policy in the United States. In *Gender and anthropology,* edited by Sandra Morgen. Washington, D.C.: American Anthropological Association Press.

Mullings, L., and I. Susser. 1992. *Harlem research and development report.* New York: Manhattan Borough President's Office.

New York State Department of Social Service. 1988. *Annual report to the government and legislature.* Albany, N. Y.: Homeless Housing and Assistance Program.

New York Times. 1987. New York City lacks space for increase of the homeless. *New York Times,* 28 May.

Piven, F, and R. Cloward. 1971. *Regulating the poor.* New York: Pantheon.

Rapp, R. 1987. Urban kinship in contemporary America: Families, classes and ideology. In *Cities of the United States,* edited by L. Mullings. Pp. 219–243. New York: Columbia University Press.

Ricketts, E., and I. Sawhill. 1988. Defining and measuring the underclass. *Journal of Policy Analysis and Management* 7, no. 2:316–325.

Sassen, S. 1991. The informal economy. In *The dual city*, edited by J. Mollenkopf and M. Castells. New York: Russell Sage Foundation..

Schneider, D. 1968. *American kinship*. Chicago: University of Chicago Press.

Sharff , J. 1981. Free enterprise and the ghetto family. *Psychology Today* (March).

Stack, C. 1974. *All Our Kin*. New York: Harper Torchbooks.

Sullivan, M. 1990. *Getting Paid*. Ithaca, N.Y.: Cornell University Press,

Susser, I. 1982. *Norman Street: Poverty and politics in an urban neighborhood*. Oxford: Oxford University Press.

———. 1986. Political activity among working-class women in a U.S. city: 1975–1980. *American Ethnologist* 13, no. 1.

———. 1989. Gender in the anthropology of the United States. In *Gender and anthropology*, edited by Sandra Morgen. Washington, D. C.: American Anthropological Association Press.

———. 1991. The separation of mothers and children. In *The dual city*, edited by J. Mollenkopf and M. Castells. New York: Russell Sage Foundation.

Susser, I., and M. Gonzalez. 1992. Sex, drugs and videotape: The prevention of AIDS in a New York City shelter for homeless men. *Medical Anthropology* 14:307–322.

Susser, I., and J. Kreniske .1987. The welfare trap: A public policy for deprivation. In *Cities of the United States*, edited by L. Mullings. New York: Columbia University Press.

Vincent, Joan. 1993. Framing the underclass. *Critique of Anthropology* vol. 13, 3: 215–231.

Wilson, W. 1987. *The Truly Disadvantaged*. Chicago: University of Chicago Press.

Wilson, W., and K. Neckerman. 1986. Poverty and family structure: The widening gap between evidence and public policy issues. In *Fighting poverty*, edited by S. Danziger and D. Weinberg. Cambridge: Harvard University Press.

TERESA P. R. CALDEIRA

3 | Fortified Enclaves
The New Urban Segregation

In the last few decades, the proliferation of fortified
enclaves has created a new model of spatial segre-
gation and transformed the quality of public life in many cities around
the world. Fortified enclaves are privatized, enclosed, and monitored
spaces for residence, consumption, leisure, and work. The fear of violence is one of their main justifications. They appeal to those who are
abandoning the traditional public sphere of the streets to the poor, the
"marginal," and the homeless. In cities fragmented by fortified enclaves,
it is difficult to maintain the principles of openness and free circulation that have been among the most significant organizing values of modern cities. As a consequence, the character of public space and of citizens'
participation in public life changes.

In order to sustain these arguments, this chapter analyzes the case
of São Paulo, Brazil, and uses Los Angeles as a comparison. São Paulo
is the largest metropolitan region (it has more than sixteen million inhabitants) of a society with one of the most inequitable distributions of
wealth in the world.[1] In São Paulo, social inequality is obvious. As a
consequence, processes of spatial segregation are also particularly visible, expressed without disguise or subtlety. Sometimes, to look at an
exaggerated form of a process is a way of throwing light onto some of
its characteristics that might otherwise go unnoticed. It is like looking
at a caricature. In fact, with its high walls and fences, armed guards,
technologies of surveillance, and contrasts of ostentatious wealth and
extreme poverty, contemporary São Paulo reveals with clarity a new

pattern of segregation that is widespread in cities throughout the world, although generally in less severe and explicit forms.

I start this chapter by describing the changes in São Paulo's pattern of spatial segregation that have occurred in the last fifteen years. Then I show how the fortified enclaves became status symbols and instruments of social separation and suggest their similarities with other enclaves around the world. I examine Los Angeles as an example both to illustrate the types of architectural design and urban planning that the enclaves use and to evaluate the effects of this design. Finally, I discuss how the new public space and the social interactions generated by the new pattern of urban segregation may relate to experiences of citizenship and democracy.

Building Up Walls: São Paulo's Recent Transformations

The forms producing segregation in city space are historically variable. From the 1940s to the 1980s, a division between center and periphery organized the space of São Paulo, where great distances separated different social groups: the middle and upper classes lived in central and well-equipped neighborhoods and the poor lived in the precarious hinterland.[2] In the last fifteen years, however, a combination of processes, some of them similar to those affecting other cities, deeply transformed the pattern of distribution of social groups and activities throughout the city. São Paulo continues to be a highly segregated city, but the way in which inequalities are inscribed into urban space has changed considerably. In the 1990s, the physical distances separating rich and poor have decreased at the same time that the mechanisms to keep them apart have become more obvious and more complex.

The urban changes that occurred in the 1980s and 1990s in São Paulo, and the new pattern of spatial segregation they generated, cannot be separated from four different processes that became intertwined during this period. First, the 1980s and early 1990s were years of economic recession, with very high rates of inflation and increasing poverty. The 1980s are known in Brazil and in Latin America as the "lost decade." Contrary to the "miracle" years of the 1970s, economic growth was very low, the gross national product dropped 5.5 percent during the 1980s, unemployment rose, and inflation went up dramatically. For several years after the mid-1980s, inflation was higher than 1,000 percent a year, and successive economic plans to deal with it failed.[3] After a decade of inflation, unemployment, and recession, poverty has grown to alarming dimensions. Recent research shows that the effects of the economic crisis were especially severe for the poor population and aggravated the already iniquitous distribution of wealth in Brazil (Rocha 1991, Lopes 1993).[4]

This process of impoverishment has had serious consequences for the position of the poor in urban space. The periphery of the city became unaffordable for the poorest. Since the 1940s, the working classes had been building their own houses in the periphery of the city in a process called "autoconstruction" (see Caldeira 1984, Holston 1991). In this process, they bought cheap lots in distant areas of the city without any infrastructure and services and frequently involving some illegality, and spent decades building their dream houses and improving their neighborhoods. In this way, they both constructed their homes and expanded the city. However, their generally successful efforts to improve the quality of life in the periphery through the organization of social movements—which I discuss below—occurred at a moment when the economic crisis denied upcoming generations of workers the same possibility of becoming homeowners, even in precarious and distant areas of town. Consequently, the poorest population had to move either to *favelas* and *cortiços* in the central areas of town, or to distant municipalities in the metropolitan region.[5] According to a study by the office of São Paulo's secretary of housing, residents in *favelas* represented 1.1 percent of the city's population in 1973, 2.2 percent in 1980, 8.8 percent in 1987, and 19.4 percent in 1993—that is, 1,902,000 people in 1993 (*O Estado de S. Paulo*, 15 October 1994, C-1).

Second, these changes during the 1980s accompanied the consolidation of a democratic government in Brazil after twenty-one years of military rule. On the one hand, elections were held peacefully, regularly, and fairly, and political parties organized freely. On the other hand, trade unions and all types of social movements emerged onto the political scene, bringing the working classes and dominated groups to the center of politics and transforming the relationship between politicians and citizens. This is not a small achievement in a country with a tradition of high social inequality, elitism, and authoritarianism. This process of democratic consolidation has had many consequences and limits (see Holston and Caldeira 1998). It is important to note the consequences of this process in terms of the urban environment. Since the mid-1970s, social movements organized by homeowners' associations in the periphery have pressured local administrations both to improve the infrastructure and services in their neighborhoods and to legalize their land. Combined with changes in political groups in office brought about by free elections, this pressure transformed the priorities of local administration, making the periphery the site of much investment in the urban infrastructure. Moreover, during two decades of land disputes, social movements forced municipal governments to offer various amnesties to illegal developers, which resulted in the regularization of lots and their insertion into the formal land market. However, these new achievements also diminished the supply of irregular and cheap lots on the market. Since legal developments and lots in areas with a better infrastructure are obviously more expensive than illegal lots in underdeveloped areas, it is not difficult to understand that the neighborhoods that achieved these improvements came to be out of the reach of the already impoverished population, who were therefore pushed into *favelas* and *corticos*.

Third, during the 1980s, São Paulo's economic activities started to be restructured. Following the same pattern of many metropolises around the world, São Paulo is undergoing a process of expansion of tertiary activities or tertiarization. In the last decade, the city lost its position as the largest industrial pole of the country to other areas of the state and to the Metropolitan Region as a whole, becoming basically a center of finance, commerce, and the coordination of productive activities and specialized services—in a pattern similar to what is happening in the so-called global cities (Sassen 1991). This process has various consequences for the urban environment. The oldest industrial areas of the city are going through combined processes of deterioration and gentrification. In some of them, especially in districts in the inner part of town where various sectors of the middle classes live, abandoned houses and factories were transformed into *corticos*. Concomitantly, the opening of both new avenues and a subway line in the eastern zone generated urban renewal and the construction of new apartment buildings for the middle classes; some of these conform to the model of closed condominiums discussed later in this chapter. The most recent process, however, concerns the displacement of services and commerce from the inner city to districts on the periphery, especially to the western and southern zones of the metropolitan region. The new tertiary jobs are located in enormous, recently built office and service centers that have multiplied in the last fifteen years. At the same time, spaces of commerce are changing as immense shopping malls are created in isolated areas of the old periphery, and as some old shopping areas are abandoned to homeless people and street vendors.

Finally, the fourth process of change relates most directly to the new pattern of urban residential segregation because it supplies the justifying rhetoric: the increase in violent crime and fear. Crime has been increasing since the mid-1980s but, more important, there has been a qualitative change in the pattern of crime. Violent crime in the 1990s represents about 30 percent of all crime, compared to 20 percent in the early 1990s. Murder rates in the 1990s are higher than thirty-five per hundred thousand people in São Paulo.[6] However, the most serious element in the increase of violence in São Paulo is police violence. In the early 1990s, São Paulo's military police killed more than one thousand suspects per year, a number that has no comparison in any other city in the world.[7] The increase in violence, insecurity, and fear comes with a series of transformations, as citizens adopt new strategies of protection. These strategies are changing the city's landscape, patterns of residence and circulation, everyday trajectories, habits, and gestures related to the use of streets and of public transportation. In sum, the fear of crime is contributing to changes in all types of public interactions.

As a result, São Paulo is today a city of walls. Physical barriers have been constructed everywhere—around houses, apartment buildings, parks, squares, office complexes, and schools. Apartment buildings and houses that used to be connected to the street by gardens are now everywhere separated by high fences and walls and guarded by electronic devices and armed security men. The new additions frequently look odd because they were improvised in spaces conceived without them, spaces designed to be open. However, these barriers are now fully integrated into new projects for individual houses, apartment buildings, shopping areas, and work spaces. A new aesthetic of security shapes all types of constructions and imposes its new logic of surveillance and distance as a means for displaying status, and it is changing the character of public life and public interactions.

Among the diverse elements changing the city, the new enclaves for residence, work, and consumption of the middle and upper classes are provoking the deepest transformations. Although they have different uses and many specializations (some for residence, others for work, leisure, or consumption; some more restricted, others more open), all types of fortified enclaves share some basic characteristics. They are private property for collective use; they are physically isolated, either by walls or empty spaces or other design devices; they are turned inward and not to the street; and they are controlled by armed guards and security systems that enforce rules of inclusion and exclusion. Moreover, these enclaves are very flexible arrangements. As a result of their size, the new technologies of communication, the new organization of work, and security systems, they possess all that is needed within a private and autonomous space and can be situated almost anywhere, independent of the surroundings. In fact, most of them have been placed in the old periphery and have as their neighbors either *favelas* or concentrations of autoconstructed houses. Finally, the enclaves tend to be socially homogeneous environments, mostly for the middle and upper classes.

Fortified enclaves represent a new alternative for the urban life of these middle and upper classes. As such, they are codified as something conferring high status. The construction of status symbols is a process that elaborates social distance and creates means for the assertion of social difference and inequality. In the next section, I examine real estate advertisements as one way of analyzing this process for the case of São Paulo's enclaves. After that, I analyze the characteristics of the enclaves that make them an urban form that creates segregation and reproduces social inequality while transforming the character of public life.

Advertising Segregated Enclaves for the Rich

Real estate advertisements tell us about the lifestyles of the middle and upper classes and reveal the elements that constitute current patterns of social differentiation. The advertisements not only reveal a new code of social distinction but also explicitly treat separation, isolation, and protection as a matter of status. The following interpretation is based on the analysis of real estate advertisements for closed condominiums published in the newspaper *O Estado de S. Paulo* between 1975 and 1995. I analyze the advertisements in order to try to discover what is capturing the imagination and desires of São Paulo's middle and upper classes and to highlight some of the main images they are using in order to construct their place in society. I am particularly interested in uncovering how, in the last twenty years, the advertisements elaborated the myth of what they call "a new concept of residence" on the basis of the articulation of images of security, isolation, homogeneity, facilities, and services.[8] I argue that the image that confers the highest status and is most seductive is that of an enclosed and isolated community, a secure environment in which one can use various facilities and services and live only among equals. The advertisements present the image of islands to which one can return every day, in order to escape from the city and its deteriorated environment and to encounter an exclusive world of pleasure among peers. The image of the enclaves, therefore, is opposed to the image of the city as a deteriorated world pervaded by not only pollution and noise but, more importantly, confusion and mixture, that is, social heterogeneity.

Closed condominiums are supposed to be separate worlds. Their advertisements propose a "total way of life" that would represent an alternative to the quality of life offered by the city and its deteriorated public space. The ads suggest the possibility of constructing a world clearly distinguishable from the surrounding city: a life of total calm and security. Condominiums are distant, but they are supposed to be as independent and complete as possible to compensate for it; thus the emphasis on the common facilities they are supposed to have that transform them into sophisticated clubs. In these advertisements, the facilities promised inside closed condominiums seem to be unlimited—from drugstores to tanning rooms, from bars and saunas to ballet rooms, from swimming pools to libraries.

In addition to common facilities, São Paulo's closed condominiums offer a wide range of services. Some of the services (excluding security) mentioned in the advertisements are psychologists and gymnastic teachers to manage children's recreation, classes of all sorts for all ages, organized sports, libraries, gardening, pet care, physicians, message centers, frozen food preparation, housekeeping administration, cooks, cleaning personnel, drivers, car washing, transportation, and servants to do the grocery shopping. If the list does not meet your dreams, do not worry, for "everything you might demand" can be made available. The expansion of domestic service is not a feature of Brazil alone. As Sassen (1991, chapters 1 and 8) shows in the case of global cities, high-income gentrification requires an increase in low-wage jobs; yuppies and poor migrant workers depend on each other. In São Paulo, however, the intensive use of domestic labor is a continuation of an old pattern, although in recent years some relationships of labor have been altered, and this work has become more professional.

The multiplication of new services creates problems, including the spatial allocation of service areas. The solutions for this problem vary, but one of the most emblematic concerns the circulation areas. Despite many recent changes, the separation between two entrances—in buildings and in each individual apartment—and two elevators, one labeled "social" and the other "service," seems to be untouchable; different classes are not supposed to mix or interact in the public areas of the buildings.[9] Sometimes the insistence on this distinction seems ridiculous, because the two elevators or doors are often placed side by side instead of being in separate areas. As space shrinks and the side-by-side solution spreads, the apartments that have totally separate areas of circulation advertise this fact with the phrase, "social hall independent from service hall." The idea is old: class separation as a form of distinction.

Another problem faced by the new developments is the control of a large number of servants. As the number of workers for each condominium increases, as many domestic jobs change their character, and as "creative services" proliferate for members of middle and upper classes who cannot do without them, so also do the mechanisms of control diversify. The "creative administrations" of the new enclaves in many cases take care of labor management and are in a position to impose strict forms of control that would create impossible daily relationships if adopted in the more personal interaction between domestic servants and the families who employ them. This more "professional" control is, therefore, a new service and is advertised as such. The basic method of control is direct and involves empowering some workers to control others. In various condominiums, both employees of the condominium and maids and cleaning workers of individual apartments (even those who live there) are required to show their identification tags to go in and out of the condominium. Often they and their personal belongings are searched when they leave work. Moreover, this control usually involves men exercising power over women.

The middle and upper classes are creating their dream of independence and freedom—both from the city and its mixture of classes and from everyday domestic tasks—on the basis of services from working-class people. They give guns to badly paid working-class guards to control their own movement in and out of their condominiums. They ask their badly paid "office boys" to solve all their bureaucratic problems, from paying their bills and standing in all types of lines to transporting incredible sums of money. They also ask their badly paid maids—who often live in the *favelas* on the other side of the condominium's wall—to wash and iron their clothes, make their beds, buy and prepare their food, and frequently care for their children all day long. In a context of increased fear of crime in which the poor are often associated with criminality, the upper classes fear contact and contamination, but they continue to depend on their servants. They can only be anxious about creating the most effective way of controlling these servants, with whom they have such ambiguous relationships of dependency and avoidance, intimacy and distrust.

Another feature of closed condominiums is isolation and distance from the city, a fact that is presented as offering the possibility of a better lifestyle. The latter is expressed, for example, by the location of the development in "nature" (green areas, parks, lakes), and in the use of phrases inspired by ecological discourses. However, it is clear in the advertisements that isolation means separation from those considered to be socially inferior, and that the key factor to assure this is security. This means fences and walls surrounding the condominium, guards on duty twenty-four hours a day controlling the entrances, and an array of facilities and services to ensure security—guardhouses with bathrooms and telephones, double doors in the garage, and armed guards patrolling the internal streets. "Total security" is crucial to "the new concept of residence." Security and control are the conditions for keeping the others out, for assuring not only isolation but also "happiness," "harmony," and even "freedom." In sum, to relate security exclusively to crime is to fail to recognize all the meanings it is acquiring in various types of environments. The new systems of security not only provide protection from crime but also create segregated spaces in which the practice of exclusion is carefully and rigorously exercised.

The elaboration of an aesthetic of security and the creation of segregation on the basis of building enclaves are part of widespread processes not necessarily occurring elsewhere in the same obvious ways as in São Paulo. Fortified enclaves are not unique to São Paulo. In October 1993, a large advertising campaign in São Paulo elaborated on the similarities with enclaves in U.S. cities. It was a campaign to sell the idea of an "edge city" (an expression used in English) as a way of increasing the appeal and price of specific enclaves. One of the main characters of this campaign was Joel Garreau, a U.S. journalist and author of the book *Edge City—Life on the New Frontier*. His photograph appeared in full page ads in national magazines and newspapers, he came to São Paulo to talk to a select group of realtors, and he was one of the main participants in a thirty-minute television program advertising some enclaves. Garreau was helping market three huge real estate developments—Alphaville, Aldeia de Serra, and Tamboré—which combined closed condominiums, shopping centers, and office complexes as if they were a piece of the First World dropped into the metropolitan region of São Paulo.

The Paulista "edge city" was not created from scratch in 1993. The Western zone in which these developments are located is the part of the metropolitan region most affected by transformations in the last two decades. Until the 1970s this area was a typical poor periphery of the metropolitan region. Since then, real estate developers who benefited from the low price of land and facilities offered by local administrations have invested heavily in this area. Over a period of fifteen years, they built large areas of walled residences adjacent to office complexes, service centers, and shopping malls. The area had among the highest rates of population growth in the metropolitan region from 1980 to 1990, a period when the growth rate in the city of São Paulo declined sharply. Because the new residents are largely from the upper social groups, this area today has a concentration of high-income inhabitants, who, before the 1980s, would have lived in central neighborhoods (Metrô 1989). In other words, this area clearly represents the new trend of movement of wealthy residents as well as services and commerce to the periphery of the city and to enclosed areas. The 1993 campaign used many images that were already old in real estate advertisements of closed condominiums, but gave them a touch of novelty by baptizing its product as "edge city." Its aim was to launch new projects in the area and for this it used Garreau's expertise on suburban development.

The television program broadcast in São Paulo on Saturday, 16 October 1993, illustrates very well the connections with the First World model as well as the local peculiarities. The program combined scenes from what they presented as U.S. edge cities (Reston, Virginia, and Columbia, Maryland) and the three developments being advertised in São Paulo. In this program, Garreau—speaking in English with Portuguese subtitles—described edge cities as the predominant form of contemporary urban growth and used Los Angeles and its multicentered form as an example. The program had interesting differences in the way it presented Brazilian as opposed to U.S. edge cities. Residents from enclaves in both countries were interviewed in front of swimming pools, lakes, and in green areas, emphasizing both the luxurious and the antiurban character of the developments. However, if the U.S. edge cities have external walls and controls in their entrance gates, they are not shown, and their security personnel is not visibly present either. In the Paulista case, on the contrary, they are crucial and emphasized. At one point, the program shows a scene shot from a helicopter: the private security personnel of a condominium intercept a "suspect car" (a popular vehicle, a Volkswagen bus) outside the walls of the condominiums and physically search the occupants, who are forced to put their arms up against the car. Although this action is completely illegal for a private security service to perform on a public street, this, together with scenes of visitors submitting identification documents at the entrance gates, reassures the rich residents (and spectators) that "suspect" (poor) people will be kept away. Another revealing scene is an interview in English with a resident of a U.S. edge city. He cites as one of his reasons for moving there the fact he wanted to live in a racially integrated community. This observation is censored in the Portuguese subtitles, which say instead that his community has "many interesting people." In São Paulo, the image of a racially integrated community would certainly devalue the whole development. For the Paulista elites, first world models are good insofar as they may be adapted to include outright control (especially of the poor) and the eradication of racial and social difference.

To use first world elements in order to sell all types of commodities is a very common practice in Third World countries. Contrasting the different situations may be especially revealing. In this case, the need to censor a reference to racial integration indicates that the Paulista system of social inequality and distance is indeed obvious and that race is one of its most sensitive points.[10] Moreover, the parallel between the Brazilian and the American examples suggests that, although the degree of segregation may vary in different contexts, it is present in similar forms in both cases. It is worth investigating, then, the characteristics of this form and its effects on the organization of public life.

Attacking Modern Public Space

The new residential enclaves of the upper classes, associated with shopping malls, isolated office complexes, and other privately controlled environments represent a new form of organizing social differences and creating segregation in São Paulo and many other cities around the world. The characteristics of the Paulista enclaves that make their segregationist intentions viable may be summarized in four points. First, they use two instruments to create explicit separation: on the one hand, physical dividers such as fences and walls; on the other, large empty spaces creating distance and discouraging pedestrian circulation. Second, as if walls and distances were not enough, separation is guaranteed by private security systems: control and surveillance are conditions for internal social homogeneity and isolation. Third, the enclaves are private universes turned inward with designs and organization making no gestures toward the street. Fourth, the enclaves aim at being independent worlds that proscribe an exterior life, which is evaluated in negative terms. The enclaves are not subordinate either to public streets or to surrounding buildings and institutions. In other words, the relationship they establish with the rest of the city and its public life is one of avoidance: they turn their backs on them. Therefore, public streets become spaces in which the elite circulate by car and poor people circulate on foot or by public transportation. To walk on the public street is becoming a sign of class in many cities, an activity that the elite is abandoning. No longer using streets as spaces of sociability, the elite now want to prevent street life from entering their enclaves.

Private enclaves and the segregation they generate deny many of the basic elements that previously constituted the modern experience of public life: primacy of streets and their openness; free circulation of crowds and vehicles; impersonal and anonymous encounters of the pedestrian; unprogrammed public enjoyment and congregation in streets and squares; and the presence of people from different social backgrounds strolling and gazing at those passing by, looking at store windows, shopping, and sitting in cafes, joining political demonstrations, or using spaces especially designed for the entertainment of the masses (promenades, parks, stadiums, exhibitions).[11] The new developments in cities such as São Paulo create enclosures that contradict both the prototype of modern urban remodeling, that of Baron Haussmann, and basic elements of the modern conception of public life. Haussmann's state-promoted transformations of Paris were strongly criticized and opposed, but no one denied that the new boulevards were readily appropriated by huge numbers of people eager to enjoy both the streets' public life, protected by anonymity, and the consumption possibilities that came with it. The *flâneur* described by Baudelaire and the consumer of the new department stores each became symbols of the modern appropriation of urban public space, as Paris became the prototype of the modern city.

At the core of the conception of urban public life embedded in modern Paris are notions that city space is open to be used and enjoyed by anyone, and that the consumption society it houses may become accessible to all. Of course, this has never been entirely the case, neither in Paris nor anywhere else, for modern cities have always remained marked by social inequalities and spatial segregation and are appropriated in quite different ways by diverse social groups, depending on their social position and power. In spite of these inequalities, however, modern western cities have always maintained various signs of openness related especially to circulation and consumption, which contributed to sustaining the positive value attached to the idea of an open public space accessible to all.

These modern urban experiences were coupled with a political life in which similar values were fostered. The modern city has been the stage for all types of public demonstrations. In fact, the promise of incorporation into modern society included not only the city and consumption but also the polity. Images of the modern city are in many ways analogous to those of the modern liberal-democratic polity, consolidated on the basis of the fiction of a social contract among equal and free people, which has shaped the modern political sphere. This fiction is quite radical—like that of the open city—and helped to destroy the hierarchical social order of feudal statuses preceding it. But, clearly, it was only with severe struggles that the definitions of those who could be considered "free and equal" have been expanded. As with the open city, the polity incorporating all equal citizens has never occurred, but its founding ideals and its promise of continuous incorporation have retained their power for at least two centuries, shaping people's experience of citizenship and city life and legitimating the actions of various excluded groups in their claims for incorporation.[12]

In sum, the images of openness, freedom, and possibilities of incorporation that constituted modernity have never been completely fulfilled, but they have never completely lost their referential role either. In cities such as São Paulo and Los Angeles, however, various aspects of public experience are now contradicting those images. One challenge to basic concepts sustaining these fictions comes from some minority groups. They question the liberal principle of universalism, arguing that the social contract has always been constituted on the basis of the exclusion of some, and that the rights of minority groups can only be addressed if approached from the perspective of difference rather than that of commonality.[13] This is what we might call a positive attack on modern liberal ideals: its aim is still to expand rights, freedom, and equality, and it searches for models that may achieve these goals in a more effective way. However, the transformations going on at the level of the urban environment represent an attack of a different kind. They reject the principles of openness and equality and take inequality and separation as their values. While minority groups criticize the limitations of liberal fictions in terms of the creation of equality and justice, recent urban transformations materially build a space with opposite values. And this new type of urban form shapes the public life and everyday interactions of millions of people around the world.

Modernist Instruments, Segregated Spaces

In order to achieve their goals of isolating, distancing, and selecting, the fortified enclaves use some instruments of design that are, in fact, instruments of modernist city planning and architectural design. Various effects of modernist city planning are similar to those of the new enclaves, suggesting that we should look at their similarities more carefully. One strikingly similar effect of both modernist city planning and the fortified enclaves is their attack on streets as a type and concept of public space. In Brazil, the construction of modernist Brasília in the late 1950s crystallized an international modernism and its transformation of public space and relayed it to the rest of the country (see Holston 1989). In modernist Brasília as in new parts of São Paulo and Los Angeles, the pedestrians and anonymous interactions in public life that marked modern Paris tend to be eliminated. However, if the results are generally the same, the original projects of modernism and current enclosures are radically different. It is worthwhile, then, to investigate how such different projects ended up producing similar effects.

Modernist architecture and city planning were elaborated on the basis of a criticism of industrial cities and societies and intended to transform them through the radical remodeling of space. Their utopian vision was clear: the erasure of social difference and creation of equality in the rational city of the future mastered by the avant-garde architect. Modernist attacks on the streets were central to its criticism of capitalism and its project of subversion. They perceived the corridor street as a conduit of disease and as an impediment to progress, because it would fail to accommodate the needs of the new machine age. Moreover, modernist architecture attacks the street because "it constitutes an architectural organization of the public and private domains of social life that modernism seeks to overturn" (Holston 1989, 103). In capitalist cities, the organization of the public and private domains is best expressed in the corridor street and its related system of public spaces, including side-walks and squares: a solid mass of contiguous private buildings frames and contains the void of public streets. Modernist planning and archi-tecture inverted these solid-void/figure-ground relationships, which have been the basis for the physical structure of western cities since the fifth century B.C.E. In the modernist city, "streets appear as continuous voids and buildings as sculptural figures" (ibid., 125). By subverting the old code of urban order, modernist planning aims to erase and succeeds in erasing the representational distinction between public and private. When all buildings—banks, offices, apartments—are sculptural, and all spaces are nonfigural, "the old architectural convention for discriminating be-tween the public and the private is effectively invalidated" (ibid., 136).

Modernist city planning aspired to transform the city into a single homogeneous state-sponsored public domain, to eliminate differences in order to create a universal rationalist city divided into functional sec-tors such as residential, employment, recreational, transportation, ad-ministrative, and civic. Brasília is the most complete embodiment of both the new type of city and the public life created by modernist city plan-ning. This new type of city space, however, turned out to be the oppo-site of the planners' intentions. Brasília is today Brazil's most segregated city, not its most egalitarian. Ironically, the instruments of modernist plan-ning, with little adaptation, become perfect instruments to produce in-equality, not to erase difference. Streets only for vehicular traffic, the absence of sidewalks, enclosure and internalization of shopping areas, and spatial voids isolating sculptural buildings and rich residential ar-eas are great instruments for generating and maintaining social separa-tions. These modernist creations radically transform public life not only in cities such as Brasília but in other contexts and with different inten-tions. In the new fortified enclaves they are used not to destroy private spaces and produce a total unified public, but to destroy public spaces. Their objective is to enlarge specific private domains so that they will fulfill public functions, but in a segregated way.

Contemporary fortified enclaves use basically modernist instruments of planning, with some notable adaptations. First, the surrounding walls: unlike examples of modernist planning, such as Brasília, where the resi-dential areas were to have no fences or walls but to be delimited only by expressways, in São Paulo the walls are necessary to demarcate the private universes. However, this demarcation of private property is not supposed to create the same type of (nonmodernist) public space that characterizes the industrial city. Because the private universes are kept apart by voids (as in modernist design), they no longer generate street corridors. Moreover, pedestrian circulation is discouraged and shopping areas are kept away from the streets, again as in modernist design. The second adaptation occurs in the materials and forms of individual buildings. Here there are two possibilities. On the one hand, buildings may completely ignore the exterior walls, treating façades as their backs. On the other, plain modernist facades may be eliminated in favor of ornament, irregularity, and ostentatious materials that display the individuality and status of their owners. These buildings reject the glass and transparency of modernism and their disclosure of private life. In other words, internalization, privacy, and individuality are enhanced. Finally, sophisticated technologies of security assure the exclusivity of the already isolated buildings.

Analyzing what is used from modernist architecture and city planning and what is transformed in the new urban form generated by the private enclaves, one arrives at a clear conclusion: the devices that have been maintained are those that destroy modern public space and social life (socially dead streets transformed into highways, sculptural buildings separated by voids and disregarding street alignments, enclaves turned inside); the devices transformed or abandoned are those intended to create equality, transparency, and a new public sphere (glass façades, uniformity of design, absence of material delimitations such as walls and fences). Instead of creating a space in which the distinctions between public and private disappear—making all space public as the modernists intended—the enclaves use modernist conventions to create spaces in which the private quality is enhanced beyond any doubt and in which the public, a shapeless void treated as residual, is deemed irrelevant. This was exactly the fate of modernist architecture and its "all public space" in Brasília, a perversion of initial premises and intentions. The situation is just the opposite with the closed condominiums and other fortified enclaves of the 1980s and 1990s. Their aim is to segregate and to change the character of public life by bringing to private spaces constructed as socially homogeneous environments those activities that had been previously enacted in public spaces.

Today, in cities such as São Paulo, we find neither gestures toward openness and freedom of circulation regardless of differences nor a technocratic universalism aiming at erasing differences. Rather, we find a city space whose old modern urban design has been fragmented by the insertion of independent and well-delineated private enclaves (of modernist design) that pay no attention to an external overall ordination and are totally focused on their own internal organization. The fortified fragments are no longer meant to be subordinated to a total order kept together by ideologies of openness, commonality, or promises of incorporation. Heterogeneity is to be taken more seriously: fragments express radical inequalities, not simple differences. Stripped of the elements which in fact erased differences such as uniform and transparent facades, modernist architectural conventions used by the enclaves are helping to insure that different social worlds meet as infrequently as possible in city space—that is, that they belong to different spaces.

In sum, in a city of walls and enclaves such as São Paulo, public space undergoes a deep transformation. Felt as more dangerous, fractured by the new voids and enclaves, broken in its old alignments, privatized with chains closing streets, armed guards, guard dogs, guardhouses, and walled parks, public space in São Paulo is increasingly abandoned to those who do not have a chance to live, work, and shop in the new private, internalized, and fortified enclaves. As the spaces for the rich are enclosed and turned inside, the outside space is left for those who cannot afford to go in. A comparison with Los Angeles shows that this new type of segregation is not São Paulo's exclusive creation and suggests some of its consequences for the transformation of the public sphere.

São Paulo, Los Angeles

Compared to São Paulo, Los Angeles has a more fragmented and dispersed urban structure.[14] São Paulo still has a vivid downtown area and some central neighborhoods, concentrating commerce and office activities, which are shaped on the model of the corridor street and, in spite of all transformations, are still crowded during the day. Contemporary Los Angeles is "polynucleated and decentralized" (Soja 1989, 208). And its renovated downtown, one of the city's economic and financial centers, does not have much street life: people's activities are contained in the corporate buildings and their under- and overpass connections to shopping, restaurants, and hotels.[15] São Paulo's process of urban fragmentation by the construction of enclaves is more recent than Los Angeles's, but it has already changed the peripheral zones and the distribution of wealth and economic functions in ways similar to that of the metropolitan region of Los Angeles. According to Soja (1989), the latter is a multicentered region marked by a "peripheral urbanization," which is created by the expansion of high-technological, post-Fordist industrialization and marked by the presence of high-income residential developments, huge regional shopping centers, programmed environments for leisure (theme parks, Disneyland), links to major universities and the Department of Defense, and various enclaves of cheap labor, mostly immigrants. Although São Paulo lacks the high-technology industries found in Los Angeles, its tertiarization and distribution of services and commerce are starting to be organized according to the Los Angeles pattern.

Although we may say that São Paulo expresses Los Angeles's process of economic transformation and urban dispersion in a less explicit form, it is more explicit and exaggerated in the creation of separation and in the use of security procedures. Where rich neighborhoods such as Morumbi use high walls, iron fences, and armed guards, the West Side of Los Angeles uses mostly electronic alarms and small signs announcing "Armed Response." While São Paulo's elites clearly appropriate public spaces—closing public streets with chains and all sorts of physical obstacles, installing private armed guards to control circulation—Los Angeles elites still show more respect for public streets. However, walled communities appropriating public streets are already appearing in Los Angeles, and one can wonder if its more discreet pattern of separation and of surveillance is not in part associated with the fact that the poor are far from the West Side, while in Morumbi they live beside the enclaves. Another reason must surely be the fact that the Los Angeles Police Department—although considered one of the most biased and violent of the United States—still appears very effective and nonviolent if compared to São Paulo's police (see Caldeira in press, chapter 5). São Paulo's upper classes explicitly rely on the services of an army of domestic servants and do not feel ashamed to transform the utilization of these services into status symbols, which in turn are incorporated in newspaper advertisements for enclaves. In West Los Angeles, although the domestic dependence on the services of immigrant maids, nannies, and gardeners seems to be increasing, the status associated with employing them has not yet become a matter for advertisement. In São Paulo, where the local government has been efficient in approving policies to help segregation, upper-class residents have not yet started any important social movement for this purpose. But in Los Angeles residents of expensive neighborhoods have been organizing powerful homeowner associations to lobby for zoning regulations that would maintain the isolation their neighborhoods now enjoy (Davis 1990, chapter 3).

Despite the many differences between the two cases, it is also clear that in both Los Angeles and São Paulo conventions of modernist city planning and technologies of security are being used to create new forms of urban space and social segregation. In both cities, the elites are retreating to privatized environments, which they increasingly control, and are abandoning earlier types of urban space to the poor and their internal antagonisms. As might be expected given these common characteristics, in both cities we find debates involving planners and architects in which the new enclaves are frequently criticized but are also defended and theorized. In São Paulo, where modernism has been the dominant dogma in schools of architecture up to the present, the defense of walled constructions is recent and timid, using as arguments only practical reasons such as increasing rates of crime and of homelessness. Architects tend to talk about walls and security devices as an unavoidable evil. They talk to the press, but I could not find academic articles or books on the subject. In Los Angeles, however, the debate has already generated an important literature, and both criticism and praise of "defensible architecture" are already quite elaborated.

One person voicing the defense of the architectural style found in the new enclaves is Charles Jencks. He analyzes recent trends in Los Angeles architecture in relation to a diagnosis of the city's social configuration. In his view, Los Angeles's main problem is its heterogeneity, which inevitably generates chronic ethnic strife and explains episodes such as the 1992 uprising (1993, 88). Since he considers this heterogeneity as constitutive of Los Angeles's reality, and since his diagnosis of the economic situation is pessimistic, his expectation is that ethnic tension will increase, that the environment will become more defensive, and that people will resort to nastier and more diverse measures of protection. Jencks sees the adoption of security devices as inevitable and as a matter of realism. Moreover, he discusses how this necessity is being transformed into art by styles that metamorphose hard-edged materials needed for security into "ambiguous signs of inventive beauty and "keep out" and design façades with their backs to the street, camouflaging the contents of the houses. For him, the response to ethnic strife is "defensible architecture and riot realism" (1993, 89). The "realism" lies in architects looking at "the dark side of division, conflict, and decay, and represent[ing] some unwelcome truths" (1993, 91). Among the latter is the fact that heterogeneity and strife are here to stay, that the promises of the melting pot can no longer be fulfilled. In this context, boundaries would have to be both clearer and more defended. "Architecturally it [Los Angeles] will have to learn the lessons of Gehry's aesthetic and en-formality: how to turn unpleasant necessities such as chain-link fence into amusing and ambiguous signs of welcome/keep out, beauty/defensive space. . . . Defensible architecture, however regrettable as a social tactic, also protects the rights of individuals and threatened groups"(1993, 93).

Jencks targets ethnic heterogeneity as the reason for Los Angeles's social conflicts and sees separation as a solution. He is not bothered by the fact that the intervention of architects and planners in the urban environment of Los Angeles reinforces social inequality and spatial segregation. He also does not interrogate the consequences of these creations for public space and political relationships. In fact, his admiration of the backside-to-the-street solution indicates a lack of concern with the maintenance of public streets as spaces that embed the values of openness and conviviality of the heterogeneous masses.

But Los Angeles's defensible architecture also has its critics. The most famous of them is Mike Davis, whose analysis I find illuminating, especially for its thinking about the transformations in the public sphere. For Davis (1990, 1991, 1993), social inequality and spatial segregation are central characteristics of Los Angeles, and his expression "Fortress L. A.," refers to the type of space being presently created in the city.

> Welcome to post-liberal Los Angeles, where the defense of luxury lifestyles is translated into a proliferation of new repressions in space and movement, undergirded by the ubiquitous "armed response." This obsession with physical security systems, and, collaterally, with the architectural policing of social boundaries, has become a zeitgeist of urban restructuring, a master narrative in the emerging built environment of the 1990s. We live in "fortress cities" brutally divided between "fortified cells" of affluent society and "places of terror" where the police battle the criminalized poor. (Davis 1990, 223–224)

For Davis, the increasingly segregated and privatized Los Angeles is the result of a clear master plan of postliberal (i.e., Reagan-Bush Republican) elites, a theme he reiterates in his analysis of the 1992 riots (Davis 1993). To talk of contemporary Los Angeles is, for Davis, to talk of a new "class war at the level of the built environment" and to demonstrate that "urban form is indeed following a repressive function in the political furrows of the Reagan-Bush era. Los Angeles, in its prefigurative mode, offers an especially disquieting catalogue of the emergent liaisons between architecture and the American police state" (Davis 1990, 228).

Davis's writing is marked by an indignation fully supported by his wealth of evidence concerning Los Angeles. Nevertheless, sometimes he collapses complex social processes into a simplified scenario of warfare that his own rich description defies. Despite this tendency to look at social reality as the direct product of elite intentions. Davis elaborates a remarkable critique of social and spatial segregation and associates the emerging urban configuration with the crucial themes of social inequality and political options. For him, not only is there nothing inevitable about "fortress architecture," but it has, in fact, deep consequences for the way in which public space and public interactions are shaped.

My analysis of São Paulo's enclaves coincides with Davis's analysis of Los Angeles as far as the issue of public space is concerned. It is clear in both cases that the public order created by private enclaves of the "defensible" style has inequalities, isolation, and fragmentation as starting points. In this context, the fiction of the overall social contract and the ideals of universal rights and equality that legitimated the modern conception of public space vanish. We should ask, then, if there is already another political fiction organizing inequalities and differences at the societal level, and how best to conceive this new configuration as the old modern model loses its explanatory value. If social differences are brought to the center of the scene instead of being put aside by universalistic claims, then what kind of model for the public realm can we maintain? What kind of polity will correspond to the new fragmented public sphere? Is democracy still possible in this new public sphere?

Public Sphere: Inequalities and Boundaries

People attach meanings to the spaces where they live in flexible and varying ways, and the factors influencing these readings and uses are endless.[16] However, cities are also material spaces with relative stability and rigidity that shape and bound people's lives and determine the types of encounters possible in public space. When walls are built up, they form the stage for public life regardless of the meanings people attach to them and regardless of the multiple "tactics" of resistance people use to appropriate urban space.

In this essay, I have been arguing that in cities where fortified enclaves produce spatial segregation, social inequalities become quite explicit. I have also been arguing that in these cities, residents' everyday interactions with people from other social groups diminish substantially, and public encounters primarily occur inside protected and relatively homogeneous groups. In the materiality of segregated spaces, in people's everyday trajectories, in their uses of public transportation, in their appropriations of streets and parks, and in their constructions of walls and defensive facades, social boundaries are rigidly constructed. Their crossing is under surveillance. When boundaries are crossed in this type of city, there is aggression, fear, and a feeling of unprotectedness; in a word, there is suspicion and danger. Residents from all social groups have a sense of exclusion and restriction. For some, the feeling of exclusion is obvious as they are denied access to various areas and are restricted to others. Affluent people who inhabit exclusive enclaves also feel restricted; their feelings of fear keep them away from regions and people identified in their mental maps of the city as dangerous.

Contemporary urban segregation is complementary to the issue of urban violence. On the one hand, the fear of crime is used to legitimate increasing measures of security and surveillance. On the other, the proliferation of everyday talk about crime becomes the context in which residents generate stereotypes as they label different social groups as dangerous and therefore as people to be feared and avoided. Everyday discussions about crime create rigid symbolic differences between social groups as they become aligned with either good or evil. In this sense, they contribute to a construction of inflexible separations as city walls do. Both enforce ungiving boundaries. In sum, one of the consequences of living in cities segregated by enclaves is that while heterogeneous contacts diminish, social differences are more rigidly perceived, and proximity to people from different groups is considered dangerous, thus emphasizing inequality and distance.

Nevertheless, the urban environment is not the only basis of people's experiences of social differences. In fact, there are other arenas in which differences tend to be experienced in almost opposite ways, offering an important counterpoint to the experience of the urban environment. This is the case of the perceptions of social difference forged through the intensification of communication networks and mass media (international news, documentaries about all types of lives and experiences), through mass movements of populations, through tourism, or through the consumption of ethnic products (food, clothes, films, music). In these contexts, boundaries between different social universes become more permeable and are constantly crossed as people have access to worlds not originally their own.

Thus, the perception and experience of social differences in contemporary cities may occur in quite distinct ways. Some tame social differences, allowing their appropriation by various types of consumers. Other experiences, such as those of emerging urban environments, characterized by fear and violence, magnify social differences and maintain distance and separateness. If the first type of experience may blur boundaries, the second type explicitly elaborates them. Both types of experience constitute the contemporary public sphere, but their consequences for public and political life are radically different. On the one hand, the softening of boundaries may still be related to the ideals of equality of the liberal-democratic polity and may serve as the basis of claims of incorporation. The tamed differences produced to be consumed do not threaten universalist ideals, and in their peculiar way put people into contact. On the other hand, the new urban morphologies of fear give new forms to inequality, keep groups apart, and inscribe a new sociability that runs against the ideals of the modern public and its democratic freedoms. When some people are denied access to certain areas and when different groups are not supposed to interact in public space, references to a universal principle of equality and freedom for social life are no longer possible, even as fiction. The consequences of the new separateness and restriction for public life are serious: contrary to what Jencks thinks (1993), by making clear the extension of social inequalities and the lack of commonalities, defensible architecture and planning may only promote conflict instead of preventing it.

Among the conditions necessary for democracy is that people acknowledge those from different social groups as co-citizens, that is, as people having similar rights. If this is true, it is clear that contemporary cities that are segregated by fortified enclaves are not environments that generate conditions conducive to democracy. Rather, they foster inequality and the sense that different groups belong to separate universes and have irreconcilable claims. Cities of walls do not strengthen citizenship; rather, they contribute to its corrosion. Moreover, this effect does not depend either on the type of political regime or on the intentions of those in power, since the architecture of the enclaves by itself entails a certain social logic.

Discussions about cities such as Los Angeles, London, or Paris, that is, cities populated by people from the most diverse cultural origins, commonly invoke the theme of the limits of modern citizenship based on affiliation to a nation-state. One might rethink the parameters of citizenship in those cities and suggest that the criterion for participation in political life could be local residence rather than national citizenship. Moreover, it would be possible to argue that this local participation is increasingly necessary to make those cities livable and to improve the quality of life of the impoverished population, increasingly consisting of immigrants. The contrast between this alternative political vision and the reality of fortified cities allows for at least two conclusions, one pessimistic and one more optimistic.

The pessimistic would say that the direction of new segregation and the extension of social separation already achieved would make impossible the engagement of a variety of social groups in a political life in which common goals and solutions would have to be negotiated. In this view, citizenship in cities of walls is meaningless. The optimistic interpretation, however, would consider that the change in the criteria for admission to political life, and the consequent change in status of a considerable part of the population, would generate a wider engagement in the search for solutions to common problems and would potentially bridge some distances. There are many reasons to be suspicious of such optimism: studies of homeowner associations in Los Angeles remind us how local democracy may be used as an instrument of segregation (Davis

1990, chapter 3). However, the boom of social movements in São Paulo after the mid-1970s suggests a cautious optimism. Where excluded residents discover that they have rights to the city, they manage to transform their neighborhoods and to improve the quality of their lives. That fortified enclaves in part counteracted this process should not make us abandon this qualified optimism. The walls were not able to totally obstruct the exercise of citizenship, and poor residents continue to expand their rights.

Notes

This chapter is based on the analysis developed in my book *City of Walls: Crime, Segregation, and Citizenship in São Paulo* (Berkeley: University of California Press, in press). I thank the University of California Press for permission to use material from the book.

1. In Brazil in 1989, the proportion of income in the hands of the poorest 50 percent of the population was only 10.4 percent. At the same time, the richest 1 percent had 17.3 percent of the income. Data are from the National Research by Domicile Sample (PNAD) undertaken by the Brazilian Census Bureau. The distribution of wealth has become more inequitable since the early 1980s (Lopes 1993, Rocha 1991).
2. For an analysis of the various patterns of urban segregation in São Paulo from the late nineteenth century to the present, see Caldeira (in press and 1996).
3. The most successful plan to fight inflation has been the Plano Real, adopted in 1994. This plan was elaborated by ex-Minister of Treasury Fernando Henrique Cardoso, who was elected president of Brazil on the basis of the success of this plan.
4. Although the Metropolitan Region of São Paulo has one of the best situations in Brazil, the Gini coefficient increased from 0.516 in 1981 to 0.566 in 1989 (Rocha 1991, 38). The Gini coefficient varies from 0 to 1. It would be 0 if all people had the same income, and 1 if one person concentrated the whole national income. For Brazil, the Gini coefficient was 0.580 in 1985 and 0.627 in 1989 (Rocha 1991, 38).
5. A *favela* is a set of shacks built on seized land. A *cortiço* is a type of tenement housing.
6. Violent crime has been growing in various metropolises around the world. In the United States, the number of violent crimes per capita grew by 355 percent between 1960 and 1990, according to FBI reports. In 1990, rates of murder per 100,000 population in several American cities were higher than or comparable to those of São Paulo. The highest rate was 77.8 in Washington, D.C. It was 36.0 in Miami. 30.6 in New York City, and 28.2 in Los Angeles (*Los Angeles Times*, 25 March 1992, A-14). However, since the early 1990s, murder rates have decreased in many American cities.
7. In 1992, São Paulo's military police killed 1,470 civilians, including 111 prisoners killed inside the city's main prison. In that year, Los Angeles police killed 25 civilians, and the New York police killed 24 civilians. For a complete analysis of the pattern of police violence and of the increase in violence and crime in São Paulo, see Caldeira (in press).
8. Expressions in quotation marks are taken from the advertisements.
9. See Holston 1989 for an analysis of this system of spatial separation in Brasília.

10. Although many people like to think of Brazilian society as a "racial democracy," any reading of available social indicators shows pervasive discrimination against the black population. For example, a study by Lopes (1993) on poverty shows that 68 percent of the urban households below the indigent line have a black or mulatto head of household, while black or mulatto households represent only 41 percent of the total urban households.

11. Analyses of various dimensions of the modern experience of urban life are found in: Benjamin 1969, Berman 1982, Clark 1984, Harvey 1985, Holston 1989, Rabinow 1989, Schorske 1961, Sennett 1974, and Vidler 1978.

12. A powerful image of progressive incorporation is offered in the classic essay by T. H. Marshall (1965 [1949]) on the development of citizenship. For recent critiques of Marshall's optimistic and evolutionary view, see Hirschman 1991 and Turner 1992; Turner also criticizes the universality of Marshall's model.

13. See, for example, the feminist critique of the social contract (Pateman 1988) and of the legal understanding of equality as sameness (Eisenstein 1988).

14. It is not my intention to give a detailed account of Los Angeles's recent pattern of urbanization. I will only point out some of its characteristics, which, by comparison with São Paulo's process, allow me to raise questions about new forms of social segregation that seem to be quite generalized. For analyses of Los Angeles, see Banham 1971, Davis 1990, and Soja 1989 and 1992.

15. See Davis 1991 and Soja 1989 on the importance of downtown Los Angeles in the structuring of the region.

16. On this theme, see de Certeau 1984, part 3.

References

Banham, Reyner. 1971. *Los Angeles: The architecture of four ecologies.* Baltimore: Pelican.

Benjamin, Walter. 1969. *Illuminations.* Translated by Harry Zohn and edited by Hannah Arendt. New York: Schocken Books.

Berman, Marshall. 1982. *All that is solid melts into air.* New York: Penguin Books.

Caldeira, Teresa Pires do Rio. 1984. *A política dos outros.* São Paulo: Brasiliense.

———. 1996. Building up walls: The new pattern of spatial segregation in São Paulo. *International Social Science Journal* 147:55–66.

———. in press. *City of walls: Crime, segregation and citizenship in São Paulo.* Berkeley: University of California Press.

de Certeau, Michel. 1984. *The practice of everyday life.* Berkeley: University of California Press.

Clark, T. J. 1984. *The painting of modern life: Paris in the art of Manet and his followers.* Princeton, N.J.: Princeton University Press.

Davis, Mike. 1990. *City of quartz: Excavating the future in Los Angeles.* London: Verso.

———. 1991. The infinite game: Redeveloping downtown L. A. In *Out of site: Social criticism of architecture,* edited by Diane Ghirardo. Pp. 77–113. Seattle: Bay Press,.

———. 1993. Who killed Los Angeles? Part two: The verdict is given. *New Left Review* 199:29–54.

Eisenstein, Zillah R. 1988. *The female body and the law.* Berkeley: University of California Press.

Harvey, David. 1985. *Consciousness and the urban experience: Studies in history and theory of capitalist urbanization.* Baltimore: The Johns Hopkins University Press.

Hirschman, Albert O. 1991. *The rhetoric of reaction: Perversity, futility, jeopardy.* Cambridge, Mass.: Belknap Press.

Holston, James. 1989. *The modernist city: An anthropological critique of Brasília.* Chicago: University of Chicago Press.

———. 1991. Autoconstruction in working-class Brazil. *Cultural Anthropology* 6, no. 4:447–465.

Holston, James, and Teresa P. R. Caldeira. 1998. Democracy, law, and violence: Disjunctions of Brazilian citizenshhip. In *Fault lines of Democracy in post-transition Latin America*, edited by Felipe Agüepo and Jeffrey Stark. Pp. 263–296. Miami: University of Miami North South Center Press.

Jencks, Charles. 1993. *Heteropolis: Los Angeles, the riots and the strange beauty of hetero-architecture.* London: Ernst and Sohn.

Lopes, Juarez. 1993. Brasil 1989: Um estudo sócioeconômico da indigência e da pobreza urbanas. NEEP: *Cadernos de pesquisa* 25.

Marshall, T. H. 1965 [1949]. Citizenship and social class. In *Class, citizenship, and social development.* New York: Doubleday.

Metrô—Companhia do Metropolitano de São Paulo. 1989. *Pesquisa OD/87: Síntese das Informações.* São Paulo: Metrô.

Pateman. Carole. 1988. *The sexual contract.* Stanford: Stanford University Press.

Rabinow, Paul. 1989. *French modern: Norms and forms of the social environment.* Cambridge, Mass.: MIT Press.

Rocha, Sonia. 1991. Pobreza metropolitana e os ciclos de curto prazo: balanço dos anos 80. IPEA: *Boletim de Conjuntura* 12

Sassen, Saskia. 1991. *The global city: New York, London, Tokyo.* Princeton, N.J.: Princeton University Press.

Schorske, Carl E. 1961. *Fin-de-siècle Vienna: Politics and culture.* New York: Vintage Books.

Sennett, Richard. 1974. *The fall of public man: On the social psychology of capitalism.* New York: Vintage Books.

Soja, Edward W. 1989. *Postmodern geographies: The reassertion of space in critical social theory.* London: Verso.

———. 1992. Inside exopolis: Scenes from Orange County. In *Variations on a theme park: The new American city and the end of public space*, edited by Michael Sorkin. New York: Noonday Press.

Turner, Bryan. 1992. Outline of a theory of citizenship. In *Dimensions of radical democracy: Pluralism, citizenship, community*, edited by Chantal Mouffe. London: Verso.

Vidler, Anthony. 1978. The scenes of the street: Transformation in ideal and reality, 1750–1871. In *On streets*, edited by Stanford Anderson. Cambridge, Mass.: MIT Press.

PART

II

The Contested City

SETHA M. LOW

4 Spatializing Culture
The Social Production and Social Construction of Public Space in Costa Rica

When Denise Lawrence and I reviewed the literature on the anthropology of the built environment and spatial form (Lawrence and Low 1990), we identified the history and the contributions of diverse theoretical and methodological perspectives on the development of an anthropological approach to the built environment, and concluded:

> [T]the most promising new direction for anthropologists lies in the area of social production theories. These approaches seek to place their understanding of built forms within the larger context of society's institutions and its history. As an object of study, the building becomes a point of spatial articulation for the intersection of multiple forces of economy, society, and culture.
>
> Further, the meaning of the built environment as revealed through its metaphorical connections and ritual practices constitutes an important but still incompletely explored dimension. The analysis and interpretation of building decisions cannot be understood apart from social and economic institutional forces that continuously influence actors, nor can the interpretation of symbolic meaning be divorced from these forces or history.

I have continued to explore these dimensions further in an effort to theorize space and spatialize human experience more effectively within cultural anthropology. By *spatialize* I mean to locate, both physically and conceptually, social relations and social practice in social space. In this chapter I use the specific analysis of two plazas in Costa Rica to explore the way that two mutually complementary perspectives of social *production* of space and social *construction* of space help us understand how public space in urban society becomes semiotically encoded and interpreted reality.

In order to clarify this discussion it is important to distinguish between these two terms, for they are often used interchangeably. The social production of space includes all those factors—social, economic, ideological, and technological—whose intended goal is the physical creation of the material setting. The materialist emphasis of the term *social production* is useful in defining the historical emergence and political and economic formation of urban space. The term *social construction* may then be conveniently reserved for the phenomenological and symbolic experience of space as mediated by social processes such as exchange, conflict, and control. Thus, the social construction of space is the actual transformation of space—through people's social exchanges, memories, images, and daily use of the material setting—into scenes and actions that convey symbolic meaning.[1] Both processes are social in the sense that both the production and the construction of space are contested for economic and ideological reasons; understanding them can help us see how local conflicts over space can be used to uncover and illuminate larger issues.

Contemporary debates concerning ethnographic methodologies and writing strategies emphasize the importance of characterizing social actors in terms of their experience of the theorized phenomena. The coproducers of the ethnography must be given a voice and a place in the written document (Appadurai 1992, Rodman 1992), and ethnographic research is increasingly judged by its ability to portray the impact of macro and micro processes through the "lived experience" of individuals. An effective anthropological theory of the spatialization of culture and human experience must therefore integrate the perspectives of social production and social construction of space, both contextualizing the forces that produce it and showing people as social agents constructing their own realities and meanings. But it must also reflect both these perspectives in the experience and daily life of public-space users.

There have been many approaches to various aspects of this problem. David Harvey (1985, 1990) and Manual Castells (1983, 1989) have examined the spatialization of social conflicts, focusing on class-based struggles with state-imposed spatial regimes. They provide historical and contemporary examples of grassroots organizations fighting to maintain control of housing (Castells 1983), urban sacred space (Harvey 1985), and neighborhood real estate (Castells 1983; Peattie 1969, 1987; see also

Smith 1991). In their analyses, they view the local population as having a role through social movements that resist the control of the dominant classes and planning elite. They fail, however, to account either for the agency of the individual actor or for the details of how spatial structures influence human behavior and, conversely, how behavior influences the experience, utilization, and allocation of space.

Michel Foucault, in his work on the prison (1975) and in a series of interviews and lectures on space (Foucault 1984, Rabinow 1984), takes a historical approach to the spatialization of social control through analysis of the human body, spatial arrangements, and architecture. He examines the relationship of power and space by positing architecture as a political "technology" for working out the concerns of government— that is, control and power over individuals—through the spatial "canalization" of everyday life. The aim of such a technology is to create a "docile body" (Foucault 1975, 198) through enclosure and the organization of individuals in space.

Continuing this approach, Paul Rabinow (1989) links the growth of modern forms of political power to the evolution of aesthetic theories and shows how French colonists sought to use architecture and city planning to demonstrate their cultural superiority. He focuses on the ordering of space as a way to understand the "historically variable links between spatial relations, aesthetics, social science, economics, and politics" (Rabinow 1982, 267). James Holston (1989) develops this argument further by examining the state-sponsored architecture and master planning of Brasilia as new forms of political domination through which the domains of daily life become the targets for state intervention. These writers successfully illustrate how architecture contributes to the maintenance of power of one group over another at a level that includes both the control of the movement and the surveillance of the body in space, but do not directly address either the lived experience of the individual or individual and group meanings of these architectural forms of social control.

Michel de Certeau (1984) takes this omission as his starting point for his attempts to show how people's "ways of operating" constitute the means by which users reappropriate space organized by techniques of sociocultural production (1984, xiv). These practices are articulated in the details of everyday life and bring to light the clandestine "tactics" used by groups or individuals "already caught in the nets of 'discipline'" (de Certeau 1984, xiv–xv). By tracing the operations of walking, naming, narrating, and remembering the city, de Certeau develops a theory of lived space in which spatial practices elude the discipline of urban planning. Thus the pedestrian's walking, like the flâneur of Walter

Benjamin (Buck-Morss 1990, 25–40), is the spatial acting out of place, creating and representing public space rather than being subjected to it.

In another effort to link human agents and domination, Bourdieu (1977) looks at the spatialization of everyday behavior and examines how the sociospatial order is translated into bodily experience and practice. He proposes the key concept of *habitus*, a generative and structuring principle of collective strategies and social practices that is used to reproduce existing structures. In his examples, the Kabyle house becomes the setting in which body space and cosmic space are integrated through metaphor and symbolic homologous structures. Through the experience of living in the spatial symbolism of the home, social structure becomes embodied and naturalized in everyday practice. Unlike the preceding theorists, Bourdieu also examines resistances and the effect of feedback on the social system. Since the concept of habitus spatially links social structure to the human body and bodily practices, the possibility of resistance to these practices becomes more apparent (Giroux 1983).

These theories of spatialization provide a basis for working out how spatial analysis would satisfy the anthropologist's need to link experience, practice, and structure. Nonetheless, it is difficult to derive ethnographic research strategies solely from these conceptual approaches. One intermediate step is to identify domains of action and endeavor that allow for empirical analysis. I have chosen to concentrate on the historical emergence of the space and on the sociopolitical ideologies and economic forces involved in its production, including the role played by planning and architecture professionals in its design, the social use of the space, and its associated affective and symbolic meanings. To categorize these domains in terms of their generative processes, historical, sociopolitical, economic, and professional understandings are matters of social production of space, while social use and affective meanings belong to the domain of social construction of space (Richardson 1982). It is always necessary, however, to keep in mind that this sorting is somewhat illusory: I agree with Lefebvre (1991) that social space is a whole, and any one event or illustration has within it aspects of that whole. The complex and contradictory nature of space is that "space is permeated with social relations; it is not only supported by social relations but it is also producing and produced by social relations" (Lefebvre 1991, 286, as cited in Hayden 1995, 31).

In this chapter, then, I examine the theorizing power of these two perspectives by focusing on the history, design, and social life of two Costa Rican plazas. Applying these analytic tools to the ethnographic material I demonstrate that there is a relationship between the circumstances of the production of public spaces such as plazas and people's experience of them; that this relationship is dialogic rather than dialectic, in spite of the high degree of conflict and contestation often found in the Costa Rican plazas; and that the plazas act as containers, thus permitting resistance, counterresistance, and change to occur publicly and with relative safety.[2] In addition, the negotiation of the form and meaning of spatial representations is illuminating as a public forum in which people work out larger conflicts stemming from the growing impact of globalization, increased tourism, and the struggle by both individuals and the state to maintain a distinct cultural identity.

I argue that ethnographic approaches to spatial analysis are crucial for any adequate analysis of the contestation of values and meanings in complex societies. Further, they highlight the most valuable anthropological contribution to the study of urban space: the ability to integrate the localized discourse with larger political and economic processes.

The Ethnography of the Spanish American Plaza

The ethnographic descriptions presented in the case studies that follow are based on long-term fieldwork that I conducted in San José, Costa Rica, from 1972 to 1974, in the summers of 1976 and 1979, and during three intensive fieldwork periods focusing only on the urban plazas (May–September 1986; December 1986–February 1987; and November–December 1993). I was able to observe differing behaviors during these visits since they were made at different times: the summer months coincide with Costa Rica's rainy season, while the winter months are dry. The rainy season is characterized by late-afternoon rain that, when heavy, interrupts plaza life for at least an hour. During these periods I would stand with other plaza occupants under the closest available shelter or visit one of the local cafés to wait for the rain to stop. During the Christmas and New Year's period, in the dry season, plaza use is at its most intense. The weather is clear, sunny, and cool, and the plazas become informal markets for seasonal gifts, nuts, and fruits.

Observation

I was concerned that participant-observation in a public space might not capture all the activities that occur, so I utilized three different observational strategies in my fieldwork. First, I observed each plaza by sector and recorded everything that occurred in that sector for a designated period of time. This time/place sampling provided a system for nonsequentially observing all the sites throughout the day on both weekends and weekdays. I also collected the data to create a series of behavioral maps locating activities and counts of people by location, sex, and age. Second, after the first month of time/space sampling a map of activity locations had emerged, so in a second set of observations I concentrated on documenting those activities and the people engaged in them throughout the plazas. Finally, during the third phase of participant-observation, I carried a camera and map, spoke to people, and became more involved in everyday plaza life. By this time plaza users were quite used to seeing me with my clipboard and pen and were delighted that I was now taking photographs and involving them in my— until then—apparently clandestine task. The camera gave many people an excuse to talk to me and to ask what I was doing. I began to make friends and hang out with some of the plaza occupants, even visiting them at home or joining them when they went for a drink or a meal.

Interviews and Historical Documentation

At the conclusion of these observations I collected a series of interviews with a variety of plaza users, asking questions that had emerged during the observational period. I completed a systematic series of interviews with the managers, owners, and directors of the relevant local institutions located on or near the plazas and collected blueprints, design guidelines, and plans for the design of the plazas. A series of interviews with local historians and archival work in the National Library and at the Universidad de Costa Rica provided documentation of the oral histories of Parque Central. Interviews with the current and previous ministers of culture (including President Oscar Arias) and the head of urban planning, as well as with the architects involved in the design of the Plaza de la Cultura, provided contextual data for the ethnographic descriptions and documentation of the processes of material production. Finally, novels, newspapers, television presentations, and conversations with friends and neighbors provided data on the broader cultural context of public life. I repeated these phases of the research project during each of the three field visits.

Analysis

This methodology was very effective in providing various kinds of data that could be compared and analyzed. The content analysis of the field notes, interviews, maps, and historical documents generated a series of themes and theoretical insights into the cultural underpinnings of plaza design and use. The observations, interviews, archival documentation, and spatial and architectural maps and drawings provided distinct "texts" that I could read in relation to one another in the search for breakdowns and incoherence that would in turn reveal areas of cultural conflict and contestation (Agar 1986, Geertz 1973).

Figure 4.1. Parque Central in San José, Costa Rica.

Setting

San José, Costa Rica, is the capital and largest city
of this small Central American nation. Costa Rica—known for its beautiful scenery, protected natural environment, friendly people, and stable
government—has become an ecotourism mecca and a desirable retirement site for middle-income North Americans who want to stretch their
dollars while living in a warm climate. The rapid increase of tourism,
the recent influx of refugees from Nicaragua and El Salvador, and the
seemingly unending economic crises are blamed for what Josefinos (San
José residents) perceive as an increase in crime and physical deterioration in the capital city of this erstwhile tropical paradise.

Two plazas in the center of the city were selected as field sites. Parque
Central, the original Plaza Mayor, is one of the oldest plazas in San José
and represents Costa Rica's Spanish colonial history in its spatial form and
context. Its relatively long history spans the colonial, republican, and
modern periods, and a number of historical photographs and portrayals
of earlier periods of plaza design and social life were available in local
archives. Parque Central remains a vibrant center of traditional Costa
Rican culture and is inhabited by a variety of largely male workers, pensioners, preachers and healers, tourists, shoppers, sex workers, and people
who just want to sit and watch the action. When I returned in 1993
it was temporarily under reconstruction: the cement kiosk was being

Figure 4.2. Plaza de la Cultura in San José, Costa Rica.

renovated and the surrounding benches, pathways, and gathering spaces had been redesigned since my previous visit.

The Plaza de la Cultura, a contemporary plaza only one block west and one block north of Parque Central, is a recently designed urban space heralded by Josefino boosters as an emblem of the "new Costa Rican culture." Because it was opened in 1982, I was able to interview individuals involved in its design and planning while at the same time I could study it as a well-established place. The Plaza de la Cultura proved to be an excellent comparison to Parque Central, providing contrasts in style of design, spatial configuration, surrounding buildings and institutions, activities, and the kinds of inhabitants and visitors. It is a site of modern consumption, an example of what Zukin (1991) calls a landscape of power. North American culture is "consumed" by Costa Rican teenagers carrying radios blaring rap music, and North American tourists "consume" Costa Rican culture by buying souvenirs, snacks, theater tickets, and artworks as well as the sexual favors and companionship of young Costa Ricans. These two urban spaces were socially produced—planned, built, designed, and maintained—in different historical and sociopolitical contexts, and both were constrained by limits imposed by the available resources as well as by the central government's political objectives. The environments thus produced are observably different: Parque Central (figure 4.1) is a furnished and enclosed space with trees, paths, and benches, while the Plaza de la Cultura (figure 4.2) is an open expanse that provides few places to sit but offers a magnificent open vista leading to a view of the National Theater.

These plazas were also socially constructed through contested patterns of use and attributed meanings. The social uses of the plazas, which at first glance appear similar, are fundamentally different according to the age, sex, ethnicity, and interests of the users. The degree and form of social contestation and conflict between the regular users and the agents of the municipal government—the police, the planning agency, and the directors of surrounding institutions—also vary, most visibly in terms of the kinds of spatial control maintained. Even the experience of being in the plaza (Richardson 1982) is distinct and voiced in different ways in the different spaces. The differences in the plazas' material production and symbolic and experiential construction have created very different urban spaces that are distinct in physical design as well as in the ways both users and nonusers control, experience, and think about them. These distinctions provide a vehicle to contrast the ways in which urban space is socially produced—both materially and symbolically—and socially constructed through experience and social interaction.

Parque Central

In 1751 Spanish colonists who had left the cacao-growing lowlands along the Caribbean coast established a new town, La Villa Nueva del Señor San José, in the central highland plateau of Costa Rica (González Víquez 1973, Vega Carballo 1981). In contrast to the Plaza de Armas, a plaza for military displays that was built a few blocks away, the Parque Central was designed as the ceremonial and civic center of the growing town. It began as a grassy, tree-covered rectangular public space that served as a weekend marketplace and was oriented as a square city block with north-south and east-west roads as its boundaries. Civic and religious institutions quickly surrounded it. The Iglesia Parroquial was built on the eastern side of the plaza in 1774 (De Mora 1973). (This church became the national cathedral after San José became the capital of Costa Rica in 1823.) The military barracks followed on the northern side, and the Casa del Cabildo (town hall) was completed on the northeast corner in 1799. At the same time, private buildings were constructed; Capitán Don Miguel Jiménez built a house on the plaza as early as 1761 (González Víquez 1973, 487). The remaining building sites were eventually filled with private residences and small businesses, including the Botica Francesa and a small hotel on the southern edge by the mid-nineteenth century. As early as the beginning of the nineteenth century, San José was a relatively urban center in comparison with other populated areas (Vega Carballo 1981).

The plan and urban design of Parque Central was part of the establishment of the Spanish American colonial empire, which repeatedly created a type of urban space that is still "produced despite the vicissitudes of imperialism, independence and industrialization" (Lefebvre 1991, 151). Its history is a perfect illustration of the production of space in Spanish American towns, based on the 1573 Orders for Discovery and Settlement as characterized by Lefebvre:

> The very building of towns thus embodied a plan which would determine the mode of occupation of the territory and define how it was to be reorganized under the administrative and political authority of urban power. . . . The result is a strictly hierarchical organization of space, a gradual progression outward from the town's centre . . . from the inevitable Plaza Mayor a grid extends indefinitely in every direction. Each square or rectangular lot has its function assigned to it, while inversely each function is assigned its own place at a greater or lesser distance from the central square: church, administrative buildings, town gates, squares, streets . . . and so on. (Lefebvre 1991, 151)

Lefebvre characterizes the building of Spanish American towns such as San José as the "production of a social space by political power—that is, by violence in the service of economic goals" (Lefebvre 1991, 151–152). While I agree with his theoretical analysis, the details of the origins of the plaza-centered grid-plan town deserve further examination.

I have argued elsewhere that the Spanish American plaza and grid-plan town are syncretic spatial forms derived from a combination of European architectural traditions of medieval *bastides* (planned agricultural towns built by the French to protect their territory) and the Mesoamerican plaza-temple complexes and urban plans of the cities encountered during the conquest of the New World (Low 1993, Low 1995). Some of the earliest Spanish American plazas were in fact superposed on the ruins of their Aztec or Maya antecedents. The European and Mesoamerican plaza designs had similar aims: both were produced to display military conquest and market domination by the conquering rulers, whether those rulers were Aztec, Mayan, or Spanish. Therefore, although the Spanish American plaza is a product of colonial control and consciously produced as a means of spatial domination, its form also derived from indigenous forms of political and economic control expressed in the Mesoamerican plaza-temple complex. Since the spatial relations of plaza to buildings, hierarchy of spaces, and functions of the plaza remained the same from the Mesoamerican models to their Spanish American successors, the symbolic meanings of the spatialized material culture reflect aspects of both cultural histories.

Parque Central retained its colonial form and meaning until the beginning of the republican era in 1823. In the mid-nineteenth century the plaza was redesigned and refurbished with all the trappings of European bourgeois elegance: a grand fountain was imported from England in 1859 to supply water to the city (and was completed in 1868); an elaborate iron fence was added in 1870; and a wooden "Victorian" kiosk in which the military band could play for the Sunday *retreta* was constructed in 1890. The plaza was also famous for its large fig, palm, and magnolia trees at this time, to the point that when one was cut down in 1902 a public protest ensued (Caja 1928).

It is in the late nineteenth century that we find textual and photographic evidence for class-based social constructions of the appropriate use (and appropriated use) of public space. The accumulated wealth of coffee growers and a republican government composed of members of the landed elite began to impose a class-biased conception of public space and spatial representation. Historical texts, retrospective interviews, and diaries from this period describe Parque Central as a place where the elite would gather and stroll in the evening and that was locked and patrolled at night (Costa Rica en el Siglo XIX 1929). This elite image, however, is contested in other sources. For instance, photographs from 1870 show workers in open shirts and boys with bare feet resting in the plaza (figure 4.3), and a well-known 1915 portrait of middle-class men with their children sitting on the ledge of the fountain captures a barefoot boy standing on the side of the scene. Photographs of street scenes along the fenced edge of the plaza in 1917 include barefoot campesinos as well as well-dressed urban business men (Banco Nacional de Costa Rica 1972), and novels of the period describe street children and poor people living in or along the edges of plaza (Trullás y Aulit 1913).

This conflict between the images of Parque Central as an elite strolling park and as a socially heterogeneous public gathering place has continued, manifesting itself most recently in the ongoing resistance to the replacement of the original 1890 kiosk. In 1944 a giant cement kiosk was donated by a Nicaraguan industrialist; this first housed a disco nightclub and later a children's library. By now, current daily users have incorporated the cement kiosk into their spatial pattern of activities. It makes a convenient stage and serves as a place to continue business on a rainy day. Children play on its ledges, and it is large enough to hold the orchestra and audience for the weekly Sunday concert.

As recently as the spring of 1992, however, a group of citizens formed a movement to tear down this cement structure and reconstruct the original Victorian one; the issue was so controversial that it provoked a series of well-attended town meetings. The cement kiosk and its current uses do not fit many Josefinos' idea of the appropriate architecture for the ceremonial and civic center of the city. The citizens who are attempting to reconstitute Parque Central in its elite turn-of-the-century image are not the daily users or the municipal designers but professional and middle-class residents who yearn for an idealized past. Thus the conflict over the architectural form of the kiosk reveals a struggle over the social construction of the meaning and appropriate use of public space. The symbolic contrasts of Victorian with modern, wooden with cement, and elite with working class provide architectural metaphors for class-based taste cultures, a forum for public conflict over appropriate modes of symbolic representation, and a convenient cover for broader class-based social meanings and conflicts.

Daily life in the Parque Central has changed over time. These changes appear in the architectural furnishings, the social class and gender composition of the users, the range of occupations and work sites, the nature of the policing and social control, and what people say about their experience of being in the plaza. Most of these changes are the end product of global economic and political forces, which have led to declin-

Figure 4.3. Youths in Parque Central, San José, Costa Rica.

ing socioeconomic conditions and increasing cultural and social diversity. Dramatic economic changes in Costa Rica since the 1950s have led
to increases in urban density as well as crowding, crime, and pollution.
Most upper-class families have left the central city and moved to the
western sector or to the suburbs, abandoning the central city—and thus
Parque Central—to the poor and the working classes. The elite residences,
symbols of the upper class's erstwhile presence in the central city, have
been replaced by the symbols of a new kind of global economy, one based
on debt and world-banking controls and dependent on foreign capital:
national and international banks, movie theaters playing English-language
movies, soda shops, and small businesses now surround Parque Central, replacing the civic and residential context of earlier plaza life. By
1985 the Latin American debt crisis had increased Costa Rica's dependence on United States AID funds (Shallat 1989), and the International
Monetary Fund (IMF) had intervened to monitor Costa Rica's economy
in order to ensure timely debt payments (Edelman and Kenen 1989).

The increase in unemployment that resulted from the decline in the
value of agricultural exports has encouraged the growth of an informal
economy. This informal economy is very visible in Parque Central. The
plaza is used as an urban workplace of exchange and coexistence:
shoeshine men control the northeast corner, ambulatory vendors use the
sidewalks and pathways, salespeople use the benches as office space,

construction workers wait for pickup jobs under the arbor, sex workers stand in the kiosk or sit on benches, and men move through the crowd selling stolen goods and gambling. The influx of refugees from Nicaragua, El Salvador, and Guatemala has increased both the number of vendors and the competition among them and has increased the presence of homeless adults and street children.

Middle-class businesspeople and nonusers, however, have used political pressure to increase the number of police in order to remove "undesirables." Concerned about the increase in crime and vagrancy that they associate with the ongoing economic crisis, the resulting numbers of people working in the plaza, homeless people, and their associated activities reflect their fears. The state is therefore attempting to constrain these uses in several ways. The police maintain open surveillance from the top of the cement kiosk, thus repeating and reiterating Parque Central's colonial history as a public space originally produced as a spatial representation of state domination and social control. In addition, plainclothes policemen look for drug transactions and the sale of stolen goods. A young couple moving through the plaza stopped to ask what I was doing; they turned out to be plainclothes police. There are also municipal agents, representing a different kind of state control; they require vendors to pay for the right to sell on city streets and in the plazas. If vendors do not have the money to pay for a license—and they frequently do not—they forfeit their proceeds for that day.

Many of the older men are pensioners who come to spend the day on their regular benches with a group of cronies. One pensioner, Don Carlos, says that he is eighty-six years old. He comes to the plaza every day at about 10:00 A.M., after having his coffee, bread, and cheese—"something to nourish one"—at home. He sits with his friends on the southwest corner until the afternoon and then returns home to eat a late meal. When he was younger, he was employed by the civil police and at one time had worked as a guard in the plaza. He opened the gates at 6:00 A.M. and closed them at 10:00 P.M. When I asked how the plaza had changed, he replied, "The plaza was more strict before; they locked the gates at night. People of all kinds can come here now, but not before. It was a very polite place then, and not everyone was allowed in." Thus control over who is in the plaza is apparently maintained less openly and more subversively than it used to be.

We can see another example of coexistence and contestation in Parque Central in the number of evangelical healers and preachers who hold prayer meetings in the arbor and healing services on the northwest corner. These Protestant practitioners and their adherents can be seen as symbolically contesting the religious hegemony of the Catholic cathedral that flanks the eastern perimeter. Although the original Parque Central was designed as the "front garden" of the Catholic church (Richardson 1982), the diversity of religious beliefs and practices has now reconstituted the space as one of broadly defined religious heterodoxy. The presence in front of the city's major Catholic institution of various religious sects, from Hare Krishna followers to born-again Christians, challenges the state Catholicism symbolized by the plaza's spatial arrangements.

The actions of the plaza users also contest the hegemony of state Catholicism. Plaza users say that they enjoy the spectacle of the healing ceremonies, to which successful cures draw large crowds of believers. One of the more successful healers—a man called "the Christian"—appears, dressed in a robe of rough sackcloth tied with animal skins, at about noon each day on the northwest corner of the plaza. A crowd of passersby quickly gathers around the raised plant bed where he stands. As the circle forms he calls out, "Who wants to receive Christ and be healed?"

There is no unified experience of being in Parque Central, but fragments of its social production are reproduced in the everyday practices and feelings of its users. Many of the older men express considerable affection for and attachment to the plaza; often the sense of being comfortable is based on memories of being in the park at an earlier time or in different circumstances. One elderly man expressed his feelings when he began to cry upon seeing a giant palm cut down and reminisced about how it felt to sit in the shade of that tree. Women, however, often express a sense of unease and are rarely found sitting for very long, especially during the week. A woman who sat down next to me gave me her explanation when I asked her if she came there often. She replied, "No, but I am resting because my package is heavy." She said that she lived in an outlying suburb and was on her way home. "I normally only come to the plaza on Sunday," she commented. I asked her why. "Because there are a lot of unemployed men here and women are usually working, or if they are not working, they are in the house. Sunday is when women come to Parque Central, with their children." Younger adult men are often found working in the plaza. One man was running his real estate business from a bench: "With the high price of rent, the electricity, water, and everything else, it is difficult to stay in business. Here my clients can find me, and I do not have all these other expenses." Other regular plaza workers include the food, candy, flower, lottery ticket, and newspaper vendors; shoeshine men; gamblers; sex workers; and day laborers waiting for casual work in the morning. These working users are territorial about their spaces and defend them both from new workers and from casual passersby. When asked about their work they express satisfaction with their working conditions, and in the case of the shoeshine men, say that they intend to hand down their work location to their children or friends.

Other plaza users come to participate in the illicit world of gambling and trade in stolen goods. One rainy day, while standing on the kiosk, I watched a well-dressed young man sit down, take off his watch, and show it to the man currently running the shell game. The man gave him some money while taking the watch. They played until the young man finally lost the game, handing the money back to the gambler, who now had both the watch and the cash. As the young man walked away I went up to him and asked him what had happened. He said that not much had occurred but that he had traded his watch for cash to gamble and had lost everything. He claimed to know that he would be more successful next time. On another rainy day one of the gamblers approached me as a mark, showing me how easy it was to win, but I never carried money to the plaza and so could not play.

According to some plaza users there is an increasing number of sex workers working in Parque Central. One afternoon I was working on a map sitting next to a man who asked me what I was doing. After I told him, I asked him who the women were in front of us. He replied, "Prostitutes, young prostitutes. They come every evening. There seem to be more [of them] than ever now for economic necessity." I also asked him about why there were so few women in the plaza. He replied that there was increasing unemployment and that the unemployed men in the plaza made women uneasy: "It is the government's fault. Have you heard that they want to build eighty thousand houses? You could not even do it physically! And the price supports for farmers and manufacturers just do not work." (Costa Rica had government subsidies for basic agricultural products such as beans, rice, and milk and high import taxes on foreign manufactured products to protect the development of local industry.)

Even the clowns who work in the Parque Central are concerned about the economic conditions of people who use it. In an interview with two clowns, I commented that they had cut their performance short the day before. The older clown responded by saying that they did not make much money in Parque Central and that they could earn more at the Plaza de la Cultura: "Because the people of the Plaza de la Cultura are of a higher social class and are richer . . . there are more tourists and foreigners. Here in the Parque Central they do not have the resources." An older man who had overheard us walked up and remarked: "I am a pensioner, and I enjoy the clowns and would like to give money, but I do not have enough to support even myself. That is how we are."

The experience of being in the plaza is sensory as well as social. When I returned to study the plaza during the dry season, I noticed that a group of pensioners had moved from the benches on the southwest corner (where I had always seen them) to the inner ring of benches near the kiosk. Until then the territories of different groups of people had been quite stable in terms of both location and time of day. When I asked them if I had been mistaken to assume that their preferred bench was on the southwest corner, they told me they had sat on that corner for the past five years but that the noise and fumes from increased bus traffic had become intolerable. The inner ring had benches where it was quieter and smelled better. I also noticed subtle sensory changes in the environment throughout the day: the bird songs early in the morning and at sunset, the bells of the cathedral at noon, and the smell of roasting candied peanuts and meats that announced the vendors who catered to the evening movie theater crowd. These sensory perceptions, although a valued part of the cultural landscape, are also undergoing change.

The ethnographic evidence for the transformation of the Parque Central into a workplace and a place mainly for pensioners and unemployed men on weekdays shows how the space is the object of conflicts over the nature of social and spatial representation in the urban center. The struggle over the design of the kiosk, the number of police and the kinds of state control, the increasing territoriality of the vendors and shoeshine men, the discomfort of women and children, and the heterodoxy of religious practitioners all illustrate how individuals and groups resist the consequences of larger sociopolitical, economic, and historical forces.

Plaza de la Cultura

The second case study, the more recently built Plaza de la Cultura, sheds further light on these processes by allowing us to observe how a new public urban space was created and defined and subsequently appropriated by a different group of users—who gave it quite distinct cultural meanings.

The Plaza de la Cultura is a modern paved plaza reminiscent of the futurist design of the Pompidou Center in Paris; it has bright chrome and yellow ventilation pipes, a shallow pool containing three water jets, metal pipe benches, and few trees. Beneath the plaza are a subterranean Gold Museum, exhibition spaces, and the Costa Rican tourist center, entered from the northern edge of the plaza by a series of grassy, sloping steps. The plaza is bordered on the south by the turn-of-the-century National Theater; on the west by the Gran Hotel, the major tourist hotel for North Americans; and on the north and east by busy shopping streets lined by McDonald's, Burger King, Pizza Hut, Sears, photographic supply stores, bookstores, and other local businesses. The few trees are in planters lining the western edge alongside the hotel shops, which include a newspaper stand carrying the *Miami Herald*, a clothing store, and a shop that sells the renowned Costa Rican ice cream, Pops.

The building of the Plaza de la Cultura was an inspiration of the minister of culture. Costa Rica's world-famous collection of pre-Columbian gold artifacts was formerly stored in the Central Bank of Costa Rica. In 1975 the head of the Central Bank convinced the Legislative Assembly to allocate funds to build a Gold Museum in order to display the collection as a celebration of indigenous Costa Rican culture. The plan was supported by the "Liberationists," the political party in power at the time. The National Liberation Party (Liberación Nacional) represents a politically liberal coalition of professional, middle-class, and working-class Costa Ricans, whereas the Social Christians' Unity Party (Partido Unidad de Social Cristianos)—a more conservative party—had grown out of earlier political coalitions that included the landed gentry and coffee-growing elite. The minister of planning and the head of the Central Bank selected the land around the National Theater, already partly owned by the Central Bank, as an appropriate site for a cultural center that would accommodate tourists and visitors to the new Gold Museum. This desire for a new cultural center was also stimulated by the changes taking place in Parque Central, which was becoming inadequate as a cultural embodiment of the National Liberation Party ideals (Low 1996). Some structures already in place would remain: the new plaza would incorporate the already existing *parquecito* (little park) Juan Mora Fernandez in front of the Gran Hotel and the shopping structure known as the Arcades (Naranjo Coto 1982). Among the many structures to be demolished, however, were the homes of a few older residents (who were to be compensated by the state) and a number of small business establishments (Archivos 1993).

This initial design was radically changed and expanded. When the minister of culture went to the site to survey the progress of the demolition, he saw the National Theater isolated in the open space created by the destruction of the surrounding buildings. In an instant, he said, he realized that it would be a much more powerful plan to have an open public plaza with the Gold Museum underground, so that there would be an unobstructed view of the National Theater—the "architectural jewel" of San José. Thus the architectural plans for the original Gold Museum were scrapped and a new phase of planning and design began. The planning, design, and building of the Plaza de la Cultura began in 1976 and culminated in the plaza's inauguration in 1982. Although some of the buildings selected for demolition were deemed of historic significance, and despite local protest, the plan moved forward. More vigorous protests appeared in the media, which criticized the government for spending money to put the Gold Museum underground (a costly and difficult feat of engineering). A particularly harsh rainy season also prevented the project from moving ahead on schedule.

Both the location and design program were produced by a combination of local sociopolitical forces and global—particularly North American—capital. When the plaza was conceived, global capital was already fueling the Costa Rican economy and the IMF restrictions would soon be in place. Foreign as well as local interests thus influenced the siting of the plaza, placing it next to the major tourist hotel and the National Theater and in the center of North American businesses (including McDonald's, Burger King, and Sears) and tourist activity. The design, on the other hand, was influenced by the political ideology of the National Liberation Party under the leadership of a new professional class, which wanted Costa Rican culture to be represented as both modern in its reliance on modern European idioms of design and indigenous in its evocation of the pre-Columbian past.

The spatial form and design, however, were ultimately determined by a team of three architects who had won the design competition for the original plan, the above-ground Gold Museum. The architects themselves, although all Costa Rican, represented Costa Rican, European, and North American design training, blended to create what they defined as a new Costa Rican design idiom. From my interviews with them, it seems that each had a different vision of the plaza. Further, they produced design features best appreciated from a male point of view.

One of them imagined the plaza to be a place where men could watch women walk past; he designed a vast paved open space, providing the longest sight line available for watching women walk in the city. Another architect saw the plaza as a meeting place, symbolically linked to other plazas in the city by a second grid, with pedestrian walkways and trees. He imagined young men leaning on the outside rails of the perimeter piping and put a foot rail just where a man's foot might rest. The third architect thought that the new plaza should be a significant open space: "Costa Ricans have their gardens and their parks, and they have their special places, but they do not have a center for jugglers, music, political meetings and large gatherings as in New York." He wanted an open space for public performances: "But we did not want a huge dry space, so we put in trees along the edges." These different social imaginings and representations of space were integrated to create a rather eclectic space with a modernist style—a design idiom that many Costa Ricans neither liked nor understood. When the plaza first opened there were spontaneous demonstrations by people who came and tore out the plantings, started fires in the trash cans, and tried to destroy as many of the furnishings as possible. There is even conflict over the meaning of these demonstrations: It is not entirely clear either from the media reports or from firsthand accounts who the demonstrators were or what exactly they were protesting, but the media interpreted this demonstration as a protest against the plaza's stark modernity.

Nonetheless, the plaza appears to be successful in terms of the architects' objectives: the unusual modern and empty urban space produced by these sociopolitical and economic forces and professional imaginings has been rapidly appropriated by groups of users. The vast open space is used by street performers, religious singing groups, political speakers, and teenagers break dancing or playing soccer (to the delight of the third architect). These are all users who did not have a public place before this plaza was constructed, since the parklike atmosphere of Parque Central does not accommodate these activities.

In addition, the small plazas created by the designers in front of the National Theater and Gran Hotel are used by officially licensed vendors who sell local crafts to tourists from their semipermanent stands. A seemingly endless stream of tourists from the Gran Hotel sit on the edges of the plaza watching people from the safety of the hotel's sidewalk café. Women and families bring their children, who run after pigeons and play in the fountain during the afternoon; in the late evening the plaza becomes a gay cruising area and social meeting place that is internationally known through guidebooks such as the *Spartacus Guide for Gay Men* (1987, 144).

From interviews with key informants and conversations with users and friends one learns that this tranquillity is contested by a number of illicit activities that contribute to the perception that the Plaza de la Cultura is an unsafe and unpleasant place. This perception is reinforced in several ways. The newspapers regularly and frequently report mishaps and transgressions and criticize the municipal government's management of the plaza. The hotel bouncer remains posted at the edge of the plaza, ready to protect his customers from the sight of beggars or poor people looking for a place to rest. Official uniformed police stand outside the National Theater and refuse entrance to anyone who looks likely to cause a disturbance; when a young man ran by and grabbed a gold chain from a girl's neck, the police were everywhere within seconds. The intensity of social and spatial control appears even greater than in the Parque Central; here it is more visible and even more intensely contested.

These conflicting forces produce an ambivalent experience of being in the Plaza de la Cultura. Nonusers uniformly describe the plaza as dangerous, frightening, and uncomfortable. The media seem to have influenced many potential users in ways I found hard to understand, inasmuch as the bright, sunlit plaza never threatened me. Mothers and children do come to this plaza to play with the pigeons or splash in the low fountain. Many more young men and women, often students, stop there to meet one another or to have lunch or an ice cream cone in the afternoon sun than in the Parque Central. Tourists seem secure and comfortable.

Yet all my students at the Universidad de Costa Rica were uncomfortable there and unwilling to visit, even for a field visit. The one female student who finally did visit was afraid the entire time that a thief was waiting to take her purse. Friends told me that there was drug dealing and that it was a terrible place. Most nonusers cited examples of robbery, pickpocketing, or uninvited sexual proposals experienced there by people they knew. For those who were unfamiliar with it, the Plaza de la Cultura was not a place to visit and was certainly not a plaza that represented the positive aspects of Costa Rican culture.

Frequent users also criticized the space, even though they admitted to spending a considerable amount of time there. For instance, an artist who said that he spent too much time in the plaza told me that he thought it was poorly designed: "It should have had a roof—a roof where artists could work and things could happen. This plaza is useless when the weather is forbidding and it is usually forbidding. We might as well have had a football stadium here."

When I asked another frequent user, a young man, how he liked the plaza, he replied that he preferred the Parque Morazon, a small park a few blocks northwest. He said that only young people came to the Plaza de la Cultura and that they made a lot of noise and commotion. "Like what?" I asked. "They have radios blaring, shout, and make a scene," he replied. He prefers the other park, where it is quiet.

Another man, sitting with his girlfriend, complained, "The plaza should be for cultured things, not for rudeness, drugs, or radios." He went on to recount all the performers who had come to the plaza: "The ball man who bounces a ball with his body. The doll, an old woman, who sells violets. A 'crazy' man who acts like a truck—these are special. But a plaza is for sitting, watching, talking—for music, meetings, and groups, but not for the rest of this stuff." He went on to say, "If you have a bar and let the wrong kind of person in, even one, then more will come and it will be too late."

People who work in the Plaza de la Cultura express some of the same ambivalence about working there. While the clowns preferred the crowd there because they could collect more money than they could elsewhere, the vendors complained that they were charged a high fee for putting up a stall in the tourist area. These stalls are carefully regulated by the municipal government and have multiplied over time. During most of the time that I observed the vendors, they sat around, talked, and smoked cigarettes while waiting for the busy Saturday craft market held in front of the National Theater. During my last visit in December 1993, however, the plaza was crammed with stalls and vendors, most of whom were illegally selling clothes and souvenirs from other Central American countries. It seems that a Guatemalan vendor, who was fined for selling without a permit, sued the city and is bringing his case to court, arguing that the plaza should be a "free market" with no charge for selling in this "democratic" country. So even the vendors are contesting the city's control of the plaza to regulate their means of making a living. The Plaza de la Cultura also has a few child workers—young shoeshine boys in front of the Gran Hotel, and children who illegally sell gum and candy. These young boys, who range in age from about seven to nine, are not found working in Parque Central.

There are nonetheless some who are happy with the plaza, often for very specific reasons. For example, two North American men whom I interviewed in the café next to the plaza said that they liked the plaza for one simple reason: it had the best girl-watching view anywhere in San José (I noted in my field notes that the designers would be pleased to hear that.) One offered this observation: "You can watch them all the way across the plaza on the left to the end of the hotel plaza. It is a long walk—and the girls are the best here, mostly upper- and upper-middle-class. . . . I mean the best for watching. I prefer the lower-class and country girls. They are friendlier, warmer, and it comes from the heart—not stuck-up like the upper-class girls."

The two men talked on, complaining that the benches in the Plaza de la Cultura were not comfortable and that there were no good places to sit, but that they met there as part of their daily routine. A retired North American commented that although the plaza pipe benches were uncomfortable, he liked the friendliness of the young girls and knew he would find young people there. The Plaza de la Cultura is also near the McDonald's, another teenage hangout: "Imagine a middle-aged guy like me hanging out in a McDonald's in Kansas City to meet girls. I would be arrested."

Probably the happiest group are the teenagers who hang out in the evenings along the pipe railing. One young man said that he found the spaciousness appealing. "Here," he said, "we feel at home." When I asked two young men what they were doing in the plaza, they replied, "Passing the time, shooting the breeze. What do young people do in the U.S.?" Before the creation of this plaza, the teenagers were not a visible part of any park or plaza. You could see them walking down the streets or in couples, kissing or quietly talking in Parque España or Parque Morazon. But now they have their own space, designed to create a stage for their nightly performances. And they have successfully appropriated this public space for their activities in the evenings.

As in Parque Central, however, the visible presence of the Gran Hotel bouncer and the *guardia civil* (civil police), who question the youths (and in some cases stop or detain them), contests their symbolic dominance. For instance, one Friday night a young man with a bottle in a brown paper bag joined the line of teenagers along the railing. I was just wondering if they realized how many police were around when two came by, took the bag, frisked all of them, took their identity cards, and lined them up along the wall.

Compared with Parque Central, this urban space represents and accommodates more modern spatial practices, based on youth, foreign capital, tourism, and an ideology of liberal modernism but contested through the localized discourse about safety and comfort. The Plaza de la Cultura seems to be more about the consumption of culture than the working landscape of Parque Central is. Most important, the forces that produced this new plaza are reflected in its design and social use as well as in the ambivalence of being there. The teenagers and tourists are comfortable, while other Costa Ricans either fear the plaza and or wish that it were quieter, calmer, more shaded, and sedate.

Furthermore, the plaza is engendered in a distinct way: there are more women and children than in Parque Central, and fewer older men, except for the male North American tourists and pensioners who are looking at (or for) young Costa Rican women. The new public space thus appears to challenge the institutionalized weekday spatial segregation of domesticated women from plaza-frequenting men, a phenomenon that remains marked in more culturally traditional settings such as Parque Central. Since spatial arrangements reproduce gender differences in power and privilege, changing spatial relations such as the creation of public spaces that women can use may potentially change the status hierarchy and improve the position of women in Costa Rica (Spain 1992, 33).

Conclusion

In both places, however, there is a hiatus between what is experienced and socially constructed by the users on the one hand, and the circumstances that socially produced the space and its current physical form and design on the other. Furthermore, the designs and material conditions of these two worlds are subject to symbolic interpretation and manipulation by the users in such a way that they themselves become cultural representations to the users. Thus the contestation of the design, furnishings, use, and atmosphere of a plaza becomes a visible public forum for the expression of cultural conflict, social change, and attempts at class-based, gender-segregated, and age-specific social control.

These examples illustrate how an anthropological approach to the study of urban space would work ethnographically. I have focused on the historical emergence, sociopolitical and economic development, patterns of social use, and experiential meanings of plaza life and design as a means of empirically working out the implications of the broader social production of space and social construction of space perspectives. The ethnographic illustrations highlight sociopolitical forces, spatial practices, and efforts at social control that provide insight into the conflicts that arise as different groups attempt to claim and define these urban spaces. Furthermore, these processes elucidate the ways in which the forces and limits of the social production of space and social construction of space are engaged and contested in public arenas.

To summarize the analytic possibilities of these complementary perspectives, I would like to return to the conflict over the design and style of the kiosk in Parque Central. As I mentioned, from 1990 through 1992 the city held a series of town meetings to discuss replacing the 1944 modernist cement kiosk with a replica of the previous Victorian wooden one. Many Josefinos argued that the Victorian kiosk was a better representation of Costa Rican cultural values because it evoked a nostalgic image of *cultura* (culture) and bourgeois decorum (see Low 1996, Richardson 1982). Others, however, argued that the 1944 cement kiosk was part of the city's patrimony and that rather than being torn down it should be preserved and improved. Ultimately, the forces for historic preservation won, and the cement kiosk was restored as the central design element in a redesigned plaza that opened in 1994. This vignette highlights the cultural importance of the design of the kiosk, a significance further demonstrated by the fact that citizens staged protests to which the government responded with a series of open town meetings. We see how these two images of a kiosk were materially produced in different historical and political periods and retained semiotic interpretations from the respective periods of their material production. Moreover, the case illustrates how these spatial representations have assumed new social meanings in the recent struggle between modernization and historic preservation forces in San José, and how this conflict highlights the importance of spatializing culture and human experience as an analytic strategy for understanding people's negotiation of cultural values and representations of those values.

Another important aspect of this sociospatial analysis is the highlighting of "visible" and "invisible" in public space. Many of the illegal activities that occurred in Parque Central—prostitution, drug dealing, and gambling—were apparently tolerated within the confines of this plaza. The dense foliage and tree cover provided places for clandestine activities that were in some sense "invisible" to the cultural gaze. But with the development of the Plaza de la Cultura as the new ceremonial and cultural center, these same activities were "exposed" by modern landscape architecture, open design, and increased social scrutiny. The increased visibility of these activities creates an atmosphere characterized by ambivalence, fear, and increasing social sanctions. It seems that when faced with the invisible-made-visible in public space, the state reacts with increased social controls; if this strategy does not work, the state abandons the space, building in its stead a new one where "culture" can be represented in a more pristine form. It leaves me wondering if public spaces in San José will become like those in New York City, with police and guard dogs to keep out homeless persons and drug dealers, benches that do not allow sleeping, and ledges topped with spikes to prevent sitting. As the complexities of modernity and urbanization become more manifest, will public spaces be so contested that they become uncomfortable places even, or especially, in a participatory democracy?

Acknowledgments

Research for the plaza studies was supported by grants from the Wenner-Gren Foundation, the National Endowment for the Humanities through the John Carter Brown Library, and the Fulbright Scholars Fellowship Program. I would like to thank Joel Lefkowitz and Laurel Wilson for their thoughtful editing and provocative discussions. I also would like to thank my colleagues Peter Marris, Robert Rotenberg, Alan Smart, Constance DeRoche, and Delmos Jones; the participants of the Columbia University City Seminar; Dolores Hayden and her graduate class on Cultural Landscape History; the participants of the faculty colloquium, particularly Fred Myers and Tom Beidelman in the department of anthropology at New York University; and the reviewers of this manuscript for their criticism, comments, and encouragement. I would also like to thank Marlene Castro and Claudio Gutierrez for their expertise about Costa Rica and for their hospitality.

Notes

1. The comments of the manuscript reviewers helped me clarify these terms..
2. I would like to acknowledge the contribution of the manuscript reviewers to this analysis.

References

Agar, Michael. 1986. *Speaking of ethnography*. Beverly Hills, Calif.: Sage.

Appadurai, Arjun. 1992. Putting hierarchy in its place. In *Rereading cultural anthropology*, edited by George Marcus. Pp. 35–45. Durham, N.C.: Duke University Press.

Archivos, Censo Municipalidad. 1993. *Municipalidad de San José*. Departamento Financiero Sec. Censo. Distrito Catedral 4, Manzana 3, Propidad 2.

Banco Nacional de Costa Rica. 1972. *La ciudad de San José 1891–1921*. San José, Costa Rica: Antonio Lehmann.

Bourdieu, Pierre. 1977. *Outline of a theory of practice*, translated by Richard Nice. Cambridge: Cambridge University Press.

Buck-Morss, Susan. 1990. *The dialectics of seeing: Walter Benjamin and the Arcades Project*. Cambridge, Mass.: Massachusetts Institute of Technology Press.

Caja. 1928. La capital de antaño. November 30, 17–19.

Castells, Manuel. 1983. *The city and the grassroots*. Berkeley: University of California Press.

———.1989. *The informational city*. Oxford: Basil Blackwell.

De Certeau, Michel. 1984. *The practice of everyday life*. Berkeley: University of California Press.

Costa Rica en el Siglo XIX. 1929. *Costa Rica en el siglo XIX*. San José: Editorial Lehmann.

DeMora, Nini. 1973. *San José: Su desarrollo. Su titulo de ciudad. Su rango de capital de Costa Rica*. San José: Universidad de Costa Rica.

Edelman, Marc, and Joanne Kenen. 1989. *The Costa Rican reader*. New York: Grove Weidenfeld.

Foucault, Michel. 1975. *Discipline and punish: The birth of the prison*. New York: Vintage Books.

———.1984. L'éspace des autres. *Architecture, Mouvement, Continuité* (October):46–49.

Geertz, Clifford. 1973. *The interpretation of cultures*. New York: Basic Books.

Giroux, Henry A. 1983. Theories of reproduction and resistance in the new sociology of education: Critical analysis. *Harvard Educational Review* 33:257–293.

González Víquez, Cleto. 1973. San José y sus comienzos. In *Obras Históricas 1*. San José: Universidad de Costa Rica.

Harvey, David. 1985. *Consciousness and the urban experience*. Vol. 2 of *Studies in the history and theory of capitalist urbanization*. Oxford: Basil Blackwell.

———. 1990. *The condition of postmodernity*. Oxford: Basil Blackwell.

Hayden, Dolores. 1995. *The power of place: Urban landscapes as people's history*. Cambridge, Mass.: MIT Press.

Holston, James. .1989. *The modernist city: An anthropological critique of Brasilia*. Chicago: University of Chicago Press.

Lawrence, Denise, and Setha M. Low. 1990. The built environment and spatial form. *Annual Review of Anthropology* 19:453–505.

Lefebvre, Henri. 1991. *The production of space*, translated by Donald Nicholson-Smith. Oxford: Basil Blackwell.

Low, Setha M. 1993. Cultural meaning of the plaza: Origin and evolution of the Spanish American gridplan-plaza urban design. In *The cultural meaning of urban space*, edited by Gary McDonogh and Robert Rotenberg. Pp. 75–94. Westport, Conn.: Bergin and Garvey.

———. 1995. Indigenous architectural representations and the Spanish American plaza in Mesoamerica and the Caribbean. *American Anthropologist* 97:748–762

———.1996. Constructing difference: Spatial boundaries in the plaza. In *Setting boundaries*, edited by Deborah Pellow. Pp. 161–178. Westport, Conn.: Bergin and Garvey.

Naranjo Coto, Manuel. 1982. *Plaza de la cultura*. Costa Rica: Litografía Trejos.

Peattie, Lisa. 1969. *View from the barrio*. Ann Arbor: University of Michigan Press.

———. 1987. *Planning*. Ann Arbor: University of Michigan Press.

Rabinow, Paul. 1982. Ordonnance, discipline, regulation: Some reflections on urbanism. *Humanities in Society* 5:267–278.

———. 1989. *French modern: Norms and forms of missionary and didactic pathos*. Cambridge, Mass.: MIT Press.

Rabinow, Paul, ed. 1984. *The Foucault reader*. New York: Pantheon Books.

Richardson, Miles. 1982. Being-in-the-market versus being-in-the-plaza: Material culture and the construction of social reality in Spanish America. *American Ethnologist* 9:421–436.

Rodman, Margaret C. 1992. Empowering place: Multilocality and multivocality. *American Anthropologist* 94:640–656.

Shallat, Lezak. 1989. AID and the secret parallel state. In *The Costa Rican reader*, edited by Marc Edelman and Joanne Kenen. Pp. 221–228. New York: Grove Weidenfeld.

Smith, Neil. 1991. New city, new frontier. In *Variations on a theme park*, edited by Michael Sorkin. Pp. 61–92. New York: Noonday Press.

Spain, Daphne. 1992. *Gendered spaces*. Chapel Hill: University of North Carolina Press.

Spartacus Guide for Gay Men. 1987. Berlin: BrunoGmÿnder.

Trullás y Aulit, Ignacio. 1913. *Escenas Josefinas*. San José: C.B.A.

Vega Carballo, José Luis. 1981. *San José: Antecedentes coloniales y formación del estado nacional*. San José: Instituto de Investigaciones Sociales.

Zukin, Sharon. 1991. *Landscapes of power: From Detroit to Disney World*. Berkeley: University of California Press.

ROBERT ROTENBERG

5 Landscape and Power in Vienna
Gardens of Discovery

On any extended stay in Europe, one realizes how much Europeans and North Americans differ in their attitudes toward environmental concerns. The mass media run documentaries and features on the destruction of rain forests, acid rain, and air quality. Environmental crises on the Continent, such as the Chernobyl disaster, directly affect people's lives. People remember them as turning points. Politicians incorporate environmental problems into their critiques of current policy and use ecological issues to attract voter allegiance. Although the Green Party, whose ideology seeks to redefine state policy around a safe and sustainable environment, exists, no party's platform explicitly assigns the environment a higher priority than economic growth. To be centrist, a party must negotiate among more radical ways of constraining the economy to benefit the environment. This broad consensus on voters' sensitivity to environmental issues is known in German-speaking Europe as the *Ekowelle*, the ecology wave.

The Ekowelle is not a coherent ideology; it is a cluster of ideas, some new, some quite old, which raise people's awareness of their relationship to nature. Underlying all of the ideas is a hermeneutic of suspicion; that is, people do not believe that their currently held ideas about nature reflect the most balanced relationship possible. Ordinarily, this uncertainty would produce a period of disinterested experimentation in word and deed among society's experts, with ordinary people watching from the sidelines until a coherent perspective emerges. This is the case with the technology-intensive revolution occurring around the organization and control of information. Ecology consciousness emerges with a heightened feeling of urgency and alarm. People believe that their children's lives, if not their own lives, hang in the balance. As a result, a low-intensity cultural crisis has arisen. People doubt the old ways of dealing with the environment, feel some urgency in discovering new ways of working with it, and are willing to experiment personally to discover the new path.

The variety of solutions is large. What they have in common is the view that once released from the constraints imposed by human agency, nature can restore its own balance. For this to occur, both states and families must become involved. At the state level, ecopolitics must prevail, which is why political parties try not to become ensnared publicly in the "ecology versus development" debate. At the family level, the actions include everything from recycling to eating more nutritious foods. The wave shares much with the reactionary antimodernism of the first few decades of the present century. The emphasis on the need to restore balance, on nature as the only reliable model for a balanced life, and on the pursuit of systemic equilibrium is strong in both movements. There are also important differences. Turn-of-the-century reactionaries had the stark and dehumanizing second industrial wave as a focus, with conditions including abject poverty, rampant tuberculosis, antidemocratic political tensions, and degradation of the environment as a backdrop for their activities.

Today in Austria, the environmental effects of economic development are occurring in a period of general public health, affluence for the overwhelming majority of citizens, and a relatively high level of consensus on democratic solutions to political issues. The present situation produces greater clarity in which to envision the environmental issues and the relationship between economic well-being and their eventual solution. No one is in a better position to envision the future than urban gardeners. They consume the products of this environment with their mouths and their eyes and spend hours each day in the urban atmosphere, digging in the urban soil.

In a 1995 study, I investigated the landscape traditions of the Viennese (Rotenberg 1995). The study involved both historical and ethnographic analysis of landscape meanings. The object of the study was to link the forces through which landscape is produced in a city with the discourse on landscape meanings that are current at different moments in time. Through this linkage, I found that landscape is a powerful language for asserting ideologically based models of community life. The models are especially energetic metaphors for the "proper" relationship of the individual to a large group. Over the last three hundred years, as groups with different ideologies ascend to positions of municipal dominance, they build public gardens and parks in specific styles in which the stylistic elements are closely associated with the group's ideology. Thus, the public landscape can be read as the modern political history of the municipality. Each of these moments in the discourse is identified through a metaphor that emerges as forty-five active Viennese gardeners talk about the meanings they find in the public gardens and how these meanings are carried over to their private gardens. There are Baroque "gardens of order," Romantic "gardens of liberty," Biedermeier "gardens of domesticity," Victorian "gardens of pleasure," turn-of-the-century "gardens of reform," labor movement–based "gardens of refuge," right-wing "gardens of reaction," and postwar "gardens of renewal." One of the conclusions that I draw in the longer study is that the meanings we attribute to the urban landscape are so closely attuned to the social production of that landscape that generalizing about these meanings from one city to another does not always succeed, even if the discourse on landscape is shared. What follows is a slightly revised reprint of the most contemporary and the most ethnographic of the book's chapters. It provides a good example of a situation where the values of the discourse, namely ecological gardening, are widely shared among Europeans, but also where the specific forces of producing such gardens that meet the criteria in Vienna are restricted to fringe elements of the social order.

I have named these "gardens of discovery" because their view of nature is that of a system independent of human will, generating novelty and variety through its own processes. Such awesome power should persuade humans to stand out of nature's way and ultimately reincorporate with it. At present, we remain alienated from nature. Our actions work counter to the environment, obstructing and interfering with the autochthonous processes. Discovering nature's unfolding can reeducate people to nature's ways; only then can they stop destroying nature and themselves.

The shapes of the discourse begin to emerge through such behaviors, but the process is ongoing. Unlike the previous uses of landscape, this discussion cannot provide a satisfying closure. What we hear in the current language of ecological gardening is a testing of the waters, a furtive searching for agreement on which way to turn. Many of the features described in the earlier formations are not yet evident, which is not to say that there is no language for the gardens of discovery. If anything, there is too much language. What is lacking is a commitment to express the underlying meanings of this language in landscape, both publicly and in domestic gardens.

Domestic gardens that employ the discourse on discovery in its fullest sense often evoke public distaste and even anger. By 1988, the owners of a domestic garden in suburban Perchtoldsdorf redesigned it as a *Wildgarten*, a garden so ecologically balanced that human cultivation was no longer necessary. It was nestled between neighboring gardens of well-manicured lawns and carefully pruned fruit trees. Compared to these, the Wildgarten was a jungle. The owners uprooted native plants from the slopes of the surrounding hills of the Vienna Woods and re-planted them in the garden in the same density as their original site. A *Biotop*, a stagnant pool, was carefully constructed with water from a town water pipe. Left to its own processes, the pool soon supported algae, a few frogs, and many mosquitoes. A sign near the garden gate proclaimed the owner's intentions to create a garden that would mirror nature's own cycles and yield the fruit that nature intended. There are a lot of messages in this garden. The most important message as far as the neighbors of the Wildgarten are concerned was the self-consumed arrogance of the garden owners who imposed this biological nuisance of weeds, pests, and chaos on others. Garden walls are relevant to humans only. Seeds, parasites, and mosquitoes pay no attention to them. The garden was the horticultural equivalent of crying fire in a crowded theater. The owners were completely surprised by their neighbors' reaction. They had assumed that everyone saw the logic of a return to ecologically balanced gardening. The rhetoric of the organic gardening movement legitimated a revolutionary praxis, the redesign of the idea of the garden in purely ecological terms. They were wrong. The logical solution for ecologically sound gardens remains as difficult to realize in landscape as equitable and sustainable habitats are to achieve nationally.

Nothing is new in the basic premises of this discourse. Francé sketched the outlines of this argument before World War I in *Law of the Forest* (1908). Although his generation left the city to find the ideal environment in which to learn about nature, members of the current generation transform their lives to discover nature within the city and within themselves. People who attempt to create gardens of discovery do so as part of an overall change in lifestyle. They begin by reorganizing their household schedules, which commonly involves commuting to work by bicycle. They favor homeopathic health systems including natural foods and a wellness-oriented lifestyle. I have also noticed that they structure their memory of the past with nuclear power plant accidents and similar man-made environmental disasters.

The most commonly expressed term for gardens of discovery is *Biogarten*, an organic garden. Organic in this case extends beyond growing vegetables without chemical fertilizers or pesticides, even though these are the first things Viennese gardeners mention when asked to define the term. Organic denotes a need to achieve a balance among plants so that the presence of some species benefits the growth of others. Animals of various kinds help check the growth of injurious pests. At this point, the gardener faces a serious design issue: human geometry itself in the laying out of beds becomes a barrier to the effective balance of the gardens, which are no longer properly Biogärten. They have become Wildgärten, whose form must revert to planned disorder. Only then is the promise of discovery possible, as this interview partner found:

> My garden contains only meadows. It is very handy. I am just drawn to the creative untidiness, the planned disorder. Anyway, it is important for my child to know that sometimes things grow which were never planted by people. No one knows where they came from. For example, I like to read the history of my garden, indeed the history of the entire settlement during the year. It is unbelievable the kinds of things that grow. In winter, you see nothing except a bizarre looking bush. Then suddenly in the spring, you see a rare Japanese plant that must have been growing for an eternity (because it grows so slowly), or a peculiar story. I am not the type who rips everything out and plants anew each year. I let everything come up, and then I select what I want. I prefer more weeds to fewer of them.[1]

Gardeners who echo these remarks are drawn to the creative untidiness— a creativity living in the garden, not in them. It is important that their children learn the lesson of the garden, that things grow even when they are not sown by people. In other words, nature has its own secrets. These are revealed, or discovered, only when one is patient enough to let the garden express itself. Nature has a history paralleling that of people; but unlike people, nature never forgets its history. Nature produces choices for us to make, and if we select correctly our lives are enhanced.

To discover what nature has built into the garden the gardeners must possess a specific set of techniques and, more importantly, they must practice a discipline. The same interview partner described it:

> If people live as we do, then the garden is a recreation space. That means it must have the components, and the care of the garden must take second place. I would not work there if it didn't bring me leisure. If I have no time or no desire, then I would do nothing. The work must be enjoyable, or it's better left alone. There must be no obligation in it. My close relationship to it is large enough that I return again and again. In the moment when I catch myself thinking about making it more beautiful than the neighbor's garden, I pull back my hand. That is no relationship. Nature is alive.

The shifting boundary between the discourse on recreation and the discourse on discovery is apparent in these first statements. The relationship of the gardener to the garden must be leisurely. The garden must not seem like an obligation, and it must never resemble work. The goal is not to create a thing of beauty, at least not as defined through comparison with the neighbors; rather, the key is *Verhältnis*, relationship, a term often associated with relations among people. For this gardener, the implication is the reciprocity he feels between his work in the garden and the garden's effect on him. If the garden were constantly being forced to higher and higher levels of performance it would impose an artificial standard on that exchange and break the balance. He explained what he meant by the idea that nature is alive:

> Well, it lives. There are earthworms, hedgehogs, butterflies, and plants of every form of being. There are cells that move. They can't speak, but they have consciousness. Therefore they are alive. And that has nothing to do with obligation. Everything must be voluntary. One must always have peace. There are so many small plants, which are so different. One must watch carefully before pulling something out. Even in mowing the meadow, you must watch out for the tiny mushrooms. You can't move quickly. I don't like this terror that comes from the illusion of making a garden beautiful. There are people who really get up three hours earlier to putter in the garden before coming to work and then putter around again when they get home. I will not be terrorized by my garden like that! I will not terrorize my garden in return.

The living garden produces variety, which is what it gives back to the gardener. To receive the gift, the gardener must observe the garden with patience and care. The gifts are both zoological and botanical. Terror not only negates the possibility of surprise, it also (in this gardener's mind) reduces enjoyment of the gift. The proper relationship between gardener and garden is filled with patience, anticipation, tender care, and respect. In the discourse on discovery, the will of the landscape is every bit as valuable as the will of the designer.

Half of the people interviewed said they tried to maintain a Biogarten, a practice hardly without controversy. The following remarks are typical of the futility some gardeners feel:

> No, [organic gardening] doesn't work. Now first, yesterday the trees were sprayed there. So, if this was an organic garden, I couldn't allow the spraying with poisons. In the spring when

they spray, we have to cover the young lettuce plants, if we have them. Besides, I'm not sure I want a garden that is completely sterile. It isn't anyhow.

Others said such an attempt is futile since the world itself is polluted:

I guess because I don't think very much of the whole movement. By my calculation organic materials no longer exist anywhere. I can do nothing about it. It doesn't matter if from today on I only use organic fertilizer or something else. If I use pure cow manure, the cow has already grazed in a chemically fertilized field. I think the whole organic gardening movement is just a big business with nothing behind it. By my estimate pure organic potatoes or organic cabbage cannot exist. And there is nothing one can do about it.

Fertilizing the garden and protecting its plants from parasites are paths for introducing artificial, and therefore harmful, elements into the garden system.

Organic gardening is certainly important, but then there is the problem that the insect pests come anyway, especially if one is not experienced. And most gardens are so infested that whatever one puts out becomes full of lice. If I don't spray with chemicals, it only gets worse. Then I don't want to eat the produce. But I won't eat insect-infested stuff either.

These contradictions force the gardener either to abandon the organic program or to permit the creative chaos of a Wildgarten. The first option forces the gardener to renege on strongly held beliefs about the enhanced quality of life that results from living in a balanced environment. It implies a reduction in the overall well-being of the domestic environment. To permit a garden to determine its own direction is so nonconforming that a gardener can expect to endure a high level of criticism for the decision. Since both solutions run counter to the contending landscape values, the solution most gardeners have worked out is to garden as organically as they can, accepting the futility of the effort, but refusing to give up entirely.

One partner refused to compromise (figure 1). With the collaboration of four other families living in the apartment house, she cultivated a Wildgarten in an area of approximately 150 square meters on the side of the Biedermeier-period house. Formerly the outdoor work area for a glass factory, the yard had been a recreational garden until the 1950s. By the time the current residents decided that they wanted to do something with the garden, it had become wild. The garden is full of trees of various ages, most of them saplings. A mixture of field plants collected

Figure 5.1. Wildgarten. This garden of discovery is appreciated for its lack of tidiness by this woman, her daughters, and a friend. The four other families who live in their apartment building supported the women's efforts to build this garden, on the condition that it would require little or no effort on their part to maintain it. This approach was well suited to the interview subject's taste for ecological gardening.

during the gardeners' frequent hikes through the Wienerwald covers the ground. The atmosphere is cool and shady. The house, which looms a few meters away, is impossible to see from the midst of the garden. Traffic noises filter in from the street, but the street itself is invisible from behind the garden fence. In the middle of the garden is a kidney-shaped plaster pool ringed with small stones and full of algae and a few water plants. This is the Biotop, the marsh element in the natural system.[2] Scattered among the trees are a few rickety chairs and a wooden table. One large tree has a few boards nailed to its limbs to form a tree house. There is no lawn to speak of, although the area next to the walk leading from the house door to the street gate has grass growing on one side. Around the street gate are a few rose plants.

The garden was designed without the help of professionals. There were no plans. A city hall initiative known as *Hofbegrünung-Förderungsaktion*, a program to support the planting of courtyards, provided funds to help the neighbors restore the garden. This program will provide up

to 20,000 schillings ($1,670) toward the cost of planting the interior court-
yard of residential buildings in the older districts of the city (Mathias
1985). In our conversation, this gardener explained how she and her
neighbors came to accept this form of a garden:

> Yeah, [it's] something not completely tame. My idea of a gar-
> den has nothing to do with mowing the grass. I prefer some-
> thing a bit more junglelike. This is more of an imitation of nature.
> One neighbor wanted everything planned, the ground leveled,
> everything pulled out, grass planted, and all the trees cut down
> and new ones planted. Then lots of the others came saying, "No,
> we want nothing other than a wilderness here, in which every-
> thing can grow." The way the garden had developed enchanted
> us. We wanted to leave everything a bit wild so we could sit in
> it. I'm not interested in technical gardening. I'm not a gardener.
> I like to work in the garden as long as it pleases me. But not
> when I must do something specific every day. The others feel
> the same way. So, the garden is half-wild. It looks quite pretty,
> but not all the time. Sure, we could do more. If the five fami-
> lies gave five hundred schillings each, it would still not be
> enough to do anything with, not so? It doesn't disturb me when
> the branches hang down. It's all the same to me. We have said
> that we like to have grass, but not a *Rasen*. We prefer plants or
> different grasses or some such. We needn't have a tidy lawn free
> of all weeds.

Her explanation of why the five families made the formal decision to
leave the garden in its wild state involved several elements: the existing state was so enchanting that no one wanted to change it; any other
kind of garden would have required more obligation than any family
was willing to undertake; the amount of money they could raise was
insufficient to make a real difference; and they had an explicit aesthetic
preference for wilderness. Among the five families there seemed to be
only one dissenter.

In spite of its small size, the garden contains a large variety of plants,
including ten different varieties of perennials, six different species of
fruit trees, grapevines on the fences, and five different flowering bushes.
The grasses and leafy ground cover are highly varied. One of the apple
trees and two of the plum trees had been so-called trellis trees—trees
forced to grow along trellis lines to create a branch pattern that conforms
to human geometry. The trees had long since become wild, but the effects of the earlier growth patterns are still apparent. The fruit trees are
both a benefit and a problem:

We benefit by letting the fallen fruit lie around. For example, many birds come and eat or pick at it. There is plenty of food for small animals there. And no one misses a few plums. We let them hang there and I think that's OK. Only lately we've had a plague of rats, and we had to spray with rat poison. Because of that we couldn't use much of the garden this summer. I was very sorry about that.

The joy of seeing the animals who come and eat the fruit is a gift from the garden to the residents, who have to do very little to receive it. But the rats also eat the fruit and then become a nuisance, a problem so severe that they had to use poison and lost the use of the garden for an entire summer. The rat poison introduced toxins into the garden, just as the chemical insecticides and acid rain interfere with the efforts of the organic gardeners. Even the committed Wildgärtner must endure the contradictions of gardening for balance in an unbalanced world.

Discourse on Gardens of Discovery

The most influential Central European designers of gardens of discovery are Louis LeRoy (1978a) and Urs Schwarz (1980). Founders of the Ekogarten movement, they insist that nature is in danger of being lost completely. Effective gardening can rescue it. Their strategy is to have gardeners protect native species of plants in home gardens until the industrially damaged and unbalanced systems can be rejuvenated. LeRoy's writings have provided the mottoes of the movement, including "Just let the weeds grow!" (1978b; cited in Burckhardt 1981, 264) and "in the garden, nature must be the master and the gardener the apprentice. The apprentice is merely a guest of the master. As a guest, he submits himself to the rules of the house" (1978a; cited in Spitzer 1981, 271). Schwarz provides the principles of the movement: "the avoidance of poison and artificial fertilizers, the replanting of native plants and the construction of specifically threatened ecological communities. The house garden can be a refuge for threatened species. But it is not enough. An entire network of ecological gardens must be developed through the city" (Breitenmoser and Schwarz 1981, 224).

Ecological gardeners argue that gardens are not natural: the variety of plants in the small space of the garden would not occur in nature. This assemblage is at war with nature, and this is the conflict that the ecological designers want to manage. The most difficult conversion from conventional to natural gardens, in their sense, is the disavowal of order. Using poisons and artificial fertilizers is only justifiable if one is trying to maintain order; and by disavowing it, the gardener gives up the need for introducing toxic materials in the garden. In time, native varieties of plants will reconquer the garden left to the creative disorder. The ecological program goes further, asking gardeners to replant regional flora actively. One must understand the regional community by observing those spaces that are still intact. Primal forests, marshlands, meadows, alms, and deserted farms are repositories of the regionally appropriate plants, and protecting them from development is to keep them as a biological trust. In the future these plants will reproduce the balanced community.

The native species requirements described in this argument are different from those developed in the reactionary movement at the turn of the century. Schwarz discusses the issue:

> By native, we mean regionally patriotic throughout. For an inhabitant of the Swiss piedmont, plants from the Alps or the Jura Mountains are no longer native, and a gardener in Cologne should not bring home plant materials from the North Sea coast or the slate mountains of the Rhine. This "narrow thinking" goes even further. Those who live in a glacial moraine should leave plants from nearby limestone hills where they are, even when the distance is only a few kilometers. There is good reason to do so: With the exception of certain universal species, plants do appear in different places by accident. This comes about through the combined special effects of climate, soil characteristics, sloop, and competition between different species. For this reason, one cannot stipulate a list here of appropriate plants for a nature garden. Every garden should look different from every other one as long as it fits with the local system. (Breitenmoser and Schwarz 1981, 226)

The reference to home plant materials is a reference to the design element known as *Bodenständigheit*, a preference for native varieties in plant selection. This element was first promulgated under reactionary design regimes. In those systems, Bodenständigheit attempted to draw a parallel between the fascist principle of "Blut and Boden," blood and soil, and the vitality of the nativist varieties of plants (Rotenberg 1995, 191, 196–197). This passage differs from the older version of Bodenständigkeit in two ways. First, it sees the native variety as adapted to a regional system. The boundaries of this system depend on the physical characteristics of the environment, not the cultural characteristics of the people. A well-defined human community can settle astride two, three, or even four different botanical communities. Gardeners get into trouble when they see the boundaries of the human communities as identical to those of plants. Thus, there are no "German" plants that grow only in Germany. Even people living in the valley of a mountain system cannot assume that the plants growing at a higher altitude are appropriate species for their garden. The earlier understanding of Bodenständigkeit narrowly mapped the human community onto the plant world. Second, there are species that thrive in every environment. They are not under threat, and no special effort needs to be made to protect them. They, too, have a role to play in the nature garden. There are no trash plants or weeds. They balance and strengthen the narrowly adapted species when they grow together. This view of the relation between the native and the cosmopolitan went unobserved in the reactionary form of Bodenständigkeit.

To execute these principles in their entirety means that one must surrender design. Throughout the early 1980s, landscape architects struggled to find a role for themselves in the creation of nature gardens. Peter Wirth provided one of the most explicit statements of the direction taken by most of the Central European designers for private homes:

> The shapes of garden design always establish themselves as a result of contemporary views of life. Our requirements for the garden today are most probably [to fortify] the individual garden life and [to facilitate] contact with living nature, The result should be a garden for daily use. The finding of a convincing overall design for a garden that organically integrates everything and connects to the house with optimal usefulness is exhausting intellectual work. It is always correct in garden planning to develop the small [landscape] from the larger one. The more one works for a simpler and more independent garden, the more difficult it is sometimes to find the way to the solution. (1984:11)

Wirth's gardens appear to be less extreme than those called for by Schwarz. For Wirth, gardens are still essentially recreational, but he also has a desire to reach a balanced natural system. By emphasizing daily use, he reproduces the symbolic forms that often compel the recreational gardener to force greater formality upon the garden. He admits that the solutions to this problem require great effort; there is no specific design principle that satisfies every case. He invalidates the pursuit of the independent garden by declaring that embedding the small garden in a wider landscape, essentially breaking down the garden walls, is always the most effective design solution.

Hans Schiller-Bütow has adapted environmental contexts for gardens in larger estates. For him, gardens are pure ornament. He makes no provision for use. Such designs must appeal to wealthier patrons who have accepted the importance of being environmentally correct. His gardens are playful and innovative but require well-defined surroundings to work effectively. In his writing on landscape, he struggles against formalism to find a connection between usefulness and the beauty of nature:

> The purpose of the garden has become ornament. Gone is the inspired woman gardener in her straw hat in a dense garden strewn with flowers and fruit. The battle against weeds, which she always lost, has become a sign of pure purposefulness. On the other side, a number of indices suggest that people seek alternative ways to live in a "healthier" world. Many abandon the city and go into the countryside. The life in the open has again become an adventure worthy of aspiration. The garden with its ancient responsibilities is an important device for achieving a new relationship to life in and according to nature. One of its original responsibilities was to collect cultigens [from the wild]. Use is not absolutely identical with edibility. Use also includes the joy that comes from working with plant materials in living green spaces, the encounter with nature, as well as the harvesting of the plants. The real desire for nature projects from the self to the naturally useful garden. The next step is from a nature garden to an artificially designed garden [that abstracts the natural forms]. (1979, 3)

Schiller-Bütow accepts the garden as the device through which people come to an understanding and respect for the workings of nature. He supports the idea of building the garden from wild, native plants and redirects the emphasis to the end rather than the means, the latter of which predominated in recreational gardening. Unlike the security of the harvest which justified the gardens of refuge, his ends include working with plants and encountering nature. Schiller-Bütow is a professional designer who must sell designs to practice. Those able to patronize him participate in the discourse on discovery but reject the creative chaos of a Wildgarten. With this in mind, he has developed a design style that incorporates native plants in local soils and local topography to create artificial gardens that borrow from the landscape outside the garden through imitation and abstraction. He selects and amplifies for the garden the features that he observes in the natural landscape. He explains how he does this:

> The naturalism of the enclosing landscape is transplanted by the planner to the garden. There nature becomes an artificial landscape. The planner sees nature from his position and ascertains the main focus. Every landscape has its special focus.

> It is this special quality, which the observer fixes on, which appeals to him, to always seek the place out again, which when it is named appears spontaneously to him as a picture. The structure of the surface of the land, the color of the materials, including the color and habitat of the plants belongs to it. (1979, 5)

The design develops from the landscape outside the garden through imitation and abstraction. Schiller-Bütow produces gardens that include mountain streams, deserts, glacial moraines, and marshlands, in each case replicating the essence of the original landscape with uncanny detail. The hand of the designer disappears. The limitations of this program lie in the location of the garden. One cannot create a desert, a moraine, or a marsh in a city. Only those who can afford to live in undeveloped regions can enjoy the artistry of Schiller-Bütow's designs.

Both Wirth and Schiller-Bütow struggle with the problem of design whose very success requires its disappearance. The last time the discourse on landscape attempted to hide the hand of the designer occurred in the eighteenth century, in the parkscapes of William Kent and Capability Brown. They, too, solved the problem by imbedding the smaller space in the larger one. As Horace Walpole put it, "[Kent] leaped the fence, and saw that all nature was a garden"(1798, 136). For Kent and Brown, nature was an unspoiled region that had escaped human intervention and rationalization (Pugh 1988, 136).[3] For Wirth and Schiller-Bütow, there is no pristine nature. There is the danger that retrieving the design of the larger environment within the smaller one will only reproduce imbalance.

This imbalance goes well beyond the condition of the environment. It is a critique of contemporary society symbolized through the degradation of nature. Nowhere is this critique more appropriate than in the domestic garden. According to critic Klaus Spitzer, there is a continuity of design from the baroque to the contemporary recreational gardens, and the outward sign of this continuity is the requirement of design, ranging from the specific imposition of geometric forms to the general compulsion to organize. The garden becomes the product of its creator. It demonstrates the triumph of the will of the individual, just as the baroque garden exhibited the overarching power of the absolutist nobility. Nature itself is lost in the process. The garden is not about nature. It is an optical illusion, a work of art employing natural materials. In this passage, which gives some hint to the passion and vehemence of the ecological gardeners, Spitzer explains how this habit to abstract nature for design purposes has undermined the sensory experience of real nature:

Before the front door of the house, as well as throughout the urban environment, people have replaced the last remnant of nature with surrogates. Our dulled consciousness doesn't react anymore if valuable open lands are rigorously planned and desolated with cotoneaster, or if a few plants are set out on the street cobbles in ungainly concrete troughs like animals in a zoo. In the balcony boxes, plastic geraniums bloom. On our streets, the leaves are coming out on the plastic trees. And deodorant sprays with forest scent replace the experience of real forests. While hybrid roses lose their scent, people have perfected the replacement: In the department stores, we sniff plastic flowers with embedded perfume. (1981, 269)

In Spitzer's view, we seem to have lost the capacity to differentiate between nature and its surrogates. For this reason, when we do encounter nature it shocks us.

This is nowhere more evident than in the definition and treatment of weeds. Weeds are uninvited guests, intruders upon the illusion of individual control in the garden. As "seeds of the devil," they symbolize nature's resistance to the gardener's will. They are polluting and must be pulled out. The tidy garden bed, the well-tended lawn, and the cared-for shrubbery are monocultural cultivations. Their value to the gardener lies in their becoming healthy specimens of their kind. All competitors, all detractors from this uniformity are useless, dangerous, and repugnant. This is why LeRoy, Schwarz, and Spitzer place so much importance on letting the weeds grow. When a gardener can perceive a bed as full of nature's variety rather than full of weeds, it is a victory for the ecological consciousness.

In these initial decades, it is hard to discern who participates and who does not. Among the generation born after 1970, the consciousness of the environment is very high. The Green Party in Austria draws its strength from the youngest voters. Among the forty-five gardeners I interviewed, only the two people quoted in the introductory section reflected the kind of commitment to gardens of discovery that these theorists demand. One social scientist who has attempted to gauge the impact of the ecological movement on public aesthetics is Werner Nohl. In a series of studies conducted primarily in Munich, he surveyed visitors to public parks to understand what it is about the contemporary experience of landscape that people find meaningful (1974, 1977, 1979, 1980, 1982).[4] Of primary concern to him and to other critics in the latter half of the 1980s was the role of aesthetic considerations in the emerging discourse on ecological landscapes. Early in his research, Nohl established that aesthetic interests accounted for 21.8 percent of responses to a survey on why people use public parks, compared with 19.3 percent for recreational interests and 17.4 percent for those seeking peace and quiet (1977, 14).

The aesthetic component in his survey focused on two verbal formulas in the discourse on landscape: the delight in the painterly character of green space (*den malerischen Charakter einer Grünlage geniessen*) and the enjoyment of the beauty of nature (*mich an der Schönheit der Natur erfreuen*). Both of these formulas have multiple resonances in the history of discourse. Both originated in the English parkscape tradition. Beauty of nature is enhanced further through association with color and variety in the Biedermeier and the reactionary yearnings for pristine landscapes at the turn of the century. The Reptonesque tradition that prevailed throughout the nineteenth century elaborated the painted character of beauty in landscape. To say that the aesthetic needs of the park visitors slightly outweigh their recreational needs and the need for quiet is the same as saying that people delight in the meaning of the parkscape to at least the same degree as they do the opportunities for movement and for resting. The message of the Reptonesque parkscape continues to speak to Viennese across the centuries.

Nohl relies on the psychology of perception research tradition to explore the aesthetic dimension of parkscape in more detail. He concludes that supporting the aesthetic needs of an urban population requires designers to install the highest degree of naturalism (*Natürlichkeit*) in the park while providing an ever-changing alternation in form between variety and novelty (ibid., 31). By *novelty* he means the perceptual comparison that discovers a break between a current structure and some previous experience. This can either be in the form of a surprise, the discrepancy between the present and the past, or uncertainty or indecision between two or more possibilities which leads to the loss of a possibility (Nohl 1977, 10). By *variety*, he means building the landscape with plants that vary in growth patterns, color, and mass. Because one moves around in the park, novelty and variety can present themselves in a temporal sequence, permitting people to develop an interest in exploring the space and discovering pleasurable perceptions. At the same time, people have a need to feel secure in public space; they do not like to become lost. This requires that the exploring movements take place in an environment that permits a certain degree of openness, with outlook points from which to survey the layout of the space. The layout itself should be simple (Nohl 1979, 638).

For Gälzer, the combination of exploratory and orientation behavior of park visitors requires contradictory design principles. Exploratory behavior demands variety and novelty, whereas orientation behavior is best served by certainty and openness. In design, it is almost impossible to be open and surprising at the same time (Gälzer 1987b, 76). Thus, no single design would completely satisfy Nohl's aesthetic requirements. The scenic qualities of a parkscape are also dependent on the visitor's ability to receive and process the information the park designer has built into it. These will vary with the visitor's age, education, and experience with landscape, as well as with the time of day, the weather, and the visitor's visual acuity and imagination (Loidl 1981, 9). All of these factors place the aesthetic qualities of the park squarely in the heads of the visitors rather than in the hands of the designers. For this reason, it should be possible for visitors to develop an aesthetic that is tolerant of the creative chaos called for by the ecological gardeners. The question that remains is how to achieve this aesthetic.

Nohl himself supplies one possible solution: the appropriation of space by visitors. The visitor identifies with well-designed spaces that are easily accessible. The descriptive term "our park" separates the merely public space and the markedly private space by providing a mediating middle ground: public space that one can appropriate for private purposes. In doing so, the visitor becomes invested in the design of the park as well as in its intended uses. The relation among design, experienced visually, and use, experienced through movement, is not a continuum. Gälzer argues that one does not attain quality in both design and function at the expense of each other. One arrives at them independently. In the appropriation of park space for personal goals, the initial attraction can be through design or use. Subsequently, the commitment to identify oneself with the space can take place simultaneously through a heightened appreciation of design and use. The key is self-involvement. Users of public gardens should be involved in the planning, building, and maintaining of their parks (Gälzer 1987b, 77–78). One historical example of the power of self-involvement in forging positive values toward the landscape is the *Pionier* movement in Vienna in the 1920s. A contemporary example is the movement to plant the courtyards and roofs of inner-city apartment buildings (see below)—principles that could apply to any design. Since the principles promulgated by the ecological school stand in such stark contrast to the values of the recreational gardeners, self-involvement appears to be the most effective way of proceeding with the revolutionary program.

Social Production of Gardens of Discovery
The program of the ecological gardeners is a ticklish political problem. No political party wants to appear openly antienvironmental. On the other hand, the forces of capital are on the side of unfet-

tered economic development. For this reason, the social production of gardens of discovery in the 1980s has continued cautiously. Since landscape planners are far ahead of most other Viennese in accepting the principles of ecological gardening, the conflicts in the public support of these gardens have taken place between government offices. Not since the 1920s, when Social Democrats controlled the Settlement Bureau and Christian Socialists controlled the Housing Bureau, has the municipal government been so divided in its approach to landscape policy. In the 1980s the split was not between political parties but between orientations of the politicians within the parties. The municipality had to appear to conduct its planning policies in ways that appealed to the environmental consciousness of the voters. In 1986, the city council approved a *Grünlanddeklaration*, or Declaration on Green Space. The declaration included the following points.

> The long-range plan of urban development in Vienna sets the financial organizational and legal resource for green space and open space as a priority. The protection of the green belt and the creation of Grünkeile are matters of special concern.
>
> The existing green space in the densely built areas where green space is scarce is to be protected from environmental threats. The green resources in these areas will be improved through systematic planning of Grünzüge and Grünverbindungen. The purchase and clearing of sites to expand the availability of green space has a special priority.
>
> In the resolution of conflicts of interest, the preservation of green space has a higher priority than any other use. Existing green space is not to be treated as marginal land or areas of future development, but should be understood as essential elements in total regional planning for the future development of the city. Planning decisions with possible negative effects on existing green space, on the goals of the city development plan for green space, or on the zoning law as it applies to green space require special justification. (Magistratsabteilung 22 19986)

It also had to avoid making planning decisions that would cripple the development potential of the edge of the city or devalue speculative investments that power interests had already made. Making such a declaration is one thing. Living up to its requirements is another. Within a year of the declaration, memos were circulating within the municipal planning department that outlines situations when the declaration could be ignored. This pattern of publicly expressing commitment to improving the city environment through the mechanism of ecological gardening and then working behind the scenes to protect the interest of economic developers is certainly not unique to Vienna or Austria. In spite of these political realities, the city has managed to produce some publicly financed projects that successfully combine the objectives of both the ecologists and the developers.

The general planning strategy for the city remains the same as that outlined in the Green Declaration. The metropolis will never become a natural ecosystem. The needs of large numbers of people, the urban ecosystem, will always overwhelm the slower-moving compensations available through nature. It is possible to establish within the metropolis a gradient in which urban ecosystems shade off into natural ecosystems. In real space, the urban population is located in the centers of activity and the natural systems on the peripheries. Current planning practice looks for ways of blending the two zones. Three different tactics are employed for this blending in Vienna. *Grünkeile* are leg-shaped continuations of green space that extend from the forest belt that surrounds the city into the densely built up inner districts. A *Grünzüge* is a strip of green of more than one hundred meters breadth that contains green space devoted to different uses. These might include small garden colonies, playing fields, public swimming pools, parks, and cemeteries. *Grünverbindungen* are small ten- to twenty-meter-wide green spaces, mostly foot paths or bicycle paths that are bordered by plantings. These may connect to larger green spaces, such as playgrounds, or even narrower ones, such as tree-planted streets. None of these forms as currently constituted lends itself to ecological gardening principles. The Grünzüge tend to be tree-lined boulevards, restricted-traffic residential streets, and similar splashes of tree plantings within the stone and stucco streetscape.

Neighbors tolerate ecological gardening within the colonies and settlements only when the gardener is highly attentive to its dangers to other gardens. People who allow their gardens to become completely wild have the gardens taken away from them. The *Gartenamt*, the municipal parks department, has the legal power to expropriate and expunge any garden on municipal land that has become a public nuisance. This situation occurs only rarely—usually when sickness or enfeeblement makes it impossible to maintain a garden. Such actions have also been threatened against gardeners who take too radical an approach to the cultivation of nature's variety. The key to responsible ecological gardening within the colonies and settlements is the perception by neighbors that the garden is under the gardener's control. If that is the case, the colonies support diversity in gardening.

Although rare in comparison with the other elements, there are areas within the Grünkeile that do lend themselves to large-scale ecological gardening. Brooks, rivulets, and marsh areas lying on the borders of colonies and playgrounds could be improved by creative neglect. The most important areas of the city for demonstrating its commitment to ecological gardening are those within the forest belt. In the 1980s, the city established as Biotop five districts within the Vienna Woods. These special preserves are not easily accessible to hikers. To permit nature's order to replace that of humans, foresters have isolated the preserves for a time. How future generations of park visitors will enjoy these preserves has yet to be determined. One thing is certain: the areas are currently not in danger of getting in the way of economic development.

The second area within the forest belt to benefit from the application of ecological gardening ideas is the riverscape. Most of the economic functions of the Danube River lie either above or below the city itself or along the canal that links the river with the center of the city. The river divides the northern, less developed half of Vienna from the traditional centers of activity. In the postwar period, expansion of public transport facilities and increased availability of subsidized housing, commercial centers, and the United Nations center have increased both the population and the importance of the northern portion. Several bridges span the river to accommodate communication between the two halves of the city. The last phase of regulating the course of the river (1972–1984) created a long sandbar in its center, which serves as a support for many of the bridges. In the 1980s, the city financed the development of the easternmost section of this sandbar and the northern riverbank it faces into three hundred hectares of recreational space. It is known as the "Donauinsel," the Danube Island.

The landscape of this island emphasizes its terrain. Rising steeply from the water's edge, the island features an edge terrace and a central terrace. Asphalt paths that permit walking and bicycling run around the circumference of the island and in gentle curves that crisscross the central terrace. A similar pattern exists on the northern riverbank as well. The center of activity is the subway station, which is itself part of a large bridge structure. The station includes a kiosk and other public amenities and provides a height from which to survey the entire layout of the park. The plantings are all indigenous to the river. There are a few stands of trees, but most of the plantings are hearty native shrubs and ground cover. Grassy areas are mixed meadows. Other areas are left as sand outcroppings and dunes. On the northern bank, there is a restaurant complex and a boat rental facility. The park is especially attractive on warm sunny days. In the summer, the slopes of the terraces fill with sunbathers. Various groups hold festivals in the area, and it is the venue for big rock concerts. What is more important, the landscape is almost self-maintaining.

Apart from tree care and the occasional sweep of debris left by park users, the ecology of the river shapes the landscape. Some complain that the landscape is so natural that all one can do is walk in it. As in many other ecological gardens, people have a hard time seeing the Donauinsel as extraordinary.

A second initiative by the city concentrated on the centers of urban activity, rather than the edge. The city invested millions of schillings in efforts to convince residents of densely populated districts to plant gardens in their courtyards, backyards, and on their roofs. It was this program that enabled the woman quoted earlier in this chapter and her neighbors to maintain their Wildgarten. The objective of this effort was to make use of greater amounts of city space for ecologically oriented gardening. Interior courtyards and roofs are an inseparable part of the city, yet planners have often ignored them as contributors to the landscape. By investing in these ordinary spaces, the city hoped to educate a greater number of residents to the responsibilities of landscape design, provide room for greater individual expression, and create the greatest impact on the Green Declaration with the least public financing (Hala, Karasz, and Kleedorfer 1988, 2).

Participants merely had to register with the parks department, which then sent an advisor to evaluate the area and make suggestions. The apartment house occupants then met, discussed the suggestions, and decided how much they were willing to contribute in time and money to building and maintaining the garden. The city would provide up to 20,000 schillings ($1,670) for the delivery and setting of earth and plants. Roof gardens, arbors, sandboxes, and play equipment could not be bought or developed with city funds. The parks department could also offer to provide plants on its initiative, and in many cases it did so free of charge. Because of the involvement of the parks department, any spaces developed under this program came under the legal protection of municipal parklands (Mathias 1985, 23).

After the program had been running for three years, the city financed a survey to see what had improved. The study noted that people had used the resources of the city in very inventive ways. The addresses of some examples of these efforts are in parentheses. People planted trees, vines, and shrubs along the alleyways leading to backyard buildings (Kirchengasse 28). Some fenced off an area and permitted it to grow wild, withdrawing the space from human use (Josefstädterstrasse 79). A less radical strategy was simply to permit overgrowth, especially of vines, to cool the southern exposure of a building (Stuckgasse 5). The simplest form of courtyard garden was a so-called pot-landscape, in which plants were set out in pots and troughs from spring through autumn. Watering the pots usually became the task of a single person (Skodagasse 21). Those lucky enough to have a fully enclosed eighteenth-century, two-story courtyard building could re-create the villagelike atmosphere of the preindustrial suburbs. These courtyards relied on one or two large trees and vines to provide collective space for several families of renters. The narrow intimate space created a feeling of intensive private use (Langegasse 29). In other courtyards, green living rooms were created, complete with outdoor furniture surrounded by a garden and potted plants (St. Ulrich's Platz 2). Some landlords divided courtyards into separate gardens, one for each apartment, a relic of a practice that seems to have begun in the eighteenth century. People rented the gardens separately from the apartment, but only apartment renters could do so (Burggasse 33). For some inner-city buildings the only possible solution was saving a single old tree in the backyard. Even here, the parks department helped to cut old branches and provided nutrients to the leached soil (Langegasse 34). Sometimes only a flower box on a windowsill was possible. Public and private office buildings also took advantage of the program, adding potted trees and gardens to the views from their windows. Even though the city did not subsidize roof gardens, some top-floor renters constructed modest gardens consisting of a few potted plants and some chairs (Hala, Karasz, and Kleedorfer 1988, 53–128). Although fewer people took advantage of the program than was hoped, it is ongoing today. The planners modified some aspects of the initial idea to make it more attractive to people with less time for gardening.

The issue of the roof gardens remains contentious. A city of roof gardens would be a spectacular sight. However, these gardens put an extra, unintended load on roofs, especially if they involve extensive building of planting beds and tree beds. Many property owners fear for the integrity of their buildings if the gardeners get too carried away. Nevertheless, a wave of penthouse building is currently sweeping the city, which may generate construction techniques that would permit the city to invest greater resources in covering the roofs of buildings with plants.

It is frankly less satisfying to discuss the current conflicts in the use of public funds to support the new gardens of discovery than it is to discuss movements with a few more decades of activity behind them. The issues seem far less clear-cut. The battle lines are less fixed. Everyone seems to be on both sides of the issue at one time or another. In witnessing the evolution of this moment in the unfolding discourse on landscape, we see new political alignments. Something is replacing the older, class- and party-based allegiances of the previous two hundred years. New interest groups are coming to consciousness. Their program is so revolutionary that sometimes it even frightens them. Should the ecological gardening movement ever come to power in Vienna, it will usher in the greatest wholesale redesign of urban space since the Ring-strasse period (1860–1914). No one I know is expecting this to happen any time soon.

The Heterotopia of Discovery

Ecological conceptions of nature create processes rather than products. Gardens of discovery do not involve making concrete plans. They unfold over time. The gardeners have no idea of what the product will look like; they simply react spontaneously and actively to the possibilities that nature presents. The garden-building process is endless. It is a form of design that works dialectically with the changeability of nature itself. In these extraordinary places we discover the formal riches of a healthy native plant community. Such terms as *health*, *balance*, *stability*, and *sustainability* all point to a view of nature that is fundamentally antimodern, standing in stark contrast to the rapid shifts in orientation and taste that characterize contemporary cultures. In surrendering one's will to dominate and giving over to nature the management of the garden's form, the gardener must also sever the link between the garden and the market, the garden and architecture, and, at least initially, the garden and the city.

Gardens of discovery dominate architecture. Roofs are covered with plants. Vines grow on the walls. If left to the will of nature, in time the building itself disappears under a cover of plants. The functions of the building remain, but the outward form that reflects the domination of humans over the material world slowly vanishes. Architecture becomes a mere human conceit, a ruin waiting to happen. The initiative of the Viennese city council to plant courtyards and walks and the efforts by some residents to plant roof gardens challenge the primacy of built form as the major component of the cityscape.

The implications of how gardens of discovery might change the lived experience of the city go even further than these challenges to the social organization of space. Such gardens can undo the link between the producer of beauty in the garden and the consumer of that beauty. Everyone who uses a garden can contribute to its design, and every active designer is simultaneously a user. Each can realize a creative potential spontaneously and playfully, free from the dictates of a fixed plan. The creation of the work lies in the creativity of everyone who works on it. Such collaboration requires a different understanding of garden "ownership" one that denotes rights of use rather than rights of disposal.

In this way, the gardens of discovery project a radical image of what the city can become. Following the lead of nature calls into question all property relations as currently constituted. In particular, the idea of the property boundary becomes meaningless. Nature ignores such arbitrary lines on maps. Even more profoundly, these gardens confound the distinction between abstract and lived space. In a landscape that develops along ecological lines, all space is lived space. Any effort to create abstract boundaries, such as zones for use, assessed value, or public access versus private preserve, conflicts with the boundlessness of the ecological garden.

Considering all of the symbolic mainstays of the discourse on landscape that the gardens of discovery reject, one might conclude that the ecological garden is devoid of human interest. Gone is the modification of nature through artificially imposed standards of formal beauty. Gone is the rule of geometry in determining the form of garden. Gone is the identification of the garden with the nongardening life of the owner, its value as a symbol of that person's character and social achievement. The symbolic valences that remain have the meditative qualities of both the deistic gardens of liberty, without the melancholia, and the mystical gardens of reaction, without the yearning for purity of essence. The meditation in the garden of discovery is one of partnership between human intellect and natural energy. Some have called it synergy and raised it to a spiritual practice, a unity between the human and universal. The efforts of the ecological gardener symbolize a willingness to engage nature first as an equal, but ultimately as the master of the garden, of the gardener's nongardening life, and of the urban community in which the gardener lives. The garden itself is the material form of the symbolic action.

The goal of ecological gardening is not seen-from-above, bounded, and closed work. Rather, it is to permit the variety contained in a miniature unit (Biotop) to reflect fully the variety of the surroundings. The creative idea never becomes frozen; it remains malleable. No condition is static. Every design form is a transition stage in an ever-changing game that increases endlessly in time and space. Temporally, the gardener experiences the garden as a series of lineal steps leading from a pre-ecological condition to one of self-sustaining balance. Whether this end is ever reached is questionable. If it is reached, the linear progression of events ceases, and the garden enters a seasonal cycle measured in geological rather than human time. History ends. Many things beyond the gardeners' control would have to change before they achieve this balance. What is different about the temporality of this garden is that one feels an acceleration toward the goal of sustainability.

Boundaries drawn on a map have no relevance to the goals of ecological gardening, but they do have relevance to the politics of gardening,

Figure 5.2. Biotop. A Biotop is a wetland system in miniature. The master gardener shown here constructed a particularly complex example of own in his backyard. The pool is home to plants, fish, and amphibians that are natural to the Danube marshlands.

especially if one's neighbors are recreational gardeners, and to the experience of the garden. Ecological gardeners must appear to confine the verdant promiscuity of plant life to their own gardens.

Viewed from outside, ecological gardens are dirty. They contain weeds, plants that are out of place in recreational gardens. If the level of maintenance appears to fall below an acceptable level, the neighboring gardeners will not tolerate the wildness in their midst. For them, the boundaries between their own garden and the outlaw are vital lines of separation. The experience of the ecological garden involves multiple sensory stimulation. All gardens awaken the eyes, ears, and nose of visitors. Gardens of discovery also reach the tactile organs. They are difficult to move around in. Everything is much closer together. There is no room to stand back from a plant and observe its individual qualities. Everything is on top of everything else. This jumble is precisely the desired effect. By combining touch with the other sensations in the garden, the visitor connects with the garden and becomes part of it. What one discovers is not a rare flower or a small animal among the plants, but rather the interdependence of the garden elements, including the humans. This feature alone would make the ecological gardens extraordinary places.

Nothing in these gardens removes from human society the fundamental imbalances that are symbolized there. The gardens are simply statements, like the slogans on the placards at a demonstration. There is no program to invest more gardens in the hands of people in return for a promise to cultivate them ecologically. Such a program would fail. It would fall into the same trap as did the city's efforts to create more recreational gardens, namely, the people who currently cultivate ecological gardens are those who have already benefited from the urban system. They alone have the freedom to reject it, since they have already gained from its strengths. We can see at the level of this individual city the same arguments that fly back and forth between developed and underdeveloped states over international agreements on the environment. Just as a poor country with severe food shortages is unwilling to forgo cheap refrigeration in the hope of slowing the deterioration of the upper atmosphere, a poor, propertyless Viennese sees the ecology movement as a propertied-class ruse to change the rules of the game just as the welfare state has achieved a modicum of social parity among all metropolitans. As these families are a decade or so away from realizing their own garden, and through it a house of their own, the ecologists are undermining the priority of gardens as recreation that ensured continued political support for increasing the supply. One implication of the movement is that these gardenless families may have to content themselves with a city-financed window box instead of the all-important parcel of land. In this sense, gardens of discovery shut out the nongardener, mystify the role of gardening in metropolitan life, and conceal the social contradictions in the politics of gardens.

Notes

1. The German transcription on which this and subsequent translations are based is available in the monograph (Rotenberg 1995, 358–361).
2. As conceived by designers, the *Biotop* is the totality of the life space for animals and plants. Its direct translation in English is *biosphere*. When used in the context of a specific location, it can also be translated as *ecological community*. In actual practice, however, when Viennese gardeners refer to their *Biotop* they mean a pool of still water in the garden. The pool is left to its own devices, and over time, a living community develops within it. In Vienna, *Biotop* have been constructed in both public and private gardens since their value in ecological landscape was first discussed by Neuenschwander (1978, 1981).
3. "The rustle of Nature's life is silenced in the stillness of thought" (Hegel 1970, 7; cited in Pugh 1988) It could be argued that even in Kent's day, the appearance of a pristine nature was illusory. If so, it was an illusion maintained by the entire culture.

4. Nohl's survey research is based on Bavarian urban populations. Viennese landscape critics accept this research as valid for Vienna as well. Whether they are justified or not is an issue that I cannot resolve. It is entirely possible for one survey result to reflect the similarity in the priority of various factors in other cities (as intuited by sensitive critics) but to obscure differences in the order of magnitude between the factors. It is also possible for the sensitive critics to read into the survey from another city the desired outcomes for their own city. Until someone actually replicates Nohl's work in Vienna, both of these possibilities make this entire discussion tentative. My reason for discussing Nohl's findings in terms of the Viennese experience revolves around the role of aesthetics in ecological gardening within the landscape discourse.

References

Breitenmoser, Urs, and Urs Schwarz. 1981. Der Naturgarten. In *Grün in der Stadt*, edited by Andritzky and Spitzer. Pp. 224–229. Reinbek bei Hamburg: Rowohlt.

Burckhardt, Lucius. 1981. Bundesgartenschau. ein Stück Showbusiness. In *Grün in der Stadt*, edited by Andritzky and Spitzer. Pp. 97–103. Reinbek bei Hamburg: Rowohlt.

Francé, Raoul Heinrich. 1908. Das Gesetz des Waldes. *Der Wandervogel. Zeitschrift des Bundes für Jugendwanderungen "Alt-Wandervogel."* 3, nos. 7/8: 100–105.

Gälzer, Ralph. 1987. Gedanken zur Gestaltqualität städtischer Grünräume. In *Gestalteter Lebensraum: Gedanken zur örtliche Raumplanung.* Festschrift für Friedrich Moser, edited by Institut für Örtliche Raumplanung, Technische Universität/Wien. Vienna: Picus Verlag.

Hegel, G. W. F., 1970, *Philosophy of Nature*, Translated by A. V. Miller. Oxford: Clarendon Press.

LeRoy, Louis G., 1978a. *Natur ausschalten—Natur einschalten.* Stuttgart: Klett-Cotta.

———. 1979b. Brennessel und Rosen. *werk + zeit* 4.

Loidl, Hans J. 1981. Landschaftsbildanalyse—Ästhetik in der Landschaftsgestaltung? *Landschaft + Stadt* 13, no. 1: 7–19.

Magistratsabteilung 22, 1986. *Grünlanddeklaration.* Vienna: Magistrat der Stadt Wien.

Mathias, R., ed. 1985. *Wieneu: Innenhofbegrünung.* Presse- und Informationsdienst der Stadt Wien. Wien: Druckhaus Vorwärts G.m.b.H.

Neuenschwander, Eduard, 1978, Sinn und Möglichkeiten der Neuanlage natürlicher Biotope im Stadtmiliew. *Deutsche Bauzeitung* 10.

———, 1981, Natürliche Biotop im Stadtmilieu. In *Grün in der Stadt.* Edited by Andritzky and Spitzer. Pp. 216–223. Reinbek bei Hamburg: Rowoht.

Nohl, Werner, 1974. *Ansätze zu einer umweltspsychologischen Freiraumforschung.* Beiheft 11 zu Landschaft + Stadt. Stuttgart.

———. 1977. *Motive zum Besuch städtischer Freiräume.* Working paper 1. Munich: Technische Universität München Weihenstephan, Lehrstuhl für Landschaftsarchitektur.

———. 1979. Der Einfluß der Ortskenntnis auf das Freiraumerlebnis. *Das Gartenamt* 28, no. 10: 638–646.

———. 1980. Visuelle Stimulation des Raumes und Aufmerksamkeitsverhalten der Benutzer als Bausteine einer Freiraumästhetic. *Garten + Landschaft.* Part 1, 3:194–198; Part 2, 4:290–293; Part 3, 6:482–488.

———. 1982. Das Naturschöne im Konzept der städtischen Freiraumplanung. *Das Gartenamt* 31, no. 9: 525–532.

————. 1987. Die Symbolnot unserer Friedhöfe: Nutzungstheoretische Überlegungen der Friedhofsplanung. *Das Gartenamt* 36, no. 5: 295–298.

Pugh, Simon. 1988. *Garden—Nature–Language.* Manchester, U.K.: Manchester University Press.

Rotenberg, Robert. 1995. *Landscape and Power in Vienna.* Baltimore, Md.: Johns Hopkins University Press.

Schiller-Bütow, Hans. 1979. *Die Landschaft als Vorbild: Gestaltungsanregungen für Landschaftsgärten.* Hannover-Berlin: Patzer Verlag G.m.b.H.

Schwarz, Urs. 1980. *Der Naturgarten. Mehr Platz für einheimische Pflanzen und Tiere.* Frankfurt am Main: Wolfgang Krüger.

Spitzer, Klaus. 1981. Gärten-Orte der Kreativität. In *Grün in der Stadt*, edited by Andritzky and Spitzer. Pp. 289–291. Reinbek bei Hamburg: Rowohlt.

Walpole, Horace. 1798. *History of modern gardening.* Pp. 517–545 in vol. 2 of *The Works.* London.

Wirth, Peter. 1984. *Hausgärtenpläne. Entwürfe und Beispiele.* Stuttgart: Verlag Eugen Ulmer.

The Global
City

JOSEPHINE SMART AND ALAN SMART

6

Personal Relations and Divergent Economies

A Case Study of Hong Kong Investment in South China

Foreword

It is 11 February 1999, as I write this foreword, twelve years after beginning formal research with Josephine Smart into the topic of this chapter, and seventeen years after we started ethnographic research in Hong Kong. The article appeared in 1991, but was completed a few months after the catastrophe of Tiananmen Square on 4 June 1989. I am now rereading it, and find myself responding "Yes, but . . . " There was so much more going on than we could know at that time. Still, I think that the tendencies identified in the article were indeed important and the basic argument still seems to stand. That is, there was a socially, rather than bureaucratically, mediated form of foreign investment used by small (and some larger) Hong Kong investors, but that was not directly used by Euro-American transnational corporations. One thing that we didn't emphasize was the way in which substantial proportions of Hong Kong investment served as disguised subcontracting for those same transnational corporations. It is still difficult to say what proportion of Hong Kong investment in China is simply channeled through Hong Kong rather than originating there.

I noticed two other limitations worth pointing out. We were wrong about Hong Kong investment in China drying up after Tiananmen. It may have slowed for a few months, but by the end of the year it was growing again, and has set new records throughout the early 1990s. We also overemphasized the prominence of investing in one's native place. While it was common, so was avoiding the village where you or your family came from for fear of entanglements. Other social ties were available, either through your native place or through those of friends of friends. In retrospect it is clear that this chapter reflects a "pioneering" stage, which has partially been replaced by a more routinized form of foreign investment, although social mediation is still crucial in many circumstances. Rules and property rights have become clearer, capitalist practices have become more routinized under the explicit acknowledgement of a "socialist market economy," and the small-scale Hong Kong entrepreneurs have become less central to the process (A. Smart 1998). Reliance on kinship and other social ties is only one option for small and medium enterprises now, rather than an almost indispensable strategy.

What I am saying here is that things were even more complicated in the real world than in our early effort to make sense of that complexity. Writing that paper crystallized our ideas and set the path for subsequent analysis and much more fieldwork. When it was written, we had only spent seven months specifically doing research for this project in Hong Kong and Guangdong province. We did, however, have the advantage of having followed the issue throughout our doctoral research. Many of our best informants are current people that we met in Hong Kong between 1982 and 1985 while doing research on Hong Kong's illegal street vendors (J. Smart 1989) and the clearance of squatter areas (A. Smart 1992).

In an ironic way, the article frequently doesn't seem very ethnographic in tone. There is considerable emphasis on statistics. Those are the parts of the paper that haven't aged well, and I have trimmed some of the less necessary ones. Newer statistics are available elsewhere (Hsing 1998, Lever-Tracy 1996, Lee 1998, G. Lin 1997). Some retain their importance, though, such as the point that in the 1980s, "only 0.6% of Chinese industrial enterprises have more than 243 workers, compared to 65.1% in Hungary and 33.5% in Yugoslavia." Surely this helps explain something about China's relative success. The regimes in the other two collapsed and are struggling with unruly capitalism and outright barbarism, while China achieved its goals of quadrupling production by the year 2000 in the early 1990s. Katherine Verdery (1996) has suggested that socialism collapsed because it could not cope with capitalism's speedup into post-Fordism. China seems an exception, and seems to have coped with late capitalism reasonably effectively, given that twenty of its thirty provinces have had real economic growth greater than any other country over the last two decades. A puzzle like this makes us wonder about what might otherwise seem certain.

Ethnography is the lifeblood of anthropology. It is the fountain of continuing surprise, and only new surprises can revitalize curiosity and inquiry. No one who does substantial ethnographic research fails to discover new interesting questions. One fieldwork project "morphs" into another through the demand for new research programmes and output, and can take strange but rewarding forms through the addiction of ethnographers to puzzles. Just like historians, when we see something we can't understand (such as why Trobrianders gave away most of their yams to their sister's family or how petty capitalists are doing something that is allegedly so hard for large multinational corporations), we can't let go of the mystery until we solve it. In researching and writing the paper you are about to read, we were constantly surprised. Trying to unravel the tangle of fascinating mysteries that we have uncovered will take us the rest of our lives.

In the rest of this foreword, I want to partially redress the lack of explicit reference to urban issues in this paper. Implicitly, of course, the paper is about Hong Kong's place in its peri-urban or rural hinterland, and the ways in which it influences what is going on in this cross-border region. But nowhere is the region adequately sketched. The following is only a few quick brushstrokes compared to what lies out there to be observed and described.

Changes in the global economy have been producing a situation in which cities will be shaped primarily by their responses to powerful global forces. The fate of individual cities is no longer primarily determined by national economies and polities. Instead, cities increasingly must forge roles for themselves in an international division of labour. At the same time that globalization has heightened the sense of cities as actors on the world stage, it has often also further reduced the viability of considering a city as a coherent and bounded unit. The same technological forces of transportation and communication that facilitate the global extension of production processes have also made possible a heightened level of contact between people separated by national borders. The recent intense interest in phenomena like transnationalism, hybridity, diasporas, virtual communities, and ethnoscapes forces us to wonder whether cities are useful arenas for anthropological inquiry, if one's community of reference and mutual aid can be spread across the globe. The decentralization of urban activities into "edge cities" and uncontrolled urban sprawl, particularly in the United States, reinforces this sense of the "urban" as diffuse and ineffable.

Nowhere, perhaps, is the classical sense of a city as a coherent, bounded, and self-governing unit more challenged than in urban agglomerations that cut across national borders, such as in the twin cities of the United States–Mexico border region. People are not citizens of these transnational urban entities, but they may experience their lives as bound up with both sides of the border that they may cross on a daily basis. Traditional models of urban governance everywhere are challenged by urban areas that sprawl beyond political boundaries, but when more than one nation-state is involved, the problems of planning and participation become much more demanding.

When we wrote this chapter, we were beginning to see the emergence of such a transborder urban region, one that cut across the boundary between communist China and hyper-capitalist Hong Kong. As a result of ethnographic research in the informal sector of Hong Kong (squatter areas and street hawkers), we serendipitously encountered small entrepreneurs who were establishing factories in China. In following the social networks of our Hong Kong informants, we explored a rapidly changing landscape of political and economic relations, and the social and cultural outcomes of those interactions.

A new kind of urban region has emerged in the Inner Delta of the Pearl River, focused at the southern poles by Hong Kong and Macau and in the north by the capital of Guangdong province of the People's Republic of China, Guangzhou. In between, there is appearing a complex amalgam of densely populated agricultural areas that are gradually being replaced by growing smaller cities, new factory towns, vast industrial development zones, new infrastructural developments, and Special Economic Zones. In the southeastern region of this zone, the impact of Hong Kong is strong enough that we can reasonably talk about the emergence of "Greater Hong Kong." The impact of Hong Kong-based property developers, the transfer of manufacturing processes from Hong Kong into China, and the profound cultural and social influence of the Hong Kong way of life are ubiquitous in this zone, although it is also extremely apparent elsewhere in the region.

There are two distinct and partially contradictory aspects of Hong Kong's role in the recent transformation of this area. One aspect concerns the areas in Guangdong that are in close proximity to the Hong Kong Special Administrative Region and can be seen as representing Greater Hong Kong. The other aspect is partially deterritorialized: the extension of Hong Kong people's networks and practices across the border, producing what we call "Hong Kong in China." Hong Kong in China can be visualized as million of lines, representing personal relationships and transactions, radiating out from Hong Kong and into China. These lines are not distributed uniformly but are concentrated in particular areas or nodes of interaction, patterned partly by proximity but also by earlier patterns of migration (predominantly from Guangdong province) and by centers of economic importance in China such as Shanghai, Wuhan,

Dalian, and Beijing. One reason why it is important to keep both dimensions (local region and fluid networks) in view is that the ability of localities in Greater Hong Kong to dictate the terms of Hong Kong investment and development is reduced by the existence of relatively dense nodes of Hong Kong in China in other parts of the Delta and elsewhere. Should the exactions and costs become too high in the nearby portions of China, enterprises can be transferred to other regions where costs are lower and local officials are more enthusiastic about the preferred investments. The result is an illustration of the worldwide tensions between localities, which are fixed in place, and the increasingly mobile capital they require to maintain or increase their prosperity. The financial crises throughout Pacific Asia in 1997 and 1998 provide clear evidence of the disruptive potential of such movements and the demands that can be generated for changing local practices to fit with the expectations of global investors.

Greater Hong Kong is an example of what has come to be called "global cities": urban places that channel and control significant portions of the world's increasingly mobile capital. We don't deal with that aspect of Hong Kong below, but for a strong case that Hong Kong can be considered a global city comparable to New York and London, see J. Lin (1997).

Introduction

Since 1978, direct foreign investment in the People's Republic of China has expanded dramatically. The largest single source of direct investment is Hong Kong, representing, with the much smaller Portuguese colony of Macao, between 60 percent and 80 percent of the total to date (Hua 1986, 67; Pan 1987, 91). Hong Kong investment also differs in character from the direct investment practices of enterprises from other capitalist nations. Although many Hong Kong investments are large-scale and negotiated with central authorities (particularly property and infrastructure projects), as with investments from other sources, a large portion of Hong Kong investment follows a different pattern rarely taken by foreign multinationals. This alternative pattern involves the establishment of small-scale enterprises that are negotiated with local authorities and are often mediated or facilitated by preexisting social connections in the site of investment.

This socially (rather than bureaucratically) mediated form of investment involves distinct relations of production and exchange, which, although not yet adequately understood, are implicated in a massive social and economic transformation occurring primarily in South China. These socially mediated investments seem to differ distinctively from the foreign investment patterns experienced so far in other socialist nations. Furthermore, the common use by Hong Kong entrepreneurs of the socially mediated, local investment form must be understood in the context of their strategies for reducing the conflicts between capitalist relations of production and the Chinese political economy. Although social mediation and the relations of gift exchange upon which it is based, create their own set of problems, they seem to play a role in reducing the incompatibilities between capitalist and socialist economic organization.

As always, the adoption of rational strategies in itself explains relatively little. What is rational, or to use a less loaded term, what makes sense, is dependent upon the context. Therefore, in order to understand the strategies adopted by Hong Kong entrepreneurs, we must examine the context of their investment in China. This task requires at least a brief sketch of the economy and society of China. In the next section, China will be examined as a social formation containing several distinct sets of relations of production and exchange. This heterogeneity of political economic organization provides the Hong Kong entrepreneur with choices about which sets of production and exchange relations to become involved with, and this choice has significant implications for the organization of production in these foreign-invested Chinese firms.

Relations of Production and Exchange in Socialist Economies

The People's Republic of China can be seen as a social formation that is dominated by a state and a party committed to preserving and extending socialist relations of production yet also contains nonsocialist relations of production. This analytical framework is useful for an examination of the forms and dynamics of capitalist involvement with and investment in China because, first, it deals with the economic heterogeneity in a consistent manner without reducing one form of economic activity to another and, second, it draws attention to the specificity of the relations of production and exchange in particular cases.

A great deal of work has been conducted upon the "articulation of modes of production" (Kahn and Llobera 1981; Foster-Carter 1978; Godelier 1972; Rey and Dupré 1978). A mode of production, such as the capitalist or feudal mode of production, is formed by a combination of "relations of production" (the forms of relationships between producers and nonproducers, if any, through which surpluses are extracted) and "forces of production" (the techniques of appropriation from nature and the organization of the work process). In the pure case, or in theoretical abstraction, a form of politics and of ideology is associated with a mode of production. Concrete societies, however, rarely have only a single model of production (Kahn 1980, 200), and this is clearly the case with existing socialist economies.

Althusser elaborated the concept of "social formation" (found in Marx's work but used in a variety of ways) as a solution. The social formation is a combination of modes of production in which one mode of production is normally dominant (Corbridge 1986, 54). Although the coexistence of two or more modes of production is normally a transitional phenomenon, from this perspective a relationship, termed "articulation," can develop between the modes so that the dominant mode can benefit and create a temporary stability. This is the case, for example, with peripheral capitalist social formations in the Third World: labor power is reproduced cheaply in the noncapitalist mode of production, reducing the costs of capitalist production.

One problem with this approach is that focusing upon modes of production reifies the modes, which are more properly abstractions to facilitate explanation (Hindess and Hirst 1977, 2; Baber 1987). The modes do not themselves interact as such; rather, individuals and institutions can be seen as participating in both modes, and through their actions, the operation of the social formations or political economies may be modified. Furthermore, within a given society, the interactions may be such that each "mode of production" is so influenced by the other(s) that it can only with difficulty be seen as a separate political economic system.

In this context, it seems preferable to focus upon distinctive *relations* of production, rather than modes of production (Hindess and Hirst 1975). In any particular case of productive activity, there will exist a set of ownership relations, so that the labor process will be controlled and the product allocated between producers and, in most cases, nonproducers. In a complex social formation, distinctive relations of production coexist and mutually influence one another.

Existing socialism likewise cannot be analyzed as a mode of production but should instead be seen as a social formation (Lane 1985, 94) in the sense formulated by Kahn (1980, 201): "The co-existence of different relations of production together with specific political and ideological forms within a single economic system."

Lane (1985, 94) saw the Soviet Union as a state socialist social formation, a social formation rather than a transition between modes of production because transitional societies are temporary and do not reproduce themselves in a stable form as had the Soviet Union (until 1991). He defined it as "state socialist" to emphasize the role of the state in dominating politics and ideology and in controlling the economy to support the goal of moving towards communism. As a social formation, the Soviet

Union involved a mixture of precapitalist, capitalist, and communist components, including relations of production. The dominant relations of production were socialist "in the sense of there being collective ownership of the means of production" (Lane 1985, 97).

The China that has been emerging since 1978 is more internally heterogeneous than the situation described by Lane, and analysts are seriously asking whether it is undergoing a process of "capitalist restoration" (Chossudovsky 1986; Petras 1988) or is entering "post-socialism" (Dirlik 1989). More positively, the growth of autonomous collectives and independent products at the expense of the state sector is seen as representing the possibility for emergence of a "society of associated producers" (Howard 1988, 175) which would provide a stronger basis for a democratic socialism.

The three main forms of relations of production found in contemporary China can be described as socialist; petty commodity-producing or petty capitalist; and capitalist.

Socialist relations of production are most clearly present in the firms that are owned by the whole people and are generally referred to as state-sector firms (Ma and Hong 1988). Despite reforms that are increasing the role of production for free markets and the director responsibility system (Walder 1989), such firms largely produce according to the plan using allocated inputs. Profits are either remitted to the state or retained for expansion, but in any case are not the legal property of those who control the productive process in an enterprise. Prior to 1978, much of the collective sector, and even the rural agricultural economy, was controlled in similar ways, but this has changed dramatically.

Petty commodity or petty capitalist relations of production are characterized by individual ownership and appropriation by the direct producers and are associated with production for the market (Kahn 1980, 133). Gates (1989) sees petty capitalism as having coexisted with a tributary mode of production in imperial China since the Song dynasty. Unlike Kahn, Gates (810) sees petty capitalism as having in some cases involved the extraction of surplus by a class of nonproducers who owned the means of production. She distinguishes this kind of production from capitalism because "China's indigenous capitalism arose in a large and strong state where the ruling class was capable of setting bounds to its expansionary tendencies" (831). This distinction seems less useful than Kahn's because it emphasizes the position of a mode of production in the society rather than the character of the relations of production: they had to be petty capitalist rather than capitalist because they were subordinate and the "laws" of capitalist accumulation and development did not apply. From a less rationalist perspective, it seems preferable to follow Kahn, who recognized the potential for some differentiation as long as the owners of the means of production retain a strong role in the actual production process. Where this condition no longer applies, we have moved from petty capitalist to capitalist relations of production.

China's collective sector now largely fits into this definition of petty commodity relations of production, although there is considerable variation. Ma and Hong (1988, 214) define collectives as enterprises "in which members own their own means of production and participate in labor as shareholders." However, in practice large collectives have been subject to planning by state ministries and workers have little control over management (Lockett 1989, 122). The responsibility system in agriculture, where individual households contract for collective land and are allowed to sell their excess production in free markets, is a clear example petty commodity or petty capitalist relations of production.

Economic reforms have also allowed the growth of individual producers and retailers in the city, who can employ up to eight workers (Gold 1989). In 1988, there were 14.13 million registered individual enterprises, employing 26.24 million people (Gold 1989, 197).

In April 1988, the National People's Congress legitimized a new ownership category, private business, for companies with more than eight employees. This size is probably a reasonable approximation of the division between petty capitalist and capitalist relations of production. By the end of 1988, there were 115,000 privately owned businesses, with 1.85 million employees (Gold 1989, 198), an average of only 16.1 per enterprise. However, in some instances private businesses may have hundreds of workers.

In addition to these domestic enterprises based upon what are essentially capitalist relations of production, there are also foreign and joint venture capitalist enterprises, the subject of this paper.

Our discussion so far has concentrated upon relations of production, but relations of exchange are also of critical importance in examining socialist social formations. Marxian analyses of social formations have tended to emphasize production over exchange. This predilection is partly a result of debates in which Marxian analysts such as Laclau (1971) criticized the work of dependency and world-system theorists such as Frank (1971) and Wallerstein (1984) for focusing upon the realm of exchange rather than production. The world-system theorists suggested that wherever imperialist nations introduced market exchange, those economies became immediately capitalist (even if peripheral or dependent capitalist). Marxians, on the other hand, focusing upon production, saw that some of the relations of production in the colonial or postcolonial societies continued to be noncapitalist. This criticism is justified, but it has had the detrimental by-product of a relative indifference to relations of exchange (Prattis 1987, 27). While production is, of course, critical, relations of exchange or distribution also have a great impact (Voss 1987). Furthermore, exchange relations are not necessarily deducible simply from knowledge of the mode of production. Following Polanyi (1944), Halperin (1988, 45) argues that production and distribution are "not only separate analytically, but can operate simultaneously with different organisational modes."

Some researchers argue that the necessity for market-oriented reforms is a result in the first place of competition with the capitalist nations, creating a need for economic efficiency. Participation in the world economy reinforces this tendency, since high levels of participation without effective reforms may lead to persistent balance-of-payments problems (Brada, Hewett, and Wolf 1988; Csikos-Nagy 1983; Csaba 1983). Furthermore, when there is an open economy policy in a socialist nation, this "means that foreign trade influences the level and structure of domestic wholesale and retail prices" (Plowiec 1988, 351–352). As a result of this, reform experiments which are targeted only for individual sectors of the economy are bound to fail due to the creation of internal conflicts between plan and market (347). Segregated reforms and two-tier (plan/market) pricing systems produce internal dynamics leading to incentives to divert output from plan to market (Byrd 1988, 10).

A common expectation ensuing from these processes resulting from foreign trade and investment is that the consequent intermediate position between an economy regulated by a plan and by a market is inherently unstable, so that economic dynamics lead toward the expansion of market regulation, but political reactions could lead back to the greater dominance of the plan (Byrd 1988, 12). Solinger (1989), however, argues that patterns of "relational contracting" between paired firms in China represent a hybrid form between plan and market that is stable and reduces the trend toward pure market regulation. The result of reforms, then, is partially dependent upon the characteristics of exchange relationships.

Often, the defining characteristic of a socialist economy is seen as the existence of a system of central planning, rather than the market, determining the allocation of resources. Even prior to 1978, China differed from other socialist economies in this regard. In 1977–1978, the central plan included only 50 to 55 percent of industrial output, and this had dropped to 30 to 40 percent by 1984 (C. P. Wong 1988, 99). Not all of the remainder, though, involves market allocation, since China has an unusually strong system of regional planning and resource allocation. Economic decentralization doesn't necessarily mean a shift to the market, since local governments can increase their control (C. P. Wong 1988, 95). Nevertheless, Byrd (9) found that in 1984, 56.1 percent of urban industrial enterprises had over 40 percent of their output allocated by free markets and 38.2 percent had 80 to 100 percent market output.

Another unusual characteristic of the Chinese economy increases the difficulty of effective central planning. China has a preponderance of small-scale enterprises. According to World Bank estimates, only 0.6 percent of Chinese industrial enterprises have more than 243 workers, compared to 65.1 percent in Hungary and 33.5 percent in Yugoslavia (C. P. Wong 1988, 97). The share of industrial output from small plants has grown from 45 percent in 1970 to about 55 percent in 1988 (97).

Even within that portion of the Chinese economy controlled by the central plan, other exchange relationships are important and modify the system. It is now a common observation that socialist systems "suffer from inherent structural flaws that force their members to engage in illegal actions to survive and pursue ordinary interests" (Oi 1989, 223). Factory managers circumvent or manipulate regulations or plans as a routine part of the performance of their duties (Walder 1989; Zafanolli 1988). This manipulation, and the diversion of goods from plan to market (Byrd 1988), are part of what is called the "second economy" or "shadow economy." The second economy involves activities that are outside the official plan, often illegally—black market, bribery and corruption, petty trade, and so on. It has been seen as the equivalent of the market in capitalist countries (Sampson 1987, 121), which "helps to alleviate consumer shortages and bureaucratic bottlenecks" (120).

The operation of this second economy is closely related to reciprocal exchange relationships, called *blat* in the Soviet Union and *guanxi* in China. Meaney (1989, 205) argues that Leninist systems are pervaded by such relationships, not just in the economic margins but also in the heart of the party bureaucracy, since "the party's monopoly over opportunities for career mobility and material reward provides the basis for clientelist patterns."

Work along these lines has greatly improved our understanding of the actual patterns of operation of socialist societies. However, Yang (1988) has criticized the concept of the second economy as a confusing catchall that includes very different types of relationships that could be better comprehended if distinguished. She suggests that at least two qualitatively distinct forms of exchange occur in the second economy: gift exchange and commodity exchange. More generally, she identifies three modes of exchange in China: the state redistributive economy; the gift economy; and the petty commodity economy (26). Yang argues convincingly that the gift economy consists of "the personal exchange and circulation of gifts, favors and banquets and the art of *guanxi* exchange lies in the skilful mobilization of moral and cultural imperatives such as obligation and reciprocity in pursuit of both diffuse social ends and calculated instrumental ends." (35) The term *guanxi* means relationships or social connections built upon preexisting relationships of classmates, people from the same native place, relatives, superior and subordinate in the same workplace, and so forth, incorporating them into its own operation (411).

Yang also argues that the gift economy "alters and weakens in a piecemeal fashion the structural principles and smooth operation of state power" in China (37). This second claim is subject to argument, since other authors suggest that the "first economy" and state power are deeply intertwined with clientelist relations of reciprocal exchange. The power differential in patron-client relationships does fit the pattern of an informal, rather than formal, redistributive relationship, but the horizontal relationships between enterprises and their managers do seem to be simultaneously gift exchanges and a fundamental part of the operation of the state-sector economy.

The value of Yang's analysis is that it identifies another mode of exchange that is of critical importance. It would be a mistake, however, to associate the gift economy with only one of the forms of relations of production found in the Chinese economy. Gift exchange is implicated in all of them, even though it may not be essential to any of them. Yang, then, misleads in her characterization of three separate economies. What she had identified are three distinct modes of exchange: Polanyi's familiar market exchange, reciprocity, and redistribution. There is no one-to-one correspondence between these modes of exchange and the coexisting relations of production found in China. As noted, the state sector is deeply influenced by gift exchange and the cultivation of *guanxi*, and this is certainly also the case for enterprises characterized by petty capitalist and capitalist relations of production. These enterprises pay taxes and informal extortion by officials, or "squeeze," and are therefore involved in relations of redistribution, and of course the reforms have brought market exchange into the operation of practically all enterprises in China. Yang's analysis is an invaluable contribution to our understanding of the pervasiveness and the distinctive characteristics of the operation of relationships based upon gift exchange, but we should not let her lapse in terminological usage lead us to think that these are distinct economies. The challenge for research on the Chinese economy is to examine how these distinctive modes of exchange interact with and influence the three forms of relations of production found in contemporary China. Gift exchange, commodity or market exchange, and redistribution influence all enterprises, but their position and role within the relations of production is not uniform.

This task is far too demanding for a single chapter. Instead, we will make a modest contribution to this endeavor by examining the way in which exchange relationships influence the decisions of Hong Kong entrepreneurs on how to invest in China, and how exchange relationships may facilitate these investments by reducing the conflicts and incompatibilities between the two divergent economies.

Foreign Investment in China

The economic restructuring of China based on the policies of the Four Modernizations (in agriculture, industry, national defense, and science and technology) and the open-door policy since 1978 has been remarkable. One of the means by which China hoped to achieve its ambitious goals of quadrupling the value of China's production by the year 2000 (Pan 1987, 4) is to abandon its long-held policy of self-reliance and isolation from the world economy. Instead of withdrawal from the capitalist world market, China would become enmeshed with it in order to develop its productive forces through controlled imports of technology and promotion of its exports (Cumings, 1989: 205; Tsao, 1987: 3). This is a dramatic break with China's Maoist past, and furthermore, "Never before has a sovereign communist state so wholeheartedly set out to attract the exponents of capitalist entrepreneurs" (Sklair 1985, 571–572).

This insertion into the world market required attention to competitive advantage. Since China's only real comparative advantage is cheap labor, the conclusion was that "China (or its coastal provinces) should be inserted into the world system at a point appropriate to its market advantage; China should be another NIC, following the path blazed by South Korea and Taiwan" (Cumings 1989, 214). The cheap labor and its appearance of unlimited supply fit in well with the global trend of relocating portions of the industrial system from the developed countries to less-developed countries.

Foreign investment comes in many forms. Equity joint ventures involve an attribution of shares to the foreign and domestic parties, with profits accruing in proportion to the shares held. Contractual joint ventures are cases "in which the profits and other rights and obligations are negotiated in the contract not necessarily in proportion to equity holdings" (N. Wang 1984, 73). Wholly owned foreign enterprises are also possible and are currently becoming more common (Hua 1986, 67). Compensation trade involves deals where the imports of machinery and technology are paid for a number of years (N. Wang 1984, 73). Finally, a significant portion of the foreign investment comes in the little-discussed

**Table 6.1   Foreign Investment in Guangdong by Investment Form:
Numbers (Percentage)**

FORM	1985		1986		1987	
Equity joint venture	487	(3.75)	369	(3.94)	607	(8.68)
Contractual joint venture	1205	(8.84)	417	(4.45)	578	(8.27)
Foreign owned	32	(0.24)	11	(0.12)	26	(0.37)
Export processing	11,780	(86.38)	8,472	(90.45)	5,622	(80.42)
Other	133	(0.97)	97	(1.03)	158	(2.17)
Total	13,637		9,366		6,991	

Source: State Statistical Bureau (1988), 318.

form of export processing, which involves the processing of materials from abroad for export, and which are usually limited-term agreements (Chan 1985, 14).

Despite difficulties in the quantification of total foreign investment in China (Sit 1988), one undisputed observation that arises is the dominance of Hong Kong and Macao investment in China. Observers suggest that 60 percent (U.S.$4.5 billion) of the total U.S.$7.45 billion direct foreign investment in China by the end of 1982 came from Hong Kong and Macao sources (Hua 1986, 67; Tong 1984, 17). The dominance of Hong Kong foreign investment in southern China is particularly impressive. Of total foreign investment in the Pearl River Delta in Guangdong, almost all came from Hong Kong and Macao. In mid-1988, Hong Kong had an estimated total direct investment of between U.S.$4.7 and U.S.$5.1 billion in Guangdong province, involving 13,000 to 15,000 enterprises (Trade Development Council 1988: 5).

In particular, Hong Kong and Macao investment more or less monopolizes the small-scale export-processing agreements in southern China. During the initial period after the open-door policy, almost all the foreign investment in Guangdong was in the form of processing agreements. The portfolio of foreign investment has since diversified, but export processing is still a significant source of foreign investment in southern China. Official statistics (tables 1 and 2) indicate that the great majority of investment projects take the export-processing form but account for a much smaller portion of capital investment: 10.6 percent in 1987, falling from 12.85 percent in 1985. In some regions of the province, export processing remains the fastest growing form of foreign investment. For instance, export-processing investment in Dongguan county in the Pearl River Delta of Guangdong province grew from U.S.$2.35 million in 1979 to U.S.$62.69 million in 1986 (Kung and Chan 1987, 17–19).

***Table 6.2 Foreign Investment in Guangdong by Investment Form:
Capital Invested in US$10,000 (Percentage of Total)***

FORM	1985		1986		1987	
Equity joint venture	11,750	(27.26)	15,365	(18.90)	19,895	(27.22)
Contractual joint venture	34,832	(53.49)	50,547	(62.19)	38,049	(52.07)
Foreign owned	851	(1.31)	1,398	(1.72)	1,452	(1.99)
Export processing	8,367	(12.85)	10,371	(12.76)	7,771	(10.63)
Other	3,341	(5.10)	3,599	(4.43)	5,912	(8.09)
Total	65,123		81,280		73,079	

Source: State Statistical Bureau (1988), 318.

One issue that is not clarified in the statistical or scholarly literature is the real status of these export-processing enterprises. Often they
are treated by the Chinese government as Chinese firms that are processing goods for foreign contractors: foreign-backed firms. In discussions with Hong Kong entrepreneurs, they are generally presented as
Hong Kong–established and –managed enterprises, although with the
assistance of a local counterpart. The situation is obviously very different if we are dealing with state-sector firms working under contract, or
if Hong Kong firms are setting up, relatively independently or coopera-
tively, new enterprises. It is likely that both patterns occur, but no information is available about which is most prevalent. From wide
discussions with Hong Kong entrepreneurs, however, it seems fairly certain that the newly established enterprise is the most common pattern,
although the enterprise may be jointly undertaken with some preexisting unit, perhaps a rural collective rather than a state sector firm. Another point that is obscured is how often the Hong Kong investor is
essentially operating as an agent for a foreign investor aware of the advantages of utilizing Hong Kong Chinese as front men.

Hong Kong Investment in Southern China

Despite the many changes in China, direct foreign
investment by foreign entrepreneurs involves a situation where capitalist
entrepreneurs are endeavoring to make profits through operations in a
nation dominated by socialist relations of production. These issues have
received some attention, although that attention is generally less academic than it is practical analysis of the potentials and perils of investment in China. These works are usually focused upon the many structural
and cultural obstacles in the path of successful joint-venture investments
in China by multinationals—the language barrier, incompatibility of management styles, the differences in negotiating practices, the distinctive

Figure 6.1. Packing goods for export from Guangdong province. *Photograph by Josephine Smart.*

bureaucratic organization of the workplace, the long time needed to ne-gotiate a contract (usually measured in years), problems with meeting production deadlines and quality control requirements, inadequacy of the legal framework, and the problem of labor productivity and management. The delineation of these various problems in multinational joint ventures suggests that the interface between the two divergent eco-nomic systems—capitalist and socialist—is riddled with tensions and contradictions that challenge the social, business, and technical sensi-bilities of participants from both sides. Seen in this context, the rela-tive ease with which Hong Kong investors have approached investment in China and their apparent greater success and efficiency (measured in start-up time at least) in their investments raises interesting questions, and not only practical ones. What is it about Hong Kong investment that gives it certain advantages over large-scale multinational investment ven-tures in China? Is there a catalytic element conducive to the effective and efficient interaction between Hong Kong investment and the socialist economy in China that is lacking in other forms of capitalist investment? Our argument is that the difference lies in the availability of preexist-ing social connections and the skilled use of reciprocal relations of gift exchange in the investment process.

Figure 6.2. Migrant workers arriving at and leaving a factory town in Guang-dong province. *Photograph by Alan Smart.*

In the early years of the open door policy, all decisions concerning foreign investment were made by central authorities or by state-owned organization. However, eventually some decision making was decentral-ized to give local authorities and enterprises the power to conduct busi-ness directly with foreign corporations (Hua 1986, 61). However, this local autonomy applies only to small or medium enterprises that do not involve key sectors of the economy, such as transportation, energy, and steel. In Guangzhou, for example, foreign investments that involve more than U.S.$10 million must still be approved by central authorities (G. Wang 1988, 173). The decentralization of the authority to negotiate agree-ments with foreign investors to individual firms or local authorities, to-gether with the availability of the export-processing form of foreign investment, provides the structural basis that makes possible the rapid expansion of small-scale investments that attract many Hong Kong in-vestors. In 1980, the average investment per processing agreement was only U.S.$11,538, increasing to U.S.$25,641 in 1981 (Sit 1985, 237). These Hong Kong investments, though small-scale in each instance, are quite significant in the aggregate, as indicated earlier.

Why do Hong Kong investors dominate small-scale investment in China? Although there are many small investors involved in investment in China, there are also many economically powerful investors who are very capable of engaging in large-scale ventures but prefer not to do so. The rationale has little to do with financial power but everything to do with strategic thinking. At the heart of the concerns about investing in China are worries about dealing with the Chinese bureaucracy: "Western traders frequently come up against what they describe as bureaucratic inflexibility or inexperience. Worse still, there are frequent allegations of corruption" (*South China Morning Post*, 22 June 1987, B1).

In the context of many problems arising from the incompatibility of the two diverse and different economic systems of socialism and capitalism, there is a risk that a single large joint venture, negotiated with central authorities, may get bogged down or aborted. Many Hong Kong investors in manufacturing circumvent such risk by setting up a number of independent units, each responsible for their own activities so that any delays in one will not affect the whole investment. In other words, small-scale investment is a strategy to reduce or minimize the economic risk associated with the problems of doing capitalist production within a socialist economy. The decentralization of decision making fits very well with this strategy, indeed largely makes it possible. Under a centralized system, a dozen small investments would have to go through the same procedure and be scrutinized by the same officials. With decentralization, however, a different authority (or enterprise or collective) is involved in each agreement, so that a bureaucratic hitch is unlikely to affect all other negotiations or agreements.

In selecting counterparts, Hong Kong entrepreneurs very frequently opt for establishing relationships with collectives or helping relatives or other contacts to establish private or collective enterprises. They frequently prefer this to dealing with state-sector firms. Although state-sector firms have superior abilities to procure resources, the bureaucratic pitfalls, such as requiring high labor compensation and closer conformity to labor regulations, are often seen as outweighing these advantages. One reflection of this is the trend toward a reduction of investment in the Shenzhen Special Economic Zone and the transfer of production into nearby counties in the Pearl River Delta. Export-processing enterprises are very commonly established in small towns or in villages rather than in the major cities such as Guangzhou.

The opportunity for small-scale export-processing investment could have existed without being so widely utilized by Hong Kong investors. The heavy participation of Hong Kong investors in this form of investment venture must be placed in the context of the macroeconomic situation in Hong Kong in particular and the global market economy in general.

Hong Kong is well known for its export manufacturing industries. Its rise from a crowded city plagued with poverty and unemployment after the Japanese occupation (1941–1945) to a major manufacturing, trading, and financial center within the short span of a few decades is a result of many interacting forces, one of which is the abundant supply of legal and illegal Chinese immigrants willing to work hard and long for a fraction of the wage that unionized western workers would get for the same work (see J. Y. S. Chen 1982; England and Rear 1975; Hopkins 1971; Lin, Mok, and Ho 1980; Sit, Wong, and Kiang 1979). As the supply of immigrant workers stabilizes and the economy of Hong Kong has diversified to offer many other economic opportunities, the manufacturing sector finds itself increasingly squeezed between the twin pressures of labor shortage and demand for higher wages. These problems are aggravated by the growing competition from other newly industrialized countries.

One way in which Hong Kong responds is by capitalizing on the relatively cheap cost of labor offered by China in an attempt to retain its export competitiveness. Taking into consideration wages and other overhead costs, the production cost in Shenzhen can be 50 percent lower than in Hong Kong, and even lower in other parts of the Pearl River Delta. Often only part of the production, the most labor-intensive processes, is shifted to China.

A number of Hong Kong entrepreneurs we interviewed clearly saw bureaucratic problems as encouraging small-scale investments rather than large-scale ones, even when the latter was financially affordable and feasible. It is generally agreed that small to medium projects are easier to manage and are less likely to suffer from bureaucratic hold-ups (*South China Morning Post*, 23 July 1987, 23). A good example of this tendency is the case of Universal Appliances. In 1988, this Hong Kong company, with market capitalization of U.S.$32 million, had 75 percent of its total output produced overseas, 70 percent of this in China. Instead of having a single large joint-venture plant in China, the company has 30 subcontracting lines in Shenzhen, Xiamen, and Hangzhou (*South China Morning Post*, 14 June 1987, M1).

One Hong Kong entrepreneur explained this tendency among Hong Kong investors to set up several small-scale ventures instead of one single major venture by using an analogy with people's war, or guerrilla warfare. This "guerilla capitalism" is a strategy to reduce or minimize the economic risk associated with the problems of capitalist production within a socialist economy (Smart and Smart 1988). A series of independent investments helps avoid crippling delays due to bureaucracy, and this strategy is made possible by the decentralization of decision making. The small-scale investment is also like people's war in that success is largely dependent upon successfully cultivating good relations with the local population in China. On guerrilla warfare, Mao Zedong commented that the forces must "disperse through all enemy-occupied areas, arouse the masses to arm themselves, and wage guerilla warfare in co-ordination with the masses" (1963, 247). The emphasis upon establishing good local social connections on the part of Hong Kong investors highlights the significance of social elements in capitalist investment in China.

Relations of Exchange in Hong Kong Investment

The heavy Hong Kong investment in southern China is most often explained on the basis of geographical and infrastructural advantages. It is true that there are certain advantages in having one's factory close to Hong Kong so that goods and materials can be transported and delivered within a short time, and one can make a quick trip into China to supervise the production at any time. The rapid expansion of Shenzhen Special Economic Zone is no doubt related to this factor (Phillips and Yeh 1989). However, not all investments are located in the closest regions: some investments are spread through more distant parts of Guangdong and in other provinces. There is a relationship between where Hong Kong entrepreneurs invest and their place of origin.

The Chinese government definitely gives great importance to the emotional link between the country and all people of Chinese ancestry outside China. The Chinese in Hong Kong, Macao, and Taiwan are called *tongbao* ("of the same biological origin"), and all other Chinese émigrés are called *huaqiao* ("overseas Chinese"). In recognition of their ancestral link to China, they are all accorded more rights and privileges than non-Chinese visitors in China. For a country with a long history of patrilineality, it is notable that children with either a mother *or* a father who is Chinese are also regarded as Chinese and accorded the same rights. In this way, a greater number of individuals can be incorporated.

The Chinese government is currently appealing to the Chinese émigrés' loyalty to China and their place of origin to encourage them to contribute to the cultural and economic well-being of their native place. Many Hong Kong Chinese have made substantial donations to construct hospitals, schools, universities, and temples for the worship of the ancestors. Many of them also have investments in their native places or in locations nearby.

The injection of capital by overseas Chinese has brought about significant economic development and cultural revival in many parts of China (Woon 1988). However, the role that their emotional loyalty to their ancestry plays in their economic participation in China should not be overemphasized. A narrow cultural approach should be expanded to include a more critical examination of how their social links and connections to a particular locality in China through kinship or ancestry can be and are actively utilized by the overseas Chinese investors toward instrumental ends.

Based on our research in 1987 and 1989, we can identify two major areas in which this occurs. First, an investment (in the form of direct investment or donations or remittances) can be made with the goal of reactivating or reinforcing an investor's social connections in China, which can later be mobilized to facilitate the successful completion of certain social ends (Smart and Smart 1988). For some older Chinese, the idea of setting up a retirement home in their place of origin can be attractive. For others, having established good social ties with their native place may prove to be useful to handle certain crises. A son in trouble with the law can be sent "home" to China temporarily; or local contacts may be utilized to find a wife for one's sons.

The effort channeled into the promotion and maintenance of social ties in China by Hong Kong residents is best illustrated by the magnitude of remittances and the number of trips made to China. It has been estimated that in the early 1970s, remittances from Hong Kong residents to China were about U.S.$100 million a year, increasing to U.S.$673.7 million in 1980. This amounted to 3.2 percent of Hong Kong's GDP (Lau 1986, 262). In 1984, Hong Kong residents made 8,036,452 trips to China, an average of 1.4 trips per year for each resident (Kwok 1986, 166).

In addition, an entrepreneur's social connections in China are a key resource in facilitating investment. The kinship and friendship relations that an investor may have in a given locality furnish him or her with initial advantages resulting from participation in relationships of gift exchange. These connections can be used to gain introductions to local officials and thus circumvent bureaucratic inefficiencies and problems of material shortages. Through participation in the "gift economy" (seen here only as a system of exchange and not as a separate economy), new social connections are cultivated and existing ones reinforced. The gifts exchanged can be in material form (such as clothes, banquets, radios, watches, computers, televisions) or in the form of services (introducing a friend to a useful local connection, acting as liaison between two parties). A Hong Kong investor may receive gifts in the form of information about who one should talk to in order to get certain requests heard, or through greater cooperation in the production and management of his or her business, or as a speedier conclusion to an investment negotiation with local officials.

Participation in this system of gift exchange certainly helps to facilitate the speedy establishment of small-scale, socially mediated investments. Paperwork can be speeded up, and negotiations are generally less detailed than in larger, bureaucratically mediated investments, since it is assumed that difficulties will arise in the future but that good social relations will allow these to be resolved. The trust that is developed through relations of reciprocity makes this kind of approach possible. The social mediation of investment and gift exchange relationships may also be instrumental in protecting the investment from the many problems encountered by most multinational joint ventures in production and marketing, personnel policy and management and so on (Gipouloux 1988, 109–111). It is suggested, then, that the prominence and greater facility of investment by Hong Kong entrepreneurs when compared to western multinationals has less to do with their greater technological expertise than with their ability to utilize a socially mediated form of investment and their ability to participate in and utilize the system of gift exchange for economic and social ends. Personal relations play the role of catalyst in facilitating a Chinese investor's easy entry in establishing enterprises in China and the subsequent successful operation of these enterprises within a socialist economy.

Yang (1989, 37) suggests that the gift economy modifies the operation of state power in China. Our case material suggests that while it may not "alter and weaken" it in the sense that Yang intends, it certainly allows individuals to tap into the system of *guanxi* in a way that may help them resolve particular problems. It also helps develop a sense of trust that the problems that are seen as inevitably developing while operating in the socialist Chinese economy will manage to be resolved in some way or other, thereby increasing the level of confidence about investing in China. In this way, involvement in the system of gift exchange bridges some of the incompatibilities between the two divergent economic systems, making possible a more effective involvement by capitalist entrepreneurs in a socialist economy.

The events in Beijing in June 1989 shook this confidence and resulted in a drying up of new investment from Hong Kong in China. This loss of confidence was not due to disillusionment with the importance of cultivating *guanxi* but with the fear that China might undergo such a massive transformation that local connections would be insufficient protection against the potential ramifications. As yet, however, local social connections and the commitment of Guangdong province to foreign investment has largely insulated existing investments from negative repercussions. Indeed, the most negative influence upon Hong Kong investments in China has come from external responses: pressure from the original equipment manufacturers for whom the production is carried out and from the sources of production finance.

In discussing the advantages of participation in the gift economy, we need to avoid ignoring its disadvantages. Although it is necessary to distinguish between gift exchange and corruption, as Yang (1989, 44) does, it is also true that widespread "squeezing" of entrepreneurs can and does occur in the guise of gift exchange. However, while the form is preserved, the distinctiveness of the exchange relationship is indicated by the absence of the quid pro quo: there is no true reciprocity, and this is really a disguised form of informal redistribution. The other drawback to the pervasiveness of the system of gift exchange and the utilization of *guanxi* is that it creates a strong incentive to invest in a place in which you have local connections, rather than in other places that may make more sense in conventional economic terms because of location, availability of infrastructure, and so on

Effective involvement in the system of gift exchange requires familiarity with the accepted practices and idiom of exchange. Yang (1989, 39–44) identifies five stages of involvement in gift exchange: transformation; incorporation; moral subordination or status antagonism; appropriation or possession; and conversion. Particularly relevant here are the first stage—transformation—and the last stage—conversion. The process of reciprocity requires that the participants be linked through shared qualities and experiences such as being classmates (*tongxue*), colleagues (*tongshi*), common native place (*tongxiang*), kinship, or other forms of commonality. Where such preexisting social commonality is absent, potential participants must become transformed through a mutual friend or acquaintance and establish a basis of familiarity before they can proceed with the other stages of gift exchange.

A large number of Hong Kong investors in the Pearl River Delta established their present investment sites through connections with friends or subordinates who either have investments in the same location or have kinship and other personal ties to local officials and interested parties. There seems to have been a pattern whereby the earliest pioneer investors utilized their own kin connections, but later investors have frequently been introduced to an investment site through the recommendation of friends who have previously established production there. To a certain extent, investment is now much more routine and standardized than it was in the earliest period. These indirect connections not only bring the Hong Kong entrepreneurs directly into contact with the necessary local parties but are also instrumental in speeding up negotiations. They also make it possible to achieve more favorable terms for the investment through a complex process of calling upon obligations built upon longstanding exchange relations between the Hong Kong intermediary and his/her local relatives and friends and establishing new *guanxi* and relations of reciprocity between the potential investors and their local counterparts.

For example, the location of a shoe factory by three partners in Baoan county (north of the Shenzhen Special Economic Zone) was determined by the fact that one of the partners is related to the principal of the local school, who happened to be agreeable to the idea of renting out part of the school's premises for industrial use. The Hong Kong investors received very favorable rental terms as a result of the close kinship relations between one of the partners and his maternal uncle, the school principal. Start-up was facilitated by allowing part of the school building to be used as a temporary factory until a new structure could be constructed. The other two partners have been brought into relations of gift exchange with the principal and other school officials through an initial round of banquets and dinner parties, subsequent occasional but regular visits to the principal at major Chinese traditional holidays with gifts of dried seafood, cigarettes, liquor, and seasonal items, and the placement of the school secretary's niece in the position of factory manager. When the school principal was on a business trip in Hong Kong, he received a twenty-four-inch color television with the compliments of the factory owners.

For the majority of the western investors in China, their participation in the gift economy is generally limited, whether as a result of their dismissal of such practices as a form of corruption or bribery (and, indeed, without facility in handling the reciprocal relationship, it can easily become such) or because they lack the "symbolic capital" (Bourdieu 1977) to enter into such exchanges effectively. In interviews with Japanese managers in Shenzhen, Andors (1988, 35) found that they resented the Hong Kong Chinese because their *guanxi* with local officials accorded them special privileges. In contrast, the Hong Kong investors and other overseas Chinese investors are furnished with the necessary symbolic capital to enter into the gift economy. Their symbolic capital comes in two forms: a general form based on their Chinese origin and a specific form based on local social ties. Most Hong Kong investors have both forms of symbolic capital, thanks to their recent departure from their home town or home village in China and/or their regular contacts with their relatives through remittances, correspondence, and occasional visits. Many also have access to local connections through friends, in-laws, or business partners.

When one receives, one becomes indebted to the giver, and repayment must be made in order to restore the balance of obligation between donor and recipient. In the last stage of gift exchange, called conversion, Yang (1989, 44) points out that "repayment may take either a material form—or a personal labour form—or more important, helping one's donor to 'accomplish a task' [*banshi*]." It is the last category of *banshi* that is of greatest interest here. It is through conversion that Hong Kong investors can skirt many of the problems faced by western investors in China.

One such problem is the increase in production costs in China as a result of the requirement that investors must remit the workers' wages, processing fees, and other costs in Hong Kong dollars through the Bank of China at the official rate of H.K.$100= RMB47. This rate is about half the black market rate for H.K.$100 of RMB90 before June 1989 and RMB82 after. Many Hong Kong investors resort to various legal and illegal measures to avoid paying the official exchange rate. One of the ways in which this can be done is by underreporting the number of workers in an enterprise, so that the total wages remitted through the Bank of China can be reduced. In order to do this effectively, a foreign investor must have the full cooperation of the local manager assigned to his or her factory, since it is this manager who keeps records of the number of workers, the total amount of materials imported and exported, and the total added value of production. In the cases we have information about, this cooperation is a product of the process of conversion in a gift exchange relationship in which a factory manager reciprocates an investor's gifts of material goods by making sure that the records are modified in the interest of the investor.

It must be emphasized that participation in the gift economy is not without its problems. First, there is the problem of who should be included in one's exchange network. It is particularly problematic for investors who have to deal with many government officials from different departments and of different ranks outside their kin-based and social-based network. Some believe that it is important to establish good *guanxi* only with senior officials who are in a position of decision making. Others suggest that it is equally important to include low-ranking officials, since they can have influence on matters directly affecting the investment.

Second, there is the widespread problem of incomplete or ineffective conversion—in other words, those who receive do not always reciprocate. This problem is most common when the exchange relationship is not bound by trust and obligation mediated through kinship and other social contacts. All other things being equal, investors with preexisting connections in the location of investment, particularly with key officials and personnel who are in a position to determine or influence the terms and management of the investment, are more likely to succeed than those who lack similar preexisting connections.

Third, what begins as a personalized, reciprocal relationship of gift exchange can become institutionalized and unilateral: squeeze rather than gift exchange. Although both are perceived from the outside as corruption, they are seen rather differently from the perspective of the investor being squeezed. This point raises the whole issue of the morality of engagement in the gift economy, which we cannot address here. Finally, there is the danger that these activities are often illegal and potentially expose the investor to legal difficulties (Myers 1989).

The argument so far has established that relations of gift exchange are pervasive in Hong Kong investment in China and that these exchange relationships may help maintain the viability of capitalist investment in a socialist economy that is diametrically opposed to the way things work in the Hong Kong economy, with all the potential for difficulties that creates. Furthermore, these relations of exchange influence decisions about the site of investment and how the investment will be organized and managed. Gift exchange is used to attempt to modify the investment context in ways that will improve the profitability of capitalist investment and reduce the risk of arbitrary bureaucratic interference (except when arbitrary bureaucratic actions are in the interests of the particular enterprise).

This paper cannot resolve the issue of the interaction between the relations of production and exchange in socially mediated Hong Kong investment. The range and quality of information that is required is simply not yet available, and the diversity is so great as to make generalization difficult. The range of variation seems to be greatest among export-processing investments, which we have concentrated upon in our research. Relations of production range from subcontracts with state-sector firms, through joint ventures (in practice if not in formal categorization) with collectives as counterparts, joint ventures with private-sector firms or individuals, to disguised, wholly foreign-managed enterprises. The shoe factory mentioned earlier was set up as an export-processing contract, but in reality it was essentially completely established and managed by the Hong Kong investors. One partner spent almost all his time at the factory, sleeping in a bunk in the office, and was responsible for all supervision of the production process. Care was taken to ensure their complete control over personnel, and relations of gift exchange were initiated with them to ensure the continuity and quality of their labor. One of the major goals of the relationships of gift exchange in which the partners participated was to maintain their autonomy over the management of labor within the factory, and they were very successful at this. As a result, the production process was little different from what it would have been in Hong Kong, except that production was much more labor-intensive than could be profitable in Hong Kong with its higher-cost labor.

Conclusion

Changes are under way in China that are only beginning to be adequately explored by social scientists, and the scale and rapidity of these changes are daunting. Foreign investment is only one of the factors implicated in these changes, and quantitatively it is dwarfed, for example, by the transformations of rural China brought about by the introduction of the responsibility system. Yet the establishment of foreign-invested firms has a qualitative dimension that makes it of great interest. New forms of relations of production are being introduced, along with the "modern" forces of production that China considers itself to require urgently. And along with new relations of production go other changes in social relations. The prevalence of Hong Kong and other overseas Chinese investment gives to these changes a particular character: an emphasis upon ties of kinship and other relations of commonality, upon locality and resistance to central control, upon the resurgence of previously repressed cultural activities, and upon social relations ordered to a much greater extent by the exchange of commodities than by collective production and political identity.

The social formation of socialist China is not homogeneous, and since the 1950s has never been less so than at present. This heterogeneity is coupled with policies that have decentralized the control over foreign investment and opened a range of types of enterprises to overseas participation previously unprecedented among socialist nations. The result of this situation is that the capitalist wishing to take advantage of China's cheap labor has a wide range of choice concerning how to go about it: what, where, with whom, and using what kind(s) of investment form. The choice between, for example, investing in a joint venture with a state-sector firm in a major city or in one or several export-processing contracts with relatives establishing new private-sector firms in rural townships or their market towns will have very different social, political, and economic impacts upon Chinese society.

Our main argument has been that Hong Kong investors are very likely to adopt a strategy of investment through the use of preexisting social connections and the reinforcement or development of relations of gift exchange to facilitate start-up and reduce risk, where this is possible. The predominance of Hong Kong investment can be explained at least in part by the availability of such connections and familiarity with the idioms and practices of the gift economy. These relations of exchange are used in the establishment of all forms of investment but seem to be less likely to degenerate into unilateral relations of squeeze when they occur in the context of ongoing social connections with close human feeling and trust.

The social mediation of investment has a number of advantages over purely bureaucratic investment in the context of an economy that is so different from that of Hong Kong, where the legal system of economic regulation is underdeveloped, unstable, and subject to unpredictable political intervention, and where the art of *guanxi* is pervasive in economic and political relationships. The small-scale Hong Kong entrepreneur does not respond to these risks by attempting to specify every possible detail in the contract, as does the multinational manager, thus producing lengthy negotiations, but by cultivating relationships and trust so that the inevitable problems can be resolved as they arise. Meanwhile, the venture has been established rapidly and is generating profits before the usually short-term opportunities in which Hong Kong business specializes have disappeared. Both forms of investment have advantages and disadvantages: social mediation fits the short-term, quick-profit business style in Hong Kong manufacturing, while bureaucratic mediation exposes the salaried multinational managers to less career risk and is more appropriate for their longer-term perspective.

Acknowledgments

We would like to thank the Social Sciences and Humanities Council of Canada, the University of Calgary, and the Centre of Asian Studies (University of Hong Kong) for supporting this research. An earlier version of this paper was presented at the Society for Economic Anthropology annual meeting in 1989.

References

Andors, P. 1988. Women and work in Shenzhen. *Bulletin of Concerned Asian Scholars* 20, 22–41.

Baber, W. L. 1987. Conceptual issues in the new economic anthropology. In *Beyond the new economic anthropology*, edited by J. Clammer. Basingstoke, U.K.: Macmillan.

Baran, P. 1985. Are toy makers moving base to China? *Hong Kong Business* (September): 12–13.

Bourdieu, P. 1977. *Outline of a theory of practice*. Cambridge: Cambridge University Press.

Brada, J. C., E. A. Hewett, and T. A. Wolf. 1988. Economic stabilization, structural adjustment, and economic reform. In *Economic adjustment and reform in Eastern Europe and the Soviet Union*, edited by J. C. Brada, EA. Hewett, and T. A. Wolf. Durham, N.C.: Duke University Press.

Byrd, W. 1988. The impact of the two-tier plan/market system in Chinese industry. In *Chinese economic reforms*, edited by B. Reynolds. Boston: Academic Press.

Chai, J. 1983. Industrial cooperation between China and Hong Kong. In *China and Hong Kong: The economic nexus*, edited by A. Youngson. Hong Kong: Oxford University Press.

Chan, T. M. H. 1985. Financing Shenzhen's economic development. Discussion paper series no. 54. Department of Economics, University of Hong Kong.

Chen, J. Y. S. 1982. *Hong Kong in the 1980s*. Hong Kong: Summerson.

Chossudovsky, M. 1986. *Towards capitalist restoration? Chinese socialism after Mao*. Basingstoke, U.K.: Macmillan.

Corbridge, S. 1986. *Capitalist world development*. Totowa, N.J.: Rowman and Littlefield.

Csaba, L. 1983. Adjustment to the world economy in eastern Europe. *Acta Oeconomica* 30:53–75.

Csikos-Nagy, B. 1983. Hungary's adjustment to the new world market relations. *Acta Oeconomica* 30:77–88.

Cumings, B. 1989. The political economy of China's turn outwards. In *China and the world*, edited by S. Kim. Pp.203–236. Boulder, Colo.: Westview Press.

Dirlik, A. 1989. Postsocialism? Reflections on "Socialism with Chinese characteristics." *Bulletin of Concerned Asian Scholars* 21:33–44.

Economic Research Department. 1987. Industrial processing in China. *Hang Seng Economic Monthly* (April): 1–3.

Economist Intelligence Unit. 1987. *Country report: Hong Kong, Macao*. London: Economist Publications.

England, J., and J. Rear. 1975. *Chinese labour under British rule*. Hong Kong: Oxford University Press.

Foster-Carter, A. 1978. Can we articulate "articulation"? In *The new economic anthropology*, edited by J. Clammer. Hong Kong: Macmillan.

Frank, A. 1971. *Capitalism and underdevelopment in Latin America*. Harmondsworth, U.K.: Penguin.

Gates, H. 1989. The commoditization of Chinese women. *Signs* 14:799–832.

Gipouloux, F. 1988. Industrial restructuring and autonomy of enterprises in China: is reform possible? In *Transforming China's economy in the eighties*, edited by S. Feuchtwang, A. Hussain, and T. Pairault. Vol. 2, *Management, industry and the urban economy*. Boulder, Colo.: Westview Press.

Godelier, M. 1972. *Rationality and irrationality in economics*. London: New Left Books.

Gold, T. 1989. Urban private business in China. *Studies in Comparative Communism* 22:187–201.

Gressel, D. 1987. People's Republic of China: The problems of structural change. *Asian Monetary Monitor* 11:2.

Halperin, R. 1988. *Economies across cultures*. New York: St. Martin's Press.

Hindess, B., and P. Hirst. 1975. *Pre-capitalist modes of production*. London: Routledge and Kegan Paul.

———. 1977. *Mode of production and social formation*. London: Macmillan.

Hopkins, K., ed. 1971. *Hong Kong: The industrial colony*. Hong Kong: Oxford University Press.

Howard, P. 1988. *Breaking the iron rice bowl*. Armonk, N.Y.: Sharpe.

Hsing, You-tien. 1998. *Making capitalism in China: The Taiwan connection*. Oxford. Oxford University Press.

Hua, G. 1986. China's opening to the world. *Problems of Communism* (November/December): 59–77.

Kahn, J. 1980. *Minangkbau social formations*. Cambridge: Cambridge University Press.

Kahn, J., and J. Llobera, eds. 1981. *The anthropology of pre-capitalist societies*. London: Macmillan.

Kung, J., and T. Chan. 1987. Export-led rural industrialization: The case of Dongguan in the Pearl River Delta in China. Paper presented at the Conference on Chinese Cities in Asian Context, University of Hong Kong, 17–19 June 1987.

Kwok, R. 1986. Regional relationships and interaction between Hong Kong and China. In *Planning and development of coastal open cities, Part II: Kong Kong section*, edited by P. Choi. Hong Kong: Centre of Asian Studies.

Laclau, E. 1971. Feudalism and capitalism in Latin America. *New Left Review* 67:19–38.

Lane, D. 1985. *Soviet economy and society.* Oxford: Basil Blackwell.

Lau, P. 1986. Economic relations between Hong Kong and China. In *Hong Kong in transition*, edited by J. Cheng. Hong Kong: Oxford University Press.

Lee, C. K. 1998. Gender and the south China miracle: Two worlds of factory women. Berkeley: University of California Press.

Lever-Tracy, C., D. Ip, and N. Tracy. 1996. The Chinese diaspora and mainland China: An emerging economic synergy. Houndmills: Macmillan Press.

Lin, G. C. S. 1997 Red Capitalism in South China: Growth and development of the Pearl River Delta. Vancouver: University of British Columbia Press.

Lin, J. 1997. Gateway in the flow of capital and culture: Hong Kong and New York as world cities. *City & Society Annual Review 1997.* Pp. 217–240.

Lin, T. B., V. Mok, and Y. P. Ho. 1980. *Manufacturing exports and employment in Hong Kong.* Hong Kong: The Chinese University Press.

Lockett, M. 1989. Foreign trade. In *China's regional development*, edited by D. Goodman. London: Routledge.

Ma, B., and Z. Hong. 1988. Enlivening large state enterprises: Where is the motive force? In *Chinese economic reform*, edited by B. Reynolds. Boston: Academic Press.

Mao, Z. 1963. *Selected military writings of Mao Tse-Tung.* Beijing: Foreign Languages Press.

Meaney, C. 1989. Market reform in a Leninist system: Some trends in the distribution of power, status, and money in urban China. *Studies in Comparative Communism* 22:203–220.

Myers, J. 1989. Modernization and "unhealthy tendencies." *Comparative Policies* 21:193–213.

Oi, J. 1989. Market reforms and corruption in rural China. *Studies in Comparative Communism* 22:221–233.

Pan, L. 1987. *The new Chinese revolution.* London: Hamish Hamilton.

Petras, J. 1988. Contradictions of market socialism in China. *Journal of Contemporary Asia* 18:3–23.

Phillips, D., and A. Yeh. 1989. Special economic zones. In *China's regional development*, edited by D. Goodman. London: Routledge.

Plowiec, U. 1988. Economic reform and foreign trade in Poland. In *Economic adjustment and reform in Eastern Europe and the Soviet Union*, edited by J. C. Brada, E. A. Hewett, and T. A. Wolf. Durham, N.C.: Duke University Press.

Polanyi, K. 1944. *The great transformations.* New York: Rinehart.

Prattis, J. 1987. Alternative views of economy in economic anthropology. In *Beyond the new economic anthropology*, edited by J. Clammer. Basingstoke, U.K. Macmillan.

Rey, P., and G. Dupré 1978. Reflections on the pertinence of a theory of the history of exchange. In *Relations of production*, edited by D. Seddon. London: Frank Cass.

Sampson, S. 1987. The second economy of the Soviet Union and Eastern Europe. *Annals of the American Academy of Political and Social Science* 493:120–136.

Sit, V. 1985. Industries in Schenzhen: an attempt at open-door industrialization.

In *China's special economic zones*, edited by Y. Jao and C. Leung. Hong Kong: Oxford University Press.

———. 1988. Industrial out-processing: Hong Kong's new relationship with the Pearl River Delta. Paper presented at the International Conference on Environment and Spatial Development of the Pearl River Delta, Hong Kong.

Sit, V., S. Wong, and T. Kiang. 1979. *Small-scale industry in a laissez-faire economy.* Hong Kong: Centre of Asian Studies.

Sklair, L. 1985. Shenzhen: A Chinese "development zone" in perspective. *Development and Change* 15:581–602.

Smart, A. 1992. *Making Room: Squatter Clearance in Hong Kong.* Hong Kong: Centre of Asian Studies.

———.1998. Economic transformation in China: Property regimes and social relations. In *Theorising transition: The political economy of post-communist transformations,* edited by John Pickles and Adrian Smith. London: Routledge.

Smart, A., and J. Smart. 1988. Guerilla capitalism: Grassroots Hong Kong investment in China. Paper presented at the Canadian Asian Studies Association Conference, Windsor.

———. 1998. Transnational social networks and negotiated identities in interactions between Hong Kong and China. In *Transnationalism from below* edited by Michael P. Smith and Luis E. Guarnizo. Pp. 103–129. New Brunswick, N.J.: Transaction Publishers.

Smart, J. 1989. *The political economy of street hawking in Hong Kong.* Hong Kong: Centre of Asian Studies.

Solinger, D. 1989. Urban reform and relational contracting in post-Mao China. *Studies in Comparative Communism* 22:171–185.

South China Morning Post (Hong Kong daily newspaper).

State Statistical Bureau. 1988. *Guangdong statistical yearbook 1988* (in Chinese). Beijing: China Statistical Information Publishing.

Tong, Z. 1984. Trade between China and Hong Kong. *Hong Kong Manager* (October):16–19.

Trade Development Council. 1988. *Survey on Hong Kong re-exports.* Hong Kong: Trade Development Council.

Tsao, J. 1987. *China's development strategies and foreign trade.* Lexington, Ky.: Lexington Books.

Verdery, K. 1996. *What was socialism and what comes next?* Princeton, N.J.: Princeton University Press

Voss, J. 1987. The politics of pork and the ritual of rice. In *Beyond the new economic anthropology,* edited by J. Clammer. Basingstoke, U.K.: Macmillan.

Walder, A. 1989. Factory and manager in an era of reform. *China Quarterly* 118:242–264.

Wallerstein, I. 1984. *The politics of the world-economy.* Cambridge: Cambridge University Press.

Wang, G. 1988. *China's new investment laws: new directions.* Singapore: Butterworth.

Wang, N. 1984. *China's modernization and transnational corporations.* Lexington, Ky.: Lexington Books

Wong, C. P. 1988. Between plan and market: The role of the local sector in post-Mao China. In *Chinese economic reform,* edited by B. Reynolds. Boston: Academic Press.

Wong, E. 1987. Recent developments in China's special economic zones. *The Developing Economies* 25:73–86.

Woon, Y. 1988. Social change and continuity in South China: Overseas Chinese and the Guan lineage of Kaiping county 1949–1987. Paper presented at the Canadian Asian Studies Association Conference, Windsor.

Yang, M. 1988. The modernity of power in the Chinese socialist order. *Cultural Anthropology* 3:408–427.

———. 1989. The gift economy and state power in China. *Comparative Studies in Society and History* 31:25–54.

Zafanolli, W. 1988. A brief outline of China's second economy. In *Transforming China's economy in the eighties*, edited by S. Feuchtwang, A. Hussain, and T. Pairault. Boulder, Colo.: Westview Press.

THEODORE C. BESTOR

7 | # Wholesale Sushi
Culture and Commodity in Tokyo's Tsukiji Market

Tokyo's Pantry

The grubby Tsukiji marketplace incongruously sits astride some of the world's most expensive real estate, a few blocks from the Ginza amidst the postindustrial glitter of central Tokyo's slick shopping districts and gleaming office buildings.[1] Six mornings a week between four and ten o'clock, the rambling sheds at Tsukiji become a swirling maelstrom of manual labor and high-tech electronics. Over 60,000 people come to Tsukiji every day to buy and sell fish to feed Tokyo's 22,000,000 residents. Boosters encourage the homey view that Tsukiji is "Tôkyô no daidokoro"—Tokyo's pantry or kitchen. It is, however, a pantry in which about $6 billion worth of fish changes hands each year. Tsukiji stands at the center of a technologically sophisticated international fishing industry, and daily the marketplace matches international supply with the traditional demands of Japanese cuisine, made ever more elaborate by Japan's prosperity and the gentrification of culinary tastes.

Seafood of every description cascades from sparkling white styrofoam boxes and across the well-worn cutting boards of the 1,677 tiny stalls that line the market's aisles. Retail fishmongers and supermarket buyers, sushi chefs and box lunch makers, hotel caterers and even a few ordinary consumers thread their way through the crowded market to pick out their day's fare from the enormous selection on display. Over the course of a year, perhaps 2,000 varieties of seafood are sold at Tsukiji;

official marketplace statistics record 450 categories of seafood, but traders recognize many more subcategories as distinct products. In any given season several hundred are available, although no single stall stocks more than a few dozen at a time. Lobsters and eels wriggle in plastic buckets; flotillas of sea bass stare blankly from their tanks; live shrimp and crabs kick tiny showers of sawdust into the crowded aisles; smooth cross-sections of dark red tuna and creamy swordfish glisten in illuminated refrigerator cases. The selection is global: slabs of Canadian and Chilean salmon; trays of Thai shrimp; Okhotsk crab; fresh bluefin tuna air-freighted from New York or Istanbul; boiled West African octopi; eels from Hamamatsu; Shikoku sea bream; and sea urchin roe from Maine repackaged in Hokkaido.

Trade in the marketplace pits hundreds of small-scale wholesalers against one another in auctions conducted in arcane hand gestures and semisecret codes. Each morning a hundred or so distinct auction arenas, each defined by and defining a singular category of commodities, attract buyers from roughly 1,500 wholesale firms. At these display auctions, the buyers crowd around open cases of fish or endless rows of whole tuna laid out across the auction floor. As the auctioneers roar on, buyers make their choices and flash their bids in flurries of rapid hand movements. At the frenetic tuna auctions, a single fresh Atlantic bluefin tuna may sell for $15,000 or $20,000 in only seconds. Elsewhere in the market—in the dried sardine and squid section, for example—where the issue of the auction is not setting price in the face of scarcity but allocating plentiful supplies among many buyers, bidding is a relaxed affair. Whether frenzied or calm, auctions are the central mechanisms for pricing and allocating seafood in the Tsukiji spot market.

As fish change hands at Tsukiji and are carted out the market's gates, the finishing touches are put on the transformation of fish into food, a process that begins when they are pulled from the water (or even before, as commercial fishers ply their craft with the market's desiderata in mind). Fish are differentiated into culturally relevant categories of commodities as they pass along channels of distribution leading to and through the complex framework of social institutions that make up the marketplace. Fish become commodities in the hands of traders whose calculations of value and utility are shaped by principles of Japanese culinary logic. The cultural valuation of commodities as they become distinctive items of cuisine is, of course, the basis for the economic valuation of these products as items of trade. The principles of Japanese food culture that dictate the menu and the market's trading mechanisms that set the table are both shaped by many factors, including the industrialization of Japan's food supply, changing patterns of domestic food preparation and consumption, and cultural concerns about culinary authenticity and national identity.

Tsukiji's auctions are pivotal in the process of defining and redefining the culturally relevant categories of commodities that are the market's stock in trade. These cultural processes are embedded in the auctions and the other social institutions of the market, which itself occupies a critical point of linkage between Tokyo's residents and the sources of their food supply, both domestic and, increasingly, global. In Ulf Hannerz's terms, Tsukiji is a central node in the networks of "provisioning roles and relationships"—the vital, yet somewhat distant, pragmatic, and instrumental connections—through which urban societies organize themselves (1980). The market and its provisioning roles are also generators of cultural meaning—they allocate and confirm the "cultural capital" of market traders, chefs, restaurateurs, and retailers who in turn fashion the social formation of "distinction" or taste (Bourdieu 1984). The relationship is threefold. Tsukiji traders possess cultural capital through their affiliation with an upscale marketplace that lays claim to great historical venerability. At the same time, their cultural positions are reproduced or reinforced daily by their central involvement in disseminating and creating the distinctions among foodstuffs upon which the restaurant trade as well as amateur connoisseurship depend (see Fine 1996). Because cuisine as a mode of consumption is so highly charged with meanings and identities that resonate with social status and hierarchy in so many realms of society at large (Bourdieu 1984, 175–201), the role of Tsukiji's traders in exercising their discrimination is an essential investment of their cultural capital, with high returns in domains of elite consumption throughout Japanese society. Thus, Tsukiji traders and the market as a whole shape and respond to the constantly shifting contexts of consumption in the daily lives of Tokyo's millions of ordinary consumers, against the backdrop of domestic change in urban Japanese society as well as its relationship to and dependence upon global supply.

Markets, Urban Life, Commodity Chains, and Consumption

Throughout history, cities and markets have sustained each other, the former providing location, demand, and social context for the latter, the latter providing sustenance, profit, and cultural verve to the former. Many anthropological studies have focused primarily on decision making within markets (Plattner 1983, 1985; Peterson 1973) or on institutional structures of market organization (Acheson 1985), although some market ethnographies relate the operations of a specific market to its urban locale and wider social-cultural milieu (Geertz 1979; Clark 1994). On a more abstract level, the interrelationships between markets and urban life along both economic and cultural dimensions have attracted much attention. Robert Redfield and Milton Singer (1954) analyzed "the cultural role of cities" and defined the marketplace as the sine qua non of what they called the "heterogenetic city," the type of city that links itself and the society of which it is a center to a wider world and, in the process, transforms the city, as well as its society more generally and the rural hinterlands that supply the city.

More recently, transnational economic, political, and social forces seem to be eroding the distinctions among cultures and societies that are implied by the Redfield-Singer perspective on cities as engines of change in the midst of distinctive and separate societies/cultures. Examining the contemporary ebbs and flows of global culture, Arjun Appadurai (1990) proposes that transnational culture today be conceptualized as "ethnoscapes," "technoscapes," "finanscapes," "mediascapes," and "ideoscapes." Very roughly, these refer to the complicated tides and undertows of people(s), of technology, of capital, of media representations, and of political ideologies that concurrently link and divide regions of the globe. Appadurai's vision of global integration (or disintegration) implies a deterritorialized world in which *place* matters little, but— viewed as a variety of "scapes"—in which there exist a series of loosely coupled domains across which this varied repertoire of influences may travel quickly, in many directions almost simultaneously. Appadurai's perspective does not give priority to one scape over another—economics need not trump media, nor need cuisine be subordinate to ethnic identity— and he recognizes that in the welter of global interactions, what may be the center or disseminator of influence in one scape may be simultaneously the periphery or recipient of influence across another scape. Ulf Hannerz (1996) makes similar points about globalization and transnationalism but refocuses them as processes mediated through world cities and the ways in which these trends of change, integration, and diversification, including the very significant impacts of trade and business, are the vehicles for massive cultural diffusion and creativity that are articulated through urban centers.

Appadurai's approach is abstract, but concrete examples of the kinds of global linkages he looks toward are easy to find (perhaps, in this chapter, as "tradescapes" and "culinascapes"). From a structural perspective, the global trade in seafood products can be seen as a complex network of "commodity chains" (Gereffi and Korzeniewicz 1994). This analysis, directly drawing on the "world systems" approach of Immanuel Wallerstein, often focuses on the production of manufactured goods through the coordinated activities of far-flung components of the so-called global factory. It examines the international division of labor into specialized realms that are integrated or coupled in multiply contingent ways, rather than by executive fiat or managerial omniscience. The structure of a commodity chain—the links, stages, phases, and hands through which a product passes as it is transformed, combined, fabricated, and distributed between ultimate producers and ultimate consumers—is a highly fragmentary and idiosyncratic social formation, itself the product of the often minutely calibrated linkages, the "provisioning relationships," that exist between every pair of hands along the way. Despite an orientation toward widely dispersed industrial production characteristic of contemporary transnational trade—Indian mills spinning cotton for Italian sweaters assembled by Latin American workers in New York—commodity chains are equally useful for understanding the fluidity of other kinds of global production and distribution, including agricultural (see Goldfrank 1994) and maritime: American fishers operating out of New England, selling bluefin tuna to American and Japanese buyers, who follow the migrating tuna up and down the Atlantic and into the Mediterranean and ship their purchases by jumbo jet to Tokyo, where they appear at auction next to tuna from the Canary Islands, Sardinia, Turkey, the Seychelles, Australia, and Fiji.

Tsukiji serves as a central node for the global seafood trade, the focal point for thousands of distinct commodity chains reaching to every corner of the global fishing industry, and the market has major influence, both domestically and internationally, on seafood prices, allocations of fishing effort, the environmental status of targeted species, and food preferences for Japanese consumers as well as for people in other countries (see Ishige et al., 1985). Analyzing the emergence of another market center, Chicago in the nineteenth century, the environmental historian William Cronon examined the reconfiguration of North American agricultural production as Chicago emerged simultaneously as both the transportation hub for the American rail system and as the production and marketing center for packed meats (Cronon 1991). These developments not only established the primacy of Chicago's markets and brought vast areas of agricultural North America into direct economic dependence on Chicago but also redefined the consumption patterns of much of the North American public with consequent realignments of local systems of production, consumption, and socioeconomic autonomy. Cronon's concrete examples of these wide-ranging processes include the ecological transformation of farming throughout the Middle West and the Great Plains, as agricultural production began to focus on supplying the stockyards, feedlots, and slaughterhouses of Chicago; the

transformation of local food production (for example, hog farming, local slaughterhouses, and local butchers) throughout the regions of the
United States served by the growing networks of railroads centered on
Chicago; and, the "industrialization of cuisine" (to use Jack Goody's
phrase—more on Goody shortly), as products manufactured far away
began to replace locally produced fresh foodstuffs, bringing changes in
the kinds and quality (nutritional as well as aesthetic) of foodstuffs as
well as in the shopping and consumption behavior of people in their
daily lives.

Similar changes continue today to alter the global production, distribution, and consumption of foodstuffs and the relationships among
different regions of the globe. The most obvious examples include the
seemingly simple, direct transplantation of elements of food culture from
one part of the world to another—sometimes called cocacolonization—
although as James Watson and his collaborators demonstrate in their
analyses of the spread of McDonald's in East Asia, local cultural and
social contexts of consumption can challenge and transform seemingly
global uniformity (Watson 1997). Other analyses of globalization and food
focus on the circulation of commodities between producer societies on
the global periphery and consumer societies of the global core. Sidney
Mintz's anthropological account of the social history of sugar places the
commodity at the intersection of imperialism, the colonization of the
Caribbean as slave societies, and Western European industrialization
(Mintz 1985). In a related vein, William Roseberry's analysis of the political economy of "yuppie coffee" in North America (Roseberry 1996)
examines the coffee trade between South and North America as it is
shaped by the growth of urban American hyper-consumerism and the
skillful marketing efforts of companies like Starbucks, thereby shaping
new structural linkages between producer and consumer societies, and
producing and reproducing new systems of cultural symbolism and identity through consumption practices.

In the latter half of the twentieth century, a variety of technological
advances—including highly efficient refrigeration and freezing technologies, the advent of global jet air cargo service, and the proliferation of
decentralized telecommunications systems such as fax, cellular telephones, and the internet—all contributed to a similar reconfiguration
of the global fishing industry, with Tsukiji as one of its major hubs. If
in the nineteenth century Chicago became Carl Sandburg's "hog butcher
for the world," at the dawn of the twenty-first century, Tsukiji has become fishmonger for the seven seas.

The role of markets is not just to organize sources of supply, however. Markets also satisfy or create demand and desire. They are the stages

upon which consumption is rehearsed and displayed. In contemporary Japanese life, consumption and commodification—displayed in consumers' shopping choices, mass media representations and promotion of consumption as essential to defining desirable lifestyles, the commodification of recreation and leisure in a mass society, the finely honed strategies of manufacturers and retailers to shape product cycles to reach increasingly finely segmented categories of consumers, and the sophisticated efforts of marketers and advertising agencies to target and reach those groups—are enormously fascinating to foreign anthropologists and sociologists. These phenomena pervade Japan today, and many recent studies demonstrate how much of contemporary Japanese society and culture can be laid bare through analyses of consumption, conspicuous and otherwise. These include White (1993) on adolescent identity, social cliques, and age groups defined in minute detail by consumption based on fads framed by media and manufacturers surfing brief product cycles; Ivy (1995) on the uncanny exoticization of Japan (to Japanese themselves) and the marketing of domestic tourism; Skov and Moeran (1995) on women, media, and consumption; Creighton (1992) on the categorical production of "Japan" and "the West" in the sales strategies of department stores; Thorn (1998) on the interactive ties among artists and fans in the production and consumption of girls' comics; Robertson (1998) on the Takarazuka musical review and the performance of gender; Kelly (1998) on regional identity and team loyalty among baseball fans; Stevens (1998) on the affective bonds between rock stars and their fans. And, of course, professional market researchers have combined practical working knowledge of product placement with insightful analyses of contemporary Japanese culture, society, and consumer behavior (e.g., Fields 1983).

Beyond these empirical examples of the complicated interplay of consumption and marketing, as meaning and commodities are framed and reframed at various levels in society, some theorists propose that consumption is the major defining social fact of contemporary Japanese life, through "the creative combining of commodities into a new pattern of signification" (Clammer 1997, 154). But such analyses often portray a disembodied late capitalism in which things are simply there for consumers to consume and to freely manipulate: "symbols not only descend from above, but are constantly reframed anew by those who consume them" (168). Yet both the consumption and production of meanings, as well as of material objects, of course, concretely take place at sites on many levels throughout society and throughout its economic system. Consumer desire may reveal cultural processes that drive consumption. But it is equally important to examine the significant ways in which markets, not only consumers, embody cultural process. Markets invest, raise, and recirculate cultural capital, even as they distribute commodities and forge linkages among different sectors of the now-global society/economy. This study examines the Tsukiji wholesale market in just such terms.

Historical Background

Institutionally the Tsukiji marketplace can trace its antecedents to the early seventeenth century, when the Tokugawa Shôgunate granted monopoly trading privileges to favored fishers who, in return for supplying the court with provisions, were allowed to establish several trade guilds at Nihonbashi at the center of Edo, as Tokyo was known until 1868. The marketplace has been at its present location in Tsukiji since 1923, when Nihonbashi was destroyed in the Kantô earthquake.

During the past century, Tokyo's fish market has undergone many radical institutional transformations. Until the 1860s it was a market constituted by feudal privilege based on guild monopolies. In the late nineteenth and early twentieth centuries until the 1920s the market operated in a highly speculative manner in the mode of unbridled laissez-faire capitalism. Seeking to curb widespread abuses of speculation in basic foodstuffs, in the 1920s the national government began to introduce a system of licensing and institutional control to create a "rational" market operating as highly regulated capitalism. This form of market was still in its infancy in the late 1930s, when militaristic regimentation introduced wartime price controls and rationing restrictions that reduced the market to little more than a distribution center. Price controls and rationing continued after World War II until the early 1950s, when these policies were rescinded and the market returned to the regulated capitalism of government licenses and institutional control that had begun in the late 1920s and early 1930s. With some minor institutional modifications, the market continues to operate within this general framework today, although the scale of operations, the value of the products handled, and the worldwide scope of Tsukiji's sources of supply all have changed radically during the past five decades.

Many present-day Tsukiji traders appropriate an aura of continuity from this rich history. This mantle of traditional identity is particularly pronounced among the small-scale traders who make up the overwhelming majority of the marketplace's intermediate wholesalers. These traders, many of whose businesses are family firms of several generations' (if not several centuries') standing, derive not only professional identity but also a more widely recognizable social identity from their claims to be direct heirs of the ancient marketplace. Most directly, some can point to their firms' standing in the fish business for four, seven, even fifteen generations. Whether "Established in 1650" or "Established in 1892," such claims carry considerable cachet. More broadly, these traders represent themselves as heirs to the mercantile traditions of Japanese business centered on small-scale family-run firms as opposed to large-scale bureaucratic, modern corporations, a contrast that has become increasingly sharp as supermarkets replace tiny grocery stores and fishmongers across Tokyo. And finally, as purveyors of fine seafoods, Tsukiji's traders—both small- and large-scale—regard themselves as stewards of Japan's culinary heritage, a significant source of cultural capital. "Traditionalism"—the appropriation of the past to cloak present-day social relations with an aura of venerable authenticity and legitimacy—is a defining feature of Japanese institutional life (Bestor 1989, 1992a, 1992b, 1996). At Tsukiji, too, reference to the past is an important component in the cultural structuring of the present.

The Social Organization of the Trade

There are two major sets of actors in the Tsukiji marketplace. One set consists of the auction houses (*oroshi gyôsha*) and their employees, including licensed auctioneers (*serinin*). The other set consists of their primary customers, roughly one thousand intermediate wholesalers and another four hundred authorized traders. Here I concentrate on the roles and organization of the intermediate wholesalers, although the analysis could be extended to include the auction houses, their suppliers, and the auctions themselves as players or mechanisms in the process of commodification.

Each night roughly 2.8 million kilograms of seafood arrive at Tsukiji, coming in tens of thousands of individual consignments ranging in size from entire truckloads of frozen tuna to shipments of only three or four small crates of fish eggs. Tsukiji's daily auctions, held six mornings a week between roughly 5:30 and 7:00, are the engines of the marketplace that reverberate throughout the entire Japanese fishing industry and reach to docks and fishing ports around the world. The auctions are highly fragmented, spatially dispersed, operationally diverse, and institutionally distinctive. There are roughly twenty major auction locations for different commodity categories scattered across the marketplace, and within each general category (e.g., tuna, shrimp, live fish) there may be several separate auctions for different grades or subcategories. The morning auctions at Tsukiji therefore comprise over one hundred distinct sales sequences that together account for between thirty thousand and fifty thousand individual transactions daily. Each separate auction is both an outcome of and a fundamentally defining force in the twin processes of cultural commodification and economic pricing. Three elements—fish, auctioneers, and intermediate wholesalers—define the auction and are in one fashion or another defined by it. Trading communities, constituted by specialist auctioneers and specialized intermediate wholesalers, define and price the fish. In turn, fish, or the seafood they are destined to become, define the trading communities.

To participate in Tsukiji's daily auctions as a buyer requires a municipal license, and there are two categories of license holders: intermediate wholesalers (nakaoroshi gyôsha) and authorized traders (baibaisankasha). The two categories are distinguished from one another by the scope of their licenses and by their typical clienteles. The intermediate wholesalers include approximately one thousand small-scale, family-held firms. Their licenses entitle them to buy at auction and to maintain stalls for reselling seafood within the marketplace.[2] Generally, the customers of intermediate wholesalers are small-scale retail fishmongers, restaurateurs, and sushi chefs. The other category, authorized traders, includes approximately four hundred buyers who are licensed to buy in bulk at auction on behalf of large consumers (such as hotels, department stores, supermarket chains, schools, and hospitals). Authorized traders are not permitted to resell products within the marketplace and may not maintain stalls there.

Although these two categories of traders are distinguished from one another by licensing and clientele, firms within both of these categories are distinguished from their peers by their individual commodity specializations and by fine-grained distinctions among the types of clientele they serve. Particularly among the intermediate wholesalers, commodity specializations are a major aspect of professional and personal identity, and these specializations form the basis within the marketplace for at least sixteen formally organized trade guilds and several dozen other subgroups, each organized by traders not only to promote friendship but also to regulate the terms of trade within a particular specialty.

The social relationships among traders, both for camaraderie and for the organization of their economic lives, suggest an important distinction which must be made between the marketplace as an institution that embodies social, cultural, and economic dimensions, and "market" in a more exclusively economic sense. Tsukiji traders use the terms ichiba (marketplace) and shijô (market) in quite distinct ways, even though both are written with the same characters and have identical underlying meanings. In a sense, ichiba is where they work each day; shijô refers to an abstract legal and economic framework for transactions. Their usage parallels my own distinction between "marketplaces" as the social institutions and physical places within which economic activity occurs (and without which real economic life cannot exist), in contrast to "markets" which I regard as the abstraction of economic activity out of its social, cultural, and spatial contexts. Thus, for example, one can speak of the market for bluefin tuna as a dispersed global network of transactions linked by common understandings and flows of information, but tuna are actually bought and sold in marketplaces, specific locations where people interact with one another in socially and culturally patterned ways.

Food Culture and Practical Reason

Clearly food culture is neither foreordained by nature nor an immutable aspect of a society's culture. Indeed, if nations are culturally "imagined communities" (Anderson 1983), then food culture equally imagines cuisines as organized around essential traits: and—other than rice—what is more essential and essentialized in Japanese cuisine than seafood? Fish and the arts associated with its preparation and consumption are central to Japan's culinary heritage. Most Japanese are highly conscious of food as an element of culture and of culture as the essential core of national identity. In English, "food culture" is a phrase used perhaps only by anthropologists and restaurant reviewers. But the equivalent Japanese expressions—*shoku bunka* and *shoku seikatsu* ("food culture" and "culinary life" respectively)—commonly appear in popular cultural commentaries on myriad details of cuisine in the Japanese press, on television, and, of course, around the marketplace. The media pay close attention to the origins of particular dishes; the harvesting and preparation of ingredients; and the proper techniques, preferred seasonal combinations, ideal implements, and appropriate accouterments for their preparation and consumption.

At Tsukiji seafood is the lifeblood of the marketplace.[3] The seas provide a seemingly infinite variety of fish, and as fish become food, they become even more intricately variegated. The marketplace plays a central role in this transformation, and not simply through the distributive processes of buying and selling fish. Rather, the Tsukiji marketplace and its counterparts throughout Japan—the fifty-six officially designated Central Wholesale Markets (*Chûô Oroshiuri Shijô*) specializing in seafood, of which Tsukiji is far and away the largest, accounting for a little more than 14 percent of the national market system's total annual tonnage (1993 figures)—are institutions where the more subtle cultural processes that differentiate fish are accomplished according to the dictates—often changing, sometimes fickle—of culinary preference. The marketplace and its daily transactions are set into motion by and delicately synchronized along cultural channels that assign meanings and uses, and hence economically calculable values, to particular species, grades, and quantities of fish. While much of the economic life of a Tsukiji trader may seem at least superficially similar to that of a trader in steel or foreign exchange or widgets, it is distinctively shaped by the simple fact that *this* marketplace revolves around perishable commodities with culturally singular connotations.

I am not talking here about the odd bits and pieces of food lore that adhere like barnacles to particular varieties of seafood. Eels served in Tokyo are slit along the back, those served in Osaka are slit along the belly. Why? Because Tokyo was a samurai town and slitting the belly was too reminiscent of ritual suicide. Why are sea bream (*tai*) so highly prized? Because of a play on words and visual imagery: *medetai* means "celebration," and the combination of the fish's reddish skin and white flesh mirrors the auspicious red-and-white color combination almost universally used on celebratory occasions in Japan, so they are served at weddings and other auspicious events. If red-and-white lobster tails are an auspicious recent addition to the celebratory menu, why aren't whole lobsters the centerpiece of wedding banquets? Because at a wedding one cannot speak of anything that cuts (the marital bond), and lobster claws look too much like scissors (which along with knives must never be given as wedding gifts). Why do so few women sell fish in the market and why are there no female sushi chefs? Because—one popular explanation runs—women's hands are warmer than men's and hence adversely affect the flavor of raw seafood.[4] Or so goes Tsukiji's folklore. Although homespun "explanations" like these give sushi chefs material for endless chatter with inquisitive foreigners, the features of culinary classification that fundamentally move the market are far more subtle and far more complex.

Writing about the process of commodification as a central feature of any economy—moral or monetized—Igor Kopytoff has argued that commodities, commonsensically defined as objects with a value both for use and for exchange, are intrinsically cultural constructions: "For the economist, commodities simply *are*. . . . From a cultural perspective, the production of commodities is also a cultural and cognitive process: commodities must be not only produced materially as things, but also culturally marked as being a certain kind of thing" (Kopytoff 1986, 64, emphasis added). Kopytoff proposes that the cultural nature of commodities and the processes of marking and classifying objects that are inherent to any system of exchange can be revealed through "cultural biographies of things." By this he means accounts of the "careers" or "life trajectories" of objects within the social contexts of their production, exchange, and consumption. Along such trajectories, objects acquire or shed meanings, identities, and implied qualities that render them worthy of use and exchange. Without this culturally constructed valuation, an object can have no value as a commodity in the sense of either social exchange or economic transaction.

This is not the place to rehearse full cultural biographies of tuna or carp or sea urchin roe. Partial biographies are nonetheless evident as one sees a fish passing from hand to hand along the channels of trade—the "commodity chains"—that lead to and from Tsukiji. The market's appraisal of a fish and its transformation into seafood reflect considerations of such diverse and culturally salient attributes as nationality, domesticity, purity and pollution (both hygienic and ritual), maturity, locality, form, and temporality (reflecting both seasonal and other calendrical concerns). These cultural markings adhere or are attached to varieties of seafood as they come forth as commodities; the details of their sale—the form, timing, and prices of transactions—reflect the outcome of this process. Tsukiji therefore constitutes a central chapter in the biographical narrative of seafood, where its varied character is constructed and embellished as fish are commodified and then consumed.

Food classifications and resulting food preferences and taboos have been the subject of much anthropological theorizing, most of it focused at the most fundamental levels. On the one hand some theorists (notably Lévi-Strauss 1966, 1970) consider classificatory schemes for foodstuffs to be manifestations of binary or triangulated structural oppositions—the raw and the cooked; smoked, roasted, or boiled; free range or genetically engineered—that represent (or simply *are*) the deep structures of human mentality. Others (e.g., Harris 1985) consider culinary preferences to be culturally explicit encodings of implicit ecological rationality. Still other theorists reject the notion that calculations of practical utility are materially based and argue instead that they are structured by the cultural or symbolic order (Sahlins 1976, 166–221). These debates are largely focused on the most basic questions posed when people encounter a potential morsel: "Is *this* food?" Such questions rarely occupy the attention of Tsukiji traders. Long before a fish has reached Tsukiji, and indeed long before the nets have even been set, Japanese food culture has resolved *that* question. My purpose is not, therefore, to test that resolution against the first principles of materialist or idealist motivation that occupy the attention of Harris or Lévi-Strauss or Sahlins.

Rather, my point is that cultural classifications of foodstuffs interact with the material circumstances of the society that produces or trades or consumes them. As Jack Goody succinctly puts it, "the presence of a concept of 'baking' [is] related to the adoption of the oven" (1982, 38).

But not only do material innovations alter the salience of food classifications; foodstuffs and the material circumstances that bring them forth are embedded in the highly fluid social, political, and economic contexts that structure both production and consumption. Food classifications do not exist entirely apart from cuisine.[5] In turn, cuisine is inextricably bound up in the complicated cultural and social contexts of eating. And neither cuisine—nor eating—can exist apart from the production and distribution of foodstuffs.

To understand how the marketplace is a cultural as well as an economic institution, closely attuned to the rhythms of metropolitan life, requires a cultural analysis of food classification applied to the institutions of trade that classify and commodify fish. Compared with the perspectives on food symbolism classically applied by anthropologists, this interpretation is a different kettle of fish.

The Industrialization of Japanese Cuisine

Since the 1940s, Japanese foodstuffs and foodways have changed enormously, following what had been already several generations of wide-ranging alterations in Japan's culinary life since the mid-nineteenth century, when Japan resumed and expanded its contacts with other societies. The recent evolution of Japanese cuisine reflects many interrelated factors, of course, including exposure to foreign cuisines, the expansion of scientific nutritional knowledge, and the development of new technologies of production, transportation, and processing.

One important result of the past few decades of dietary change in Japan is the creation of a homogenized national fare that has gradually replaced regionally varied ones based on traditional foodstuffs and locally idiosyncratic techniques of preparation. The resulting Japanese diet is often represented as the product of "Westernization." To be sure, the introduction of foreign foodstuffs and dishes—by no means exclusively Western—has had tremendous impact on the diet of the average Japanese. More fundamentally, however, the evolution of Japanese cuisine reflects the industrialization of the food supply; a phenomenon that Jack Goody (1982, 154–174) identifies for Western Europe and North America as well as for colonial Africa, whereby the entire character of a society's sustenance—selections of crops; methods of production and processing; techniques of distribution, sales, and advertising; daily rhythms of eating; and nutritional content of the daily diet—is adapted to and shaped by industrial, capital-intensive production. Typically, this "industrialization" of food results in the increasing substitution of highly standardized processed and manufactured foodstuffs for highly varied, locally produced raw and semiprocessed ones in the repertory of goods available to consumers.

This industrialization of the food supply affects both the production and processing of foodstuffs, and the economic and social institutions that distribute them. On one side of the equation, Goody points out that the nineteenth-century industrialization of food production in the West centered on new processing techniques for canning, baking, preserving, and flavoring. On the other hand, developments in food processing were inextricably linked with the creation of new forms of retailing and advertising. Proprietary brand names were attached both to newly developed products and to products that previously had been generic items in the culinary public domain. Advertising promoted brand name goods. Wide-spectrum grocers replaced specialized provisioners.

On the production side, the Japanese case includes excellent examples of traditional foodstuffs developing into industrialized products widely marketed under proprietary brand names. Kikkoman soy sauce is a case in point: Kikkoman became the world's leading producer of soy sauce by creating a nationally standardized manufactured product out of what was traditionally an item of local craft production (Fruin 1983). A more recent and more highly technological example is the transformation of traditional fish pastes into a virtually new industrial foodstuff, *surimi*, known to American consumers as "imitation crab meat," to those in the trade as "extruded pollock." At the retail level, industrialization heralds a shift away from products sold generically (e.g., soy sauce, soy paste, or *miso*, and rice), as a commodity in the economist's sense of the term, possibly distinguished by the merchant's house brand name or that of a local producer, toward brand-name goods (e.g., Kikkoman soy sauce) distributed regionally, nationally, or internationally in standardized form, interchangeably available from one retailer to the next.

Most of the effects of industrialization on Japanese seafood have been concentrated on the technologies of catching, transporting, and storing fish rather than on the creation of entirely new products. The results, therefore, are relatively invisible to consumers who find familiar seafood available for consumption in seemingly unchanging ways—although perhaps more cheaply, in greater quantity, and of higher quality than before. Of course, even if developments in production (such as fish farming) or in transportation (such as bringing fresh fish from international sources to market in Japan) are not immediately obvious to the consumer, they are linked to major transformations in the institutional structure of the fishing industry, of distribution channels such as those that converge on the Tsukiji marketplace, and of the retail sectors of the food business. As the repertoire of products available to consumers changes, so too do the sellers.

Among the institutional changes closest to the experience of consumers are the growth of supermarkets at the expense of small-scale retailers (Bestor 1990). Home cooking and home dining have declined in contemporary life as restaurants (especially large chains) have flourished. To address for the moment only the first of these trends, as standardized packaged goods become increasingly the staple products, wide-spectrum grocery stores displace narrowly specialized purveyors in all but those fields where freshness is paramount and brand names almost irrelevant. Clearly greengrocers, fishmongers, and butchers are, for several reasons, among the culinary specialists best able to resist the encroachments of supermarkets. Their fresh products are not particularly susceptible to direct displacement by industrialized foods; canned and fresh tuna are hardly interchangeable, especially in Japanese cuisine. Because the products undergo relatively little industrial processing, it is difficult to establish brand names for otherwise undifferentiated generic products (e.g., Mrs. Paul's Golden Fish Fillets versus Atlantic flounder). And because fresh products usually remain generic commodities, the skills and reputation of the individual purveyor as judge of quality remain central, their ability to discriminate and validate distinction being an important source of their cultural capital. For all these reasons, although wide-spectrum grocery stores and supermarkets can try to duplicate the specialties of the greengrocer, the fishmonger, and the butcher, even a deluxe superstore cannot redefine all culinary specialties so completely that the skills of the independent merchant are rendered obsolete.

Domesticity and Cuisine

Against the changing supply side of the Japanese seafood business, shaped by industrialization (including aquacultural technology) and international trade, the consumption patterns of ordinary Japanese also have changed enormously in recent decades. But culinary homogenization, rising standards of food preference, the renewed celebration of fresh ingredients and of regional cuisine, and other changes in the Japanese diet have not occurred solely because of technological advances in production, supply, or distribution. They result particularly from wider social changes in Japan over the past generation or so, many of which at first glance bear little direct relationship to food culture. A few examples may sketch some of the ways in which Japanese culinary habits are shaped by the changing social contexts of cuisine that result from other, much more general changes in the lives of ordinary Japanese.

Rising levels of per capita income have led to greater disposable income and the greater consumption of "luxury" foods, both domestic and imported, as well as to what Japanese marketers like to call the "gourmet boom" (*gurume bûmu*). In the seafood realm, for example, live fish have become extremely popular in the past decade, and trendy restaurants and retail fish markets flaunt their expensive fare with large, well-stocked tanks from which a patron may select a specific fish to be prepared for the coming meal or packaged to take home.

In the past few decades, the palate of Japanese tastes has broadened to include an ever widening array of foreign culinary specialties. These changes have coincided with the expansion of Japan's role as a global economic superpower and the increasing opportunities for international travel by ordinary Japanese for both business and recreation. At the same time, foreign restaurant chains (such as Kentucky Fried Chicken and McDonald's [see Ohnuki-Tierney 1997]) have aggressively entered the Japanese domestic market, and Japanese food producers have themselves eagerly promoted new foodstuffs and new dishes.

Many nominally foreign dishes have become so much a part of prevailing Japanese mass market tastes as to be now virtually indigenous: curried rice, kimchee (*kimuchi*), and McDonald's hamburgers are obvious illustrations. In Japan, unlike the United States, immigration and urban ethnic diversity have not been major sources of culinary innovation. A recent exception is the increased popularity of Southeast Asian cuisine as immigrants from that region have become numerous. And, of course, Korean and Chinese cuisine are widely available in Japan, a legacy of Japan's imperial expansion before 1945 and, in the case of Korea, the large numbers of Koreans who were brought, sometimes forcibly, to Japan and whose descendants still form a distinct minority population.

In some cases, dishes from other culinary traditions, while retaining a "foreign" label, have been thoroughly adapted to Japanese tastes: sea urchin pizza, for example, or hearty fish sausages. But international culinary cross-fertilization is not one-sided; "Japanese" cuisine has simultaneously diffused abroad and sometimes rediffused back "home." Even as sushi has become an icon of North American yuppie tastes, and as *nouvelle cuisine* has become a major influence at the highest echelons of the international cuisine, the "Franco-Japonaise" culinary style currently popular in New York and Los Angeles has swept *haute* Tokyo as well.[6]

Japanese domestic living arrangements have also affected the social context of cuisine. Since the mid-1950s, the appliance revolution in home furnishings has saturated Japanese homes with everything from refrigerators, gas ranges, and electric rice cookers to microwave ovens, automatic bread makers, and devices that can make rice cakes (*mochi*) from scratch. The high-tech inventory of an ordinary Tokyo domestic kitchen today stands in stark contrast to the meager lists of household goods compiled by Dore in the early 1950s, when only 12.6 percent of households owned iceboxes (not refrigerators) (Dore 1958, 51–52).

Households—and hence the domestic hearth—have themselves changed considerably. Throughout urban and rural Japan, nuclear and quasi-nuclear families have become the norm even if not the universal ideal. Not only are family units smaller on the average, they are less likely to include members of several generations. Even when extended families live together, it is not uncommon for the generations to maintain somewhat separate cooking facilities and eating schedules (Kelly 1986). The increasingly individualistic schedules of young and old alike have eroded patterns of family dining. Children returning late from cram-schools may eat separately from their parents and siblings, and numerous surveys show that the average urban male white-collar employee eats dinner at home less often than he eats out.[7] Particularly in urban areas, single-person households—of the very old and of those just coming of age—have become common. Recently, in some urban areas, so-called one-room mansions (condominium studio apartments) have almost entirely replaced family dwellings. Taken together, the culinary impact of these trends is profound. More and more foodstuffs consumed at home are commercially prepared fast foods for the home microwave packaged in single-serving portions. And fewer and fewer home cooks learn or feel comfortable with traditional culinary skills. Tsukiji traders joke about possibly apocryphal young brides who do not own an ordinary kitchen cleaver or who misconstrue the standard culinary techniques of *sanmai oroshi* (filleting a whole fish) and *daikon oroshi* (grating a radish) as the same thing.

As the culinary connotations of home and hearth have diminished, the range of domestic responsibilities—or at least expectation of their accomplishment—has been altered. Traditionally, women were expected to take charge of all aspects of household food preparation, and Japanese women typically have been highly concerned with their families' diet, nutrition, and health (Lock 1980, 73–74, 104–106). Although contemporary women may be expected to know more than their mothers or grandmothers about a much wider and more varied range of culinary styles (e.g., domesticated versions of Chinese, Indian, Italian, and French cuisine) and to have a repertoire of fancy dishes for special occasions, in other senses women today neither know, nor need to know, as much about basic foodstuffs or start-from-scratch culinary techniques as did females in earlier generations. Many ordinary consumers with whom I have talked admit freely that they do not know how to make many of the dishes they ate as children (although they can put together much fancier meals with the aid of prepared and semiprepared ingredients from grocery stores). Both male and female workers at Tsukiji express similar though more pointedly negative opinions about the cooking abilities of most Tokyo women today.[8]

Suzanne Vogel's essay (1978) on the "professional housewife" points out that bridal training classes (*hanayome shugyô* or *o-keikogoto*) generally include education in culinary arts. Rather than focusing on everyday skills of domestic cooking, however, the training often revolves around preparation of special dishes for formal events—such as the elaborate, highly stylized cuisine, known as *o-sechi ryôri,* for the New Year holiday. But today there is no need to make this cuisine from scratch. *O-sechi* dishes are widely available commercially, from traditional mom-and-pop purveyors and increasingly from supermarkets, convenience stores, and department stores as entire packaged banquets. The 7–11 chain does a booming business catering urban family New Year parties. Millie Creighton (personal communications) has mentioned one department store that provides a total package for the home holiday banquet that includes not only the food but also housecleaning beforehand!

Although commercial alternatives to home cooking are ever increasing, the popularity of cooking classes at private academies as well as at municipal adult education centers suggests that many Japanese women at one point or another in their domesticated careers as brides-to-be, wives, and mothers enroll in formal culinary training. Culinary competence appears, at least in some cases, to be intensely competitive. For example, Anne Allison's analysis (1991) of mothers preparing box lunches (*o-bentô*) for their nursery school children illustrates that the task is framed on the one hand by enormous social pressures to prove one's mothering skills and on the other hand by cultural constraints that resonate with issues of culinary nationalism in the selection and presentation of "appropriate" foods.

As the industrialization of food diminishes this aspect of women's traditionally defined roles as "good wives and wise mothers" (*ryôsai kenbo,* to use the ideologically charged phrase for women's expected roles in the period before World War II), it accentuates the alienation of women from the world of professional culinary accomplishment and specialized knowledge that characterizes Tsukiji, from which the largely male population of Tsukiji traders draws considerable professional pride. It also alters some of the criteria by which Tsukiji traders themselves judge food.

One comment frequently made to me at Tsukiji is that women (that is, housewives; an equation almost universally held by workers at Tsukiji, both male and female) are neither familiar with raw ingredients nor particularly comfortable with them. An easy familiarity with ingredients and a willingness to substitute or make do based on what the marketplace can provide does not characterize the ordinary consumer's approach to grocery shopping. As one supermarket executive put it to me, many Japanese consumers are "uneasy" about fresh foods. To the "nervous" eyes of a shopper, this executive grumbled, even blemishes having no possible link to either the food value or the usability of the product may damn it: cucumbers must be straight, the cherries' stems must be uniform in length, the fish's tail must be unscarred, a package of several sardines must not be mismatched by size. Many shoppers have highly detailed ideas about what constitutes idealized perfection for any given item of fresh food. That is, the executive told me, his suppliers constantly have to worry about ideal outward form, an attribute known as *kata*.[9]

If the role of food preparation within the home is being redefined, so too is the relationship between home and food consumption. Car culture—what David Plath (1992) calls "my-car-isma"—increasingly drives domestic groups to meals at "family restaurants." The American restaurant chain Denny's and its many Japanese clones now have thousands of such restaurants in urban areas and along major highways. Not only do they promise an enjoyable meal as part of a simple outing in the family car but their varied menus allow guests to order individualistically, anything from grilled fish (*yakizakana*) to beef stroganoff. Some major chains, such as Kyôtaru, however, offer fare from a single culinary spectrum with menus almost entirely devoted to seafood—mostly in "traditional" Japanese dishes—extending from sushi to *nabemono* (a sort of bouillabaisse, often but not always made with seafood).[10] Whether their menus are confined to a "Japanese" culinary realm or are more "international" in their appeal, all such restaurants offer a range of dishes far more eclectic than do traditional Japanese restaurants, which typically specialize in a particular culinary genre, whether *tonkatsu* (pork cutlets), sushi, tempura, or *râmen* noodles. Customers in these new-style family restaurants are much more likely to order individually—grilled fish for Dad, coquille St. Jacques for Mom, cod roe spaghetti for the kids—in marked contrast to traditional restaurants where customers frequently match their orders to those of their tablemates.

The growth of these "family restaurants" is only one facet of what those in the food business call the "eating-out boom" (*gaishoku bûmu*). Trade publications regularly report surveys that show rapid increases in the percentage of meals eaten outside the home and in the percentage of total household food expenditures spent on meals in restaurants.

Retailers naturally view this trend with alarm; restaurateurs compete more fiercely for market share.

Although the "eating-out boom" is a current buzz word, it is really little more than a blip within much larger changes that are reshaping the retail world, the restaurant industry, the food processing industry, and Japanese culinary habits generally. These include such trends as the spread of convenience stores and large-scale supermarkets at the expense of old-fashioned small-scale local retailers and the growing popularity of convenience foods and newly developed industrial foods that are replacing the traditional raw or only semiprocessed ingredients upon which earlier generations of consumers relied.

The burden (and the profit) of provisioning the urban Japanese household has begun to shift from neighborhood mom-and-pop stores to convenience stores and supermarkets. The old-fashioned local shops are often quite specialized, dealing in *saké*, or fish, or rice, or vegetables, or pickles. Although such shops, of course, handle at least some nationally known brand-name goods, their stock in trade is frequently items that are almost generic commodities for which the merchant's reputation (either as processor, for example, of home-made pickles, or as knowing buyer, for example, of fresh fish or produce) is important to the shop's clientele. That is, one buys from Mr. Saito's fish shop with the knowledge—or at least the hope—that Mr. Saito personally selected only good quality fish when he visited the Tsukiji marketplace, and perhaps because Mrs. Saito's homemade pickles are your family's favorite; the fact that they are neighbors and know your children adds to the relationship.

On the other hand, supermarkets deal largely in brand-name merchandise, where the reputational stakes are held more by manufacturers and less by merchants; the supermarket's stock in trade is the promise of convenience and greater variety for the daily diet, and, sometimes, a lower price. As a shopper, you bypass the Saito shop for the Daiei supermarket (maybe returning along a back street to avoid flaunting your purchases), hoping to shave a few yen off your bill, knowing that the freezer case is full of Nichirei's ready-to-heat fish cakes and that at the fresh fish counter something of everything—not Mr. Saito's more limited and idiosyncratic selection—will be available, even if each fish was weighed to the closest gram after it was cleaned, labeled, and wrapped several hours earlier.

But other countertrends help sustain traditional, small-scale merchants and restaurateurs in the face of supermarkets and franchised family restaurants. The "eating-out boom" parallels a "gourmet boom" for high-priced and often esoteric foodstuffs. As what were formerly considered luxury foods are increasingly ordinary items in the daily diet of many if not most Japanese, the frontiers of conspicuous consumption are pushed back. One trend, therefore, is to create demand for ever higher standards of freshness, a trend that has led Japan Air Lines to develop anaerobic technology to transport jet loads of live fish in hibernation with almost no water. (Jet cargoes of fresh fish have become so common, the stale joke at Tsukiji runs that Japan's leading fishing port is now Narita International Airport.)

Not surprisingly, another fertile field for epicurean imagination is to search for the culinary authenticity of the past. In what I call the gentrification of taste, regional culinary styles have been rediscovered by urban restaurateurs and retailers. The hallmarks of such cuisines—emphasis on fresh, locally produced foodstuffs, often prepared in locally idiosyncratic combinations or manners—amply meet the demands for fresh and "natural" food that is culturally authentic, yet esoteric enough to have cachet. Of course, for those in the business, the ingredients can command a hefty premium.

Goody's analysis of cuisine discusses the relationship between class structure, the existence or elaboration of "high" and "low" cuisines, and the forms of food production common within a society (1982, 97–153). Not surprisingly, industrial food is deeply embedded in class structures, and although Goody does not address the gentrification of taste or the re-discovery and elevation of regional cuisine, it is simple to extrapolate the phenomenon that Appadurai (1986) identifies as concern with "culinary authenticity" as a postindustrial response to what Goody identifies as an earlier "industrialization" of food. On the one hand, this process shifted the balance away from locally available, rather generic or anonymous forms to nationally known brand-name commodities; on the other hand, in the postindustrial economy, formerly anonymous local foodstuffs have now acquired cachet as brand-name merchandise. One Japanese example is the recent renaissance in locally brewed *saké* (known as *jizake*), which has—as a genre of brand-name goods—limited distribution but national (if esoteric) prestige among connoisseurs, somewhat analogous to the recent popularity of local microbreweries in the United States. As yet, although seafood has not yet undergone the same brand-name transformation, the reinvigorated popularity of particular local specialties seems to be roughly parallel.

But as I have emphasized earlier, the industrialization of the food supply (or in this case reactions against it) not only shapes products but also affects its purveyors. As the "gourmet boom" and the gentrification of taste reshape Japanese preferences, they also refocus attention on the independent merchant whose implicit stock in trade is the specialized knowledge and discernment that enables a merchant to supply the newly minted connoisseur with items of appropriate quality. As the "gourmet boom" intersects with the "eating-out boom," both old-fashioned retail fishmongers and their supermarket competitors strive to position themselves to meet consumers' varied and often contradictory demands. Retail fishmongers struggle to improve the quality of the fish they sell and to stock increasingly fancy and exotic species, as well as to instruct consumers both in basic culinary techniques and in the familiar uses of unfamiliar varieties. Supermarkets put increasing emphasis on selling seafood that is already cleaned, sliced, and even arranged on platters, accompanied with the necessary condiments to make home cooking as simple as possible; some try to reduplicate the service traditionally provided by the old-fashioned neighborhood fishmonger.[11] Traders at Tsukiji try to adjust their product mix and their clientele base accordingly, wondering if the future holds a system of brands for fresh seafood and, if so, whether they, like retail merchants, will find the real value of their reputations as judges of seafood deflated.

Culinary Authenticity and International Dependency

Foreigners and Japanese alike generally regard raw seafood as one of the pillars of "authentic" Japanese cuisine. Inverting Claude Lévi-Strauss's famous dichotomy, Emiko Ohnuki-Tierney observes, "For the Japanese raw or uncooked food is *food*, while in other cultures food usually means *cooked* food. The raw in Japanese culture thus represents culturalized nature; like a rock garden in which traces of [the] human hands that transformed nature into culturalized nature have been carefully erased, the raw food of the Japanese represents a highly crafted cultural artifact presented as natural food" (1990, 206, emphasis added). Arjun Appadurai ascribes concern over "culinary authenticity" to outsiders rather than to "native participants in a culinary tradition" and goes on to say that "the concern with authenticity indicates some sort of doubt, and this sort of doubt is rarely part of the discourse of an undisturbed cuisine" (1986, 25). Yet doubt need not be an outsider's prerogative. Doubt and its attempted resolution are pervasive features of Japanese cultural encounters with themselves-as-others throughout the postwar period (Bestor 1989, 1996; Gluck and Graubard 1992; Kelly 1990; Ivy 1995). And cuisine appears to offer ample and authentic grounds for cultural concern.

Despite the enormous culinary changes of the past generation— or perhaps precisely because of them—many Japanese maintain a strong conceptual sense of "Japanese cuisine" as a distinct category: *wa-shoku* ("Japanese food") as opposed to *yô-shoku* ("Western food"). The identification of a distinctive Japanese cuisine, of course, is an allegation of historical continuity and stability (see Bestor 1989, Kelly 1990).

Yet like all other aspects of "tradition," food culture constantly evolves. Many dishes and delicacies now widely regarded as hallmarks of Japanese cuisine—by foreigners as well as by Japanese—are actually of relatively recent introduction or invention. For example, even the basic form of sushi, a thin slice of fish atop a compact oblong block of vinegared rice—the style of sushi characteristic of Tokyo's cuisine and now the world's de facto sushi standard—was an innovation of the mid-nineteenth century. The particular style of Edo-Tokyo sushi, called *nigiri-zushi* ("squeezed" or "hand-molded" sushi) or *Edomae-zushi* (sushi from "in front of Edo"), was developed only in the 1820s or 1830s (Omae and Tachibana 1981, 105; Yoshino 1986, 16).

One common story of *nigiri-zushi*'s origins puts it in the hands of a famed sushi chef, Hanaya Yohei (1799–1858), who invented or perfected the technique in 1824 at his shop in Ryôgoku (then one of Edo's major entertainment districts), a shop that survived until the 1930s.

Omae and Tachibana quote a nineteenth-century verse celebrating the shop:

Crowded together, weary with waiting
Customers squeeze their hands
As Yohei squeezes sushi

Sushi shops named Yohei Zushi are still common. Presumably the name is meant to imply descent from the eponymous ancestor by suggesting that the shops were established by apprentices of the original Yohei who were permitted to retain and use their master's name.

Many of the present varieties of *nigiri-zushi* made with extremely fresh seafood were not even possible until the advent of mechanical re-frigeration in the mid-twentieth century. And tastes in toppings have changed dramatically, as well: until about a generation ago *toro*—the fatty flesh from tuna bellies that is now the quintessential high-priced sushi topping—was held in such low regard that it was given away as cat food (Omae and Tachibana 1981, 12, 104–105; Watanabe 1991, 26). To appreciate fully what a lowly status this implied for *toro*, one must know that the Japanese "cultural biography" of cats casts them not as adorable house pets but as necessary domestic nuisances, useful for catching rats but otherwise pests themselves (see Smith 1992, 23–24). Worse yet for *toro*'s status, even at Tsukiji until the 1950s *toro* was referred to as "fish that even a cat would disdain" (*neko-matagi*) (Watanabe 1991, 26).

As Japanese cuisine (in the marked sense of "Japanese") has evolved, it has done so within a context of increasing dependence on imported foodstuffs. Japan's dominant position in international trade flows is, in a sense, another dimension of the industrialization of Japan's seafood supply. Developments in transportation as well as Japan's economic power have created systems of trade capable of supplying Japan with large amounts of imported fresh and frozen fish, but their reception is distinctly ambivalent. Japan has long since ceased to be self-sufficient in any category of foodstuff except rice.[12] Imported fish supply basic protein and calories to a food-poor country but also provide one of the centerpieces of Japanese cuisine. Although Japan's food dependency is unavoidable and makes policy sense in terms of comparative and absolute trade advantages, it is a trade imbalance fraught with cultural tension.

The mass media have made the issue of food dependency widely known. A recurrently popular topic for newspaper articles around the New Year is to illustrate Japanese food dependency by cataloging the extent to which preparation of even the most resolutely traditional of Japanese feasts, the distinctive cuisine for the New Year's holidays (*o-sechi*), now relies largely on imported basic foodstuffs. The question of food dependency, of course, has practical political and economic dimensions involving the reliability of Japanese allies and the international flow of trade.[13] As such, protectionist responses—expressed through vigorous defense of Japanese agricultural and fisheries producers—often take the potent form of defending Japanese economic interests by linking them with Japanese cultural identity and its culinary components.

Many foodstuffs now or recently the subjects of recurring trade disputes—such as rice, beef, citrus fruits, and seafood—are also the subjects of intense cultural commentary in contemporary Japan. Some—oranges and beef are notable examples—have become rallying symbols for Japanese economic and cultural nationalism largely because they are focal points for disputes in international trade, not because of any particularly significant cultural overtones related to traditional aspects of their production and consumption. Other foodstuffs, like rice and seafood, are invested with pervasive cultural symbolism that is almost instantly evoked when foreign challenges arise (see Ohnuki-Tierney 1993).

Seafood derives some of its symbolic salience in the eyes of contemporary Japanese from its position in the contemporary political economy of world trade and marine resource management, and the disputes that rage around whales, tuna, dolphins, squid, and the tangled issues of drift-net fishing. Like rice, seafood occupies a special symbolic niche in Japanese cuisine both because of long history and because it is so frequently marked—by foreigners and Japanese alike—as an essential and distinctive element of Japanese cuisine, and by extension, of fundamental orientations embodied in Japanese culture itself.

Since cuisine is central to cultural identity, imported foodstuffs—though vital to the national diet—perhaps seem less culturally filling, but other issues are raised as well. Concerns about freshness and purity are a normal part of any food culture. In Japan, however, purity and pollution both have multiple meanings, and unease over dietary matters is widespread. The Japanese public in the past generation or so has repeatedly come up against environmental, social, and political issues involving the fundamental integrity and viability of Japan's food supply. On the one hand extensive folklore on links between cancer and the diet have been at least partially borne out in scientific studies that suggest such Japanese favorites as flame-grilled fish (*yakizakana*) may contribute to the incidence of stomach cancer. On the other hand, the horrendous pollution cases of the 1960s and 1970s frequently first came to public attention through contaminated fish.

During the late 1980s, concern over food preservatives and additives used in American processed foods became an issue around which Japanese agricultural protectionists were able to rally widespread support in opposition to liberalizing food imports from the United States. Even the Japan Socialist Party, long dependent on urban voters who might be expected to favor agricultural trade liberalization as a means to lower food costs, managed to straddle the issue by opposing liberalization, nominally on the grounds of protecting Japanese consumers from food adulterated with excessive preservatives and other contaminants.

Along yet another dimension, foreign foods are often regarded as simply inferior. All other things being equal, *kokusan* ("domestically harvested or produced") foodstuffs will be favored over imports. Thus, although sea urchin roe from Hokkaido and from Maine are indistinguishable, Hokkaido roe command a premium at Tsukiji. (And, of course, the indistinguishability and the premium give rise to grumbling by American producers that some Japanese importers repackage Maine roe in Hokkaido before sending it to the marketplace.) The preference for domestically produced foodstuffs may in part reflect fundamental Japanese parochialism, but it also reflects the issue of "idealized form," *kata*, and the inability of foreign producers to live up to Japanese standards. The ideal of perfect external form adds an extra dimension to assessing foodstuffs. The slightest blemish, the smallest imperfection, or the most trivial deviation from a foodstuff's idealized form can make a product—or entire shipment—languish unsold. That is, the product's outward form, its *kata*, must be perfect, since imperfection outside may signal imperfection within, just as the etiquette of wrapping gifts communicates the ritual as well as hygienic purity of a package's contents (Hendry 1990).

Even where concern over the integrity of the inner product is not directly at issue, the question of *kata* bedevils the international fish trade.

An American lobster producer from California once told me that he had given up trying to ship lobsters to Japan. Apparently his Japanese broker rejected sample shipment after sample shipment, complaining that the individual lobsters in each lot were too varied in size. "I gave up. I don't sort that carefully for anybody," the American exporter told me disdainfully. Instead, he concentrates on the American restaurant market, where the normal lobster dinner is served individually and often priced according to the weight of the lobster. Even if people dining together all order lobster, they are unlikely to compare their individual lobsters closely, and if they do, the differences in price by size will usually account for any obvious disparities.

Across the Pacific, a Tsukiji lobster trader tells another side to the story. "Hotel banquet halls buy almost all the lobsters at Tsukiji. The auspicious red-and-white color of lobster tail makes it very popular at wedding banquets. Everybody's plate has to look exactly like the one next to it. If a guest sees that his lobster tail is smaller than the person sitting next to him, everyone gets uncomfortable."

Almost every Tsukiji trader who deals in imported fish has his favorite horror story about the improper handling of fish by foreign producers and brokers; in retelling these tales they return again and again to issues of Japanese food preferences as they are made manifest through "Tsukiji specs," the demanding specifications that the Tsukiji auction houses expect suppliers to adhere to—and which foreign exporters often seem to ignore or dismiss, according to Tsukiji traders. One salmon dealer, for example, recounted with dismay his visit to an Alaskan fishing port where salmon were being unloaded by crew members wielding pitchforks, rendering the lacerated fish unsalable in Japan. He went on to show me how even the size and placement of an external scar could make a difference. A scar running lengthwise along a salmon (parallel to the spine) would make the fish unsalable as a filet; on the other hand, a fish scarred at right angles to the spine could be salvaged because it could be cut into slices or salmon steaks and the portion with the damaged skin simply discarded.

Finally, although the Japanese appetite for fish is enormous, and enormously varied, Japanese consumers are conservative in adopting new species of seafood. As one Tsukiji broker, with long experience in managing imports, told me, "I always tell foreign producers who want to sell at Tsukiji to look carefully at what is on sale here, then go home and find the fish that is closest to what you saw here. Send us that one, don't send us anything unfamiliar." Far from breeding contempt, familiarity makes for peace of mind, for an acceptance bred by the reassurances of safety and predictability that are encoded in preferences for domestic products and in the reliance on *kata* as an index of both purity and culinary authenticity.

The Wild and the Caged

Fish cultivation, or aquaculture, has been practiced for centuries in Japan, and in recent decades Japanese developments in aquacultural technology have been enormously successful, both in increasing domestic production of species (such as eels and shrimp) that have long been cultivated and in exploring techniques for cultivating species that are generally free-ranging. Vast amounts of salmon, for example, are raised through aquaculture. And although tuna is a highly migratory fish that normally ranges across broad swaths of the ocean, in the past decade Japanese researchers have come close to producing cultivated tuna in quantities and qualities suitable for commercial exploitation; other Japanese fisheries scientists are even more ambitious in attempting to cultivate whales in captivity for food production.

As a form of industrial food, cultivated fish have been particularly popular in the supermarket and mass-market restaurant industries, where there is great year-round demand for large quantities of highly standardized seafood. Cultivation is popular among producers and shippers as well, for it regularizes capital expenditures and product flows and at least gives the appearance of minimizing risks associated with other forms of fishing. But Tsukiji traders and their professional customers, like sushi chefs, draw an important conceptual distinction between "wild" or "natural" fish (that is, those hunted and caught by fishers operating in open waters) and cultivated fish.[14] Tsukiji traders usually regard cultivated fish as inferior to their "wild" cousins, and all other things being equal, a wild fish (whether live, fresh, or frozen) will command a premium over its comparable cultivated cousin. The conceptual dimension of wild versus cultivated roughly parallel to distinctions between pure and impure, and to domestic versus foreign.

Generally, cultivated fish are thought to be inferior in such things as fat content, firmness and tone of flesh, and flavor; all these are regarded as consequences of raising fish in captivity where they eat an unvarying diet of prepared feed and cannot range freely. Their image in the marketplace is also tainted by fears of the potential hazards posed by contaminated feeds; the fact that much aquaculture takes place in Japanese coastal waters, which, at least in popular thinking, are likely to be contaminated by various forms of perhaps as yet undiscovered industrial pollution; or the possibility that illness may spread throughout an entire batch kept in close captivity. These very real environmental dangers, along with the effects of speculative investments that have cre-

ated an overcapacity for some forms of cultivation, actually make aquaculture a highly risky venture. Adding insult to market risk is the fact
that even if a producer gets cultivated fish safely to market, they may
be disdained and devalued by traders and culinary professionals.

Although the average consumer might well share environmental fears
over the purity of cultivated fish—and perhaps would hold them more
strongly than professionals—the typical shopper or restaurant guest is
unlikely to know much about aquaculture or be able to distinguish a
cultivated from a wild fish. Under such conditions, the snob appeal of
connoisseurship flourishes. Premier sushi bars and elite restaurants
(*ryôtei*) that specialize in classical Japanese cuisine make a point of *not*
serving cultivated seafood, and some, to underscore their elite menus,
will even avoid serving the "wild" versions of seafood that are widely
available in cultivated form. Cultivated seafood thus ends up in processing plants, supermarkets, and the kitchens of large restaurant chains.

Time to Eat

The cultural beliefs and social practices that define
foodstuffs and shape their consumption are also embedded in temporal
patterns of Japanese life, some that are quite contemporary and others
that have venerable pedigrees; some linked to rites of passage and cycles
of holidays and others to the flow of secular time. In the contemporary
commercialized culture of consumption, time plays an important role
in defining tastes and preferences among consumers, and therefore in
shaping conditions of supply and demand in the marketplace.

Some secular patterns are immediately obvious. Weekends stimulate demand across the board; bars and restaurants stock up for their
increased trade, and retailers buy heavily on Fridays and Saturdays, both
because weekends are busy shopping days and because the marketplace
is closed on Sundays.[15] The major monthly paydays for salaried employees also stimulate demand at Tsukiji for somewhat fancier than average grades of seafood.

The political calendar plays its role, too. When Tokyo is the site of
a major international summit meeting or when an important head of state
pays a visit to Tokyo, the demand for expensive seafood drops. Why?
Because the tight security imposed on central Tokyo encourages ordinary citizens to stay at home and not frequent the entertainment districts. And the exclusive Japanese-style restaurants (*ryôtei*) and sushi bars
of the major hotels suffer a loss in business as high-rolling Japanese guests
are replaced by foreign dignitaries with little appetite for the more exotic and expensive seafood delicacies that are these restaurants' normal
stock in trade.

Similarly, the cultural politics of contemporary life makes itself felt. When the pall of the Shôwa Emperor's impending death lingered over Tokyo from September 1988 until early January 1989, many normal recreational activities were curtailed in the name of "self-restraint." Along with other industries, the restaurant trade suffered, and demand by hotels, ryôtei, and sushi restaurants dropped dramatically for several months.

The annual cycle of holidays and festivals also underscores links among time, food culture, and consumption. The New Year, O-Shôgatsu, is the most prominent example, with virtually its own distinctive cuisine for the holiday (more distinctive than, say, an ordinary American Christmas or Thanksgiving dinner, which includes many elements of cuisine that are typical of many other meals of the year). The typical New Year's banquet, an elaborate buffet of traditional delicacies, makes great use of seafood, including some varieties, such as herring roe (kazunoko), that are virtually synonymous with the New Year's holidays. But throughout the year, dozens of other holidays, both national and local, have a culinary component, and even those not explicitly associated with any specific cuisine stimulate demand for the festive meals that normally accompany any holiday.

The simple passing of the seasons is, of course, obvious in almost any food culture. Little explanation is needed to account for varying tastes that reflect the bounty of harvest times, the seasons in which particular kinds of seafood are freshest and most plentiful, the depths of winter when hearty soups and stews are preferred, or seasons of scarcity when pickled dishes take the place of fresh ones.

But Japanese culture marks the passing of time even more finely. Each day of the Japanese year has its unique constellation of cultural undertones that can, at least potentially, shape its culinary character. Several sets of calendrical considerations—seasonal and ritual—can interact to define the types of foodstuffs appropriate or ideal for that particular day. Obviously no individual in his or her own domestic life is likely to give thought to—let alone base a daily diet on—all the possible permutations. But the arcane complexities of the calendar as it relates to food consumption exist nonetheless, and they form part of the background against which patterns of consumption and of marketplace demand ebb and flow.

One feature of this calendrical precision is the system of rokuyô, a six-day cycle of ritually lucky and unlucky days; these days are listed in almanacs and on many calendars as an aid to determining appropriate days for funerals, weddings, and other ritual events. The day known as Taian ("Great Peace"), for example, is favored for weddings; Tsukiji wholesalers who supply hotels and catering firms in the wedding business can thus roughly anticipate that the demand for sea bream, lobster, and other seafoods popular for wedding banquets will fluctuate more or less predictably according to the complicated intersections of this ritual cycle with other secular cycles (such as weekends and national holidays).

Another aspect of the passing of time is the customary Japanese division of the year into twenty-four segments of roughly two weeks apiece. Each such mini-season (*sekki*) has its own distinctive name, evocative of weather conditions or agricultural phenomena. And each mini-season is marked by a vast array of such things as appropriate greetings, artistic motifs, poetic allusions, recreations, festivities, rituals, styles of traditional clothing, and of course cuisine. Particular kinds of seafood or specific dishes are often regarded as hallmarks of a mini-season.

An especially apt example is the midsummer Day of the Ox (*doyô no ushi no hi*), a day that falls sometime in late July or early August, traditionally considered the hottest period of the year, when one is supposed to eat eel to maintain one's stamina against the withering heat. A dish of broiled eel filets, called *kabayaki*, is the particular specialty of the Day of the Ox. On this day, eel restaurants have lines of waiting customers stretching around the block, supermarkets schedule special sales of eel, and the eel trade is in full frenzy. One common explanation for the popularity of eel on this particular day holds that the high oil and protein content of grilled eel especially fortifies the stomach against the midsummer heat. The calendrical symbolism that reinforces this set of beliefs and sustains consumption is complex, involving the intersection of several different aspects of marking time, including the twenty-four mini-seasons, as well as a further division of the year into phases that correspond to the five elements of Chinese cosmology: wood, fire, earth, metal, and water. Although the origins and symbolism of the custom are arcane, the Day of the Ox is obviously not an obscure consideration for any Tsukiji dealer in eels, for any restaurateur, or for any supermarket manager planning July's sales campaigns, since the period around the Day of the Ox accounts for about one-third of annual eel sales.[16]

Culinary calendars are culturally constructed in other ways as well. Particularly with seafood, seasonality (known as *shun*, a term that also indicates a traditional measure of time, equivalent to one-third of a month) of course is a significant temporal feature of cuisine.

"First things" (of the year or the season), called *hatsumono*, are the flagships of seasonality, setting the values (both economic and cultural) that are assigned to commodities in the marketplace. The first catches arriving in the marketplace (known to market insiders as *hatsuni* ("first shipments")) are heralded with high prices and intense competition among wholesalers eager to obtain scarce supplies. First shipments arrive accompanied by ceremonial fanfare, banners, and delegations of fisheries representatives; the beginning of the market year each January 5 is celebrated by traders who perform complicated clapping rhythms (based on traditional rituals of Edo's merchant quarters) that precede the auction for the year's first tuna, all recorded by television cameras for the national evening news broadcasts.

Retail shops and restaurants mark the seasons of *hatsumono* with special sales and special menus, and the availability of a particular seafood marks the passing of the seasons in the public eye as well in the market's calendar. For Edokko (the stereotypical denizen of Edo's merchant districts, born and bred in the city), the first bonito of the year—*hatsugatsuo*—was emblematic of civic identity (and masculinity). One seventeenth-century verse exulted: "To be a man, born in Edo, and eat the first bonito." (Of course, eager anticipation of the first of a new crop is hardly unique to Japanese culinary habits. And today, just as jumbo jets arrive at Narita airport with cargoes of fresh seafood from around the world, they also arrive in season laden with nouvelle Beaujolais to ensure that Tokyo's sommeliers are among the first to decant the new vintage.)

Seasonality plays an important role in defining varieties of seafood, not just by availability and quality but by their essential characteristics. That is, fish of the same species may be known by different names depending on the time of year they are caught, their size, their maturity, or the location in which they are caught—all of which may, of course, be closely interrelated. Yellowtail, for example, is known variously (depending on the maturational level) as *hamachi, mojako, wakashi, inada, warasa,* and *buri.* Each is regarded as distinctive, with particular strongpoints and ideal culinary niches (Yoshino 1986, 40). As one sushi chef carefully explained to me, to his palate (and to the palates of the consumers he instructs) these are distinct varieties of seafood, each with its own characteristic flavors and textures, each with its own best methods for preparation and consumption, and each to be judged by its own standards of quality. Since they are not necessarily interchangeable, to substitute *meji* (an immature tuna), for example, for *maguro* (a mature tuna) would be to miss the point of the cuisine. *Meji* is neither more nor less delicious than *maguro*; each size or season of a given fish species has its own unique flavors and qualities that are exploited in Japanese cuisine according to their own perceived merits. Popular guides to sushi, for consumer and professional alike, focus on the repertoire of sushi toppings, known by cognoscente as *tane* or *sushidane*; they list seventy, eighty, or one hundred distinct varieties and the seasons of the year in which they are at their peak of perfection.[17]

Back to the Market

Tsukiji's auction arenas are defined first and foremost by the different commodities they handle. Fresh tuna; frozen tuna; fresh fish from the waters near Tokyo versus fresh fish from the waters off Northern Honshû or the Sea of Japan; live fish; salted salmon; sushi toppings; live shrimp; dried sardines; shark; or fresh sea urchin roe are simply a few examples. At first glance the categories seem wildly inconsistent and by no means mutually exclusive. Some are constituted around particular species of fish; others are based on the method of processing that fish have undergone; some are organized around fish caught in particular locales; others represent particular quality grades or culinary end uses. Fish do not end up in a particular auction arena by some automatic process. Rather, they are directed to one of several possible auction arenas by routinized chains of decisions made by auctioneers who divert shipments based on their knowledge of the buying habits—the commodity specializations—of the trading community of intermediate wholesalers who frequent a particular auction arena. But decisions about which commodity categories each auction arena handles, and hence the working definitions of the boundaries of the individual auction arenas, are constantly renegotiated within the formal institutions of market governance maintained among the dozen-and-a-half specialized trade guilds, the seven auction houses, and the municipal authorities.

From day to day the cast of characters at any given arena is roughly the same, and each arena is a tight cluster of familiar faces and established trading customs. Intermediate wholesalers who specialize in supplying sushi chefs and those who fill orders for supermarket chains, for example, may participate in different auctions and may operate almost in different worlds. Likewise, intermediate wholesalers whose clients are hotel chefs and those whose clients are hole-in-the-wall restaurants rarely compete with one another. These market niches are buffeted in different ways by the enormously varied pressures that drive trends in consumption: the "eating-out boom" that stimulates sales of low-cost high-volume fish, and the "gourmet boom" that has the opposite effect; trends that promote the growth of supermarket sales versus those that sustain market niches for specialty fishmongers; consumption styles that promote the use of wild fish and those that depend on cultivated ones. It is these often conflicting trends that shape the specialties of intermediate wholesalers and affect their long-term decisions about which auction arenas they call home.

On the one hand, commodity specialties are a major defining force in the professional identities of intermediate wholesalers, from which they derive great pride and reflected glory as stewards of particular aspects of culinary tradition. A tuna trader and a shellfish dealer, a blowfish (*fugu*) trader and an eel merchant all inhabit very different historical and cultural spaces, quite self-consciously so and proud of it. On the other hand, their actual businesses are based on the combination of a commodity specialization that they may share with dozens of other traders and a specialized clientele whose own market niches are defined not by commodity but by entirely different sets of criteria. After all, few restaurants or retailers can stay in business selling only tuna or shrimp or whale meat. Restaurateurs and retailers define themselves—and constitute identifiable market segments—on the basis of such things as location, scale of operations, socioeconomic standing of their desired customers, and only sometimes by culinary specialty. The real specializations of intermediate wholesalers take shape—their real cultural capital is on the line and their real abilities to discern and to transmit the essence of distinction is on display—where these two dimensions intersect: at this point the market's specialties resolve into tuna dealers who cater to sushi chefs versus those who cater to supermarkets; shrimp traders who sell to walk-in trade versus those whose orders come by facsimile from department stores; fish pâté (*kamaboko*) merchants whose clients are small fishmongers versus those who sell to box-lunch makers. And it is in this intersection of commodity specialization (on the supply side as a tuna dealer or a whale merchant, for example) and the structural niches defined by market segmentation (on the demand side as a supplier of supermarkets or *sushi* shops, for example) that the real tensions in the marketplace arise.

The commodity specializations of intermediate wholesalers reflect their traditional definitions not only of themselves but also of the spectrum of culinary commodities. At the same time, the market segments that constitute their clients very concretely represent the demands generated by wider social, political, and economic trends in society at large, as well as the versions of culinary reality that motivate the ultimate consumers of seafood.

It is in this intersection of the internal structure (both institutional and cultural) of the marketplace with the changing social context of consumption that individual traders rise or fall as supermarket and restaurant chains create demands for particular kinds of products at the expense of other kinds. (Or, if a chain is large enough it may bypass the market altogether, by setting up supply relationships directly with producers and importers.) It is here that carving out a new specialty serving upscale Franco-Japonaise bistros rather than old-line sushi chefs offers enormous opportunities and equally large risks. It is here that the rising demand for whale meat, a result of the public's response to the moratorium imposed by the International Whaling Commission, creates pressures to maintain market specialties that seem to have no future. It is here that the forces that define fickle demand outside the market's gates compel Tsukiji traders to reconsider and reevaluate their own commodity specializations and therefore to redefine incrementally what is good to eat and good to think.

Of course, the traders of the Tsukiji marketplace have an array of technical information and professional skills related to seafood on a level far above that of the general public. From this position of cultural capital in the bank, so to speak, they are at times quietly scornful of the public's naive assumptions about the foodstuffs they purvey, and cynical about the cultural attitudes and processes that govern demand if not supply. Yet they still know, in their merchants' hearts, that the customer is always right. And they, too, enjoy the romance of food culture that not only shapes the profiles of demand for their products but also gives them a role in the great chain of Japanese tradition.

Clifford Geertz argues that "man is an animal suspended in webs of significance he himself has spun" (1973, 5). Tsukiji's traders have hardly spun all the webs of food culture themselves; in fact, many view their occupation instead as suspended on strings pulled by the fickle tastes of consumers, the social forces that drive the "eating-out boom" and other such trends, and the political and economic policymakers whose actions enable supermarkets to spread. Rarely do they consider themselves masters of these webs of significance. But as they manipulate their expertise and embellish the cachet of culinary authenticity their products carry in order to catch particular waves of demand, they play central roles in mediating a process of commodification—perhaps arbitrage—between the changing cultural significances and the more wildly fluctuating economic values that are at the heart of contemporary Japanese consumption.

Each morning at six, as Tsukiji's traders flash their bids, their hands produce prices even as they reproduce and construct commodities and culinary categories. Their work is the cultural work of the marketplace, creating meanings as it feeds the city, and linking global and domestic in complex and not always obvious ways. To paraphrase Stuart Hall (1992), it is they and thousands of others in markets, freight depots, fishing boats, and processing plants who stock the shelves of "the global cultural supermarket."

Notes

1. This chapter is based on extensive fieldwork at Tsukiji, including participant-observation, formal and informal interviews with many market participants, and analysis of documents on the historical development and the contemporary institutional structure of the marketplace. Readers interested in more detailed analyses of Tsukiji's current structure and history should consult Bestor (1995, 1997, 1998, forthcoming); these include references to the extensive range of Japanese-language publications on Tsukiji, food culture, and Tokyo's history, which I have largely excluded from this chapter in the interests of brevity.

   I conducted fieldwork at Tsukiji and other markets in Japan during academic year 1988–89; January, July, and September–November 1990; May–June 1991; December–January 1991–92; May–June 1994; and June–July 1995; and during a number of brief visits to Tokyo between July 1997 and July 1998. I am grateful for the generous support of a number of organizations, including at various times the Japan Foundation, the Social Science Research Council, the U.S. Department of Education's Fulbright Program, the National Science Foundation (Grants: BNS 90–08696 and SBR 94–96163), the Abe Fellowship Program of the Japan Foundation's Center for Global Partnership, the New York Sea Grant Institute (Grants R/SPD-3 and R/SPD-4), the East Asian Institute and the Center on Japanese Economy and Business, both of Columbia University, and the East Asia Program of Cornell University.

   Many people associated with Tsukiji generously gave me their time and their knowledge about the marketplace. The members, officers, and staff of the Tôkyô Uoichiba Oroshi Kyôdô Kumiai (the Tokyo Fish Market Wholesalers' Cooperative Union) and of Ginrinkai (the Silver Scale Society), and officials of the Tokyo Metropolitan Government's Bureau of Markets deserve special thanks.

   Dorothy Bestor, Keiko Ikeda, David Koester, Emiko Ohnuki-Tierney, and especially Victoria Lyon Bestor made many constructive suggestions on earlier drafts of this chapter, for which I am extremely grateful. Of course, the responsibility for facts, interpretations, and opinions expressed here is mine alone.

2. Since the late 1950s there have been 1,677 licenses for midlevel wholesalers. Each license permits one auction buyer and one market stall; some wholesale firms control more than one license—in 1992 the largest firm controlled 16 licenses—and can field another buyer and operate an additional stall with each additional license.

3. The Tsukiji Central Wholesale Market (*Tsukiji Chûô Oroshiuri Shijô*) comprises two major divisions, one specializing in fresh produce (*seikamono*), the other, and larger, division specializing in seafood (*suisanbutsu*, itself a category that includes freshwater fish and seaweed, in contrast to commonplace English meanings of "seafood"). This chapter focuses only on Tsukiji's seafood division (*suisan-bu*).

4. Although in some human populations minute differences in the average body temperatures of males and females indeed are found (Ralph Holloway, personal communications), there is no evidence that differences in skin temperature—whether between males and females, or among handlers of seafood of the same sex—have any effect on seafood or other food products.

5. A cuisine, according to one definition (Messer 1984, 228), is distinguished by its selection of sets of basic staple and secondary foods; its characteristic forms of flavoring; its characteristic methods of preparing ingredients; and its rules that dictate acceptable foodstuffs, appropriate combinations of foods, festive and symbolic uses of foods, and the social context of eating.

Although this definition of cuisine does, in its first and fourth clauses, encompass the discriminations that contribute to the identification, classification, and selection of things as foodstuffs, it does not address the production and distribution—that is, the actual availability—of commodities.

6. Tobin's analysis of provenance and cultural meaning in "Franco-Japonaise" cuisine in Honolulu (1992) and Dorinne Kondo's work on Japanese designers in the international high fashion industry (Kondo 1992, 1997) both explore similar questions about the attribution of "national" identity to stylistic developments in transnational expressive contexts.

7. In the early 1990s, only 11 percent of Tokyo elementary schoolchildren ate dinner with both their parents every evening, according to a survey conducted by a major manufacturer of instant curry mix, the House Food Industrial Company (reported in *The Japan Digest,* 25 July 1991). On average their fathers ate at home only three nights a week, and 12 percent of the children reported that they preferred meals without father. Twenty-seven percent of the children reported that they sometimes missed family meals because of extra classes at cram schools.

8. The extensive literature on gendered differentiation of roles and responsibilities in contemporary Japanese society is surprisingly mute on the subject of women and cooking. Bernstein (1983, 72–74) gives a brief account of cooking in the context of the much larger repertory of domestic tasks in the daily life of a contemporary rural woman. R. J. Smith (1978, 143–147) outlines general changes in the domestic diet, also in a rural setting. *Makiko's Diary* (Nakano 1995), a journal kept by the wife of a merchant family in Kyoto in 1910, makes detailed references to the elaborately differentiated cuisine and heavy cooking duties of women at that time. Cwiertka (1999) outlines the emergence of cooking as an urban middle-class hobby and element of cultivated leisure during the first three decades of this century. Other major English-language works on Japanese women's roles in the domestic realm say little about either cooking or meals (e.g., Bernstein 1991; Imamura 1987; J. Lebra et al. 1976; T. Lebra 1984; Smith and Wiswell 1982; E. Vogel 1991).

9. For a more detailed discussion of *kata* as an aspect of food culture, see Bestor (1995b; forthcoming, chapter 4).

10. The popularity of the new restaurants can be seen in the scale of the Kyôtaru chain. At its peak in 1989, it operated 752 shops nationwide (using several related names and similar culinary themes), 346 of them in Tokyo alone. Not all were auto-oriented; some were located at major shopping districts in front of railway stations; some were sit-down restaurants; others specialized in take-out orders. (Figures from Kyôtaru's official filing with the Ministry of Finance, December 1989). The chain later filed for bankruptcy, primarily because of its real estate investments, a victim of the so-called Bubble Economy rather than a lack of culinary appeal.

11. The philosophical struggle between supermarkets and old-fashioned purveyors of foodstuffs—efficiency versus service; assembly line versus individual expertise—is at the heart of the hit comedy movie, *Suupaa no Onna* (The Supermarket Woman) by the late director Itami Jûzô.

12. Even rice production has proven problematic. A poor harvest in 1993 forced the Japanese government to authorize the first rice imports in decades. In the face of widespread revulsion at the prospect of eating foreign rice, the government required rice dealers to blend domestic and foreign rice so that consumers could not pick and choose which varieties to purchase.

13. On this score, the United States has generally done poorly, being regarded as an unreliable supplier of basic foodstuffs and one that is likely to hold

food supplies hostage to other political and trade issues. President Nixon's sudden embargo on soybean exports to Japan in the 1970s, for example, was regarded by most Japanese as an unwarranted assault. Similarly, the linkages the United States draws between fisheries and other trade issues are frequently seen, particularly at Tsukiji and in the Japanese fishing and food industries more generally, as imperiling Japanese food supplies for reasons having little or nothing to do with fisheries issues.

14. Fish raised through aquaculture are referred to as "cultivated" or "cultured" (*yôshoku*), the term also used to refer to cultured pearls or silkworm culture. In contrast, wild fish are referred to as "natural" (*tennen*, literally "natural" or "spontaneous"). In the trade, all fish are presumptively *tennen* unless otherwise stated, so *yôshoku* constitutes the linguistically marked category, the one that requires special comment or labeling. The coincidental homonyms *yôshoku* ("cultivated") and *yô-shoku* ("Western-style food") mentioned elsewhere in this chapter bear no etymological relationship.

15. The Sunday closure of the Tsukiji marketplace is itself a relatively recent historical development, reflecting the pressures in the past generation or so on marketplace firms as employers to conform to the rhythms of the wider labor market and thus to give workers at least one day a week off. Historically, the market operated throughout the year, closing only for a few days around the New Year's holiday; workers were also given a few days off around the mid-summer O-Bon holiday, customarily the time to return to one's ancestral village and tend to the spirits of one's deceased ancestors.

16. A more detailed explanation of the background of the Day of the Ox appears in Bestor (forthcoming, chapter 4). Margaret Lock (1980, 27–49) outlines the five elements of Chinese cosmology and their relationship to health and nutrition. She also describes the importance of the stomach (*hara*) in traditional Japanese beliefs about health and illness, and the deleterious effects that temperature is supposed to have on the stomach (86–88).

17. Examples include Rakugo (1990), in a popular book on *sushi*, and Honda (1997), a restaurant guide, published in conjunction with a leading gourmet magazine.

References Cited

Acheson, James. 1985. Social organization of the Maine lobster market. In *Markets and marketing*, edited by Stuart Plattner. Lanham, Md.: Society for Economic Anthropology. pp. 105–130.

Akimichi, Tomoyo et al. 1988. *Small-type coastal whaling in Japan*. Occasional Publication No. 27. Boreal Institute for Northern Studies, University of Alberta. Edmonton.

Allison, Anne. 1991. Japanese mothers and obentos: The lunch-box as ideological state apparatus. *Anthropological Quarterly* 64, no. 4:195–208.

Anderson, Benedict. 1983. *Imagined communities: Reflections on the origin and spread of nationalism*. London: Verso.

Appadurai, Arjun. 1986. On Culinary Authenticity. *Anthropology Today* 2, no. 4:25.

Appadurai, Arjun. 1990. Disjuncture and difference in the global cultural economy. *Public Culture* 2, no. 2: 1–24.

Bernstein, Gail Lee. 1983. *Haruko's world*. Stanford, Calif.: Stanford University Press.

Bernstein, Gail Lee, ed. 1991. *Recreating Japanese women, 1600–1945*. Berkeley: University of California Press.

Bestor, Theodore C. 1989. *Neighborhood Tokyo*. Stanford, Calif.: Stanford University Press.

————. 1990. Tokyo Mom-and-Pop. *Wilson Quarterly* 14, no. 4:27–33.

————. 1992a. Conflict, legitimacy, and tradition in a Tokyo neighborhood. In *Japanese Social Organization*, edited by Takie S. Lebra. Honolulu: University of Hawaii Press. pp. 23–47.

————. 1992b. Rediscovering *Shitamachi*: Subculture, class and Tokyo's 'traditional' urbanism, In *The cultural meaning of urban space*. edited by Gary McDonogh and Robert Rotenberg. North Hadley, Mass.: Bergen and Garvey.

————. 1995. What shape's your seafood in? Food culture and trade at the Tsukiji market. *American Seafood Institute Report* (September).

————. 1996. Forging tradition: Social life and identity in a Tokyo neighborhood. In *Urban life: Readings in urban anthropology*, edited by George Gmelch and Walter P. Zenner. 3d ed. Prospect Heights, IL. Waveland Press. pp. 524–47.

————. 1997. Visible hands: Auctions and institutional integration in the Tsukiji wholesale fish market, Tokyo. In *Japanese Business: Critical perspectives on business and management*, edited by Schon Beechler and Kristin Stucker. London: Routledge, pp. 229–54.

————. 1998. Making things clique: Cartels, coalitions, and institutional structure in the Tsukiji wholesale seafood market. In *Networks, markets, and the Pacific Rim: Studies in strategy*, edited by Mark Fruin. New York: Oxford University Press pp. 154–180.

————. Forthcoming. *Tokyo's marketplace: Culture and trade in the Tsukiji wholesale fish market*. Berkeley: University of California Press.

Bourdieu, Pierre. 1984. *Distinction: A social critique of the judgement of taste*. Cambridge: Harvard University Press.

Clammer, John. 1997. *Contemporary urban Japan: A sociology of consumption*. Oxford: Blackwell.

Clark, Gracia. 1994. *Onions are my husband*. Chicago: University of Chicago Press.

Creighton, Millie R. 1992. The *Depâto*: Merchandising the West while selling Japaneseness. In *Re-Made in Japan: Everyday life and consumer taste in a changing society*, edited by Joseph J. Tobin. New Haven, Conn.: Yale University Press. pp. 42–57.

Cwiertka, Katarzyna. 1999. *The making of the modern culinary tradition in Japan*. Doctoral dissertation, Center for Japanese Studies, University of Leiden, the Netherlands.

de la Pradelle, Michèle. 1995. Market exchange and the social construction of a public space. *French Cultural Studies* 6:359–371.

Dore, R. P. 1958. *City life in Japan*. Berkeley: University of California Press.

Dore, Ronald. 1987. Goodwill and the spirit of market capitalism. In *Taking Japan seriously: A confucian perspective on leading economic issues*, by Ronald Dore. Stanford, Calif.: Stanford University Press, pp. 169–192.

Douglas, Mary. 1966. *Purity and danger: An analysis of the concepts of pollution and taboo*. London: Routledge and Kegan Paul.

————. 1971. Deciphering a meal. In *Myth, symbol, and culture*, edited by Clifford Geertz. New York: Norton, pp. 61–81.

Douglas, Mary, ed. 1984. *Food in the social order: Studies of food and festivities in three American communities*. New York: Russell Sage Foundation.

Fields, George. 1983. *From bonsai to Levi's*. New York: Macmillan.

Fine, Gary Alan. 1996. *Kitchens: The culture of restaurant work*. Berkeley: University of California Press.

Fruin, Mark W. 1983. *Kikkoman: Company, clan, and community*. Cambridge: Harvard University Press.

Geertz, Clifford. 1973. *The interpretation of cultures*. New York: Basic Books.

Gluck, Carol, and Stephen R. Graubard, eds. 1992. *Showa: The Japan of Hirohito*. New York: Norton.

Goldfrank, Walter L. 1994. Fresh demand: The consumption of Chilean produce in the United States. In *Commodity chains and global capitalism*, edited by Gary Gereffi and Miguel Korzeniewicz. Westport, Conn.: Praeger, pp. 267–79.

Goody, Jack. 1982. *Cooking, cuisine and class: A study in comparative sociology*. Cambridge: Cambridge University Press.

Hall, Stuart. 1992. The question of cultural identity. In *Modernity and its futures*, edited by Stuart Hall, David Held, and Tony McGrew, Cambridge UK: Polity Press and the Open University.

Hannerz, Ulf. 1980. *Exploring the city*. New York: Columbia University Press.

———. 1996. The cultural role of world cities. In *Transnational connections*, by Ulf Hannerz. London: Routledge, pp. 127–139.

Harris, Marvin. 1985. *The sacred cow and the abominable pig: Riddles of food and culture*. New York: Simon and Schuster.

Hendry, Joy. 1990. Humidity, hygiene, or ritual care: Some thoughts on wrapping as a social phenomenon. In *Unwrapping Japan*, edited by Eyal Ben-Ari, Brian Moeran, and James Valentine. Manchester, U.K.: Manchester University Press, pp. 18–35

Honda, Yukiko. 1997. *Sushi neta zukan* (The illustrated book of sushi toppings). Tokyo: Shogakkan.

Imamura, Anne E. 1987. *Urban Japanese housewives: At home and in the community*. Honolulu: University of Hawaii Press.

Ishige, Naomichi et al. 1985. *Rosuanjerusu nihon ryôriten* (Japanese restaurants in Los Angeles). Tokyo: Domesu Shuppan.

Ivy, Marilyn. 1995. *Discourses of the vanishing*. Chicago: University of Chicago Press.

Kelly, William W. 1986. Rationalization and nostalgia: Cultural dynamics of new middle-class Japan. *American Ethnologist* 13, no. 4: 603–618.

———. 1990. Japanese No-Noh: The crosstalk of public culture in a rural festivity. *Public Culture* 2, no. 2:65–81.

———. 1998. Sense and sensibility at the ballpark: What fans make of profesional baseball in modern Japan. Paper presented at the Fandom in Japan conference, Yale University, New Haven, Connecticut. Sept. 18–19.

Kondo, Dorinne. 1992. The aesthetics and politics of Japanese identity in the fashion industry. In *Re-Made in Japan: Everyday life and consumer taste in a changing society*, edited by Joseph J. Tobin. New Haven, Conn.: Yale University Press. pp. 176–203.

———. 1997. *About face: Performing race in fashion and theater*. London: Routledge.

Kopytoff, Igor. 1986. The cultural biography of things: Commoditization as process. In *The social life of things: Commodities in cultural perspective*, edited by Arjun Appadurai. Cambridge: Cambridge University Press, pp. 64–91.

Lebra, Joyce et al., eds. 1976. *Women in changing Japan*. Boulder, Colo.: Westview Press.

Lebra, Takie Sugiyama. 1984. *Japanese women: Constraint and fulfillment*. Honolulu: University of Hawaii Press.

Lévi-Strauss, Claude. 1966. The culinary triangle. *The Partisan Review* 33:586–595.

———. 1970. *The raw and the cooked*. New York: Harper and Row.

Lock, Margaret. 1980. *East Asian medicine in urban Japan*. Berkeley: University of California Press.

Messer, Ellen. 1984. Anthropological perspectives on diet. *Annual Review of Anthropology* 13:205–249.

Nakano, Makiko. 1995. *Makiko's diary*. Translated by Kazuko Smith. Stanford, Calif.: Stanford University Press.

Ohnuki-Tierney, Emiko. 1990. The ambivalent self of the contemporary Japanese. *Cultural Anthropology* 5, no. 2:197–216.

———. 1993. *Rice as self: Japanese identities through time.* Princeton, N.J.: Princeton University Press.

———. 1995. Structure, event and historical metaphor: Rice and identities in Japanese history. *Journal of the Royal Anthropological Institute.* 30, no. 2:1–27.

———. 1997. McDonald's in Japan: Changing manners and etiquette. In *Golden arches east: McDonald's in East Asia*, edited by James L. Watson. Stanford, Calif.: Stanford University Press. pp. 161–82.

Omae, Kinjiro, and Yuzuru Tachibana. 1981. *The book of sushi.* Tokyo: Kodansha International.

Peterson, Susan B. 1973. Decisions in a market: A study of the Honolulu fish auction. Ph.D. dissertation, department of anthropology, University of Hawaii.

Plath, David W. 1992. My-Car-isma: Motorizing the Showa self. In *Showa: The Japan of Hirohito*, edited by Carol Gluck and Stephen R. Graubard. New York: Norton.

Plattner, Stuart. 1983. Economic custom in a competitive market place. *American Anthropologist* 85:848–858.

———. 1985. Equilibrating market relationships. In *Markets and Marketing*, edited by Stuart Plattner. Lanham, Md.: Society for Economic Anthropology. pp. 133–52.

Rakugo, Shin'ichi. 1990. Sushidane saijiki (Annual chronicle of sushi toppings). *Taiyo: Tokushu—Sushi Dokuhon* no. 343 (February): 38–51.

Redfield, Robert, and Milton Singer. 1954. The cultural role of cities. *Economic Development and Cultural Change* 3 (October): 53–77.

Robertson, Jennifer. 1998. *Takarazuka: Sexual politics and popular culture in modern Japan.* Berkeley: University of California Press.

Sahlins, Marshall. 1976. *Culture and practical reason.* Chicago: University of Chicago Press.

Skov, Lise, and Brian Moeran, eds. 1995. *Women, media, and consumption in Japan.* London and Honolulu: Curzon Press and the University of Hawaii Press.

Smith, Robert J. 1978. *Kurusu: The price of progress in a Japanese village.* Stanford, Calif.: Stanford University Press.

———. 1992. The living and the dead in Japanese popular religion. Unpublished paper presented to the Columbia University Modern Japan Seminar.

Smith, Robert J., and Ella Lury Wiswell. 1982. *The women of Suye Mura.* Chicago: University of Chicago Press.

Stevens, Carolyn. 1998. Buying intimacy: Proximity and exchange at a Japanese rock concert. Paper presented at the Fandom in Japan conference, Yale University, New Haven, Connecticut. Sept. 18–19.

Thorn, Matthew. 1998. Girls and women getting out of hand—the pleasure and politics of Japan's amateur comics community. Paper presented at the Fandom in Japan conference, Yale University, New Haven, Connecticut. Sept. 18–19.

Tobin, Jeffrey. 1992. A Japanese-French restaurant in Hawai'i. In *Re-Made in Japan: Everyday Life and Consumer Taste in a Changing Society*, edited by Joseph J. Tobin. New Haven, Conn.: Yale University Press. pp. 159–75.

Vogel, Ezra F. 1991. *Japan's new middle class.* 3d ed. Berkeley: University of California Press.

Vogel, Suzanne H. 1978. Professional housewife: The career of urban middle class Japanese women, *Japan Interpreter* 12, no 1:16–43.

Watanabe, Fumio, ed. 1991. *Maguro o marugoto ajiwau hon* (The complete book of tuna tasting). Tokyo: Kobunsha.

Watson, James L., ed. 1997. *Golden arches east: McDonald's in East Asia*. Stanford, Calif.: Stanford University Press.

White, Merry. 1993. *The material child: Coming of age in Japan and America*. New York: The Free Press.

Yoshino, Masuo. 1986. *Sushi*. Tokyo: Gakken.

PART
IV

The Modernist City

JAMES HOLSTON

8

The Modernist City and the Death of the Street

The discovery that Brasília is a city without street corners produces a profound disorientation. At the very least, the realization that utopia lacks intersections means that both pedestrian and driver must learn to renegotiate urban locomotion. In a larger sense, it may signal that "the man multiplied by the motor"—to use a shibboleth of futurism—has at last realized his utopia. In other Brazilian cities, the pedestrian strolls to the corner of almost any street, waits for the light, and with some security ventures to the other side. In Brasília, where the *balão*, or traffic circle, replaces the street corner and where there are therefore no intersections to distribute the rights of way between pedestrian and vehicle, this passage is distinctly more danger-ous. The resulting imbalance of forces tends, simply, to eliminate the pedestrian: everyone who can drives. The absence of the rite of passage of street corners is but one indication of a distinctive and radical fea-ture of Brasília's modernity: the absence of streets themselves. In place of the street, Brasília substitutes high-speed avenues and residential cul-de-sacs; in place of the pedestrian, the automobile; and in place of the system of public spaces that streets traditionally support, the vision of a modern and messianic urbanism (fig. 8.1–5).

At the scale of an entire city, Brasília thus realizes one of modern architecture's fundamental planning objectives: to redefine the urban function of traffic by eliminating what it calls the corridor street, the street edged with continuous building façades. In its critique of the cit-ies and society of capitalism, modern architecture proposes the elimi-nation of the street as a prerequisite of modern urban organization.[1] It

Figure 8.1. Salvador: Largo do Pelourinho, view of the museum of the city on the left and the former slave market on the right, 1980.

Figure 8.2. Brasília: Praça dos Três Poderes, view of the Palace of the Planalto and the Museum of Brasília, 1980.

Figure 8.3. Ouro Preto: Praça Tiradentes, view of the former Municipal Palace and Jail, and the Monument to Tiradentes, 1980.

Figure 8.4. Brasília: Praça dos Três Poderes, view of the National Congress and the monument of "The Warriors," 1980.

Figure 8.5. Brasília: aerial view of the Praça dos Três Poderes and the Esplanade of the Ministries.

attacks the street for a number of reasons. On the one hand, it views the corridor street as a cesspool of disease. On the other, it considers the street an impediment to progress because it fails to accommodate the needs of the machine age.

Yet modernist planning derives only in part from public health concerns and technological innovations. More profoundly, modern architecture attacks the street because, as we shall see in this chapter, it constitutes an architectural organization of the public and private domains of social life that modernism seeks to overturn. In the type of city modernism attacks, the street is both a particular type of place and a domain of public life. The architectural organization of this domain structures the entire cityscape in terms of a contrast between public space and private building. In sustaining this contrast, the street embodies the concept of the public defined in relation to the private. Thus, the street is not simply a place where various categories of activity occur. It also embodies a principle of architectural order through which the public sphere of civic life is both represented and constituted.

That the street embodies such a discourse between the public and the private will become clear when we examine its structure in the preindustrial city and its elimination in the city of modern architecture.

Accordingly, in this chapter we shall consider the street (and what has replaced it) in two contrasting types of urbanism, that of preindustrial Rio de Janeiro and Ouro Preto and that of Brasília. We shall ask what the design and planning of streets in these examples may tell us about the structure of urban organization in different types of cities. In addition, we shall ask what this organization may tell us about the nature of ruling political regimes and about their relations to society. I shall suggest that to compare the structure of public space in the preindustrial cities of a colonial empire and in the administrative capital of a modern bureaucratic state is to reveal different types of urban order as concretizations of contrasting political regimes. Furthermore, it is to expose very different conceptions of what constitutes the public and the private in the relations between civic authority and civil society.

I contrast modernist with preindustrial urbanism in Brazil because Brasília was designed to transform, both architecturally and socially, an urban way of life established in preindustrial cities. Thus, European modernism attacks the nineteenth-century city in large measure because its preindustrial physical foundations, dominated by the "ruthless rule" of private property, does not meet the requirements and consequences of industrialization. In Brazil as in Europe, we must therefore assess the structure of preindustrial urbanism to understand the significance of modernist transformations.

Preindustrial urbanism in Brazil crystallized into a national pattern during the late eighteenth and early nineteenth centuries, and I focus on Ouro Preto and Rio de Janeiro because they were capitals, respectively, of these centuries. During this period, Brazil's large cities emerged as dominant, radiating centers of cultural, social, and attitudinal influence, establishing regional (in the case of Ouro Preto) and national (in the case of Rio) patterns of urban form as well as of urban society.[2] As urban life crystallized and expanded in Ouro Preto around its gold production and in Rio around the arrival of the Portuguese court from Lisbon, both capitals became exemplary centers for their respective domains. They served as vehicles for change in the hinterland and projected their patterns of urban organization to other cities. Thus, in the periods in which we shall look at them, Ouro Preto and Rio express dominant patterns of preindustrial urbanism in Brazil. These patterns are the final result of three centuries of colonial endeavor. They reveal a synthesis of the most characteristic and fundamental features of preindustrial urbanism, one no longer dependent either socially or culturally on rural patrimonial society and one not yet transformed by industrialization.

While industrialization certainly changed this synthesis, it continues to represent a basic pattern of social life and spatial organization in many if not a majority of small Brazilian cities. This pattern remains important because although it is often assumed that urbanization is a product of industrialization, there is in fact a lack of correlation between the two processes in Brazil.[3] Since 1940, cities in the nonindustrial regions have been growing about as fast as cities in the industrial regions. Essentially, these cities remain pre- or nonindustrial, expanding on the foundations of the early nineteenth-century urban pattern. Thus, the contrast I shall draw between modernist and preindustrial urbanism is not simply an exercise in historical analysis but addresses the issues of urbanization in contemporary Brazil.

The corridor street is basic to these issues because it constitutes the architectural context of the outdoor public life of Brazilian cities. In its preindustrial form, this context is defined in terms of a contrast between the street system of public spaces and the residential system of private buildings. It is this relation between the public and the private, with its consequences for social life that Brasília subverts.

To understand how the street orders the public and private domains and how its elimination in Brasília affects this order, we must first determine how the street can mean anything at all. One way of doing this is to identify the architectural conventions that architects and planners use in designing urban spaces—of which the street is the principal type—and that are experienced in everyday life as an architecture already built. If we analyze these conventions in preindustrial Rio de Janeiro and Ouro Preto, the significance of the death of the street in Brasília will become apparent.

The Architectural Context of Street Life

One of the most profound shocks of migrating to Brasília is the discovery that it is a city without crowds. It is not the absence of crowding that migrants complain of, but rather the absence of the social life of crowds that they expect to find in the public places of a city. In interview after interview comparing Brasília with hometowns of all sizes, Brasilienses register this basic difference: in Brasília "there are no people in the streets," the city "lacks crowds" and "lacks the bustle of street life." The absence of an urban crowd has earned Brasília the reputation of a city that "lacks human warmth."

Brasilienses consistently attribute this lack of street life to several factors, such as the enormous distances separating buildings and the segregation of activities into discrete urban sectors. But the most common explanation is at the same time the most profound. It is that Brasília "lacks street corners." This observation refers to the absence in Brasília of the entire system of public spaces that streets traditionally support in other

Brazilian cities, to the absence not only of corners but also of curbs, side-walks edged with continuous façades of shops and residences, squares, and streets themselves. It is an explanation that uses the corner as a metonym for the street system of exchange between people, residence, commerce, and traffic. It is one that explicitly draws a connection between the public spaces of a city and the public life streets support.

The nature of this connection is suggested in the following typical comparison of a hometown and Brasília, given by an official of the capital's development corporation (Novacap). This civil engineer was born in a small city in the interior of the northeastern state of Ceará. He moved to the state capital, Fortaleza, for his university studies and remained there for many years after completing his degree. For better employment, he moved to Brasília in the mid-1960s. Describing his first year in the city as a period of *brasilite*, "estrangement," he attributed his "allergy to Brasília," as he called it, to the absence of the kinds of "traditional public places of encounter" he was used to, especially the neighborhood street corner. He defined the social importance of corners by calling them "points of sociality" in the neighborhood (*pontos de convivência social*). These were the most important places of (generally male) encounter and public activity in the residential community. In his neighborhood in Fortaleza, for example, he described "X's corner," named after a store-restaurant-bar that occupied a corner building site, as the place to go whenever he wanted to meet a friend, pass the time, find a neighbor, or hear the news. This corner was his neighborhood's information nexus, its outdoor living room so to speak.

In Brasília, however, he found that the lack of corners (i.e., of the street system of public spaces) had an interiorizing effect; it forced people to remain in their apartments and replaced the spontaneity of street encounters with the formality of home visits. "To meet a friend I practically had to go to his house or he to mine." As people are often more reluctant, he claimed, to receive friends in their homes than to meet them in a public place, this interiorization of social life had the effect of restricting, and ultimately constricting, his social universe. To one accustomed to an outdoor public, to the sociality of the corner, its elimination produced not just an interiorization of social encounters but also a profound sense of isolation. In planned Brasília, there are no urban crowds, no street corner societies, and no sidewalk sociality, largely because there are no squares, no streets, and no street corners.

Brazilians expect to experience the daily life of crowds in cities not only because they anticipate a larger population in cities than in the country, but even more because they expect to find streets in a city and because the street is the customary arena of *movimento*—of the public display and transactions of crowds. This expectation is based on the distinction that the very existence of *ruas*, "streets," makes between urban life and rural life. Rural communities (*aldeias*, *povoados*, *fazendas*, and *roças*) do not have *ruas*; rather they have *estradas*, "roads," and *caminhos,* "paths." Only cities—those settlements officially classified, regardless of their size, as *cidades* and *vilas*—have *ruas*. Thus, one of the urbanite's expressions for going downtown, to the commercial center of the city, is *vou à rua*, "I'm going to the street," and the peasant's expression for going to town from the hinterland is exactly the same. Therefore, the word "street" signifies "city" because it refers to a particular type of place that only cities have.

This type of place has a distinctive physical form that constitutes a fundamental difference between urban and rural architecture. This difference is most clearly perceived in preindustrial Brazil, but it applies equally to the physical foundations of industrialized, though not modernized, communities. In rural settlements, the basic pattern of land use is one of detached buildings separated from each other on all sides by open space, some of which is used for circulation. In contrast, the preindustrial city is, from an architectural perspective, a solid mass of contiguous buildings out of which the spaces for circulation are carved. The buildings are not freestanding (with significant exceptions discussed later), and the bounded spaces are streets used primarily for circulation (see fig. 8.1). Moreover, the preindustrial city generally expands by enclosing the open, rural space around it with buildings. Even where city space is progressively filled in, new buildings usually maintain this spatial sense of enclosure that defines the street.

The street is not, however, just a passage for traffic. Its space is only one element of a complex form. As an architectural configuration, the street comprises a space open to the sky and the physical frame that contains and shapes it, that is, the façades of the buildings, and a floor. The latter is usually paved and differentiated into two or more levels: the base level of the buildings and the roadway proper, at a lower level, the two being mediated by a third level of curb, sidewalk, and steps that differentiates the street into distinct but interpenetrating zones of activity. The interplay of the expansion of this floor and the height and character of the surrounding buildings gives the impression that the sky has a defined height. The street system of public spaces comprises all the elements of this architectural configuration.

The urban square is a special case of the street defined in these terms.[4] It is evident in Jean Baptiste Debret's 1839 plan of Rio de Janeiro that the square in Brazilian cities typically develops in relation to the street in one or a combination of ways, for example, as a widening or lateral expansion of main thoroughfares, usually called a *largo*; as a point of access to main thoroughfares at the city gate or port; at the intersection of principal radiating streets, often distinguished by the term *praça*; as an outlying piece of land that the city eventually absorbs and frames into a square, called *rocio* or *rossio*; or, as a parvis, an area in front of a church that eventually becomes surrounded by buildings and connected to the street system. In all of these cases, the square is defined by the same architectural features as the street.

To see how these features constitute the architectural context of street life in the preindustrial city, we may look at Debret's illustrations of nineteenth-century Rio (figs. 8.6–7). But for obvious changes in such things as dress and transport, these scenes of the street and square present a remarkably contemporary view of street life in Rio and especially in smaller cities throughout Brazil. With great ethnographic accuracy, they depict the life of Rio's outdoor public domain—the daily and ceremonial activities of its crowds, the habits of its strollers, shoppers, vendors, and paupers.[5]

Debret's illustrations portray Rio during its initial period of cultural and political primacy, after the relocation of the Portuguese court from Lisbon in 1808 had transformed it from a sleepy colonial city of 60,000 inhabitants into Brazil's most influential city and the capital of an empire. What is especially important for our purposes is that the presence of the court engendered an urban crowd unlike any previously found in Brazilian cities—a vast body of all classes of people permanently residing and working in the capital. By the time Debret arrived nearly a decade after the royal hegira, Rio's population had doubled. The afflux of 24,000 Portuguese and numbers of other Europeans metamorphosed the life of the capital. The Crown embarked on a project of institution building. It created numerous institutes of higher education (including those of military science, engineering, medicine, and fine arts), a national library, and a myriad of government bureaus, all of which were new to Brazil. These institutions required new buildings, and the resulting public works gave a definitive character to the civic, commercial, and residential domains of the city. As the titles and offices of the court attracted wealthy Brazilian families to the capital, Rio became in turn a condensor and relay of an idealized pattern of urban life, its physical form serving as a recognizable setting for its crowds, customs, fads, and peculiar synthesis of European and African sensibilities.[6]

If we compare Rio's principal civic square, a street in the downtown area, and a street in a residential neighborhood (figs. 6–7), we see that a limited number of factors define and mediate the contrast between the street's solids and voids. These establish a characteristic pattern of forms and massings throughout the city. The appearance of the architectural frame of public space is similar in each case. Its most significant feature is the street's lining of contiguous façades: each building adjoins the next, and each is built exactly in line with its neighbor in relation to the sidewalk. Thus, the public space of the street and square is contained by a solid front of buildings. Although most buildings have a backyard, or *quintal*, which serves as a *private* outdoor space, there are no front yards of any kind to separate their façades from the public outdoor space. Rather, their aligned façades are built flush with the sidewalk, and their doorways give out immediately onto the public street.[7]

A number of architectural elements mediate this opposition between the street's wall lining of façades and its passage of space. These elements relate the private domain behind the wall to the public domain in front of it. The first such elements that come to our attention are doors, windows, and balconies. It is important to note that because the façades are flush with the sidewalk, these openings provide a means of direct visual, vocal, and even tactile communication between the two domains, as is evident in the exchanges of conversation, food, service, money, and gestures (fig. 8.6). Thus, the street façade's function is complex: it defines by containment and separation interior and exterior, private and public, house and street (and all that is associated with these contrasting domains of social life) and yet provides for numerous kinds of passages between them.

As a selectively porous divider, therefore, the street façade constitutes a liminal zone of exchange between the domains it holds apart. It not only serves the need to negotiate boundaries but also stimulates our fascination with liminality in that its passageways are usually marked for special public attention. Apertures are distinguished by the ornaments of carved lintels, entablatures, window frames, and balustrades; by the signboards of places of business; and by escutcheons displaying coats of arms and other emblems that announce family status in the public world. As a liminal zone, the street façade is on the one hand the exterior wall of the private domain and on the other the interior wall of the public.

In the latter sense, it defines the space of the street as a room, akin to the living room of a house, which is marked as such by what we might call street furniture. Thus, not only the wall's apertures but also its surfaces are ornamented—by volutes, rosettes, stone drapery, and the like, which appear as wall hangings of the public room. A feature typical of interior design that appears on the façade is the wainscot, the lower three feet of an interior wall finished differently from the upper part (fig. 8.6). At waist height, the wainscot generally distinguishes the level of sitting

Figure 8.6. Jean Baptiste Debret: The Barber Shop. Rio de Janeiro (1816–1831). The area surrounding the civic square in Brazilian cities, the *centro*, is the commercial domain of the city, its downtown. It is a warren of streets devoted to commerce, shopping, and services, and its streetlife revolves around the economic. In Debret's time as well as today, an illustration of one of Rio's principal downtown streets, such as the Rua do Ouvidor, would show wall-to-wall commercial establishments at street level, and warehouses, manufacturers, hotels, and residences on the floors above. This figure portrays the mixed residential and commercial use of the ground level typical of its side streets. In the *centro* of the city, many people earn their living on the pavement: the peddlers, musicians, knifesharpeners, bootblacks, beggars, and the like. Literally, one step removed from this economy of the pavement are the stall holders, exemplified in the illustration by the barbers. The stall is little more than a hole-in-the-wall, and its activities invariably spill out onto the pavement. Even today, stalls are rarely shut off from the pavement by a barrier, such as glass. Rather, the activities of the street flow into and out of them through a permeable building façade, which thus creates a liminal space neither precisely public nor private.

This barbershop is a typical stall of many services. Its signboard reads "Barber, Hairdresser, Blood-letter, Dentist, and Applier of Leeches." The barbers are shown preparing for the day's labor. They are former slaves who have purchased their freedom. One is sharpening the razors with his helper; the other is mending the stockings of their clients. He is seated on a bench that straddles the threshold, where the clients will wait for their turn in the barber chair inside the stall. At the end of the day, the barbers will bring their street furniture inside, lower the curtain over the doorway, and sleep on straw mats at the back of the stall. Thus, the illustration portrays and essential feature of the Brazilian downtown street: it is a domain of mixed, and mixed-up, use; one of commerce, residence, and work.

Figure 8.7. Jean Baptiste Debret: The Refreshments of the Largo do Polacio. Rio de Janeiro (1816–1831). As much as the square is a stage for formal ceremony and political assembly, it is also the city's *sala de visitas*, its public visiting room. It is a realm of informal encounter and congregation, a place for leisure-time socializing, a place to see and be seen. In this aspect, the square's activities are informal, quotidian, and essentially noncommercial. People gather to socialize away from the restraints of the home. Their activities consist principally in the varieties of conversation: in discussion, exchanges of opinion, news, and information, anecdote, and flirtation. The former are, of course, indispensable to the political life of citizens, and the square provides the setting for the formation and exercise of public opinion. These informal activities occur among and between all classes of people as all have free access to the square. It is the heterogeneity and voluntarism of the square's encounters that distinguish the social activity of its room from that of the house.

As this figure illustrates, the square's conversations are usually abetted by some form of refreshment and entertainment, services that make the social hour of the square pass agreeably but that do not constitute business. The square is not the domain of the economic; it is the domain of informal and extradomestic sociality, of conversation and pastime. Debret portrays the habits of one of the groups that frequents the square every day: the "middle class of little capitalists," as he (1978: 202) calls them, those who own one or two slaves whose daily earnings, collected weekly, are sufficient income for their masters to enjoy leisure time. The afternoons of this leisure time are spent in the square. After the midday siesta, these "little capitalists" habitually gather in the square from 4 o'clock until the Ave Maria at 7. By 4:30, every seat along the quay wall (street furniture) is taken. Debret (1978: 202–203) relates that the conversations of this leisured class are punctuated by "a little ritual" of purchasing a sweet and a swig of fresh fountain water from the street vendors. The game is to become widely recognized as a big spender on sweets, a favorite and flirtatious client, and so become feted by all the vendors of the square. Just as the "little capitalists" have their corner of the square, other groups have by informal agreement and by habit marked out their areas of congregation. Thus, the background of the illustration reveals merchants, shopkeepers, street vendors, ship captains, shipbrokers, sailors, foreigners, court officials, dockworkers, and a policeman whose responsibility it is to maintain the peace of the square.

in a room from that of standing. On the exterior façade, it functions to emphasize the street's character as a room and also to establish the zone where benches, seats, and tables are either built into the wall or placed on the pavement. The quay wall of the civic square (figure 7) was constructed as a two-tiered bench for sitting in the city's most public outdoor room.[8]

Thus far, we have discussed a number of architectural attributes that characterize the street as a domain of public life. The most important attribute is the opposition between the street's frame and its space, which the others mediate in a variety of ways. This opposition is itself the basis of a fundamental convention of architectural order that structures the entire cityscape into a coherent and predictable pattern of solids (buildings) and voids (spaces). What is important about this convention for the study of cities is that it organizes the perception of solids and voids into a system of information, a legible code, about what the relations between them signify. In the case of the preindustrial city, this is a system of information about the meanings of public space and private building, and more generally about the articulations between the public and the private domains of city life. This architectural codification of the "brute facts" of perception occurs in two situations: in design, when architects make spaces and objects, defining one in relation to the other; and, in the everyday experience of an architecture already constructed. In both cases, the same perceptual categories are brought into meaningful relation through the conventions of architecture.

The Solid-Void/Figure-Ground Convention

Conventions are culturally recognized and socially sanctioned relationships between expressions and what these expressions stand for.[9] The conventions of architectural design are the elements of composition codified into norms and prescriptions of information. For example, the plan of a building is a conventional representation in two dimensions of a three-dimensional structure. To knowledgeable readers it contains a code of building instructions and aesthetic relations. The use of classical pediments and columns on building façades is an easily recognized convention: that of quoting from the past as a way of indicating affinities with the idealized virtues of ancient republicanism. In each case, the convention is essentially a principle of difference— two dimensions opposed to three; the past opposed to the present. Architectural legibility, like any other, pivots on this principle: opposition creates a structure of signification capable of being invested with contrasting values, the identity of which history and prevailing ideology determine.

The principal convention of difference ordering the street in both perceptual experience and architectural composition is the organization of its solids and voids into figure and ground relations.[10] We perceive the city street as both a void and a volume of space contained by surrounding solids (fig. 8.1). As a void, it reveals these solids; as a volume it takes the shape of its container. The street thus constitutes a special kind of empty space; it is a void that has a defined shape, usually a rectangular volume. From the context of its containing solids, the street emerges as a distinct and recognizable figure, one that is empty but that has form. We may therefore consider the corridor street as a figural void.

The recognition of a figure requires the presence of a context, its ground, from which it appears to stand out. As studies in Gestalt psychology have shown, the figure stands out because it appears to possess a contour that separates it from the ground. As a common boundary between two fields, a contour can appear to shape one field more than the other. The field most shaped by the contour is perceived as the figure; the other is the ground. A figure is therefore a noncontinuous field against which the ground is perceived as a continuous field.[11] In the case of the street, the ground consists of the buildings—or any other visual boundary, such as trees—that give shape to the void. For example, in figure 8 the street is represented in two dimensions as one of the white stripes. From these examples, the pattern is evident: where streets are perceived (and designed) as figural spaces, the buildings surrounding them function as ground. This pattern organizes the experience of urban space in three dimensions and in two, that is, from the perspective of the person in the street and from that of the plan as in (fig. 8.8).

These figure-ground relations present a visual paradox that confirms the character of the street as a room. When buildings are ground to the figural space of the street, their walls must end at the space but paradoxically can have no boundary because the contours belong visually to the figure (the space) and not to the ground (the wall). In other words, the plane of the façade (its surface and edges) belongs visually to the space and not to the wall. The space of the street "steals" the façades of surrounding walls for its contours. This paradoxical condition creates the impression that the building façades are the interior walls of an outdoor room. The traditional architectural solution to this paradox of the wall that must stop but that has no boundary is to create a border around it that acts as an area of transition between figure and ground. This is done by applying ornament to the wall surface and by framing its edges and openings with a sidewalk along the bottom edge, a cornice along the top, pilasters at the sides, and window and door frames around the apertures. In addition to serving as decoration for the outdoor room, these

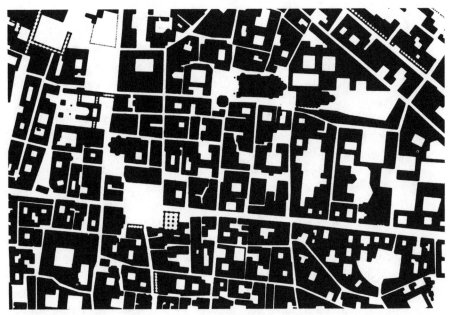

Figure 8.8. Parma: figure-ground plan, 1830. Figures 8 and 9 show approximately the same area (350m x 530m) in the same scale (1:3,460).

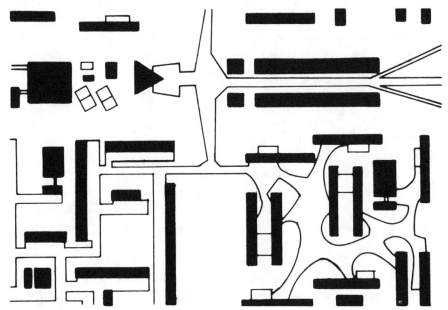

Figure 8.9. Brasília: figure-ground plan of an east-west section of the South Wing, showing residential *superquadras* and commercial sectors, c. 1960.

framing elements have an important perceptual function: they confirm the figural character of the street and provide raised surfaces behind which the wall can comfortably end. They create a border condition in which their inner edges will be perceived as belonging to the ground (the wall) and their outer edges to the figure (the street) as its defining contour.

One of the most significant architectural features of the solid-void/figure-ground convention is its reversibility: figures may be either solids or voids, as one is but the negative of the other. In figures 8 and 9, consider the blacks as solids and the whites as voids, and compare the two figures. In the latter, the solids are figural and the voids ground, whereas in the former these relations are reversed. Thus, buildings may be perceived and indeed designed either as ground (as in our previous example) or as figure (consider a cathedral standing in a square for instance). In sum, solids may constitute the perceptual ground in contrast to which voids emerge as distinctive figures, or voids may constitute the ground in contrast to which solids appear as distinctive figures. There is in all of this a discourse of perception, if you will, between solids and voids and figures and grounds. Each exists only in its relation to the other, forming a structured set of perceptual differences. As the analysis of the street in Ouro Preto will demonstrate, it is the possibility of reversing these differences that gives the solid-void/figure-ground convention great semantic utility in distinguishing architecturally the public and the private domains.

The analysis of this street convention has special relevance to the study of the city for a simple reason. Insofar as a circulation system of streets forms the anatomy of a city, its representational structure characterizes the urban order as a whole. This is so because the organization of the city's solids (buildings) and voids (principally streets and squares, but also courtyards) into figure-ground relationships promotes a perceptual order of these relations among the totality of architectural elements (fig. 8.8). Thus, the semantic structure of the street organizes the entire cityscape into a coherent and predictable order. This order serves both architects and inhabitants alike as a system of simple oppositions for elaborating aesthetic, political, and social values, as the comparison of Ouro Preto and Brasília will show.

Architects study this order through an analytical device known as the figure-ground plan. It represents the three-dimensional solid-void structure of the city in two dimensions, and architects use it both in evaluation and in design. The plan consists of a blackening or hatching of either the solids or the voids—but typically the solids—to reveal their organization into figure and ground relations (figs. 8.8–9). Considering this analytical use, we may say that the solid-void/figure-ground convention has a special status in our investigation: based in the physics of perception, it is both fundamental to the everyday experience of objects and spaces and a convention that specialists use as a means of analysis and design.

When we compare, in approximately the same scale, the figureground plan of a typical preindustrial city with that of a modernist city, we make a startling discovery: these simple figure-ground relations produce strikingly *inverse orders of solids and voids* (figs. 8.8 and 9). As Rowe and Koetter (1978, 62–63) observe in their study of these Gestalt patterns, the preindustrial city is almost all black in the plan; the modernist almost all white. The former presents a manipulation of defined voids (streets, squares, and courtyards) in largely unmodulated solids; the latter a manipulation of solids (buildings) in largely unmodulated voids. Each features an entirely different category of figure: in one, space; in the other, object. In the preindustrial city, streets read as figural voids and buildings as continuous ground (fig. 8.8). In the modernist city, streets appear as continuous void and buildings as sculptural figures (fig. 8.9). In the former, bounded spaces are defined by a solid mass. In the latter, isolated buildings stand free in boundless space.[12]

These comparisons are enormously suggestive about the principles of urban order. They demonstrate that even in supposedly unplanned cities, object-space relations are not produced haphazardly, Rather, they manifest a coherent order, a constructed logic, which is to say, an architectural convention worked out in different historical contexts. Like any other domain of cultural activity, architecture is never in this sense unplanned. There is no such thing, therefore, as the so-called organic or spontaneous city. Those cities which do not result from planners' decisions are only in the most narrow sense unplanned. They are not unordered or even unthought.

Moreover, it should now be evident that the formal conceptualization of the preindustrial city as a solid mass in which the public spaces of streets and squares are figural voids is not unique to the Brazilian cases we are considering. This elemental urban form of solids and voids has had an enduring presence in the occidental experience of city life. The figural street system developed its recognizable Western character as the arena of public commerce and congregation in Greece and her colonies from the fifth century B.C.E. onward, when especially the square—as an elaboration of the street—appeared as the outdoor forum for the ritual and political affairs of citizenship. It was formalized and carried to northern Europe by the Romans and, after the eclipse of urbanization during the Dark Ages, again became the prominent form of urban organization as variously embodied in late medieval, Renaissance, and baroque interpretations. During the sixteenth century, the Spanish and the Portuguese transported their colonial version to Latin America, where they established the principal city square as the domain of the most important institutions of church and state. Thus, in various incarnations and with somewhat different but related political meanings, it has been basic to the physical structure of Mediterranean, northwestern and central European, and Latin American cities.[13]

We are, therefore, considering a conception of urban order and a system of representing it that have dominated the Western experience of cities without serious challenge for twenty-five hundred years. I am not claiming that this system is somehow a generalized, ahistorical structure of perceptual experience. Rather, I suggest that it is a structure of signification maintained over a very long period of time by professional education and practice in architecture, one with a history of use and value (especially as reinterpreted in early modern Europe) prevailing in the institution of architecture until twentieth-century modernists advanced a radically alternative conception. In the following discussion, therefore, the cities of Ouro Preto and Brasília serve as representative examples, and their comparison as a contextualized instance, of a more global antagonism between opposing conceptions and representations of urban order.

Most important for our purposes, the striking inversions of the modernist and preindustrial figure-ground plans suggest a way of studying the transformation of city and society in terms of the order architecture creates. They suggest that this perceptual order is also an ordering of social relations and practices in the city. As such, architecture constitutes a system of conventions that may be used to stand for something else. What it stands for can only be determined through an ethnographic and historical study of how it is used.

The Street in Ouro Preto: Private Property and Public Display

During the eighteenth century, the city of Ouro Preto emerged as a center of fabulous gold wealth six hundred miles inland from Rio de Janeiro (fig. 8.3). As a result of its riches, it became the capital of Brazil's mining economy in the present-day states of Minas Gerais, Bahia, Goiás, and Mato Grosso. The settlement of the city parallels the growth and decline of its gold production.[14] In 1700, pioneers from São Paulo established a mining camp called Vila Rica de Ouro Preto, the "Rich Town of Black Gold." By 1750, the population reached its peak of 95,000 inhabitants, 25,000 of whom lived in the city center and 70,000 in the immediately surrounding *comarca*, "county." Slave labor powered the mining economy. In 1796 there were 5.2 nonwhite inhabitants for every white, a ratio giving a rough idea of the master-slave coefficient in the economy. Its major social groups consisted of entrepreneurs with large-scale mining operations, city officials representing the Portuguese Crown, wildcat prospectors and merchants, indentured servants, and slaves.

According to Furtado (1971, 79–82), the Brazilian mining economy afforded people of limited means unusual prospects for wealth and status because it was not an economy based on large mines, but rather on the less capital intensive system of alluvial panning. It was a lucrative situation for all, including the slaves, many of whom managed to work for their own account. As a result, migrants flocked to the new Eldorado. At mid-eighteenth century, gold production and population peaked. Gold output reached 1,770 kilos of refined ore. By 1777, however, production was down to 1,050 kilos, by 1811 to 360 kilos, and by 1820 to a mere 120 kilos. From the mid-century high of 95,000 inhabitants, the population declined drastically to 8,000 by 1816, at which level it remained for the next hundred years. With Ouro Preto's mines exhausted, the inhabitants regressed into subsistence agriculture or simply abandoned the city for other promised lands, leaving behind a gold-plated testament to mercantile enterprise.

In its glory, the city displayed its riches in classic fashion: through grand architecture. By the end of the eighteenth century, thirteen major churches, a palatial city hall, state capital, and treasury had been constructed in a blaze of public building projects that—considering the size and isolation of Ouro Preto—rival those of Periclean Athens in conspicuous consumption of vast resources, liturgical splendor, and elaborate celebration of civic accomplishments. Yet, for all its monumental opulence and political prominence, Ouro Preto was also a residential and working city for all classes of inhabitants. How, then, were these two elements of the urban order, the public and the private, architecturally related?

If, in a most general sense, political discourse is about such things as private gain and public good, how does the urban order represent the relationship between the public and the private in a city dominated by the politics of capital accumulation? A detailed analysis of this urban order would have to relate its architectural evolution to the various phases of capital accumulation and consolidation of power: from the collective settlement of a pioneer camp, to the main-street free-for-all of many individual competitors, to the grandiloquent public display of political and financial elites. I shall focus on this final grandiloquent phase of Ouro Preto's development to consider the following question. In Ouro Preto, as in most occidental cities, the private accumulation of wealth is paramount in defining both the physical and the political structure of the city (see fig. 8.3). In what specifically *architectural* ways is private property the source of public order in such a city, and in what ways is wealth represented as civic display in public buildings and monuments?

In cities such as Ouro Preto the solid mass of buildings constitutes the perceptual ground in contrast to which the voids of streets and squares emerge as figures (fig. 8.3). As most private activity occurs inside buildings and most (but not all) public activity occurs in streets and squares, the figure-ground conventions of the street provide a means of distinguishing the two domains. In such cities, the experience of a figural void predictably signals that one is in the public domain, in a street or square; this in turn cues certain kinds of behavioral expectations. Similarly, when perceiving an anonymous ribbon of street façades, one knows that these are private properties, unless otherwise informed by a flag or a signboard, for example. The public and private domains are thus distinguished by a simple and legible architectural convention:

solid = ground = private
void = figure = public

But, of course, not all buildings are private. How then are public buildings and monuments recognized in terms of this convention? The semantic solution is remarkably simple: the opposition between figure and ground is reversed to signal buildings that are in fact public. These buildings (churches, government institutions, museums, monuments, and the like) are designed not as continuous ground but as sculptural figures (fig. 8.3). They are broken away from the context of private buildings (the solid fabric of the city) through a combination of design strategies. They are generally set in the void of a square or a green that serves as the ground against which they are perceived as monumental figures. Often they are also heavily ornamented, sculpturally massed, and massively scaled. Thus, civic buildings stand out as great public gestures, figures in space, against the surrounding field of more uniform, contiguous, and in this case whitewashed façades. The repetitive forms and massings of these everyday structures constitute the ground out of which monuments to city, nation, God, and private wealth literally arise. The reversal of figure and ground thus provides the architectural means of transforming wealth into public display. In this way, the street code of figure-ground and solid-void conventions systematically relates civic architecture and the architecture of everyday life. In doing so, it presents an extremely simple and legible ordering of the public and private domains.

We can summarize the fundamental architectural structure of public display and private property in Ouro Preto as follows. In this preindustrial baroque city, both space and building are reversibly both figure and ground. Although space is consistently figure and building ground, these relations are easily reversed to signify public monuments and civic institutions. This reversal of figure and ground is the key rhetorical principle of the architectural discourse—literally a "running back and forth," as the etymology of the word *discourse* suggests—between the public and the private. The ambivalence of the system loads each element of the figure-ground convention with alternating values:

solid = ground = private

void = figure = public

The Modernist Inversion

Modernism breaks decisively with this traditional system of architectural signification. Whereas the preindustrial baroque city provides an order of public and private values by juxtaposing architectural conventions of repetition and exception, the modernist city is conceived of as the antithesis both of this mode of representation and of its represented political order. By asserting the primacy of open space, volumetric clarity, pure form, and geometric abstraction, modernism not only initiates a new vocabulary of form, more radically it inverts the entire mode of perceiving architecture. Recognition, the activity of perceiving meanings and relationships, is turned inside out—as if the figural solids of the modernist city had been produced in the mold of the figural voids of preindustrial urbanism.

Basic to modernism's doctrine of salvation is the elimination of the figural street. This it condemns as the bastion of a corrupt civic order of stagnant public and private values, imposed on the city through an architecture of antiquarian monuments, chaotic streets, decadent ornament, and unsanitary dwellings. Modern architecture eliminates the corridor street by inverting the baroque planning convention of figure and ground and by rupturing its discourse of reversals. A comparison of the figure-ground plan of preindustrial cities such as Parma and Ouro Preto with that of Brasília reveals this inversion clearly (figs. 8–9). In the modernist city, vast areas of continuous space *without exception* form the perceptual ground against which the solids of buildings emerge as sculptural figures. There is no relief from this absolute division of architectural labor: space is always treated as continuous and never as figural;

buildings always as sculptural and never as background. In the modernist inversion of the figure-ground convention,

solid = figure (never ground)
void = ground (never figure)

The consequences of this inversion are profound. It eliminates the reversals of the traditional code by insisting on the immutability of the terms: by establishing the absolute supremacy of continuous nonfigural void, it transforms the ambivalence of baroque planning into a monolithic spatial order. Reversals are now impossible. In effect, it abandons the discourse of reversals in favor of an uncompromising clarity of function. The perceptual structure of the street in Ouro Preto has thus been doubly inverted in Brasília. On the one hand, the broad avenues of the new city are unsubordinated to any other spatial or volumetric entity. Without architectural containment and without visible destination, they rush past the monumental buildings they isolate in space. On the other hand, as isolated sculpture, *every* building now vies to be recognized as a monument. Each competes for attention, each immortalizes its creator, and each celebrates the "beauty of the speedway" leading people and machines to apparently limitless horizons.

The motivations and consequences of these polemical inversions are essentially of two types. One involves the conventions of architecture, addressing the process of signification itself. The other involves a reevaluation of the social and political values signified. Modern architecture institutes its distinctive mode of recognition by refashioning old conventions into new conceptual devices. The success with which modernism breaks with the past in advancing its claims is in large part due to the simplicity of these formal solutions. By inverting the poles of the traditional oppositions between figure and ground, and neutralizing their reversal, it brings a radical unfamiliarity to in architectural code *the terms and values of which we already know.* It retains the terms of the baroque "argument" (i.e., solid, void, figure, ground) but presents them with a different logic so as to bring their established values (i.e., public, private) under new scrutiny. By holding the terms constant but defamiliarizing their relations, the modern code explicitly exposes the process of architectural signification, that is, the process of investing empirical categories (the terms) with significance. In the strange steel-and-glass landscape of the modern city, the inverted figures and displaced voids call attention to themselves as convention. They shock us into an awareness of the process of saying something about something in stone, of inscribing social values in an architectural code. Thus, through inversion, neutralization, and defamiliarization, modern architecture deliberately lays bare its own devices and intentions for restructuring our perception.

Yet, it does more than just unmask convention. Having exposed the process of inscribing social discriminations in architecture, it attempts to efface the inscription and to write a new one in which private property in real estate is no longer a source of public order, and traditional discriminations between the two no longer the focus of architectural comment and convention. If architectural inscription in capitalist cities constitutes a discourse (in the sense of a going back and forth) between "public figures" and "private ground," the modern project is therefore nothing less than the total transformation of this civic discourse in which the very distinctions between the public and the private disappear.[15]

How is such erasure possible? Modernism's power as a conquering vision results from its ability to translate its objectives for a new institutional order into simple conventions of architectural defamiliarization. These conventions impose a totality of perceptions in which identification of the public and the private cannot be made, and in which—in theory—a way of life based on such discriminations is therefore negated. In large measure, this semantic erasure is a direct and unavoidable consequence of eliminating the figural street through the inversion of the figure-ground convention. In the ideal modern city where *all* buildings are figures, the code of recognizing public institutions as *exceptional* figures in the common ground is rendered irrelevant. Public institutions are reduced, paradoxically, to sculptural anonymity: as sculptural objects in a vast field of sculptural objects, they are indistinguishable. Thus, the efficacious reversals of the traditional code have now become a semantic impossibility. If we know that all buildings are not private, yet cannot distinguish which are public, the old architectural convention for discriminating between the public and the private is effectively invalidated.

Transforming Civic Discourse: The New Public of Brasília

The modern city that emerges from these transformations is in theory an entirely public city. Its utopian design eliminates private property in real estate as an institutional basis of urban order for both family and civic life. However, as the public is defined in relation to the private, the elimination of the latter does not leave the former unchanged. Therefore, the modernist city features a new kind of public domain. The example of Ouro Preto suggested that the type of urban order whose basic unit is an opposition between public street and private building expresses a type of political order that is grounded in preindustrial capitalist relations between public affairs and private interests. If, in this sense, urban order is a concretization of political order, what kind of public city is the one that eliminates private realty?

In Brasília's Master Plan, the city's architecture and organization constitute an argument for egalitarianism:

> The four-by-four grouping of the superblocks will, while favoring the coexistence of social groups, avoid any undue and undesired stratification of society. And, in any case, variations in the standard of living from one superblock to another will be offset [*neutralizadas*, in original] by the organization of the urban scheme itself and will not be of such a nature as to affect that degree of social comfort to which all members of society have a right (Costa 1957, art. 17).

The egalitarian discourse thus maintains that the architectural conventions themselves ("the four-by-four grouping," "the urban scheme itself," and others developed in the Master Plan) will produce a communitarian political order. The city is to belong "to the people" (a category that originally included ministers of the government and their chauffeurs living in the same superblock) regardless of socioeconomic differences. As an inscription in space, all of the city's buildings and all of its spaces are to signify the public good. By eliminating market competition and profit from architecture, state-sponsored total design intends that collective and not private enterprise will generate this public good. Where there is to be little profit from city-building and where all construction must be referred to a Master Plan, an inequitable distribution of urban amenities will not occur. Moreover, where all buildings are monuments to this plan, class domination will not be able to mystify itself in the form of individual monuments to profit and privilege that dissimulate the private conquest of the public realm.[16] Instead, the totality of Brasília will be a monument to the collective efforts of master planning and to the state, which sponsors it. Thus, the Master Plan—"the urban scheme itself"—stands behind the new secular order as its motivation and ultimate reference. As the plan speaks through architecture, the city itself becomes the oracle of its egalitarian intentions.

To understand the nature of Brasília's new public, we shall look at what has taken the place of the old street and its public domain. The modernist alternative is the "local commercial sector," intended to provide the same commercial services as the traditionally mixed residential-commercial street and square (examples of which can be seen in figures 1 and 6). We shall consider the initial concept of the commercial sector, its evolution, and, most important, its reception by Brasilienses since the city's inauguration in 1960.

Nowhere in Costa's plan does the word *rua*, "street," appear. We can, therefore, assume that its absence is deliberate and corresponds to the elimination both of the concept of the street and of the physical fact itself.[17] Modernist Brasília (the Plano Piloto) is organized around the crossing of two "radial arteries": super-speedways called the Residential-Highway Axis and the Monumental Axis. The former encompasses fourteen contiguous traffic lanes. These are divided into center lanes for fast traffic and side lanes for local traffic. The side lanes connect to the residential units on either side through ramps, underpasses, and cloverleaf interchanges. While somewhat less symphonic in traffic flow, the Monumental Axis features eight lanes, four in each direction, separated by the enormous Esplanade of the Ministeries.[18] Neither axis has a single traffic light or stop-and-go intersection, for the objective of this circulatory scheme is the "unimpeded flow of traffic through the central and residential sectors" (Costa 1957, art. 7). That this objective will result from the elimination of streets is a basic contention of the plan: in article three, Costa defines *its idée maîtresse* as the application of "the free principles of highway engineering—*including the elimination of intersections* [i.e., street corners]—to the technique of urban planning" (emphasis added).[19]

On either side of the Residential Axis, Costa (ibid., art. 16) interpolates a ranked series of *vias*, "ways," today numbered L1 to L5 and W1 to W5, to serve the residential superblocks. The plan calls for *faixas*, "bands," of community facilities and local commerce, alternately intersecting these service ways, to be developed between the *superquadras*. Each band of commerce, called a "local commercial sector," is reached by a *via de acceso motorizado*, "motorized access way"—a choice of terms carefully and consistently avoiding any reference to "street."

In fact, Costa's original proposal (art. 16) assiduously denies any reference to the old marketplace: store entrances and display windows are to front onto the *superquadras* and not the accessways. Thus, the scheme links commerce and residence by way of the arcadian park of each superblock and not the "dirty, hazardous street." The latter is architecturally segregated and restricted to functions of vehicular supply, access, and parking. With unflappable faith in the power of words and architecture to change the world, the Master Plan transforms the age-old institutions of the marketplace and the market street into a "commercial sector" and a "motorized service way."

The absence of the word *street* in the plan is thus prophetic: it reveals an attempt to dismantle the traditional urban market by reordering relations of commerce and residence, pedestrians and transport. However, it is more than simple lexical proscription that eliminates the market street from Brasília. The street has also been transformed architecturally from a figure carved out of a solid mass into an unbounded throughway. It is no longer recognizable as a figural void in a discourse of figure-ground relations. The serviceways of Brasília can only be perceived as asphalt strips catering to the needs of machines in motion. They bear no relation to the street as a socializing space for pedestrians. Similarly, the marketplace has been architecturally reconceived as a single building, a sculptural block, which is to say, a figural object in the void—or, in the words of Lúcio Costa (1957, art. 16), "a single body only" set out starkly against the trees on one side and against the service access on the other. This reconceptualization of the commercial street effects a fundamental change in the relationship between urban commerce and residence. For Costa's plan accomplishes a radical functional differentiation of commercial space and thereby of exchange: streets have become entirely identified with the functions of transport and supply; distribution with detached buildings.

Having considered the prehistory of the "street" in Brasília, it is revealing to see how Brasilienses have responded to its elimination. The commercial sector developed in three phases. These correspond to the major division of the city into Asa Sul (South Wing) and Asa Norte (North Wing), the former constructed well before the latter, which still remains incomplete. In the first phase, the commercial sectors of the South Wing were built according to plan. However, the antistreet conception of these sectors proved untenable: in defiance of the Master Plan, the residents rejected it. Some planners argue that because the city was unfinished at the time of its inauguration, the total vision could not be implemented, let alone appreciated. However, the true explanation for the plan's failure is perhaps less apocalyptic. The first inhabitants of Brasília's *superquadras* simply rejected the antistreet because it contradicted social practice. Constituting a cross-section of the bureaucracy, these settlers were predominantly from urban Brazil, where the street is the focus of public activity.[20] As people accustomed to the bustle of the street, they quickly grasped and repudiated the radical intentions of the Master Plan. They refused the proposed garden entrances of the commercial units and converted the service backs into store fronts. Associated with sidewalks, traffic, and *movimento,* the original backs were perceived as customary areas of exchange and sociality. As a result, habit reproduced the street in practice where it had been architecturally denied.

To this day, the garden sides of most of the commercial units in Asa Sul remain undeveloped. The result is what one might call a front-back problem. Reversal has returned but in the form of confusion. Façades obviously designed as fronts are masked by storage crates, locked gates, and general neglect. Although some stores "solve" the problem by constructing two entrances, the one on the "street" always reads as the front door. The reinversion has thus been complete. Although the street itself had been architecturally denied and remains legally proscribed in Brasília (as city ordinances based on the Master Plan establish uniform heights, setbacks, openings, displays, etc.), the inhabitants of Asa Sul resuscitated its semantic code. They put their shops back on the street in contact with curbs and traffic. Not surprisingly, the signs of the popular street reappeared: mixed-up functions (cars and people), uncoordinated signs, colors, and displays, window shopping, sidewalk socializing, loitering, and even littering. The riot of urban codes reasserted itself in spite of the best attempts yet devised to prevent it.

However, both the extent and the effectiveness of this rebellious revival are limited at best. First and most important, Brasília does not have a genuine system of streets. Therefore, any attempt to recreate one is doomed to relative isolation within the totality—in this case, limited to the older commercial sectors of Asa Sul. Second, officialdom was not pleased with this turn of events. One administrator claimed that the popular street code reemerged because the central planning agency, Novacap, was unable to effect total control over commercial development (interview, October 1980). He argued that because of an initial lack of financial resources, Novacap could not develop the commercial sectors as coordinated wholes. Instead, it was forced to contract individually. The absence of a "guiding hand" led to uncontrolled development and competition among proprietors, with the resulting street riot of signs and symbols. Faith in "total design" was not easily discouraged, however, and the government resolved to give it a second chance in the construction of Asa Norte.

The design of commercial units in the north appears as an attempt to preclude by architectural and legal means a recurrence of the kind of street behavior that "deformed" the southern units. Each local commercial sector is now broken up into separate pavilions standing thirty to fifty feet apart. Each pavilion is composed as a two-story cubic loggia having two or three shops per side below and offices above. The second story protrudes over the first, creating a perimeter arcade tucked well into the body of the building. Their square plan somewhat resolves the front-back problem of Asa Sul by allowing shops to occupy all sides of the structure. Equilateral symmetry thus solves the problem by turning each side into a front.

In the new solution, however, the pavilions have also been pulled back about twenty-five feet from the curb and constructed several feet above street grade. One must now traverse a flight of stairs to reach each one. The sidewalk, that traditional ribbon of social exchange, has now been irretrievably severed from the street, broken into discrete lengths, and wrapped around each pavilion as an arcade. While it might be argued that these arcades simply replace the sidewalk with a protected passage, their effects are quite different. On the one hand, protection is actually minimal. On the other, this design precludes the possibility of street life by severing the street from the place of exchange. It eliminates sidewalk contact between the two and considers each separately, demoting the street to the single function of transport and sequestering all commerce into self-contained, detached mini-malls. In the absence of a continuous sidewalk edged with façades, not only is "strolling down the avenue" impossible, but, moreover, the urban flâneur is now confronted with extinction.

Recently, city officials unveiled the "final solution" to neighborhood shopping in the modern city, inaugurating the third phase of local commercial development in Brasília. Twenty years late, Local Commercial Sector 205/206 North finally and totally realizes the ultimate projections of the Master Plan. Conceived as a totality and constructed as a single megastructure, it represents "the way all of Brasília was supposed to have been built," in the words of one city administrator (interview, March 1981). Not surprisingly, the official media presents it as a model of urban development. As the architects and planners of the building explained, it represents a "return to the principles of the Master Plan" (interview, March 1981). It is deliberately designed to pull all shopping activity away from the "street" and "return" it to the sides facing the *superquadras*. No longer conceived as a simple block of stores or even as discrete pavilions, the project engulfs the entire site, on both sides of the road, into one palatial structure.

Locally referred to as Babylonia, 205/206 North is a veritable palace of consumption: a ziggurat *qua* mall complete with arched windows, roof terraces, scissor ramps, labyrinthine corridors lined with expensive shops and play areas for the toddlers of Brasília's new elite. As a final solution, it eliminates beyond doubt, recall, or even memory all traces of the traditional shopping street. With its stores internalized into the bowels of the building, the mall's façades appear as high, blank white walls, above and behind which the arched windows of the internal corridors rise. To let the road pass through it, the structure divides in half, turning the public accessway into a speedway connector. Parking is no longer available along the accessway but is relegated to the sides of the structure. A landscaped mini-lawn replaces the sidewalk, leaving hazardously little space for pedestrians to walk between the building's flanks and the road. Perhaps having realized that there are so few pedestrians in Brasília, architects have simply ceased making traditional gestures to them—like store windows and sidewalks.

As if to confirm the architectural elimination of the street in Brasília, Brasilienses do not use the word *rua* in address terminology. Using the city's impeccably rational address system, they say, for example: *na Comercial 103 Sul*, "in the Commercial [Sector] 103 South," and *na SQS 407*, "in Superquadra South 407." The one exception proves the case: Local Commercial Sector 107/108 South is commonly referred to as the Rua da Igrejinha, the "Street of the Little Church." It is named after the only recognized landmark in the residential areas of the city, the Igrejinha da Fátima, the "Little Church of Fátima." Designed by Oscar Niemeyer, it was the first church constructed in the city. Although there are many other churches, two striking Buddhist temples, and other exceptional structures (like mammoth supermarkets) in other commercial sectors, only the Igrejinha is considered enough of a landmark to be immortalized as a street name in the public memory.

The reason for its commemoration is obvious in light of our analysis of the preindustrial street: from the perspective of the shopping sector, the church is perceived in relation to its context according to the rules of traditional and not modern urbanism. It is in fact the only instance in Brasília of a traditional figure-ground relation between a public monument and a public street. Urbanistically, it follows the model of churches in cities like Ouro Preto: it crowns the street leading to it as a figural object set in a defined void. Thus, in relation to its commercial sector, the design of the Little Church of Fátima recapitulates the monument-street complex of preindustrial cities, and, for a moment, the public memory of it.

Notes

This essay is excerpted from *The Modernist City*, chapter 4, pages 101–144. As originally published, the chapter had forty-three illustrations, most of which had to be cut for this excerpt. The text is modified accordingly. All illustrations are by the author unless otherwise indicated.

1. Le Corbusier proclaimed the death of the street in an article first published in the French syndicalist newspaper *L'Intransigeant* in 1929. A slightly different and expanded version was republished in the syndicalist review *Plans* 5 (May 1931). This version is reprinted in Le Corbusier's *Radiant City*.

2. The Crown's instructions of 1548 to Tomé de Sousa, first governor general of Brazil, contain stipulations regarding the site selection and planning of urban settlements that recall earlier and later Spanish master plans. However, it was not until the period under consideration that a pattern emerged throughout Brazil of orthogonal planning with baroque embellishments, regularizing the architectural and planning conventions that concern us in this

chapter. For an overview of Brazil's urban development as colony and empire, see Morse 1974. A study of city plans and planning in eighteenth-century Brazil may be found in Delson 1979.

3. See Schmitter 1971, 35–36 for a discussion of this point.

4. For a historical and morphological study of the square from antiquity to the nineteenth century, principally concerned with Europe but with some attention to the New World, see Zucker 1959.

5. Published in France between 1834 and 1839 as *Voyage Pittoresque et Historique au Brésil*, Debret's illustrations were the product of fifteen years of continuous research and documentation in Brazil. As a member of the French Artistic Mission invited by the Crown to found the Academy of Fine Arts, Debret arrived in 1816, eight years after the flight of the Portuguese court from Lisbon to Rio and one year after the elevation of Brazil to the status of a kingdom. When his work appeared, the official Brazilian Institute of History and Geography condemned it as "shocking that it should depict customs of slaves and scenes of popular life with such realism" (Debret 1978, 13). It is of course precisely this condemnation that confirms our interest in Debret's ethnography today.

6. Walsh wrote in 1830 that "old and respectable creole families . . . repaired to the capital, where frequent galas, levees, and birth-day ceremonies at court, attracted crowds together. Here, from mixing with strangers, both Portuguese and English, they soon rubbed off the rust of retirement, and returned home with new ideas and modes of life, which were again adopted by their neighbours" (cited in Morse 1974, 65).

7. In contemporary Brazilian cities that still feature the preindustrial pattern of solids and voids, the immediacy of contact between house and street distinguishes the *casa colonial*, "colonial house" (a type referring to new as well as old houses), from the *casa moderna*, "modern house." It is perhaps an even more significant distinction than the one between pitched (colonial) and flat (modern) roofs. Thus, in these cities, Brazilians classify houses that have any space between their façades and the sidewalk as *tipo moderno*, the "modern kind." My study of this distinction confirms similar observations by Wagley (1963, 152) and Harris (1971, 30, 34).

8. People quite consciously experience the street and square as a room. For example, to indicate the place where people socialize in Rio, its inhabitants have the popular expression "the living room is in the street" (*a sala está na rua*). Or again, in his study of Rio's civic square (fig. 7), Ferrez (1978, 9) calls the Largo do Carmo (Praça XV) "for three centuries the parlor of our city" (*a sala de visitas*). Thus, the house and the city stand in a reiterative relation to each other, in which the rooms and corridors of the one are conceived of as a reiteration (in plan, section, and elevation) of the squares and streets of the other. One of the earliest theoretical statements on this relation of house and city is found in Alberti's *Ten Books on Architecture*, a work that decisively influenced the design and conceptualization of Western cities after its publication in Italy in 1485. For a complementary analysis of the "house and the street" as domains of Brazilian society, see Da Matta's (1978, 70–95) insightful discussion.

9. The notion of convention in semiotic theory is discussed in Eco 1976 and Lyons 1977, 99–109.

10. For an extremely useful analysis of the visual world in terms of these perceptual relations and others, see Arnheim 1974.

11. A classic discussion of the figure-ground relationship and its complexities is Ruben 1958.

12. With important exceptions that we shall consider in a moment, the blackened solids of the figure-ground plans of preindustrial cities (e.g., fig. 8) do

not represent *single* buildings. Rather, they represent entire blocks of many, *contiguous* buildings, none of which has an individuating shape in plan (with the exceptions noted). This representation should be compared to the modernist plan in which the blackened solids normally represent single buildings, each a freestanding object in space. This contrast is clearly shown in Le Corbusier's Plan Voisin. It presents both orders of solids and voids in the same drawing. Le Corbusier uses the figure-ground plan to emphasize the inversion of object-space relations in his plan for a new Paris as compared with that in the plan of old Paris. Note that each Cartesian cross in his new Paris represents a single building.

13. However, with some notable exceptions, it is not an essential feature of North American cities, where buildings tend to be freestanding in their lots and separated from the street by a front yard.

14. Population and gold statistics from Vasconcellos 1977, 35–36, 50.

15. The possibility of effacing the "old order" and inscribing a new one complements, at an architectural level, the possibility of a development leap proposed in the theory of the modernist city. It is this aesthetic of erasure and reinscription that makes modernist architecture especially appealing both to radical Right and to radical Left political ideologies.

16. Private buildings, especially bourgeois urban villas, become such monuments by using the figural conventions of public architecture for private aggrandizement. For the architectural basis of this appropriation, see the discussion above on the reversal of figure and ground as a means of transforming wealth into public display.

17. This relation between lexical proscription and physical elimination was made explicit in Le Corbusier's 1946 proposal: "The word street nowadays means chaotic circulation. Let us replace the word (and the thing itself) by the terms *footpath* and *automobile road* or *highway*" (Le Corbusier 1971, 59).

18. The organization of the city into a Monumental Axis and a Residential Axis does not represent a public-private division. In Brasília, the Monumental and the Residential are different types of public spaces, both sponsored by the state.

19. At the heart of the city, the axial crossing itself consists of a series of under- and overpasses creating a multilevel highway platform. Here, the high-speed center lanes of the Residential Axis pass under the Monumental Axis while the side lanes designated for local residential traffic pass over it. The two axes communicate through a series of ramps and cloverleaf interchanges. This assemblage of interconnecting speedways defines the area of the platform and constitutes its ceilings, floors, and walls. The platform is thus neither all building nor all roadway, but a carefully orchestrated fusion of the two. Its upper level contains parking lots and the Touring Club and features an unobstructed view of the eastern axis. On the west, it is contiguous with the Entertainment sectors, and on the east it provides stair access to the National Theater. Its lower level contains its prime function, that of the Interurban Bus Terminal, the hub of Brasília's commuter bus service between the Plano Piloto and the satellite cities.

20. Moreover, contrary to popular belief, most of the preinaugural settlers (construction workers, merchants, engineers, and administrative staff) were also from cities. In fact, about 79 percent were urban migrants.

References

Arnheim, Rudolph. 1974. *Art and visual perception.* Berkeley: University of California Press.

Costa, Lúcio. 1957. O relatório do Plano Piloto de Brasília. *Módulo* 8.

Da Matta, Roberto. 1978. *Carnavais, malandros e heróis: Para uma sociologia do dilema brasileiro.* Rio de Janeiro: Zahar Editores.

Debret, Jean Baptiste. 1978.*Viagem pitoresca e histórica ao Brasil.* São Paulo: Editora da Universidade de São Paulo. [1834–39].

Delson, Roberta Marx. 1979. *New towns for colonial Brazil: Spatial and social planning of the eighteenth century.* Ann Arbor: University Microfilms International.

Eco, Umberto. 1976. *A theory of semiotics.* Bloomington: Indiana University Press.

Ferrez, Gilberto. 1978. *A praça 15 de Novembro, antigo Largo do Carmo.* Rio de Janeiro: Riotur.

Furtado, Celso. 1971. *The economic growth of Brazil.* Berkeley: University of California Press.

Harris, Marvin. 1971. *Town and country in Brazil.* New York: Norton. [1956].

Le Corbusier. 1967. *The radiant city: Elements of a doctrine of urbanism to be used as the basis of our machine-age civilization.* New York: Orion Press [1933].

———.1971 *Looking at city planning.* New York: Grossman. [1946].

Lyons, John. 1977. *Semantics.* Vol. 1. Cambridge: Cambridge University Press.

Morse, Richard M. 1974. Brazil's urban development: colony and empire. *Journal of Urban History* 1, no. 1:39–72.

Rowe, Colin, and Fred Koetter. 1978. *Collage city.* Cambridge, Mass.: The MIT Press.

Ruben, Edgar. 1958. Figure and ground. In *Readings in perception,* edited by D. C. Beardslee and M. Wertheimer. Pp. 194–203. Princeton, N.J.: Van Nostrand.

Schmitter, Philippe C. 1971. *Interest conflict and political change in Brazil.* Stanford, Calif.: Stanford University Press.

Vasconcellos, Sylvio de. 1977. *Vila Rica.* São Paulo: Editora Perspectiva.

Wagley, Charles. 1963. *An introduction to Brazil.* New York: Columbia University Press.

Zucker, Paul. 1959. *Town and square: From the agora to the village green.* New York: Columbia University Press.

DEBORAH PELLOW

9 The Power of Space in the Evolution of an Accra *Zongo*

This chapter analyzes the impact of exogenous forces on the social institutions and the physical space of the community known as Sabon Zongo, "new stranger community."[1] Pursuant to the thesis that control over land carries political power, I shall explore the issues of community development and political legitimacy when rights to land are absent or expropriated and indigenous leaders are constrained by colonial and indigenous authority systems. One aim is to analyze changes or persistence in the culture of space and in the development of a *zongo*, using Sabon Zongo as a case example. The primary focus is the chieftaincy of Sabon Zongo, which had no basis for legitimacy in land.[2] Indeed, a central consideration is the legitimacy of a nonindigenous chief in Ghana in the past and today: "They make me *Sarkin Banza* [useless, illegitimate chief]," complained Sha'aibu Bako, the Hausa chief of Accra's Sabon Zongo. "The family regard me as a chief but do not respect me as a chief." When his brother, and before him his uncle, was chief, the position carried respect and the power and authority to affect behavior and enforce decisions. Has the chieftaincy devolved to powerlessness, as Sha'aibu implies? Is this specific to Accra's zongo, or are there larger issues affecting West African chieftaincies? Besides these issues, I hope to demonstrate the importance of wealth as a continuing basis of patronage and thus a criterion for leadership.

My second aim is to explore a community's spatial history, its organization, location, and operation, to demonstrate the reflexivity of social and physical space. Moreover, I shall show how the organization of physical space is ordered by and reflects the power structures to which the community is subordinated and within which its leadership operates.[3]

At the turn of the century, there were at least two power structures in Accra involving immigrant groups—the British and local landowners. In this essay, I shall examine how the strangers established claims to place and leadership and how the community's social and spatial evolution was influenced both by outside forces and by internal needs and constraints.

I chose Sabon Zongo for several reasons. It was the first Accra stranger enclave created by the group for whom it was intended. The son of the man thought to be the first Hausa landlord in Accra created this community to maintain Hausa institutions without interference from other stranger groups. Nearly one hundred years of archival evidence survive on the interfamily dispute that has figured centrally in the establishment of the community and current community relations.

The Power of Place and the Place of Power in Place

Social and cultural factors are inherent in the perception and use of space: space affects the organization of groups, individual and group status, and intergroup relationships (Ardener 1981). Social systems have structural properties, which "exist only in so far as forms of social conduct are reproduced chronically across time and space" and "social activities become 'stretched' across wide spans of time-space" (Giddens 1984, xxi). The contextuality of social life and social institutions is composed of strips of time and space, within which social activities take place. The physical environment not only is the locus of interaction but is implicit to the social system (ibid.). One may think of space and its design as "sets of social relations [that] introduce and legitimize ways and forms of life. In such circumstances, space and programme either maintain the status quo, or they can be formulated to express alternative social relationships" (Clarke and Dutton, quoted in Anthony Ward 1991, 98).

Like the authority system that governs it, a community's space is political: territory, land, planning, division and subdivision, appropriation, and use involve relations of power. Individual or group access to space, and the nature of space, can empower or disempower (Weisman 1981), just as the category of people who inhabit a space affects its valuation.

Kuper (1972, 420) defines a space as a site—"a particular piece of social space" socially and ideologically separated and demarcated from other places—as "a symbol within the total and complex system of communication in the total social universe." Moreover, sites may signify values, and "transactions that constitute the totality of social life may be spatially mapped with specific sites expressing relatively durable structured interests and related values" (ibid., 421). Thus a Swazi politician held meetings in the *sibaya* (an open-air arena, used for important gatherings) rather than the *lihovisi* (office, built according to British stipulation, and ideologically opposed to the *sibaya*) as an assertion of identity: "We are Swazi and we meet in the *sibaya* for affairs of our nation" (ibid., 418).

British control of land and political power was not merely symbolic but was apparent in the spatial delineation of their administration and the space they accorded local peoples. The British used space as a means to their political ends by appropriating and redefining ownership, especially on the Gold Coast. Colonial domination meant control of the means of production, and in West Africa this included British ownership of land (Kaniki 1985, 384). "In theory all lands in the conquered areas of British West Africa . . . or lands ceded to the British Crown . . . were owned by the Crown" (ibid., 390). Despite this, the British were unsuccessful in establishing direct control over land in West Africa.[4] In the Gold Coast, the development of modern gold mining increased land values and brought in considerable wealth to the affected villages. The Government Lands Bills of 1894–1897 attempted "to control excessive alienation and facilitate approved expatriate enterprise" (Kimble 1963, 21). The laws also instigated much indigenous opposition from the chiefs and the people because they altered "natural rights of absolute ownership into that of mere holders and settlers. . . . [T]he [1897] Bill would destroy the control exercised by headmen over villages and families" (ibid., 345). Ultimately, the Bill was withdrawn, and in the Colony and Ashanti specifically, the British left untouched traditional systems of landownership (Harvey 1966, 81).

The British did succeed, however, in developing their West African space—dividing it, building it up and building on it, and increasing its value. They recognized the importance of erecting and maintaining an infrastructure—roads, railroads, harbors, and telegraph lines—to facilitate the export of products (Hart 1982, 44f.). The emerging process of urbanization and colonial domination became "the expression of this social dynamic at the level of space," functioning to administer and fix political sovereignty and exploit the colony's resources (Castells 1979, 44). In colonial settlement, urban districts reproduced the cities of the home country, effecting a standardized colonial plan (ibid., 45).

Colonial impact on an indigenous people's social and physical space is most evident in the colonial city, consisting of two or three major parts: the indigenous often precolonial, settlement; the oft-termed "modern," "western," or "European" sector, which King refers to as the "colonial urban settlement; and in some colonial territories, a "stranger" sector, occupied by migrants (King 1976, 33).[5] In West Africa, the colonial city was intended for a principally African population and served as a nodal point within the export-based colonial spatial economy (Mabogunje 1970, 346). The social organization of the colonial city reflected the spatial organization of the colonial society, a "pastiche of zoned functions, land uses and populations" (Blair 1971:229), with six typical zones—five controlled by Europeans, one encompassing the old city and stranger community.

The Yoruba cities in Nigeria illustrate the introduction of a European presence through institutions and physical morphology, including the administrative apparatus and the railway: "It was inevitable that they could not be integrated into, or contained within, the old city" (Mabogunje 1967, 39). Thus new locations for these institutions carried new meanings; they were different and separate in appearance, ideology, ranking, from the indigenous space.

Accra, Ghana, exemplifies the spatial impact of the colonial system of organization on the urban landscape, with regional inequalities complemented by socio-spatial inequalities of density, modernization, and residential exclusion in the capital city. Like other colonial cities, Accra is a product of cultural interaction between two or more systems of culturally specific values, technology resulting in the separation of home and work, and the development of new institutions, methods, technologies, and roles to deal with the change in knowledge and organization. It is more significant, King asserts, that "physical space in the colonial settlement and between it and the indigenous city, is organized according to mid- and late nineteenth century scientific and especially medical theories which, in brief, assume a causal connection between aerial distance and bacterial infection" (1976, 37).[6]

Accra sits on the Atlantic Ocean, at the base of the Akwapim-Togo mountain range; much of the city's distinctiveness is tied to the history of settlement of Ghana's coastal areas in general and of Accra's in particular (Acquah 1958; Bosman 1967; William E. F. Ward 1948). Until the fifteenth century, after which great migrations brought new African populations coincident with the arrival of the Europeans, the Kpesi were the Gold Coast's only known inhabitants. The Africans established territorial rights and hierarchies and competed over trading links with the Europeans. By 1600, the Ga people had settled in, with Accra on the way to becoming capital of their federation. European trade was based in the Europeans' forts (most built in the 1600s to accommodate the slave trade) and continued until the nineteenth century. The forts became centers of economic and political power, often stronger than the traditional capitals. Three were built in Accra: Crèvecoeur (renamed Ussher Fort), James Fort, and Christiansborg Castle.

In 1850, the Gold Coast was separated from Sierra Leone as a distinct colony; the governor and his administrators resided at Cape Coast. The British transferred their administrative headquarters to Accra in 1877, and the growth of population through migration to this business center necessitated expansion of both business and residential space. As Accra expanded, neighborhoods similar to the old Ga towns, with distinct locations and names, grew up, including the Ussher Fort-James Fort area in the oldest part of town. In the 1890s, the British built up Victoriaborg as a European quarter and, being aware of subtle and not-so-subtle differences among the indigenous people,[7] cordoned off other sections for various groups. This created a de facto social and spatial compartmentalization of the town (Brand 1972),[8] including the establishment of zongos. The marginal zoning of the zongos reflected the separateness and powerlessness of the component populations, "accounted for not simply in terms of cultural differences but in terms of the distribution of power" (King 1976, 40).

Access to Power over People in Place

In precolonial Africa, the authority of the chief derived from three sources: lineage membership (ascription), a contest among eligibles (partial achievement), and possession of the best qualities (total achievement) (Mair 1971, 167). The chief's legitimacy derived from the indigenous African community, either through a hereditary system or, as in West Africa, through the conciliar systems, where "wealth was the dominant criterion of fitness" (ibid.). In Ghana, where hereditary systems of leadership persist, chieftaincy is symbolized by the right to sit on the stool in the south or on the skin in the north. All land and authority over that land's inhabitants, is held by people of the stool or skin, yet chiefs remain in power only as long as they have the people's support.

The establishment of colonialism, whether in Africa or South Asia (King 1976), introduced a foreign component into the sociospatial equation, the colonial powers' domination over indigenous peoples. In West Africa, the British played a role in who would become chief and how far his powers would extend; on a larger scale, they renewed towns and built commercial, mining, plantation, and urban centers. Economic development brought large numbers of Africans to these foreign areas, and they fell under the aegis of the Europeans (Skinner 1963, 308f.). One focus of this chapter is the extent to which the Accra zongo chief's perceived lack of authority is a carryover from the colonial period, or whether his predecessors exercised greater authority. An interesting debate in the literature questions how African indigenous leadership fared during the colonial period. Were the outside powers interventionist or supportive? Did their impact reinforce or undermine the chief's authority?

Conventional wisdom suggests that "the British practiced a non-interventionist indirect rule system of administration, especially in the Muslim emirates, which did not entail the introduction of drastic changes in the traditional political institutions" (Tibenderana 1987, 231). Thus, in Northern Nigeria, the prototype for indirect rule in Africa,[9] traditional political institutions were allowed to function as they had earlier. Moreover, while the emirs' appointments were subject to colonial confirmation, the appointment of "legitimate" claimants (Crowder and Ikime 1970, xii; see also Miles 1987, 238)—those recognized by the local people—continued, and these were elected by the "traditional kingmakers" (Tibenderana 1987, 232). Paden (1970) suggests that colonialism did not change formal procedures for selection to emirship. The corollary to this non-intervention position is that the British did not undermine the chiefs but, in certain cases at least, enhanced their authority and power: "Not only did they now have the force of the British Empire behind them, but in certain cases their territorial jurisdiction was enlarged. . . . In their portion of Hausaland, the British conferred hierarchical ranks and symbols of authority upon the *sarkuna* (chiefs), reinforcing their already high esteem in the eyes of the *talakawa* (commoners)" (Miles 1987, 238).

French colonialism, on the other hand, is thought to have greatly weakened traditional political institutions. Miles (ibid.), for example, follows Crowder (1968) in distinguishing French colonialism from British along this axis. "The French were determined to eliminate any conceivable challenge to their own authority, and trod quite harshly upon the indigenous rulers. . . . whereas the British tended to reinforce the authority of chiefs through territorial grants, the French tended to carve up large dominions into smaller administrative districts, thereby diminishing chiefly powers" (Miles 1987, 239). In turn-of-the-century Senegal, the administration was explicitly interested in controlling chiefly succession, taking away traditional titles, and controlling the courts (Klein 1971). Many French officials, through their desire for simple and clearly articulated lines of authority, wanted to make the chief an official completely dependent upon them. "In doing so, the French may well have undermined the chief and prepared the way for changes they did not want." Because the chief was entrusted with unpopular tasks, "he increasingly lost his standing with his own people . . . By strengthening the chief, the French prepared the way for his downfall (ibid., 70).

Other scholars view British indirect rule in the same light as French direct rule. Tibenderana, for instance, rejects British benevolence, concentrating on Sokoto Province in Nigeria to show that "the kingmakers' right to elect emirs was not generally recognized by the Administration until the 1930s, and that most of the emirs who were appointed in the province during the period 1903–30 were selected by British administrators and not by the kingmakers" (1987, 233). Others suggest, countering Paden, that in Northern Nigeria, the British made and broke leaders (Salamone 1978, 45) and changed territory to alter its administration (Smith 1960, 223, 211).

In the Gold Coast after 1904, chiefs and headchiefs could apply to the governor to be recognized, and, if satisfied that the candidate had followed native custom, the governor could confirm him "thus determining the lawfulness of his status in all courts of the Colony" (Harvey 1966, 83). Writing about Asante under the British, Busia (1951) demonstrates that government support of the chiefs, typical of indirect rule in Asante, did not support traditional legitimacy. For example, in Juaben in 1906, when the chief died, the Queen Mother and members of the royal lineage were opposed to the succession of his younger brother. After investigating the matter, the chief commissioner retained the man, stating that "the constitutional custom which governed the election of chiefs did not now depend solely on the will of the people, but also on the will of Government." This became a consistently followed policy (ibid., 106). The 1906 chief commissioner's report on the Southern Province makes note of the people's recognition of the government as their chief guardian, whose advice they sought on the smallest matters. This "index of the success of the Administration, is the index of the decreasing authority of the chief over his subjects. . . . Under the British Administration, the chief has become a subordinate authority" (ibid., 110).

In the North Eastern Province of the Northern Territories of the Gold Coast, "many of the colonial chiefs did not spring from the traditional clan organization, rather they were the recent creation of the British; others held traditional offices that the administration had vested with vastly extended or modified executive powers" (Thomas 1983, 59). In sum, to serve European needs, the authority of and traditional respect for the native rulers were often undermined in the Gold Coast as elsewhere (Smith 1960; Kuklick 1979, 44f.; Betts 1978, 132), albeit in two different ways. [10]

Leadership Among Strangers

For hundreds of years, West Africans had moved from one area to another, creating stranger communities and deriving their political rights from local African authorities, whose rules they were expected to obey. As in the northern Ghanaian town of Salaga, stranger communities had their own leaders who were responsible for maintaining order and who communicated the wishes of the local rulers (Sudarkasa 1979). Under colonialism, European administrators made the laws. While the British avoided European landownership in West Africa, they parceled out and developed urban and regional space, creating spatial and social entities for the strangers (zongos), whose residents wanted chiefly representation. But the British had the right to recognize (if not determine) that representation; thus, the stranger communities' relationships with the local African political authorities became secondary to those with Europeans.

As early as the eighteenth century, Muslims resided in the southern Ghanaian city of Kumase, where they held prominent advisory positions in the Asantehene's court and were protected by the Asante ruler. The origins of the present Kumase zongo, however, can be traced back only to the late nineteenth century (Schildkrout 1970a; 1978), having developed from the multiethnic settlement of Muslim traders—Hausa, Yoruba, and Mossi—and of Northern Territories (Ghana) migrants—Frafra, Grusi, Kuasasi, and others (Schildkrout 1978, 73). Zongos were also created by other means: Sabo Gari, Ibadan Nigeria's zongo, was not established until 1916, by the British, and then as a Hausa "village." All Hausa resident in Ibadan were ordered to move there, and Hausa exclusiveness was formally institutionalized (Cohen 1969).

In coastal Accra, Muslim settlement began about one hundred years ago, developing a "stranger" collectivity—made up of Yoruba, Hausa, Nupe, Fulani, Wangara, and others—in the old Ga section of town, although alliances were situationally defined and ever shifting.[11] In Accra, as in Kumase, the Hausa perceiving themselves to be superior to all other Muslim ethnic groups (Geoffrey 1982),[12] had a disproportionate influence on them in dress, language, roles, and offices. Zongo leadership positions (*sarauta*) may have been borrowed from Hausa state tradition, but the structure in its constituent units, their articulation and functions, was quite different. Because the Hausa and other Muslims in Accra and Kumase were strangers, there was no endowment of fiefs as a condition of eligibility and tenure, for example.

According to Gold Coast customary law, there is a close relationship between land tenure and patterns of authority, of land trusteeship and chieftaincy. In the Gold Coast (and Ghana), the stool or skin, representing the collective authority of the community, is the absolute owner of the collectivity's land; the occupant of the stool or skin "is a trustee holding the land for and on behalf of the community, tribe, or family"

(Ollennu 1962, 6). Formerly, as in Ghana today, a stranger had no inherent right to occupy land, although he might obtain land "by gift or grant upon payment of a prestation" to the owner (Pogucki 1954, 32). In Accra, the Ga or a specific Ga stool, were the owners, with land allotments by them subject to British approval.

Early colonial and later independence governments ruled the heterogeneous stranger community through a single recognized leader.[13] Thus, the British and the Ga controlled the land on which the *zongo* could be located and the selection and authority of the leader, because the headman did not carry the power of office vested in land. As in Chad's Muslim migrant communities (lacking hereditary chiefs or appointed title holders), the strangers created their own organized hierarchy, and the headman of a stranger group, lacking stool or skin, was dependent upon an informal relationship with colonial and indigenous authorities (Works 1976). In the Gold Coast, unlike Northern Nigeria, the British were interested primarily in supporting the authority of the traditional stools rather than newer Muslim hierarchies (Hiskett 1984, 278).

The position of the stranger headman was structurally unsound, making him dependent on the continuing support of his constituency.[14] In Muslim enclaves—Sabon Zongo, Kumase (Hill 1966), Nigeria's Sabo Gari in Ibadan (Cohen 1969), and Mushin in Lagos's migrant (settler) villages (Barnes 1986)—the patron (*mai gida*) was an internal source of authority, a man who cared for and was championed by his people, his clients. Defined as a landlord or settled stranger (Cohen 1965), the mai gida accommodated long-distance stranger-traders and assisted them (Hill 1966).

The position of mai gida supported and was in turn sustained by the exogenous authorities of the colonial and indigenous structures: precolonial chiefs, the British during the colonial era, the postcolonial independence government. In the Hausa "diaspora," "the chief *mai gida* ... if he is Hausa, is likely ... to be chief of the Hausa stranger-community" (ibid., 365), yet anyone with power and influence could vie for leadership and the position of patron. Because access to power and influence was not ascribed, disputes were common. In Sabo Gari, for example, until 1930, power was divided between the chief of Sabo, the chief of the cattle market, and the chief of the butchers; from 1930 on, rivalry, machinations, and political subversion continued among the three for leadership status. The man holding the dual posts of chief of the quarter and chief of the cattle market wielded considerable power (by owning houses and starting clients in business), played a judicial role, and had symbolic indicators, such as loud *maroka* (praise-singers) (Cohen 1969).

In Mushin, the strangers could establish permanent ties by assuming a territorial identity, purchasing or leasing plots of land, and moving into the position of patrons. Land and housing became sources of power (Barnes 1986, 48ff.)

Birth of a Zongo

Sha'aibu Bako, current chief of Sabon Zongo, is the grandson of Malam Bako and great-grandson of Malam Idris Bako Nenu. Nenu arrived from Katsina around 1860 and is described apocryphally as the first "Hausa man" in Accra (according to various members of the Bako; see also Odoom 1971, 5; Adamu 1978, 166).[15] In 1881, taking on the role of one of Accra's first mai gida, Malam Nenu acquired a piece of property from the local Ga Manche, which came to be known as Zongo Lane.

After 1874 Accra became a magnet for Hausa as a result of four factors: the establishment of the Gold Coast Hausa Constabulary, the lifting of the Asante ban on northern traders travelling to the coast; the breakup of Salaga as a major market, and the recruitment of Hausa into the Asante army (Adamu 1978, 166). Some Hausa, like Nenu, also came as itinerant teachers. Trade, especially in kola and cattle, was an important source of wealth in Accra, as elsewhere in the Hausa diaspora (Cohen 1965), and thus a basis for patronage. Many Hausa migrants brought wives and families. Rather than integrate with the growing cosmopolitan community of Accra, the Hausa stayed within their own domain and worked as individual entrepreneurs. Malam Nenu took in and helped settlers and transients alike, becoming Accra's Chief Imam in 1891. Following his death in 1893, Nenu was succeeded by Malam Garuba. Malam Bako, Nenu's son and Garuba's nephew, became Garuba's assistant (Case No. 1331/07, 29 May 1909, ADM 11/1502, NAG).[16] In 1899, Malam Bako became sole heir to Nenu's land, inheriting the role of patron as well.

After the death of Tackie Tawiah, the Ga chief in 1902, Muslim leadership and disunity became problematic. Tackie Tawiah selected Alhaji Ibrahima "Butcher" Braimah, a Yoruba from Ilorin and the Yoruba headman in Accra, to succeed him.[17] But the Ga chief died before he could have Braimah installed.[18] The acting governor met with Native Officer (N.O.) Ali (a soldier, reputedly Hausa, in the Gold Coast Hausa Constabulary and an antagonist of Braimah), Harri Zenua (another former soldier, a Kanuri from Bornu), Braimah, and Captain Kudjo (Tawiah's primary advisor) informing them that Braimah could not be recognized by the British as headman. [19] Moreover, he reminded Braimah that only with the sanction of the Colonial Government could the Ga Manche make him a chief (quoted in Dretke 1968, 44), emphasizing the limited authority of local powers.

In matters of religious leadership, the government also got involved (ibid., 46) when political pressure within the native community demanded it. Malam Garuba was charged with adultery and was removed from office in 1900 by the British governor, Sir F. M. Hodgson. Malam Osumanu was placed in his stead. Two years later, Sir Matthew Nathan had Garuba reinstated when the government, under community pressure, reinvestigated and found the charges to be false. British involvement helped incite religious disturbances; supporters of Garuba and Osumanu waged their war in the mosque (ibid., 48–50).[20] To alleviate tensions, the government enlisted the support of the Yoruba, Braimah, and of Native Officer Ali in bringing Fulata Boronu from Cape Coast as chief imam.[21] N.O. Ali failed to influence Garuba and his followers, but Fulata Boronu was presented to the people by Deputy Governor Hunter on 14 March 1903.[22] Garuba and Bako made a clean break, defiantly building a mosque in Bako's zongo. While Fulata Boronu was recognized by the government, Bako became the leader of a separate group after the deaths of Garuba and Osumanu.

Braimah suggested that Fulata Boronu be housed with N.O. Zenua, but the new imam acknowledged colonial dominion by requesting help from the government, because "when occasion arose for him to punish anyone for misconduct, he would not be independent. He desired to be under no obligation to the Mohammedans who had called him to Accra, and thus be in a position to deal impartially with them" (memo to His Excellency, 6 August 1903, SNA 2288/07, NAG). The British agreed to rent him a site on government land.

A kind of fragile peace settled on the Muslim population. In 1907, representatives of the Hausa asked the government to recognize N.O. Ali as a headchief of the Hausa section, in order to provide "an effective channel for communication with the Governor" (letter to the colonial secretary, 20 September 1907, SNA 1331/07, NAG). Support came from Fulata Boronu, Harri Zenua, Abubakar, and other Fulani malams (letter to Acting Governor Bryan, 16 June 1909, SNA 1331/07).[23] The request was granted, but N.O. Ali died within a few months.

In 1903, Bako and N.O. Ali had been on opposite sides regarding the imamship. Bako had retired to his own space, where he in effect played both religious and secular leadership roles. When a move was made to ensconce N.O. Ali as headchief in 1907, Malam Bako decided to relocate his zongo: he reasoned that his people had outgrown the space, but N.O. Ali's changing role may have been a factor.[24] As a recognized leader, Bako was given a plot by Tackie Obile, the Ga chief; despite the fact that the British wanted it for a railroad station.[25] Another Ga man[26] approached the Jamestown (Alata) chief, Kojo Ababio IV, on Bako's behalf for another piece of land, and in September 1907 Ababio and seven of his advisors witnessed the transferral of a portion of land, "six acres more or less to Malam Bakoe for building purposes and farm—and not for sale."[27] At that time, the Alata, Sempe, and Akumaje chiefs were part of English Accra or Jamestown, one of six stools among the Accra Ga; Asere (Usshertown) was the senior stool (Field 1940, 146ff.). After initially agreeing to the sale of land, Sempe reneged.

Once again, the colonial government played a crucial role, for the British worked alongside the Ga in the allocation of land. In this instance, the case was brought before the Supreme Court of the Gold Coast Colony in 1910. Malam Bako and his people were restrained from putting up or continuing to put up any buildings until the question of ownership and title to the land was determined. In the course of the initial case, Kojo Ababio IV testified that when he was enstooled, the Alatas, Sempes and Akumajes entrusted the lands, which belonged to the Sempes, to his care.[28] The Asere Manche was induced to sue for declaration that the land was attached to the Asere stool.[29] The court ruled that the land in dispute belonged to Jamestown, not to Usshertown, and awarded Malam Bako proprietary rights, as founder of the Hausa settlement there. He named his portion Sabon Zongo, "new zongo."[30]

In 1908, plague hit Accra, affecting all quarters, with the exception of those living in "good" houses. The British evicted the residents at Bako's *zongo* so that it could be rebuilt (1 December 1909, ADM 11/1/32, SNA 21/09, NAG), upholding the idea of a new zongo "so that all the Muhammedans can have a place to live together" (palaver held on 9 July 1908, Case No. 1331/07, ADM 11/1502) and proposing as one site the plot Ababio promised to Malam Bako. While they supported Bako's plan for a new zongo, they saw it as a heterogeneous stranger enclave rather than for the Hausa alone, as was the case in Ibadan's Sabo Gari.[31] In 1909, while Malam Bako was engaged in engineering a move for his family and followers, the aging Fulata Boronu decided to resign and return to Cape Coast. He recommended his former antagonist Bako as his successor; this appointment was defended by Braimah, Zenua, and Bako's people. Braimah was again nominated as chief (since no one was appointed to replace N.O. Ali after his untimely death), and had the majority of people behind him, including Bako and his followers.[32] The British perceived Bako's faction as the more important one, in part because "they were numerically superior to any one single section of the Muhammedan community with the exception of the Yorubas" (letter to the acting governor, 16 June 1909, SNA 1331/07), and agreed to recog-

nize Braimah as chief. In July 1909, Bako and Braimah thus became, respectively, the Muslims' head imam and head chief. The British viewed
this as a way of uniting the two strongmen in the community. The government was also sanctioning Braimah's role as a patron, since he helped
maintain the mosque and poorer Muslims.

By 1912, Malam Bako, his family, and his adherents had established
themselves at Sabon Zongo, where Bako informally played the role of
headman, continuing as chief imam for the Accra community. The death
of the conciliator Braimah on 1 May 1915 was the catalyst for ethnic
disturbances in the Muslim community. When they reached a climax
in the central mosque, the government ordered the building closed on
3 September 1915, and Bako's imamship ended (Dretke 1968).

Malam Bako's New Zongo

Although it lies only two miles northwest of Zongo
Lane, Sabon Zongo was at first a town apart, outside Accra's city limits
(see fig. 9.1). It was described as "bush": "They had animals, bad animals even . . . wolves. . . . At that time, if you were going to Sabon Zongo,
you came to a river—they called it Korle. You paid a penny before you
could cross. At that time, there was no street" (Braimah 1982).

The impediments of the natural environment telescoped the separateness of Sabon Zongo. Some Hausa chose not to come because of the
physical wildness of the new community, others because they chose to
follow Alhaji Kadri English, a kola trader from Kano who became a *mai
gida* for visiting Hausa traders in central Accra. Successful *masu gida*
could organize demonstrations, thereby advancing their election to
headmanship. Once Malam Bako left for Sabon Zongo, Kadri English
became the Accra Central Hausa chief (ibid.; Sha'aibu Bako 1982; English 1982).

About a hundred people settled at Bako's new zongo, no longer forced
to live among, pray with, and trade with the embattled members of
Accra's ethnically diverse downtown Muslim community.[33] Sabon
Zongo's separateness from Central Accra facilitated the founder's express
desire to avoid "any contradiction in our religion which is Islam."[34] The
Sabon Zongo people built their own mosques; the first, Masalaci Malam
Bako, was constructed adjacent to the palace.

In 1921, Malam Bako wrote to the Colonial Office, informing the government that he was no longer associating with the other Hausa chiefs
(letter of 5 June 1921, ADM 11/1502, NAG). When the Accra Central
mosque reopened in April 1922, Malam Bako declined the role of imam,
though he did gain political backing through the outside help of the colonial government and the Jamestown stool. (The Ga political structure

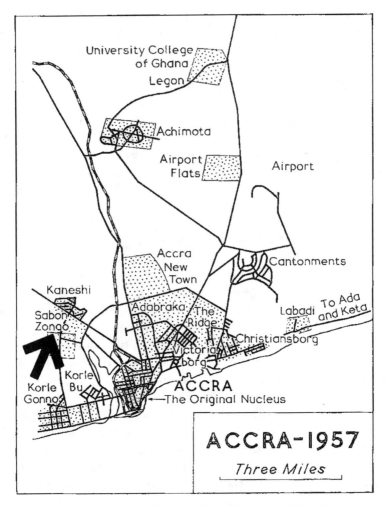

Figure 9.1. Location of Sabon Zongo in Accra (Booteng 1959:148).

was intact, yet the British assumed the higher authority.) Bako's chiefly legitimacy derived from access to social capita—the support of his people—based in turn on material resources (see Pellow 1985, 430–436). He could support clients, rally his people in response to a government request, and, for his people, provide land. Since the Hausa were strangers, they could not aspire to true land ownership, that is, ownership of stool land, but the Bako family could divide and distribute the land given them by the Ga and rule over it (English 1982; Sha'aibu Bako 1982; Braimah 1982).[35] Ga families living on the Sabon Zongo land and cultivating cassava relinquished their farms, and Bako allocated the space to his people, who raised cassava and corn as well as cows.[36]

Table 9.1 Ethnic Compostion of House Owners

Hausa	175
Fulani	7
Yoruba	8
Wangara	5
Mossi	4
Kanuri	1
Nupe	1
Zabrama	2
Ga	1
Benin	1
Zugu	1
Unknown	3
	209

Malam Bako also demarcated living space. While Sabon Zongo has been characterized as Hausa, it may not have been exclusively so, because the British collapsed strangers into one category and housed them together. When first surveyed, the acreage was subdivided into thirty-two portions, varying somewhat in size and greatly in the number and dimensions of compounds. According to the current chief and his elders, the ethnic variability of houseowners was minimal, the Hausa constituting almost 85 percent (table 9.1).[37] Seventeen parcels had no non-Hausa owners; another ten each contained only one each. Ethnically mixed houseownership was confined to four sections, adjacent to one another at the far northern edge.

In the 1930s, some twenty years after its founding, the vast majority of Sabon Zongo's people were Hausa, and all spoke the Hausa language. The current sarkin fada (the Hausa chief's main counselor) recalls that when he was a boy, the immediate neighborhood was Hausa, with the exception of a few Zabrama and Adar tenants. Moreover, most people owned their own homes, which became family homes owned and inhabited by extended kin. In 1933, Malam Bako stated that there were "600 persons in this zongo and about 160 Rate payers" (taxpayers or property owners), composing 27 percent of the total, with part of the balance being renters.[38]

Malam Bako built in other categorical and spatial subdivisions (aside from ethnicity), which were common in Hausa towns. Blind people (makafai) were given an area to stay in (ungowan makafai) under the leadership of a sarkin makafai provided with a "palace" with rooms for blind visitors. For obvious reasons, lepers (kutare) were allotted a separate area (ungowan kutare), in a subarea of Ayigbetown. A sarkin kutare was only appointed by the third headman of Sabon Zongo, Malam Bako's

Figure 9.2. Map indicating informal socio-spatial subdivisions in Sabon Zongo (superimposed on Survey of Ghana 1969, sheets 71, 72).

grandson Lebbo. There is also a crippled population (*gurgu*) scattered throughout Sabon Zongo; in 1994, Sha'aibu appointed a Sarkin Gurgu. While he lives in *makafai*, his constituents meet in Ayigbetown, at the home of his imam.

Malam Bako appointed a chief barber (*sarkin aski*), Wansa Damaley, and gave him a house. Such chiefs, who oversaw their constituents and advocated for them, were ultimately responsible to Malam Bako.

The zongo headman fell under the authority of the British and the Ga, and those within the zongo fell under the headman's authority. As in Kumase's zongo (Schildkrout 1970a, 373), the Sabon Zongo headman's authority held only for the zongo. His judicial powers were confined to his own people and limited in scope; for instance, he lacked the power to arrest. Moreover, he owed his tenure in office to the beneficence of his subjects. As the son of N.O. Ali wrote to the Secretary for Native Affairs, W.J.A. Jones, in 1930, "Our status [as Muslim chiefs in Accra] is only determined by the Subjects who agree to serve us and [we] have practically no effective or absolute control over them if they resent to be our subjects. . . . Our position is only as you know Sir, to conserve peace among our subjects and to guide and protect them in cases of difficulty (letter of 5 May 1930, ADM 11/1446, 5 May 1930). As a headman, Malam Bako looked after those who were ailing and without family, buried the dead, and arbitrated disputes. He also recruited workers for government-initiated tasks—maintaining the condition of the main road running by Sabon Zongo,[39] informing reservists of the Gold Coast Regiment to report to the district commissioner, and recruiting others to serve in the regiment.[40]

Other pieces of land were part of the same Ga stool and fell within the sway of the Sabon Zongo headman. One such place was a village in a rural area about five miles west of Zongo Lane, adjacent to the contemporary Dansoman Estates.[41] Malam Bako appointed the first *sarki* there.

Malam Bako was never installed as a Hausa chief, and Wansa Damaley, the former chief barber appointed by Malam Bako, tried to undermine Bako's position by acting like a village headman: solemnizing marriages, granting divorces, having drums beaten and horns blown on his behalf; the talking drums announced, "This is the Senior chief . . . here is a chief, here is a chief."[42] According to his grandson Adamu (Damaley 1982), he was given the space (and the legitimation to rule) Sabon Zongo in 1918 by Kadri English, the downtown patron and Hausa chief. However, Malam Bako was acknowledged by the majority of Ga stools and British as leader of the community, and he dismissed Wansa as chief barber for "bad conduct." The chieftaincy was established in Bako's line and given "the proprietary rights of the Bako family in Sabon Zongo lands as Founders of the Hausa settlement thereon."[43]

Changes in Leadership

Malam Bako's eldest son, Idrissu, was formally installed as *sarkin zongo* (chief of the *zongo*) in July 1933. Five years later, Malam Bako died. Despite his formalization as a stranger headman, Idrissu owed his position to the continuing support of his people, to the local "owner of the land" (the Ga chief), and to the colonial government. Like his father (and other earlier Accra Muslim leaders), Idrissu Bako faced problems within the zongo regarding his leadership. As chief, Idrissu was empowered to beat the gong whenever any public work was required to be done. Damaley refused to join Idrissu's gang to clear the road and weed, as requested by the district commissioner, but persisted in engaging in headmanlike activities, even beating the gong to have his followers clear the road. To resolve the issue, Idrissu took Damaley to court on 28 September 1933; the case was argued before Nii Ababio, chief of the Tribunal of the (Ga) Jamestown Division, which had jurisdiction over Sabon Zongo. In his defense to the court, Damaley asserted that he was headman "only for such people who love him at Sarbon [sic] Zongo and not over all the community of Sarbon Zongo."[44] (The patronage of Kadri English allowed Damaley his *own* followers.)

The tribunal found Damaley guilty of defying Idrissu's authority and attempting to usurp his position, ordered him to desist from such activities, and fined him twenty-five pounds. Damaley appealed the decision. Once again, the stranger's case was taken to an outside "higher" authority. Fearing the Ga Manche's prejudice against him, Damaley appealed to the Supreme Court of the Gold Coast Colony, bringing the colonial government into the fray. The judge, District Commissioner Rutherford, upheld the judgement of the tribunal, making several noteworthy points: that Sabon Zongo lay within the Jamestown jurisdiction; that its headman could be appointed only with the consent of the Jamestown chief and elders; and that they had confirmed Idrissu. Damaley also said he had been appointed by the late Chief Kadri English, to whom he had attached himself after his dismissal by Malam Bako. According to the Court, Kadri English "never had authority over or in Sabon Zongo. . . . [I]t is a matter of record that Kadri English was head of the Hausas in *Accra* Town only, and that Malam Bako, now succeeded by [Idrissu Bako] was head of Sabon Zongo and entirely independent of Kadri English. . . . Kadri English therefore could not have had authority to appoint Headman in Sabon Zongo.[45] Thus the British reinforced Sabon Zongo's spatial and political separateness, the right of the Jamestown Ga to acclaim its headman, and of a Bako family member to be that headman, with all of the office's responsibilities, pomp, and circumstances. However, the Hausa headman's authority was also circumscribed by the colonial government. The District Commissioner reminded the Sabon Zongo headman in a letter dated 27 May 1940 that "you with your Elders are at liberty at any time to endeavour to Settle disputes and quarrels by arbitration. . . . I must however point out that you have no legal right or other power to enforce any finding of such arbitration neither can you charge fees nor can you inflict fines" (No. 879/36/33).

Political parties, burgeoning during the 1950s in the transition from colonial rule to independence, also legitimated native leadership. In Sabon Zongo, as in the Kumase zongo, there was great opposition to Nkrumah's Convention Peoples Party (CPP) (see Schildkrout 1978, 208). Many people supported the Moslem Association Party (MAP), founded in 1954, and the United Party (UP), which succeeded it in 1957; this included Idrissu Bako and the rest of his family. But Damaley had supported the CPP, and with Nkrumah's accession to the presidency, Damaley was made chief.[46] On his death in 1962, his son Sanni succeeded him—although, according to the current sarkin zongo Sha'aibu Bako, they were chiefs only in their house.

Ga politics also entered the picture to legitimate the Sabon Zongo chief. Prior to the unification of Sempe, Akumaje, and Alata as the

Jamestown stool, the land Chief Ababio had granted to Malam Bako had belonged to the Sempe stool. An appeal of the 1912 judgment while Idrissu was headman confirmed the proprietary rights of the Bako family to Sabon Zongo, "subject to the allodial rights therein of the Sempe stool."[47] In 1969, the same year that Idrissu's son Lebbo Bako was installed as *sarkin zongo*, Sanni Damaley died and his brother Adamu succeeded him; the next year, another appeal recognized the Bako family's rights in Sabon Zongo lands and "jurisdictional rights as Sarikin or subchiefs of Sabon Zongo."[48] Each appeal supported the Bako family, yet the Damaleys continued to challenge the headmanship; each had ample popular support. Bako B. K., a local supporter of Adamu Damaley, phrased it as follows: Mallam Bako (and his heirs) had the land; Damaley (and his) had the people.

Like his father Wansa, who had a patron in Kadri English, Adamu Damaley was sponsored by Alhaji Maicancan, a wealthy Hausa trader and a modern mai gida. Maicancan was chairman of the new mosque building committee and the cattle dealers' association and, as a generous contributor, was made advisor to the Council of Muslim Chiefs. According to Chief Braimah (1982), chairman of the Council of Muslim Chiefs, this allowed Maicancan to insist that Damaley sit on the Council, even though Sha'aibu Bako already did so as chief of Sabon Zongo. Thus Bako's strong family background was consistently pitted against Maicancan's backing of Adamu Damaley. Until his sudden death, members of the Council felt that Damaley's connections enabled him to approach government functionaries for favors for the Muslims. Indeed, upon Damaley's death, Braimah sent out an announcement characterizing him as chief of the Hausa community at Sabon Zongo, infuriating Sha'aibu.

On 23 December 1981, Adamu Damaley and the acting Sempe chief were taken to court by Lebbo Bako to straighten out Ga rights to land and the appointment of a chief on that land.[49] The justice of the high court, K. A. Agyepong, ruled that while the Sempe Stool had allodial rights to the Sabon Zongo land, it had no rights to other property, or to install Adamu Damaley in place of Lebbo Bako. Notwithstanding, after Lebbo's death in 1981 and the installation of Sha'aibu Bako, Damaley took a more strident position than his father, asserting his claim to the Sabon Zongo headmanship. After his brother's death, Nii Amane Akwei, Sempe Mankralo and Acting Sempe Manche, and the principal elders of the Sempe Stool, presented "Adamu Damale [sic] Sarkin of the Sabon Zongo power of attorney to act as caretaker on behalf of the Sempe stool in safe guarding the interest of the Sempe stool, in matters pertaining to Sempe lands at Sabon Zongo at Abossey Okai not without power of sale nor negotiation for sale or grant of such lands."

Upon Damaley's death in April 1982, funerary arrangements were overseen by Alhaji Ali Kadri English, chief of the Accra Central Hausa and grandson of the chief who had anointed Adamu Damaley's father some fifty years earlier. "The Hausa elders of Sabon Zongo in Accra. . . . appointed Salifu Baha Kowa Adamu Damaley [Adamu's twenty-two year old son] regent of the area pending the installation of a substantive chief" (*Daily Graphic* 1982). The Acting Sempe Manche gave the tribute, calling for unity among the people. Sha'aibu Bako's side did not attend.

Since 1912, the various Bako headmen have appealed to outside authorities—colonial, Ga, Ghanaian—to legitimate their position, and these courts have ruled consistently in favor of the Bako family. Yet Adamu, the most recent member of the Damaley family to arrogate the Sabon Zongo headmanship, used the Ga stool disagreement to question Bako and to rally support for his position. The controversy has proved irrelevant to members of Accra's Muslim leadership, concerned with other, more convertible resources to which Damaley has access: money and connections.

The original Damaley/Bako dispute has been inherited, as were the respective criteria for success in the community—a kind of clientage based on exogenous support that could be parlayed into material resources to attract internal support. Sha'aibu Bako does not have Damaley's money; his chieftaincy has barely any revenue, and there is no land left in Sabon Zongo to distribute. In any case, the status of even a stool-sitting chief in Ghana today "is reduced to that of a stipendiary of the central government, dependent in fact for official recognition, limited to meeting in bodies many of which have no traditional base, under procedures and to perform functions defined by statute" (Harvey 1966, 121f.).

Zongo and the Chieftaincy Today

Spatially and socially, Sabon Zongo has changed considerably from its early days. It is no longer "bush": there is now a road bridge over the lagoon, and no toll is exacted from the masses who travel it daily in buses, trucks, taxis, and private cars or on foot. The inhabitants have allowed leafy trees to remain, but there are far fewer of them. Sheep, popular in all of Accra's Muslim areas, are generally confined to pens or empty lots, rather than being left to wander in the streets. In place of the maze of alleys characterizing the downtown zongo, there is a gridlike pattern of roads, some suitable for motorized traffic. The original compounds still stand, joined by additional buildings—houses, mosques, schools, shops, and a movie theater.

There are currently ten Muslim areas in the Accra district: Sabon Zongo, Accra Central, Nima, Newtown (Lagostown), Adabraka, Alhamdu,

Figure 9.3. An east-west lane in Sabon Zongo.

Abeka, Darkoma, Shukura, and Madina, each with a Muslim headman. The residents of Sabon Zongo are more integrated with Accra's other Muslim/Hausa communities, especially that of Accra Central, than in the days of Malam Bako (when there was only Accra Central). On Fridays, most of the men go to the main Accra mosque, walking distance from Sabon Zongo since it was constructed in 1982. Id il Fitr (the celebration of the ending of the fast of Ramadan) is observed citywide, with the Sabon Zongo Muslims marching as a group in a route that takes all afternoon, snaking from the main mosque through their community. Different women's groups wear distinctive cloth. Chief Sha'aibu Bako, the current chief of Sabon Zongo, has strong political ties to the other Muslim chiefs and automatically belongs to the Council of Muslim Chiefs. He also has strong ties to a select group of chiefs, descendants of the "first families of Islam" in Accra (including Yoruba, Wangara, and Nupe), and unlike his grandfather, involves himself in parochial Muslim affairs external to Sabon Zongo.

The 1970 population census of Sabon Zongo (which includes Lartebiokarshie and Town Council Line) lists 24,245 residents; in 1996, there were 14,000 registered voters. By my reckoning, there are nine subdivisions in Sha'aibu Bako's Sabon Zongo that house around 25,000 adults. People particularly began moving into rented rooms in Sabon Zongo in the 1950s. During the flurry of modernization that followed

World War II, part of the ambitious program of the First Republic, increasing numbers of ethnically diverse renters moved there (Hamidu 1982).

Sha'aibu's perception is that more Hausa live in Sabon Zongo than elsewhere in Accra. Certainly they have an overarching influence. Compounds are still overwhelmingly owned by descendants of the original Hausa families. And yet, my census of 18 compounds produced 700 adults, most of who are tenants and only 289 of whom (or 41 percent) are Hausa. The many non-Hausa who have swelled the ranks include Kanuri, Zabrama, Wangara, Fulani, Busanga, Chamba, and Kotokoli, from neighboring African countries, and the Frafra, Wala, Sisala, Dagarti, Mossi, Ga, and various Akan subgroups from Ghana. Most, but by no means all, are practicing Muslims; many of the Muslims identify themselves as Hausa, perhaps as a result of the perception of Sabon Zongo as a Hausa community but probably also because of that ethnic group's flexible boundaries and continued importance as a model of orthodoxy.

In the past, four ethnic groups have had chiefs in Sabon Zongo—the Mossi, Wangara, Chamba, and the non-Muslim Ewe. Many Wangara live in that group's original section (*ungowan wangarawa*) created by Malam Bako and where its chief, when they had one, resided.[50] The last leader, Malam Maman Ibrahim, was the son of the first Wangara chief in Sabon Zongo, selected by Idrissu Bako to succeed to the post. Maman Ibrahim supported Sha'aibu, because Malam Bako chose his father as Wangara chief and gave him a house: "If someone gives you your place, you can't then take that person as your enemy. If anyone in Sabon Zongo tells you Malam Bako didn't give him his house, he is telling lies" (Ibrahim 1982). There is also a house for a Chamba chief, who, when alive, met there with his people and heard disputes. Unlike Wangara, however, he equivocated on the Sabon Zongo chieftaincy dispute. While Maman Ibrahim clearly stated that cases beyond his power went to Bako, Malam Halidou said he sent them to "the Hausa chief"—meaning Bako *and* Damaley, both of whom he recognized (Dedji 1982).[51] The Ewe live near their chief's house in what is known as Ayigbetown (Ewetown). The Mossi chief's house is in the Mossi area; he has been dead for about twenty years and has not been replaced. It is telling that the only ethnic chief being maintained in Sabon Zongo is that of the Hausa, who is also recognized as the chief of the whole community.

The growth of the community has led to other divisions as well: one area in Ayigbetown is called *ungowan katifa* (mattress area), due to its occupational specialty; another, in Kan Tudu near the chief's house, is *makwala* (tureen), because it is an area of much food-selling activity. Both are primarily Hausa, while Ewe also inhabit ungowan katifa.

The seeming non-Ghanaian behavior of residents, in dress, religion, and cultural orientation generally, is intriguing, since according to the 1970 census of the total Sabon Zongo area 76 percent of the population was born in Ghana and only 6 percent in Nigeria (Ghana Government 1978, 194, table 9). Those identifying themselves as foreign nationals numbered 5,742, of whom 1,401, or 24 percent, were Nigerian. And of those 24 percent, 45 percent stated they were born in Ghana, (ibid., 374, table 23).[52]

Islam is the centripetal force for community identification and continuity in Sabon Zongo: there are twenty-seven roofed and two unroofed mosques. Churches and mosques are both found elsewhere in Accra, but as Ojo (1968) noted for Yorubaland, in the zongo one finds mosques only. Moreover, many people at least pay lip service to the insignificance of ethnicity compared to religion. Indeed, over the years there have been several traditional associations. *Zumunci* and *zumunta*, both inactive for the last ten years, were Islam-based and ethnically mixed. Bako B.K., the chairman of Sabon Zongo's branch of zumunta, indicated that the membership, while mainly Hausa, also included Zabrama, Kotokoli, Chamba, and a couple of Akan and Ga. Predominantly male, it was said to be open to unmarried women. Zumunci, an Accra-wide women's association, had many members in Sabon Zongo. Its ethnic admixture was neither a unifying nor a dividing factor, overridden as it was by the binding nature of a northern ethos (Pellow 1987). Both were mutual aid societies.

Currently, there are women's associations (*minti* = meeting) that crosscut Sabon Zongo; there are also neighborhood-based women's associations. All are mutual aid societies, and members come together for life events. They are age-graded: *Sweet Aminchi* (trusting, trustworthiness) is for girls and young unmarried women; *Expensive Ladies* are older than Aminchi but still young; *Personality* is for those too old to be in Aminchi, and some are married, some not; *Happiness*—for newly married women; *Young 16*—married but not too long; *Challenger*—thirty years-plus; *Wonderful*; *Commander*; *Turmi* (mortar): first formed for women about thirty, the membership are now in their forties, and a thirty-year-old can't join; at a baby outdooring or wedding, this group brings a mortar and pestle (female and male) and sings risqué songs; *Shin fi da Fuska* (spread your face, the old ladies); *Sha Hudu*; *En Ashirin* (old yet feel like a twenty-year-old). At Id, members of each group often dress in the same cloth and walk/dance together under an association flag. Groups are forming all the time and while they are age-graded to start, they stay together indefinitely. Only for Aminchi or other young never-marrieds does membership have to change.

Figure 9.4. A Hausa (Muslim) bride ceremonially reciting a portion of the Koran for the men, with women and children looking on.

All Muslim Sabon Zongo parents send their children to *makaranta*, Quranic school. There are currently eight operating in Sabon Zongo. They are teaching approximately eleven hundred children; the others are sent to makaranta outside. With the exception of one, which is not functioning well at the moment because it has lost its teachers, all are melting pots of ethnicities. In the approximate numbers obtained, 60 percent of the children are Hausa. The balance includes not only Kotokoli, Zabrama, Fulani, Yoruba, and Busanga—generally considered to have Muslim affiliation—but also small numbers of the southern Ghanaian Ga, Akan, and Ewe (who are usually Christian-affiliated). In the past, those girls who were sent to Quranic school received a minimal course of study until they married at about age thirteen. With the dilution of custom, all Muslim girls are given some Quranic schooling, while values associated with Islam have fed resistance to Western schooling in Sabon Zongo, and education of adults and children is well below the urban average, especially for females. Three of the eight Quranic school in Sabon Zongo now offer a combined English/Arabic curriculum, on top of the regular Western primary-plus schooling that children attend elsewhere. There is one secular primary school on the edge of Sabon Zongo; youth attend JSS (Junior Secondary School) and SS (Secondary School) outside the community.

Among the adult population, many of whom have had minimal secu-

lar education, professional expertise is low, there has been severe unemployment among men, and there are fewer women than in the wider
society in the wage-earning labor force (Brand 1972, 288). The remarks
of one elder was recapitulated by Alhaji Sule Bako, a college graduate
and son of the current chief: "[I]f the children of our fathers had gone
to school, there would be many many Hausa in educated positions." In
the early days, according to Alhaji Hamisu (1982), men worked primarily as traders (in cows, sheep, goats, or kola nuts), Quranic teachers,
tailors, butchers, retailers, *wanzamai* (traditional doctors/barbers), and
maroka (praise-singers); among the Hausa, as in Hausaland, these occupations were ranked. There were also beggars, lepers, cripples, and the
blind. Today, these traditional occupations and their organization, like
the chieftaincy and its offices, persist. According to the insider stereotype, all the men in Kan Tudu ("up on top," at the core of Sabon Zongo)
are Quranic teachers, while the men in Gangari ("downhill," the area
abutting the northern boundary of a major Accra road) are tailors and
mechanics. In fact, even for the Hausa, the occupational range is considerably broader. Among the 302 men of mixed ethnicities I sampled,
19 percent are tailors, 30 percent are in commerce, and 17 percent are
in transport (as drivers or repairmen). Commercial enterprises span mobile traders in watches and used cloth to wholesalers and large-scale
merchants. Traditional service roles for illiterates, like carrier ("kaya-
kaya"), watchman, and messenger, have been transposed to the modern
sector, in government and private business. Carpentry is, following the
ethnic stereotype, still overwhelmingly Ewe, charcoal sellers Sisala or
Grunshie, corn sellers in the market Zabrama, butchers and Quranic
teachers Hausa. But men are also white-collar workers and businessmen—
all indications of slowly penetrating change as the social and spatial
boundedness of the community has eased. Seventy years ago, owning
cows was a sign of prestige in Sabon Zongo; while this continues to be
true among the Hausa, it is no longer legal to raise them within the city
limits. And a cash economy has spawned other displays of wealth—cars,
ownership of homes elsewhere, household consumer items, multiple trips
to Mecca.

For Sabon Zongo women, the changes have been greater. The married Hausa women are far more mobile than they were in Malam Bako's
day. Like most of the other Sabon Zongo women, they engage in money-
earning activities, almost all of them in trade of one sort or another. While
the Queenmother of Sabon Zongo's Freedom Market, Letitia Tetteh, has
Hausa zongo women listed on her rolls, in fact none of them do sell
there—perhaps because of the deteriorated state of the market, although
other traders have not been deterred: there are between eighty-nine and

one hundred market traders there on a daily basis: 35 percent are Sabon Zongo dwellers; 38 percent are Ga, 26 percent Ewe, and the balance are primarily Akan. Many Hausa women engage in what the Yoruba call *jojoma:* they give something to the market women to sell. "Credit" women pay for the items gradually, so those who left them to be sold must return every day to collect payments from the traders selling for them. Jojoma traders sell cloth, petty goods, and jewelry. In my 18–compound sample, 18 out of 174 traders do jojoma. Twenty-four percent of the other traders sell their goods in the house or very nearby outside. In other words, one-third of the traders does not sit out in what is construed as the public space. More than half of the traders deal in food, 36 percent in *cooked* food. The nontraders are predominantly seamstresses.

Fewer girls than boys are sent for *Western* schooling beyond the primary grades; thus, even if they are free to work, assuming opportunities exist, they lack job skills for work in the modern sector. The persistence of northern traditionalism underscores the marginality of the community.

The spatial segregation, tied in with the economy and the inherent inequalities built in by the colonial government, has been exacerbated by age. Described as one of the "highly traditional tracts" and a "low status migrant sink" (Brand 1972:296, 292), Sabon Zongo is still spatially peripheral to the city, and poverty there is extreme. Unlike the suburban areas that grew out of the elite colonial neighborhoods, Sabon Zongo is also densely populated. Its shabby nature reflects the early ecological effect of European influence, which fostered a pattern of neglect by municipal authorities, traditional leaders, and private houseowners in the years that followed.

Despite its physical shabbiness, the Hausa, other Muslims, *and* Christians like to live in Sabon Zongo. Beyond economics, for the Hausa and Muslims, it is the pull of network coherence; for the Christians, it is the peacefulness and nondanger that are appealing. Well-to-do men reside there but do not own homes, simply because they are not heirs to early houseowners and there is no place to build. Some build houses in Shukura, Lagostown, and Abossey Okai but rent rooms in Sabon Zongo. They do not move into their owned properties outside Sabon Zongo, because "if you go live there, people take it like you want to go out from Muslim society. There are no mosques around there. And then if anything happens, you don't hear it quick. Things will happen, and then they will just pass before you hear it. [Within the zongo it is] easy for you to hear, because you are with the people and then people still regard you as being with them. As soon as you go [to the suburbs] then they think that you are making yourself too big for your people" (Hamidu 1982; see also Bako and Alkali 1982).

Chiefly Meaning

The Bako family chieftaincy persists, despite its unstable underpinnings and changing function. Sha'aibu's role and jurisdiction are no greater than those of his predecessors; they may be less, following the community's evolution, decreased isolation and insulation, greater diversity in population, and acculturation to the wider society. He is still an arbitrator, but members of the *fadawa* (the chief's officers, or cabinet) work outside the community, and it is difficult to hear cases regularly during the day. Nonetheless, the people do not view their access to outside civil courts as a viable alternative for resolving their quarrels.

The zongo chief's importance is tied to the functions he performs for his people, either directly or indirectly. Idrissu Bako, the first installed headman of Sabon Zongo, set up a court of offices, choosing the *galadima* and *ciroma* from among the family: the galadima was an important pre-Fulani position reserved for son or brother of the emir, and the *ciroma* is a title given to a son of the paramount chief (Schildkrout 1978, 92). In Zazzau, before the arrival of the British, it was rare for the sons of one father to succeed to the chieftaincy. With the British came changes in rules, form, and direction; for example, the British dropped the rule that only sons of kings could succeed to office (Smith 1960). In Accra, either galadima or ciroma could become chief, depending upon who was older, a practice that persists. The *sarkin fada* (chief's main counselor), *madawaki* (title of importance), and *maaji* (treasurer) were and still are chosen from other families, although of Hausa background.

Sha'aibu Bako became the ciroma. After Idrissu's death in 1969, his son Lebbo Bako was installed as chief.[53] Under Lebbo, Inussa (son of Lebbo's father's brother Hamisu) became galadima, while Sha'aibu (Lebbo's brother), continued as ciroma. Three years after assuming the headmanship (1969), Lebbo became ill, and Sha'aibu took over his duties. Lebbo died in 1981, and Sha'aibu was formally installed as sarkin zongo, while Inussa remained as galadima and Inussa's younger brother Yehaya became ciroma.

Like those who preceded him, Sha'aibu's role authorizes marriages (which the imam performs), grants divorces, and judges disputes. His fadawa advise him. The *alkali* (judge) consults the Quran for aid in coming to a just resolution. Most of Sha'aibu's cases involve domestic problems, including paternity suits. Some disputes occur between residents of differing ethnicity. In such situations, they go to their chiefs first, only coming to Sha'aibu as a court of last resort. In effect, the zongo has a pyramidal structure of chiefs and linkages between them: the Sabon Zongo chief is at the top and under him Kotokoli, Wangara, Chamba, and Ewe. Moreover, there are the traditional Hausa subchiefs of barbers, butchers, blind, and lepers, who oversee their constituents. When resolution of a problem is difficult, the subchief brings it to the Sabon Zongo headman.

As in times past, the chief also serves as a link between the government and the community. If Sabon Zongo needs certain services, the chief makes the request, for instance, to have better roads laid, new gutters dug. To expedite his "green revolution," Rawlings notified Sha'aibu, as one of the chiefs, to get his people involved. As chief, Sha'aibu is also informed of occasions, of rites of passage in the community; for example, he is presented with kola prior to a wedding, and he leads his people during festivals, including the annual Salla procession at the end of Ramadan.

The chief clearly serves a more informal role as well. Sha'aibu's house sits on one of the main streets in Sabon Zongo, in the *makwala* section, where there is much food selling. He is about seventy and has given up working as a "businessman." Shops flank his entrance hall (*zaure*). When he is not out, he sits in his *zaure*, the door open. Joined by individual advisors who may be free and by male friends who drop in to spend time with him he is available to advise his constituents. As it happens, like his father's brother Alhaji Hamisu, Sha'aibu is also recognized as a "healer": people suffering from aches and pains from various joint problems come to him.

The bulk of the Sabon Zongo people are Bako supporters. As chief, he is a symbol for them: his chieftaincy represents the founding of the community and provides grounds for ethnic continuity, for example in times of crisis or celebration. In fact, Alhaji Futa (1982), an educated and prominent member of Accra's Hausa community, speaks of things falling apart for the Hausa: they are unsure of their identity and support Muslim unity. As a consequence, symbols take on great import: while the chief is not empowered to do much, the continuing existence of the chieftaincy is indicative of the persistence of the group.

But Chief Sha'aibu feels his dignity and the authority he wields are demeaned and resents the way he is treated in his own house. His advisors do not show up for important meetings; when they intended to meet to appoint officers to five vacant posts, only one of the advisors showed up. In a child custody dispute that Sha'aibu was judging, the putative father refused to attend. After discussing the case, Sha'aibu said, "The Hausa chieftaincy is finished. Small boy, he doesn't come" (Sha'aibu Bako 1982). Sha'aibu is also disturbed by Bako family behavior: there is no unity among members, and they cannot be depended upon to attend as a group, only "one by one" (ibid.). And while Sha'aibu performed as acting chief while Lebbo was sick, he was challenged by Inussa.

Internal politics do not help in the continuing battle with the Damaley family. Sha'aibu points to the strategic importance of land as a source of chiefly authority: "If let's say you own this land and you are the chief here, that is more respectable at the same time comfortable because you can control everybody. Why? Because it is yours. But if this land is not yours and you are a chief, somebody can come and challenge you." But he does not understand the inherent weakness in his family's claim to Sabon Zongo's acreage: "At Zongo Lane they can challenge the chief, because the land is Accra chiefs' land. But here. . . . The land is ours, it is our *property*, nobody can come and say he will be the chief unless from our family" (ibid.). As strangers, they do *not* own the land. They were merely granted custodial privileges, and even that has been called into question, due to the dissension within the Ga stool. Schildkrout's work on the Kumase zongo shows that under colonialism "the headmen had no clearly defined position in the formal structure of government" (1970b, 266) and the relationships of the strangers with the colonial government, the traditional local authorities, and elected or party officials "have always been characterized by patronage rather than by the formal devolution of authority" (ibid., 258). From the foregoing material, we see that this has also been the case in Accra.

Sha'aibu's sense that the chieftaincy has suffered a loss of respect and power may in part be a mythologizing of the past—of the ethnic "purity" of the community, the rights of the Bako line, the legal victories that have provided immunity to challenge, and the authority of the chief. It may also be a metaphor for the alterations that have affected Sabon Zongo—the decreased separateness of men and women, the changes in housing composition, diversity of occupations, and education—Western as well as Quranic—for girls as well as boys. Yet, certainly, from the start, the stranger chief was cast in the role of the *mai gida*, the patron to his people, who himself needed patronage from formal governmental structures. This has not changed.

Competing sources of authority within the *zongo* have been critical. When they reached a disturbing pitch downtown, in concert with other pragmatic concerns, Malam Bako sought a new location for his community with support from within, from the British, from the Ga. Some Ga and Accra backing were shaky, and independence and party politics affected the balance of power. The current chief found himself a chief in name only.

Conclusion

This chapter has examined the culture of space and its relationship to the development of a community and its leadership.

Power is grounded in space, space encapsulates social values, and the design of space can alter the political status quo. It then follows that the spatial and social dispositions of the community, over which a leader holds sway, are mutually reflexive.

While the argument has focused on the example of the community of Sabon Zongo in Accra, it is by no means confined to it. During the colonial period, the British arrogated rights over territory wherever they were—in the Gold Coast and other African and South Asian colonies—determining who could claim territory and its use. They redesigned the spatial power relations tied up in the space and influenced the social composition of the community, exemplified by colonial cities, and their spatial organization, as in Accra and New Delhi.

Accra began not only as an administrative center but also as a commercial entrepôt. Increasing migration, especially to the growing urban areas, led to the development of differentiated enclaves, including a European sector, indigenous areas, and zongos. Examining the initial development of the downtown zongo and the creation of a new one provides insight into the clientage supporting the leader (patron), that leader's access to resources, and how resources are constituted. Malam Nenu, as the first Hausa mai gida, received land from the Ga; Malam Bako, his son, inherited Nenu's mantle. He gained credibility within the community as his father's son, as a scholar like his father, and as one who had claim to land that he could allocate. Public and British perception of him as a leader were mutually reinforcing; it was only with the sanction of the British that the Ga could acknowledge him.

According to native Gold Coast law, land trusteeship was tied to political leadership, that is, to chieftaincy, and because the Sabon Zongo people did not own the land, they were beholden to the Ga and to the British in power when Sabon Zongo was established. Thus, the stranger groups, like the constituents of the zongo who lacked traditional land rights, also looked to the British for access to land and headmanship over it. The British parceled out Ga space and decided who would reside there. But both the British and the Ga constituted a resource, a venue to legitimacy for those people desiring to be leaders. With the country's move to independence, political parties wielded influence regarding rights to chieftaincy. Clearly, landownership was not the only element needed to legitimize a group and its leader, and alternative means existed both internally and externally. In Sabon Zongo, as in Ibadan's Sabo Gari, the patron has always played a strong role, controlling clients and *zongo* leaders through considerable trade capital and through the help he provides. Patrons hoping to gain official leadership recognition depended upon their constituency and exogenous sources of authority. The choice, tenure, and effectiveness of leaders have been influenced by is-sues of authority both internal and external to the zongo in Accra and elsewhere.

Once colonialism entered the non-Western scene, chieftaincies in general were affected, with colonial powers, French or British, strength-ening or more likely weakening indigenous leadership. In any case, co-lonialism unquestionably had an impact upon power relations, and this did not cease with the end of the colonial era; it carried over into inde-pendence, with the "new elites" in Africa often moving into the social and physical spaces previously occupied by the foreign power. This per-petuated the confusion of social and political hierarchy—indigenous, stranger, European, independence, party, de facto, de jure. In Africa, and specifically Ghana, custom as represented by attachment to a traditional chieftaincy, or the idea of a traditional chieftaincy, also persists. In Chad, Nigeria, and Ghana, where zongo residents differ in background and ori-entation from those outside but are also more acculturated to the broader society than earlier residents are, the chief reminds them of their roots. Resources are important to these people who feel marginal to the local power structure, and zongo dwellers still want powerful patrons who can help them. As in the past, a community representative is necessary to deal with higher officials, but the man with the title and the man with the power may not be the same. While the titleholder glorifies the past, his title may be only symbolic to his subjects—something that provides continuity with the past, like the community, in its social and spatial aspects, where many have chosen to stay.

Notes

This chapter was originally published as an article in 1991 in *Ethnohistory* 38, no. 4:414–450. In 1995 and 1996, I did further research in the commu-nity of Sabon Zongo. I have incorporated data from these two field trips into this chapter, especially updating material in the "Zongo and the Chieftancy Today" section.

The research was carried out in 1982, 1995, and 1996 in Accra and was supported by grants from Syracuse University's Senate Research Fund, the Appleby-Mosher Foundation, and the American Philosophical Society. I read an earlier version, "Chieftaincy and the Evolution of an Accra *Zongo*," at the Center for Africa Studies at Yale University, in a workshop entitled "Un-planned Urbanization in Tropical Africa" in October 1986, and at the an-nual meeting of the African Studies Association in Madison, Wisconsin, also in October 1986. I would like to thank John M. Middleton, Frank A. Salamone, Naomi Chazan, Jon Kirby, Aidan Southall, Rhoda Howard, Shepard Krech III, and several shadowy reviewers for their comments. David Cole provided wonderful editorial advice. I alone am responsible for any inaccuracies.

1. The residents in the zongo are referred to as "strangers"—not so much non-Ghanaians as northerners, people from ethnic groups that are Muslim and inward-looking, whose cultural orientation contrasts with that of the "southerners," who are Christian and outward-looking.

2. My primary focus in this project was Accra's Hausa community and the manner in which it has maintained its identity over the past century. My methodology combined anthropology's traditional method of participant observation with more structured interviewing of Accra's Muslim chiefs and luminaries, the Sabon Zongo chiefs, members of (the recognized Hausa Sabon Zongo chief) Sha'aibu Bako's cabinet and family, and residents of Sabon Zongo. The Hausa speakers were interviewed in Hausa with the help of an interpreter. I collected family histories and accounts of the settlement of Sabon Zongo and the power struggles that precipitated its establishment, which I corroborated through research in Accra's National Archives. In order to pin down dates, for example that of the relocation to Sabon Zongo, I went to the Lands Department to search land titles for the construction of the railroad station and the main mosque. Some of the archival materials were extraordinary; for example, the account of the Bako family's political struggles follows several generations and is remarkably complete. But the state of the National Archives was chaotic, and one potentially crucial file (on Accra's Muslim community in the last quarter of the nineteenth century) could not be found.

Sha'aibu Bako introduced me to the lawyer representing his claim to the Sabon Zongo chieftaincy, James Glover-Amoako, who gave me all of the relevant court transcripts, as well as a survey map of Sabon Zongo. Sha'aibu also had old letters from the colonial government to Malam Bako and other members of the family, which he allowed me to photocopy.

3. Elsewhere I have dealt with the Accra-wide political struggles of the Muslims in relation to the central mosque (Pellow 1985).

4. Prevention of wholesale alienation of land was due to its not being very rich in minerals and to failure to institute plantations (Kaniki 1985).

5. It is clear from the literature that the migrants may have come to Ghana (the Gold Coast) not only as recruits (for example, in the military) but for idiosyncratic entrepreneurial reasons.

6. For example, when New Delhi was being planned as the capital of India, some British officials had suggested that it be placed in the hills of Simla, the hot-weather capital, in part because it would be remote from the indigenous people (Irving 1981). This is not only true in India; Spitzer (1974) documents the British creation of a hill station in Freetown, Sierra Leone, as a means of health segregation—to protect the Europeans from an unsalubrious climate and malaria-carrying mosquitoes by housing them in their own enclave above Freetown.

7. For example, the Hausas continually violated Ga traditions by killing crocodiles and cutting down mangrove trees by the Sakum River. Then the Ga would complain to the British ("A Report of Ga Chief Tackie's Complaints," 27 January 1893, SNA 1086, NAG).

8. As Leys (1975) notes for Kenya, indigenous people interested in organizing and facilitating the new economic activities became the mediating elite, and in Accra, upon independence, they moved into the physical and leadership spaces vacated by the British.

9. Through indirect rule, the British Crown created a façade of native rulers. "The 'Chief' [often indiscriminately designated] and the local colonial administrator were bound together officially in a pact of cooperation," the authority of each clearly dependent upon the will of the other (Betts 1978, 132).

10. Crowder and Ikime (1970, xv) agree that the chief lost his sovereignty to the colonial authorities in British West Africa but "nevertheless increased his power over his subjects because he was no longer restrained by the traditional checks and balances from below."

11. Much of the early material is based upon Dretke's (1968) account of the growth of Accra's Muslim community.

12. Junius Geoffrey is former secretary of the Ghana Muslim Mission.

13. Schildkrout (1970b, 258) describes this situation for Kumase.

14. In fact, even traditional Gold Coast chiefs who succeeded to office through ascription were judged on their performance by their subjects and needed popular approval to stay in office (Chazan 1983, 91).

15. Adamu may have consulted British records for this information, which throws into suspicion what is meant by *Hausa*. Is it simply a general term for "Muslim stranger"? I use the term as my informants presented it: their "forefather" who came from Katsina, one of the Hausa Bekwai.

16. Odoom (1971) has Abu Bakr next in line.

17. Ibrahima Braimah was a cattle dealer. His middle name apparently refers to his occupation, which, among the Hausa, is ranked at the bottom of the occupational ladder.

18. As Ga Manche, and thus owner of the land, he had the right to accept or reject a candidate for chieftaincy over any resident stranger tribal group (memo, 28 November 1902, SNA file 2288/01, NAG).

19. Tackie Tawiah told him "as his last words in the presence of witnesses, that he believed he will not live long, and in case he dies, the things [state sword and messenger cane] he had made for Mr. Braimah, must be taken by me with witnesses, and present [them] to him in the presence of his people" (letter from Captain Cudjoe to Acting Governor L. R. Arthur, 11 March 1902, ADM 11/1502, NAG).

20. Cohen (1969, 136f.) delineates the political nature of Friday prayer disputes common in the history of many Islamic communities.

21. On the 14 March 1903 meeting at Old Government House, Victoriaborg (Accra), between colonial government representatives and members of the Muslim community, see SNA 2288/01, NAG.

22. On the 5 March 1903 palaver held with Acting Secretary for Native Affairs Fell and N.O. Ali, Zenua, Garuba, Bako, and others, see SNA 2288/01, NAG.

23. Abubakar was the imam who catered to the men fighting in Captain Glover's force (from Nigeria) against the Asante, and who has also been listed by Odoom (1971) as one of Accra's chief imams.

24. Malam Bako recounted this episode in a letter to the district commissioner dated 10 July 1933. I obtained a copy from Sha'aibu Bako.

25. The land was so designated on 9 July 1907 in a certificate of title registered 28 March 1913, by A. White. I obtained a copy of it from Sha'aibu Bako.

26. According to Nii Sampah Kojo (1982), the Oshiahene [the man who conducts enstoolment for the Jamestown stool], he was Adjaben Ankrah; according to Idrissu Bako, former chief of Sabon Zongo, he was Quansah (*Manche D. P. Hammond v. Manche Kojo Ababio and Anor*. I hold the transcripts of this and all subsequently cited court cases.).

27. In fact, in the 25 April 1912 judgment of *Hammond v. Ababio* in the dispute regarding the land, 1909 was given as the date of the grant. Moreover, according to the map of this land drawn on August 25 1945 for a judgment in the dispute regarding the land given to Malam Bako, the size of the parcel was 71.2 acres. James Glover-Amoako, Sha'aibu Bako's lawyer, gave me a copy of the map.

28. *Tetteh Kwaku v. Kpakpo Brown and Ors*, 16 February 1910.

29. *Mantse D. P. Hammond of Asere, Ussher Town as Mantse of Asere v. Mantse Kojo Ababio IV and Chief Malam Bako*, 7 June 1910–25 April 1912.

30. *Chief Lebbo Baako v. Alhaji Adamu Damanley [sic] and Anor.*, 23 December 1981.

31. Correspondence from 1907 reveals that the British were involved in negotiations to survey a zongo outside of town, which was the section of land that became Sabon Zongo (letter to Y. Ex., 10/24/1907, ADM 11/1502, NAG).

32. N.O. Ali's eldest son, Mama Ali, was also nominated by Malam Abubakar and his "Fulani" followers.

33. Malam Bako's testimony, *Hammond v. Ababio*, 12 April 1912, p. 61.

34. See letter cited in note 24.

35. Kimble (1963, 18) notes that customary law provided for a permanent grant of land to a whole group of strangers who wished to settle; it did not need to be renewed upon the chief's death.

36. *Idrissu v. Damaley*,6 June 1982.

37. I derived the breakdown in table 1 from a survey map, which actually lists the names of the owners on each compound delineation. The copy I acquired was traced on 25 August 1945. I do not know when the original was drawn, but according to the chief and his elders, the listing is an early one, from Malam Bako's time.

38. *Hammond v. Ababio*, 25 April 1912, p. 75.

39. Letter from the DC [District Commissioner]'s Office, Victoriaborg, 18 April 1939. I obtained a copy from Sha'aibu Bako.

40. Letter from District Commissioner, Victoriaborg (Accra), to Hausa Chief, Sabon Zongo, 17 July 1940, No.1329/263/1939. I obtained a copy from Sha'aibu Bako.

41. Some refer to it as Toonga (Moro 1982; ADM 11/1502; SNA 2288/01), which corresponds to what others call Jonkobli. In his statement as the defendants' lawyer, Mills makes reference to "Jogobli" as a Hausa village (*Mantse D. P. Hammond of Asere, Ussher Town as Mantse of Asere v. Mantse Kojo Ababio IV and Chief Malam Bako*, 7 June 1910); Daniel Armatey Sampah, in his testimony, refers to Jonkobli as one of the villages founded on the disputed land (Supreme Court, Ghana, on appeal from the High Court, Lands Section—Accra; Tr. L. Suit No. 22/1948; Tr. L. Suit No. 25/1948; Tr. L. Suit No. 30/1953; 18 May 1962).

42. Abudu Razarku testimony, appeal proceedings *Idirisu Bako v. Wansa Damaley*, 4 November 1933.

43. *Chief Lebbo Bako v. Alhaji Adamu Damanley [sic] and Anor.*, 23 December 1981.

44. *Idrissu v. Wansa*, 29 September 1933.

45. *Idrissu Bako v. Wansa Damaley*, 20 February 1934.

46. Its leaders were violently anti-CPP because they backed age and traditional authority, which the CPP did not, and because they feared bad treatment of minority communities (Austin 1964, 188f.).

47. *Malam Idrissu Baako v. J. E. K. Djan*, Civil Appeal No. 72/69.

48. *Nii Yao Duade Crabbe III & Anor. v. J. A. Quaye and Anor.*, Civil Appeal No. 50/66, O. S. 22/80, 23 December 1981.

49. *Chief Lebbo Baako v. Alhaji Adamu Damaley and J.P. Allotey (Alias) Nii Amane Akwai II.*

50. The main Wangara chief, Jimala, lived in Accra Central.

51. Malam Halidou Atcha Dedji is the Chamba chief.

52. The 1970 census was taken shortly after the enactment of the Aliens' Expulsion Act (1969), and it is impossible to know to what extent fear of deportation affected the truthfulness of the responses regarding nationality and place of birth.

53. According to Alhaji Hamisu (1982), the succession "normally" goes from son to son of different wives, but all were too old.

References

Acquah, Ione.1958. *Accra Survey.* London: University of London Press.

Adamu, Mahdi. 1978. *The Hausa factor in African history.* London: Oxford University Press.

Ardener, Shirley, ed. 1981. *Women and space: Ground rules and social maps.* New York: St. Martin's Press.

Austin, Dennis. 1964. *Politics in Ghana: 1946–1960.* London: Oxford University Press.

B. K., Bako. 1982. Interview with author, 7 May, Accra, Ghana. Transcribed notes in possession of author.

Bako, Sha'aibu. 1982. Interviews with author, 4 March, 22 March, 23 April, 5 June. Accra, Ghana. Transcribed notes in possession of author.

Bako, Sha'aibu and Alkali. 1982. Interview with author, 4 May. Accra, Ghana. Transcribed notes in possession of author.

Barnes, Sandra T. 1986. *Patrons and power: Creating a political community in metropolitan Lagos.* Bloomington: Indiana University Press.

Betts, Raymond F. 1978. Imperialism and colonialism. *In African society, culture, and politics: An introduction to African studies,* edited by Christopher C. Mojekwu, Victor C. Uchendu, and Leo Van Hoey. Pp. 120–137. Washington, D.C.: University Press of America.

Blair, Thomas L. 1971. Shelter in urbanising and industrialising Africa. In *Shelter in Africa,* edited by Paul Oliver. Pp. 226–139. London: Barrie and Jenkins.

Boateng, E. A. 1959. *A geography of Ghana.* Cambridge: Cambridge University Press.

Bosman, William. [1705] 1967. *Description of Guinea.* London: Frank Cass.

Braimah, Amida. 1982. Interview with author, 18 January, 3 March, 30 March. Accra, Ghana. Transcribed notes in author's possession.

Brand, Richard. 1972. The spatial organization of residential areas in Accra, Ghana, with particular reference to aspects of modernization. *Economic Geography* 48:284–298.

Busia, K. A. 1951. *The position of the chief in the modern political system of Ashanti.* London: Oxford University Press.

Castells, Manuel. 1979. *The urban question: A Marxist approach.* Cambridge, Mass.: MIT Press.

Chazan, Naomi. 1983. *An anatomy of Ghanaian politics: Managing political recession, 1969–1982.* Boulder, Colo.: Westview.

Cohen, Abner. 1965. The social organization of credit in a West African cattle market. *Africa* 35:8–20.

———. 1969. *Custom and politics in urban Africa: A study of Hausa migrants in Yoruba towns.* London: Routledge and Kegan Paul.

Crowder, Michael. 1968. *West Africa under colonial rule.* Evanston, Ill.: Northwestern University Press.

Crowder, Michael, and Obaro Ikime, eds. 1970. *West African chiefs: Their changing status under colonial rule and independence.* New York: Africana Publishing.

Daily Graphic, The. 1982. Regent appointed for Sabon Zongo. April 16. Accra, Ghana.

Damaley, Adamu. 1982. Interview with author, 28 January. Accra, Ghana. Transcribed notes in possession of author.

Dedji, Malam Halidou Atcha. 1982. Interview with author, 12 June. Accra, Ghana. Transcribed notes in possession of author.

Dretke, James P. 1968. The Muslim community in Accra: An historical survey. M.A. thesis, University of Ghana, Legon.

English, Ali Kadri. 1982. Interview with author, 11 February. Accra, Ghana. Transcribed notes in possession of author.

Field, Margaret J. 1940. *Search for security: An ethno-psychiatric study of rural Ghana*. London: Faber and Faber.

Futa, Alhaji. 1982. Interview with author, 27 April. Accra, Ghana. Transcribed notes in possession of author.

Geoffrey, Junius. 1982. Interview with author, 21 June. Accra, Ghana. Transcribed notes in possession of author.

Ghana Government. 1978. *1970 Population Census of Ghana*. Special Report A. *Statistics of Towns with Population 10,000 and Over*. Accra: Census Office.

Giddens, Anthony. 1984. *The constitution of society: Outline of the theory of structuration*. Berkeley and Los Angeles: University of California Press.

Hamidu, Safianu. 1982. Interview with author, 6 February and 23 July. Accra, Ghana. Transcribed notes in possession of author.

Hamisu, Alhaji. 1982. Interview with author, 5 April and 13 May. Accra, Ghana. Transcribed notes in possession of author.

Hart, Keith. 1982. *The political economy of West African agriculture*. Cambridge: Cambridge University Press.

Harvey, William B. 1966. *Law and social change in Ghana*. Princeton, N.J.: Princeton University Press.

Hill, Polly. 1966. Landlords and brokers: A West African trading system. *Cahiers d'etudes africaines* 6:349–366.

Hiskett, Mervyn. 1984. *The development of Islam in West Africa*. London: Longman.

Ibrahim, Maman. 1982. Interview with author, 16 May. Accra, Ghana. Transcribed notes in possession of author.

Irving, Robert Grant. 1981. *Indian summer: Lutyens, Baker, and imperial Delhi*. New Haven, Conn.: Yale University Press.

Kaniki, M. H. Y. 1985. The colonial economy: The former British zones. In *General history of Africa*. Vol. 7, *Africa under colonial domination, 1880–1935*, edited by Adu Boahen. Pp. 382–419. Berkeley: University of California Press.

Kimble, David. 1963. *A political history of Ghana: The rise of Gold Coast nationalism, 1850–1928*. Oxford: Clarendon.

King, Anthony D. 1976. *Colonial urban development: Culture, social power and environment*. London: Routledge and Kegan Paul.

Klein, Martin A. 1971. Chiefship in Sine-Saloum (Senegal), 1887–1914. In *Colonialism in Africa: 1870–1960*. Vol. 3, *Profiles of change: African society and colonial rule*, edited by Victor Turner. Pp. 49–73. Cambridge: Cambridge University Press.

Kojo, Nii Sampah. 1982. Interview with the author, 29 April. Accra, Ghana. Transcribed notes in possession of author.

Kuklick, Henrika. 1979. *The imperial bureaucrat: The colonial administrative service in the Gold Coast, 1920–1939*. Stanford, Calif.: Hoover Institution Press.

Kuper, Hilda. 1972. The language of sites in the politics of space. *American Anthropologist* 74:411–425.

Leys, Colin. 1975. *Underdevelopment in Kenya: The political economy of neo-colonialism, 1964–1971*. London: Heinemann.

Mabogunje, Akin L. 1967. The morphology of Ibadan. In *The City of Ibadan*, edited by Peter C. Lloyd, Akin L. Mabogunje, and B. Awe. Pp. 35–56. Cambridge: Cambridge University Press.

———. 1970. Urbanization and Change. In *The African experience*. Vol. 1, *Essays*, edited by John N. Paden and Edward W. Soja. Pp. 331–358. Evanston, Ill.: Northwestern University Press.

Mair, Lucy. 1971. New elites in East and West Africa. In *Colonialism in Africa: 1870–1960*. Vol. 3, *Profiles of change: African society and colonial rule*, edited by Victor Turner. Pp. 167–192. Cambridge: Cambridge University Press.

Miles, William F. S. 1987. Partitioned royalty: The evolution of Hausa chiefs in Nigeria and Niger. *Journal of Modern African Studies* 25:233–258.

Moro, Hamidu. 1982. Interview with author, 24 January. Accra, Ghana. Transcribed notes in possession of author.

Odoom, K. O. 1971. A document on pioneers of the Muslim community in Accra. *Institute of African Studies Research Review* (Accra) 7, no. 3:1–31.

Ojo, G. J. Afolabi. 1968. Hausa quarters of Yoruba towns with special reference to Ile-Ife. *Journal of Tropical Geography* 27:40–49.

Ollennu, Nii Amaa. 1962. *Principles of customary land law in Ghana.* London: Staples Printers Ltd.

Paden, John. 1970. Aspects of emirship in Kano. In *West African chiefs: Their changing status under colonial rule and independence,* edited by Michael Crowder and Obaro Ikime. Pp. 162–186. New York: Africana Publishing.

Pellow, Deborah. 1985. Muslim segmentation: Cohesion and divisiveness in Accra. *The Journal of Modern African Studies* 23:419–444.

———. 1987. Solidarity among Muslim women in Accra, Ghana. *Anthropos* 82:489–506.

———. 1988. What housing does: Changes in an Accra community. *Architecture et Comportement* 4:205–220.

Pogucki, R. J. H. 1954. *Report on land tenure in customary law of the non-Akan areas of the Gold Coast (now Eastern Region of Ghana). Pt. 2, Ga.* Accra: Government Publishing.

Salamone, Frank A. 1978. Early expatriate society in Northern Nigeria: Contributions to a refinement of a rheory of pluralism. *The African Studies Review* 21, no. 2:39–54.

Schildkrout, Enid. 1970a. Government and chiefs in Kumasi Zongo. In *West African chiefs: Their changing status under colonial rule and independence,* edited by Michael Crowder and Obaro Ikime. Pp. 370–392. New York: Africana Publishing.

———. 1970b. Strangers and local government in Kumasi. *The Journal of Modern African Studies* 8:251–269.

———. 1978. *People of the Zongo: The transformation of ethnic identities in Ghana.* Cambridge: Cambridge University Press.

Skinner, Elliot P. 1963. Strangers in West African societies. *Africa* 33:307–320.

Smith, M. G. 1960. *Government in Zazzau: 1800–1950.* London: Oxford University Press.

Spitzer, Leo. 1974. *The Creoles of Sierra Leone: Responses to colonialism, 1870–1945.* Madison: University of Wisconsin Press.

Sudarkasa, Niara. 1979. From stranger to alien: The socio-political history of the Nigerian Yoruba in Ghana, 1900–1970. In *Strangers in African Societies,* edited by William Shack and Elliot Skinner. Pp. 141–67. Berkeley and Los Angeles: University of California Press.

Survey of Ghana. 1969. Accra: Government Publishing.

Thomas, Roger G. 1983. The 1916 Bongo "riots" and their background: Aspects of colonial administration and African response in eastern Upper Ghana. *Journal of African History* 24:57–75.

Tibenderana, Peter Kazenga. 1987. The role of the British administration in the appointment of the emirs of Northern Nigeria, 1904–1931: The case of Sokoto Province. *Journal of African History* 28:231–57.

Ward, Anthony. 1991. Biculturalism and community: A transformative model for design education. *Journal of Architectural Education* 44, no 2:90–109.

Ward, William E. F. 1948. *A history of the Gold Coast.* London: George Allen and Unwin.

Weisman, Leslie K. 1981. Women's environmental rights: A manifesto. *Heresies* 5, no. 3:6–8.

Works, John. 1976. *Pilgrims in a strange land: Hausa communities in Chad.* New York: Columbia University Press. Original edition 1972.

Archival Resources

NAG (National Archives of Ghana)
  ADM (Administration) 11/
    SNA (Secretary for Native Affairs) 1086 Accra Native
  Affairs: 1878–1903 (Case No. 271/1900)
  ADM 11/1
  ADM 11/1502 Hausa Community—Accra (Case No. 86/1912—SNA Board 133)
    SNA 1331/07
    SNA 2288

PART
V

The Postmodern City

CHARLES RUTHEISER

10 Making Place in the Nonplace Urban Realm

Notes on the Revitalization of Downtown Atlanta

Numerous recent chroniclers of the urban landscape have commented that the sociospatial processes of late capitalism have rendered contemporary cities less unique and more "a-geographic" (e.g., Zukin 1991, Sorkin 1992). Atlanta is in many ways paradigmatic of what Melvin Webber three decades ago termed "a nonplace urban realm" (Webber 1964): a sprawling, polycentered landscape characterized by the steady erasure of locality by the generic forms of a diversified yet ultimately homogenizing market culture. Since 1960, Atlanta has consistently ranked among the fastest-growing metropolitan areas in the United States. Between 1990 and 1995, the population of the twenty-county Atlanta metro area increased by 100,000 residents a year and led the nation in job growth. The benefits of this expansion have been most unevenly distributed, however, with the lion's share of growth concentrated in the suburban and exurban fringes that lie beyond the Perimeter beltway (see Hartshorn and Ihlanfeldt 1993; Rutheiser 1996, 74–138).

By contrast, with the exception of a few majority-white elite enclaves, such as Buckhead, Midtown, and a handful of gentrified "Intown" neighborhoods, the central city of Atlanta has seen its social and physical infrastructure further deteriorate in recent decades. Unlike those of other Sunbelt cities, such as Houston, Charlotte, and Memphis, Atlanta's efforts to expand via annexation have been unsuccessful. Its current municipal boundaries have remained essentially the same since 1952.

Consequently, by 1995, the city of Atlanta was home to approximately only 425,000 of the metro region's more than 3.5 million residents (*Atlanta Constitution,* 24 August 1995). Despite its progressive reputation as "the city too busy to hate," Atlanta nonetheless experienced massive "white flight" during the 1960s. In 1960, whites constituted two-thirds of the city's population; by 1970, they were less than half. In 1980, nearly two-thirds of the city's population was African American, a proportion that has remained stable to this day.

During the 1970s and 1980s, the suburban exodus expanded to include much of the city's much-celebrated African American middle class as well as some of the African American poor. The departure of many of Atlanta's most affluent African Americans helped to contribute to extreme income inequality along racial lines. In 1990, for example, white median household income was $61,691, while for African Americans it was only $22,372 (Hartshorn and Ihlanfeldt 1993, 41). During the early 1990s, while the Atlanta metro area enjoyed the status of being one of the most hospitable for business in the world, the city at its core enjoyed the dubious statuses of being one of the poorest and most violent in the nation.

No one area better exemplifies the city of Atlanta's decline and fall than its central business district, an area that takes its name from a crucial street juncture known as "Five Points." Once known as the "Times Square, the Hollywood and Vine, the Singapore of the South" because of its bustling mix of commercial, retail, and entertainment functions (Sindeman 1991, 13), by the early 1990s the Five Points area was a vacant shell of its former self, a void at the center of the ring of growth. In 1992, downtown Atlanta was no more than an archipelagic assemblage of fortified enclaves inhabited in the daylight hours by government office workers, conventioneers, and college students, and in the night by a substantial population of homeless persons.

In 1990, the city's selection to host the 1996 Olympic Games raised hopes among many Atlantans that the Olympics would be a catalyst for redevelopment of its moribund core and its surrounding ring of depressed residential neighborhoods. Indeed, the prospect of a material Olympic legacy helped to minimize organized opposition to the city's bid. Most of the major Olympic venues were to be located in a five-kilometer-wide "Olympic Ring" centered on downtown. Despite these expectations, however, the mostly white, suburban corporate mandarins atop the summit of the Atlanta Committee for the Olympic Games, or ACOG, modeled their operations on the highly profitable Los Angeles Games of 1984, rather than on the more lavishly state-subsidized ventures in Seoul (1988) and Barcelona (1992). Despite Mayor Maynard Jackson's call for exten-

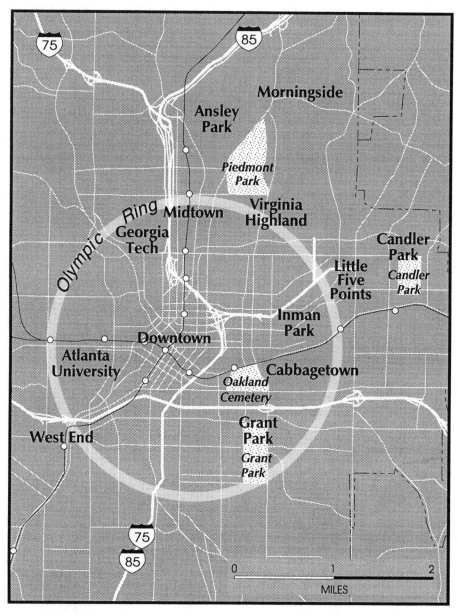

sive redevelopment projects in connection with the Games, ACOG limited its vision, money, and responsibility to "inside the fences" of the stadia and other venues, rather than the entire extent of the Olympic Ring.

The responsibility for creating a meaningful Olympic legacy thus fell to the city government and the business community, two entities that in the past had enjoyed a close working relationship often described

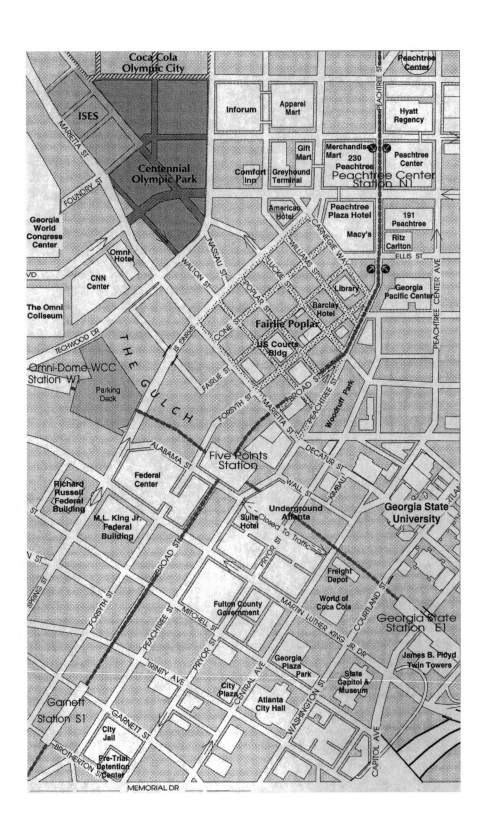

as a marriage of white money and black political power (see Stone 1989). Visiting Barcelona as honored guests during the 1992 Olympics, Atlanta's civic and business leaders were reminded that the center of their city lacked a sense of what they referred to as "traditional urbanity." Given the vast amount of academic ink that has been spilled over what terms like "city" and "urban" mean, I was naturally intrigued by what the power elite meant by "traditional urbanity" and how it could be realized through what they termed "the renovation of the public character of the city." Their emphasis on the "public character" of the city was especially significant given the current tendencies toward the eradication of public space in contemporary North American cities (see Sorkin 1992, Boyer 1993), as well as the exceptional degree to which past patterns of urban development had eviscerated Atlanta's public spatial domain.

The Whole in the Center

Atlanta's current concern with fabricating a sense of urbanity needs to be seen in the context of a century and a half of efforts to enhance its image and reputation. While campaigns of organized and systematic promotion are an integral part of the history of virtually every U.S. city, few cities can match Atlanta's giddy and fervid boosterism. Under the influence of the mystical "Atlanta Spirit," generations of profit-minded visionaries have transformed a once provincial railroad hub into a putatively "world-class" postindustrial metropolis. As measured through its official slogans, in the course of this century Atlanta has evolved from the "Gate City" and "Capital of the New South" to a "Major League" or "National City," that was "Too Busy to Hate" to the "World's Next Great International City" (see White and Crimmins 1980). The current efforts of Atlanta's boosters celebrate a neutered vision of a bland, techno-oriented, generic urbanity that downplays or outrightly excludes reference to the city's two principal and conflicting historical legacies: one, the segregated white southern city that once served as world headquarters of the revived Ku Klux Klan; the other the "Black Mecca" of African American educators, entrepreneurs, and civil rights leaders.

An orientation toward the future helps Atlantans ignore the contradictory complexities of their multiple pasts that continue to be manifest in the present. Since the 1960s, these technopolitan visions have been inscribed, sometimes rather brutally, on the physical body of the city, and have served to help eradicate, or at best obscure, the material manifestations of Atlanta's divided and contested history. As historian Clifford Kuhn has noted, the segregation of collective memory in Atlanta has far outlasted the formal-legal segregation of its physical landscape (Kuhn et al. 1990). Although they might seem otherwise, current efforts to renovate the public character of downtown mark the latest elaboration of, rather than a sharp break from, a generically urban technopolitan mentality.

Appropriating a term from Walt Disney, I like to refer to those actors and institutions who are reshaping the image and built form of downtown Atlanta as "imagineers." This is more than a glib metaphor, for their wistful visions of Atlanta as a "safe, clean, and user-friendly city" (Central Atlanta Progress 1987), resonate rather strongly with the programmed totalizing environments encountered in one of Disney's theme parks. Indeed, the Disney-fied notion of a city as a kind of theme park has, through the practices and publications of the Rouse Corporation and the Urban Land Institute, increasingly been assimilated into mainstream practices of urban design and have been made manifest in cities from San Diego to Boston. Still, I am using "imagineering" in a much looser way than the strict Disney-ite sense of designing "futuristic solutions to theatrical and infrastructural problems" (Fjellman 1992), to encompass the activities of all those cultural producers who create the discursive fields in which the practices of urban redevelopment and revitalization are conceptualized, discussed, and turned into facts on the ground. These include journalists and academics as well as politicians, developers, business leaders, and their hired cadres of architects, designers, engineers, and public relations specialists. These imagineers in no way constitute a unified group. Indeed, they do not recognize themselves as such, and relations among some of them are better described more in terms of conflict than consensus. Nonetheless, differences of professional identity and conflicts of interest are frequently transcended by belief in the same strategic myth of Atlanta as a socially progressive, racially harmonious, world-class city with a high-tech future. In addition, the imagineers often reach some agreement about the tactics necessary to turn this myth into concrete realities.

As Paul Virillio (1983), Nell Smith (1986, 1992), and Mike Davis (1990), among others, have noted, contemporary practices of urban redevelopment frequently employ the rhetoric, if not the outright methods, of military conquest and colonial settlement. The proposed redevelopment of downtown Atlanta provides yet another example of efforts to pacify and resettle a threatening and unruly urban frontier. Indeed, the frontier mythos of virtuous pioneers civilizing a savage urban landscape has been well established for over a decade and provides a ready-made vocabulary to authorize the process of gentrification and revitalization. The frontier replaces social hygiene as the paradigmatic referent for an earlier set of loaded metaphors that accompanied the successive waves of urban renewal that took place from the late 1930s to the late 1960s. By conceptualizing poor neighborhoods in terms of "blight," the then-dominant vernacular of social pathology legitimated dramatic intervention to check the spread of contagion and ensure the vitality of the urban organism. Regardless of the differences between these two sets of authorizing metaphors, however, the underlying aim has been the same: the revitalization of real estate values rather than of communities. Indeed, many of the assumptions and images of urban pathology remain in our popular cultural consciousness.

Restructuring the Center: The Urban Renewal Years

Although many Atlantans like to joke that Sherman's sacking of the city in the late fall of 1864 constituted its first instance of urban renewal, the federally sanctioned and subsidized spasm of demolition and displacement did not take place until the 1930s. During the throes of the Depression, downtown property owners successfully lobbied the Roosevelt administration for funds to raze poor neighborhoods on the periphery of the central business district and replace them with low-cost public housing (see Palmer 1955; Stone 1989). In 1936, Atlanta became the site for the first federally funded public housing project in the United States: Techwood Homes. Located just northwest of downtown and immediately south of the campus of the Georgia Institute of Technology, Techwood was soon joined by nine other public housing projects on the southern, eastern, and western edges of downtown by 1942.

During World War II, Atlanta's largest downtown businesses and property owners created a formal organization—the Central Atlanta Improvement Association, later known as the Central Atlanta Association, or CAA—to advance their collective interests and plan for the city's future. In large measure, the city administration deferred to the interests and visions of the CAA, especially its most powerful member, the Coca-Cola Corporation. As one commentator put it, "The business elite ran the city as a benevolent oligarchy with a practically telepathic link to city hall" (Powledge 1975, 46). After the war, Atlanta's civic-business elite abandoned its support for close-in public housing and utilized federally subsidized highway construction and urban renewal to create a *cordon sanitaire* around the central business district and to raze some of the adjacent, largely African American residential neighborhoods for new development. In 1952, the elite's vision for the city was formalized in Atlanta's first master planning study, conducted by the newly created Metropolitan Planning Commission. The nonbinding plan called for a network of connecting and perimeter highways linking the center to the growing suburbs, the extensive rebuilding of downtown in a style of megalomaniacal modernism that Jane Jacobs later referred to as the "Radiant Garden City Beautiful" (Jacobs 1961), and the relocation of African Americans living on the peripheries of downtown to new public housing built in the far southern and western reaches of the city (Metropolitan Planning Commission 1952, i)

In the course of the next two decades, the vision of the Metropolitan Planning Commission was largely, although not completely, realized. In the late 1950s and early 1960s, the "Downtown Connector" expressway forcefully disconnected the central business district from the surrounding neighborhoods. Mayor Ivan Allen, a scion of the "benevolent oligarchy," made extensive use of federal urban renewal and other public monies to build the necessary public infrastructure to attract private investment and put Atlanta on the map as a city of national significance, a "major league city" (Stone 1989). These features included a stadium for major league sports teams, extensive hotel and convention facilities, and a mass transit system focused on downtown. Together with freeway construction, urban renewal projects demolished more than thirty thousand units of low-income housing and displaced at least 20 percent of the central city's population between 1958 and 1968, nearly all of whom were African American (Stone 1989). Meanwhile, the dynamic growth of suburban counties siphoned off the retailing and commercial office activity of the central business district, leading to massive vacancy, demolition, and disinvestment in ensuing decades.

While urban renewal was creating free-fire zones for private capital just outside the walls, behind the battlements of the expressway downtown was turned inside out in the late 1960s and early 1970s by a series of enclaved mixed-use developments (or MXDs) that embodied the first principles of an essentially generic urbanism. Whereas the Metropolitan Planning Commission had envisioned the continued centrality of the Five Points area, the new MXDs were all located on the peripheries of the central business district. The mother of all these MXDs was Peachtree Center, a networked realm of convention hotels, trademarts, office buildings, and shopping galleries covering more than ten square blocks a quarter-mile north of Five Points. Built piecemeal between 1966 and 1992, Peachtree Center was intended by its architect/developer, John Portman, to be a "new downtown" for the "national" or major league city that Atlanta had become. By the mid-1980s, Peachtree Center was the recognized core of a dedicated hotel-convention district that lay at the heart of the central city's economy.

During the 1970s, a number of other MXDs were built on the fringes of the central business district. The largest and most important of these was the Omni International complex, which arose along the southwestern edge of downtown on a platform built in the air rights over the Norfolk and Southern rail lines. Like Peachtree Center, the Omni originally featured a mix of office, shopping, hotel, and entertainment facilities, including a sports arena, ice rink, and amusement park. However, unlike Portman's "new downtown," the Omni project was beset by massive cost overruns and opened just as its intended market (the city's white upper middle class) was completing its exodus to the suburbs. The failure of the Omni mall was somewhat offset by the state-subsidized construction of the Omni Arena for professional basketball and ice hockey and the elephantine Georgia World Congress Center, a successful convention and trade show facility. In 1987, the bunkered, debt-ridden, and partially vacant Omni International complex was acquired by media mogul Ted Turner, who turned it into the headquarters for his Cable News Network. Now known as CNN Center, the former Omni is currently one of the city's major tourist attractions. The mixed-use megastructure was further strengthened with the completion of the Georgia Dome in 1990 and the construction of the Georgia International Plaza in 1996.

The recentering of downtown Atlanta was driven by the competitive efforts of rival groups of private developers rather than by coordinated planning. Although the city government developed its planning capacity during the late 1960s, it continued to defer to the visions of the business community when it came to downtown. In 1967, the Central Atlanta Association was transformed into a nonprofit corporation known as Central Atlanta Progress, or CAP, so as to better leverage public subsidies for private development. In 1971, CAP released its first master plan for the downtown area. Essentially a transportation plan, the Central Area Study, as it was known, called for the massive expansion of the expressway and mass transit systems to better link downtown with the airport and the expanding suburbs (Central Atlanta Progress 1971). Aside from calling for the development of the area around Peachtree Center as a hotel-convention district, it was short on specifics and gave a mostly unimpeded hand to private developers. Although community opposition stymied the construction of new expressways through residential neighborhoods, much of the Central Area Study found its way into official city development policy.

Outside the enclaves formed by Peachtree Center and the CNN Center/World Congress Center/Dome complex, the remainder of downtown Atlanta deteriorated markedly in the 1970s and 1980s. The case of Underground Atlanta provides a good example of this process, as well as an early effort to re-create a nostalgic simulation of urbanity. During the 1920s, the city government had constructed raised viaducts over the railroad tracks south of Five Points to relieve traffic congestion. In the late 1960s, local entrepreneurs adaptively reused some of this forgotten space for a popular subterranean entertainment venue, featuring bars, restaurants, and live music, in a simulated 1890s streetscape. However, as Atlanta became a majority black city in the 1970s, Underground Atlanta was increasingly perceived as a dangerous area by white suburbanites, who stayed away in droves. Together with the disruptions caused by construction of the city's central mass transit system, the disruption of business by racially coded perceptions of crime and danger helped to drive Underground into bankruptcy in 1982.

For the remainder of the 1980s, two successive mayoral administrations negotiated with the Maryland-based Rouse Corporation in an effort to revive Underground. Developer James Rouse had by the middle of the decade risen to national prominence on the success of a series of "urban festival markets," such as Boston's Faneuil Hall and Baltimore's Harborplace. Characterized by slick marketing and a highly romanticized and selective use of history, the festival market married the consuming imperatives of the shopping mall with the programmed feel of the theme park. Indeed, James Rouse made no bones about his admiration for, and intellectual debt to, Walt Disney (see Fjellman 1992, Sorkin 1992). Housed in decayed port areas and other spaces made obsolete by the relentless march of market-driven change, Rouse's creations were heralded as postmodern miracles of adaptive reuse. After years of complex negotiations and subsidized by nearly $200 million in loans, city bonds, and federal Urban Development Action Grants, the new Underground Atlanta reopened as just such a Rouse-ified zone in 1989.

Unlike Faneuil Hall and Harborplace, however, Underground failed in its intended role as an anchor for downtown redevelopment. Part of this problem is the nature of the site. The most successful of Rouse's markets were located in harbor or riverside locations with dramatic views of the skyline. While railroads were to Atlanta what ports were to many other cities, the analogy was not as amenable to adaptive reuse. Underground was exactly what its name implied: a claustrophobic subterranean space with no views, light, or air that no amount of attention to the fine-grained historical details could overcome. Bad space was the least of Underground's problems, however. Between 1989 and 1992, the Five Points business district suffered the departure of nearly ten thousand jobs (Haddow and Company 1991, 1A), as downtown department stores, banks, and law, architecture, and accounting firms flocked to the prime new spaces arising outside the central area. A near mortal blow was delivered in late April, 1992, when large-scale rioting and looting by African American teens after the announcement of the Rodney King verdict helped to reconfirm in the minds of white suburbanites and corporate leaders the status of Five Points (and Underground) as a dangerous area. Swimming in red ink and beset by high rates of vacancy and tenant turnover, Underground's management company was obliged to seek a massive restructuring of its debt payments in 1995. On the eve of the Olympics, many in the business community and even city government had grown pessimistic about Underground's chances for survival.

The second coming of Underground Atlanta, though, was more a creation of the city government than of the business community. While CAP gave the project its reluctant endorsement, its main concerns lay north of the Five Points area. Underground, for example, did not figure prominently in the second Central Area Study that CAP published in 1987. Just as the first Central Area Study reflected the autocentric obsessions of late modernist city building, CAS-II embodied the postmodern, Rouse-ian turn toward making place through a concern for the specific details of the urban landscape. CAS-II was concerned with filling in the gaps and softening the hard edges of the urban surface encouraged by its predecessor with mixed-income housing and better security, maintenance, marketing, and design. The shared vision it articulated for Atlanta (without bothering to specify who it was that shared it) was of a safe, clean, "user-friendly," "twenty-four hour city" (see Central Atlanta Progress 1987).

Of all these notions, that of the "user-friendly city" is the most revelatory about the imbedded assumptions of CAP's imagineers. The term "user-friendly" is most often encountered in the realm of computers, where it refers to an interface carefully designed not to intimidate or confuse the user. What makes the interface "friendly" is that all the potentially problematic and complicated choices have been worked out for the users in a simple, persuasive, and clearly rendered manner. Of course, this is not in and of itself a bad thing; we can all appreciate legible street signs and buildings that inspire, uplift, and empower, but user-friendliness also has the tendency to program out certain kinds of knowledge, constrain choice, and assume a certain standardization of needs and experiences. There is a world of difference between making cities "legible" (see Lynch 1960) and turning them into the kinds of edutainment theme parks that sell a sterilized essence of urbanity.

The characterization of the urban population as "users," rather than as residents, taxpayers, citizens, or voters, is even more telling. The term may imply that the city is more oriented to visitors than residents, or rather, that the line between residents and visitors is no longer that significant, that even natives are strangers who need guidelines, and better yet, guides. In 1996, downtown property owners levied a tax on themselves to create a Downtown Improvement District and fund the creation of a private security patrol: the Downtown Ambassadors Force. In addition to policing "quality of life" crimes like panhandling and graffiti, one of the most important functions of the pith-helmeted Ambassadors is to provide directions and other information to the legitimate users of the city's sidewalks. The notion of user-friendliness also assumes that all users have the same needs and identities, or that certain groups, such as the poor or homeless, are excluded outright from the category of desired users.

Indeed, CAS-II ushered in the beginning of an institutionalized crackdown on Atlanta's homeless that continues unabated into the present. The study proposed a "safeguard" or "hospitality" zone for downtown in which a wide range of homeless behaviors, such as panhandling, loitering, and sleeping on park benches, would be forbidden. Recent city policy has gone considerably beyond CAS-II recommendations, with the homeless viewed as "predatory" rather than a victimized population. By the mid 1990s, even putatively liberal newspaper columnists blamed the homeless for almost single-handedly causing downtown's decline, conveniently overlooking the wider socioeconomic forces at play in motivating the corporate exodus from downtown. Rather than provide training, jobs, and housing for the homeless, both the city government and the business community are more interested in making downtown less amenable to these undesirable users. Actually, the homeless are not users at all, since users "use" the city by spending money.

The development of middle- and upper-income housing was another key element of CAS-II, with no less than ten thousand new units of market-rate housing to be built in the central area by private developers heavily subsidized by public loan guarantees, state-backed bonds, tax abatements, and the like. Between 1988 and 1990, the city government created eleven housing enterprise zones on the periphery of downtown. Developers building in these zones qualified for tax-exempt bond financing from the city's Urban Residential Finance Authority and long-term abatements on property taxes. Six of these zones were located just to the northeast of the central business district in an area known as Bedford-Pine. Originally a poor African American neighborhood called Buttermilk Bottom, the area had been razed during the 1960s, but redevelopment had been stymied by the opposition of adjacent neighborhood leaders. During the latter half of the 1980s, a for-profit subsidiary of Central Atlanta Progress aided private developers in constructing a series of gated town-home communities in Bedford-Pine. While successful, the enclaved developments did little to revitalize the surrounding area.

As with previous "plans" for the city, CAS-II was a rough guide rather than a detailed blueprint for action. The emphasis was on creating an alluring investment climate rather than a set of coordinated and regulated actions that limited the prerogatives of private developers. More important, it failed to link the redevelopment of the central area with the poorer residential neighborhoods that surrounded it. In any event, the implementation of its vision was severely limited by several developments. The most important of these were the post-1987 recession and the legacy of a decade of speculative overbuilding, which left downtown glutted with vacant luxury office space and put many developers in dire financial straits through the early 1990s. Compounding these troubles was the unavailability of the necessary public subsidies for private development. Burdened by a long-term debt load second only to New York City (Stone 1989), and with federal aid to cities reduced to a trickle of its former flow, the city of Atlanta was (and remains) hard-pressed to provide the kind of corporate welfare demanded by potential investors.

Far more significant than the shortage of necessary capital, though, was a breakdown of the city's biracial civic-business coalition. During the late 1980s and early 1990s, many of downtown's corporate fixtures were acquired by national firms and/or divested themselves of their sunk investments in downtown, while for its part the city's political establishment was paralyzed by internecine conflicts and revelations of corruption. in short, by 1990, what Logan and Molotch have called Atlanta's "urban growth machine" (Logan and Molotch 1987) had been driven straight into the ground.

The Politics of Olympic Redevelopment, 1990–1995

The awarding of the Olympics in September of 1990 thus came at a very awkward time, as both the city government and the business community were in a profound state of disarray. With the unraveling of the biracial civic-business partnership and the active support of then-mayor Andrew Young, ACOG was able to carve out a protected sphere of maneuver free of any meaningful public oversight. With its hiring of Young and legions of other city hall insiders, ACOG in some ways constituted a private-public partnership in and of itself. By limiting its responsibility to inside the fences of the venues themselves, ACOG relegated everything else to a city government that lacked the fiscal and human resources to deal with it.

Despite much talk of an impressive Olympic legacy during the bid process, after the awarding of the Games in 1990 ACOG announced that it would focus its attention, and its money, only on the Olympic venues themselves. Any and all responsibility for plans "outside the fence," as they called it, rested with the city. During the fall of 1992, the city government belatedly mobilized to realize this aim. A crack team of nationally known architects and planners, the Rural/Urban Design Assistance Team, or R/UDAT, was brought in to consult. Their report argued against initiating any major new construction and focused instead on building pacified pedestrian corridors between already existing nodes of development, such as Peachtree Center, Underground Atlanta, and the CNN/World Congress Center area (R/UDAT 1992). These corridors were to be created by new street lighting, pavements, and street furniture and were intended to stimulate pedestrian traffic both during and after the Olympics. Indeed, a more pedestrian-friendly streetscape, along with downtown housing for aspiring urban gentry, is what many city and business leaders meant by the term "traditional urbanity": a stage set with the look and feel of an older city. The R/UDAT recommendations corresponded rather neatly with the streetscape plans of the 1987 Central Area Study. Nonetheless, many Atlantans, especially those in the poorer neighborhoods, were deeply disappointed by the modesty and limited extent of R/UDAT's urban redecorating plans.

Shortly after the release of the R/UDAT report, the city established the Corporation for Olympic Development in Atlanta, or CODA, to oversee "outside the fence" development. In a flurry of Olympic-sized rhetoric, Mayor Maynard Jackson envisioned CODA spending several hundred million dollars to redevelop Atlanta's poorest neighborhoods. However, unlike ACOG, CODA was severely limited in its ability to acquire either public or private financing. After its appeals for funding to the state legislature and the local business community were rebuffed, and facing opposition from justifiably suspicious neighborhood leaders, CODA soon abandoned plans to undertake large scale revitalization of depressed inner city neighborhoods within the Olympic Ring and instead essentially adopted the corridor strategy as outlined in the R/UDAT report. In the end, CODA expended only $70 million on new downtown streetscapes, sculpture, and the renovation of two small parks before disbanding in December 1996.

Although CODA's vision languished for lack of funding, the city of Atlanta was able to obtain federal funding for three other ambitious projects, none of which was completed before the Olympics. In 1993, the city-owned Atlanta Economic Development Corporation won approval for the construction of a $300 million federal office complex adjacent to Underground Atlanta. Located on the former site of the landmark Rich's Department Store, the Atlanta Federal Center would house up to 8,000 federal employees when it was completed in 1997. While heralded by city officials as the savior of the southern central business district, the

Federal Center is another enclaved mini-arcology like Peachtree Center that has little physical linkage to the surrounding area. More important, the transfer of federal employees to the new complex emptied eight older, or "Class B," office buildings in the downtown area.

In 1994, the city of Atlanta was selected as one of six cities in the United States to qualify for the federal Empowerment Zone project. Quite probably, the last big disbursement of federal urban development monies, the Empowerment Zone is a Clintonian reinterpretation of the notion of urban enterprise zones. The Department of Housing and Urban Development will provide Atlanta's Empowerment Zone Corporation (EZC) with $100 million to enhance housing, childcare, and job training in a nine square mile area to the south, east, and west of downtown where over half the population live below the poverty line and more than a fifth are unemployed (*Atlanta Journal Constitution*, 3 June 1994). In addition, businesses choosing to invest in the area will receive $150 million in tax breaks. As the Empowerment Zone project is to take its lead from projects generated by the communities themselves, it offers the prospect of true "bottom-up" rather than "top-down" development. The extent of community participation in this process is questionable, as control of the EZC is vested in the hands of the mayor and his hand-picked appointees. As of late 1996, however, the only major project to receive the approval of the EZC board was the reconversion of an abandoned textile mill into a mixed-use loft/studio development.

In October 1993, the Atlanta Housing Authority received a separate grant of $42 million from the Department of Housing and Urban Development to convert the Techwood/Clark Howell housing projects into a privatized mixed-income community. Located just south of the Georgia Tech campus and the world headquarters of the Coca-Cola Corporation, Techwood/Clark Howell had long posed a problem for Central Atlanta Progress and other members of the business community. Previous efforts to raze the complex had been stymied by the political problems associated with the displacement and relocation of several hundred poor African American families. In 1992, a small section of Techwood was demolished to make way for housing for Olympic athletes. Shortly thereafter, pressure from ACOG, together with the sacking of the AHA's director and the timely provision of federal funding, proved sufficient to overcome resistance to the conversion project. Since then, nine other public housing projects in Atlanta have been slated for conversion into privatized mixed-income communities.

While the replacement of these decrepit, poorly maintained establishments constitutes a significant improvement, the end result of these conversions will be a significant decrease in the number of low-income housing units in the city of Atlanta. The new communities will have fewer overall units than the projects they replace, and only 60 percent of those units will be dedicated for low-income households. Residents displaced by construction, and those unable to be accommodated in the new communities, will be relocated in private housing with Section VIII vouchers. As these vouchers only provide from three to five years of subsidized rent, this relocation strategy provides only a temporary fix to the problem of low-income housing. Indeed, according to Empty the Shelters, a local homeless advocacy group, a significant number of those families displaced from Techwood/Clark Howell have become homeless.

Despite these three projects, it has been the private sector that proved most energetic in renovating the public character of downtown prior to the Olympics. The most spectacular project in this regard was the construction of the Centennial Olympic Park by a joint partnership of ACOG, the Atlanta business community, and the State of Georgia. Less than a month after HUD awarded the money for the reconversion of Techwood/Clark Howell, ACOG erased the line it had drawn between inside and outside the fence, and proposed the construction of a privately funded park located on seventy-two acres just south of Techwood. This expanse of parking lots, single-room occupancy hotels, homeless shelters, and small manufacturing enterprises had long been re-visioned by architects and coveted by speculators, but the depressed state of the downtown real estate market throughout much of the 1970s and 1980s, not to mention the existence of the nearby Techwood/Clark Howell housing projects, stymied efforts at redevelopment.

In October 1993, HUD removed this latter impediment by allocating the funds to demolish Techwood /Clark Howell and replace it with a smaller, privately managed mixed-income community. Although the project would not be completed until 1997–1998, the demolition of the offending residences would be completed well before the world's media arrived to cover the Olympic Games. A little more than a month later, astonished Atlantans picked up their morning paper to read about ACOG's plan to replace what the then-president of the Chamber of Commerce called a "cancer on the body of the city" with a vast new green space. No group of Atlantans were more surprised that Thanksgiving Day morn than the mayor, the mayor-elect, the planning commissioner, and the rest of the political establishment, none of whom had been consulted. ACOG's explanation for its silent maneuvering was that it wanted to work out all the details and financing before revealing it to the public. However, it is clear that ACOG wanted to minimize any potential opposition to its plans by keeping the project secret as long as possible.

By contrast, ACOG leaders had no compunction about quietly meeting with the president of Coca-Cola and governor of Georgia, although they saw no need to inform the city government of its plans. ACOG and the business community were determined to keep the city as far out of "their" park as possible. In January 1994 Georgia Governor Zell Miller authorized the state-owned World Congress Center Authority to oversee the effort to build the park, although funding would come exclusively from private sources, including ACOG, major local corporations, and philanthropic foundations.

For a city that prided itself on the harmonious marriage of civic and business interests, the park project marked a major refiguring of the concept of the public-private partnership. In this case, the "public" in the partnership was constituted by the State of Georgia and its quasi-public entities like the World Congress Center Authority, not the city government, much less the citizenry the latter represented. Rather than being players, the city and its panoply of development agencies were reduced, essentially, to benchwarmers at best, mere spectators at worst.

City officials did not contest their role and, instead, publicly embraced the park concept. Indeed, given the lush, water-colored renderings of a sylvan paradise of trees, fountains, pavilions, and a thirty-acre lake, it was difficult not to. Exhibiting their usual Atlanta-spirited exuberance, numerous city and business leaders reiterated the claim that such a park would serve as a catalyst for post-Olympic development and prove beyond a doubt that Atlanta was a world-class city on par with New York, London, and Paris. One of the most compelling aspects of the plan was that the area was widely perceived as an empty, decayed, and pathological space and that nobody would be displaced. But, as Gary McDonogh has noted, paraphrasing Benjamin Lee Whorf, empty spaces are rarely "empty", rather, they are usually full of undesirable and/or unacknowledged users (McDonogh 1993).

Protests by small-business owners and homeless advocates subsequently demonstrated that the area was not empty after all, although with scant result. Almost one thousand homeless-shelter beds were lost to the park and, as of this writing, have not been replaced. Opposition from community activists who argued that the money would be better spent revitalizing their nearby ravaged neighborhoods also fell on deaf ears. The lack of recognition given to concerns of the urban poor and the homeless indicate that these groups do not constitute part of "the public" in whose name the park was being constructed. In fact, the park's builders were quite clear about their intentions to make the park unamenable to these undesirable users. Not surprisingly, the most effective, if only temporary, opposition to the park was provided by property owners within the proposed park area. These owners included old-guard Atlanta families and foreign speculators. They succeeded in getting top dollar for their parcels, raising the cost of land acquisition, which, along with a halving the development budget to $50 million, greatly reduced the size of the park area. In the end, only twenty-two of the originally specified seventy-two acres were incorporated into the Centennial Olympic Park.

The balance of the original park area was divided up among other interested parties. Chief among these was the Coca-Cola Corporation, whose international headquarters were located just to the northwest of the site. Coke acquired eleven acres just north of the park for a temporary amusement/ promotional venue called "Coca Cola's Olympic City." The $20 million site featured a twelve-story Coke bottle, a miniaturized replica of the Olympic Stadium, and facilities in which visitors competed against video footage of famous athletes. Despite its $13 admission tariff, Olympic City proved to a be a very popular attraction with visitors. At the close of the Olympics, it was carefully disassembled and packed away until the year 2000, when it will be shipped to Sydney for their Olympic Games.

The downsizing of the Centennial Park also freed a large section of land along the western edge of the original parcel. This fifteen-acre site was designated as a "special district" by the Immigration and Naturalization Service as part of an immigrant investor program that sought to attract foreign, particularly Hong Kong, capital in exchange for green cards for themselves and their families. It was acquired by a syndicate of local developers who planned to build a luxury hotel on the site with capital attracted through the immigrant investor program. However, lack of interest by prospective foreign investors dashed hopes that the hotel would be built before 1996. Instead, part of the area was leased to Nike Corporation, which constructed a temporary museum/shrine to its sports shoes in a derelict parking garage.

Actually, the Centennial Olympic Park proved not to be too dissimilar from the Nike venue and Coke's Olympic City, as all three were conjured realms in which the boundaries between advertisement, entertainment, and education were effaced by a more profound "pecuniary truth" (see Henry 1963). During the Olympics, more than one-third of the park was leased to such official corporate sponsors as ATT, Anheuser-Busch, Swatch, and General Motors, who erected large pavilions celebrating their products. Together with the plethora of food and souvenir stalls that sprouted on privately owned parking lots just outside its boundaries, the park constituted a luridly literal display of commodity fetishism. Indeed the tacky banality of Atlanta's hyper-commercialism was one of the enduring motifs in the Olympic coverage of both the United States and foreign media.

Midway through the Olympics, however, media critiques of Atlanta's crass commercialism were offset and partially effaced by the tragedy of the Olympic Park bombing. While ACOG officials had always intended the park to be a centerpiece of media attention, they could have scarcely anticipated what followed this act of terrorism. In the days after the bombing, the park became a stage on which the mythology of Atlanta rising triumphantly from tragedy was re-enacted for the global media. The ritual cleansing of a sunrise rededication ceremony led by ACOG cochair, the Rev. Andrew Young, was a perfectly stage-managed example of the biracial city overcoming adversity. The ceremony, coupled with the swift apprehension of the lone alleged suspect, allowed the festivities to resume with minimal disruption. As with many things in Atlanta, however, this proved only a temporary fix. Long after the Olympics had ended, the bombing continued to raise unsettling questions, such as why the city's 911 system failed to pass on warning of the bomb and, with the absolving of suspect Richard Jewell, who indeed planted the bomb? By then, however, few outside Atlanta were paying attention.

Notwithstanding the problems associated with the still-mysterious park bombing, the end of the Games brought with it a collective sense of post-Olympic depression. The 1996 Games were the most transient ever, as many of the Olympic venues were temporary constructions. The most tangible physical legacies were a new stadium for the Atlanta Braves, new dorms for Georgia State University, and several athletic facilities at the Atlanta University Center and Georgia Tech. Prior to the Games, ACOG officials argued that the most important Olympic legacy would be in the form of Atlanta's enhanced global reputation rather than bricks and mortar. However, given the critical tone of much of the foreign media coverage, it is questionable if this ephemeral and admittedly hard to measure aim was realized. Retailers and homeowners anticipating an Olympic windfall from increased business and home rentals were also greatly disappointed, with many vendors experiencing catastrophic losses.

Nowhere was the gap between hype and reality displayed more clearly than in the Centennial Olympic Park. Even before the closing ceremonies had started, workers were already removing the temporary corporate pavilions. Aside from the central plaza, as of this writing, much of the park remains a vacant, detritus-strewn lot of red Georgia clay. The $15 million necessary to repair the park has yet to be secured. More important, even before it was completed, the park had raised adjacent land values to the point where extensive public subsidies, such as written-down land costs and other incentives, would be necessary to attract prospective developers. Still, as one Atlanta developer noted: "Just by demolishing [the area] and building the park we are improving that area a hundredfold" (see Rutheiser 1996, 269–270). Neither he nor any of his other colleagues so concerned with a sense of traditional urbanity, seem to have read their Jane Jacobs very carefully, for as the author of *The Death and Life of Great American Cities* notes, parks are only as successful as the neighborhoods around them (Jacobs 1961).

Imagineering the Future

Despite the whirlwind of pre-Olympic hype, the Park project is nothing more than urban renewal with a happy face, a crafty way of assembling more than one hundred separate parcels into a post-Olympic playing field for what Mike Davis has called "the infinite game" of downtown redevelopment (Davis 1991). Although there was considerable pre-Olympic talk of the park being a major catalyst for a post-Olympic revitalization of the central city, six months after the Olympics, the post-Olympic future remains highly speculative.

The most detailed vision was recently revealed in a conceptual plan commissioned by Central Atlanta Progress. This nonbinding prospectus suggested combining the area occupied by Coke's Olympic City and the Techwood /Clark Howell public housing projects and building a series of diverse residential neighborhoods clustered around small village greens and squares, along with an entertainment zone and a high-tech office park. While the neighborhoods are envisioned as mixed-income, the mix is envisioned more in terms of middle and upper income, than middle, upper, and low. Rather than redevelopment or revitalization, the consulting designers (a number of whom had previously worked for the Disney Corporation) referred to their task as "re-neighboring." Whatever one wishes to call the process, it still adds up to displacement: very few of those families who currently live in the area will be able to return. Rather, the whole point of the exercise is to bring the "right" sort of people back downtown. As with the park project itself, it appears that the city government will play no more than a supporting role during the post-Olympic period. In fact, shortly after the Olympics ended, Central Atlanta Progress created a nonprofit corporation called Centennial Olympic Park Area, Inc., or COPA for short, to fine-tune the design plan and market the area to prospective developers, including, it is rumored, the Disney Corporation, MCA, and other theme park developers.

While plans for the park area remain in the conceptual phase, other developers used the Olympics to begin ambitious adaptive reuse projects in the heart of the old central business district itself, an area now known as the Fairlie-Poplar Historic District. Fairlie-Poplar provides a good example of neo-Rouse-ian strategies of "making place." Until 1978, the twenty-three-block area, which made up the smallest of the city's original nineteenth-century street grids, was not distinguished from the wider Five Points business district. As in the urban renewal era, the first step in redevelopment was a kind of symbolic cleansing through the renaming of the area. Between the 1920s and early 1960s, the area now known as Fairlie-Poplar was characterized by a lively diversity of uses and users: prestigious office and retail to the south and east, bustling hotels, bars, restaurants, and theaters in the central area. By the end of the 1960s, however, the fringes of the area were razed for parking lots and new office buildings, while the hotels and entertainment facilities began to cater to a much more déclassé clientele. In 1978, Central Atlanta Progress, together with the Rouse Corporation's Land/Design Research subsidiary, sought to revitalize the area through the creation of a mall-like atmosphere that would link the Rich's department store south of Five Points with the Macy's on Peachtree. Designers talked of creating something along the lines of New York's Greenwich Village and SoHo or New Orleans's French Quarter, an exciting mix of housing, retail, and office space (Robert and Company 1978).

Despite the initial enthusiasm and some minor streetscape improvements, neither the city nor Central Atlanta Progress made the area a priority. Instead, Fairlie-Poplar became an unsupervised playground for a diverse mix of speculators seeking to take advantage of the tax incentives that accompanied the rehabilitation of historic structures. Property values in the area rose steadily until 1986, when changes in the federal tax code greatly reduced the tax benefits and sent prices falling. Once renovated, many of the buildings had difficulty attracting tenants. Although the original redevelopment plan indicated that creation of a new attraction was vital for the success of redevelopment, there was no central coordination of efforts, and developers acted as if the renovated buildings themselves would be their own attraction. Prospects for Fairlie-Poplar hit rock bottom when three major projects ended in lawsuits or arrests for fraud or securities violations in the late 1980s. Many in the business community like to place blame for Fairlie-Poplar's initial failure on the presence of homeless persons and drug dealers, but attributing the principal cause of failure to crime and undesirable users denies the role of other fundamental causes that lie in the realms of market forces, poor planning, and political neglect.

In 1992, however, Fairlie-Poplar was given new life as the exodus from the adjacent Five Points area reached biblical proportions. A new plan, inspired by the National Trust for Historic Preservation's Main Street program, received the blessing of both city and business leaders. In large measure, the new plan echoed the themes of the 1978 vision. Once again, the image of New York's loft-living, art-dealing SoHo district was invoked, but the comparison is misleading. As Sharon Zukin and Neil Smith have documented, the gentrification of SoHo and of the nearby Lower East Side of Manhattan was initiated by poor artists and bohemians seeking cheap rents, with both pioneer groups being displaced as the area was discovered and taken over by the more established real estate and culture industries (Zukin 1986, Smith 1986). Lacking this crucial first wave, prospective redevelopers of Fairlie-Poplar have sought to seed "Culture" directly to stimulate the simultaneous growth of retail and residential development. In this case, "Culture" takes the form of Georgia State University's Rialto Theatre and School of Music, as well as the Atlanta Arts Festival.

The inclusion of Georgia State University (GSU) marks a critical departure from GSU's own past pattern of development as well as the direction of downtown redevelopment more generally. Located just to the east of the Five Points area, GSU occupies a 1960s-era "platform campus" that is raised above street level and interconnected by pedestrian skyways. As the enclaved campus indicates, GSU has historically considered itself to be in downtown but not quite of it. With the departure of the long-time corporate tenants from Five Points, it now finds itself in the awkward position of being the anointed savior of downtown. In the years just prior to occupying the Rialto Theatre and the new home for the School of Music, GSU had acquired a number of commercial office buildings, including the landmark Citizens and Southern Bank Building, which now houses its College of Business. In the fall of 1996, Nationsbank donated the Commerce Club Building to GSU. Earlier plans for dormitories, however, have been scrapped for now.

Instead of attracting a low-rent student population, developers have gone completely upmarket in their adaptive reuse of three buildings near the Five Points intersection and the Rialto Theatre. These three projects give something of a new twist to gentrification as a process in which the symbolic capital of central location is appropriated to revitalize depressed property values. Whereas gentrification usually involves the conversion of working-class spaces (in the form of either factories or warehouses) or decayed middle-class residential space, and the displacement of the poor residents of these now marginal spaces, these projects seek to use vacant and formerly prestigious office and retail space.

The decision to go exclusively upmarket and not to provide student dormitories undermines an earlier vision of creating "a sort of Greenwich Village-Washington Square, Hyde Park-University of Chicago environment" in the Five Points/GSU area (Creative Loafing, 19 November 1994). Such an outcome is not surprising, as the last thing that either GSU or Central Atlanta Progress is interested in fostering is anything remotely resembling these legendarily urbane domains. Homeless encampments, drug dealers, skateboarders, radical political activists, and other denizens of the urban demi-monde do not have a place in the elite's vision of traditional urbanity. Indeed, given the frequency and ease with which Atlanta boosters conjure up visions of SoHos and Washington Squares in their midst while also holding to the orderly vision of a safe, clean, and graffiti free, user-friendly city), it is clear that they are content to sell only the sanitized look and feel, rather than the gritty realities, of the urban lifestyle.

It remains an open question if enough of the right people can be attracted to live downtown. Although a survey of downtown office workers commissioned by CAP in 1995 indicated that as many as twenty-five thousand persons would be willing to live downtown (AAREASG 1995), these numbers were considered by even a number of normally Pollyanna-ish real estate professionals to be rather soft. Even so, such numbers have prompted other developers to embark on more than a dozen new loft conversions in rundown industrial areas on the periphery of downtown. In contrast to "loft-style" units in Five Points, these adaptively reused factories and warehouses are the "real" thing, even down to the blasted, postapocalyptic ambience of their surroundings. In addition, Fairlie-Poplar continues to face steep competition from more established midtown and intown neighborhoods that gentrified a decade ago. Whether the promised safety and cleanliness of the new developments in Fairlie-Poplar (not to mention the Centennial Park area) will be enough to overcome the area's lack of energy and excitement, not to mention secure parking, is unclear at this point.

One thing that is clear, however, is the effect of redevelopment on the homeless persons who formerly occupied the streets, doorways, and parks of the Five Points area after five in the evening. The conversion of office space into residences has intensified the crackdown on the city's most unfortunate. In the fall of 1996, the Atlanta city council passed a series of ordinances dedicated to eradicating the homeless problem from downtown. These included a ban on loitering and "urban camping," and the absolute prohibition of panhandling within a certain radius of pay phones, automated teller machines, public buildings, and other designated establishments. The city council has not acted, however, to provide facilities for treating, training, and housing the homeless. Instead, as with residents displaced during the privatization of public housing, the homeless are being pushed further into the interstices of the urban landscape.

The current direction of downtown redevelopment continues the texture and trajectory of Olympic redecorating efforts: the creation of an alluring tapestry of "ornamental nodes" (Boyer 1993) that it is hoped will confirm Atlanta's self-ascribed status as a "world-class city." Having for the most part eradicated the physical residues of its multiple less-than-storybook pasts, Atlanta is obliged to recreate in their place spurious and less-than-compelling simulations. The visions for Underground Atlanta, the Centennial Park area, and the Fairlie-Poplar district all conjure a traditionally urban past that never quite existed in Atlanta. They are examples of the contemporary paradigm of urban revitalization that privileges the artful design of secure, simulated, and resegregated environments over the articulation of comprehensive plans for dealing with uneven development, homelessness, poverty, crime and unemployment in the city as a whole.

Of course, what is taking place in Atlanta is of a piece with what is occurring in New York, Los Angeles, Baltimore, San Diego, Cleveland, and dozens of other medium- and large-sized American cities. Indeed, Atlanta has sought to emulate what has proven successful in other places: the festival market place, the historic, gentrified residential district, and so on. There is, then, nothing particularly southern about what is happening in Atlanta. Despite the city's association with *Gone with the Wind*, Atlanta has more often than not been in the South, but not of it, or as W. E. B. Du Bois put it: "[S]outh of the North, but north of the South" (Du Bois 1965, 262). Atlanta's ageographia, or at least its geographical liminality, is nothing new. Atlanta's in-betweenness of place is thus part of its very identity, perhaps even its most stable and consistent part. As with its erstwhile Olympic mascot Whatizit (subsequently renamed "Izzy"), Atlanta's most defining characteristic has been its ability to redefine itself to make it more appealing to outsiders. As the mascot's ignominious fate has demonstrated, however, this is a strategy of dubious value.

References

AAREASG. 1995. Downtown Atlanta housing study. Arthur Anderson Real Estate Advisory Group.

Bover, M. C. 1993. The city of illusion. In *The restless urban landscape*, edited by P. Knox. Pp. 112–126.Englewood Cliffs, N. J.: Prentice Hall.

Central Atlanta Progress. 1971. *Central area study*. Atlanta: Central Atlanta Progress and Bureau of Planning, City of Atlanta.

———. 1987. *Central area study II*. Atlanta: Central Atlanta Progress and Bureau of Planning, City of Atlanta.

Davis, M. 1990. *City of quartz: Excavating the future in Los Angeles*. London: Verso.

———. 1991. The infinite game: Redeveloping downtown L.A. In *Out of site: A social criticism of architecture*, edited by D. Ghirardo. Seattle, Wash.: Bay Press.

Du Bois, W. E. B. 1965. *The souls of black folk*. New York: Avon Books. Original edition 1903.

Fjellman, S. 1992. *Vinyl leaves: Walt Disney World and America*. Boulder, Colo.: Westview Press.

Haddow and Company. 1991. *Revitalization plan for Fairlie-Poplar district*. Atlanta: Haddow and Company.

Hartshorn, T, and K. Ihlanfeldt. 1993. *The dynamics of change: An analysis of growth in metropolitan Atlanta over the past two decades*. Atlanta: Research Atlanta, Inc., Policy Research Center, Georgia State University.

Henry, J. 1963. *Culture against man*. New York: Vintage.

Jacobs, J. 1961. *The death and life of great American cities*. New York: Doubleday.

Kuhn, C., et al. 1990. *Living Atlanta: An oral history of the city, 1914–1948*. Athens: University of Georgia Press.

Logan, J., and H. Molotch. 1987. *Urban fortunes: The political economy of place*. Berkeley: University of California Press.

Lynch, K. 1960. *The image of the city*. Cambridge, Mass.: MIT Press.

McDonogh, G. 1993. The geography of emptiness. In *The cultural meanings of urban space*, edited by R. Rotenberg and G. McDonogh. Pp. 3–16. South Hadley, Mass.: Bergin and Garvey.

Metropolitan Planning Commission. 1952. Up ahead: A regional land use plan for metropolitan Atlanta. Atlanta.

Palmer, C. 1955. Adventures of a slum fighter. Atlanta: Tupper and Low.

Powledge, F. 1975. Atlanta begins to sense the loss of its seeming immunity to urban problems. *AIA Journal* 34:40–51.

Robert and Company. 1978. Fairlie-Poplar planning report. Manuscript in possession of author.

R/UDAT. 1992. Atlanta: Report of the rural/urban design assistance team. Xerox copy.

Rutheiser, C. 1996. *Imagineering Atlanta: The politics of place in the city of dreams*. London: Verso.

Sindeman, M. 1991. The William-Oliver building's Five Points role. *Atlanta Business Chronicle*, 1 April 1991, 13–14

Smith, N. 1986. Gentrification, the frontier, and the restructuring of urban life. *In Gentrification of the city*, edited by N. Smith and P. Williams. Pp. 15–34. Boston: Allen and Unwin.

_____. 1992. The Lower East Side as wild, wild West. In *Variations on a theme park: The new American city and the death of public space*, edited by M. Sorkin. Pp. 61–99. New York: Hill and Wang.

Sorkin, M., ed. 1992. *Variations on a theme park: The new American city and the death of public space*. New York: Hill and Wang.

Stone, C. 1989. *Regime politics: Governing Atlanta, 1945–1988*. Lawrence: University of Kansas Press.

Virillio, P. 1983. *Pure war*. New York: Semiotext(e)

Webber, M. 1964. The urban place and the nonplace urban realm. In *Explorations into urban structure*, edited by M. Webber et al. Pp. 79–153. Philadelphia: University of Pennsylvania Press.

White, D., and T. Crimmins. 1980. How Atlanta grew. In *Urban Atlanta: Redefining the role of the city*, edited by A. Hamer. Pp. 7–33. Research Monograph No. 84. Atlanta: Georgia State University, College of Business Administration.

Zukin S. 1986. Loft living: Culture and capital in urban change. Baltimore: Johns Hopkins University Press.

———. 1991. *Landscapes of power: From Detroit to Disney World*. Berkeley: University of California Press.

GARY MCDONOGH

11 Discourses of the City
Policy and Response in Post-Transitional Barcelona

Contemporary urban planning in Barcelona reflects both a historical process through which the city has been defined and a rapid political and metropolitan evolution since the end of the Franco regime, during which urban interests have been debated intensely. This chapter focuses on the emergence of new discourses about the city in the 1970s and 1980s that laid the foundations for the Olympic and global city of the 1990s. It also contrasts hegemonic models, as realized in rhetoric, planning, and construction, with other voices from the Raval, a marginal downtown neighborhood that has become a particular focus of urban renovation.[1] The chapter argues that analysis of the formation of an elite orthodoxy in city planning must be nuanced both by critical readings and by appreciation of alternative urban models and experiences.

Setting the Stage

In the introduction to a 1983 collection on recent urban projects in Barcelona, Socialist Mayor Pascual Maragall extolled the complexity of neighborhoods within his city: "The city is a sign of identity, a historic testimony of social and economic transformation and a demonstration of the production of culture. Barcelona, in this sense, is a transparent city: its neighborhoods, its growth, its great complexity are without doubt, a discourse about the social tensions it has lived and, definitively, the most complete image of our past, recent and remote" (1983, 9).[2] Yet, when I returned to Barcelona in June 1987 to continue research on ideology and marginality in the downtown portside quarter, the Raval, I encountered barrio residents in revolt against the elected Socialist administration of the city. Frustrated residents had launched a vociferous campaign to force city authorities to attend to their concerns about crime, drugs, unemployment, poor housing, and lax sanitation. Inhabitants had already invaded streets in a late-night *tamborada*, beating pots and pans in a call for attention well noticed by urban news media (*El Periódico*, 13 May 1987; *Avui*, 13 May 1987). Shortly after my arrival, Raval merchants went on strike for an afternoon, shuttering their businesses and emptying the streets. Some residents exulted at the prospect of change; others, especially those who lived in areas considered to be hard-core drug and prostitution zones, remained suspicious. Finally, on 12 June, a choral society band and the president of the neighborhood association led residents through dark, narrow streets lined with bars, along the Rambles and the portside Moll de la Fusta, Barcelona's central promenades, and finally to the Governor-General's palace. There, they presented their demands for reform of the state.

During this imbroglio, Mayor Maragall admitted that the neighborhood had suffered: "In the last seven years [those of democratic government], the rhythm of degradation has been superior to that of improvement in the *Ciutat Vella*. I will recognize that we have failed, if this means that things will begin to achieve order" (*El Periódico*, 7 May 1987). Before and after these dramatic incidents, I discussed neighborhood concerns with residents and social workers, examining planning materials and projects of the last two decades as well as the rhetoric of reform. In this study, it became apparent that the revolt of the Raval was a piece in a larger debate over the nature of the Spanish city and over who holds the right to define and reform it.

The Raval, especially in its notorious *barrio chino*—long famous for prostitution and illicit activities—has a history of marginalization under monarchic, parliamentary, nationalist, leftist, fascist, and democratic regimes. Raval residents have challenged outside opinions on their neighborhood and its role in the city, but rarely have they successfully communicated these views to urban authorities. This, too, was challenged as Spain moved toward democracy. One strong spokesman, the Associació de Veïns del Raval (AV-Raval), had coalesced in 1974 with socialist support after a conflagration in an illegal factory ravaged a residential block. The fire incited widespread neighborhood anger, raising demands for enforcement of laws on zoning and property use (*Diario de Barcelona*, 6–15 September 1974). Throughout Spain in this late Franco period, neighborhood associations had emerged as parapolitical organizations in the absence of authorized parties (Alibes et al. 1975; Carbonell et al. 1976). Manuel Castells highlighted this process in Madrid in the 1970s

(1983, 215–288). In the years immediately after Franco's death, however, the AV-Raval, like many other national organizations, faded from view. Political-party activity and revitalized urban governments undercut grassroots organizations and co-opted public forums. The 1987 incidents exposed smoldering discontent and renewed the AV-Raval. This response challenged twelve years of democratization and eight years of socialist planning by questioning the nature of the city itself. Neighborhood leaders complained that new democratic institutions lacked sensitivity to neighborhood problems in planning, forcing a grassroots response. Indeed, the problems of the Raval in the late 1980s spoke to a new era that replaced early post-Franco years of hope and experimentation in both municipal and state politics throughout Spain. These problems, in turn, provide critical illumination of the culture of planning that created the Olympic and global city of the 1990s (Borja 1996, McDonogh 1997).

This chapter poses interlocking questions about the nature of contemporary Spain and about theoretical issues of urban planning that have been tested there. Primarily, I ask how we may characterize ways of talking about and acting on the city exemplified in late twentieth-century Barcelona in both diachronic and synchronic terms. While Barcelona as a center for the Catalan polity, especially as repressed by the Franco regime, is unique, its pressing issues of controlled growth, gentrification, globalization, expanded services, and care for marginal groups have become equally present in other Spanish metropoles, including Madrid, Sevilla, Basque cities, Valencia, and Tarragona (see Fernández Alba and Gavira 1986; Pujadas and Bardají 1987; Rispa et al 1992). At a more general level, I ask how discourses about the city encompass principles and practices, and how these can be situated in terms of long-term development as well as periods of intensive changes. In particular, I am concerned with the ways in which dominant ideals of the city interact with alternative visions, where case materials from the Raval counter the privilege of the planner's urban texts. While this coincides with the work of Castells in Madrid, it seeks to be more inclusive of the fragmentary ideas voiced and enacted by residents themselves, which forms a growing concern of urban analysts worldwide (see Fincher and Jacobs 1998; Gregory 1998).

My discussion begins with an overview of the emergence of city planning in Barcelona within its Spanish and European context, and the models of the city that have guided it. The interpretation of the Raval within successive plans provides a foundation for analysis of contemporary problems. I then examine the establishment of institutions and canons of urbanism in the 1970s and 1980s. By the time of the Socialist reelection campaign of 1987, the stability of renewal programs and physical intervention in the city clearly dominated any debate and shaped Olympic triumphs and subsequent actions, including the ongoing demolition of the Raval (Ajuntament de Barcelona 1983, 1987; Maragall 1986). A discourse formed by texts, rhetoric, actions, and constructions had emerged, with key speakers who generally agreed on their premises for the city to the exclusion of other voices, such as those of Raval residents. Despite differences among parties, for example, dominant strata with a shared ideology of the city control both policy and means of persuasion in electoral campaigns.

On this basis, I return to the Raval and its citizens to examine the strains in the changing city of the 1980s. In this third section, I explore municipal planning from the viewpoint of interviews with residents, neighborhood leaders, and social service workers, through journalism, and through participant-observation in the neighborhood over the past twenty years. Housing reform, social services, citizen security, the transformation of social space, and the linkage of neighborhood and city provide specific thematic materials. These do not constitute a holistic ethnography of the Raval, yet by asking how Raval residents participate in the city, we balance silenced voices against a shared public model in order to see how a dominant discourse defined both citizenry and problems, Finally, in the epilogue, I relate these discourses to further transitions in the city for the beginning of the twenty-first century.

Urban Planning in Barcelona: An Overview

Contemporary Barcelona manifests the relics of planning by successive regimes since Roman times. Roman foundations shaped the city for centuries: "For nearly two thousand years, from 1 BCE to 1860, the entire order of the city referred to that cross of 'Cardos' and 'Decumanus' that the legion's geometers traced on the highest point of Taber Hill" (M. Solà-Morales i Rubió 1985, 5). From this classic crossroads, Barcelona expanded to become a major medieval capital in which fortification and harbor construction dominated planning. Urban growth, however, was constrained by the political-economic decline of Catalunya against the centralizing Spanish state and by the shift of world economic power from the Mediterranean to northern Europe (Vilar 1962; Elliott 1963, Wallerstein 1974; Amelang 1986; Carreras 1993.)

After Barcelona had remained relatively stable in population for centuries, economic and cultural expansion in the eighteenth century fueled massive growth in the city (Vilar 1962). Population tripled to 111,000 between 1717 and 1787. Eighteenth-century innovations ranged from Europeanized hygienic excisions, such as the removal of parish cemeteries (McDonogh 1986; also see Ariès 1981), to direct political intervention by the state. After the War of Spanish Succession, for example, the Spanish military leveled the lively and resistant Ribera neighborhood, replacing it with a military fortress. Some Ribera inhabitants were later settled in the Barceloneta, a port addition now recognized as a monument of Baroque city planning in Spain (Tatjer 1973; M. Solà-Morales i Rubió 1985, 6; Ajuntament de Barcelona 1985, 14–15).

As industrial growth and commercial expansion continued in the nineteenth century, new yet piecemeal projects were implemented. These included the redesign of the seafront, the urbanization of the central promenade (Rambles), and the development of parks, lighting, and transportation (Ajuntament de Barcelona 1985). More significantly, the dominant cultural goals of urbanism become focused, accommodating Barcelona to ideals of the rationalized industrial city that spread through Europe in this period: "An urban fabric in which diverse uses and tenants alternated, where streets branched, forming characteristic medieval cul-de-sacs was progressively replaced by a new spacial order. . . . State public power, through a more or less articulated local delegation, took possession of street space, as it did with large plazas and urban services. The street would no longer be a space annexed to the house but an area of diverse urban services" (Adjuntament de Barcelona 1985, 29; also see Hohenberg and Lees 1985). These changes came in response to the needs and values of the emergent industrial bourgeoisie. The annexation of streets to bars and shops, as well as to children's play space, still remains a marked characteristic of working-class neighborhoods.

Finally, Barcelona began to challenge the urban walls and surrounding demilitarized plain that had constricted it for centuries. In 1854, the Spanish state granted permission to demolish the constraining early modern walls of the city. This physical opening of the city provided a unique opportunity for a renewed interest in systematic planning. After municipal competitions, the state chose a rectilinear model for urban growth that had been submitted by the engineer Ildefons Cerdà. His *Teoría de la Urbanización* (1968–1971; originally proposed 1859) shifted the weight of the urban core away from the vested interests of the old city but was resisted by local architects as well as by dominant residents (Cerdà 1996). This conflict sketched the two general models that have subsequently vied for domination in the city's planning:

> the Cerdà (1859), Macià (1933) and Torres i Clavé plans (1971) [are] structured on some determined common points which we can define as their profoundly transformative character vis-à-vis urban reality, their progressivism, their belief in adaptation

Figure 11.1. Barcelona 1891. Contrasts between the medieval city and the rectilinear Cerda plan. (The Raval is the pentagonal area to the left side of the dense inner core.) *Courtesy of the Institut Municipal d'Historia.*

> to and definition of the urban-topographic-geographic structure of Barcelona, etc., are counterpoised to the plans of Rovira i Trias (1859), of Jaussely (1905), of Rubió i Tuduri (1929), the Comarcal plan of 1953 and the Porcioles plan (1971). These latter traced another, more conservative tradition, with more academic, technical foundations, legalizing forms of urbanistic action already consummated and as the expression of an idea of the bourgeois city par excellence. (Tarragó 1978, 24)

Urban practice during Barcelona's industrial-period growth challenged rationalized planning. Cerdà, for example, had envisioned octagonal housing blocks sheltering interior parks, which would create a regular yet verdant expansion of the urban core. Although new building would concentrate on the Eixample, Barcelona's bourgeois expansion zone, Cerdà had studied urban lower classes and sought to improve their lives within a general expansion of open space for the city (Cerdà 1996). Nonetheless, property developers overbuilt inner blocks, dramatically reducing green space per inhabitant. Automotive encroachment and capitalist

exploitation of space distort Cerdà's goals today, although his planning
has experienced renewed interest in the 1980s. Market forces also den-
sified housing in core areas like the Raval through the subdivision of
buildings. As the city grew through expansion and consolidation of the
suburbs in its hundred-square-kilometer plain, it reached a population
of five hundred thousand by the end of the century. By 1930, Barcelona
held more than one million inhabitants.

As the critic Salvador Tarragó suggested, the twentieth century has
brought continual reevaluation of planning models by academics and
politicians. Some plans have elaborated on Cerdà's framework while incorporating expanded transportation and services. Others would demolish
the urban core in a more rationalized city, as evident in the influence
of Le Corbusier and his Catalan disciples (the Grup d'Arquitectes i
Tècnics Espànyols per al Progrès de l'Arquitectura Contemporània) on
the 1932–1934 Plà Macià (Mackay 1989, 93–113; Ucelay Da Cal 1997).
Despite a wide spectrum of political positions, however, four characteristics apparent in capitalist planning emerged to dominate discussion
of the fabric of the two-thousand-year-year-old city: order, control, efficiency, and speed (see Lynch 1960, 1981). In addition, technology, as
much as capitalist efficiency and rationalization, began to challenge
heterogeneity.

The Franco regime (1939–1975) interrupted systematic planning,
opening the city to speculators who profited from economic recovery
in the 1950s and 1960s, intense immigration, and the urbanization of
satellite cities in the metropolitan area. While comprehensive urban plans
were proposed in 1953, 1971, and 1976, the realities of urbanization were
conveyed by the constant abuse of norms, whether in violation of building
and use codes, misappropriation of resources, privatization of public
space (parks into parking lots), or uncontrolled mushrooming of housing (Bohigas 1963, Terán 1969; Ynfante 1974, Ferras 1977, Tarragó 1978;
Ajuntament de Barcelona 1987, 1, 83–93, Carreras 1993). While similar
processes took place in other Spanish cities, Franco's distaste for the "enemy" Catalan was also apparent (see Castells 1983 on Madrid and Fernández Alba and Gavira 1986 on Spain in general). Systematic values, social
services, and citizen comfort were generally disregarded by mayors dependent on the central state, and this corrupted the city within this state.
Political security was the priority of the regime. Mayor Maragall, early
in his tenure, epitomized the feelings of many Barcelonins about this
earlier era: "We have closed a long tradition of 'exceptions,' both in urban expansion and in the renovation of its structures" (Ajuntament de
Barcelona 1983, 9).

Within overall city planning, the Raval has long provided a primary metaphoric counterpoint to dominant ideals of "the good city." As early as the seventeenth century, city leaders identified this portside extra-mural zone as an area of danger, pollution, and disease. Catalan elites in the late nineteenth century voiced a social-reformist concern, but this was eclipsed by erotic voyeurism toward the *barrio chino* in the 1920s (McDonogh 1987, 1992; González 1997). The overriding planning concern for the Raval, as for shantytowns on the urban fringe, was cleaning and excision. Thus, radical civil war preaching about such neighborhoods would have been as familiar to earlier Catalan nationalists as to Francoist managers in the 1950s: "They should be destroyed as prophylactic measures. The revolutionary picks should scrape the sorrowful entrails that have developed roots in our city. . . . From today, slums no longer exist" (Balius 1936, 4). In the civil war, however, inhabitants would have been relocated in bourgeois apartments rather than in the satellite cities of the 1960s.

The Raval nonetheless continued to grow, packing over one hundred thousand people into a one-square-kilometer area by the peak of post–civil war migration. Population fell to fifty thousand in the 1980s as a consequence of both urban reform and new areas of worker housing. Where the Raval was once an independent political unit with one-tenth of the city's population, it is now a neighborhood in a changing downtown core, and part of an old city district housing less than 1 percent of the greater metropolitan population.

Raval residents saw the barrio as both problematic and structured. While aware of the larger city's beliefs that only vice and poverty abound there, Raval dwellers recall the neighborhood as a mixed zone in the 1930s, 1940s, and 1950s. One woman in her seventies in 1985 told how working families and Andalusian immigrants resided "amid thieves and pickpockets. We were so happy." An elderly druggist defensively compared his neighborhood to the barrios of the dominant classes: "the escapades of this barrio are the same of those with hat and cocktail." Yet dominant ideologies generally eclipse these memories in planning debates.

The construction of two parallel arteries through the city core to unite the port and the bourgeois expansion areas epitomizes the effects of outside decisions on the Raval. The construction of the Via Laietana, begun in 1907 on the east side of the city, demolished a warren of medieval streets as well as generations of artisanal and shopkeeper society; 412 streets and nearly 4,000 buildings were affected in this creation of an "American" avenue. The contemporary Avinguda de Drassanes in the heart of the Raval advanced only fitfully.[3] In the 1920s and 1930s (*La Vanguardia*, 9 January 1936), as in the postwar period (*Solidaridad*

Figure 11.2. The old Raval and the new, 1998. Aging housing stock meets new open spaces created by demolition.

Nacional, 20 July 1941), planners evoked Drassanes as an antidote to the cramped housing and the flea market that formed a social center for the barrio chino. Yet critics could also be oblivious to the barrio itself: "There, where there was a huddled and unhygienic array of shocks and shanties, there will soon open a wide and luminous highway so that Mediterranean breezes will reach the heights of the city" (J. S. A. 1947:2). Eradication become the symbol of a "new Barcelona" (*Diario de Barcelona*, 27April 1962; Guallar 1963). The appointed Francoist mayor of Barcelona (Porcioles) lauded the avenue even as he noted that "the urban conditions in which the area's inhabitants live will disappear totally" (*Diario de Barcelona*, 26 April 1962). The demands of the city as a whole, especially its elite, "higher" barrios, overwhelmed the social integrity of the Raval.

Again, barrio residents had different perspectives. A female now in her forties recalled the *market* fondly while noting, "Ten years ago there were more people. Our zone has disappeared." The older woman cited previously was less nostalgic about what had been lost: "a nursery for evil . . . old houses, no bath, no toilet." Both women, however, felt themselves passive observers of a process rather than protagonists of change.

The Drassanes project continued to be discussed into the final decades of Franco's rule. Journalist Angel Guallar, while favoring the plan, noted that seven thousand families would be affected. He cited the personal cost for an elderly man who had lived there fifty years: "You can imagine how much I loved these streets and houses. We know nothing about what the mayor will do. But what he does must be for the good of the city" (Guallar 1964). The journalistic anecdote become an emblem of individual acquiescence and neighborhood subordination in the predemocratic period. Other critics, including the AV-Raval, argued that Drassanes would hurt seventy thousand people instead of the projected thirty thousand (Alibes et al. 1975). Ultimately, apathy and economic crisis halted the project as much as did numbers and citizen outcry. For decades, Drassanes remained a short broad avenue lined by military and public buildings that dead-ended, literally and metaphorically, after one hundred meters. In 1988, work began on a revised continuation that will create a new pedestrian plaza in the Raval while eliminating a zone of prostitution and cheap residential hotels. This plan, in fact, has subsequently reshaped the entire barrio.

Planning for the Raval has been torn between the romanticization of its past and the nightmare of its actual living conditions in many areas. Neither representation, however, has listened to the inhabitants of the area. Through much of the history of planning in Barcelona, the city has imposed problems and solutions. Thus the Raval has come to embody ongoing tensions between freedom and a technocracy of order. This dialectic also opposes the demands and models of the city as a whole against the values of segments, classes, or neighborhoods.

After the Transition: Establishing Discourses

The waning years of the Franco regime permitted limited urban action by such groups as neighborhood associations. Even for urban bureaucrats, the 1970s offered possibilities to control the overt exploitation exemplified by the Porcioles administration (Ynfante 1974; Castells 1983; Carreras 1993). The Plà General Metropolità (PGM) of 1976, for example, proposed a striking new vision of the city: "Despite the rarefied politics and the speculative pressure amid which it arose, [the plan] become in many respects an intelligent vision, due, without a doubt, to some "infiltrating" technicians who were able to work a little, thanks to the circumstances of late Francoism which suggested an apparent opening as well as by the imposition of their will to correct the situation visible to their professional and disciplinary perspectives" (Ajuntament de Barcelona 1983, 12). Oriol Bohigas, the dominant socialist planner writing here, valued technologization and professionalization of planning above all else as the aperture of the PGM. Professionalization, indeed, has become an important theme throughout Spain as not only political elites but also bureaucrats and architects have gained cohesion and status (Solà-Morales 1986, 14–15, Ucelay Da Cal 1997).

The PGM laid the groundwork for planning public space; proposed guidelines for density, use, and local zoning; and dealt with the relations of center and periphery that were crucial to the growth of the metropolitan area. Despite its advances, the project was constrained by its technology and information processing in comparison with its modern epigones. It also, in Bohigas's view, favored "the concept of the city as a unitary ideal system" over "the concept of the city as a conflictive sum of real places" (Ajuntament de Barcelona 1983, 12–13). An architectural critic of the planning process bluntly attacked "the persistence of a mistakenly megalomaniac attitude towards the destruction of the urban fabric, by which it ends up subordinating the city to the requirements of traffic. It also continues to insist on lengthy projects which will be difficult to realize in the medium term but which have negative effects on the city of today" (I. Solà-Morales 1986, 12).

After Franco's death in 1975, by contrast, discussions exulted in the city as a "conflictive sum of real places." Many groups battled for their interests without any clear shared orthodoxy except for a rejection of the Francoist post. Questions were debated through a media spectrum ranging from Falangist holdovers to communist dailies. Academic and professional panels argued that Barcelona could "not grow anymore as it does now or it faces disaster" (*La Vanguardia*, 26 May 1976); new and revived political parties took up a range of urban themes. What stands out impressionistically from this transitional period is its extraordinary level of enthusiasm and argument. Little effective action was inaugurated in most barrios that I knew, for lack of structure, consensus, or leadership. Nor was urban reform per se the central theme of the bars and shops that I knew in the Raval. Yet throughout Spain, and particularly in such oppressed national capitals as Barcelona, the rejection of the past brought a search for more complex, new urban models. In

Barcelona, models were sought to express the city and Catalunya as a polity, as well as to express its "Europeanness," in contrast to the rest of Spain.

By 1979, the Socialist Party was victorious in municipal elections and issued a paradigmatic statement on urbanism:

> A fundamental objective will be the attainment of a balanced Barcelona, eliminating segregation, seeking social and territorial equality for all citizens in access to social equipment and in the levels of urbanization of their *barrios*, avoiding the expulsion of popular sectors from the center city. . . . [Our plan] tries to preserve the historic artistic patrimony of Barcelona understood not as a catalogue of edifices and monuments, but as a conjunct of historic centers, unique ambiences resulting from the union of generations which we must transmit not as museum pieces but by using them as living things integrated into the community. The ordering of Barcelona, the improvement of living conditions, demands the development of standing plans. (Ajuntament de Barcelona 1983, 10)

This statement combines an appreciation of the history of the city with a promise for both equality and development through planning. Its apparent valuation of neighborhoods as social-historical formations, however, would soon come into conflict with the demands of the rationalized metropolis.

In this post-transitional phase, planning was no longer a reaction to Franco or a search for alternatives but a system based on careful research and development. Three lavish volumes published by the municipal administration chronicled current actions as well as the historical planning whose traditions planners claim to continue (Ajuntament de Barcelona 1983, 1985, 1987). In addition, a glossy trimestral journal, *Barcelona: Metròpolis Mediterrània,* featured reports on planning alongside popular articles. The Olympic games in Barcelona for 1992 and the potential for new capitals within reorganization of a united Europe that same year also gave planning a visible public orientation that sustains commitment to new museums and cultural facilities, new leisure centers, and a stream of international events.

Exhibits, historical research, criticism, and construction transcended simple design; more than in any previous period, plans in the 1980s were linked to direct and efficient implementation. Buildings have been renovated, transportation ordered, public spaces created or altered. The complex of perspectives and plans, and their execution shaped a new universe

of discourse apparent in the 1987 municipal elections, where the Socialist programs effectively set the stage for all discussion of the city as
a system, while other parties fought to control it.

In these elections, the Socialists presented a fifteen-point plan for
the city, including: finishing the beltway system; extending the subway;
establishing local security juntas and more police barracks; recuperat-
ing the urban core at a cost of 5 billion pesetas ($33 million) in credit
for private rehabilitation in the old city (which included movement of
part of the university to the Raval and of institutional and business headquarters to the historic core); managing and expanding public education; establishing a drug center in the Raval; integrating the urban health
system; creating new high technology centers; expanding parks and zoo
facilities; implementing the direct election of district councilors and the
passing of 90 percent of operations to local councils within the city; increasing the social service budget front 3 billion to 8 billion pesetas ($20
million to $53 million) through joint funding; extending the Diagonal,
a major cross-town thoroughfare, to the sea (and to the Olympic village);
improving modes of transport, including plans for port reforms, high-
speed trains, and modernization of the airport "to capture international
flights"; encouraging managerial pacts between city and industry to create
new jobs; and increasing funding from the state and region to 90 billion
pesetas ($600 million) *(El País,* 5 June 1987). Mayor Maragall synthe-
sized these themes in his vision of a city that "transcends its frontiers,
which consolidates social welfare as the fruit of the alliance of workers
with the entrepreneurial middle classes, the Barcelona of always . . . *La
Barcelona gran*" (ibid.; also see Maragall 1986).

The second-place Catalanist centrist-rightist (Convergència i Unió
[CiU]) candidate, Josep Maria Cullell, supported these emphases while
calling for "a rigorous design of solutions for all these problems" in campaign flyers. Again, "the opportunity and challenge that the Olympic
Games of 1992 represent" appeared as a point of reference. Communist
presentations concurred in the need for planning for an advancing city.
During the campaign, Communists even proposed putting aside "the
poor" as a political issue, a remarkable acquiescence of the Left to the
silences of urban domination (DiGiacomo, personal communication to
author, September 1989).

Ruling parties, in fact, would be dealing with the same planning and
building establishment. They were also linked by the need for institutional cooperation between the CiU Catalan government of the Generalitat,
and the Socialist Ajuntament. Autonomous institutions moved in lockstep
despite endless wrangles about responsibility for such mutual concerns
as subway improvement. A ruling discourse, as both model and plan of

action, had come into place. Nonetheless, this does not imply total harmony, even among competing elites. A 1984 article in the Convergentist newspaper *Avui*, for example, excoriated the Socialist model of the city, which "prioritizes great achievements, plazas and Olympic rings that later appear photographed in international architectural magazines." If plans fail, then it was not simply residents' opposition, but "because they are too utopian. Or because they cost more than the city can spend" (Fava 1984, 3). Nonetheless, while the inhabitants' opposition was mentioned, it was also discounted; the weight of policy making remained with political and financial elites.

This hegemonic discourse generally shared six central characteristics that can be distilled from the rhetoric and action of the 1980s: "completion," balance of regions, balance of classes, renovation for order and efficiency, technology as a solution, and internationalization as a reward. Each demands more critical elaboration.

Barcelona was planned as a "full-grown" city in both administrative and research bureaucracy. This image, from architect Ignasi de Solà-Morales (1986), reflects the partial and individualizing outcomes under which the city functioned in the Franco years, in comparison to other capitals viewed through continuous data and analysis that shape a totalizing urban plan. Many specifics of the 1987 Socialist platform and subsequent actions, for example, refer to the articulation of the city as an organic whole (subway, beltways). This image also underlies the concept of a neighborhood as a cell within the city and the identification of a barrio like the Raval with specific functions, whether for drugs or culture.

Planning, secondly, sought a balance between center and periphery, a dichotomy that related core areas and political-economic centralization to perceived alternative interests. Barcelona was conceived of as a decentralizable unit in which neighborhoods or localized councils would have power in relation to the total city. The center-periphery model was extended to encompass concerns with the order of suburban workers' cities (Ajuntament de Barcelona 1987, 83–93). This model also embodies an implicit relationship between Barcelona as capital and the rest of Catalunya. Both city-suburb and city-region relations generate major political issues focused on the extent of socialist power outside of the city of Barcelona. Finally, the model of center and periphery expresses the relationship of Barcelona and Catalunya to the European Economic Community and the world (Carreras 1993; McDonogh 1997; Solà-Morales 1986).

Third, planning was proclaimed as a check on the internal divisions of the city. Despite these programmatic statements, elites and workers have warred repeatedly throughout the century, and class tensions remain apparent albeit muted in the 1990s city, focused on consumption more than production. Administrative decentralization, managerial pacts, and bureaucracies, while proposed as solutions to disparities, reinforce inherited structures of silence and control. Here, discourse was more programmatic than descriptive.

Fourth, the general discourse of the urban future was based on a commitment to renovation to clarify order and efficiency in the city as machine. Intervention was the thrust of action rather than new initiatives. Renovation focused on the downtown area, and involved rephrasing plans of the past century. It accepted that the urban core was the "most degraded area" of the city, while at the same time envisioning its potential for the city and the world. Meanwhile, other projects have developed parks, social centers, and Olympic facilities throughout the metropolitan area while stressing the connection of systems within the metropolis.

In all these areas, technologization became the solution, whether presented as a specific feature or as part of general concerns for transport, construction, or social services. Technology was the fix for urban information and planning at all levels, which continued in rapid adoption of internet sources for urban discourse in the 1990s (www.seebcn. com).[4] Thus, I have seen little public reflection on the non-neutrality of technical solutions within planning, whether by leaders or by those receiving the model.

Finally, internationalization was held out as a reward. The image of an Olympic city, both in specific projects and in the general representation of a cosmopolitan center, answered the centuries-old problematic status of Barcelona as a primate city that is not a state capital. Thus, the new airport would capture international flights (which previously transferred through Madrid), and technology would win international commerce. Architecture, old and new, would become world famous. If Barcelona could not escape Spain, it might transcend it—an especially popular point in public opinion.

This vision of the city was not limited to electoral rhetoric; it underpinned the formation of district councils as well as massive Olympic construction. As a discourse on the city, it defined a new orthodoxy of theory and praxis, established on its own rather than reacting to the Franco regime. This way of talking about and acting on the city, in fact, developed as clearly from a general European drive toward planning, order, and efficiency in cities since the eighteenth century as from distinctly partisan values. It proved a restoration instead of a revolution in the image of the city, especially in relation to technocratic planning

(Ucelay Da Cal 1997). This discourse must be contextualized in terms of the lives of residents who did not fully participate in it, including those who marched in protest in the Raval.

Urban Policy and the Post-Transitional Raval

Within the range of projects that reshaped Barcelona in the Raval and the old city in general, I treat five specific areas: housing, social services, security, the formation of social space, and the relationship of the barrio and the city. These do not fully characterize the neighborhood, leaving aside such major themes as health care (Ros Hombravello 1986), drugs (Romaní 1982), and new immigration (McDonogh 1991, 1993a). Nonetheless, they suggest shared and divisive concerns of both residents and administrations, as well as the impact of the discourse of the 1980s on the neighborhood into the 1990s.

Housing

Raval reformers have long voiced concern with the housing infrastructure of the neighborhood, which deteriorated with the aging of buildings, 90 percent of which were built before 1900 (*El Periódico*, 22 March 1983, also see Artigues Vidal, Mas Palahi, and Suñol Ferrer 1980). By the end of the Franco period, the population was extremely dense (777 inhabitants per hectare), despite a deficit of four thousand units and a proliferation of inexpensive resident hotels, subleasing, and illegal overcrowding (*Diario de Barcelona*, 6 September 1974). Ten years later, only 3 percent of the housing in the Raval had water, electricity, gas, heat, toilets, and showers. Planners estimated that 22 billion pesetas ($147 million) would be necessary for rehabilitation (*El Periódico*, 22 March 1983).

New public ventures were lauded as replacements to this housing stock in the 1950s under the Franco regime (*Correo Catalán*, 7 February 1950). Nonetheless, the idea of the greater city and the thrust for control overrode neighborhood reform in this period. Eviction and destruction were not met with new opportunities for resettlement in the barrio. Instead, both evictees and new immigrants scrambled toward residential-industrial complexes in the metropolitan fringe (see Castells 1983 on Madrid). These emigrants were followed by longer-term residents whose businesses had depended on the dense population of the Raval. In the 1980s, the Generalitat and the Ajuntament reemphasized concern with housing as a physical and a human problem. In the *barrio chino*, a large public housing block was completed, as well as an edifice for the elderly. Demolition of substandard housing, blocks of bars, and *pensiones* (cheap hotels) continued through the 1990s, although many pensiones were simply closed in a massive sweep in the fall of 1988; houses of assignation were eliminated later (*El Periódico*, 17 January 1994). In most cases, housing replacement called for plans to relocate residents in the barrio if they chose. Significantly, this often did not apply to those who rented rooms in hotels, including the poor and the most recent immigrants from Africa and Asia. Yet, in the late 1980s, social service workers noted government surprise at the numbers who chose indemnification and departure from the neighborhood over relocation in new local housing.

Part of the problem here sprang from the multiple transformations that new housing brought. The decreasing density of the barrio, which these plans encouraged, destroyed past opportunity structures and social ties. Residents increasingly felt that there was no future for the older *barrio chino* (McDonogh 1992; González 1997). New housing also responded more to the perception of lifestyles of citizens in the idealized larger city than to the specific needs of the Raval. This produced a paradox in terms of use versus design apparent in Maragall's interpretation of urban renovation in the old city: "Old Barcelona will recover a tone of grand category. It will be necessary to remake housing adapted to the ambiance, to permit among other things the rehousing of people who have been expropriated in the same neighborhood" (1986, 26). Hence, in the 1990s, housing has been oriented toward cultural fortunes of the center city and populations of students, artists, and urban gentrifiers.

Problems arose in meeting specific barrio needs and adaptations. Early replacement apartments for the many elderly residents of the barrio, for example, appeared too large for those who lived alone. While this was taken into account in subsequent planning, smaller units paradoxically destroyed a primary survival strategy of other older residents who lived in rent-controlled apartments on small pensions: they rented their homes at rents fixed for decades at eighty to two thousand pesetas per month (eighty cents to twenty dollars) and sublet rooms illegally at competitive contemporary rates to cover living expenses.

Major housing units completed by 1989 also made strong architectural statements of security and isolation. One residential block eliminates street-level interaction via bars and shops with a blank wall and garage broken by heavily fortified entrances sheltering an inner patio. This contravened social patterns of the area, especially for the immigrants who constituted a large part of its earlier population. The security seemed so forbidding that neighbors nicknamed the building *la quinta galeria*, labeling the apartments as an extension of the city's prison. In another residence, social services rather than shops and bars control street interface. Techno-imagery and consumption rather than traditions of human spacial interaction shaped the new neighborhood; design imposed from outside redefined the nature of the house and street. Even if residents do not critique the planning process, their departures and their nicknames embody cultural responses.

The 1988 closing of the pensiones epitomized the ambiguities of housing reform. The boarding houses, many of which lacked basic sanitation, provided refuge for the poorest groups of the barrio. Control of disease, drugs, and crime become the rationale for their elimination in sweeps that evicted residents into an expensive and crowded housing market. Social service workers scrambled to help, but could not offer autonomy or neighborhood relocation for those who had adjusted for decades to their own room. Barcelona appeared, in 1989, to be re-creating the process of developing a homeless problem that the United States had already experienced.

Social Services

While housing evoked concern on the part of urban authorities as early as the 1920s, social services (in the sense of government intervention to deal with urban problems and planning) were much more limited and erratic. Under Franco, minimal social services were channeled through the Sección Feminina (the women's service auxiliary to the Falange) and the Catholic Church (Rubio 1951). The reestablishment of democratic regimes fostered an elaboration of competing social services by both the conservative Catalanist Generalitat and the Socialist Ajuntament. Each represented different ideals of the city and varying identification of its problems and solutions, although neither actually corresponded completely to the ideas or demands of Raval residents.

My discussion with youth service representatives of the Generalitat in the barrio in 1986, for example, revealed an emphasis on bonding the immigrant population of the barrio to the Catalan polity and the rural heartland of modern nationalist symbolism. A counselor explained at length the importance of taking youth out of the barrio to experience the countryside—a historic and politicized tradition of *naturalisme* in Catalonia. Other programs underscored this linkage of the Raval (which is Castilian-dominated except in the most settled areas) and a Catalan-speaking polity, reflecting the ambitions and politics of the Generalitat in reconstructing the polity of which Barcelona is capital.

The central and district city governments also offer a wide range of services for youths, as well as family planning, elder care, and general neighborhood activism. The program of *educadores de calle*, for example, has placed social service workers in the street to organize peer groups

and bring counseling to those who would not generally enter bureaucratic offices (Guerau de Arellano 1985). In a decade of cooperation with
these workers, I repeatedly witnessed this spirit of flexibility and openness in confronting municipal problems at the grassroots level, as residents have appropriated service centers as urban spaces. It is striking
also to watch *educadores* learn from the barrio, as evidenced in the increasing incorporation of existing popular sports clubs into programs for
the socialization of barrio youths (Maza, personal communications to
the author, June 1998).

Both regimes remained constrained by lack of capital and infrastructure to deal with past problems, much less adapt to growing new ones.
The wildfire spread of cocaine and heroin through the neighborhood in
the early 1980s—in which the Raval once again served the rest of the
city—was first met with only scattered and ill-coordinated competing
agencies dealing with control, education, and treatment. Prostitutes, who
have worked in the barrio chino for decades, also have tended to be defined as outside the range of social services unless they qualify for youth
services. For example, no nighttime day care centers were available
through the late 1980s, forcing prostitute mothers to leave their children
in infamous centers managed by former prostitutes. Only nuns worked
specifically with prostitute counseling. This was an ironic reflection on
the past triumphant posture of the church, as a neighborhood cleric noted,
and a striking intervention in a barrio where "they are believers but do
not believe in priests." In addition, the Catholic Church, divorced from
its power and responsibilities since the end of the Franco regime, took
the initiative in working with Arab, African, and Filipino immigrants
to the barrio, while political authorities debated their ambiguous status
(McDonogh 1991, 1993a). Within limited resources then, administrators
promoted urbanistic values of the good (e.g., elderly) or the redeemable
(e.g., child, young family) citizen rather than the anticitizen (e.g., prostitute) or the noncitizen (McDonogh 1997). The Raval itself, however,
has included those who take a more marginal position and viewpoint
with regard to such shared urban norms.

The participation of the Raval within a decentralizable city also affected social services. In 1984, the Ajuntament threatened to close, for
the summer, the Casal d'Infants del Raval, a holistic education center
for neighborhood children. The AV-Raval president exclaimed, "It is
inconceivable . . . that given the conditions children live in, in this barrio, youth services can close the Casal d'Infants in summer, as it does
in the rest of Barcelona" (*Noticiero Universal*, 3 October 1984). Municipal districts and programs maintain an overall parity, which may mean
that resources seem more scarce in the Raval, as one part of Ciutat Vella,

than in upper-class barrios with fewer problem cases. Thus, by being defined as a cell in the city, the Raval's problems are recategorized as competitive bookkeeping entries.

Citizen Security

Raval residents in the 1980s often associated the presence of illegal Arab and African immigrants in the downtown area with a strong threat of crime and assaults. Friends in middle-class neighborhoods also complained increasingly about break-ins and muggings, which they interpreted in class or ethnic terms. When I heard similar complaints in the Raval, however, I confronted a paradox in an area where tolerance for illegal activities has been part of a culture of a resistance (McDonogh and Maza forthcoming). Residents of the *barrio chino* used to boast of areas that the police were afraid to enter, much less control, in the barrio's heyday. This autonomy was challenged, though, in December 1985, when the city administration approved an integrated security, social service, and youth service program for the old city (Maragall 1986, 33). In the 1987 marches as well as in many discussions with me in subsequent fieldwork, Raval residents defined drug addicts, dealers, and immigrants as a new, dangerous category to be excised. While many of these residents were themselves immigrants or children of immigrants from the 1930s, 1940s, or 1950s, their tolerance had been strained by a new "other." A woman born in the 1940s commented: "See how the neighborhood has changed? Now we have nothing but thieves, junkies, addicts." The 1987 neighborhood petition to the government stressed strict implementation of immigration laws, while other petitions have appealed for increased police action.

In the 1987 municipal campaigns, candidates for political office vied to offer increased security in the downtown area of which the Raval is part. Pascual Maragall wrote in his programmatic statement, "Old Barcelona merits the efforts of all Barcelona. It is too important, it has too much historical and human value to not do so" (1986, 33). Subsequently, new police centers were built on the border of the barrio and the Rambles; mobile police stations were added in principal plazas in 1988 and 1989; and patrols increased in visibility. A new headquarters for the Guardia Civil also has been built on a central street. Many Raval residents were skeptical that increased visibility on the part of police was a solution. This response seemed more appropriate for an overtly law-abiding, bourgeois neighborhood than for an area with a tradition of extralegal activity where police were suspect and foreign. Thus, when police questioned me in 1986 about my presence in a bar in the barrio, this formed an immediate narrative shared among friends, renewing my bonds there. In 1989, one of the mobile police stations was even set ablaze in a main plaza. Yet, later that summer, a friend whose bar had been an erstwhile hangout for drug dealers looked at the station down the street and said, "Don't you see, Gary, it's for the better?" Discourse can be met with ambivalence as well as resistance.

Other interpretations of the police response by residents and workers in the Raval extended the range of suspicion. For some, increased patrols seemed to keep malefactors out of public tourist areas such as the nearby Rambles, following the orientations of the dominant city rather than responding to the needs of the barrio. Since police were frequently walking past known sites of drug dealing and prostitution, they also were suspected of complicity. Finally, in the late 1980s and 1990s, I personally witnessed police harassment of African immigrants in the Raval, an ambivalent response to the requests of older residents that isolated new immigrants clustered in these marginal districts. Yet it appears that residents were internalizing the surveillance model, absorbing the discourse of security they or their ancestors had resisted. Still, they did not read security as police, in the way urban administrators do, so much as the removal of threats and disruptions, which might include police. The external drive for control and order still clashed with some aspects of barrio life (McDonogh 1993a).

Green Space

The construction of new urban open spaces and the refurbishment of existing spaces has also been a priority within the new discourse of the ideal city. Here, urban planning took advantage of a historical irony of the transition: "[T]hanks to a slump in the private property market and an increase in the strength of the new democratic administrators, it has been possible to make greater allowance, in recent town-planning laws, for transfer of land in public use, infrastructures, parks, and all those parameters that predate current urban development. Even though these do not correspond to more recent trends in urban design, they had been transformed into genuine objectives of the urban struggle which had assumed so great an importance during the lost years under Franco" (I. Solà-Morales 1986,13). Striking in Solà-Morales's statement is the equation of goals that had been "transformed into genuine objects of the urban struggle," with their categorization as antiquated design elements, "predating" contemporary discourse. This duality permeated 1970s and 1980s processes of appropriation and transformation of urban space that became evident citywide, in such projects as the development of the Parc de L'Espanya Industrial, on the grounds of a former cotton factory (Carreras Verdaguer 1980; Adjuntament de

Barcelona 1983, 186–189; Maragall 1986, 66; Borja 1996); the renovation of the downtown Plaça Reial (Ajuntament de Barcelona 1983, 129–133); and the redevelopment of the Maritime promenade (Ajuntament de Barcelona 1983, 37–53; Solà-Morales 1986, 65–70; Maragall 1986, 5–18). While revindication of urban space has been a dominant theme throughout post-Francoist Spanish cities, large and small, Barcelona became a self-conscious vanguard, proud of its world image as a new cosmopolis. Most of these projects share visible planning ideals: the ordering of space within an urban fabric, the valuation of art and monumentality, the triumph of concrete over greenery and an overall concern with "design" (Remassar 1997). As the 1984 *Avui* editorial charged, these can easily be critiqued as spaces designed to be photographed, as they are, in fact, presented in many glossy publicity materials. Some places and parks gave concrete evidence of the urban discourse realized at the microlevel: *places dures* (hard plazas) were immediately noticeable and widely criticized by urban residents.

Later, the theme of protection favored dramatic separations of urban open space from potential trouble. The Maritime promenade is separated from the old downtown by a highway and a parking "moat." Carnival, a historic opportunity for critique and upheaval, was celebrated by 1989 in the Poble Espanyol, a walled, imitation Spanish village originally built on Montjuïc for Barcelona's 1929 International Exposition and refurbished for the Olympics as a nightspot, protected by its distance from public transport and by paid and guarded admission. The Olympic Village and Maritime Port to the north of the Central Business District, and Maremagnum, a mall built *in* the old harbor, have continued this new geography of entertainment in the 1990s.

Two major open-space projects, under the aegis of the Ajuntament and the Generalitat, were realized early in the Raval, while others are in progress. Plaça Salvador Seguí, named for a revolutionary hero murdered in the 1920s, reused a space that had previously served as a prison and a cinema. Under the Franco regime and in the early transition, the space was dominated by illegal parking demanded by Barcelona's automotive overcrowding. In the 1980s, the square, hemmed in by buildings on three sides and a major thoroughfare on the fourth, was paved and playground equipment was added, as was a fringe of trees along contiguous streets. The playground equipment was later replaced with hard flagstones and fixed benches. In 1989, a mobile police station was added. By the late 1990s, it lost its "sheltered" character as streets were demolished around it

Extensive observations that I conducted with Gaspar Maza, and later with students in 1986, 1987, and 1989, suggested that the early social

Figure 11.3. The forbidden space: Placa Emili Vendrell, 1996. *Photography by Gary McDonogh.*

patterns of this plaza were limited. The openness of the plaza to sun and wind confined most daytime activities to sheltered side areas. Rather than transforming the surrounding areas, the square became part of their primary function: a locale for prostitution and a residence for transients. One of the area's most regular social structures in 1986 and 1987 was a crap game conducted near one of the benches. Homeless people would sleep there at night. In the winter, the *plaça* often was deserted and torn up, piled with garbage at night; in the summer, pickup soccer games were played in front of the anti-AIDS Keith Haring mural adorning the back wall. By the late 1990s, even the mural was removed to the Museu de l'Art Contemporani.

Plaça Emili Vendrell, in the northern and more stable section of the Raval, has a more complicated history. This small corner garden takes the form of a preexisting building with one-story arched walls and a shaded, fountained interior. The ruined building the *plaça* replaced had become a haven for squatters; local merchants were instrumental in its transformation, asking for a *plaça* that could be locked at night. Yet, within a few months of its inauguration, the square was identified as a plaza that "serves for everything except to walk in" (*Noticiero Universal*, 12 November 1983). Alcoholics, drug addicts, and children playing hookey took advantage of its hidden spaces, excluding and alarming neighborhood residents, who detoured around it. For decades, this *plaça* has generally been empty during the day, when I have passed it, and locked at night (McDonogh 1993b).

These two projects again patterned the values of a dominant city onto the spacial relations of another realm. For generations, inhabitants of the Raval have taken over public streets and semipublic bars for life activities that could not be conducted in crowded, inadequate private housing. In contrast to the urban planning ethos of the city since the 18th century, the Raval street is an intrinsic social space, despite the multiple transit plans of the municipality. Open spaces, however, with little linkage to social networks, have been neither part of barrio history nor valued by inhabitants. Such spaces, indeed, are also potential areas of conflict between groups, generations, or uses that erupted into gang warfare between gypsies and Africans over drugs in the 1980s. The order and control of the city as a whole, again, was inimical to the values of the barrio.

Barrio residents do consistently demand more sports facilities. Such places, while generally on the fringes of the Raval, show intensive use, unlike any other open spaces. This has been an area of slow development in urban planning, with facilities slowly replacing crumbling older playgrounds. New concrete plazas do not lend themselves well to such actions, even if children transform the concrete floors of Salvador Seguí into a makeshift soccer field.

Open spaces also challenge the articulation of barrio and city. A new park around the Romanesque church of Sant Pau united and revitalized parking and play zones that barrio residents have used in a new complex and eliminated a famous area of prostitution. Yet it also provided vistas and underground parking for an area of luxury hotel development for the Olympics. This dualism can be further explored by reference to other Raval projects linked to the city as a whole.

The Barrio and the City

The major current renovation project in the Raval since the 1970s entails the construction of the broad esplanade that will be a pedestrian continuation of the Avinguda de Drassanes. While this space will no longer serve for automotive transit through the Raval as it was envisioned decades earlier, the space it creates does not correspond to traditional residential or open-space use in the area either. Its parallelism to the Rambles suggested to social service workers in the 1980s the possibility of a separate promenade to "clean up" the more public area: a *rambla dels marginats* (Rambla of the marginal). This project destroyed major streets of prostitution and marginal housing in the barrio, while opening the neighborhood up to potential gentrification. Still, some prostitutes and their clients mingle in a new *plaça dura* named for Pierye de Mandiargues, author of a famous French novel about the depraved *barrio chino.*

Even more controversial is the relation of the barrio and the city made manifest in the placement of urban cultural capital in the Raval. For years, the space around the Convent dels Angels and the Casa de Caritat in the northern Raval was a de facto playground and green space for the surrounding areas. This goal was specifically espoused by a mural, over-looking its dirt fields, claiming the territory for the neighborhood. To-day, these structures constitute the center for a network of museums, libraries, and educational institutions convenient to the rest of the city. The city's plan *Del Liceu al Setmanari* links monuments to bourgeois prestige and cultural capital within the barrio (such as the Liceu opera house or Biblioteca de Catalunya, the national library) and to new projects (such as the Museum of Contemporary Art). The Faculty of Geography and History of the University will also be located in this area. Such uses serve a population outside the barrio—few residents go to the library, much less the university or opera—while changing the infrastructure of services for the neighborhood. The mentality of planning for urban cul-ture is suggested by a comment concerning a historic antituberculosis clinic and its surroundings in the northern Raval in Maragall's *Refent Barcelona*: "This is another zone that can become monumental (*pot mounmentalitzar-se*) within the global plan. . . . It is very close to the traditional epicenter of the city and only needs psychological implemen-tation of access routes" (1986, 25, emphasis in original). Maragall saw this as an attraction to be appropriated by the city rather than a con-cern of the barrio to which it creates access.

The execution of these changes made more prescient the 1981 con-cerns of a barrio spokesman to the discourses he perceived to be form-ing around the disposition of the Convent dels Angels: "Admitting the installation of cultural activities of this caliber must carry the conscious assumption of transformations in the urban and social structure that will be produced in the great spaces destined for accesses and parking as well as in the impulse it will give to the specialization of the barrio in activities at the level of the city, favoring the tertiarization and concen-tration of services which could brusquely revalue the zone (look at the Barrio Gótico) with a consequent expulsion of the population through an increase in the rents" (Artigues Vidal 1981, 24).[5] Artigues, in fact, voiced for the Raval's residents the primary alternative to the history of planning that has consistently made the barrio a subordinate service area for the changing dominant ideology of the city: "We must respect the decision of the population that wishes to remain, favoring it through rehabilitation, the continuity of customs and activities. The contrary will be to abandon the Raval to degradation or, in its place, through an artificial conservation, to its transformation into a new 'historical-cultural-commercial' center" (1981, 24). This complex, however, now embodies the vision of the city that characterized late twentieth-century Barcelona. The underlying unity of this project entails planners acting as agents of the dominant political discourse and vision, rather than as facilitators of a pluralistic urban model that includes neighborhood concerns.

Amidst the election frenzy of 1987, a *Diario de Barcelona* editorial entitled *"El Raval no vol ser el cul de Barcelona"* ("The Raval Does Not Wish to Be Barcelono's Ass") challenged planning, its models and its deafness:

> The Raval and its conscientious residents have decided not to let the occasion of elections pass and attacks with force to see if any compromises can be reached. The more *normal* residents, those who have spent almost their whole life without any changes, ignore it, and little has been done to change intolerable living conditions to make an old city worthy of living. And there are fewer opportunities to do so all the time.
>
> To complete the politics of a *gran Barcelona*—like that of the Del Liceu al Setmanari project—with a search for a plan that resolves daily problems of a degraded neighborhood as they have in other countries—definitively, to apply a model on a human scale, starting with residents who live in the Raval, is more and more necessary. (5 June 1987, emphasis in original)

The recurrent question in interpreting many reforms thus becomes not only their abstract value within urban revitalization but also their response to social groups who will actually construct their lives among these projects. Reform programs, as we have seen, have emerged from a shared hegemonic discourse about the city. Plans were projected at the level of the city or the metropolitan areas, and reform was subsequently imposed. In some cases, residents were brought into agreement; in others, they were simply dominated. Despite an ostensible valuation of a city of neighborhoods, planning arises from the city of elite discourse and its ideals of neighborhood and citizens, which ignores—perhaps no longer hears—some grassroots values (McDonogh 1997). Yet residents, by their uses, comments, and occasional manifestations, still convey their fragmentary alternate visions.

Reflecting on Urban Discourses

In this chapter, I have proposed an interlocking analysis of questions concerning the nature of urban planning in Barcelona and, indeed, for general planning of late-industrial cities. City planning in Barcelona, as in most of Spain, entered a new phase at the end of the Franco regime and the era of immediate reaction to it. This period was defined by the establishment of institutional action, by core thematics of discourse about the city, and by the relationship between this period and continuities in the historical dynamics of urbanism in modern Spain. While I have highlighted them only for Barcelona, similar yet localized transformations are apparent in Madrid, Sevilla, Valencia, Tarragona, and Santander, among cities I have visited or studied.

In a more general sense, this chapter also has examined the relationship between dominant discourses of urban planning and the beliefs and actions of those who live in the city, especially in a "problem zone." My analysis of residents of the Raval in speech and action has looked through the structural silence of the city to tease out the clashes of planning and values that have emerged as problems in the framework of a reestablished planning regime.

In the 1980s, urban planning in Barcelona, in both the implementation of design and the stability of debate within a democratic framework, constituted new discourses of the city. Participants in this hegemonic dialogue valued the city as an ordered, efficient unit in which parts co-exist with each other rather than living in conflict, and in which recognition of success would be national and international, as well as local. The "post-transitional" era grew out of the history of conception and action about the city that had developed since the eighteenth century. Planning maintained a dialogue with the past more than with some residents of the present. Comparison with the Franco regime and its aftermath shows that the new discourses did not spring from a simple continuity but from a reassertion after the intrusion of alternate and imposed models. The transitional period offered alternative visions of grassroots participation to the pattern of acquiescence and response that Castells also glimpsed in his analysis of citizens' movements in Madrid (1983), but these, too, changed over time.

Continuity and the institutionalization of an ideal of the city in planning take on different meanings if we compare urban philosophy with the living conditions and values of different urban groups. In the Raval, despite a public commitment to listen to voices of the neighborhood, competing political parties and administrative units have stressed to classic models of who may be considered a citizen (good citizen), of what citizens' problems should be, and of how citizens are to appreciate solutions for their neighborhoods and city. As this discourse was solidified among competing elites, challenges from below became less audible. The possibility this article explores, by critique and observation, was encapsulated by a social service worker as "unir el humano y el desarrollo en la planificación" (to unite that which is human with development in planning). The alternative seems to be a reification of division and subordination in the city.

These interpretations do not condemn the Socialist regime or its planning, which has attempted to be responsive and even corrective with regard to responsibilities in the Raval. This regime has, in fact, avoided many problematic interventions that had been practiced by a variety of previous governments, and has expanded services throughout the Raval. Rather, this chapter asks planners, politicians, and social scientists studying the city to step back and ask what cultural baggage Barcelona—or other cities—may carry unexamined as "second nature." This entails a critical perspective on the nature of the city, of conflict, and of power in planning as criticisms to be applied to the institutions and analysis who work with the city. Urban anthropology in such a setting must become both more reflexive and more extensive—looking at the peoples and structures of small units we have traditionally worked with and questioning in a dramatic way other metaphors of the city present in mass media, bureaucracy, and politics. Urban anthropology, while often outside traditional realms of planning, has unique resources to discuss the sociocultural production of the city not only at the grassroots level but also among dominant strata, and these must ultimately encompass our fellow intellectuals and our own discourse. The effects of "invisible" ideologies of the city must be questioned for cities throughout the modern world, while alternatives are attended to and brought into discussion. By so posing a critical reading of the discourses of the city in a period of crucial transformation in Barcelona, I hope to continue the debate that the post-transitional period has already built upon, and perhaps to temper a new discourse of the city to contribute to the Barcelona of the future.

Epilogue 1999: Discourses, Development, and Fragmentation

A version of this article first appeared on the eve of Barcelona's Summer Olympic Games of 1992, an event whose success provided a capstone for the transformations of the city after Franco. Barcelona subsequently has become a frequent destination for global visitors and a model for postindustrial urban reform. Recognition by architects and planners worldwide also has affirmed urban projects of decentralization, linkages and new monuments. Moreover, the city continues to reconstitute itself actively as a discursive universe. The government still publishes the glossy review *Barcelona Metropòlis Mediterrània* (BMM) alongside journals for civil servants, shopkeepers, and neighborhoods residents that all extol the city, and exhibits in museums, universities, and municipal centers constantly discuss the city. Newspapers and television refer frequently to architecture, planning, and identity as well as global perceptions of the city; hence, these media and ideas filter into everyday discussion in bars, at home and at school. And the Centre de Cultura Contemporània de Barcelona (CCCB), housed in the former Casa de Caritat of the Raval, has become a center for exhibits about the city, ranging from the massive overview of modern planning that greeted ten thousand participants in the International Union of Architects meetings of July 1996 to smaller installations on the Raval or the Sustainable City, both held in the summer of 1998).

Meanwhile, the Raval has continued to change. As the CCCB, Richard Meier's Museu de l'Art Contemporani de Barcelona (MACBA) and other cultural institutions replace older edifices, they become nuclei for further gentrification. The construction of the as yet unrealized broad central plaza continues to eviscerate the barrio's older urban fabric. There remain those in the Raval who speak out against this technocratic urban cleansing: in June 1998, for example local anarchists staged a rally in a new open space, sarcastically labeled the Black Square, to protest displacement. Yet there are fewer and fewer older residents for whom to speak, as outmigration, controls on illegal immigrants, and planned replacements of both buildings and people have fostered a nostalgic disappearance of the *barrio chino* (González 1997).

Barcelona's very success has created a new discursive universe. With the Olympics as history, new goals must be formulated. Moreover, Barcelona is no longer a regional industrial capital but a global city, closely linked to European metropoles and other service centers. Competition now takes place not only in politics (where relations of Catalunya and the Spanish state continue to be negotiated) but also through media imagery. Bilbao, for example, which once vied with Barcelona in industrial production, is now perceived as a threat because of its architectural/cultural investments, including its new branch of the Guggenheim Museum, designed by Frank Gehry (Zulaika 1997), and its subway stations designed by Sir Norman Foster, whose communications tower is an emblem of the new Barcelona.

Despite the recent retirement of Pascual Maragall, different, fragmented discourses have emerged that are not embedded in competing political agendas so much as in organizations, institutions, and public intellectuals. This new universe also incorporates the criticism of the recent past: Josep Miró Ardevol, for example, complained in *La Vanguardia,* "What Cerdà did was to start with detailed study of the conditions of the concrete life of the people, and put the most attention where there were greatest human needs. He thought of the people in terms of persons, necessities and justice—themes that now, among us, we find too distant. Too often the valorization of Barcelona is made "from outside" the conditions of real life of its people—an error which must be corrected in the future" (1997). Critics, including those, like Oriol Bohigas, who were deeply involved in the 1980s transformations, are also formulating new discourses—after modernity. These can be illustrated through an examination of the use of "sustainability," "diversity," and "culture" as new discursive threads.

Interest in a balance of energy inputs and uses that would constitute "urban sustainability" led to a 1998 CCCB exhibit where videos, computers, and interactive installations highlighted world problems of pollution, consumption, and sprawl (Ciutat Sostenible 1998). It also constructed an image of Barcelona as a potential paradigm for sustainable design, given its density and pedestrian scale as well as its mild climate and architectural creativity. While Catalunya has longstanding concerns with nature, I do not believe sustainability emerges "organically" from local environmental discourse, which has focussed on the countryside as the site of a true Catalan national identity in opposition to the city. It may reflect new urban groups opposed to the material development of the 1970s and 1980s, but direct stimulus also came the 1994 Aalborg Letter, in which eighty European local authorities committed themselves to move toward sustainability. This pits Barcelona against other cities whose plans are more advanced, while offering rewards that ecological entrepreneurs are already pursuing. The architects and projects of a new sustainability are local, yet their discourse is more directly tied to other European cities than anything projected in the 1980s.

Globalization also permeated "diversity" as an urban characteristic in the CCCB's exhibit on "Scenes of the Raval." The exhibit, itself an artistically fragmented interactive installation, included interviews with Moroccan merchants, presentations by local mosques, and representations by local Filipino groups who used the center's internet connections to follow Filipino elections (Madueño 1998). On the tour that accompanied the exhibit, the shops and institutions of these groups were indicated as the guide explained that Barcelonins choose to live in the Raval "because of its diversity." This signals a sea change since the mid-1980s, when new immigration produced racial tensions throughout Catalunya, including angry confrontations among Africans, Arabs, and

Gypsies and other Spanish groups in the Raval (McDonogh 1993a). Part of the transformation seems to have come through a shift in the visibility of ethnic groups—Chinese, Filipinos, and Indians are perceived as less aggressive than the earlier African populations, whom the press consistently associated with drugs and violence. As bars, rooming houses, and other centers for marginal immigrants have been closed, moreover, an image of bourgeois immigrants with shops, mosques, and restaurants has taken their place. Finally, diversity has been constructed as a necessary feature of the globalism to which Barcelona aspires. In a 1996 speech at the MACBA, for example, Pascual Maragall claimed that "we want to be capital of Catalunya and the European capital of culture. We want to be the site where diversity is revindicated as a cultural value" (Aragay 1996). In 1997, *BMM* introduced a new section called Plural Barcelona. Among its first profiles were Argentines and Japanese, with the latter introduced as "rich immigrants, directors of multinationals, young artists or professors of Japanese. They come from a rich country and stay here voluntarily, knowing that they can return to their country when they wish" (Pernau and Luque 1997, 79).

Diversity is also linked to "culture," used in an embracing albeit vague sense mingling art/high culture, belief, lifestyles, language, and oppositional creativity; hence the Raval exhibit of cultural history was explained as "the people of the Raval, artistic object" (Madueño 1998). While debates over class and power through the prism of culture have a long history in Catalunya, both in internal struggles and in the definition of polity vis-à-vis the Spanish state, "culture" has gained new power as a symbol of urbane commodities and erudite attractions that consolidate Barcelona's position on a global stage. For years after the Olympics, in fact, Barcelona sought recognition as a European Capital of Culture, a title already held by Athens, Amsterdam, Dublin, and Glasgow. In the 1995 candidate dossier *El Temps de la Imaginació* (The Time of Imagination), Maragall situated culture within a sequence of urban development: "After a stage characterized by urbanistic renovation, and another characterized by the creation of great infrastructures that have made the city more habitable and accessible, now . . . is the time to enjoy the city and to develop its quality of life: the hour of urbanitat (urbaneness), we ourselves say, of which culture is a fundamental element" (Mascarell, 1995, 21–22). Culture also becomes a vital feature for Barcelona's entry into global prestige: "There is a network of cities from Saint Petersburg and Oslo to the North, including London and Berlin, Paris and Amsterdam, Vienna and Frankfurt, Barcelona and Florence, Rome, Madrid, Sevilla, Athens . . . into which we must insert ourselves powerfully" (ibid., 24).

In June 1998, the title of European Capital of Culture was awarded instead to Salamanca. Yet politicians and civic groups had already prepared another vaguer but locally generated Forum of World Cultures for 2004. This year-long exposition proposes goals ranging from development of the Besòs river to "bringing together 150,00 people (intellectuals, politicians, anthropologists, and religious, among other collectives) to look for permanent peace in the world" (Marín 1997). A 1999 visit to the city's Web site shows Mayor Joan Clos claiming that "During the summer months of 2004, Barcelona will become the world's capital of culture" (www.seebcn.com/welcome.htm). Yet even these features are often contested among participants worried about cost and scale (*El País*, 23 January 1998). Meanwhile, a June 1998 panel discussion at the CCCB announced that the Forum would incorporate solar-powered housing for participants, among other ecological features, although members of the audience pointed out contradictions between sustainability and the influx of hundreds of thousands of visitors and participants.

Forum 2004 nonetheless underscores a further transformation of discourse in and about the city in the past decade from a city of process to a city of events, indeed, of spectacle. Hence the International Architects meeting received remarkable press coverage, and the empty title of Capital of Culture was coveted to program another year of recognition. While some worry about both the demands of the city-theater on urban life and the scarcity of such events, these events also structure the ways in which Barcelonins ask what the city is and what it will be. These new discourses, in turn, tell us about a complex contemporary society moving beyond the construction of modernity.

Acknowledgment

This article is based primarily on fieldwork in Barcelona's *barrio chino* in 1986, 1987, and 1989 as part of a larger project on the interaction of ideology and society in the formation of the late-capitalist city (1993, 1994, 1995, 1998). Research support has been provided by the American Council of Learned Societies, the National Endowment for the Humanities, and the New College Anthropology Endowment and by Bryn Mawr College through the Hewlett and Pew Foundation programs. It also draws on extensive previous fieldwork in Barcelona that began at the beginning of the transitional period and has continued into the present (McDonogh 1986, 1997).

This article has profited by comments from Donald Moore, Hing Yuk Wong, Susan DiGiacomo, Geoffrey Mohlman, Gaspar Maza, Josep Maria Gallart, and the New College Urban Studies Reading Group (especially Olga Ronay and Ron Annis). Carles Carreras Verdaguer gave a careful reading to a final draft within the context of seminars that he offered at New College and Bryn Mawr College. I also owe a debt of gratitude to colleagues in anthropology, geography, architecture, and urban planning in Barcelona who have shared and debated ideas.

I am grateful to the Hemeroteca de Barcelona and the AV-Raval for periodical resources, including articles from *Solidaridad Obrera*, *Avui*, *Diari(o) de Barcelona*, *Lo Vanguardia*, *Correo Catalan*, and *El Periódico*.

Notes

1. The Raval designates a one-kilometer area of the urban core formerly bounded by inner and outer walls. While it was an administrative district itself until the 1980s, it has now been merged with other urban core areas and is referred to globally as Ciutat Vella (the old city). In the 1920s, the most infamous section of the Raval, its southern tip near the port, became known as the *barrio chino* for prostitution, crime, and adventure. This section differed from the northern Raval, which housed workers and some bourgeois families, but urban decay has moved northward in recent years. Generally, I use *Raval* to describe the entire neighborhood, situating specific problems of loci as appropriate.
2. All quotations are the translations of the author, emphasis added unless otherwise noted.
3. Avenida García Morato under the Franco regime.
4. Solà-Morales, however, suggests that this technology also partakes of specifically Catalan experiences of technique (1986).
5. Barrio Gótico is a central neighborhood that includes many historic monuments and is increasingly being defined as a tourist-amusement center for the city.

References

Adjuntament de Barcelona. 1983. *Plans i projectes per a Barcelona 1981/82.* Barcelona: Ajuntament, Area d'Urbanisme.

———. 1985 *Inicis de la urbanística municipal de Barcelona: Mostra dels fons municipal de plans I projectes d'urbanisme, 1750–1930.* Barcelona: Ajuntament.

———. 1987 *Urbanisme a Barcelona: Plans cap al 92.* Barcelona: Ajuntament.

Alibes, R., et al. 1975. *La lucha de barrios.* Barcelona: Aedos.

Amelang, James.1986. *Honored citizens of Barcelona.* Princeton, N.J.: Princeton University Press.

Aragay , Ignasi. 1996. "Maragall: 'La nostra patria és el llenguatge europeu.'" *Avui* (July 3), 1.

Ariès, Phillipe. 1981. *At the hour of our death.* New York: Knopf.

Artigues Vidal, Jaume. 1981. Análysis urbanístico de los barrios de Barcelona (2). El Raval (Distrito V): Un suburbio en el centro. *Noticiero Universal,* July 7.

Artigues Vidal, Jaume, Francesc Mas Palahi, and Xavier Suñol Ferrer. 1980. *El Raval: História d'un barri servidor d'uno ciutat.* Barcelona: Colecció el Raval, Number 1.

Balius (pseud.) 1936. La ciudad de Barcelona. *Solidaridad Nacional,* August 16.Barcelona

"El barrio no es chino: el ayuntamiento ha cerrado los 'meublés.'" *El Periódico,*17 January 1994.

Bohigas, Oriol. 1963. *Barcelona entre el plan Cerdà i el barrâquisme.* Barcelona: Edicions 62.

Borja, Jordi. 1996. *Barcelona: An urban transformation model 1980–1995.* Quito, Ecuador: Urban Management Programme.

Carbonell, Joume, and equipos de estudios. 1976. *La lucha de barrios en Barcelona.* Madrid: Elias Querejeta.

Carreras Verdaguer, Carles. 1980. *Sants: Analisi del procès de l'espai urbà de Barcelona.* Barcelona: Serpa.

————. 1993. *Geografia general de Barcelona: Espai Mediterrani, temps Europeu.* Barcelona: Oikos-Tau.

Castells, Manuel. 1983. *The city and the grassroots: A cross-cultural theory of urban social movements.* Berkeley: University of California Press.

Cerdà, Ildefons. 1968–1971. *Teoría de la urbanización y aplicación de sus principios y doctrinas a la reforma de Barcelona.* Barcelona: Instituto de Estudios Fiscales.

Cerdà: Urbs i territori. 1996. Barcelona: Generalitat.

La Ciutat sostenible. 1998. Barcelona: Centre de Cultura Contemporània.

Elliott, J, H. 1963. *The revolt of the Catalans: A study in the decline of Spain (1598–1640).* Cambridge: Cambridge University Press.

Fava, Maria. 1984. Els barris denuncien la frenada als plans de reforma interior: El model socialista de la ciutat oblida els PERIS. *Avui*, 8 February.

Fernández Alba, Antonio, and Carmen Gavira. 1986. *Crónicas del espacio perdido: La destrucción de la ciudad en España, 1960–1980.* Madrid: Dirección General de Arquitectura y Edificación.

Ferras, Robert. 1977. *Barcelone.* Paris: Anthropos.

Fincher, Ruth and Jane M. Jacobs, eds. 1998. *Cities of difference.* New York: The Guilford Press.

González, Dolors. 1997. "Temps del Raval." *Descobrir Catalunya,* no. 2 (May–June): 44–48.

Gregory, Steven. 1998 *Black Corona: Race and the politics of place in an urban community.* Princeton, N.J.: Princeton University Press.

Guallar, Angel. 1963. Barcelona: Distrito par distrito. El Distrito V será del conglomerado más moderno de Barcelona: Juan Abellán, concejal-presidente, paladín de este milagro. *Diario de Barcelona,* 22 May.

————. 1964 Siete mil familias afectadas por una mejora urbana. La avenida García Morato aniquilará definitivamente al famoso "barrio chino." *Diario de Barcelona,* 25 August.

Guerau de Arellano, Faustino. 1985. *La vida pedagógica.* Barcelona: Roselló Impressions.

Hohenberg, Paul M., and Lynn Hollen Lees. 1985. *The making of urban Europe, 1000–1950.* Cambridge, Mass.: Harvard University Press.

J. S. A. 1947. Relieve de la ciudad: À golpe de piqueta. *La Prensa,* June 12.

Lynch, Kevin. 1960. *The image of the city.* Cambridge, Mass.: MIT Press.

————. 1981. *A theory of good city form.* Cambridge, Mass.: MIT Press.

McDonogh, Gary. 1986. *Good families of Barcelona: A social history of power in the industrial era.* Princeton, N. J.: Princeton University Press.

————. 1987 The geography of evil: Barcelona's barrio chino. *Anthropological Quarterly* 60:174–184.

————. 1991. Terra de Pas: Reflections on new immigration in Catalunya. *Contemporary Catalonia in Spain and Europe,* edited by Milton Azevedo. Pp. 70–97. Berkeley: International Studies Center, University of California, Berkeley.

————. 1992. "Gender, bars and virtue in Barcelona." *Anthropological Quarterly* (January): 19–33.

————. 1993a. The face behind the door: European integration, immigration and identity. In *Anthropological perspectives on European economic integration,* edited by T. Wilson and M. Estellie Smith. Pp. 143–166. Boulder, Colo.: Westview Press.

————. 1993b. "The Geography of emptiness." *Cultural meaning of urban space,* edited by Robert Rotenberg and Gary McDonogh. Pp. 3–16. Westport, Conn.: Bergin and Garvey.

————. 1997. "Citizenship, locality and resistance." *City & Society Annual Review,* 5–34.

McDonogh, Gary, and Gaspar Maza. Forthcoming. Mean streets: Childhood and values in Barcelona's barrio chino. *Arxiu d'Etnologia Catalana.*

Mackay, David. 1989. *L'arquitectura moderna a Barcelona (1854–1939).* Barcelona: Edicions 62.

Madueño, Eugenio. 1998. La gente del Raval, objetivo artístico. *La Vanguardia* 22 May.

Maragall, Pascual. 1983. Presentació. In *Plans i projectes per a Barcelona 1981/ 82.* Ajuntament, Area d'Urbanisme. Pp. 9–10. Barcelona: Ajuntament, Area d'Urbanisme.

―――. 1986. *Refent Barcelona* (Remaking Barcelona). Barcelona: Planeta.

Marín, Angel. 1997. La Unesco aprobará el Foro Universal de las Culturas 2004. *ABC Cataluna,* November 12.

Mascarell i Canalda, Ferran, ed. 1995. *El temps de la imaginació.* Barcelona: Candiature per Barcelona 2001.

Miró Ardevol, Josep. 1997. La ruidosa Barcelona de Maragall. *La Vanguardia,* 13 January.

Pernau, Gabriel, and Carmen Luque. 1997."Arigato, Barcelona. *Barcelona Metròpolis Mediterrània* (September-October):79–85.

Pujadas, J., and F. Bardají. 1987. *Los barrios de Tarragona: Una aproximación antropologica.* Tarragona: Ajuntament.

Remassar, A., ed. 1997. *Urban regeneration: A challenge for public art,* Monografies Psico-Socio Ambientals, 6. Barcelona: Universitat

Rispa, Raul, Cesar Alonso de los Rios, and Maria Jose Aguaza. 1993. *Expo '92 Seville: Architecture and design.* Milan: Electa.

Romaní, Oriol. 1982. Droga i subcultura: Una història cultural del "haix" a Barcelona (1960–1980). Tesis doctoral, departmento de antropologia cultural, Universitat de Barcelona.

Ros Hombravello, J. 1986. Torno la tuberculosis a la ciutat vella. *Avui,* January 26.

Rubio, Enrique. 1951. Habla el párroco de San Pablo del Campo. *Solidaridad Nacional,* 11 November.

Solà-Morales, Ignosi de. 1986. *Architettura minimale a Barcelona: Costruire sulla citta costruita.* Milano: Electa.

Solà-Morales I Rubió, Manuel de. 1985. Barcelona, taller d'urbanisme. In *Barcelona, Inicis d'urbanisme. Adjuntament de Barcelona.* Pp. 5–7. Barcelona: Ajuntament.

Tarragó, Salvador. 1978. *En defensa de Barcelona.* Barcelona: Adeos.

Tatjer, Mercé. 1973. *La Barceloneta del segle XVIII al plan de la Ribera.* Barcelona: Salurno.

Terán, F. 1969. *Ciudad y urbanización en el mundo actual.* Madrid: Blume.

Ucelay Da Cal, Enric. 1997. "Le Corbusier i les rivalitats tecnocràtiques a la Catalunya revolucionaria." *Le Corbusier y Espana,* edited by J. J. Lahuerta. Pp. 121–189. Barcelona: Centre de Cultura Contemporània.

Vilar, Pierre. 1962. *La Catalogne dans l'Espagne moderne.* Paris: SEVPEN.

Wallerstein, Immanuel. 1974. *The modern world system: Capitalist agriculture and the European world system.* New York: Academic Press.

Ynfante, José. 1974. *Los negocios de Porcioles: Las sagradas familias de Barcelona.* Toulouse: Midi-Livre.

Zulaika, Joseba. 1997. *Guggenheim Bilbao: Crónica de una seducción.* Madrid: Nerea.

MATTHEW COOPER

12 Spatial Discourses and Social Boundaries
Re-Imagining the Toronto Waterfront

In contemporary North America, spatial discourses play an important part in the construction and reconstruction of social space. In this chapter, I will be particularly concerned with the emergence of a new kind of spatial discourse in a planning context. I will argue that focusing on changing forms of discourse opens a window on the historical processes through which spatial meanings and the experience of space change. A useful area in which to observe such processes is the social construction of transitional zones and boundaries. The work of a Canadian royal commission from 1988 to 1991 investigating the future of the Toronto waterfront provides an interesting case study of this process. This chapter begins with a brief discussion of spatial discourses, followed by a description of the context in which this new discourse emerged. I then analyze the discourse and consider some of its implications for perception of the area, definition of the issues, and planning strategies. I argue that the Toronto waterfront, both physically and conceptually, is an historical and social product.

Discourses of space and the ideologies they manifest help constitute social reality, including the human environment, and shape cultural change and the experience of place. However, it is crucial that they be viewed in relation to the material practices in which they are embedded and which they also affect (Cosgrove 1984, Harvey 1989). A number of writers concerned with spatial issues have turned to the study of discourse as a way of understanding the social production of space. Henri Lefebvre has been one of the most influential. He relates spatial practices to "representations of space" (e.g., discourses) and to kinds of spaces (especially "representational spaces"), that is, the triad of the *perceived*, the *conceived*, and the *lived* (1991, 40)—or, as David Harvey (1989, 219) perhaps more usefully interprets the terms, "the experienced, the perceived, and the imagined." James Duncan and associates (1990, J. Duncan and N. Duncan 1988, Barnes and J. Duncan 1992) have explored discourse, text, and metaphor in the representation of landscape. In a collection entitled *The Cultural Meaning of Urban Space*, Rotenberg (1993a, xiv) argues that discourse provides entrée into a topic of crucial concern to urban anthropologists: the historical emergence of spatial meanings in relation to change in the built environment. "As people participate in the discourse, they act on their understanding to disproportionately shape to their purposes the urban places they control. These places then enter the historical development of spatial meaning as artifacts, preserving forever after the moment when a meaning was given concrete form in space." Margaret Rodman and I (1995), in studying housing designed to be accessible for people with disabilities, have argued that some spatial discourses inscribe both difference and the attempt to efface it in the human environment.

Rob Shields argues that "social spatialization" is a useful conceptual tool for thinking about the means by which spatial processes emerge in relation to changes in the human environment. By that term he means the overarching "social construction of the spatial which is a formation of both discursive and non-discursive elements, practices, and processes" (1991, 31). "Social spatialization" occurs, he says, "[a]t the level of the social imaginary (collective mythologies, presuppositions) as well as interventions in the landscape (for example, the built environment). This term [social spatialization] allows us to name an object of study which encompasses both the cultural logic of the spatial and its expression and elaboration in language and more concrete actions, constructions and institutional arrangements" (ibid., 31). Through spatial discourses, people elaborate ideologies of place, which variously and ambiguously help/lead/force them to think and act in certain ways. In my summary formulation, using ideologies of place people describe the kinds of places that exist, explain their nature, evaluate them (employing cognitively and emotionally salient imagery to create a symbolic landscape), identify with them, and imagine places as they ought to be (thus creating moral landscapes). It is also relevant to take into account that discourses of space are themselves spatialized. David Harvey, for example, points out, "We learn our ways of thinking and conceptualizing from active grappling with the spatializations of the written word, the study and production of maps, graphs, diagrams, photographs, models, paintings, mathematical symbols, and the like" (1989, 206).

The forms in which space is represented in such discourses are crucial to the ways in which ideologies are expressed (Barnes and Duncan 1992). A number of scholars have analyzed spatial representation, the organization of space, and ideology. For example, Dolores Hayden's *Seven American Utopias* (1976) brilliantly explores the relation between utopian visions and the attempt to realize them, at least in part, through built form. Rotenberg (1993b) finds interesting parallels between the discourse of the Roman architect Vitruvius and contemporary residents of Vienna about the healthfulness of urban places. Bowden argues that "major American beliefs about the pre-American environment were all created successively as myths after settlement in each ecological zone" (1992, 3). In the *Journal of Historical Geography*, he and his associates explore the invention of American traditions of landscape and settlement in relation to settlement history and the interests of those involved.

In thinking about Western spatial discourses, I find it helpful at a general level to distinguish discourses that are *transcendental* from those that are *humanistic*. Transcendental discourses ground their analysis and prescriptions in allegedly universal and immutable characteristics of the world or Being. Humanistic ones ground theirs in human characteristics, needs, and aspirations, however conceived. Clearly, these categories overlap; they are not meant to be watertight only to help in thinking about the phenomena.

Humanistic discourses of space figure, for example, in the writings of many geographers (e.g., Harvey 1989, Duncan 1990, and Shields 1991), as well as in anthropological discussions of the relation between the organization of space and cultural meaning (Lawrence and Low 1990). No matter the other differences in these writings, all ground their spatial discourse in an analysis of human society and culture. David Harvey (1989, 206), for example, rejects an "absolute" characterization of space or time. He argues that their very nature is socially and historically constituted, thus relative. Most urban planning rests on explicit though variable conceptions of human needs and proclivities, and how the built environment can serve or affect them (see Hall 1988 for many examples).

Transcendental spatial discourses appear in many forms. A well-known example is the discourse of European neoclassicism. Aesthetic norms of regularity, uniformity, simplicity, and balance prevailed as ways of representing nature. The key, as Lovejoy (1960a, 1960b, 1960c) argued many years ago, was in the definition and connotations of "nature" and "natural." The regular was thought to be more "natural" because it reflected the underlying mathematical principles thought to order the world. It represented reality rather than mere appearance.

Another example of a very different sort, as Cosgrove (1984) has argued, is the attempt in academic geography to substitute "region" for "landscape." The latter implies a viewer, someone who perceives and organizes a view. But, as an analytical category, "region" does not depend on there being humans from whose viewpoint the world is to be perceived. It thus substitutes a seemingly transhistorical, nonsocial concept for one that is preeminently historical and cultural.

For Foucault (1980), revealing how such transcendental discourses attempt to naturalize ideology and power relations is critical. By so doing, one can bring to light the intersections of power and knowledge crucial to the constitution of modern societies. Mitchell's (1988) analysis of the reorganization of space in colonial Egypt is a fascinating attempt to apply some of Foucault's ideas. Similarly, Paul Rabinow (1989) situates French colonial urban planning in the context of the development of a French social science that attempted to naturalize and absolutize ideology.

I have found the distinction between humanistic and transcendental spatial discourses useful analytically. But like any dichotomy, it should alert us to look for emerging discourses that reject its polarities. In the remainder of this chapter I will focus on a spatial discourse that has emerged recently, based on radically different presuppositions. I will do so by considering a new social spatialization of the Toronto area waterfront and how it may affect perception and the representation of space. While I will not consider the social and material determinants of this change here, I will describe some of the context in which it emerged and its potential consequences for planning.

From Waterfront to Watershed

Changes in the political economy of Toronto's waterfront provide some of the context for the emergence of this new social spatialization. Since the mid-1970s the Toronto waterfront has been the focus of controversy (Cooper 1993). By the 1960s, container ships had became increasingly common and the old port facilities fell into disuse. Meanwhile, the Regional Municipality of Metropolitan Toronto (RMMT), which includes the City of Toronto and the four surrounding municipalities, undertook a major waterfront planning exercise. This led to waterfront development at the eastern and western sides of Metro Toronto. It also produced a futuristic recreation complex built on artificial islands near the central waterfront in the City of Toronto. The central waterfront itself, however, had been excluded from this 1967 plan. A high-rise development of offices, hotel, and luxury apartments rose massively at the very center of the city waterfront. But the rest of it was deserted and rapidly became derelict.

In 1972, the Canadian federal government gave a thirty-five-hectare parcel of central waterfront land to the City of Toronto for redevelopment as mixed-use green space. Thus began the development of what I have called a landscape of consumption (Cooper 1993).The Harbourfront Corporation, a federal government corporation, was created to redevelop and administer the area. Its board of directors saw it as "an urban meeting place with a waterfront flavour, providing opportunity to display, enrich and share the diverse cultural traditions of the people of Toronto" (Harbourfront Corporation 1978, 2). This early park plan gave way in 1980 to a scheme approved by the Toronto City Council and the Ontario Municipal Board to take the city to the water's edge by including a mix of recreational, commercial, and residential uses. Harbourfront Corporation developed the central waterfront into a major cultural and touristic attraction, programming thousands of cultural events there. But the redevelopment that actually took place, especially in the 1980s, produced a wall of mostly upscale high rise condominiums, hotels, and shopping along the lake shore.

Desfor, Goldrick, and Merrens (1988, 100–102; 1989) have suggested a political economic context for these events. They saw the Harbourfront plan as a response to the interaction of complex political and economic forces affecting the redevelopment of the waterfront. Toronto's economy had become more oriented toward services in the 1970s and 1980s, especially finance and information processing. Furthermore, high-order information-based services tended increasingly to concentrate in the city's central area. Thus, the city's occupational structure also changed, with the rapid growth of managerial, technical, and administrative jobs.

Many relatively affluent white-collar workers preferred to live near where they worked. Thus, extensive gentrification occurred in older, working-class districts near the central area, and many expensive condominium projects went up. At the same time, established middle-class residential areas were able to win exclusionary zoning regulations to protect themselves against redevelopment. The upshot was rapidly rising land rents throughout the central area and adjacent parts of the city. One of the few areas that could be redeveloped was the waterfront. Given the general level of land rents, for developers only the construction of high-density, luxury commercial and residential space made sense economically.

Controversy over the scale and kind of development as well as Harbourfront's role in it led to the demand for a public inquiry. Several planned projects, especially condominiums, had been caught in a crossfire between residents of the area, private developers, and a number of agencies concerned with land use planning. The issue of the waterfront's future was further complicated by jurisdictional squabbles among a host of governmental players, each with its own agenda. In addition to the federal and Ontario governments, the City of Toronto, the Regional Municipality of Metropolitan Toronto, and a number of more or less autonomous agencies, especially the Toronto Harbour Commission, were involved. Waterfront redevelopment thus had become a true political football.

Hence, on 30 March 1988, the Government of Canada appointed a royal commission, the Royal Commission on the Future of the Toronto Waterfront (RCFTW), to inquire into the future of the Toronto waterfront. David Crombie, former mayor of Toronto and at the time a federal cabinet minister, was named as sole commissioner. The royal commission was federally appointed because harbors fall under federal jurisdiction in Canada. However, in early 1989, recognizing its own interest, the Ontario government appointed Crombie to serve concurrently as commissioner for its own inquiry. The Order-in-Council establishing the royal commission noted that "there exists a historic opportunity to create a unique, world class waterfront in Toronto" but also noted that there were "a number of urgent matters that must be studied and dealt with" (Royal Commission on the Future of the Toronto Waterfront [RCFTW] 1990, 161).

Initially, the royal commission was instructed to consider a range of issues that fell under federal jurisdiction. Staff began to study the future of the port of Toronto, a small airport on the Toronto Islands, as well as land use and development activities of federal agencies on the waterfront. During its first year alone, more than three hundred groups and individuals made submissions during public hearings. It soon became clear to the commission that waterfront issues were both broader and deeper than the list in its initial mandate. The issues "stemmed from historical forces related to the way society and the economy had evolved over the past 200 years, and to [sic] the impact each had on the waterfront and on the local and regional environment of which the waterfront is a part" (RCFTW 1992, 2).

Thus, the very nature and scope of the waterfront had to be rethought. Geographers had likened the waterfront of Toronto and other port cities to an urban "frontier" (Desfor, Goldrick, and Merrens 1988, 1989). By this they meant that the course of change on the waterfront reflected more pervasive changes in the city, in the larger political economy, and in culture. But the image also has other implications that are useful to consider.

As a kind of social spatialization, a frontier appears to be an edge between two zones whose use and users differ markedly, whether for political, sociocultural, or ecological reasons. Thus talking of a waterfront as a frontier or edge highlights discontinuity. Frontiers may be "crossed," "pushed back," or "opened up;" they may be "moving" or even "vanishing." Such metaphors suggest that the imagery used to figure frontiers helps to constitute them and thus is important for understanding them. Like most other social boundaries, frontiers are socially and culturally constructed.

I suggest that a different image may be more useful; we should see a waterfront not as an edge but as a zone of transition. Thus, we would have to think about it in terms of continuity and widened context, both historical and ecological. Historically, we would see a waterfront as having been an ambiguous zone, one whose physical form and meaning has shifted in relation to geomorphological processes, diverse interests, technology, and changing patterns of use. Furthermore, it would become apparent that the waterfront's use and meaning often have been contested.

For example, as Edward Relph pointed out, the Toronto landscape one sees today did not always appear as it now does. "Probably the most distinctive thing about Toronto's geomorphology now is how much of it is artificial, or has been profoundly altered by humans—streams buried, ravines filled, lake shore extended, spits constructed. Even the Islands . . . have been raised and extended with landfill. The Leslie Street Spit to the east of [the] Islands is an entirely artificial geomorphological project, one of a series of pseudo-spits intended to change the patterns of erosion and deposition along the lake shore" (1990, 26).

Figure 12.1 shows natural and human changes to the Toronto waterfront between 1834 and 1988. The history of Toronto's waterfront can be divided into several periods: aboriginal (until approximately the 1790s); early commercial and military settlement (before 1850); dominance of the railways (1850–1909); commercial and industrial dominance (1909–mid 1960s); the era of consumption (early 1970s–present) (Desfor, Goldrick, and Merrens 1988, 1989; RCFTW 1989b, 1989c, 1990; Cooper 1993). The landscape, uses, and meaning of the waterfront differed during each period but in ways that reflected the different interests and perceptions of those most concerned with it. The crucial point is that "the Toronto waterfront" is not a naturally given phenomenon, a line neatly separating the land from Lake Ontario. Rather it is a historical and social product, and by no means a finished one.

After its first year of work, the royal commission made what turned out to be its most important decisions. At first the commission had focused on the waterfront of Metropolitan Toronto, its actual mandate. But by 1989 it had decided that its scope must be the entire watershed of the Toronto-centered region (RCFTW 1989c). Even more important, it adopted an ecosystem approach.

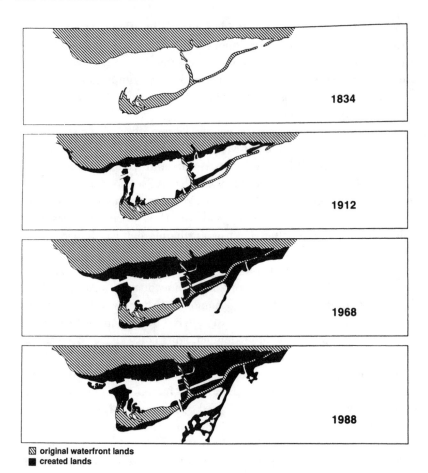

original waterfront lands
created lands

Figure 12.1. Toronto's changing waterfront

[I]t became apparent that the Toronto waterfront could not be viewed as simply a narrow band along its shore; it is linked by Lake Ontario to the other Great Lakes, by rivers and creeks to the watersheds, and by water mains, storm and sanitary sewers, and roads to homes and businesses.... The air along the lake shore is influenced by emissions from local and regional sources . . . and distant sources in the United States and beyond. [The diverse habitats of the waterfront] are linked to the hinterland through the movement of people and wildlife, via the river valleys, to Lake Ontario. Human uses of the land . . . tie the waterfront economically and socially to the larger region in which it is located. . . . These examples illustrate a fundamental point—everything is connected to everything else. (RCFTW 1990, 17)

These shifts in focus were strongly backed by the province of Ontario, which gave the commission a complementary mandate to report on waterfront issues along the entire northern shore of Lake Ontario (RCFTW 1992, 9). The royal commission now came to advocate a bioregional perspective (see, e.g., Sale 1985). Crucially, this approach defines regions in terms of "natural boundaries, rather than political jurisdictions," that is, in this case in terms of landforms, Lake Ontario, and the watersheds (RCFTW 1992, 21).

However, as defined by the royal commission, this bioregion does not coincide with existing political jurisdictions. Metropolitan Toronto and parts of the eight adjoining regional municipalities were included in the bioregion. Another planning unit, however, the Greater Toronto Area (GTA), had been set up in the late 1980s by the government of Ontario to try to coordinate planning for Metro Toronto and the surrounding four regional municipalities (which themselves contain thirty local municipalities). As if this were not complicated enough, Statistics Canada gathers information based on the Toronto Census Metropolitan Area, which does not coincide with the GTA. In a recent speech, David Crombie complained, "We have four levels of government and endless agencies. We have created a jurisdictional gridlock which denies the ability of ordinary people to understand who is responsible for what" (Coutts 1993). Furthermore, the Greater Toronto bioregion does not coincide exactly with any or all of these political units which form the basis for ordinary government data collection and decision making. Rather, the latter is defined by its major natural characteristics: the Niagara Escarpment to the west, the Oak Ridges glacial moraine to the north and east, and the Lake Ontario shoreline to the south (figure 12.2). Thus, the royal commission argued that to "truly understand the waterfront itself, we must gain an understanding of the biological region . . . in which it lies" (RCFTW 1990, 22).

This bioregion is almost two hundred kilometers from east to west and forty kilometers from north to south; its population is about four million and rising. Its landforms and soils are based on the glacial deposits of the Lake Ontario plain, which rises from the lake shore to the Oak Ridges moraine. The latter is an important hydrogeological resource—the site of the headwaters of the rivers flowing north and south in the area. Within the Greater Toronto bioregion, there are sixteen major rivers and numerous smaller creeks flowing south into Lake Ontario. In all, there are about sixty-five river valley systems in the region.

Pulling together studies of the air, land, water, wildlife, and human activities in the bioregion, the royal commission revealed that the ecosystem was under considerable stress. The waters were unfit for swimming

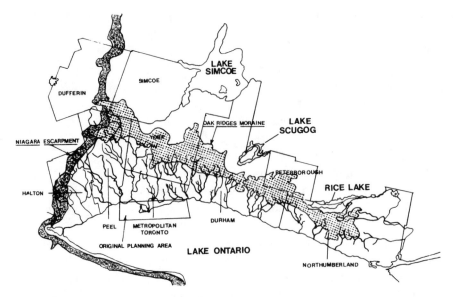

Figure 12.2. Greater Toronto bioregion

or drinking without treatment. Persistent organic chemicals and heavy metals were widespread in the soils, waters, and air. Development pressures threatened wildlife habitats. Sewage and solid waste disposal presented increasing problems. Transportation systems were at or above capacity. Seemingly relentless development had overtaken prime agricultural land and green space (RCFTW 1990, 21–47, 1992, 19–31). New approaches were needed to deal with this multitude of different, but interconnected problems.

Thus, by the expiry of its mandate on 31 December 1991, the royal commission had succeeded in redefining the scope and nature of the "future of the Toronto waterfront." In addition to its final report, the royal commission had published fifteen major discussion papers, two interim reports, eleven working papers, and twelve technical papers. (An annotated bibliography of its publications can be found in RCFTW 1992, 483–488). A new Waterfront Regeneration Trust, headed by David Crombie, was charged with carrying out the many recommendations made by his royal commission. No longer could it be considered adequate to examine only a narrow strip of land just within Metropolitan Toronto. Nor could the human uses any longer be treated in isolation from the natural systems of which they are a part.

Reestablishing Connections

This section discusses some of the consequences of the royal commission's adoption of bioregionalism. I am especially concerned with how it helped to create a new social spatialization, that is, how it affected both the "social imaginary" and interventions in the landscape (Shields 1991). While bioregionalism as such is not new (e.g., Sale 1985, Andruss et al. 1990, Wilson 1991), its application to planning in this area is. One of the reasons the royal commission's work was so significant is precisely that it rejected previously obvious boundaries. It literally redrew those boundaries and reimagined the Greater Toronto waterfront as a place. It rejected the more traditional approaches that isolated areas and segmented problems. Thus, it offered a different description of the nature of places, explained their nature differently, evaluated them differently, and used this new vision to recommend potentially far-reaching changes in policy. Before analyzing bioregionalism as discourse in this case, however, I will briefly describe some of its discursive context. This is what Judith Kenny, in analyzing the Portland, Oregon, comprehensive plan of the 1970s as text, calls a "discursive field," that is, a "range of competing discourses that are relevant to a particular realm of social practice" (1992, 179).

Canadian urban planning began early in this century, but it is only since the end of World War II that it has become a regularized and highly institutionalized part of Canadian life. In the main, it has been concerned with two general issues: planning for urban expansion—including growth management, regional planning, and suburban development—and urban redevelopment issues (Smith and Moore 1993, 344). While there are many differences between Canadian and American urban areas (Goldberg and Mercer 1986; Mercer 1991), as in the Portland case described by Kenny (1992), planning from the 1960s on incorporated a liberal ideology. As Michael Dear (1986, 377) has pointed out, it consisted of a "new scientism" on the one hand, and "the rise of popular planning" on the other. This somewhat uneasy marriage linked faith in technical expertise and rational management to popular participation. As Kenny puts it, "Conflicts in land use decisions could be eliminated, it was assumed, through the technical skills of the professional planner and the guidance of an active citizenry" (1992, 181–182) On the other hand, as Perks and Jamieson argue, after the 1960s a system developed in Canada of pragmatic working relationships between public planners and private developers. Indeed, Perks and Jamieson refer to these relationships as "interlocking institutions and professional practices" (1991, 488). A "social liberal" discourse of the public good thus coexisted with an increasingly powerful "economic liberal" discourse that reduced public planning to a technical support for private enterprise.

Given the scope of this chapter, I can comment on only two aspects of this planning. One is that comprehensive metropolitan-regional planning achieved considerable popularity, especially in the 1960s, but faded in the 1970s. The most notable example is the "Toronto-Centred Region" (TCR) plan promulgated in 1970; it proposed to secure balanced growth of the region within a radius of about 120 kilometers from downtown Toronto, including reserving lands for parkways, green belts, agriculture, and recreation, while channeling growth to new centers. As Smith and Moore remark, "The TCR experience was admittedly extreme, both in the scale of the plan's conception and in its utter collapse" (1993, 349). Such comprehensive planning was undermined by the fragmentation of planning jurisdictions and, especially, by the growing power of large private development corporations. The latter "brought into the planning system . . . a highly-integrated financial and production industry with the power to undertake development projects of a scale and complexity hitherto not encountered by municipal administrations. . . . In negotiations, public planners faced highly-trained and politically-sophisticated business teams possessed of immense financial power and influence" (Perks and Jamieson 1991, 506).

The second is that all such planning, regardless of scale, invoked a "master narrative" of progress. Social and individual betterment would be achieved through the growth of knowledge and the improvement of technology. The story assumed, among other things, that conflict is not fundamental to the nature of society and that human reason will prevail over action based on nonrational motives. Important here is that this narrative involved the reduction of nature to a set of resources. That is, the natural world has no value, except in relation to human purposes. These purposes might differ, as do the proposed means to realize them, but all are grounded in conceptions of an exclusively human good.

In comparison with such planning discourses, bioregionalism is both new and very old. It tells a large story that rests on several striking premises. The story begins with an indivisible though constantly changing whole: the ecosystem in which animate and inanimate nature are inseparably connected. The plot turns on a charge of hubris, the overweening pride that has led people to exalt themselves over nature. Because people have tried to dominate nature, they have made it and themselves sick. To restore themselves and the planet to health, people must gain self knowledge. They must learn that their dreams of being exceptional (that is, apart from nature and able to dominate it) not only were illusions but have turned into nightmares. Heightened self-knowledge teaches people humility as they learn to accept their diminished place in the world. But it also leads to right action, steps taken to regenerate or heal a disintegrated but still viable body.

Put briefly, this story embodies an ideology that has at least the following features. One is an organic analogy, that is, ecosystems at varying scales up to and including the planet often are likened to living bodies. The second is a sort of dynamic holism. The ecosystem, as a whole, metaphysically is prior to its parts, which constantly are changing. Yet at the same time, bioregionalism emphasizes pluralism. Within those wholes there is great and necessary diversity. Thus, bioregionalism focuses on and employs an imagery of connectedness and mutual dependence. It rejects dualism and, especially, the opposition of humankind and nature. Rather, it celebrates both diversity and unity. Because of its use of an organic analogy, it assesses the state of the whole in terms of sickness and health. Sickness manifests itself as disintegration, that is the breakdown of some parts which increasingly affects other parts. Thus, the discourse of bioregionalism often includes a therapeutic stance (using imageries of "stress," regeneration," "healing," and so forth).

In the interests of brevity, I deliberately treat bioregionalism here as a unitary discourse. However, there are many differences of opinion and emphasis among environmentalists (see, for example, Evernden 1993, Miller 1991, Roszak, 1992, and Wilson 1991 for useful bibliographies). Oelschlaeger (1991, 316–317) situates bioregionalism in the range of environmental philosophies. He characterizes it as a kind of "deep ecology," which he feels "although [it] has exposed many of the anomalies of Modernism, . . . provides no philosophically adequate undergirding (ontological, cosmological, epistemological) for a postmodern project. Foundational ecology is now more multifaceted process than finished paradigm."

The Toronto waterfront has been redefined not only in shape but in its very nature. From this new perspective, the essential characteristics of the newly defined bioregion are natural rather than social. Yet planners argued that the nature of the region was the complex result of the interplay, over long periods of time, of physical, biological, and social factors. None of these could be eliminated from the description. Indeed, new vocabularies would be needed to describe features that traditional land use planning lumps together. For example, the royal commission pointed out that traditional land use plans generally use only one term—open space—for all unbuilt lands in an area. Yet they have many terms describing settled areas (RCFTW 1992, 78). Nor could explanation of the nature of the region be reduced to only one of these sets of factors (or worse, to one factor in a set, for example, economics). Evaluation must take into account all of these factors and, especially, their interconnections. Thus, the new perspective requires that planning rest on more holistic and less wholly human-centered principles.

Based on its new bioregional perspective, the royal commission thus laid out a set of nine planning principles. The central metaphor was "regeneration as a healing process." At the level of the "social imaginary," the public and planners were urged to connect the new description and explanation of the nature of the waterfront with interventions in the landscape. As summarized in its final report, these guiding principles were: "clean, green, connected, open, accessible, useable, diverse, affordable, and attractive" (RCFTW 1992, 60). Existing land uses and new development should all contribute to the health, diversity, and sustainability of the whole ecosystem. The tasks before the planning community, thus, were to "translate ecosystem theory into pragmatic methods of improving quality of life; establish land-use patterns; balance demand, capacity, and technology; accommodate economic development; and evaluate possible scenarios for the future. This must be done for natural and built environments at all planning scales, from region to individual site, for both public- and private-sector activities" (ibid., 76; see also RCFTW 1990, 1991; Davies 1991).

To meet these challenges, the royal commission made a large number of recommendations. One of the most significant involved the concept of greenways, that is, corridors of green space throughout the region. The greenways concept emerged in the 1960s and has been implemented recently in a number of American urban centers, most notably the San Francisco Bay area, as well as in the Ottawa area in Ontario (Little 1990). "The idea behind greenways is elegantly simple: link existing green spaces to create interconnected corridors, thereby increasing their usefulness for both people and wildlife" (RCFTW 1992, 177). "The essence of greenways is connections—not simply connecting recreational areas through trails, but connecting wildlife habitats to each other, human communities to other human communities, city to country, people to nature" (ibid., 179). A proposed waterfront trail would link together thirty-four major parks, seventy-four small waterfront parks and promenades, forty significant natural habitats, and twenty-five marinas (ibid., 178). Running along the southern edge of the bioregion, it would connect with other trails along the river valleys, the Bruce Trail that runs for 725 kilometers along the Niagara Escarpment, and another long-distance trail to be developed along the Oak Ridges Moraine (see figure 12.3). Crucially, the greenway would be a continuous corridor of natural vegetation and open space, though parts of it might vary in width and in whether the trail through them was continuous. It would be divided into

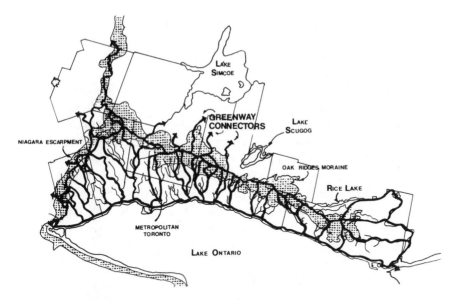

Figure 12.3. Proposed greenways for the Greater Toronto bioregion

two tiers: arterial greenways (for example, following the waterfront and river valleys) across the entire region and local connectors. Given the difficulty of acquiring much additional land in the region for traditional parks, the greenway would provide substantial ecological and social benefits at reasonable cost.

The general planning strategy put forward by the royal commission and its successor agency, the Waterfront Regeneration Trust, however, must be developed into actual plans and implemented at regional and local levels. It is at this point, though, that one of the chief weaknesses of the royal commission's approach becomes clear, perhaps reflecting the fact that the royal commission speaks from a position of influence. After all, it was attempting to apply bioregionalism to planning not to employ it as part of an oppositional discourse. The bioregion is represented as an interconnected ecosystem with diverse parts. However, the constitution of society, and especially the nature of power in it, is conspicuous by its absence from the analysis. That is, the systemic character of natural parts of the ecosystem is delineated but there is no serious analysis of social components of the system, except for transportation. If this approach is seriously intended to interconnect the social, historical, and natural components of the ecosystem, it needs that kind of analysis. Furthermore, there is no serious attention given to the nature of power and power relations. Implementing such wide-ranging proposals will depend on overcoming powerful interests and understanding power relations in our society. Clearly, decisions made by the various municipalities and regions provide opportunities for some, while potentially endangering the interests of others.

The advent of this new spatialization also raises the more general question of how changing discourse relates to people's experience of place. This large issue has occasioned considerable discussion (e.g., Cosgrove 1993, 1984, Barnes and Duncan 1992, Lefebvre 1991, Shields 1991, Harvey 1989). Like any land use planning discourse, bioregionalism asserts similarity and difference. Places are grouped together or separated as part of a system defined by certain criteria. While such criteria often are presented as natural or apolitically technical, it is clear that control over their choice and definition gives power to planners but more especially to the interests that they often serve, for example, the "urban growth machine" (Logan and Molotch 1987). The discourse may lead to interventions in the landscape that structure many of the parameters of people's daily lives. But as Harvey points out in a somewhat different context: "This does not mean that practices are determined by built form (no matter how hard the planners may try); for they [i.e., the practices] have the awkward habit of escaping their moorings in any fixed schema of representation. New meanings can be found for older materializations of space and time" (1989, 204). That is, people's experience of place and its meanings for them are too diverse to be reducible in such terms.

The city of Burlington (a Toronto suburb with both urban and rural areas at the southwestern end of the bioregion) provides examples of some of the issues that arise. A Draft Greenway and Trail Strategy was prepared by a firm of planning consultants in the spring of 1993, following earlier city decisions to "naturalize" and "green" the city, including developing a linked natural trail system (City of Burlington 1993). The proposed system provided a four-level hierarchy of components, from intermunicipal trails connecting Burlington with adjoining jurisdictions, through community and local trails, down to "bikeway connectors." At public open houses held in the fall of 1992 and spring of 1993, city residents considered the proposals.

The major concerns raised by attending residents revolved about the rights, obligations, and fears associated with landownership. One of the problems presented by the greenways proposal is that only some of the lands affected are already in public hands. For example, currently 54 percent of the 133 kilometers of proposed waterfront greenway outside of Metro Toronto is publicly owned, but 17 percent of the total is not publicly accessible. In rural areas away from the actual lake shore much of the land through which the greenways would pass is privately held. The royal commission proposed a variety of ways of dealing with this problem, including the suggestion that some lands with particular biological or visual significance might be better protected by remaining in private hands (RCFTW 1992, 192). The Burlington Draft Strategy clearly indicated that no expropriation was contemplated. The planners hope that access can be obtained through more cooperative means such as access agreements, incentives for developers, purchase/saleback, and conservation easements, although fee simple acquisition of land or property rights from willing owners might be necessary "in some high priority cases" (Hough Stansbury Woodland Ltd. 1993). However, many residents refuse to believe that expropriation will not occur. Other resident concerns have to do with security, potential damage to crops and animals, "the population of Toronto walking through our backyards," and resident liability if trail users trespassed and got hurt (City of Burlington 1993; Burlington Greenways and Trail System Study Public Open House number 2, 15 April 1993). A final strategy, incorporating most of the proposals laid out in the Draft Strategy, was approved in June 1993.

The actual waterfront of Burlington is largely in private hands. As a matter of policy, when waterfront redevelopment takes place Burlington does not require that a strip of land be given to the town. In neighboring Oakville, which has had such a requirement since the 1970s, the public has extensive access to the lake shore. But, as a 1991 study showed, in Burlington only about eight percent of a waterfront trail would run on the optimal route along the shoreline (RCFTW 1992, 271). Waterfront properties in these two municipalities tend to be among the most expensive in the entire region. Burlington waterfront residents protested vociferously against what they saw as proposals to run a public trail through their backyards. Because of resident protest the consultants came up with a simple solution. By the time the Draft Strategy appeared, the waterfront greenway had been demoted to a bikeway (which already existed) running along a fairly heavily traveled paved road rather than on the lake shore itself. Given that the trail system as proposed is hierarchical and contains bikeways as low-level connectors, this change appeared logical and relatively insignificant. In fact, though, its effect was to make it appear that a waterfront trail was being provided when nothing actually was planned. This example shows, ironically, that while the greenway proposal talks of connecting communities it also has the potential to divide those with different interests within them.

It also shows how such issues provide a niche for mediators such as planning consultants. Through their ability to deploy maps, drawings, written, and oral descriptions in a variety of contexts (meetings with the city council and parks department, public meetings, and so on) they can control the representation of space and the flow of information, and thus influence decision making. For example, in the Burlington case they were able to exploit some of the discursive tools provided by the greenways proposal (and the broader discourse of which it is a part). Local political pressures required that the waterfront trail be dropped. The rhetoric of the proposal (especially its stress on connectedness within a hierarchical network) made it relatively easy to accomplish this end by making the already existing bikeway appear to be part of the greenway system. Yet will *calling* the current bicycle path that runs along the sidewalk of a road a *connector* and thus part of the larger greenway system change how people perceive and experience it? It seems doubtful that those who favored a real waterfront trail in Burlington will be fooled.

In the Toronto-area waterfront case, planning for implementation of the proposals has only begun. As the Burlington example illustrates, there likely will be considerable variability in how the waterfront strategy is realized. Partly this will follow from the royal commission's redefinition of the area with which it was concerned. The Greater Toronto Bioregion covers a large number of sometimes overlapping planning jurisdictions, on at least four levels. Furthermore, implementation of the proposals may take up to twenty years and will be contingent on the outcome of many local political struggles. Changing economic and political circumstances and cultural understandings will have a great deal to do with the ways in which the general proposals are translated into interventions in the landscape.

Conclusions

It seems reasonable to conclude that the many studies and recommendations made by the Royal Commission on the Future of the Toronto Waterfront have produced a new social spatialization of the region. They have changed the way the region is represented, both verbally and graphically, as well as the principles that underlie planning for the region's future. In this spatialization new boundaries have been drawn while old ones have been effaced, or, at least, connections made across them. As we have seen, boundaries were redrawn between nature and human society, among sociopolitical units, and in the disciplines concerned with understanding and planning for the region. Using the new spatial discourse, planners thus have attempted to alter perception especially through the mediation of new representations. The royal commission's work laid the basis for material consequences that began with writing and map making and are continuing, among other things, into trail construction and habitat restoration. Yet, with implementation of the proposals only beginning, it is clear that the nature and scope of these material consequences will depend on political struggles, at varying scales, over many years.

Finally, I would like to return to the earlier discussion of kinds of spatial discourses. If the characterization of Western spatial discourses as being either humanistic or transcendental is accurate, then bioregionalism represents a significant departure. On the one hand, it defines places in terms of natural characteristics, derived from the universalizing discourse of science. The bioregion is explicitly not defined from the perspective of a human perceiver (as a landscape would be) or in terms of some subset of human activities (as would be the case in regional analysis, for example). Yet this discourse need not imply another attempt to naturalize social inequities in the name of some higher good. Like the related discourses of "biocentrism" and "ecocentrism," bioregionalism deliberately rejects the implied dualism of nature and humankind (Oelschlaeger 1991, 292–319). It also rejects the privileging of human values over those of nature. The bioregion, in its very physical nature, is constituted both by natural forces and by human activity. Some versions of bioregionalism, as oppositional discourses, privilege the "natural" environment over human activities. But the Toronto royal commission, from its institutional position, adopted the view that in planning, environmental, economic, and social problems must be thought about simultaneously. The commission's approach, therefore, is necessarily historical. Followed to its logical conclusion, its version of bioregionalism, by including human interests and activities at its center, also should recognize that knowledge, power, and social conflict are constitutive of social reality.

While the language of bioregionalism often employs medical images, it can be argued that the sort of medicine it implies is more holistic than most contemporary North American practice. It seeks to reintegrate, to reestablish broken connections, especially those between humankind and nature. As Alexander Wilson put it:

> Restoration actively seeks out places to repair the biosphere, to recreate habitat, to breach the ruptures and disconnections that agriculture and urbanization have brought to the landscape. But unlike preservationism, it is not an elegiac exercise. Rather than eulogize what industrial civilization has destroyed restoration proposes a new environmental ethic. Its projects demonstrate that humans must intervene in nature, must garden it, participate in it. Restoration thus nurtures a new appreciation of working landscape, those places that actively figure a harmonious dwelling-in-the-world. (1991, 115)

Afterword

Many developments have occurred in the Toronto waterfront story since the paper on which this chapter is based was written in early 1994. I will limit myself to discussing two kinds of developments here: implementation of some of the plans put forward by the Waterfront Regeneration Trust and changes in the definition of the area included.

From 1992 onward, the Waterfront Regeneration Trust has worked with a broad group of stakeholders to develop a strategy for the future of the Lake Ontario Waterfront from Burlington to Trenton. The Lake Ontario Waterfront Network was established in 1996 to provide leadership and coordinate project implementation. This group includes more than ninety representatives from the waterfront municipalities, conservation authorities, provincial and federal ministries, community groups, and the private sector. Since 1992, the Trust has facilitated the implementation of more than eighty projects on the Waterfront Trail and other waterfront sites. The Trail now links hundreds of parks, natural areas, and marinas, and more than twenty-five communities. Of the $37 million invested in these projects, $12 million was contributed by the provincial government of Ontario directed through the Trust. The remaining $25 million was contributed by municipalities, conservation authorities, service clubs, and the private sector. Projects include, for example, construction of new sections of the Waterfront Trail, restoration and protection of wetlands, a Toronto Bay initiative to create a greener, more accessible harbor, and the remediation and development of so-called "brownfield" sites. The latter are locations, generally in urban centers, where commercial and industrial uses have left a legacy of contaminated soil and groundwater. The Waterfront Trust has worked with various stakeholders, such as owners, regulators, investors, lenders, and communities, to address the challenges posed by brownfields. To help with this work, the Waterfront Trust established a round table involving municipal and provincial regulators and representatives from Imperial Oil, GE Capital Canada, the Canadian Imperial Bank of Commerce, and various technical firms. The Trust is also working closely with the Toronto Economic Development Corporation to develop a soil and groundwater strategy for the remediation of the Port Lands area of Toronto's waterfront.

Interestingly, the Waterfront Trust also has extended the scope of its work. Its predecessor, the royal commission, had been charged with considering the state of the waterfront in Toronto itself. With the adoption of a bioregional perspective, the scope was broadened to encompass a bioregion (defined in terms of major geomorphological features) that ran from Burlington in the west to Trenton, east of Toronto. Recently, however, the Trust has changed its goal: it now proposes to link Niagara-on-the Lake at the mouth of the Niagara River in the west with Gananoque on the St. Lawrence River southwest of Montreal. That is, its new projects go far beyond the boundaries of the previously defined Toronto bioregion. Yet there appears not to have been any formal attempt to redefine the nature or extent of the area in which it operates.

Much of the Waterfront Regeneration Trust's work remains to be done. It seems fair to say, however, that it continues to attempt to implement a strategy based on the environmental ethic described in this chapter. Its future success, like its success to date, will depend on its ability to negotiate deals that bring together a wide variety of collaborators who can be persuaded that their otherwise divergent interests can find common cause in restoration and enhancement of the waterfront.

Acknowledgments

I would like to thank Margaret Rodman, Setha Low, Connie deRoche, and two anonymous reviewers for *City & Society* for helpful comments on earlier versions of this chapter. Thanks also to the Royal Commission on the Future of the Toronto Waterfront for permission to reprint the figures used as illustrations.

References Cited

Andruss, Van, Christopher Plant, Judith Plant, and Eleanor Wright. 1990. *Home! A bioregional reader.* Philadelphia: New Society Publishers.

Barnes, Trevor, and James Duncan. 1992. *Writing worlds: Discourse, text and metaphor in the representation of landscape.* London: Routledge.

Bowden, Martyn J. 1992. The invention of American tradition. *Journal of Historical Geography* 18:3–26.

City of Burlington. 1993. Burlington's greenway and trail strategy nearing completion. Burlington, Ont.: Parks and Recreation Department.

Cooper, Matthew. 1993. On the waterfront: Transformations of meaning of the Toronto lakeshore. In *The cultural meaning of urban space*, edited by Robert Rotenberg and Gary McDonough. Pp. 157–172.Westport, Conn.: Bergin & Garvey.

Cosgrove, Denis. 1984. *Social formation and symbolic landscape.* London: Croom Helm.

———. 1993. *The Palladian landscape.* University Park: Pennsylvania State University Press.

Coutts, Jane. 1993. Crombie urges streamlined services. *Toronto Globe and Mail*, 15 June, A12.

Davies, K. 1991. *Towards ecosystem-based planning: A perspective on cumulative environmental effects.* Toronto: Royal Commission on the Future of the Toronto Waterfront.

Dear, Michael. 1986. Postmodernism and planning. *Environment and Planning D: Society and Space* 4:367–384.

Desfor, Gene, Michael Goldrick, and Roy Merrens. 1988. Redevelopment on the North American water-frontier: The case of Toronto. In *Revitalising the waterfront: International dimensions of dockland redevelopment*, edited by B. S Hoyle, D. Pinder, and M. S. Husain, Pp. 92–113. London: Belhaven Press.

————. 1989. A political economy of the water-frontier: Planning and development in Toronto. *Geoforum* 20:487–501.

Duncan, James. 1990. *The city as text: The politics of landscape interpretation in the Kandyan kingdom.* Cambridge: Cambridge University Press.

Duncan, James, and Nancy Duncan. 1988. (Re) reading the landscape. *Environment and Planning D: Society and Space* 6:117–126.

Evernden, Neil. 1993. *The natural alien: Humankind and environment.* 2d ed. Toronto: University of Toronto Press.

Foucault, Michel. 1980. *Power/knowledge.* New York: Pantheon.

Goldberg, Michael, and John Mercer. 1986. *The myth of the North American city.* Vancouver: University of British Columbia Press.

Hall, Peter. 1988. *Cities of tomorrow.* Oxford: Basil Blackwell.

Harbourfront Corporation. 1978. *Harbourfront, site history.* Toronto: Harbourfront Corporation

Harvey, David. 1989. *The condition of postmodernity.* Oxford: Basil Blackwell.

Hayden, Dolores. 1976. *Seven American utopias.* Cambridge, Mass.: MIT Press.

Hough Stansbury Woodland Ltd. 1993. *Greenways and trails system study for the City of Burlington, Parks and Recreation Department.* Toronto: Hough Stansbury Woodland.

Kenny, Judith. 1992. Portland's comprehensive plan as text. In *Writing worlds,* edited by Trevor Barnes and James Duncan. Pp. 176–192. London: Routledge.

Lawrence, Denise, and Setha Low. 1990. The built environment and spatial form. *Annual Review of Anthropology* 19:453–505.

Lefebvre, Henri. 1991. *The production of space.* Oxford: Basil Blackwell.

Little, Charles. 1990. *Greenways for America.* Baltimore, Md.: Johns Hopkins University Press.

Logan, John, and Harvey Molotch. 1987. *Urban fortunes: The political economy of place.* Berkeley: University of California Press.

Lovejoy, Arthur. 1960a. The Chinese origin of a romanticism. In *Essays in the history of ideas,* edited by A. Lovejoy. Pp. 99–135. New York: Putnam.

————. 1960b. The first Gothic Revival and the return to nature. In *Essays in the history of ideas.* Pp. 136–165.

————. 1960c. "Nature" as aesthetic norm. In *Essays in the history of ideas.* Pp. 69–77.

Mercer, John. 1991. The Canadian city in continental context. In *Canadian cities in transition,* edited by Trudi Bunting and Pierre Filion. Pp. 45–68.. Toronto: Oxford University Press.

Miller, Alan. 1991. *Gaia connections.* Savage, Md.: Rowman & Littlefield.

Mitchell, Timothy. 1988. *Colonising Egypt.* Cambridge: Cambridge University Press.

Oelschlaeger, Max. 1991. *The idea of wilderness.* New Haven, Conn.: Yale University Press.

Perks, William T., and Walter Jamieson. 1991. Planning and development in Canadian cities. In *Canadian cities in transition,* edited by Trudi Bunting and Pierre Filion. Pp. 487–518. Toronto: Oxford University Press.

Rabinow, Paul. 1989. *French modern: Norms and forms of the social environment.* Cambridge, Mass.: MIT Press.

Relph, Edward. 1990. *The Toronto guide.* Prepared for the annual meetings of the Association of American Geographers, Toronto, April 1990.

Rodman, Margaret and Matthew Cooper. 1995. Accessibility as a discourse of space in Canadian housing cooperatives. *American Ethnologist* 22, no. 3:589–601.

Roszak, Theodore. 1992. *The voice of the earth.* New York: Simon and Schuster.

Rotenberg, Robert. 1993a. Introduction to *The cultural meaning of urban space,* edited by Robert Rotenberg and Gary McDonogh. Pp. Xi–xix. Westport, Conn.: Bergin & Garvey.

———. 1993b. On the salubrity of sites. In *The cultural meaning of urban space.* Pp. 17–29. Westport, Conn.: Bergin & Garvey.

Royal Commission on the Future of the Toronto Waterfront. 1989a. *Interim report, 1989.* Toronto: The Royal Commission.

———. 1989b. *Parks, pleasures, and public amenities.* Report no. 4. Toronto: The Royal Commission.

———. 1989c. *Persistence and Change: Waterfront issues and the board of Toronto Harbour Commissioners.* Report no. 6. Toronto: The Royal Commission.

———. 1990. *Watershed. Interim report, August.* Toronto: The Royal Commission.

———. 1991. *Planning for sustainability: Towards integrating environmental protection into land-use planning.* Toronto: The Royal Commission.

———. 1992 *Regeneration: Toronto's waterfront and the sustainable city: Final report.* Toronto: The Royal Commission.

Sale, Kirkpatrick. 1985. *Dwellers in the land: The bioregional perspective.* San Francisco: Sierra Club.

Shields, Rob. 1991. *Places on the margin.* London: Routledge.

Smith, P. J., and P. W. Moore. 1993. Cities as a social responsibility: Planning and urban form. In *The changing social geography of Canadian cities*, edited by Larry Bourne and David Ley. Pp. 343–366. Montreal: McGill-Queen's University Press.

Wilson, Alexander. 1991. *The culture of nature.* Toronto: Between the Lines.

Biographical Notes

THEODORE C. BESTOR is professor of anthropology and Japanese studies at Harvard University. He has spent eight of the last twenty-five years in Japan doing research on contemporary urban life. He is the author of *Neighborhood Tokyo* and the forthcoming *Tokyo's Marketplace* and coeditor of the forthcoming volume, *Japanese Cuisine, Consumption and Culture*.

TERESA P. R. CALDEIRA teaches in the departments of anthropology at the University of California, Irvine and at Unicamp (State University of Campinas, São Paulo). Her book *City of Walls: Crime, Segregation, and Citizenship in São Paulo* is forthcoming. Her current research focuses on the constitution and expansion of citizenship rights from a comparative perspective and on the association of these processes with notions of the body and of racial relations.

MATTHEW COOPER is professor of anthropology at McMaster University. He is interested in the anthropology of space and place and is undertaking continuing research on housing and urban change. He is coauthor of *New Neighbors: A Case Study of Cooperative Housing*.

STEVEN GREGORY is associate professor of anthropology and Africana studies at New York University. He is the author of *Black Corona: Race and the Politics of Place in an Urban Community* and the coeditor of *Race*.

JAMES HOLSTON is associate professor of anthropology at the University of California, San Diego. His research focuses on citizenship and democratic change in the Americas, especially Brazil, and transformations in the social and spatial organization of cities. He is the author of *The Modernist City* and coeditor of *Cities and Citizenship*.

SETHA M. LOW is professor of environmental psychology and anthropology and director of the Public Space Research Group at the Graduate School and University Center at the City University of New York. Her research focuses on theorizing space and culture through ethnographic analyses of housing, parks, public places, and historic preservation in Costa Rica, Guatemala, Mexico, and the United States. She is the author of *On the Plaza: the Politics of Public Space and Culture*, *Children of the Urban Poor*, and *Culture, Politics and Medicine in Costa Rica*, and coeditor of *Place Attachment*, *Housing, Culture and Design: A Comparative Perspective*, and *Gender, Health and Illness: The Case of Nerves*.

GARY MCDONOGH is professor of anthropology and chair of the program Growth and Structure of Cities at Bryn Mawr College. He has focused on issues of urban form, imagery, and the nature of conflict in two decades of work in Barcelona, Savannah, Philadelphia, and Hong Kong. He is the author of *Good Families of Barcelona*, *Black and Catholic in Savannah, Georgia*, and coeditor of *The Cultural Meaning of Urban Space* and *Encyclopedia of Contemporary American Culture*.

DEBORAH PELLOW is professor of anthropology at Syracuse University. She was trained as an Africanist and most of her research has been in Ghana focusing on issues the social organization and social structure of residential space. She is the editor of *Setting Boundaries: The Anthropology of Spatial and Social Organization*.

ROBERT ROTENBERG is professor of anthropology and director of international studies at DePaul University. He has focused on issues of metropolitan knowledge in Vienna and how this knowledge is expressed in the time schedules, public spaces, and identities of city inhabitants. He is the author of *Landscape and Power in Vienna*, and *Time and Order in Metropolitan Vienna* and coeditor of *The Cultural Meaning of Urban Space*.

CHARLES RUTHEISER is assistant professor of anthropology and geography at Georgia State University. He has conducted research on a wide variety of urban issues in Israel, Venezuela, Belize, the United States, and, most recently, Cuba. He is the author of *Imagineering Atlanta: The Politics of Place in the City of Dreams* and the forthcoming *After Babylon: Cities in a Post-urban World*.

ALAN SMART is associate professor of anthropology at the University of Calgary. He has conducted research in Hong Kong and China since 1982. He is the author of *Making Room: Squatter Clearance in Hong Kong.*

JOSEPHINE SMART is associate professor of anthropology at the University of Calgary. Her research focuses on the informal economy, foreign investment in China, migration of Hong Kong Chinese to Canada, and gender relations and development in post-1978 China. She is the author of *The Political Economy of Street Hawkers in Hong Kong.*

IDA SUSSER is professor of anthropology at Hunter College and the Graduate School and University Center of the City University of New York. Her research focuses on issues of social inequality, homelessness, and urban poverty in Puerto Rico and the United States. She is the author of *Norman Street.*

Index

Note: Page numbers in italics indicate figures and tables.

Aalborg Letter (1994), 371
Ababio, Kojo, IV, 288, 309n. 26, 309n. 27, 309n. 29
Ababio, Nii, 293
Abubakar, 287, 309n. 23, 309n. 32
Abu-Lughod, J. L., 11
Abyssinian Baptist Church (New York City), 42
Academy of Fine Arts (Brazil), 274n. 5
Accra (Ghana): chief imam in, 286–289; colonial system in, 16, 281, 306–307; history of, 280–281, 286; plague in, 288–289; power structures in, 278. *See also* chiefs/headmen; *mai gida* (patron); Muslims; Sabon Zongo (Accra)
ACOG. *See* Atlanta Committee for the Olympic Games (ACOG)
Adamu, Mahdi, 286, 309n. 15
ADC (Aid to Dependent Children), 69, 78
advertisements/advertising: for fortified enclaves, 88–92; industrialization of food supply linked to, 215. *See also* brand names
aesthetics: park use and, 152–154; security and, 87. *See also* design
AFDC (Aid to Families with Dependent Children), 69, 78
Africa: British social anthropology in, 4; expanding population of, 3. *See also specific countries*
African American community: civil rights activism in, 45–48; class stratification in, 37–41, 44–45, 49–50, 53, 60–62; "golden age" of, 41–45; homeownership in, 50–62; issues in, 37–38; median household income of, 318; neighborhoods, 323, 328. *See also* Corona-East Elmhurst (N.Y.); divided city
African American middle class: emergence of, 37–41, 44; as homeowners, 44–45, 51–62; outmigration of, 39–40; political participation of, 42–48, 51–52; quality-of-life politics of, 58–60. *See also* Corona-East Elmhurst (N.Y.)
African Americans: activism and, 39–40, 50–53; Atlanta's importance to, 321; boycotts by, 43; displacement of, 324, 331–332, 336; ghetto experience of, 2; outmigration of, 39–40, 318, 337–338; social services and, 43, 47, 49–50, 63n. 5; stratification of, 37–41, 44–45, 49–50, 53, 60–62

age, shelter system divisions by, 73. *See also* children; older people; teenagers

age-grading, in women's associations, 299

agriculture: Chicago as market center for, 205–206; petty commodity production in, 177; protection of Japanese, 225, 226. *See also* fishing industry; food culture; livestock

Agyepong, K. A., 295

Aid to Dependent Children (ADC), 69, 78

Aid to Families with Dependent Children (AFDC), 69, 78

airports: construction of, 43, 57–58; marketplace's link to, 222, 232; modernization of, 354, 356

Ajuntament (Barcelona): cooperation of, 354–355; housing and, 357; open spaces and, 363; social services and, 359, 360

Akan people, 299, 300, 302

Akumaje, 288, 294

Akwei, Nii Amane, 295

Alata, 288, 294

Alberti, Leon Battista, 274n. 8

Aldeia de Serra (closed condominium), 91–92

Ali, Mama, 292, 309n. 32

Ali (Native Officer), 286–288, 309n. 32

Aliens' Expulsion Act (Ghana), 310n. 52

Allem, Walter R., 63n. 3

Allen, Ivan, 323–329

Allison, Anne, 219

Alphaville (closed condominium), 91–92

Althusser, Louis, 175

Amsterdam (Netherlands), as capital of culture, 372

Anderson, E., 2, 19

Andors, P., 192

annexation, use of, 317

antimodernism, ecology wave compared to, 139, 160

Appadurai, Arjun, 14, 204–205, 222, 223

aquacultural technology, 228–229, 238n. 14

arcades (San José), 128

architecture: colonial city and, 15–16; conference on, 370, 373; debate over defensible, 100–102; elements and conventions in, 254, *255, 256;* erasure and reinscription in, 267; European influence in, 120–121; figure-ground/solid-void in, 257–267; fortress city and, 18–19; function of, 262–265; modernist city and, 15–16, 95–98, 99–100; postmodern city and, 16–18; power wielded through, 113–114; streets and, 248–257. *See also* built environment; design; fortified enclaves; housing; plazas

Ardener, Shirley, 278

Arias, Oscar, 116

Artigues Vidal, Jaume, 366–367

Asante people, 283, 284, 286

Asere stool, 288

Associació de Veïns del Raval (AV-Raval), 343–344, 351, 360

associations: age-grading in, 299; homeowners', 44–45, 50, 52–62, 85–86, 99, 104; institutions vs., 47–50. *See also* neighborhood associations; East Elmhurst-Corona Civic Association

Athens (Greece), as capital of culture, 372

Atlanta Arts Festival, 338

Atlanta Committee for the Olympic Games (ACOG): Centennial Olympic Park and, 332–334; focus of, 329–331; limited vision of, 318–319, 335–336

Atlanta Economic Development Corporation, 330

Atlanta Federal Center, 330–331

Atlanta (Ga.): characteristics of, 317–318, 325; civic-business relations in, 319, 321, 329–336; economy of, 329; future of, 336–340; housing in, 323–324, 328, 330–334, 336–339; as nonplace, 317–321; outmigration from, 318, 337–338; past in, 321–323, 340; plans for, 323, 325, 327–328, 330, 336; "public character" of, 321–322, 332; recentering of downtown, 323–329; renewal/redevelopment of, 17, 322–323, 329–334; reputation of, 335–336; riots in, 326–327. *See also* Five Points (Atlanta); Olympics (1996); Underground Atlanta

Atlanta Housing Authority, 331
Atlanta University Center, 335
auctions/auctioneers: function of, 202–203; social organization of, 209–210; specialization in, 210, 232, 233–235
Austria, environment of, 139–140. *See also* Vienna (Austria)
authenticity, food culture and, 203, 222, 223–228
authorities (local), investment negotiations and, 173, 185, 189–190, 193
authority: in chieftancy/headmanship, 281–282, 285; constraints by, 277
"autoconstruction," concept of, 85, 87
automobiles. *See* car culture; highways
AV-Raval (Associació de Veïns del Raval), 343–344, 351, 360
Avui (newspaper), 355, 363
Aztecs, influence by, 121

Bako, Alhaji Sule, 300–301
Bako, B. K., 295
Bako, Idrissu, 293–295, 298, 303
Bako, Inussa, 303, 304
Bako, Lebbo, 291, 294–295, 303, 304, 309n. 30
Bako, Malam: counselors appointed by, 291–292, 298; death of, 293; descendants of, 286; leadership of, 286–293, 306; records of, 307–308n. 2; Sabon Zongo and, *290, 291*
Bako, Sha'aibu: background of, 286; leadership of, 292, 295, 298, 302–305; on legitimacy, 277; political ties of, 297; records of, 307–308n. 2; status of, 296, 304–305
Bako family: disunity in, 304–305; political party of, 294; proprietary rights of, 294–296; records on, 307–308n. 2
Balius (pseud.), 349
Baltimore (Md.): festival market in, 326; perception of violence in, 19
Banck, G. A., 10, 19
Bank of China, 193
banshi, role of, 193
barber, appointment for, 292
barber shop, Debret's drawing of, *256*

Barberton (Ohio), deindustrialization in, 12
Barcelona: Metropolis Mediterrania (journal), 353, 370, 372
Barcelona (Spain): highways constructed in, 349–351, 354; history of, 345–347, 353; internationalization of, 356, 369–373; land and labor control in, 10; models for, 353, 355–357; old city in, 343, 374n. 1; plans for, 346–348, *347,* 352, 354, 355, 366; politics in, 345, 353–355, 361–362, 367; population of, 348; success of, 369–373; urban planning in, 342, 344–351, 368–369; urban policy components in, 357–367; Web site of, 373. *See also* Catalunya; discourse; Olympics (1992); Raval (Barcelona neighborhood)
Barrio Gótico (Barcelona), 374n. 5
barrios: area of, 374n. 1; attitudes toward, 349–350, 370; city's link to, 365–367; discourse on city in, 352–354; function of, 355; novel about, 366; tolerance in, 361–362. *See also* Raval (Barcelona neighborhood)
bars, as social space, 361–362, 365
baseball, identity and, 207
bastides, influence by, 121
Baudelaire, Charles, 94
Bavaria, park use in, 164n. 4
Benjamin, Walter, 113–114
Berlin (Germany), divisions in, 7
Bernstein, Gail Lee, 237n. 8
Bestor, Theodore C., 13, 20–21
Betts, Raymond F., 308n. 9
Bhaktapur (India), as sacred city, 20
Biedermeier (designer), 153
Bilbao (Spain), 370
Biogärten, concept of, 141–144. *See also* private gardens, of discovery; Wildgärten
bioregionalism: approach of, 383–386; discourse on, 388–395
Biotop, concept of, 141, 145, 157, 161, *162,* 163n. 2
Black Belt (South Side Chicago): isolation of, 19; racial division of, 8–9
black market: in plazas, 126, 132; as second economy, 179–180
black middle class. *See* African American middle class

Black Panther Party, 46
Blair, Thomas L., 280
blat (reciprocal relations), 179
Blim, M. L., 13
block associations. *See* neighborhood associations
boarding houses, closure of, 359
Bodenständigkeit (design element), 148–149
Bohigas, Oriol, 352, 371
Bolivia, domestic workers in, 9
"border metropolis," concept of, 13, 171–172
Boronu, Fulata, 287, 288
Boston (Mass.), festival market in, 326
Botica Francesca (building), 120
Bott, E., 2–3
boundaries: natural, of region, 384–386; social construction of, 377; social type of, 102–105
Bourdieu, Pierre, 114, 203
Bourgois, P., 1, 19
Bowden, Martyn J., 379
Boyer, M. C., 16
Boyz N the Hood (film), 18
Braimah, Alhaji Ibrahima "Butcher": on Damaley, 295; as head chief, 288–289; leadership disputes and, 286–287; occupation of, 309n. 17
brand names: absence of, 216; emergence of, 215, 221, 222
Brandywine Museum (Chadds Ford), 17
Brasília: civic discourse transformed in, 267–273; figure-ground plan of, *260;* highways in, 269, 270, 272, 275n. 18, 275n. 19; hometown compared to, 251; as modernist city, 15, 96; planning and design of, 3, 4, 245, 248–249, 268; public space eliminated in, 95, 97, 250–251; state intervention in, 113; street corners/streets absent in, 245, 248–251, 269–273; views of, *246, 247, 248*
Brazil: cities' emergence in, 249–250; democratic consolidation in, 85–86; economic crisis in, 84–85, 105n. 3, 105n. 4; fortification in, 19; mining economy in, 262–263; politics in, 253, 274n. 5; racial discrimination in, 106n. 10; religious discourse in, 20; social and income inequality in, 83, 105n. 1; urban development in,

273–274n. 2. *See also* Brasília; Ouro Preto (Brazil); São Paulo (Brazil)
Brazilian Institute of History and Geography, 274n. 5
Breitenmoser, Urs, 147, 148
brigas, concept of, 19
Brighton Beach, film set in, 5–6
British colonialism. *See* colonialism
Brooklyn (N.Y.), parade as resistance in, 10
Brown, Capability, 151
built environment: "autoconstruction" and, 85, 87; colonial vs. modern, 274n. 7; gardens' domination of, 160; as monument, 268–269, 275n. 16; perspectives on, 111; on plaza edges, 120, 127–128; as private, juxtaposed to public street, 97, 100–101, 254, *255, 256,* 257; private vs. public, 264–265; rural vs. urban, 252; solids and voids in, 257–267, 274–275n. 12; street façade in, 254, *255, 256,* 257. *See also* architecture; housing; public space; walls; *zongos*
Burawoy, M., 11
Burdick, J., 20
Burger King, in Costa Rica, 127, 129
Burlington (Ont.), greenways and, 392–394, 396
Busanga people, 298, 300
Busia, K. A., 283
businesses: black boycotts of white-owned, 43; influence by, 323; on plaza edges, 123–125, 127–128; size of, 177; studies of global, 13; tradition of small-scale, 208–209, 221. *See also* entrepreneurs; fishing industry; industrial enterprises; shoeshine men/boys; trade; vendors
Byrd, W., 179

CAA (Central Atlanta Association), 323, 325
Cable News Network (CNN), 325, 330
Cairo (Egypt), women's protests in, 10
Caldeira, Teresa P. R., 9
California: ethnic politics in, 6; greenways in, 390; as postmodern center, 16. *See also* Los Angeles (Calif.)

Canada, urban planning in, 387–388. *See also* Toronto; Toronto waterfront

Canadian Imperial Bank of Commerce, 396

CAP. *See* Central Atlanta Progress (CAP)

capitalism: controlled in China, 176–177; impact of international, 14; market regulation and, 208; modernist critique of, 95–96; socialism vs., in investment, 174–175, 178, 183–188, 194; speedup in, 170

car culture: effects of, 220–221; streets made for, 245, 248. *See also* highways

Cardoso, Fernando Henrique, 105n. 3

Carnival, violence during, 19

Casa de Caritat (Barcelona), 366, 370

Casa del Cabildo (town hall), 120

Casal d'Infants del Raval (school), 360

Castells, Manuel: on informational city, 14–15; on neighborhood associations, 344, 368; on social movements, 10; on space, 279; on spatialization of social conflict, 112–113

Catalunya: Barcelona's relation to, 355, 359, 370, 371; discourse in, 372; Franco's repression of, 344, 348; models for, 353. *See also* Barcelona (Spain)

Catholicism: contestation of, 124–125; social services and, 359, 360

cemeteries, removed from urban area, 346

Centennial Olympic Park Area, Inc. (COPA), 336

Centennial Olympic Park (Atlanta): development of, 332–334; future of, 336–337, 340; hype vs. reality of, 335–336; ritual cleansing of, 335

Central Area Studies (Atlanta), 325, 327–328, 330

Central Atlanta Association (CAA), 323, 325

Central Atlanta Progress (CAP): adaptive reuse and, 337; goals of, 325, 336, 338–339; housing development and, 328; Underground Atlanta and, 327

Central Bank of Costa Rica, 128

Central Wholesale Markets (Japan), 211

Centre de Cultura Contemporània de Barcelona, 370, 371, 373

Cerdà, Ildefons, 346–347, *347,* 347–348, 371

Chad: migrant communities in, 285; tradition's persistence in, 307

Chadds Ford (Pa.), study of, 4, 16–17

Chamba people, 298, 299, 303

Chaubes (priests), 20

chefs, 203, 210, 212, 224

Chicago (Ill.): deindustrialization in, 12; ethnic politics in, 6; as market center, 205–206; outmigration in, 39–40. *See also* Black Belt (South Side Chicago)

Chicago School, 2

chiefs/headmen: British recognition of, 282–287, 288–289, 303, 308n. 9; current situation for, 296–302; function of, 303–304, 307; as healers, 304; hierarchy of, 288, 291–293, 303; popular approval needed by, 308n. 14; status of, 296, 304–305; tasks of, 290–293, 303–304

chieftancy/headmanship: authority of, 281–282, 285; disputes over, 287–288, 293–296; legitimacy of, 277, 281, 290, 293, 306; persistence of, 302–305; structure of, 291–293

children: day care for, 47, 74, 76, 79; diagnostic center for foster, 53–56; gardens and, 142; meals for, 218, 219, 237n. 7; plazas used by, 122, 125, 130, 132, 364–365; recreational facilities for, 63n. 5; in shelter system, 73–79; social services for, 360; as workers, 132

China: banks in, 193; bureaucracy in, 186, 190; cosmology of, 231, 238n. 16; cuisine of, 217; cultural revival in, 189; decentralization in, 185–188; development in, 16, 170; economic restructuring in, 176–181, 195; Hong Kong's link to, 172–173, 188–189; immigration from, 188; production in, 174–177; reciprocal relations in, 179–180; responsibility system in, 195; second economy in, 179–180; as social formation, 174–175, 195;

China (*continued*)
social hierarchy in, 21; urban
studies in, 4, 21. *See also* Guangdong province (China); Hong Kong
investment
Christian Democratic Party (Austria),
155
Christiano, Anne, 80n. 1
Christiansborg Castle (Ghana), 281
churches: civil rights activism and,
45–46; commemoration of, 273;
community role of, 42–43, 47, 49;
development of local, 9, 42; social
class in, 49–50
CIAM (Congrès Internationaux
d'Architecture Moderne), 15
Citizens and Southern Bank Building
(Atlanta), 338
citizens/citizenship: definition of,
104–105; security and, 361–362; in
transnational cities, 172. *See also*
discourse; political participation;
public space
city: as commodity, 16; contested
meanings in, 10–11, 22; cultural
role of, 204; as divided, 7–9, 37–
41; ethnicity in, 5–7; as fortress,
18–19; as gendered, 9–10;
globalization and, 12–14, 171–172;
historical theorizing on, 2–4; ideal
vs. real, 352–353; images of, 5–21;
as informational, 14–15; as
machine, 356; modernist, 15–16;
nature discovered within, 141;
postmodernist, 16–18; preindustrial, 249–250, 253–254, *255,
256,* 257, 261–262; public
character of, 321–322, 332;
representational, 4; as sacred, 20;
social boundaries in, 102–105;
tradition in, 20–21; "user-
friendly," 327–328. *See also* urban
anthropology; urban planning;
urban renewal; urbanism
City Planning Commission (Corona),
43, 45
Ciudad Guyana, planning of, 3
Ciutat Vella (Barcelona), 343, 374n. 1
Civic Association. *See* East Elmhurst-
Corona Civic Association
civil rights-era reforms: increased
stratification due to, 37–41, 50–51,
62, 64n. 8; political participation
and, 45–50

Clammer, John, 207
class. *See* social class
Clos, Joan, 373
closed condominiums, ads for,
88–92
clothing, in religious practices, 297
clowns, in plazas, 126, 131–132
CNN Center (Atlanta), 325, 330
Coca-Cola Corporation, 323, 331, 333,
334
cocacolonization, 206
CODA (Corporation for Olympic
Development in Atlanta), 330–331
collectives, 177, 186
"colonial city," concept of, 15–16
colonialism: city in, 279–281, 380;
indigenous leadership under, 281–
289, 292, 294, 303, 306–307;
indirect rule of, 282–283, 308n. 9;
land ownership under, 279;
location of cities and, 308n. 6; in
urban renewal rhetoric, 322–323
Columbia (Md.), as edge city, 92
Columbus (Ohio), homeownership in,
52–53
Comarcal plan, 347
comics, consumption of girls', 207
commerce: move to periphery, 86;
sector for, 268–273. *See also*
businesses; industrial enterprises;
investment
Commerce Club Building (Atlanta),
338
Commission on Human Rights, 64n.
10
commodities: circulation of, 205–208;
cities as, 16; exchange of, 179–181;
food culture as, 212–213, 233–235;
seafood as, 201–203, 205, 210;
trading specializations in, 210,
233–235. *See also* consumption
commodity chains, concept of, 204–
205
communications media. *See* media
Communist Party (Barcelona), 354
communities: associations vs.
institutions in politics of, 47–50;
chief as link between government
and, 303–304; concept of, 55;
decentralization of, 48; development assistance for, 48, 49–50, 51;
divisions/connections among, 393;
facilities for "special populations"
in, 53–56, 60–61; maintaining

identity of, 307–308n. 2; planned change in, 3; rural vs. urban, 252; space of, as political, 278; strangers,' 283–284; studies of, 2–3, 11; as vulnerable extension of home, 57. *See also* African American community; leadership; neighborhoods; *zongos*

compensation trade, role of, 181–182, *182*

conciliar systems, as source of legitimacy, 281

condominiums (closed), ads for, 88–92

Congrès Internationaux d'Architecture Moderne (CIAM), 15

conquest, in urban renewal rhetoric, 322–323

consumption: celebration of, 334; changes in Japanese, 216–217; Costa Rican, of North American goods, 119; foodstuffs' classification and, 213–214; industrialization of food supply linked to, 214–216, 219, 222–223, 228–229; in spatializing culture, 119; landscape of, 381; marketing and, 205–208; social class and, 19; temporality and, 229–232. *See also* cuisine

Convent dels Angels (Barcelona), 366–367

Convention Peoples Party (CPP, Ghana), 294

Convergència i unié (CiU, Barcelona), 354–355

cooking. *See* chefs; food preparation

Cooper, Matthew, 17

COPA (Centennial Olympic Park Area, Inc), 336

Corona Congregational Church: civil rights activism and, 45–46; founding of, 42

Corona-East Elmhurst (N.Y.): civil rights activism in, 45–48; color line in, 44; "golden age" in, 41–45; homeownership in, 50–62; issues in, 37–38; organizations in, 44–48, 49–50, 52–56; politics restructured in, 46–50; social services in, 43, 47, 63n. 5; "special populations" in, 53–56, 60–62; stratification in, 37–41, 44–45, 49–50, 53, 60–62

Corporation for Olympic Develop-

ment in Atlanta (CODA), 330–331

cortiços: definition of, 105n. 5; poor relegated to, 85–86

Cosgrove, Denis, 379–380

Costa, Lúcio, 269–270

Costa Rica: banks in, 128; economy of, 123–124, 126, 129; ecotourism in, 117; politics in, 128, 129; seasons in, 115; tourist center for, 127. *See also* Parque Central (Costa Rica); Plaza de la Cultura (Costa Rica); San José (Costa Rica)

Council of Muslim Chiefs (Ghana), 295, 297

Cox, Kevin R., 52–53

Creighton, Millie R., 207, 219

Crèvecoeur, 281. *See also* Ussher Fort-James Fort area (Accra)

crime: block associations and, 56, 59–60; in plaza, 124, 130–131, 135; São Paulo's rates of, 86–87; talk about, 103. *See also* violence

Crombie, David, 382, 385, 386

Cronon, William, 205–206

Cross, M., 7

Crowder, Michael, 282, 308n. 10

Cuban Americans, political power of, 6

cuisine: as consumption, 203; definition of, 236–237n. 5; domesticity and, 217–223; food classification and, 214; Franco-Japonaise, 217, 236n. 6; high vs. low, 222; industrialization of, 214–216, 219, 222–223, 228–229; national vs. regional, 214–216, 222. *See also* Japanese cuisine

culinary life, use of term, 211, 213

Cullell, Josep Maria, 254

cultural capital: of cities, 372–373; concept of, 8; markets' role in, 208; of traders, 203, 235

culture: diversity's link to, 372–373; sacred city and, 20; spatialization of, 11; traditional city and, 20–21; transnationalism's impact on, 203–206. *See also* food culture

Cumings, Bruce, 181

Cwiertka, Katarzyna, 237n. 8

Dagarti people, 298

Daiei (supermarket), 221

Dalits (group), 11

Damaley, Adamu, 293–295

Damaley, Salifu Baha Kowa Adamu, 295–296
Damaley, Sanni, 294–295
Damaley, Wansa, 292–294, 309n. 30
Damaley family, Bako family vs., 304–305
Dansoman Estates (Accra), 293
Danube (river), 157–158
Davis, Mike, 18, 101–102, 322, 336
day care: in shelter system, 74, 76, 79; sponsored by civic association, 47
Day of the Ox (Japan), 231, 238n. 16
dchefs: sushi invented by, 224
Dear, Michael, 387
Debret, Jean Baptiste, 252–254, *255, 256,* 274n. 5
de Certeau, Michel, 113–114
decision making: decentralization of, 185–188; in markets, 203; professional influence on, 394
Declaration of Green Space (Austria), 155–160
Dedji, Malam Halidou Atcha, 310n. 51
deindustrialization, studies of, 12
democracy: in Brazil, 85–86; components of, 104; in Spain, 343–344, 359
Democratic Party (U.S.), black involvement in, 42–43, 47, 51
Denny's (restaurant), 220
Denton, Nancy A., 7
dependency, cultural authenticity and, 224–228
Desfor, Gene, 381
design: continuity in, 151; gardens and, 149–154; solids and voids in city, 257–267; spatial form in, 111
development: block associations' impact on, 57–59; components of, 16; enterprise zones in, 331; environment vs., 138–139, 154–156, 163. *See also* Atlanta (Ga.); Barcelona (Spain); Brasília; discourse; investment; Toronto waterfront
Diario de Barcelona (newspaper), 367
difference: eroded by transnationalism, 204–205; exposure to, 102–105; inscription of, 378; in public vs. private sphere, 96–97
Dinkins, David, 72
discourse: bioregionalism in, 388–

395; characteristics of, 355–357; development, fragmentation, and, 369–373; on egalitarianism, 268; experience of place and, 392–394; forms of space in, 379–380; on healthfulness and urban space, 379; on landscape, 147–154; as model for understanding, 368–369; modernist transformation of, 267–273; participants in, 342, 344–345, 352–355; role of, 377–378; on Toronto waterfront, 381–382; on trail system proposal, 392–394; transcendental vs. humanistic, 379–380, 395; on urban policy components, 357–367
disease: antituberculosis clinic and, 366; colonial city and theories of, 248, 280, 308n. 6; plague, 288–289; in Sabon Zongo, 291–292; in social-reformist rhetoric, 349; in urban renewal rhetoric, 323, 333, 359
Disney, Walt, 322, 326
Disney Corporation, 336
District of Columbia, migration to, 9–10
Ditmars Boulevard Block Association, 59
diversity: globalization and, 371–372; limits on, 64n. 10; visibility of, 372–373. *See also* bioregionalism; difference
domesticity, cuisine and, 217–223, 237n. 8. *See also* public/private sphere
domestic service, 89–90, 90, 99
Dore, R. P., 218
Dorst, J. D., 4, 16–17
Dovey, K., 18
Downtown Ambassadors Force (Atlanta), 328
Downtown Improvement District (Atlanta), 328
Drassanes, Avinguda de (Barcelona), 349–351, 365–366
drop-in centers, 72–73
drug dealing/drug use: countermeasures to, 60, 360–361; in homeless hotels, 77; in plazas, 124, 131, 135, 364–365; police complicity in, 362; study of, 14
"dual city," concept of, 13

Dublin (Ireland), as capital of culture, 372

Du Bois, W. E. B., 340

Duncan, James, 378

East Elmhurst-Corona Civic Association: community decay monitored by, 64n. 12; day care sponsored by, 47; on facilities for "special populations," 53–56, 60–62; formation of, 44–45; meeting of, 58–60; members of, 64n. 7; power and function of, 57–60

East Elmhurst (N.Y.): block associations in, 52–56; boundaries of, 63–64n. 6; issues in, 37–38; settlement of, 43; stratification of, 44. *See also* Corona-East Elmhurst (N.Y.), 37–38

Ebenezer Missionary Baptist Church (Flushing), 64–65n. 14

ecology wave (Ekowelle): concept of, 138–139, 140; gardens of discovery in, 140–147, 154–163; impact of, 152–153, 159–160; sustainable city in, 370–371. *See also* bioregionalism; Ekogarten movement; environment

economy: centralized planning in, 178–179; deindustrialized city and, 12; food culture and, 217; global city and, 12–14; growth of informal, 123–124; homelessness from crisis in, 70–71; informational city and, 14–15; second, in China, 179–180; structural changes in, 39–40, 123–124. *See also* investment; markets

ecotourism, Costa Rica, 117

"edge city," use of term, 91–92, 171

Edo. *See* Tokyo (Japan)

educadores de calle (program), 359–360

egalitarianism, discourse on, 268

Egypt: colonialism and space in, 380; religion as resistance in, 20; women's protests in, 10

Ekogarten movement: green space and, 156–159; politics of, 154–156; principles of, 147–149, 160–163

Ekowelle. *See* ecology wave (Ekowelle)

El Barrio (East Harlem), fear of violence in, 19

Elmcor Youth and Adult Services, 47, 55

El Salvadore: migration from, 9–10; refugees from, 117, 124

Emergency Assistance Bureaus (EABs), 71–72

Empowerment Zone Corporation (U.S.), 331

England, social networks in, 2–3. *See also* colonialism; London (England)

English, Kadri, 289, 293–294

English, Kadri (grandson), 295

enterprise zones, 331

entrepreneurs: exchange relations and, 181–183; local mediators used by, 174; on small-scale investments, 187–188; social networks of, 172; "squeezing" of, 191, 194. *See also* Hong Kong investment

environment: attitudes toward, 138, 152–153; development vs., 138–139, 154–156, 163; fish cultivation and, 228–229; international agreements on, 163; politics of, 138–139, 152, 154–155. *See also* bioregionalism; ecology wave (Ekowelle); Ekogarten movement

Esplanade of the Ministries (Brasília), *248*, 269

ethnic enclave, concept of, 6

ethnicity: political development and, 6; in Sabon Zongo, 290–291, *292*, 296–299; studies of, 5–7; visibility of, 372–373

Europe: Americanization of poverty in, 8; capitals of culture in, 372–373; ecology wave (Ekowelle) in, 138–139; sustainability and, 371. *See also specific countries*

European Economic Community, 355

Ewe people, 298, 300, 301, 302, 303

exchange: modes of, 179–181; relations of, 177–183, 188–196

export processing, 182–187, 194–195

Fainstein, S. S., 18

Fairlie-Poplar Historic District (Atlanta), 336–340

faixas (bands), 269

family: ecopolitics of, 138–139; meals for, 218, 220–221, 237n. 7, 237n. 10; models of, 68–69, 72; in shelter

family (*continued*)
system, 73–79. *See also* children; household structure; mothers
Faneuil Hall (Boston), 326
Farley, Reynolds, 63n. 3
fashion industry, Japanese designers in, 237n. 6
fast food restaurants: in Costa Rica, 127–128, 129, 132; in Japan, 217
fathers, defined out of shelter system, 73–79
Fava, Maria, 355
favelas: definition of, 105n. 5; fortified enclaves next to, 87, 99; poor relegated to, 85–86
Fernandez-Kelly, M. P., 8
Ferrez, Gilberto, 274n. 8
festival markets, development of, 326
Field Associates, 58–59
figure/ground. *See* built environment, solids and voids in
films: *Boyz N the Hood,* 18; *Little Odessa,* 5; *Mad Max,* 18; *Mad Max Beyond Thunderdome,* 18; *Pulp Fiction,* 16; *The Road Warrior,* 18; *Roger and Me,* 12; *Suupaa no Onna,* 237n. 11; *Twelve Monkeys,* 18
fire, 343, 362
Firestone Tire and Rubber, 12
fish. *See* fishmongers; seafood
fishing industry: commodity chains in, 205; institutional structure of, 215–216; protection of Japanese, 225; social organization and, 209–211; technological advances in, 206, 224, 228–229, 238n. 14. *See also* seafood; Tsukiji marketplace (Tokyo)
fishmongers, 210, 216, 221, 223
Five Points (Atlanta): adaptive reuse projects in, 336–339; description of, 318; deterioration of, 326–327; mixed-use developments in, 324–325; renewal/redevelopment of, 322–323, 328–331; riots in, 326–327; security for, 328; university's role in, 338–339
Fjellman, S. M., 17, 322
"flexible body," concept of, 14–15
Flint (Mich.), deindustrialization in, 12
Flushing (N.Y.), facilities for "special populations" in, 61, 64–65n. 14
food culture: authenticity in, 203, 222, 223–228; commodification in, 212–213, 233–235; globalization of, 206; practical reason and, 211–214; social changes and, 216–217, 221–222; temporality and, 229–232; use of term, 211. *See also* fast food restaurants; Japanese cuisine
food preparation, 202–203, 218–220, 237n. 8. *See also* chefs
foodstuffs: beef, 225; coffee, 206; cultural classification of, 212–214; fish pastes, 215; foreign vs. domestic, 226; kata of, 220, 225–228; luxury (gourmet), 221–222; oranges, 225; pizza, 217; raw vs. cooked, 223; rice, 211, 225, 237n. 12; saké, 222; sausages, 217; soy sauce, 215; sugar, 206. *See also* fishing industry; seafood; sushi
food supply: commodity chains in, 205–206; industrialization of, 214–216, 219, 222–223, 228–229; purity and pollution concerns in, 226
Fortaleza (Brazil), Brasília compared to, 251
fortified enclaves: advertisements for, 88–92; characteristics of, 93–95; context of, 84–87; debate over, 99–102; emergence of, 83–84; in films, 18; modernist instruments used in, 95–98; role of, 9; social differences hardened by, 103–105. *See also* São Paulo (Brazil); security
Forum of World Cultures (2004), 373
Foster, Sir Norman, 370
foster children, diagnostic center for, 53–56
Foucault, Michel, 113, 380
fountains, 121, 130
Four Modernizations (China), 181
Fox, R., 2
Frafra people, 284, 298
France, colonialism of, 282, 306–307. *See also* Paris (France)
Francé, Raoul Heinrich, 141
Franco, Francisco: aftermath of, 342, 368–369; Catalan repressed by, 344, 348; death of, 352; housing under, 357; neighborhood associations under, 343; open space under, 363; social services under, 359; waning years of regime of, 357–358

Franco-Japonaise cuisine, 217, 236n. 6

Frank, A., 177

Friedmann, J., 13

frontier: as social spatialization, 382–383; in urban renewal rhetoric, 322–323

Fulani people, 284, 298, 300

Furtado, Celso, 263

Futa, Alhaji, 304

Gälzer, Ralph, 153–154

gambling, in plazas, 124, 125, 126, 135

gangs, spatial patterns and, 19, 365

Ga people: associations of, 299; Hausa differences with, 308n. 7; land ownership and, 285, 288, 306; leadership and, 286–288; occupations and, 301; politics and, 294–295; schools for, 299–300; settlement and, 280, 290, 298

Garden City (Kans.), ethnic politics in, 6

gardens. See Ekogarten movement; open spaces; private gardens; public gardens

Garreau, Joel, 91–92

Garuba, Malam, 286–287

Gates, H., 176–177

GE Capital Canada Corporation, 396

Geertz, Clifford, 235

Gehry, Frank, 370

gender: body temperature differences by, 236n. 4; city images and, 9–10; food lore and, 212, 218–220, 237n. 8; public space and, 133; in Sabon Zongo, 300–302; in shelter system, 72–79

General Electric Company, 12

Generalitat (Barcelona): cooperation of, 354–355; on housing, 357; open spaces and, 363; social services and, 359

General Motors, 12

gentrification: effects of, 338; impetus for, 366, 370, 381; jobs generated by, 89–90

Geoffrey, Junius, 308n. 12

geography: academic training and, 4; in bioregion definition, *384*, 384–386, *386;* humanistic discourse in, 379, 395; region vs. landscape in, 380

George, L., 8, 9

Georgia Dome (Atlanta), 325, 330

Georgia International Plaza (Atlanta), 325, 330

Georgia State University, 335, 338

Georgia Tech University, 331, 335

Georgia World Congress Center (Atlanta), 325, 330, 333

Germany, divisions in Berlin, 7

Ghana: customary law in, 284–285, 290, 305, 306, 310n. 35; development in, 16; healers in, 304; indigenous leadership in, 281–289, 292, 294–307; migrants to, 280, 308n. 5; political parties in, 294–295; space's meaning on, 279; "strangers" in, 284, 307n. 1; tradition's persistence in, 307. *See also* Accra (Ghana); chiefs/headmen; Sabon Zongo (Accra)

Ghana Muslim Mission, 308n. 12

Giddens, Anthony, 16, 278

gift exchange: benefits of, 190–191; components of, 13, 189–190; problems in, 191, 193–194; role of, 179–181, 184–185, 195–196; stages of, 191–193

Glasgow (Scotland), as capital of culture, 372

Glazer, Lisa, 64n. 10

global city, Hong Kong as, 173

global culture, 203–206

"global factory," concept of, 13, 205

globalization: capital's mobility in, 173; as challenge to cities, 171–172; diversity and, 371–372; of food culture, 206; industrialization and, 13; local forces and, 15; studies of, 12–14, 22

global trade: China's move into, 181; commodity chains in, 204–206

Glover-Amoako, James, 307–308n. 2, 309n. 27

Gold Coast. *See* Ghana

gold mining, 262–263, 279

Gold Museum (San José), 127, 128–129

Goldrick, Michael, 381

Gonzalez, Alfredo, 80n. 1

Goode, J., 6

Goody, Jack, 206, 213, 214–215, 222

Govan, Jacob, 41–42

Government Lands Bills (Gold Coast), 279

Grand Central Terminal (New York), 72

Gran Hotel (San José), 127, 128, 130, 132, 133

Great Britain. *See* colonialism; England; Glasgow (Scotland)

Greater Toronto Area (GTA), 385

Greece, street system in, 261. *See also* Athens (Greece)

Greenbaum, S. D., 7

Green Party (Austria), 138, 152

green space. *See* open spaces

Greenway and Trail Strategy (Burlington), 392–394

Greenwich Village (N.Y.), parade as resistance in, 10

Gregory, Steven, 7

grid-plan town, concept of, 121

Grünkeile (green space), 156–157

Grünlanddeklaration (Declaration of Green Space, Austria), 155–160

Grunshie people, 301

Grünverbindungen (green space), 156

Grünzüge (green space), 156

Grup d'Arquitecetes i Tènics Espànyols per al Progrès de l'Arquitectura Contemporània, 348

Grusi people, 284

Guallar, Angel, 351

Guangdong province (China): foreign investment in, *182,* 182–183, *183,* 185–188, 190–192; Hong Kong's influence on, 172–173; migrant workers in, *185;* packing export goods in, *184;* research in, 170, 172; shoe factory in, 192, 194–195

guanxi (reciprocal relations), 13, 179–180, 190–193, 196. *See also* gift exchange

guardia civil (civil police). *See* police

Guatemala: refugees from, 124; vendors from, 132

Guest, Avery M., 57

Guggenheim Museum (Bilbao), 370

Gulick, J., 2

habitus, concept of, 114

Halidou, Malam, 298

Hall, Stuart, 235

Halloween Parade, 10

Halperin, R., 178

Hamisu, Alhaji, 301, 302, 304, 310n. 53

Hanaya Yohei, 224

handicapped people: facilities for, 53–56, 60–62, 64–65n. 14; in Sabon Zongo, 291–292

Hannerz, Ulf, 3–4, 15, 203, 204

harbor area, restoration of, 363. *See also* waterfront

Harborplace (Baltimore), 326

harbors, jurisdiction over, 382

Harbourfront Corporation (Toronto), 381–382

Hare Krishna followers, 125

Haring, Keith, 364

Harlem (New York): Corona's links to, 42; hats sold in, 14; identity politics in, 9

Harris, Marvin, 213

Hart, Keith, 279

Harvey, David: on chiefs' recognition, 283, 296; on discourse, 378, 379, 392; on postmodern city, 16; on representation of space, 378; on spatialization of social conflict, 112–113

Harvey, William B., 279

Hausa people: associations of, 299; Ga people's differences with, 308n. 7; identity of, 304, 307–308n. 2; leadership of, 286–288; *mai gida* of, 285; migration of, 286; occupational hierarchy of, 301; schools for, 299–300; use of term, 309n. 15; *zongo* for, 284. *See also* Sabon Zongo (Accra)

Haussmann, Georges-Eugène, 93

Hayden, Dolores, 10, 379

health issues, 226, 245, 248. *See also* disease

Hegel, G. W. F., 163n. 3

hereditary systems, as source of legitimacy, 281

Heron, Sheryl, 80n. 1

heterogeneity, 100–101, 204. *See also* difference; diversity

highways: in Barcelona, 349–351, 354; in Brasília, 269, 270, 272, 275n. 18, 275n. 19. *See also* streets

Hill, Harriet, 42

Hinduism, city as mesocosm and, 20

Hinton, Rev. George W., 42–43

historical preservation, modernization vs., 134–135

Hodgson, Sir F. M., 287

Hofbegrünung-Förderungsaktion (program), 145–146

Holiday Inn Corporation, 58

holidays: in Barcelona, 363; in Ghana, 297, 304; in Japan, 219, 225, 229–232; parades and, 10

Holston, James, 4, 15, 96, 113

homeless hotels: description of, 71–74; families at, 73, 75–79

homelessness: experience of, 67–70, 78–79; history of, 70–72; renewal/redevelopment's impact on, 328, 339, 358–359; spatial patterns and, 19. See also shelter system

homeownership: activism linked to, 52–53, 85–86; associations for, 44–45, 50, 52–62, 85–86, 99, 104; politics of, 50–62; renters vs., 64n. 11; in Sabon Zongo, 290–291; via "autoconstruction," 85, 87

homosexuality, plaza use and, 130

Honda, Yukiko, 238n. 17

Hong, Z., 177

Hong Kong: China's link to, 172–173, 188–189; postmodernity in, 17–18; postwar transformation of, 187; research in, 170; skyscrapers in, 18. See also entrepreneurs; Hong Kong investment

Hong Kong investment: after Tiananmen Square, 169–170, 190–191; area of, 172; Atlanta's encouragement of, 334; character of, 173–174; context of, 171–181; as disguised subcontracting, 169; dominance of, 181–188, 195–196; in export processing, 182–183; reciprocal relations and, 13, 179–180, 190–193, 196; relations of exchange in, 188–196; small-scale, 185–188, 190, 196; for social connections, 189–190; socially vs. bureaucratically mediated, 169–170, 173–174, 196. See also entrepreneurs

Hong Kong-South China region: as "border metropolis," 13; border of, 172; Hong Kong investment in, 182–188; transformation of, 173

Honolulu (Hawaii), cuisine popular in, 237n. 6

Horton, J., 6

House Food Industrial Company, 237n. 7

household structure: analysis of, 67–69; food culture and, 218–219, 221; institutional expectations of, 68–69, 72

housing: Barcelona public policy on, 357–359; colonial vs. modern in Brazil, 274n. 7; control of, 10, 48; discrimination in, 64n. 10; "doubling up" in, 70, 72; funds for improvements in, 45; middle- and upper-income, 328, 381; migration's impact on, 43; models of family used in, 68; public, in Atlanta, 323–324, 331–332; public, in Barcelona, 357; public, in U.S., 72; racial divisions and, 7; as source of power, 286; studies of, 3; tenure in, 52–53; transitional, 73, 74–75, 77. See also fortified enclaves; homeownership; household structure; shelter system

Houston (Tex.), ethnic politics in, 6

Hungary, industrial enterprises in, 170, 179

Hunter (deputy governor), 287

hyper-commercialism, Atlanta's, 334

hyperghetto, concept of, 8

Ibadan Nigeria, zongo in, 284, 285

Ibrahim, Maman, 298

identity: food culture and, 203, 211, 225; maintaining community, 307–308n. 2; regional, 207; space linked to, 19; symbol's role in, 304; trading specializations and, 210, 233–235

ideologies of place: bioregionalism's impact on, 388–395; expression of, 378–380; role of, 377

Iglesia Parroquial (church), 120

Igrejinha da Fátima (Little Church of Fátima), 273

Ikime, Obaro, 308n. 10

imagineers, use of term, 322, 327, 336–340

IMF (International Monetary Fund), 123, 129

immigrants: attitudes toward, 371–373; police harassment of, 362; security issues and, 361–362; social services for, 360. See also migration; outmigration

Imperial Oil Corporation, 396

India: city location in, 308n. 6; sacred cities in, 20; urban sociology in, 21. See also Dalits (group)

indigenous people, leadership among, 281–289, 292, 294–307, 308n. 8. *See also specific groups*

industrial capitalism, studies of, 4

industrial enterprises: allocation of output of, 179; foreign-owned, 181, *182, 183;* gift exchange and, 180–181; investment in, 173–174; newly established vs. state-sector, 183; size of, 170, 177, 179

industrialization: of food supply, 214–216, 219, 222–223, 228–229; preindustrial urbanism and, 249

informational city, concept of, 14–15

inner-city buildings, plantings for, 154, 158–160

Institute of Community Studies, 2–3

institutions: vs. associations in community politics, 47–50; buildings for, 253; cooperation of, 354–355; experience of poverty and, 67–68; markets as, 203; models of family used in, 68–69; on plaza edges, 120, 127–128. *See also* Tsukiji marketplace (Tokyo)

internationalization: of city, 356, 369–373; in urban planning, 356

International Monetary Fund (IMF), 123, 129

International Union of Architects conference, 370, 373

International Whaling Commission, 235

Internet: Barcelona on, 373; diversity and, 372; urban planning and, 356

investment: encouragement of foreign, 334; forms of, 181–182; negotiation of, 13; routinization of, 191; socially vs. bureaucratically mediated, 169–170, 173–174, 196; state control of, 185; by western companies, 192. *See also* Hong Kong investment

Islam. *See* Muslims

Itami Jûzô, 237n. 11

Ivy, Marilyn, 207

Jackson, Maynard, 318–319, 330

Jackson, P., 2

Jackson Heights (New York City), discrimination in, 64n. 10

Jacobs, Jane, 4, 324, 336

Jamaica, street vendors in, 9

James Fort (Ghana), 281

Jameson, F., 16

Jamestown (Alata): components of, 294; leadership of, 288, 293–294

Jamieson, Walter, 387–388

Japan: cats in, 224; central market system in, 211; Chinese investment by, 192; consumption and commodification in, 207–208; cultural time in, 229–232; eating-out boom in, 220–221, 223, 233, 235; economy of, 237n. 10; gourmet boom in, 221–223, 233; imports of, 225–228, 237n. 12; neighborhoods in, 20–21; purity and pollution in, 226, 228–229; status maintenance in, 21; temporality in, 229–232; work organization studies in, 4. *See also* Tokyo (Japan); Tsukiji marketplace (Tokyo)

Japan Air Lines, 222

Japanese cuisine: authenticity and, 203, 222, 223–228; changes in, 223–225; domesticity and, 217–223; foreign dishes in, 217; industrialization of, 214–216, 219, 222–223; international dependency and, 224–228; principles of, 202–203; seafood's centrality in, 211–212, 223, 225; stewards of, 209; temporality and, 229–232; women and, 218–220, 237n. 8. *See also* sushi

Japan Socialist Party, 226

Jaussely plan, 347

Jencks, Charles, 100–101, 104

Jewell, Richard, 335

Jimala (chief), 310n. 50

Jimenez, Capt. Don Miguel, 120

joint ventures: investment through, 181–182, *182, 183,* 195; problems for multinationals in, 183–184, 186, 190

Jones, D. J., 8

Jones, W. J. A., 292

Jonkobli (Ghana), 310n. 41

Journal of Historical Geography, 379

Juan Mora Fernandez park (San José), 128

Julian I. Garfield Democratic Association, 51

Kabyle house, 114

Kahn, J., 175, 176–177

Kaniki, M. H. Y., 279
Kanuri people, 298
Katznelson, Ira, 48
Keith, M., 7
Kelly, William W., 207
Kenny, Judith, 387
Kent, William, 151
Kentucky Fried Chicken, 217
Kenya, mediating elite in, 308n. 8
Kikkoman soy sauce, 215
Kimble, David, 279, 310n. 35
King, Anthony D., 16, 280, 281
King, Martin Luther, Jr., 45
King, Rodney, 326–327
kinship, investment and, 170
kiosks: contested meaning of, 122,
    134–135; on Danube River, 157;
    import of, 121; police surveillance
    from, 124; renovation of, 117, 119
knowledge: conflicting forms of, 11;
    control of, 14–15
Koch, Edward, 72
Koetter, Fred, 261
Kojo, Nii Sampah, 309n. 26
Kondo, Dorinne, 21, 237n. 6
Kopytoff, Igor, 212–213
Korea, cuisine of, 217
Kotokoli people, 298, 299, 300, 303
Kpesi people, 280
Kuasasi people, 284
Kubitschek, Juscelino, 15
Kudjo (captain), 286
Kuhn, Clifford, 321
Ku Klux Klan, 321
Kumase (Ghana): *mai gida* in, 285;
    Muslim influence in, 284; *zongo*
    in, 292, 305
Kuper, Hilda, 278–279
Kyôtaru (restaurant), 220, 237n. 10

labor: cheap, 181, 187, 194–195; in
    gift exchange, 193; Hong Kong
    dollars for, 193; international
    division of, 205; migrant, *185;* in
    mode of production, 175
labor unions, 12
Laclau, E., 177
Lagos (Nigeria), slum clearance in, 2–
    3
La Guardia Airport Holiday Inn, 58
La Guardia Airport (New York City),
    43, 57–58
Lake Ontario Waterfront Network,
    396. *See also* Ontario, Lake

Lamphere, L., 6
land: as source of power, 277, 286;
    studies of access to, 10; tenure
    rights to, 3
land ownership: control of, 279;
    customary laws on, 284–285, 290,
    305, 306, 310n. 35; leadship
    disputes and, 287–288, 293–296;
    public discourse on, 392–394
Landry, Bart, 42, 63n. 1
landscape: along Danube, 157–158;
    alteration of, 383, *384;* of con-
    sumption, 381; discourse on, 147–
    154; inventing traditions of, 379;
    as lived space, 161; as model of
    community life, 139–140; moral,
    378; novelty and variety in, 153;
    region vs., 380; representation of,
    378, 394; sensory experience of,
    127, 162–163; social production
    of, 140, 154–160; state policy on,
    155; Viennese traditions of, 139–
    140. *See also* open spaces; plazas;
    private gardens; public gardens;
    trees
land use: bioregionalism and, 392–
    395; disputes over, 387–388;
    terminology of, 389–390
Lane, D., 175–176
Largo do Carmo (Rio), 274n. 8
Largo do Pelourinho (Salvador), *246*
LaSalle, Yvonne, 80n. 1
Las Fallas (event), 10
Latin America: colonial power
    relations in, 15–16; debt crisis in,
    123; divided city image in, 9; "lost
    decade" in, 84; population of, 3;
    street system in, 262; studies of, 4.
    See also specific countries
Lawrence, Denise, 111
laws: colonialism's preempting of,
    284; customary, in Ghana, 284–
    285, 290, 305, 306, 310n. 35;
    indigenous response to colonial,
    279. *See also* zoning laws
lawsuits, over leadership, 293–295
leadership: current (Ghana), 296–307;
    disputes in (Ghana), 287–288,
    293–296; expectations in (U.S.
    neighborhood), 58; indigenous
    (Ghana), 281–289, 292, 294–307;
    power of place and, 305–307;
    wealth as criterion in (Ghana),
    277, 281

League for Better Community Life, 60

Le Corbusier, 273n. 1, 274–275n. 12, 275n. 17, 348

Leeds, A., 3

Lefebvre, Henri, 114, 120–121, 377–378

Leninism, reciprocal relations in, 179–180

lepers, in Sabon Zongo, 291–292

LeRoy, Louis, 147, 152

Lévi-Strauss, Claude, 213, 223

Levy, R., 20

Leys, Colin, 308n. 8

liberal ideology, in Canadian planning, 387–388

Lin, J., 173

Lindsay, John, 47

Linger, D. T., 19

Little Odessa (film), 5

lived experience: gardens' impact on, 160; spatial practice and, 112–114

lived space, theory of, 113–114

livestock, 296, 301

local governments, control by, 179. See also specific cities

local interests, role of, 16. See also associations; specific groups

localized friendships, concept of, 57

Lock, Margaret, 238n. 16

Logan, J., 329

London (England): as fortress city, 18; as global city, 12–13; slum clearance in, 2–3

Lopes, Juarez, 106n. 10

Los Angeles (Calif.): cuisine in, 217; as edge city, 92; as fortress city, 9, 18; peripheral urbanization in, 98–99; police violence in, 99, 105n. 7; as postmodern center, 16; public space eliminated in, 95; São Paulo compared to, 83–84, 98–102; urban planning debates in, 99–102; violent crime in, 105n. 6; women's contributions in, 10. See also South Central (Los Angeles)

Los Angeles Police Department, 99, 105n. 7

Lovejoy, Arthur, 379

Low, Setha M., 11, 15–16

Lower East Side (New York), community study of, 11

Luque, Carmen, 372

Lynch, O., 20

Ma, B., 177

Mabogunje, Akin L., 280

Macao, China's link to, 173, 182, 188

MacCannell, D., 16

Macià plan, 346–347

Macy's Department Store, 337

Mad Max Beyond Thunderdome (film), 18

Mad Max (film), 18

Maicancan, Alhaji, 295

mai gida (patron): role of, 285–286, 305, 306; for traders, 289. See also chiefs/headmen

Main Street program (NTHP), 337

Makiko's Diary (Nakano), 237n. 8

Malcolm X, 14, 46

Mandiargues, Pierye de, 366

Manhattan, gentrification in, 338

Mao Zedong, 188

Maragall, Pascual: on Barcelona, 342, 354, 366; on diversity, 372; on politics, 348; on Raval, 343; retirement of, 370–371; on security, 361; on urban renovation, 358

Maremagnum (Barcelona), 363

Marin, Angel, 373

Maritime promenade (Barcelona), 363

marketplace: in barrio, 351; commercial sector vs., 269–272; definition of, 203–204, 210–211; plazas as, 120, 126, 132; tensions of, 234–235; women's role in, 9, 301–302. See also black market; supermarkets; traders; Tsukiji marketplace (Tokyo)

markets: niches in, 233–235; role of, 205–208; use of term, 210–211

Marshall, Helen, 47, 52, 54, 61–62

Marshall, T. H., 106n. 12

Martinez, Gwendolyn, 80n. 1

Marxism, production as focus of, 177

Masalaci Malam Bako (mosque), 289

Massey, Douglas S., 7

Mathura (India), as sacred, 20

Maya, influence by, 121

Maza, Gaspar, 363–364

MCA (corporation), 336

McDonald's: in East Asia, 13, 206, 217; in San José (Costa Rica), 127, 129, 132

McDonogh, Gary, 7, 11, 17, 333

Meaney, C., 179–180

media: control of, 14–16; on environment, 138; on food culture, 211, 225; on fortified enclaves, 91–92; on plaza safety, 130–131; on social difference, 103. *See also* advertisements/advertising

Meier, Richard, 370

memory, segregation of, 321

men: organizations of, 299; in shelter system, 73–79

mental illness, shelter system and, 73

Merrens, Roy, 381

Merry, S., 18–19

Mesoamerica, plaza designs in, 121

methodology: analysis as, 116; debates over, 112; ethnography's role in, 170–171; innovations in, 11; interviews and historical documentation in, 116; observational strategies in, 115–116, 307–308n. 2; setting in, 117–119; in shelter system research, 80n. 1; statistics as, 170

Metropolitan Planning Commission (Atlanta), 323–324

Miami (Fla.): development of, 6; violent crime in, 105n. 6

Miami Herald (newspaper), 128

middle class: ads geared to, 88–92; fortified enclaves for, 87–88; housing for, 328, 381; as "little capitalists," *256;* NIMBY attitudes of, 55; outmigration of, 39–40; plazas used by, 122, 124, 125, 132; social networks of, 2–3. *See also* African American middle class; homeownership

migration: of Chinese illegals, 187; community change due to, 43; gender-specific, 9–10; studies of, 14

Miles, William F. S., 282

Miller, Zell, 333

Mingione, E., 8

mining, 262–263, 279

minority groups, challenge by, 94–95

Mintz, Sidney, 206

Miró Ardevol, Josep, 371

Mitchell, Timothy, 15, 64–65n. 14, 380

mixed-use developments (MXDs), 324–325

modernism: demonstration against, 129–130; discourse transformed in, 267–273; inversion by, 265–267; open spaces in, 93–95; planning objectives in, 245, 248–250, 265–267; urban planning and, 15–16

modernization, historical preservation vs., 134–135

Moeran, Brian, 207

Moll de la Fusta (Barcelona), 343

Molotch, H., 329

Montbach, J., 8

Monterey Park (Calif.), ethnic politics in, 6

Monument to Tiradentes (Ouro Preto), *247*

Moore, Michael, 12

Moore, P. W., 388

Moslem Association Party (MAP, Ghana), 294

Mossi people, 298

mothers: children separated from, 8; in shelter system, 72–79

Mullings, L., 3–4

multinationals, joint ventures as problems for, 183–184, 186, 190. *See also* transnational corporations

Mummer's New Year Parade, 10

Museu d'Art Contemporani (Barcelona), 364, 366, 370, 372

Museum of Brasília, *246*

museums, areas for, 366, 370

Mushin (Nigeria): establishing permanence in, 286; *mai gida* in, 285

Muslims: disputes among, 289, 309n. 20; leadership of, 285–288; political struggles of, 308n. 3; sacred cities and, 20; schools for, 299–300; settlement of, 284. *See also* Hausa people; Sabon Zongo (Accra); Yoruba people

mutual aid societies, in Ghana, 299

Narita International Airport, 222, 232

Nash, J., 12

Nathan, Sir Matthew, 287

National Association for the Advancement of Colored People (NAACP), 43, 45, 47

National Congress (Brasília), *247*

nationalism, food culture and, 225. *See also* nation-state

National Liberation Party (Costa Rica), 128, 129

National Library (Costa Rica), 116
National People's Congress (China), 177
National Theater (Brazil), 275n. 19
National Theater (Costa Rica), 119, 127, 128–129, 130, 132
National Trust for Historic Preservation, 337
Nation of Islam, 46
Nationsbank, 338
nation-state: central planning by, 178–179; city as monument to, 268; environmental commitment of, 138–139, 155–156; as imagined community, 211; social formation and, 175–176, 195. *See also* state-sector firms
nativity, investment and, 169–170, 188–190, 193–194
natural disasters, 3
naturalism, in parkscape, 153
nature: abstracted for design, 151–152; as alive, 142–143; antimodern view of, 139, 160; balance and, 139, 147–149, 160–161, 388–389, 395; beauty of, 153; gardens as mirror of, 141, 150–151, 160; as independent of human will, 140; preserves for, 157; in progress narrative, 388; in transcendental discourse, 379–380, 395
neighborhood associations: African American middle class, 44–48, 49–50, 52–53; in Barcelona neighborhoods, 343–344, 351–352, 360, 368; community decay monitored by, 64n. 12; community role of, 56–58; political activism of, 53–56; power and function of, 57–60. *See also* East Elmhurst-Corona Civic Association
neighborhoods: as cells within city, 355, 361; decline in, 51; divisions of, 7–9; middle-class activism in, 52–53; regulations for, 18–19; shitamachi, 20–21; shopping in, 272–273, 358–359; as socio-historical formations, 353; streets in working-class, 346; studies of, 3–4. *See also* Corona-East Elmhurst (N.Y.); fortified enclaves; neighborhood associations; Raval (Barcelona neighborhood)
Nenu, Malam Idris Bako, 286, 306

neoclassicism, as transcendental discourse, 379–380
New Delhi (India), planning and location of, 308n. 6
Newman, K. S., 1, 9
New York City Human Resources Administration, 54–55, 71, 73
New York (N.Y.): cuisine in, 217; "doubling up" in, 70, 72; as fortress city, 18; gentrification in, 338; as global city, 12–13; homelessness in, 67–72, 78–79; land and labor control in, 10; police violence in, 105n. 7; shelter system in, 68–69, 71–79; violent crime in, 105n. 6; women's protests in, 10. *See also* Harlem (New York)
New York State Assembly, 47
Nicaragua, refugees from, 117, 124
Niemeyer, Oscar, 273
Nigeria: colonial rule of, 280, 282–283; tradition's persistence in, 307; *zongo* in, 284
Nihonbashi, trade guilds at, 208
Nike Corporation, 334
NIMBY attitude, 55
Ninety-ninth Street Block Association, 53–56
Nixon, Richard M., 237–238n. 13
Nkrumah, Kwame, 294
Nohl, Werner, 152–154, 164n. 4
North Corona (N.Y.): block associations in, 64n. 9; class stratification in, 44; crime in, 56; issues in, 38; migration's impact on, 43–44; settlement of, 41–43; as urban renewal area, 45. *See also* Corona-East Elmhurst (N.Y.)
Novacap (Brasília's development corporation), 251, 271
novelty, use of term, 153
Nupe people, 284

Obile, Tackie, 287–288
occupations: changes in black, 38–40, 50–51, 63n. 1; hierarchy in, 309n. 17; of homeless, 70; men's, in Ghana, 301; tradition vs., 21; training for, 47; urban location and, 298
Ocean Hill-Brownsville school crisis, 46
Oelschlaeger, Max, 389

O Estado de S. Paulo (newspaper), 88–92

office buildings, plantings for, 159

Ogbu, J., 8

Ohnuki-Tierney, Emiko, 223

Oi, J., 179

Ojo, G. J. Afolabi, 299

older people: plaza used by, 124, 125–127, 133; retirement homes for, 189; social services for, 359–360

Ollennu, Nii Amaa, 285

Olympics (1984), 318

Olympics (1988), 318

Olympics (1992, Barcelona): Atlanta leaders at, 321; context of, 344–345; luxury hotel for, 365; nightspot at, 363; as opportunity for planning, 353–354, 356; planning's link to, 17, 353; state-subsidized, 318; success of, 369–370

Olympics (1996, Atlanta): Atlanta repackaged for, 17, 329–334; bombing in, 335; corporate pavilions in, 334; hype vs. reality of, 335–336; limited vision of, 318–319, 335–336; mascot of, 340; post-games depression after, 335

Olympics (2000, Sydney), 334

Olympic Village and Maritime Port (Barcelona), 363

Omae, Kinjiro, 224

Omi, Michael, 50, 64n. 13

Omni International complex (Atlanta), 325

Ontario, Lake, in bioregion, 384–386, 396–397. *See also* Toronto waterfront

Ontario Municipal Board, 381

open-door policy (China), 181, 182, 185

open spaces: Barcelona public policy on, 362–365; conflict over, 11; convent as, 366; on Danube River, 157; greenways as, 390–394, *391;* in modernism, 93–95; plaza as, 129–130, 135, 362–365, 370; public response to plan for, 392–394; use of term, 389–390. *See also* plazas; parks

Orange County (Calif.), as post-modern center, 16

organic gardening: rejection of, 143–144; strategies of, 141–143

Oropesa, R. S., 57

Ossman, S., 16

Osumanu, Malam, 287

Other, poor as, 56

Ottawa (Ont.), greenways in, 390

Ouro Preto (Brazil): Brasília compared to, 265–267; preindustrial urbanism in, 249–250; street system in, 259–260, 262–265; view of, *247*

outmigration: effects of, 39–40, 44, 123; by race, 39–40, 318, 337–338; of role models, 40, 63n. 2

overseas Chinese, 188

Paden, John, 282–283

Page, H., 8

Palace of the Planalto (Brasília), *246*

Palace Square, refreshments of, *256*

Pappas, G., 12

parades, as resistance, 10

Parc de L'Espanya (Barcelona), 362–363

Paris (France): as model, 93–94; Pompidou Center in, 127; racial division of, 8

Parish, S. M., 20

parks: aesthetics and, 152–154; Barcelona public policy on, 362–365; as residential-commercial link, 269–270; success of, 336. *See also* plazas; theme parks; Toronto waterfront

Parma (Brazil), *259,* 265

Parque Central (Costa Rica): contested meaning of, 122, 128, 134–135; daily social life in, 122–126, 135; description of, 116–117, *117,* 119; planning and design of, 120–121; Plaza de la Cultura compared to, 130–131, 133; sensory experience of, 127; social construction of, 121–123, *123,* 133–134; social production of, 120–121, 124, 125, 133–134. *See also* kiosks

Parque España (San José), 133

Parque Morazon (San José), 131, 133

Peachtree Center (Atlanta), 324–325, 330–331, 337

Pellow, Deborah, 16

People's Republic of China. *See* China

Perks, William T., 387–388

Pernau, Gabriel, 372

Philadelphia (Pa.): deindustrialization in, 12; ethnic politics in,
6–7; parade as resistance in, 10;
"streetwise" residents in, 19
Pionier movement, 154
Pittsfield (Mass.), deindustrialization
in, 12
Pizza Hut, 127
Plaça Emili Vendrell (Barcelona), *364,*
364–365
Plaça Pierye de Mandiargues (Barcelona), 366
Plaça Reial (Barcelona), 363
Plaça Salvador Seguí (Barcelona),
363–364, 365
place: access to power over people in,
281–283; discourse and experience of, 392–394; in nonplace,
317–321; power of/in, 278–281,
305–307. *See also* ideologies of
place; space
Plà General Metropolità (PGM,
Barcelona), 351–352
Plà Macià (Barcelona), 348
Plano Real (Brazil), 105n. 3
Plath, David, 220
Plaza de Armas (Costa Rica), 120
Plaza de la Cultura (Costa Rica):
contested meaning of, 129–134;
description of, *118,* 119, 127–128;
experience of, 130–131; Parque
Central compared to, 126;
planning and design of, 116, 128–
130; safety at, 130–131; social
construction of, 129–130, 133–
134; social production of, 129,
133–134
Plaza Mayor. *See* Parque Central
(Costa Rica)
plazas: approach to understanding,
114–115; colonial power relations
reflected in, 15–16; contested
meanings of, 11; criticism of, 363;
ethnography of, 115–119; for
military, 120–121; as open spaces,
129–130, 135, 362–365, 370; role
of, in empire, 120–121; social
construction of, 121–122; social
production of, 120–121, 124; as
workplace, 123–127, 130, 131. *See
also* kiosks; Parque Central (Costa
Rica); Plaza de la Cultura (Costa
Rica); squares
plaza-temple complex, 121

Plowiec, U., 178
Poble Espanyol (Barcelona), 363
Pogucki, R. J. H., 285
Polanyi, Karl, 178, 180
police: for control of barrios, 361–
362; for control of plaza, 124, 130,
133; violence by, 87, 99, 105n. 7
political economy: in gendered city,
9–10; studies of, 3–4. *See also*
exchange; production
political participation: African
American, 42–48, 51–52; citizenship's definition and, 104–105;
on civil rights, 45–48; of homeowners, 44–45; introduction to,
56–57; motivation for, 57; of
neighborhood associations, 53–56;
overlapping organizations for, 58–
59. *See also* neighborhood
associations
political parties: forums coopted by,
344; in Austria, 138, 152, 155; in
Barcelona, 352–355; in China, 179;
in Costa Rica, 128, 129; in
discourse on city, 352–355; in
Ghana, 294–295; in Japan, 226; in
the United States, 45–50; leadership legitimated by, 294–295;
reciprocal relations in, 179. *See
also* National Liberation Party;
Social Christian Union Party
politics: associations vs. institutions
in, 47–50; class stratification's
impact on, 41, 59–62; of environment, 138–139, 152, 154–155; of
gardening, 161–163; of homeownership, 50–62; patron-client
relationships in, 42–43; of poverty,
49–50; public space linked to, 94;
quality-of-life, 58–60; restructured
in civil rights era, 46–50
pollution: bioregional planning and,
385–386; as food supply concern,
226
poor people: fortified enclaves next
to, 87, 99; housing for, demolished, 358–359; ignored in park
plans, 333–334; plazas used by,
122; social networks and, 3; urban
space and, 85–86, 102. *See also*
underclass
Porcioles plan, 347
Port Authority Bus Terminal (New
York), 72

Portes, A., 6
Portland (Ore.), planning in, 387
Portman, John, 324–325
postmodernism, urban planning and, 16–18
pot-landscape, 158–159
poverty: as administrative problem, 49, 51; components of, 51, 56; concentration of inner-city black, 38–41; expansion of, 84–85; experience of, 67–68, 71; race linked to, 106n. 10. *See also* homelessness; poor people; underclass
power: absent in urban plan, 391–392; access to, 281–283; housing as source of, 286; land as source of, 277, 286; of/in place, 278–281, 305–307; political, 113; resistance to, 10–11; spatial organization and, 277–278. *See also* leadership
Powledge, F., 323
Praça dos Três Poderes (Brasília), *246, 247, 248*
Praça Tiradentes (Ouro Preto), *247*
praise-singers, 285
Pred, A., 10
privacy, enforcement of, 18–19
private gardens: conflict over, 11, 141; control of, 156; design and, 149–152; discourse on, 147–154; of discovery, 140–147, 154–163; funding for, 145–146, 158–159; native species in, 147–149; politics of, 161–163; as process, 160; as recreation space, 142–143, 149, 150, 162; sensory experience of, 162–163; social production of, 140, 154–160; temporality of, 161; weeds and, 152–153, 162. *See also* public gardens
private property: elimination of, 267–268; streets and, 263–265. *See also* homeownership; land ownership; property relations
production: colonial control of, 279; dispersed, in transnationalism, 205; foodstuffs' classification and, 213–214; increased, via capitalist involvement, 181; industrialization of food, 214–216, 219, 222–223; modes of, 174–176; relations of, 176–178, 180–181, 194–196; terminology in, 174–175

progress, master narrative of, 388
property relations: nature's challenge to, 160; urban planning and, 333–334. *See also* homeownership; landownership; private property
prostitution: in barrios, 351, 365–366; in plaza, 124, 125, 126, 135; police complicity in, 362; social services to combat, 360
Protestantism, Catholicism contested by, 124–125
public gardens: design and, 153–154; as models of community life, 139–140; reason for using, 152–154; visitors' investment in, 154. *See also* private gardens
public policy: barrios and city in, 365–367; on citizen security, 361–362; on green space, 362–365; on housing, 357–359; limited anthropological influence on, 1; on social services, 359–361. *See also* decision making
public/private sphere: difference between, 96, 97; modernist inversion of, 265–267; modernist rejection of, 248–250; of street/interior, 254, *255, 256,* 257–262; urban order and, 263–265
public space: appropriated by users, 154; changing character of, 83–84, 87–88; comparisons of, 249–250; creation and appropriation of, 99, 114, 127; as display area, 263–265; encoding of, 112; as engendered, 133; fortified enclaves as attack on, 93–95, 101–102; modernist instruments for attacking, 95–100; planning, 352; role of, 250–251; security in, 130–131, 153; social construction of, 121–122, 129–130; social difference in, 102–105; street corners as, 245, 248–251; street system of, 252–254; urbanism vs., 245, 248–249; visible and invisible in, 135. *See also* plazas; public gardens; squares; streets
Pulp Fiction (film), 16

quality of life: politics of, 58–60; studies of, 10
Queens (N.Y.): black community in, 37–38; King's speech in, 45

Rabinow, Paul, 15, 113, 380
race: depoliticization of, 48, 50;
    stratification's impact on issue of,
    60–62; urban divisions and, 7–9,
    92
racial discrimination: African
    American activism and, 39–41,
    50–53l, in Atlanta, 321–322; in
    Brazil, 106n. 10; in housing, 64n.
    10
racial integration, censoring of, 92
racism: class stratification's link to, 41,
    44, 51–53, 60–62; effects of, 7–9
Rakugo, Shin'ichi, 238n. 17
Rambles (Barcelona), 343, 346, 361–
    362, 365
Raval (Barcelona neighborhood): area
    of, 374n. 1; characteristics of, 349–
    351; city's link to, 365–369;
    demolition in, 345, 349–350, 350,
    357–358; exhibits on, 370, 371–
    372; green space in, 362–365;
    highways in, 349–351; housing in,
    348, 357–359; marginalization of,
    343–344; old vs. new, 350;
    outmigration from, 357–358;
    population of, 349, 357; protests
    in, 343, 357, 361, 370; role of, 342,
    368–369; romanticism vs. reality
    of, 351; security in, 361–362;
    social service in, 359–361. See
    also barrios
RCFTW. See Royal Commission on
    the Future of the Toronto Water-
    front (RCFTW)
rearticulation, definition of, 64n. 13
reciprocity. See gift exchange; social
    networks
recreation: for children, 63n. 5;
    private gardens for, 142–143, 149,
    150; public parks for, 153, 157–
    158
Red Belt (Paris), racial division of, 8
Redfield, Robert, 204
redistribution, as exchange mode,
    180–181
Reed, Adolphe, Jr., 63n. 2
Reeves, E. B., 20
region, use of term, 380. See also
    bioregionalism
Regional Municipality of Metropoli-
    tan Toronto (RMMT), 380, 382
religion: community identity and,
    299–300; contestation of, 124–125;
schools linked to, 299–300;
    traditional city and, 20–21. See
    also Catholicism; churches;
    Protestantism
religious practices: disputes over,
    309n. 20; in Ghana, 297, 304;
    leadership and, 287; in plaza, 124–
    125
Relph, Edward, 383
re-neighboring, use of term, 336
Repak, T. A., 9–10
Repton, Humphrey, 153
resistance: nonviolent, to segregation,
    45; as possibility, 114; to power,
    10–11; religion's role in, 20; to
    urban planning, 270–271; to walls,
    105
restaurants: family meals at, 220–221,
    237n. 10; fast food, 127–128, 129,
    132, 217; increased use of, 216;
    lobsters for, 227; peak times for,
    229; seasons and, 232; social
    changes and, 221; wild vs.
    cultivated fish in, 229, 233
restaurateurs, 203, 210, 234
Reston (Va.), as edge city, 92
retailers: cultural capital of, 203, 235;
    gourmet boom and, 222–223; in
    marketplace organization, 234;
    peak purchases by, 229; seasons
    and, 232; social changes and, 221;
    supermarkets as replacement for,
    216, 221
Rialto Theatre (Atlanta), 338
Ribera neighborhood (Barcelona), 346
Rich's Department Store (Atlanta),
    330, 337
Rio de Janeiro (Brazil): Debret's plan
    for, 252–254, 255, 256, 274n. 5;
    diversity of, 253, 274n. 6; pre-
    industrial urbanism in, 249–250
riverscape, ecological gardening and,
    157
RMMT (Regional Municipality of
    Metropolitan Toronto), 380, 382
The Road Warrior (film), 18
Robertson, Jennifer, 20–21, 207
Rodman, Margaret, 378
Roger and Me (film), 12
role models, outmigration of, 40, 63n.
    2
Rome, Barcelona influenced by, 345
roof gardens, support for, 154, 159,
    160

Roosevelt, Franklin D., 323
Roseberry, William, 206
Rotenberg, Robert, 11, 148, 378, 379
Rothstein, F. A., 13
Rouse, James, 326–327
Rouse Corporation, 322, 326, 337
Rovira i Trias plan, 347
Rowe, Colin, 261
Royal Commission on the Future of
    the Toronto Waterfront (RCFTW):
    accomplishments of, 386; ecosys-
    tem/bioregional aproach of, 383–
    386, 394–395; establishment of,
    382; recommendations of, 389–
    392, *391;* tasks of, 382; weaknesses
    of plan of, 391–392
rua. See streets
Rubió i Tuduri plan, 347
Ruble, B., 17
Ruddick, S., 19
Rural/Urban Design Assistance Team
    (R/UDAT), 330
Russia, postsocialist transition in, 17
Rutheiser, Charles, 16, 17
Rutherford (judge), 294

Sabo Gari (Ibadan Nigeria), 284, 285
Sabon Zongo (Accra): approach to,
    307–308n. 2; changes in, 305;
    court of offices in, 303; description
    of, 289–290, 302; establishment
    of, 278, 288–289, 306, 309n. 31;
    ethnicity in, 290–291, *292,* 296–
    299; exogenous forces on, 277;
    gender in, 301–302; leadership of,
    291–302; maps of, *290, 291;*
    modernization of, 297; population
    of, 297; religion in, 289, 299–300;
    schools in, 299–301; spatial
    history of, 277–278; specific areas
    in, 291–292. *See also* chiefs/
    headmen; *mai gida* (patron)
Sacks, K. B., 8
Sahlins, Marshall, 213
Salaga (Ghana): as market, 286;
    stranger communities in, 284
Salamanca (Spain), as capital of
    culture, 372
Salvador (Brazil), view of, *246*
Sampah, Daniel Armatey, 310n. 41
Sampson, S., 179
Sandburg, Carl, 206
San Francisco (Calif.), greenways in,
    390

San José (Costa Rica): description of,
    117–119; establishment of, 120;
    fieldwork in, 115; social conflicts
    in, 11; upper-class outmigration
    in, 123. *See also* Parque Central
    (Costa Rica); Plaza de la Cultura
    (Costa Rica)
Sant Pau (church, Barcelona), 365
São Paulo (Brazil): approach to, 83–
    84; fear of violence in, 86–87; Los
    Angeles compared to, 83–84, 98–
    102; police violence in, 87, 99,
    105n. 7; public space eliminated
    in, 95; race as issue in, 92; real
    estate ads in, 88–92; spatial
    segregation in, 84, 87–88, 97–98;
    tertiarization in, 86, 98–99; urban
    planning debates in, 99–100. *See
    also* fortified enclaves
sarkin (counselor), appointments for,
    291–295
Sassen, Saskia, 12–13, 89
Savannah (Ga.), urban divisions in, 7
"scape," concept of, 204–205
Schildkrout, Enid, 305
Schiller-Bütow, Hans, 149–151
Schneider, J. A., 6–7
School of Music (Atlanta), 338
schools: Afrocentric, 9; building for,
    360; civil rights activism and, 46;
    failure of, 8; gender and, 300, 302;
    importance of, 300–301; for
    Muslims, 299–300; political
    control of, 48; silencing in, 10–11;
    as social services, 360
Schwarz, Urs, 147, 148, 149, 152
seafood: centrality of, 211–212, 223,
    225; as commodity, 201–203, 205,
    210; in culinary cycle, 229–232;
    cultural biography of, 212–213;
    imports of, 225–228; industrializa-
    tion of, 215–216, 228–229, 238n.
    14; *kata* of, 226–228; marketplace
    for, 201–203, 205; popularity of,
    217; purchases of, 221; seasonality
    and, 231–232; transportation of,
    222. *See also* fishing industry;
    sushi
Sears (store), 127, 129
Sección Feminina (Spain), 359
security: Barcelona public policy on,
    361–362; for insuring segregation,
    93, 97, 99, 101; necessity of, 100–
    101, 103; new aesthetic of, 87;

security (*continued*)
open spaces and, 363; tactics in,
90–92, 99
segregation: African American
activism, 39–40, 45–50; as city's
legacy, 321; effects of, 102–105;
fortified enclaves as, 18–19, 83–
88, 93–98, 101–102; in Atlanta,
321–322; in Barcelona, 353;
nonviolent resistance to, 45;
persistence of residential, 63n. 3;
violence linked to, 102–103. *See
also* fortified enclaves; civil rights-
era reforms
Seguí, Salvador, 363
Sempe, 288, 294–296
Senegal, colonialism in, 282
Seoul (Korea), Olympics in, 318
7–11 (chain store), 219
sex workers. *See* prostitution
shelter system: establishment of, 71–
72; gender and, 72–79; model of
family in, 68–69, 72; number of
homeless in, 70–71; park's
encroachment on, 333; transitional
housing in, 73, 74–75, 77. *See also*
homeless hotels
Shenzhen Special Economic Zone,
186, 188, 192
Sherman, William Tecumseh, 323
Shields, Rob, 378
shoe factory, in China, 192, 194–195
shoeshine men/boys, in Costa Rica,
123, 125–126, 132
Shulman, Steven, 62
sidewalks, reconfiguration of, 272–
273
Sieber, R. T., 17
Sierra Leone, early trade and, 281
silencing, concept of, 10–11
Singer, Milton, 204
Sisala people, 298, 301
Sklair, L., 181
Skov, Lise, 207
slavery, in Brazil, 263
Smart, Alan, 13
Smart, Josephine, 13
Smith, Neil, 338
Smith, Nell, 322
Smith, P. J., 388
Smith, R. J., 237n. 8
social capital, concept of, 8, 63n. 2
social change: food culture linked to,
216–217, 221–222; tradition vs.,
20–21

Social Christians' Unity Party (Costa
Rica), 128
social class: consumption and, 19; in
"dual city," 13; identifiers of, 42;
increased stratification in, 37–41,
44–45, 49–50, 53, 60–62; industrial food and, 222; institutional
connections among, 67; maintenance of, 21; planning as tool in
cooperation among, 355–356;
politics of homeownership and,
50–62; public space and, 121–122;
spatial segregation and, 84–90;
urban divisions and, 7–9. *See also*
middle class; poor people;
underclass; upper class; working
class
social construction: of boundaries,
377; concept of, 112; of plazas,
119, 121–123, *123*, 129–130, 133–
134; of space, 112, 121–122, 134–
135, 378; of transitional zones, 377
Social Democratic Party (Austria),
155
social formation, concept of, 175–176,
195
socialism: capitalism vs., in investment, 174–175, 178, 183–188, 194;
collapse of, 170; relations of
exchange and, 177–178; relations
of production and, 176–177;
second economy in, 179–180; as
social formation, 175–176, 195
Socialist Party, 353–355
social movements: emergence of, 85–
86; spatialization and, 112–113
social networks: guanxi (reciprocal
relations) in, 13, 179–180, 190–
193, 196; between Hong Kong and
China, 172–173; Hong Kong
investment and, 184–185, 188–
196; studies of, 2–3. *See also*
social relations
social organizational paradigm, 3–4
social production: concept of, 112; in
empire, 120–121; of landscape/
gardens, 140, 154–160; of plazas,
119, 120–121, 124, 125, 129, 133–
134; of private gardens, 140, 154–
160; of space, 112, 134–135,
377–380
social relations: contested city and,
9–11, 22; divided city and, 7–9;
ethnic city and, 5–7; public spaces

for, 251–254, *255, 256,* 257; urban renewal as interruption in, 358–359. *See also* ethnicity; social networks

Social Security Act (1934), 69

social services: African Americans and, 43, 47, 49–50, 63n. 5; Barcelona public policy on, 359–361; bureaucratization of, 48, 49–50, 56; in closed condominiums, 89–90; to combat prostitution, 360; for immigrants, 360; location of, 86; in N.Y. neighborhood, 43, 47, 63n. 5; for older people, 359–360; schools as, 360; for teenagers, 359–360, 361

social spatialization: analyses of, 379–380; bioregionalism's impact on, 388–395; frontier as, 382–383; use of term, 378. *See also* spatialization; Toronto waterfront

SoHo, gentrification of, 338

Soja, Edward W., 16, 98

Solà-Morales, Ignosi de, 352, 355, 356, 362

Solà-Morales I Rubió, Manuel de, 345

Solinger, D., 178

Sousa, Tomé de, 273–274n. 2

South Central (Los Angeles): identity politics in, 9; riots in, 18

Southeast Asia, cuisine of, 217

Soviet Union: reciprocal relations in, 179; as socialist social formation, 175–176

space: complexity of, 114; identity linked to, 19; meanings assigned to, 102, 278–279; reflexivity of, 277–278; representation of, 377–378, 394; social practice and, 11, 93–95, 102, 113–114. *See also* fortified enclaves; place; public space; spatialization; streets

Spain: democratic government in, 343–344, 359; neighbohood associations in, 343–344, 351–352; professionalization in, 352–354; urban planning in, 344–345, 368–369. *See also* Barcelona (Spain); Catalunya

Spanish American empire, plaza's role in, 120–121. *See also* plazas

Spanish Civil War, 349

Spartacus Guide for Gay Men (guidebook), 130

spatialization: culture and, 11; theories of, 111–115. *See also* social spatialization

Special Economic Zones (China), 172, 186, 188, 192

"special populations," facilities for, 53–56, 60–62, 64–65n. 14

Spitzer, Klaus, 151–152

Spitzer, Leo, 308n. 6

sports teams, 325, 360, 365

squares: definition of, 252–253, 274n. 8; in Greece, 261; in Latin America, 262; in Rio de Janeiro, 253–254, *255, 256,* 257. *See also* plazas; streets

squatter areas, clearance of, 170

Stack, C., 1

stall holders, in Rio de Janeiro, *256. See also* vendors.

Starbucks, 206

state. *See* nation-state

state-sector firms, 176–177, 180, 186

Statistics Canada, 385

status: of chiefs/headmen, 296, 304–305; maintenance of, 21; of strangers, 305; symbols of, 88–92, 99

Stepick, A., 6

stereotypes, 77, 78, 103

Stevens, Carolyn, 207

Stone, Clarence N., 58

strangers: status of, 305; use of term, 290, 307n. 1. *See also* zongos

streets: as anatomy of city, 260–262; architectural context of, 250–257; commercial sector as replacement for, 268–272; contested control of, 10; in conventions of solids and voids, 257–267; elimination of, 245, 248–251, 269–273; fortified enclaves vs., 93–95, 100–101; modernist attack on, 95–97, 265–267; names of, 10; patterns of, 253–254; in preindustrial urbanism, 249–250, 253–254, *255, 256,* 257, 261–262; private property vs. public display and, 263–265; as public/private discourse, 248–249; role of, 251–252; shopping separated from, 272–273; as social space, 252–254, 258–262, 274n. 8, 358–359, 365; in working-class neighborhoods, 346; in *zongo,* 296. *See also* highways; homelessness; squares; walking

Stull, D., 6
suburbanism, central business vs., 324
subways, as city competition, 370
Sudan, women's protests in, 10
supermarkets: film about, 237n. 11; growth of, 216, 221; sales strategies of, 223
sushi: authenticity and, 223–225; guides to, 238n. 17; preferences in, 220, 229; seasonality and, 232
Susser, Ida, 1, 3–4, 8
sustainability, city and, 370–371
Suupaa no Onna (film), 237n. 11
Swazi, space's meaning for, 279
symbolic capital, in gift economy, 192

Tachibana, Yuzuru, 224
Taiwan, China's link to, 188
Takarazuka musical review, 207
tamborada, as tactic, 343
Tamboré (closed condominium), 91–92
Tarantino, Quentin, 16
Tarragó, Salvador, 348
Tavistock Institute of Human Relations, 2–3
Tawiah, Tackie, 286, 309n. 19
taxes, for development, 328
TCR plan, 388
technology: in fishing industry, 206, 224, 228–229, 238n. 14; food preparation and, 218–219; urban planning and, 352, 356, 387. *See also* security
Techwood Homes (Atlanta), 323, 331–332, 336
teenagers: consumption by, 207; hangouts for, 132–133; perception of violence, 19; social services for, 359–360, 361
Tetteh, Letitia, 301
theme parks: cities as, 322, 327; influence of, 17; redevelopment and, 336
Thomas, Roger G., 283
Thorn, Matthew, 207
Tiananmen Square, 169–170, 190–191
Tibenderana, Peter Kazenga, 282, 283
time: food culture and, 229–232; in social systems, 278
Tobin, Jeffrey, 237n. 6
Tokyo (Japan): cuisine in, 217; as global city, 12–13, 14; restaurants

in, 229, 237n. 10. *See also* Tsukiji marketplace (Tokyo)
Toonga (Ghana), 310n. 41
Toronto (Ont.): altered geomorphology of, 383, *384, 386;* economy of, 381–382; planning for, 385, 388; spatial ideologies in, 17. *See also* Toronto waterfront
Toronto Census Metropolitan Area, 385
"Toronto-Centred Region" (TCR) plan, 388
Toronto City Council, 381
Toronto Economic Development Corporation, 396
Toronto waterfront: as ecosystem/bioregion, 383–386, *384, 386,* 389–392, 394–395; as historical/social product, 377; nature and scope of, 382–383; political economy of, 380, 381; recent developments in, 396–397; recommendations for, 389–392, *391,* 394
Torres i Clavé plan, 346–347
Touring Club (Brazil), 275n. 19
tourism: barrio as center for, 374n. 5; ecological focus in, 117; exoticization in, 207; middle-class images in, 17; plaza use and, 126, 131, 133; vendors and, 130
towns. *See* communities
trade: centers for in Africa, 280–281; as source of wealth, 286
trade guilds: regulations of, 233; role of, 208; specializations of, 210, 233–235
traders: at auctions, 209–210; cultural capital of, 203, 235; food culture and, 212; licenses for, 210; *mai gida* for, 289; social relations among, 210–211; on Tsukiji specs, 227; women as, 9, 301–302. *See also* retailers; wholesalers
tradition: invention of, 379; maintenance of, 20–21, 209; persistence of, 302, 307. *See also* food culture
traditional urbanity, use of term, 321, 330
trails, in ecosystem-oriented plan, 390–391, 392–394, 396
transitional zones: social construction of, 377; waterfront as, 383
transnational corporations, subcontracting by, 169. *See also* multinationals

transnationalism: cities and, 171–172; global culture and, 203–206

transportation: industrialization of food supply linked to, 215–216, 222, 225; of live fish, 222; market center and railroad, 205–206; streets identified with, 270, 272, 275n. 18, 275n. 19; in urban planning, 323–327. *See also* airports; streets

trees: cutting of, 121, 125; on Danube River, 157–158; planting of, 121, 128, 129, 158; saving old, 159; in urban and ecozones, 156–157; in Wildgärten, 146–147

Trenton (Ont.), green space discourse and, 396

Tsukiji marketplace (Tokyo): description of, 201–203, 236n. 3; history of, 208–209; lobster sales at, 227; in market structure, 233–235; regulations of, 233; sales strategies and, 223; as seafood center, 205, 206, 211–213; social organization of, 209–211; Sunday closure of, 229, 238n. 15; wild vs. caged fish in, 228–229, 233, 238n. 14

tuna, 202, 205, 211, 228, 232

Turkey, pieceworkers in, 9

Turner, J., 8

Turner, Ted, 325

Twelve Monkeys (film), 18

underclass: context of term, 67; emergence of, 39. *See also* poor people

Underground Atlanta: development of, 325–326; failure of, 326–327, 340; redevelopment of, 330

Union of Soviet Socialist Republics. *See* Soviet Union

United Nations, Vienna center for, 157

United Party (UP, Ghana), 294

United States: edge cities in, 91–92; food exports of, 237–238n. 13; fortified enclaves in, 91; streets/buildings in, 275n. 13; violent crime in, 105n. 6. *See also specific cities and states*

USAID, Costa Rica's dependence on, 123, 129

U.S. Department of Housing and Urban Development, 331–332

U.S. Immigration and Naturalization Service, 334

United States-Mexico border, 13, 171–172

Universal Appliances, 187

universalism: challenge to, 94–95; discourse based in, 379–380

Universidad de Costa Rica, 116, 131

University of Chicago, 2

University of Manchester, 3

upper class: advertisements geared to, 88–92; fortified enclaves for, 87–88; housing for, 328, 381; plazas used by, 121–123, 132; privatization as theme of, 101–102. *See also* fortified enclaves

urban anthropology: directions in, 111, 369; dominant trends in, 21–22; historical overview of, 2–4; theoretical impact of, 1–2

Urban Development Action Grants (U.S.), 326

urban ethnography, focus of, 4, 11

urbanism: cultural goals of, 346; discourse on, 352–355; meaning of, 4; public space vs., 245, 248–249; streets in preindustrial, 249–250, 253–254, *255, 256,* 257, 261–262

Urban Land Institute, 322

Urban League of Greater New York, 63n. 5

urban planning: bioregionalism's impact on, 388–395; business control of, 323–329, 332–334; centralization of, 178–179; characteristics discussed in, 348; effects of, 353, 355–356; egalitarian discourse in, 268; elite orthodoxy in, 342; emergence of, 344–351; implementation of, 353–354; liberalism and economic interests linked in, 387–388; modernist, 15–16, 95–98, 99–100; professionalization of, 352–354, 393–394; resistance to, 270–271; technologization of, 352, 356, 387; on urban zone and ecozone blends, 156–160; "user-friendliness" and, 327–328; weak links in, 391–392. *See also* Atlanta (Ga.); Brasília

urban policy. *See* public policy

urban renewal: cleansing via renaming, 337; homeowners' role in, 45; reasons for, 323, 356; rhetoric of, 322–323. *See also* Atlanta (Ga.); Barcelona (Spain)

Urban Residential Finance Authority (Atlanta), 328

urban space. *See* public space

Ussher Fort-James Fort area (Accra), 281

Valencia, parade as resistance in, 10

variety, use of term, 153

vendors: in Costa Rica, 124–127, 130, 132; in Hong Kong, 170; in Jamaica, 9; in Rio de Janeiro, *255, 256*

Vendrell, Emili, 364–365

Verdery, Katherine, 170

vias (ways), 269

Victoriaborg (Accra), 281

Vienna (Austria): conflict over open spaces/gardens in, 11, 141; discourse on gardens in, 147–154; discourse on healthfulness and urban space in, 379; ecopolitics in, 138–139, 154–156; funding for gardens in, 145–146, 158–159; gardens of discovery in, 140–147, 154–163; landscape traditions in, 139–140; urban and ecozone blends in, 156–160

Vienna Woods, 141, 157

violence: fear of, 19, 83, 86–87, 90, 103–104, 124, 131; in homeless hotels, 77; by police, 87, 99, 105n. 7; segregation linked to, 102–103; white on black, 53, 65n. 15. *See also* crime

Virillio, Paul, 322

Vitruvius (architect), 379

Vogel, Suzanne, 219

Voyage Pittoresque et Historique au Brasil. See Debret, Jean Baptiste

Wacquant, Loic J. D., 2, 8, 9, 19, 63n. 2

Wala people, 298

walking: esplanade for, 365–366; pedestrian rights of, 245; sidewalks and, 272–273; as spatial acting out of place, 113–114; women, 129, 132

Wallerstein, Immanuel, 177, 204

walls: function of, 96–97, 102, 104; gardens and, 141, 149; necessity of, 100–101; resistance to, 105

Walpole, Horace, 151

Walsh (scholar), 274n. 6

Walt Disney World (Fla.), 17

Wang, N., 181

Wangara people, 284, 298, 303

Ward, Anthony, 278

War of Spanish Succession, 346

War on Poverty, 47, 49–50

"The Warriors" (Brasília), *247*

Washington (D.C.), crime in, 105n. 6

waterfront: as ecosystem/bioregion, 383–386, *384, 386,* 389–392, 394–395; jurisdiction over, 382; nature and scope of, 382–383; promenades/trails along, 363, 390–391, 392–393, 396; as tourist site, 17. *See also* Toronto waterfront

Waterfront Regeneration Trust, 386, 391, 396–397

Watson, James L., 13, 206

Webber, Melvin, 317

weeds, treatment of, 152–153, 162

Weisman, Leslie K., 278

West Africa: colonial city in, 279–280; colonialism in, 281–282; land ownership in, 279; market women in, 9; stranger communities in, 283–284. *See also* Ghana

West Indian Labor Day Parade, 10

whale meat, demand for, 235

White, Merry, 207

"white public space," concept of, 8

wholesalers: at auctions, 202, 209–211; cultural capital of, 203, 235; food culture and, 212; licenses for, 210, 236n. 2; social relations among, 208–211; specializations of, 210, 233–235

Whorf, Benjamin Lee, 333

Wildgärten: concept of, 142, 144; example of, 141, 144–147, *145,* 158; rationale for, 146; rejection of, 150, 156; tolerance for, 162–163

Williams, Brett, 7, 64n. 11

Wilson, Alexander, 395

Wilson, E., 9

Wilson, William Julius: on black class structure, 38–41, 50, 62, 63n. 1; critique of, 9; on social capital, 63n. 2; terminology of, 67

Winant, Howard, 50, 64n. 13

Wirth, Peter, 149, 151

women: consumption and, 207; food culture and, 212, 218–220, 237n. 8; in gendered city, 9–10; organizations of, 299; plazas used by, 125, 126, 129–133; protests of, 10; schools for, 300; in shelter system, 73–79; as traders, 9, 301–302

working class: deindustrialization and, 12; homes built by, 85, 87; outmigration of, 39–40; plazas used by, 122, *123*, 132

workplace, plaza as, 123–127, 130, 131

World Bank, 179

"world city," concept of, 13

world market. *See* globalization

World's Fair (1939), 42

world-systems theory, 177–178

Wyeth, Andrew, 17

Yang, M.: on gift economy, 190, 191–193; on modes of exchange, 179–181

Yohei Zushi shops, 224

Yoruba people: colonial city and, 280; leadership disputes and, 287; schools for, 299–300; *zongo* for, 284

Young, Andrew, 329–330, 335

youth. *See* teenagers

Yugoslavia, industrial enterprises in, 170, 179

yuppies, food preferences of, 217

Zabrama people, 298–301

Zenua, Harri, 286–288

Zongo Lane (Accra), 286

zongos: development of, 277, 281, 284, 286–289; leadership in, 284–289, 292, 293–302. *See also* Sabon Zongo (Accra)

zoning: for enterprise areas, 331; political control of, 48, 381. *See also* Special Economic Zones (China); transitional zones

zoning laws: in Atlanta, 324–326; in Barcelona, 352–355; in Toronto, 381–386

Zukin, Sharon, 16, 119, 338

zumunci/zumunta (associations), 299